The Dark Side of
Close Relationships

The Dark Side
of Close Relationships

Edited by

Brian H. Spitzberg
San Diego State University

William R. Cupach
Illinois State University

Routledge
Taylor & Francis Group
New York   London

First published by Lawrence Erlbaum Associates
10 Industrial Avenue
Mahwah, NJ 07430

Cover design by Kathryn Houghtaling Lacey

Library of Congress Cataloging-in-Publication Data

The dark side of close relationships / edited by Brian H. Spitzberg and William R. Cupach
    p. cm.
Includes bibliographical references and indexes.
ISBN 0-8058-2486-3 (cloth : alk. paper). —ISBN 0-8058-2487-1 (pbk. : alk. paper)
    1. Interpersonal communication. 2. Interpersonal conflict. I. Spitzberg, Brian H. II. Cupach, William R.
    BF637.C45D335 1998
    158.2—dc21

98–9549
CIP

ontents

reface

This volume represents a follow-up to our 1994 publication, *The Dark Side of Interpersonal Communication* (Lawrence Erlbaum Associates). In the preface to that volume, we argued, "To fully understand how people function effectively requires us to consider how individuals cope with social interaction that is difficult, problematic, challenging, distressing, and disruptive" (p. vii). In this companion volume, we expand our focus from interaction to close relationships (although it is obvious that the two foci overlap).

Aside from the inherent need to investigate the bad as well as the good of interpersonal relationships, we and our colleagues simply find the dark side metaphor to be intellectually arousing: It is intriguing, heuristic, and provocative. It stimulates investigation of important, yet often neglected, phenomena and it especially encourages consideration of the hidden and forbidden and the paradoxical and ironic, elements of human relating.

The current volume once again assembles the cutting edge work of first rate scholars. As in *The Dark Side of Interpersonal Communication*, the subject matter and stylistic approaches are diverse, reflecting the broad and interdisciplinary domain that is the dark side of human affairs. Our selection of topics is somewhat arbitrary, reflecting only a sample of emerging scholarship in the interdisciplinary study of relationships. The authors come from the ranks of communication, psychology, sociology, and cognate disciplines.

In the brief opening chapter, we present a philosophical frame for investigating the darker sides of interpersonal behavior. Here, we briefly explore some of the meanings, assumptions, and implications associated with employing the dark side metaphor. We pick up where we left off in our epilogue to the previous *Dark Side* volume. Between the lines it should be apparent that human interest in the dark side is timeless and may itself be suggestive of something in human nature.

In chapter 1, Felmlee extends her provocative work regarding fatal attraction. She reviews previous and current research demonstrating that the very features that attract us to another individual, sometimes lead to disaffection and relationship dissolution. Felmlee explores theoretical explanations of this phenomenon and suggests implications for theories of relational development and dissolution.

Chapter 2 offers an in-depth view of the dark side of jealousy and envy. Guerrero and Andersen concisely situate these complex emotions in a larger context of relationship emotions, focusing on the negative psychic and interpersonal consequences surrounding the experience and expression of jealousy and envy. They also discuss ways in which communication can be used to cope with jealousy and envy.

In chapter 3, Sillars considers how properties of communication and relationships figure into the complex concepts of understanding and interpersonal perception. Sillars identifies many of the key features of perception in close relationships en route to examining the nature of understanding. Drawing on recent empirical data, he discusses common sources of misunderstanding in relationship conflict.

In chapter 4, Jaeger, Skelder, and Rosnow present an explication of the functions and consequences of gossip in interpersonal relations. Framing gossip in the context of larger networks of interaction, these authors provide data that support some common beliefs about gossip while debunking other cherished assumptions.

Patterns of conflict in romantic and family relationships are considered by Messman and Canary in chapter 5. Unlike most examinations of conflict that focus on styles, strategies, and tactics, this chapter takes a look at what is known about sequences and extended patterns of conflict. The authors offer some novel insights into the nature and occurrence of entrenched, interlocking sequences of interaction that relationship members coproduce.

Chapter 6 portrays the paradoxical features of codependent relationships. Le Poire, Hallett, and Giles adopt a relational conceptualization of codependency. Using the theory of inconsistent nurturing as control, they demonstrate that the attempts of codependent partners to control the adverse behavior of afflicted (e.g., alcoholic) partners may actually reinforce and perpetuate the undesirable behavior. Important implications for both research and treatment are derived.

Spitzberg, in chapter 7, reviews diverse and copious literatures bearing on the incidence of sexual coercion among courtship couples. He carefully elaborates the notion of coerciveness and reviews various theories that account for its occurrence. Then, he explicates an interactional approach to understanding coercion—an approach that focuses prominently on the role of miscommunication.

We lay the foundation in chapter 8 for our own program of research regarding stalking and obsessive relational intrusion. Specifically, we review empirical evidence concerning individuals who receive unwanted pestering or harassment by another person who desires relational contact. After outlining the diverse profiles of intrusion perpetrators, we attempt to clarify the nature and incidence of various forms of intrusion behavior. Then, we consider the consequences for and coping responses of victims of unwanted pursuit.

Weber tackles the subject of nonmarital break ups in chapter 9. With style and flair, she weaves an engaging tale about the occurrence and aftermath of relationship uncoupling. Weber persuasively demonstrates the importance of sense-making processes and offers practical observations about overcoming (and even benefiting from) relationship loss.

In chapter 10, Bratslavsky, Baumeister, and Sommer provide a synthesis of research on the trials and tribulations of unrequited love and they characterize the respective experiences associated with the roles of the rejector and the would-be lover. Interdependence theory is employed to explain differences in the emotional outcomes for rejectors and would-be lovers. The authors conclude that mutuality of love, rather than giving or receiving of love, is what is required for happiness and fulfillment.

Segrin, in chapter 11, reviews a vast literature to show how disrupted and distressed interpersonal relationships can both lead to and result from various mental health problems. He explores the complex links between psychological and relational spheres, elaborating specifically on schizophrenia, depression, loneliness, alcoholism, and eating disorders. Such disorders often represent a sense of losing one's senses, or losing one's place in relationships.

In chapter 12, Rook critically inspects the body of research that investigates the relative impact of positive and negative experiences in personal relationships. On one hand, research suggests that relationships meaningfully contribute to the psychological and physical well-being of individuals. On the other hand, several studies indicate that negative aspects of relationships tend to cancel or outweigh the benefits. Rook carefully dissects this literature, showing methodological weaknesses that undermine our ability to draw strong inferences. These limitations are then used to fashion an agenda for more rigorous future research into the relative importance of positive and negative events in relationships.

Collectively, the scholarly journeys made in this volume are intended to illustrate the complexities, both moral and functional, involved in close relationship processes. The intent is neither to valorize nor demonize the darker aspects of close relationships, but rather, to emphasize the importance of their day-to-day performances in relationships. Only by accepting such processes as integral to relationships can their role be fully understood.

Finally, we would like to express our gratitude to Tonya Felder, Katherine Ferrer, Jacqueline Post, and Michelle Schroeder for their invaluable assistance in the preparation of the indexes.

—*Brian H. Spitzberg*
William R. Cupach

Introduction: Dusk, Detritus, and Delusion—A Prolegomenon to the Dark Side of Close Relationships

All life is a struggle in the dark.

—Lucretius (*The Nature of Things*, circa 45 BC)

Life may indeed be a struggle in the dark, but a few years hence from our first venture into the shadowlands, the metaphor of the "dark" side of human behavior (or perhaps human nature) continues to intrigue. We began our journey with a collection of chapters on the dark side of interpersonal communication (Cupach & Spitzberg, 1994). This previous collection included chapters on such topics as incompetence, equivocation, paradox, dilemmas, predicaments, transgression, privacy violation, deception, hurtful messages, abuse, and the darkness of normal family interaction. Our original impetus was the belief that the social sciences were overly pollyanna-like in perspective. This is perhaps most evidenced by the contents of most undergraduate textbooks, littered with commendations to be attractive, open, honest, self-confident, assertive, visionary, good-humored, supportive, cooperative, empathic, clear, polite, competent, and to develop and maintain normal friendships, heterosexual romances, and resilient nuclear families. Our argument was not to usurp these maxims of social preference, as much as to provide a more balanced understanding of some of the paradoxes of such morally muddled principles when examined in the functional fabric of interaction. Attractiveness can be a curse (Tseëlon, 1992), openness can be costly (Bochner, 1982), honesty is often more destructive than deceit (Barnes, 1994; Bavelas, Black, Chovil, & Mullet, 1990; DePaulo, Kashy, Kirkendol, Wyer & Epstein, 1996; Rodriquez & Ryave, 1990), self-esteem can be self-absorbing (Gustafson & Ritzer, 1995) and a source of aggression (Baumeister, Smart, & Boden, 1996). Assertiveness tends to be unlikable (Spitzberg, 1993), visionary leadership can be misguided (Conger, 1990), humor can be violent and oppressive (Dundes, 1987; Jenkins, 1994; Keough, 1990), supportiveness can aggravate rather than heal (LaGaipa, 1990, Ray, 1993; Rook & Pietromonaco, 1987), cooperation and empathy are susceptible to exploitation (Tedeschi & Rosenfeld, 1980), clarity is often the least functional form of communication (Cerullo, 1988; Kursh, 1971; Nyberg, 1993; Rue, 1994; Tooke & Camire, 1991), politeness can be a reflection of oppression (Janeway, 1987; Kasson, 1990), and competence in one's communication can backfire in myriad ways (Spitzberg, 1993, 1994a). Friendships are often fraught with difficulties (Fehr, 1996; Rawlins, 1992; Rook, 1989; Wiseman, 1986) and same sex romantic relationships (Huston & Schwartz, 1995) and alternative models of families (e.g., Altman, 1993) often are quite functional compared to their "normal" alternatives (e.g., Blount, 1982; Finkelhor, Gelles, Hotaling, & Straus, 1983; Moltz, 1992; Poster, 1978).

> It is possible to know, albeit harder to accept, the shadow side of ourselves, the essential darkness that breeds ill will. Envy, greed, and jealousy are the fundamental components of this malice. ... when the negative components of our emotional life are denied or ignored (because of guilt or fear), the positive ones suffer, too. As always, love and hate are inexorably intertwined—Berke (1988, p. 12, 13)

The obverse of looking on the bright side of life is that the things we often consider dark in their moral or functional implications are instead valuable in surprising ways. Gossip (Bergmann, 1993), obscenity (Allan & Burridge, 1991), embarrassment (Miller, 1996), humiliation (Miller, 1993), paradox (Palazzoli, Boscolo, Cecchin, & Prata, 1978; Weeks & L'Abate, 1982), narcissism (Emmons, 1984; Watson & Biderman, 1993), jealousy (Fitness & Fletcher, 1993; Pines & Aronson, 1983; Stearns, 1989), envy (Schoeck, 1966), anger (Averill, 1993; Canary, Spitzberg & Semic, 1998; Stearns & Stearns, 1986), aggression (Gilmore, 1987; Twitchell, 1989), violence (Spitzberg, 1997; Tedeschi & Felson, 1994), enmity (Volkan, 1988), hate (Schoenewolf, 1991), regret (Landman, 1993), failure (Payne, 1989); cultism (Festinger, Riecken & Schachter, 1956; Galanter, 1989; Keiser & Keiser, 1987), sadomasochism (Chancer, 1992), child abuse (McMillen, Zuravin, & Rideout, 1995), and many other presumptively "dark" traits, states, and processes all have their adaptive potential (see Cupach & Spitzberg, 1994; Spitzberg, 1994b). At a truly systemic (and theoretical) level, for example, a certain degree of dishonesty and exploitation in a society may create some level of consumer caution, and therefore less overall exploitation, compared to systems in which consumers presume honesty, and thereby suffer from unchecked and wide-scale exploitation (Schotter, 1986). Relationships obviously come replete with costs as well as rewards (Rook & Pietromonoco, 1987; Sedikides, Oliver & Campbell, 1994). As Duck (1994) emphasized, any comprehensive approach to human relationships requires not only an understanding of the darker aspects of relationships, but the integration of these aspects into theories of relating and into an understanding of the entire relational system. Love and hate are indeed impossible to disentangle.

> *Modern political science owes a great deal to Machiavelli's ... insights ... that the traditional concentration on the "ought," on the manner in which princes and statesmen ought to behave, interferes with the fuller understanding of the "is" that can be achieved when attention is closely and coldly riveted on the ways in which statecraft is in fact carried on—*Albert O. Hirschman (1981, pp. 294–295)

> *If evil is imagined as other than who or what we are, then it will remain an aspect or segment of life and experience denied to us by the limitations of our imagination. Somehow all that is dark and objectionable has to be seen as material for a full experience of quintessential human life, as well as for the unfolding of our own individual natures—*Moore (1994, p. 186)

The dark side is hardly a novel concept (Pratt, 1994). Many observers of the human condition have drawn attention to the more suboptimal (Coupland, Wiemann, & Giles, 1991), asynchronous (Mortensen, 1997), morally ambiguous (Sabini & Silver, 1982), inept (Phillips, 1991), challenging (Duck & Wood, 1995), absurd (Lyman & Scott, 1970), troublesome (Levitt, Silver, & Franco, 1996), stigmatized (Goffman, 1963), perverted (Peak, 1996), relationally exploitative (Fillion, 1996; Goldberg, 1993), destructive (Fromm, 1973), hateful (Berke, 1988), punishing (Ferraro & Johnson, 1983; Long & McNamara, 1989; Rosen, 1996), criminal (Katz, 1988), and intrinsically darker sides of our behavior (Adams, 1977) and nature (Anders, 1994; Harper, 1968; Watson, 1995). What has often been missing in the social sciences, taken broadly, is the examination of the dark side as not just a Gordian knot of paradoxes, but also an integrative theoretical metaphor. A more complete understanding and appreciation of the dark side of human action requires an examination of certain propositions about the nature of this darkness (i.e., what this darkness is, and who or what we are, rather than what it, or we, ought to be). We believe that the dark side metaphor implies and means many things for social science.

> *There are many darknesses. There is the darkness of creative solitude and revery. There is the darkness of loving adoration and satisfying supplication and thanksgiving, existential and mystical, human and divine. There is the darkness of tragic suffering and watching, the sudden end of life and hope and virtue. There is the darkness of premonition of evil, depression, and then demoralization. There is the loss of love and the certainty of death*—Harper (1968, p. 7)

There are indeed many darknesses. First among the many shades of darkness is perhaps the most obvious. The dark side is concerned with the dysfunctional, distorted, distressing, and destructive aspects of human action. Charny (1996) and Baumeister (1997) described such features as forms of evil. These forms of evil are so characterized because they systematically diminish one's own (or another's) ability to function.

Second, the dark side is concerned with deviance, betrayal, transgression, and violation. Behavior that is awkward, rude, and disruptive can annoy, and behavior that boldly transgresses can disintegrate. Enculturation designs a preference for continuity and comfort. Activities that run counter to the normative, the taken for granted, the expected, and the preferred represent pursuits that strike at the core of the dialectic between autonomy and communal consciousness. One person's criminality can be another person's cry for freedom. Violation of norms and preferences is often a source of darkness.

Third, the dark side is concerned with exploitation of the innocent. Excessive extraction of valued or valuable resources, manipulation of the ignorant, cruelty toward the helpless, and constraint of basic freedoms reflect many of the fundamental egocentrisms of social life, and the difficulties of promoting collective welfare in a cultural climate of individualism. Harming those who have little power to protect themselves from harm is another source of darkness.

Fourth, the dark side is concerned with the unfulfilled, unpotentiated, underestimated, and unappreciated in human endeavors. The loves lost and the loves never found, the things we should have said, the paths we could have taken, the regrets and resulting self-recriminations all describe worlds we wish we had created and are painfully aware of having (just) missed. Eden was in our grasp and darkness is now a constant shadow on a world ensnared by a serpent.

Fifth, the dark side is concerned with the unattractive, unwanted, distasteful, and repulsive. Those people deemed unattractive are often normatively shunned, alienated, and isolated. Such symbolic imprisonment can serve to bind group identity, but it can also create a type of hell for those individuals disavowed by the collective.

Sixth, the dark side is concerned with objectification. The treatment of people's basic humanity as if inhuman, diminishing a person's personhood, and categorically reducing an individual to the status of thing are all ways of deanimating humans. Animals we may be, but our capacity for symbolism, creativity, humor, self-reflection, conceptualization, and moral perspective provide us with potential far beyond the level of the inanimate. One need not presume a spirit to be spiritual, but one must be more than a mere object to discover anything worthwhile beyond the objective.

Finally, the dark side is concerned with the paradoxical, dialectical, dualistic, and mystifying aspects of life. Things are seldom entirely what they seem—and when they are, we often refuse to accept them as such, often creating another level of paradox. Excavations of paradox, dilemma and dialectic reveal the complexities of our symbolicity and our seemingly limitless capacity for folly, error, conflict, capriciousness, and entanglement.

As far as we can discern, the sole purpose of human existence is to kindle a light in the darkness of mere being—Carl Jung *(Memories, Dreams, Reflections,* 1963, as cited in Prott, 1994, p. 260)

These seven "deadly sins" of darkness are probably neither comprehensive nor mutually exclusive. They do, we hope, begin to enlighten some of the topography of the dark side. However, being able to see the terrain still does not necessarily reveal much in the ways in which the terrain should best be traversed. Here, we recommend that people who journey to the dark side keep two suggestions in mind. First, excursions into the dark side are often attempts to understand those domains of human activity that are still unexplored, lying in the shadows, and waiting for the enlightenment of scholarly investigation. Second, investigations of the dark side should be about the virtuous, as well as the venal, vexing, and venomous aspects of human nature. Indeed, the dark side is about the ironies involved in discovering that what is presumed to be evil often has moral and functional justification; likewise, what is presumed to be satisfying, legitimate, and righteous often is reprehensible and prone to abuse and destructiveness.

In maps from antiquity, the edge of the enlightened, known universe is often noted by some foreboding to the effect that "beyond here, there be dragons." A study of the dark side is a boundary-spanning endeavor that must ignore the imaginary dangers of disciplinary and moral edges, requiring instead that scholars intrepidly sail beyond the comforts of their own disciplinary maps and ideological homelands to discover the new domains that lie beyond ordinary and normative pursuits.

It is in Morality as it is in Nature, there is nothing so perfectly Good in Creatures that it cannot be hurtful to any one of the Society, nor any thing so entirely Evil, but it may prove beneficial to some part or other of the Creation: So that things are only Good and Evil in reference to something else, and according to the Light and Position they are placed in—Bernard Mandeville (1732, p. 367)

The study of the dark side often ends up blurring the distinction between good and evil or the bright and the dark of the human condition. There are those who find such endeavors to lack moral perspective and therefore, intellectual gravity (e.g., Rawlins, 1997). The argument is twofold. First, the juxtaposition of investigating topics such as gossip and embarrassment next to rape, violence, and deadly activities (e.g., unsafe sex) trivializes the notion of darkness in general, and the seriousness of the darker topics therein. Second, if all darkness has a silver lining and if this silver lining is viewed solely in the language of functionalism, then we lose our moral bearings and perpetuate a science without an ethical voice. We believe such a critique entirely misses the point.

We do not apologize for what is often a functionalist rhetoric of science. We could have pursued the construction of an ideological and critical architectonic in which to judge the human praxis examined in this and our previous text. However, it is obvious that the functionality of behavior must be at the root of any ethical system, unless we buy into the ontological philosophies that have wreaked such ideological repression and inevitably reflect ethnocentric concepts of right and wrong. Reductionistic moral maxims and universals have wonderful idealistic rings of assent, but their operationalizations in the variegations of human activity become far more problematic and often do not lend themselves to simplistic assessment of implications. The study of the dark side is, in part, a recognition of this moral complexity and ambivalence and constantly cautions us against advancing our ethical forays in the dark.

Second, the very issue of the moral implicature of human behavior can only be questioned competently when people are aware of the nature of the dark side (e.g., Makau, 1991). To the extent that a polyannish rhetoric has infected our textbooks, studies, and teachings, we are hardly able to escape our prevailing ideologies to occupy a vantage point from which moral issues are examined (Burgoon, 1995; Lannamann, 1991; Parks, 1982, 1995). Social behavior is multifunctional, and moral judgments of such behavior are conceptually and empirically independent of its functioning (Wojciszke, 1994). Therefore, only by delving into the dark side of human behavior and discovering its functions are we likely to develop an informed sense of the possible moral issues implicit and explicit in social action.

Furthermore, the notion that only aspects of humanity that threaten life and limb deserve the moniker of *darkness* ignores the lifetimes of quiet struggle, dissatisfaction, and sense of frustration, anger, and despair that result from merely suboptimal forms of human endeavor in our significant (and even mundane) relationships with others. For example, Marshall's (1994) finding that psychological abuse tends to be more predictive of trauma than of physical abuse does not morally excuse physical abuse. Yet, enormous efforts of public policy, expenditures of social resources, and an almost endless number of psychological interventions effectively ignored the dynamics of psychological abuse under the overly simplistic ethical assumption that physical abuse is the most significant problem. Any critique of a functionalist examination of the dark side (on the grounds that it trivializes the true dark side) creates an overly dichotomous separation of dark and light that we reject. A primary rationale for our excursions into the dark side is to discover that the boundaries between light and dark are amorphous and are seldom as distinct as commonly presumed by our sciences and ethical commentaries.

We believe there are moral issues involved in the study of the dark side and that such investigations raise moral questions—both about the phenomena studied and the process of investigation itself. However, we also believe such moral debates are best engaged when informed by sound functionalist scholarship. For example, research that investigates the potential positive functions of child abuse (McMillen et al., 1995) raises obvious moral issues (e.g., Does conducting such research provide potential legitimization of the act it is studying? Does the suggestion of positive functions trivialize or minimize efforts to eradicate such tragic actions or increase societal tolerance for the act of child abuse itself? Does asking the question imply an overly paternalistic, functionalist, and insensitive scientific ideology?). However, if such investigation uncovers characteristic differences between victims who do and do not reveal resilience and self-actualization despite their tragedy, then modes of intervention, and perhaps prevention, are much better informed and vast realms of human suffering are eventually eradicated. Moral censure of such lines of investigations thereby runs the risk of running afoul of its own best intentions. Moral debate without a functionalist science to inform the issues of the debate risks reducing rhetoric to its mere status, with no lessons for the actual habitus and praxis of human pursuits. In essence, science without ideology, if such can be envisioned, lacks a moral compass; yet, morality without science is dangerously disconnected from the empirical world. Furthermore, positing such dichotomies itself unnecessarily exaggerates the schism between principle and practice at a time when common ground is needed most (Parks, 1995).

Darkness is very close by, at all times. We learn the ambiguity of darkness. There is a cold dark, full of fear and loneliness, and a warm dark for embracing and acceptance. ... There is "the dark side of the earth" and "the theoretic bright one." *... Darkness has its advantages*—Harper (1968, p. 4, 5)

In conclusion, there is a sense of seduction regarding the forbidden, the deviant, and the destructive (Goldberg, 1993; Katz, 1988). There is fascination in the human psyche with those things that nature, nation, and relationships have forbidden or made taboo. This collection of essays continues the journey begun by many others through time and the journey we began in earnest in our earlier collection. The current selection of topics is intended to be neither comprehensive nor fully representative of the dark side of close relationships—indeed, we continue to search the shadows for the next venture into the dark side. Perhaps paradoxically, we hope that many more dark journeys still await us.

All nature is but art unknown to thee;
All chance, direction which thou canst not see;
All discord, harmony not understood;
All partial evil, universal good.

—Pope (1733, p. 249)

REFERENCES

Adams, R. M. (1977). *Bad mouth: Fugitive papers on the dark side.* Berkeley: University of California Press.

Allan, K., & Burridge, K. (1991). *Euphemism and dysphemism: Language used as shield and weapon.* New York: Oxford University Press.

Altman, I. (1993). Challenges and opportunities of a transactional world view: Case study of contemporary Mormon polygynous families. *American Journal of Community Psychology, 21*, 135–163.

Anders, T. (1994). *The evolution of evil.* Chicago: Open Court.

Averill, J. R. (1993). Illusions of anger. In R. B. Felson & J. T. Tedeschi (Eds.), *Aggression and violence: Social interactionist perspectives* (pp. 171–193). Washington, DC: American Psychological Association.

Barnes, J. A. (1994). *A pack of lies: Towards a sociology of lying.* Cambridge, England: Cambridge University Press.

Batsche, G. M., & Knoff, H. M. (1994). Bullies and their victims: Understanding a pervasive problem in the schools. *School Psychology Review, 23*, 165–174.

Baumeister, R. F. (1997). *Evil: Inside human violence and cruelty.* New York: W. H. Freeman.

Baumeister, R. F., Smart, L., & Boden, J. M. (1996). Relation of threatened egotism to violence and aggression: The dark side of high self-esteem. *Psychological Review, 103*, 5–33.

Bavelas, J. B., Black, A., Chovil, N., & Mullett, J. (1990). *Equivocal communication.* Newbury Park, CA: Sage.

Becker, E. (1968). *The structure of evil.* New York: George Braziller.

Bergmann, J. R. (1993). *Discreet indiscretions: The social organization of gossip* (J. Bednarz, Jr., Trans.). New York: Aldine De Gruyter.

Berke, J. H. (1988). *The tyranny of malice: Exploring the dark side of culture*. New York: Summit Books.

Bernstein, J. Y., & Watson, M. W. (1997). Children who are targets of bullying: A victim pattern. *Journal of Interpersonal Violence, 12*, 483–498.

Blount, F. (1982). *The subversive family: An alternative history of love and marriage*. London: Jonathan Cape.

Bochner, A. P. (1982). On the efficacy of openness. In M. Burgoon (Ed.), *Communication yearbook 5* (pp. 109–124). New Brunswick, NJ: Transaction/International Communication Association.

Burgoon, M. (1995). A kinder, gentler discipline: Feeling good about being mediocre. In B.R. Burleson (Ed.), *Communication yearbook 18* (pp. 480–497). Thousand Oaks, CA: Sage.

Canary, D. J., Spitzberg, B. H., & Semic, B. A. (1998). The experience and expression of anger in interpersonal settings. In P. A. Andersen & L. K. Guerrero (Eds.), *Handbook of communication and emotion* (pp. 189–213). San Diego, CA: Academic Press.

Cerullo, K. A. (1988). What's wrong with this picture? Enhancing communication through distortion. *Communication Research, 15*, 93–101.

Chancer, L. S. (1992). *Sadomasochism in everyday life: The dynamics of power and powerlessness*. New Brunswick, NJ: Rutgers University Press.

Charny, I. W. (1996). Evil in human personality: Disorders of doing harm to others in family relationships. In F.W. Kaslow (Ed.), *Handbook of relational diagnosis and dysfunctional family patterns* (pp. 477–495). New York: Wiley.

Conger, J. A. (1990). The dark side of leadership. *Organizational Dynamics, 19*, 44–55.

Connell, A., & Farrington, D. P. (1996). Bullying among incarcerated young offenders: Developing an interview schedule and some preliminary results. *Journal of Adolescence, 19*, 75–93.

Coupland, N., Wiemann, J. M., & Giles, H. (1991). Talk as "problem" and communication as "miscommunication": An integrative analysis. *"Miscommunication" and problematic talk* (pp. 1–17). Newbury Park: Sage.

Crant, J. M. (1996). Doing more harm than good: When is impression management likely to evoke a negative response? *Journal of Applied Social Psychology, 26*, 1454–1471.

Cupach, W. R., & Spitzberg, B. H. (Eds.). (1994). *The dark side of interpersonal communication*. Hillsdale, NJ: Lawrence Erlbaum Associates.

DePaulo, B. M., Kashy, D. A., Kirkendol, S. E., Wyer, M. M., & Epstein, J. A. (1996). Lying in everyday life. *Journal of Personality and Social Psychology, 70*, 979–995.

Duck, S. (1994). Stratagems, spoils, and a serpent's tooth: On the delights and dilemmas of personal relationships. In W.R. Cupach & B.H. Spitzberg (Eds.), *The dark side of interpersonal communication* (pp. 3–24). Hillsdale, NJ: Lawrence Erlbaum Associates.

Duck, S., & Wood, J. T. (1995). For better, for worse, for richer, for poorer: The rough and the smooth of relationships. In S. Duck & J. T. Wood (Eds.), *Confronting relationship challenges* (pp. 1–21). Thousand Oaks, CA: Sage.

Dundes, A. (1987). *Cracking jokes: Studies of sick humor cycles and stereotypes*. Berkeley, CA: Ten Speed Press.

Emmons, R. A. (1984). Factor analysis and construct validity of the narcissistic personality inventory. *Journal of Personality Assessment, 48*, 291–300.

Ewart, C. K., Taylor, C. B., Kraemer, H. C. & Agras, W. S. (1991). High blood pressure and marital discord: Not being nasty matters more than being nice. *Health Psychology, 10*, 155–163.

Fehr, B. (1996). *Friendship processes*. Thousand Oaks, CA: Sage.

Ferraro, K. J., & Johnson, J. M. (1983). How women experience battering: The process of victimization. *Social Problems*, 30, 325–339.

Festinger, L., Riecken, H. W., & Schachter, S. (1956). *When prophecy fails*. Minneapolis: University of Minnesota Press.

Fillion, K. (1996). *Lip service: The truth about women's darker side in love, sex, and friendship*. New York: HarperCollins.

Finkelhor, D., Gelles, R. J., Hotaling, G. T., & Straus, M. A. (Eds.). (1983). *The dark side of families: Current family violence research*. Newbury Park, CA: Sage.

Fitness, J., & Fletcher, G. J. O. (1993). Love, hate, anger, and jealousy in close relationships: A prototype and cognitive appraisal analysis. *Journal of Personality and Social Psychology, 65*, 942–958.

Fox, S. A., & Giles, H. (1996). Interability communication: Evaluating patronizing encounters. *Journal of Language and Social Psychology, 15,* 265–290.

Fromm, E. (1973). *The anatomy of human destructiveness.* New York: Holt, Rinehart, & Winston.

Galanter, M. (1989). *Cults: Faith, healing, and coercion.* New York: Oxford University Press.

Gemen, J. (1997). Dangerous liaisons: On the systematic self-production of codependent identities. *Journal of Applied Communication Research, 25,* 132–149.

Gilmore, D. D. (1987). *Aggression and community: Paradoxes of Andalusian culture.* New Haven, CT: Yale University Press.

Goffman, E. (1963). *Stigma: Notes on the management of spoiled identity.* Englewood Cliffs, NJ: Prentice-Hall.

Goldberg, J. G. (1993). *The dark side of love: The positive role of our negative feelings—anger, jealousy, and hate.* New York: Putnam.

Gustafson, S. B., & Ritzer, D. R. (1995). The dark side of normal: A psychopathy-linked pattern called aberrant self-promotion. *European Journal of Personality, 9,* 147–183.

Harper, R. (1968). *The path of darkness.* Cleveland, OH: Case Western Reserve University Press.

Hirschman, D. O. (1981). *Essays in trespassing: Economics to politics and beyond.* Cambridge: Cambridge University Press.

Huston, M., & Schwartz, P. (1995). The relationships of lesbians and of gay men. In J.T. Wood & S. Duck (Eds.), *Under-studied relationships: Off the beaten track* (pp. 89–121). Thousand Oaks, CA: Sage.

Janeway, E. (1987). *Improper behavior.* New York: Morrow.

Jenkins, R. (1994). *Subversive laughter: The liberating power of comedy.* New York: The Free Press.

Kasson, J. F. (1990). *Rudeness and civility: Manners in nineteenth-century urban America.* New York: Hill and Wang.

Katz, J. (1988). *Seductions of crime: Moral and sensual attractions in doing evil.* New York: Basic Books.

Keiser, T. W., & Keiser, J. L. (1987). *The anatomy of illusion: Religious cults and destructive persuasion.* Springfield, IL: Thomas.

Keough, W. (1990). *Punchlines: The violence of American humor.* New York: Paragon House.

Kursh, C. O. (1971). The benefits of poor communication. *Psychoanalytic Review, 58,* 189–208.

LaGaipa, J. J. (1990). The negative effects of informal support systems. In S. Duck (Ed.), *Personal relationships and social support* (pp. 122–139). Newbury Park, CA: Sage.

Landman, J. (1993). *Regret: The persistence of the possible.* New York: Oxford University Press.

Lannamann, J. W. (1991). Interpersonal communication research as ideological practice. *Communication Theory, 3,* 179–203.

Levitt, M. J., Silver, M. E., & Franco, N. (1996). Troublesome relationships: A part of human experience. *Journal of Social and Personal Relationships, 13,* 523–536.

Long, G. M., & McNamara, J. R. (1989). Paradoxical punishment as it relates to the battered woman syndrome. *Behavior Modification, 13,* 192–205.

Lyman, S. M., & Scott, M. B. (1970). *A sociology of the absurd.* New York: Meredith Corporation.

Makau, J. M. (1991). The principles of fidelity and veracity: Guidelines for ethical communication. In K. J. Greenberg (Ed.), *Conversations on communication ethics* (pp. 111–120). Norwood, NJ: Ablex.

Mandeville, B. (1732/1924). *The fable of the bees* (Part I, A search into the nature of society). London: Oxford University Press.

Marshall, L. L. (1994). Physical and psychological abuse. In W.R. Cupach & B.H. Spitzberg (Eds.), *The dark side of interpersonal communication* (pp. 281–312). Hillsdale, NJ: Lawrence Erlbaum Associates.

McMillen, C., Zuravin, S., & Rideout, G. (1995). Perceived benefit from child sexual abuse. *Journal of Consulting and Clinical Psychology, 63,* 1037–1043.

Miller, R. S. (1996). *Embarrassment: Poise and peril in everyday life.* New York: Guilford.

Miller, W. I. (1993). *Humiliation, and other essays on honor, social discomfort, and violence.* Ithaca, NY: Cornell University Press.

Moltz, D. (1992). Abuse and violence: The dark side of the family–An introduction. *Journal of Marital and Family Therapy, 18,* 223.

Moore, T. (1994). *Dark eros: The imagination of sadism* (2nd ed.). Woodstock, CT: Spring Publications.

Mortensen, C. D. (1997). *Miscommunication.* Thousand Oaks, CA: Sage.

Nyberg, D. (1993). *The varnished truth: Truth telling and deceiving in ordinary life.* Chicago: University of Chicago Press.

Palazzoli, M.S., Boscolo, L., Cecchin, G., & Prata, G. (1978). *Paradox and counterparadox: A new model in the therapy of the family in schizophrenic transaction.* New York: Aronson.

Parks, M. (1982). Ideology in interpersonal communication: Off the couch and into the world. In M. Burgoon (Ed.), *Communication yearbook 5* (pp. 79–108). New Brunswick, NJ: Transaction.

Parks, M. R. (1995). Ideology in interpersonal communication: Beyond the couches, talk shows, and bunkers. In B. R. Burleson (Ed.), *Communication yearbook/18* (pp. 480–497). Thousand Oaks, CA: Sage.

Payne, D. (1989). *Coping with failure: The therapeutic uses of rhetoric.* Columbia: University of South Carolina Press.

Peak, K. J. (1996). "Things fearful to name" An overview of sex crimes and perversions. *Journal of Contemporary Criminal Justice, 12,* 204–214.

Phillips, G. M. (1991). *Communication incompetencies: A theory of training oral performance behavior.* Carbondale: Southern Illinois University Press.

Pines, A., & Aronson, E. (1983). Antecedents, correlates, and consequences of sexual jealousy. *Journal of Personality, 51,* 108–136.

Poster, M. (1978). *Critical theory of the family.* New York: Seabury.

Pratt, A. R. (1994). *The dark side: Thoughts on the futility of life from the ancient Greeks to the present.* New York: Carol Publishing Group.

Putney, M. J. (1992). Welcome to the dark side. In J. A. Krantz (Ed.), *Dangerous men and adventurous women* (pp. 99–105). Philadelphia: University of Pennsylvania.

Rawlins, W. K. (1992). *Friendship matters: Communication, dialectics, and the life course.* New York: Aldine De Gruyter.

Rawlins, W. K. (1997). Review: *The dark side of interpersonal communication. Communication Theory, 7,* 89–93.

Ray, E. B. (1993). When the links become chains: Considering dysfunctions of supportive communication in the workplace. *Communication Monographs, 60,* 106–111.

Rodriquez, N., & Ryave, A. (1990). Telling lies in everyday life: Motivational and organizational consequences of sequential preferences. *Qualitative Sociology, 13,* 195–210.

Rook, K. S. (1989). Strains in older adults' friendships. In R. G. Adams & R. Blieszner (Eds.), *Older adult friendship: Structure and process* (pp. 166–194). Newbury Park, CA: Sage.

Rook, K. S., & Pietromonaco, P. (1987). Close relationships: Ties that heal or ties that bind? In W. H. Jones & D. Perlman (Eds.), *Advances in personal relationships* (Vol. 1, pp. 1–35). Greenwich, CT: JAI.

Pope, A. (1733/1966). *Pope poetical works* (Essay on man, Epistle I). Oxford: Oxford University Press.

Rosen, K. (1996). The ties that bind women to violent premarital relationships: Processes of seduction and entrapment. In D. D. Cahn & S. A. Lloyd (Eds.), *Family violence from a communication perspective* (pp. 151–176). Thousand Oaks, CA: Sage.

Rue, L. (1994). *By the grace of guile: The role of deception in natural history and human affairs.* New York: Oxford University Press.

Sabini, J., & Silver, M. (1982). *Moralities of everyday life.* Oxford, England: Oxford University Press.

Schoeck, H. (1966). *Envy: A theory of social behavior* (M. Glenny & B. Ross, Trans.). New York: Harcout Brace.

Schotter, A. (1986). On the economic virtues of incompetency and dishonesty. In A. Diekmann & P. Mitter (Eds.), *Paradoxical effects of social behavior* (pp. 235–241). Heidelberg, Germany: Physica-Verlag Heidelberg Wein.

Schoenewolf, G. (1991). *The art of hating.* Northvale, NJ: Aronson.

Sedikides, C., Oliver, M. B., & Campbell, W. K. (1994). Perceived benefits and costs of romantic relationships for women and men: Implications for exchange theory. *Personal Relationships, 1,* 5–21.

Spitzberg, B. H. (1993). The dialectics of (in)competence. *Journal of Social and Personal Relationships, 10,* 137–158.

Spitzberg, B. H. (1994a). The dark side of (in)competence. In W. R. Cupach & B. H. Spitzberg (Eds.), *The dark side of interpersonal communication* (pp. 25–49). Hillsdale, NJ: Lawrence Erlbaum Associates.

Spitzberg, B. H. (1994b). The dark side metaphor. *International Society for the Study of Personal Relationships Bulletin, 11*, 8–9.

Spitzberg, B. H. (1997). Intimate violence. In W. R. Cupach & D. J. Canary (Eds.), *Competence in interpersonal conflict* (pp. 174–201). New York: McGraw-Hill.

Stearns, C. Z., & Stearns, P. N. (1986). *Anger: The struggle for emotional control in America's history.* Chicago: University of Chicago Press.

Stearns, P. N. (1989). *Jealousy: The evolution of an emotion in American history.* New York: New York University Press.

Tedeschi, J.T., & Felson, R.B. (1994). *Violence, aggression, and coercive actions.* Washington, DC: American Psychological Association.

Tedeschi, J. T., & Rosenfeld, P. (1980). Communication in bargaining and negotiation. In M.E. Roloff & G. R. Miller (Eds.), *Persuasion: New directions in theory and research* (pp. 225–248). Beverly Hills, CA: Sage.

Tooke, W., & Camire, L. (1991). Patterns of deception in intersexual and intrasexual mating strategies. *Ethology and Sociobiology, 12*, 345–364.

Tseëlon, E. (1992). What is beautiful is bad: Physical attractiveness as stigma. *Journal for the Theory of Social Behavior, 22*, 295–310.

Twitchell, J.B. (1989). *Preposterous violence: Fables of aggression in modern culture.* New York: Oxford University Press.

Volkan, V.D. (1988). *The need to have enemies and allies: From clinical practice to international relationships.* Northvale, NJ: Aronson.

Watson, L. (1995). *Dark nature: A natural history of evil.* New York: HarperCollins.

Watson, P. J., & Biderman, M. D. (1993). Narcissistic personality inventory factors, splitting, and self-consciousness. *Journal of Personality Assessment, 61*, 41–57.

Weeks, G. R., & L'Abate, L. (1982). *Paradoxical psychotherapy: Theory and practice with individuals, couples, and families.* New York: Brunner/Mazel.

Wiseman, J.P. (1986). Friendship: Bonds and binds in a voluntary relationship. *Journal of Social and Personal Relationships, 3*, 191–212.

Wojciszke, B. (1994). Multiple meanings of behavior: Construing actions in terms of competence or morality. *Journal of Personality and Social Psychology, 67*, 222–232.

I

SEDUCING

Fatal Attraction

Diane H. Felmlee
University of California, Davis

"... the traits that make him appealing can make him appalling in the flash of an eye."

—*New York Times* article describing
President Bill Clinton (Purdum, 1996, p. 36)

It begins with an attraction; two people are drawn inexorably to one another and an intimate relationship ensues. More often than not, however, it ends with disillusionment and heartbreak; the relationship does not work out. In such instances, a person's perceptions of a romantic partner shift from that of idealization and infatuation to irritation and resentment. In discussing the causes of a breakup, for example, divorced individuals often mention that their former partners were flawed, or lacking in desirable attributes (Goode, 1956; Spanier & Thompson, 1984). The implication is that they did not get what they wanted in a romantic partner. What happened? What went wrong? How is it that a once beloved partner is now viewed in such a negative light?

The answer proposed here suggests that for some, the process of attraction is less straightforward and more paradoxical than is usually assumed. The central focus of this chapter is that there are often close links between the qualities in a partner that initially allure us, and those that we later find problematic. Like a moth to a flame, individuals are drawn to the very aspects of another individual that they eventually will dislike. This process is termed *fatal attraction*, where *fatal* is used in the dictionary sense not of "deadly,"

3

but of "foretelling a sequence"; in this case, the initial attraction foretells a relationship sequence that ends in disenchantment (Felmlee, 1995).

The purpose of this chapter is to provide an in-depth investigation of the process of fatal attractions in intimate relationships. First, related research is discussed in the areas of interpersonal attraction and personal accounts of relationship breakups. Next, theoretical explanations for fatal attractions are described and previous research on the topic is summarized. New information and analyses on this relationship issue are then presented in which the dark and corresponding light sides to fatal attractions are examined. Finally, this chapter ends with a discussion of the implications of this pattern of romantic disenchantment for theories relevant to the initiation and dissolution of intimate relationships.

THE SUNNY SIDE OF ATTRACTION

The process by which one person is attracted to another receives considerable attention in literature. A number of factors were found to play a significant role in interpersonal attraction, including proximity (e.g., Festinger, 1951), physical attractiveness (e.g., Hatfield & Sprecher, 1986), similarity (e.g., Newcomb, 1961), and familiarity (e.g., Zajonc, 1968).

One factor that was the focus of extensive research, for example, is physical attractiveness. Many studies on this topic find support for the *matching hypothesis*, that is, that attractiveness is significantly correlated among members of romantic couples (e.g., for a meta-analysis, see Feingold, 1988). Other studies conclude that there is a social stereotype that links beauty and goodness, whereby physically attractive people are thought to possess a number of positive characteristics relating to social and/or intellectual competence (for meta-analyses, see Eagly, Ashmore, Makhijani, & Longo, 1991; Feingold, 1992; Jackson, Hunter, & Hodge, 1995). Finally, there are also gender differences in the salience of physical attractiveness. Mate selection studies find that physical attractiveness is more important in a prospective mate for men than it is for women, whereas women are more likely than men to prefer an ambitious, educated, intelligent, and/or dependable partner (e.g., Buss, 1994; Sprecher, Sulllivan & Hatfield, 1994; for a meta-analysis, see Feingold, 1990).

The role of similarity in attraction has also gained considerable attention. There is a link between attraction and similarity on a number of dimensions, such as demographic characteristics (e.g., Surra, 1991), attitudes (e.g., Byrne, 1971), personality traits, such as extreme gender role adherence (Smith, Byrne, & Fielding, 1995), cognitive traits, such as cognitive complexity (e.g., Neimeyer, 1984), and social–cognitive and communication skills (e.g., Burleson & Denton, 1992).

Nevertheless, research on the role of similarity in the attraction process is not without its critics. Rosenbaum (1986), for instance, argued that rather than similarity leading to attraction, dissimilarity in another is avoided (i.e., the *repulsion hypothesis*). Others maintained that the link between attitude similarity and attraction is greatly overestimated (Sunnafrank, 1991). Finally, scholars also note that the process of becoming attracted to another person occurs in an interactional context and that a dynamic communication perspective is needed to understand the intricacies of attraction (Bell, Tremblay, & Buerkel-Rothfuss, 1987; Burleson & Denton, 1992).

Stage models represent an additional line of development in the field of interpersonal attraction. These models delineate sequential steps in the selection of an intimate partner (e.g., Kerchoff & Davis, 1962; Lewis, 1973; Murstein, 1970), with most models maintaining that one of the steps is based on similarity. In the premarital dyadic formation framework, for instance, Lewis (1973) proposed that the attraction process goes through five stages, beginning with "perceiving similarities" and ending with "achieving dyadic crystallization." In an alternative model, Duck (1977) argued that attitudinal similarity predicts interpersonal attraction early on in acquaintance. In the later stages of a relationship, however, similarity in the context of interpersonal constructs (i.e., one's worldview) becomes more important than attitudinal similarity.

In general, the emphasis in the attraction literature is on the positive and appealing qualities of a potential mate or on the relatively smooth, sequential stages by which the attraction process progresses.

Relatively little work, however, attempts to examine potentially troublesome aspects of the attraction process. Two exceptions that relate most directly to fatal attractions are: the clinical literature, which introduces the concept of *disenchantment*, the process by which individuals in serious relationships become disenchanted with partner characteristics that they initially found appealing (Hatfield & Rapson, 1993) and a small study of married couples in which Whitehouse (1981) examined not only the positive aspects of partner characteristics, but also those that are negative. She found that the qualities reported as most annoying in a spouse were either an exaggeration, implication, or the opposite of those that were most appealing. Despite these types of exceptions, our knowledge of the dark side of attraction is comparatively meager (cf. chaps. 2 and 8, this volume; Freeman, 1985; Goldberg, 1993; Tseëlon, 1992).

THE CIRCUMSTANTIAL NATURE OF BREAKUPS

Another relevant area of inquiry examines the so-called "grave-dressing phase" of relationship dissolution (Duck, 1982), that is, the public story that each partner constructs about how and why a relationship ended (e.g., Harvey, Orbuch, & Weber, 1992). One of the most common reasons given for breakups in such accounts concerns some type of dissimilarity in the interpersonal characteristics of the dyad. Different interests, for example, was the most common reason given for the demise of a relationship in a recent study of couples (Sprecher, 1994). Communication problems, desire for autonomy or independence, and problematic characteristics of the partner (e.g., lack of supportiveness and lack of openness) are other typical rationales (e.g., Baxter, 1986; Cupach & Metts, 1986, Sprecher, 1994; Stephen, 1987). These personal accounts suggest that the ending of a romantic relationship is relatively opaque and unpredictable—differences surface between partners, communication problems arise, someone needs more autonomy or has undesirable traits. Such explanations make the romantic attraction process more intriguing and complex. After examining these breakup accounts, for example, the question arises: "Why is a person attracted in the first place to an individual who has different interests, is difficult to communicate with, or possesses undesirable qualities?" The answer proposed here is less circumstantial and implies that sometimes individuals are attracted to those potentially vexing aspects from the beginning.

THE DARK SIDE OF ATTRACTION

There are a number of ways in which the attraction process has a contradictory or problematic side, although such negative issues in close relationships generally receive relatively little regard in literature (Duck, 1994b). To begin, research on interpersonal attraction proposes that the norm of *homogamy*—in which like attracts like—is dominant. Nevertheless, countless individuals defy this norm and are attracted to those whose demographic characteristics differ from their own. Other societal norms are ignored in attractions to individuals who are already married or to those of the same gender. Given that society often deems such pairings as inappropriate, couples in these situations are likely to encounter difficulties in their dealings with the larger society, if not in their own interactions. Furthermore, attractions can have a seriously dark side to them, in the case of individuals who are attracted to those who would do them harm—either emotionally or physically—or to those whom they would harm (Marshall, 1994; Spitzberg, 1997).

Unlike these obvious dark sides of the initiation of romantic liaisons, the phenomenon of fatal attraction is more subtle. Yet, it may also be more common. In fatal attractions, individuals are drawn to partners because of certain pleasing qualities, but they later dislike aspects of those same qualities. Examples of such attractions include a woman who was interested in a man because he was "funny and fun," but disliked his "constant silliness," and a man who was attracted to his girlfriend's "refreshing innocence," yet found her "lack of maturity" problematic (Felmlee, 1995). In such cases, the characteristics that individuals disliked in their former companions were closely related to those that attracted them in the first place.

FATAL ATTRACTION: THE THEORY

Why does such a pattern of disillusionment with a partner occur? At least three different factors help explain the emergence of fatal attractions. First, a person's virtues and vices may be one and the same. Such a conclusion is implied in the clinical psychology literature, where we see discussions of the shadow side of personality (Goldberg, 1993; Jung, 1973; Moore, 1992). According to Goldberg (1993), in her discussion of the dark side of love: "The line that separates normal from pathological is, at times, frighteningly thin. Protectiveness can easily turn into possessiveness; concern into control; interest into obsession" (p. 8). Popular literature also reiterates such a message. A *New York Times* reporter summed up his assessment of President Clinton as: "His strengths and weaknesses not only spring from the same source, but could also not exist without one another. In a real sense, his strengths are his weaknesses, his enthusiasms are his undoing and most of the traits that make him appealing can make him appalling in the flash of an eye," (Purdum, 1996, p. 36). If it is true that virtues and vices are inextricably linked, this means that when people are drawn to the strengths of another, they encounter that person's shadow side as well. Given such reasoning, it is not surprising, then, if people dislike the very qualities they once found alluring in a partner.

A second explanation for fatal attractions operates at the dyadic, rather than the individual, level. This explanation focuses on the fact that intimate couples develop their own interactive system that evolves over time (Felmlee & Greenberg, 1996) and that such a system can facilitate the development of fatal attractions. Dialectical theorists, for example, argue that individuals in close relationships confront ongoing tensions between pairs of contradictory forces, such as those of autonomy and connection, novelty and predictability, and closedness and openness (e.g., Altman, Vinsel, & Brown, 1981; Baxter & Montgomery, 1996). According to such perspectives, a couple's experience pulls from both poles of forces simultaneously; that is, they feel the need for both autonomy and connection, novelty and predictability, as well as closedness and openness in their relationships. One reason that fatal attractions occur, therefore, is that individuals choose a partner on the basis of qualities that exemplify one pole of a dialectical force (e.g., novelty), but then they find that their relationship is lacking in the opposing pole (e.g., predictability).

Finally, the concept of fatal attraction is also informed by relationship theories that focus on the construction of meaning. Duck (1994a), for example, maintained that giving meaning to one another's behavior is one of the central purposes of personal relationships and this task constantly evolves and is never completely finished. From this perspective, a fatal attraction is seen as a shift over time in the meaning of a partner's characteristic, a shift that represents only one moment of what is, in fact, a fluid, ongoing transformation.

The theoretical arguments regarding the shadow side of personality, opposing relationship tensions, and the plasticity of meaning help explain why fatal attractions occur; that is, they provide an explanation as to why someone would reject the characteristics that initially attracted them to a romantic companion. Nevertheless, these arguments do not address questions concerning the over-time psychological process involved in such an attraction. Why aren't the negative dimensions of the positive qualities of a partner rejected immediately? How does a fatal attraction unfold over time?

FATAL ATTRACTION: THE PROCESS

There are several possible scenarios by which the type of disenchantment involved in a fatal attraction could occur. These scenarios are labeled as follows: time will tell, sour grapes, rose-colored glasses, people pleasing, and familiarity breeds contempt.

Time Will Tell. One possible fatal attraction process is that individuals are initially drawn to certain aspects of another person, but the individual does not reveal the negative sides of those qualities until some amount of time has passed in a relationship. This happens if people try to put their "best face" forward and attempt to hide or alter the less attractive elements of their personality at the start of a romantic liaison, but then are unable to maintain this facade over time.

Sour Grapes. A second possibility is that individuals attempt to reduce the cognitive dissonance (Festinger, 1957) generated by the demise of a once close, intimate relationship by denigrating their former partner's character. Of course, they can denigrate an ex-partner in many ways that would not be defined as fatal attractions. Nevertheless, it may be cognitively easier to recast a former partner's attractive qualities in a negative light (i.e., a fatal attraction) than it would be to claim that a partner never possessed those qualities at all or to maintain that a partner had weaknesses that were completely unrelated to his or her strengths.

Rose-Colored Glasses.   A third possible scenario is that individuals are romantically drawn to the strengths of another person and they are aware of the associated weaknesses from the very beginning, but choose to ignore or downplay these weaknesses. When infatuation fades, however, it becomes difficult to ignore the other person's weaknesses and to overlook related relationship tensions, and thus, a fatal attraction becomes evident. Certain vices are probably harder to disregard than others (e.g., those that are different from one's own and those that are extreme) and so, disenchantment with an intimate companion is especially likely in such cases.

People Pleasing.   Another possible explanation for fatal attractions is that people in a relationship actually change and they may alter in ways that cause their own attractive trait to turn into a liability. Suppose, for instance, that individuals unwittingly or intentionally reinforce the appealing qualities and actions of a partner by complimenting and giving attention to these qualities. Their partner then attempts to intensify or amplify these characteristics and related behaviors. Someone aware that his romantic companion likes humor, for example, then tells so many jokes and acts so funny, that he appears silly. Another may exude arrogance and a "know-it-all" attitude when she attempts to further impress a boyfriend who originally found her intelligent and confident manner pleasing. (See chap. 6, this volume, on the paradoxical reinforcement involved in codependent relationships.)

Familiarity Breeds Contempt.   A final possibility is that there is a saturation effect of partner attributes over time, and that a partner's endearing qualities can get old and become annoying. Certain relationship stage models (e.g., Huston, McHale, & Crouter, 1986), as well as theories of emotion (Berscheid, 1983), suggest that either arousal potential diminishes over time for routine or familiar activities or the things that were once rewarding can lose their reinforcement value over time.

The various theoretical arguments discussed thus far help explain why fatal attractions might occur and what might transpire in the over-time process of such attractions. Yet, how prevalent is this particular type of disillusionment? Do fatal attractions occur in a substantial number of couples? To answer these questions, we turn to previous empirical work on romantic relationships.

EXAMINING FATAL ATTRACTIONS

Research Design

A sample of 301 individuals (200 females and 101 males), who were attending one of three lower-division courses in a West Coast university, provided information on a past romantic relationship. Six respondents reported on homosexual relationships. The ethnic composition of students in the department from which the data were collected was relatively diverse, with Caucasians representing less than one half of the population: 43% Caucasians/Whites, 23% Asian Americans, 20% Mexican Americans/Latinos, 10% African Americans/Blacks, and 4% other ethnicities.

Participants were given a questionnaire in which they were asked to think about the most recent, serious romantic relationship they had that ended. Next, they were asked to respond to a series of open-ended questions, two of which were used to determine whether a fatal attraction occurred: "Describe the specific qualities that *first attracted* you to that individual" and "In retrospect, what were the qualities about that individual that you found *least attractive?*" Responses to these two open-ended questions were placed by coders into general categories of "liked" and "disliked" partner qualities.

Previous Results

Previous research (Felmlee, 1995) found that for both men and women, the four most common categories of characteristics mentioned as attractors, in order of those most frequent, were "Physical" (27.5%, e.g., attractive, eyes, and sexy), "Fun" (17.8%, e.g., fun, and funny), "Caring" (15.6%, e.g., caring, nice, and attentive), and "Competent" (11.7%, e.g., intelligent, confident, and powerful). Qualities that they did not like, on the other hand, were most frequent in the categories of "Selfish"

(28.3%, e.g., selfish, and insensitive), "Insecure" (22.5%, e.g., possessive, and insecure), "Undependable" (12.1%, e.g., dishonest, and immature), and "Physical" (10.7%, unattractive, and short), respectively.

Fatal attractions were defined as occurring when a quality reported by a respondent to be least attractive in a former partner was similar to (e.g., a synonym), or a negative interpretation of, a quality reported as being initially attracting. Arrogance, for example, was defined as a negative interpretation of the quality of confidence. Each of the cases was evaluated by the author and two independent coders, and an intercoder reliability of $\kappa=1.76$ was obtained for the 301 cases.

Fatal attractions occurred for 88 of the 301 individuals (29.2%). This means that at least one of the qualities listed as "least attractive" was directly related to one or more of those reported as initially attracting for a little less than one-third of the participants. Fatal attractions occurred among all categories of partner characteristics, but some types were more predominant than others. An intimate companion's qualities were significantly more likely to be fatal attractions when they were in the categories of "Fun" (e.g., funny, and fun), "Competent" (e.g., intelligent and confident), "Excitement" (e.g., exciting and spontaneous), "Easy-Going" (e.g., laid-back), or "Different" (e.g., different interests), than those not in these categories, according to univariate, chi-square tests. Characteristics in the "Similar" (e.g., common interests and similar values) and "Physical" (e.g., attractive and smile) categories, on the other hand, were significantly less likely to be later disliked (i.e., have fatal attractions).

Thus, previous research shows that fatal attractions occur in a substantial number of romantic relationships and that a variety of partner qualities are vulnerable to this type of disenchantment. However, we still do not know what shadow sides surface in these types of romantic pairings. Therefore, in the following section, a new analysis is undertaken in which the light sides and corresponding dark sides of fatal attractions are delineated.

THE LIGHT AND DARK SIDES OF FATAL ATTRACTIONS

There are numerous pairs of positive and negative components to close relationships that emerge from an examination of the data. Three of the most common are described in the following.

Fun to Foolish.   The most prevalent dark side to personality reflected in fatal attractions was foolishness, with fun as its corresponding light side. One attraction of this type involved a woman who was drawn to her partner because he was "extremely funny and spontaneous." In retrospect, however, she said that what she least liked about this man was that he "would embarrass me in public by throwing himself on the floor or exhibiting really STRANGE behavior." In another case, a man's "I don't care ... I'll have fun anyway" attitude attracted a woman, but she then disliked his "immaturity." Thus, the implication is that the downside of a fun and humorous relationship is its frivolity and lack of seriousness.

Strong to Domineering.   There were also a number of examples of fatal attractions in which domineering behavior was mentioned as a negative quality. One man, for instance, was drawn to his former girlfriend because of her "strong character and beliefs." He disliked, however, that she was "pushy, loud, domineering, and always took the initiative." In another relevant example, a woman was attracted to a "strong-willed" man whom she later judged to be "domineering and macho." In such cases, pushiness or domineering behavior, appears to be the vice associated with the virtue of character strength.

Spontaneous to Unpredictable.   A dark side of personality that emerged in fatal attractions to spontaneous partners was unpredictability or irresponsibility. In one such case, a woman disliked that her "spontaneous" ex-boyfriend was "flighty." In another instance, a man was of interest to a woman because he was "impulsive," but subsequently, she was bothered by his tendency to "blow at any moment."

Numerous additional positive and negative themes occur in this data set. Examples of some of these can be seen in the illustrations of fatal attractions listed in Table 1.1. Like the previous examples, these illustrations contain verbatim quotes from respondents regarding the qualities that initially attracted them to a partner and those they later disliked.

Taken together, the findings discussed yield evidence of a dark side to certain romantic attractions. They do not identify, nevertheless, the conditions under which fatal attractions are particularly probable. In the next section, factors that potentially influence the chances of this type of disenchanting encounter are discussed and the effects of these factors are investigated.

TABLE 1.1

Illustrations of the Light and Dark Sides of Fatal Attractions, Based on Direct Quotes Describing an Attracting Partner Quality and Its Corresponding Disliked Quality

Light Side	Dark Side
Nurturing	Smothering
Confident	Acted like a god
Offbeat personality	Too hippie
Intense interest in me	Jealous & possessive
Spontaneity, fun	Irresponsibility
Strong-willed, persistent	Domineering, persistent
Shy and timid	Insecure
Very unique	No common interest
She would have sex	She couldn't say no to sex
Relaxed	Constantly late
Older	Too mature
Successful and focused	Work commanded him
Flattering	Superficial
Sense of humor	Played too many jokes
Sweet and sensitive	Too nice

FACTORS AFFECTING FATAL ATTRACTIONS

Theoretical Arguments

Given the ironic and potentially frustrating nature of fatal attractions, it is important to understand the circumstances under which they are more, or less, likely. There are several factors thought to influence fatal attraction propensities, four of which are discussed as follows:

Similarity–Dissimilarity. One factor that affects the probability of a fatal attraction is whether the attraction is based on similarity or dissimilarity. One major determinant of interpersonal attraction is similarity (e.g., Newcomb, 1961), as discussed earlier. Similarity between partners can have a dark side, however, if it results in too much predictability in a relationship or too little excitement and challenge. Similarity, as a basis of attraction, is also problematic when it is debilitating to the individual or dysfunctional to the relationship. A relationship between two extreme introverts, for example, might suffer from insufficient open communication.

Nevertheless, similarity is likely to play a role in attraction because it is rewarding in a number of ways. Similarities with another person validate our own perspectives (Byrne & Clore, 1970) and encourage expectations that the other person will like us (Aronson & Worchel, 1966). Characteristics of a romantic companion that are similar to those of an individual, therefore, are apt to be positively regarded. In addition, similar characteristics are unlikely to be subject to subsequent negative reinterpretation because people are less harsh when examining the qualities of a partner that they also share. For these reasons, then, fatal attractions are expected to be relatively infrequent when an individual is attracted to qualities in another person that are similar to his or her own.

In some cases, dissimilarity in a potential mate is appealing because encountering differences can lead to an expanded sense of self (Aron & Aron, 1986) or because it fosters feelings of uniqueness or specialness (Snyder & Fromkin, 1980). Nevertheless, dissimilarity is a much less likely source of attraction than is similarity (Byrne, 1971). Dissimilarity is also associated with strong disliking (Byrne, 1971) and is a frequently cited rationale for divorces and breakups (Hill, Rubin, & Peplau, 1976; Spanier & Thompson, 1984).

Clearly intracouple dissimilarity is often problematic and there are a number of reasons. First, unlike similarity, differences challenge one's views of the world and they also raise fears that this dissimilar person to whom one is attracted will be rejecting. Second, differences between partners are troublesome because they lead to disagreements and conflict. Dissimilar communication skills, for example, make it difficult for members to resolve disagreements (Burleson & Denton, 1992). Finally, discrepancies between partners in demographic characteristics, personality, or attitudes, heighten resistance to the relationship from family and friends because couples are expected to be similar in a variety of sociodemographic characteristics (Kerchoff, 1974).

Because of the problems inherent in differences among a couple, qualities in a partner that are viewed as dissimilar are susceptible to disillusionment. A difference that is initially appealing is likely to wear thin over time. In fact, dissimilarities that are attractive at the start of a relationship can be particularly fatal because they are likely to be immediately noticed, suggesting that the size of the discrepancy is considerable. Considerable differences result in considerable disagreements, thereby facilitating the disenchantment process.

Extreme Traits. A second factor that is thought to influence the chances of disenchantment is the intensity or the extremity of an attractive quality of a partner. Virtues of a partner that are intense in nature are especially likely to have clearly associated vices. For example, an extremely confident person is more susceptible to arrogance than a person who is only moderately confident. Likewise, perhaps an individual who is unusually humble is more insecure than someone who is only somewhat humble. Furthermore, when an individual is attracted to qualities in a partner that are extreme, this indicates that one relationship dimension is being emphasized at the expense of another. The focus of a relationship is likely to be on autonomy, rather than on connection (e.g., when the basis of an attraction is extreme independence in a romantic companion). Such an intense focus on autonomy should produce a desire for more connectivity or interdependence, according to dialectical theorists. In other words, qualities in an intimate partner that are intense or extreme are particularly likely to have a downside and to be involved in fatal attractions.

Atypicality Gender Qualities.   Previous research considered the contention that atypical gender qualities are over represented in fatal attractions. Atypical gender qualities refer to personality characteristics that are unrepresentative of traditional gender stereotypes, such as gentleness or expressiveness in a man or confidence and assertiveness in a woman. Atypical gender characteristics, it was argued, are not widely supported in the general culture and thus, are especially disillusioning. Nevertheless, findings indicated that atypical gender partner characteristics are not overrepresented in fatal attractions and attractions to intimate companions with qualities that were gender typical (e.g., an aggressive man, or a caring woman), rather than atypical, could also end in disenchantment (Felmlee, in press, a).

Multiple Indicators of a Fatal Quality.   Certain individuals also have a tendency to report a series of attractive partner qualities that are later disliked (i.e., fatal), most of which are synonyms for, or variations of the same general quality, according to earlier work (Felmlee, in press, a) . For instance, one man listed numeroust physical traits of a woman (e.g., face, legs, hair, body, etc.) as the qualities that initially attracted him, but later disliked that his relationship was "too physical" and based only on "lust, not love." Reporting so many physical aspects of this woman as appealing suggests that he found her to be extremely physically attractive. Therefore, this tendency to describe multiple dimensions of the same general attracting characteristic (e.g., physical attractiveness) in a fatal attraction provides additional evidence for the argument that attractions based on qualities of a partner that are extreme are vulnerable to disillusionment. This particular case also shows that physical traits can become a source of fatal attractions.

New Research Agenda

A number of interesting questions remain unanswered in fatal attraction research. Here two are examined: the role of positive partner qualities that are physical in fatal attractions and how the responsibility for the breakup idea might influence such encounters.

Physical–Personality Qualities. Previous multivariate work on fatal attraction predictors used data on only nonphysical (i.e., personality) partner characteristics (Felmlee, in press, a). It is not known if the same influences affect the chances of a fatal attraction based on the physical aspects of a love object. Yet, the most common category of attractor in the data discussed here is physical—both for women and men—and physical fatal attractions do transpire, as was previously shown. It is important to determine whether the main factors of extremeness and dissimilarity, for instance, influence the likelihood of fatal attractions for all types of partner qualities—physical as well as personality. It is also of interest to examine whether traits that were once enticing in a loved one are less likely to be disliked (i.e., fatal) later if they are physical rather than nonphysical.

Theoretically, it is possible that certain physical features of an individual, such as general attractiveness, could result in fatal attractions. An example of such a fatal attraction would be an individual who is drawn to a partner's physical beauty, but who does not appreciate the time and money spent on make-up and clothing designed to highlight that beauty. Another example might be someone who finds the physique of a body builder appealing, but who resents the time that person spends in the gym.

On the other hand, physical attributes are less susceptible to reinterpretation over time than personality characteristics of a partner because most are probably more difficult to change. Specific physical virtues do not always have corresponding physical vices. For instance, having pretty eyes or nice hair does not have a clear downside that would be obvious to a partner; a person is unlikely to be judged as having eyes that are too pretty or hair that is too nice. This is not to say that more generally, beauty lacks a dark side. Physical attractiveness has negative as well as positive (e.g., vain or snobbish) connotations (Freeman, 1985), and it acts as a stigma by which the beautiful, especially women, are viewed as objects (Tseëlon, 1992). Nevertheless, these drawbacks are probably more salient to those who exhibit physical attractiveness than they are to those who admire it.

Whose Idea Was the Breakup? We know that termination of a relationship is unlikely to be mutual, that one member of a couple often desires a breakup more than the other, and that one peron is more likely to initiate the breakup (Vaughan, 1986). Whether an individual is the initiator of a breakup probably influences the likelihood of disenchantment, although this issue was never investigated.

Two differing scenarios concerning the role of responsibility for the breakup idea in fatal attractions can be described. First, suppose that an individual's partner is the one who initiated the idea of ending the relationship. That person may then justify being the victim of the breakup by impugning the instigator's virtues. A fatal attraction in such situations would be a case of "sour grapes." In one case from this data set, for example, a woman said that her boyfriend ended their relationship because, "He got back together with his previous girlfriend. I learned about it from mutual friends." She said that what originally attracted her, however, was that he had "an intense interest in me." In retrospect, what she did not like about him was that he was "jealous and possessive," as well as insincere and dishonest. The fact that her boyfriend ended the relationship may have caused this woman to reinterpret her boyfriend's initially positive trait of "intense interest" in her as the negative trait of jealousy.

Second, the individual himself or herself initiates the breakup. In this scenario, that person may have wanted to breakup precisely because he or she became aware of drawbacks to the other person's virtues. In fact, individuals who take responsibility for a breakup can be especially disillusioned with their partner's appealing traits, implying that these cases will become prominent in fatal attractions. In one such example, a man broke up with his girlfriend and said that what he liked least about her was her "lack of maturity." On the other hand, he reported that he was initially drawn to his former girlfriend because, "She had an innocence about her that was refreshing." This man's negative appraisal of his girlfriend's trait of innocence appeared to be one reason that he stopped seeing her.

The next section of this chapter addresses these previously unanswered issues in an examination of empirical data. An analysis of fatal attractions is conducted, using new information from physical and personality attractors taken from the data set described earlier in this chapter (Felmlee, 1995). This analysis determines whether the factors previously found to influence fatal personality attractions remain significant in analyses of attractions due to either personality or physical attributes. In this investigation, the role of an additional factor is also examined—responsibility for the breakup idea.

PREDICTORS OF FATAL ATTRACTIONS

A Multivariate Analysis

The determinants of fatal attractions are investigated in a multivariate, logistic regression analysis. The unit of analysis is the attracting quality listed by each respondent, and the dependent variable measures if the attracting quality is later disliked (i.e., a fatal attraction). The final sample consists of the 1,416 physical and nonphysical positive partner characteristics listed by the 301 study participants. Logistic regression analysis is used—rather than ordinary least squares—because the dependent variable is a skewed, dichotomous variable (fatal–not fatal). The independent variables include the following measures, of which the first five are intended to examine various theoretical issues and the last three are control variables.

Respondent's Breakup Idea.   This variable is included in order to examine the effect of initiation of the breakup on the likelihood of a fatal attraction. Respondents were asked the following open-ended question: "Whose idea was it to end the relationship?" Answers to this question were placed into five categories: *completely partner's* (1)—e.g., "hers," or "the other person's," 14.8%, *mostly partner's* (2)—e.g., "mostly hers/his," 4.9%, *mutual idea* (3)—e.g., "mutual" or "both of ours," 24.8%, *mostly respondent's* (4)—e.g., "mine, but we agreed," 9%, *completely respondent's* (5)—e.g., "mine," 46.5%.

Extreme Partner Quality.   This variable measures the degree to which an attracting quality of a partner was described in an extreme or intense manner. If an extreme adjective, such as "extremely," "unusually," or "incredible" was used, then this variable was given a value of 2 (12.6%). If a more moderate adjective was used, such as "very," "really," or "lots," then this variable received a value of 1 (10.9%). If no special modifiers were used to describe a partner's positive trait, then a value of 0 (76.5%) was given to this variable (i.e., *not extreme*). Two coders (one male and one female) read the verbatim descriptions of the attracting qualities and determined which of the three categories was appropriate, with an intercoder reliability of $\kappa = .79$.

Different Partner Quality.   This variable measures whether the attracting quality is in the category of *Different*. A quality of a partner is coded as *1* (*Different*) if the respondent used words such as "different" or "unique" when describing the characteristics that attracted him or her (1.1%); otherwise, it is coded 0 (98.9%).

Similar Partner Quality.   This variable measures whether the attracting quality is in the category of *Similar*. A quality of a partner is coded as *1* (*Similar*) if the respondent used phrases such as "similar interests" or "common values" in describing the characteristics that attracted her or him (5.2%); otherwise, it is coded 0 (94.8%).

Physical Partner Quality.   Attracting qualities that are physical traits or physical characteristics are coded 1 (27.5%); those that are nonphysical characteristics (i.e., personality traits) are coded 0 (72.5%). Two new coders (one male and one female) verified the validity of this category, *Physical*, as well as the validity of the other two categories of qualities, *Different*, and *Similar*, with an overall intercoder reliability of $\kappa = .82$.

Female Respondent.   This variable is coded 1 if the respondent is female (69.9%); it is coded 0 for males (30.1%).

Duration of Relationship.   This variable measures the total length of the relationship in months ($M = 9.5, SD = 18.9$).

Number of Qualities.   This variable is the total number of attracting qualities mentioned by the respondent ($M = 5.6, SD = 2.3$). It is possible that a person's propensity to experience a fatal attraction is directly related to the number of attracting qualities in a partner that an individual reports. Therefore, this variable is included to control statistically the tendency of respondents to be at a high risk of a fatal attraction simply because they list numerous positive partner qualities.

Results

Initiating the idea of a relationship breakup is positively and significantly associated with the likelihood of a fatal attraction, even when controlling for a number of other factors in the multivariate analysis, as shown in Table 1.2. Respondents who reported that the idea to end the relationship was theirs are approximately 1.8 times more likely than those who said the idea was the other person's to later dislike a quality that they were initially attracted to (i.e., a fatal attraction). Thus, those who initiate a breakup are almost twice as likely as those at the recipient end to have a fatal attraction.[1]

Another new finding is that physical traits are less likely to be fatal than

---

[1] The antilog coefficient for a one unit change in the variable Respondent's Breakup Idea is 1.15, which means that a change of one unit in Respondent's Idea multiplies the likelihood of a fatal attraction by 1.15. The antilog for a four unit change is 1.8; that is, a change from the value 1 (*completely partner's idea*) to the value 5 (*completely respondent's idea*) multiplies the rate of a fatal attraction is by 1.8.

TABLE 1.2

The Effects of Predictors of Fatal Attractions in a Logistic Regression Analysis of 1,410 Physical and Nonphysical Attracting Partner Qualities

Independent Variable	Beta Coefficient	Standard Error	Antilog Coefficient
Respondent's breakup idea	.14*	.07	1.15
Extreme partner quality.	.71***	.10	2.03
Different partner quality	1.43**	.55	4.17
Similar partner quality	-1.60*	.73	.20
Physical partner quality	-.94***	.26	.39
Female respondent	.49*	.22	1.64
Duration of relationship	-.01	.01	.99
Number of qualities	.01	.04	1.01
Constant	-3.14	.38	
Model Chi-Square	100.89***		

Note. $*p < .05$, $**p < .01$, $***p < .001$

personality characteristics, as can be seen in the negative, highly significant coefficient for the Physical variable. The size of the effect is also large. Fatal attractions are close to one-third less probable when the attracting quality in a partner is physical, rather than nonphysical.

Additional results show that the rate of a fatal attraction increases when individuals use extreme, rather than less extreme, adjectives to describe a partner's qualities and when respondents view these qualities as "different" or "unique." However, when the appealing characteristics of a companion are similar to those of the respondent, the likelihood of a fatal attraction decreases. These effects are all large in magnitude, with the chances of a fatal attraction being four times more likely when a quality appears to be extreme (as opposed to not extreme) or when it is in the category of *Different* rather than another category. However, when a partner's characteristic is *Similar*, the probability of a fatal attraction is only one fifth of what it would be otherwise. Therefore, whether a positive partner quality is extreme, different, or similar, has large effects on fatal attraction propensities.

Finally, although the effect size is not large, females are more likely than males to have fatal attractions, with a ratio of female to male attractions of this type of 1.64 to 1. In addition, respondents who mention many attracting qualities are not significantly more prone to fatal attractions than those listing fewer qualities.[2] Finally, regarding length of involvement, short relationships are not significantly more likely than longer ones to be fatal, although it should be noted that the range of relationship length is relatively limited in this sample.[3] With the possible exception of gender, then, control variables have little effect on the probability of a fatal attraction in these data.

DISCUSSION

The findings reported in this chapter help to clarify a picture of the phenomenon of fatal attraction. First, illustrations of individual cases show that there are light and dark sides to these attractions (e.g., nurturing vs. smothering). These results reinforce the possibility that one's virtues and vices emanate from a common source and that this shadow side to personality helps explain why fatal attractions might occur. In addition, these light and dark dimensions are reminiscent of some of the opposing relationship forces discussed by dialectical perspectives. The corresponding positive and negative qualities of spontaneity and unpredictability, for example, imply that tensions emerge in some fatal attractions between the dialectic forces of novelty and predictability. The possibility of new, unidentified dialectical tensions, such as those between relaxation and motivation (e.g., easygoing to lazy) also emerges in these data (Felmlee, in press, b).

A second set of results, based on the statistical analysis of predictors of fatal attractions, confirm the proposed theoretical arguments. Findings indicate that when individuals are attracted to qualities in another person that are extreme or different, they are especially prone to fatal attractions (as hypothesized). However, attractions to others because of similarities

---

[2]In order to control for the possibility of correlated errors within individuals, an analysis was conducted in which dummy variables were included in the model for each individual in the sample. Due to redundancies among independent variables, some of the variables in the model had to be dropped (e.g., number of fatal qualities, or breakup idea). The general substantive conclusions regarding the effects of the remaining variables in the model (e.g., *Similar, Different, Extreme*) remained the same as those reported in this chapter.

[3]The sample here contains relationships of moderate length at best, when compared with a 20-year marriage. Perhaps if longer relationships were included in the data, fatal attractions would be confined mostly to relatively short-lived relationships. On the other hand, if vices and virtues are indeed one and the same, then fatal attractions could occur in lengthy relationships as well as brief ones. In other words, one could dislike the downside of a partner's initially appealing virtues even after many years.

are much less likely to be fatal. These results replicate previous findings conducted on a more limited data set consisting only of personality-based attractions (Felmlee, 1996). According to the analyses reported herein, all types of attractions—physical as well as personality—have an increased chance of being fatal when the appealing physical or personality characteristics of the particular love object are viewed as being extreme or different.

Extreme partner qualities are particularly prone to disenchantment for a couple of reasons. First, extreme qualities are inherently more problematic than moderate qualities, as mentioned earlier. Even the trait of honesty, for example, might lead to blunt and untactful behavior when displayed indiscriminately. In other words, any virtue taken to excess has its limitations. Second, labeling a partner's quality as extreme means that the individual views it as different from his or her own qualities. When a woman describes her partner as extremely funny, for instance, she may see herself as being less humorous than he is. As previously discussed, differences can be intriguing in a partner, but they can also be a source of dyadic conflict. Finally, extreme partner qualities may signal an imbalance in dialectical relationship tensions. Extreme openness on the part of a partner, no matter how appealing, may imply that a partnership with that person is lacking in the opposite dialectical pole of closedness.

Initiation of the Breakup

This statistical analysis also addressed a previously uninvestigated determinant of relationship disillusionment: responsibility for the breakup idea. Fatal attractions are significantly more likely in cases in which respondents report that the breakup was their own idea rather than their partner's or a mutual idea. This is an important result because it suggests that fatal attractions are not simply instances in which scorned lovers recast their ex-partner's appealing characteristics in an unflattering light (e.g., the Sour Grapes hypothesis). Instead, fatal attractions are much more prevalent when individuals themselves are the initiators of a breakup.

Note that this does not mean that rejected lovers look favorably on their former partners, but simply that they do not express their dislike in terms of fatal attractions. For example, one man whose girlfriend went back to her previous boyfriend complained that she "lie[d], cheat[ed], and tried to deceive me." A woman whose partner broke up with her described him, in retrospect, as "selfish, temperamental, cynical, and not very sexually satisfying." The qualities that first attracted these two to their partners (e.g., physical attributes), however, were unrelated to those they disliked.

These negative evaluations of their former companions may be cognitive reinterpretations (i.e., sour grapes), but they are not reappraisals of originally appealing qualities.

It should also be pointed out that only a minority of respondents report that their partner was responsible for the breakup (19.9%). Perhaps a larger sample size is needed to find fatal attractions in such instances. Furthermore, if individuals who are at the receiving end of a breakup reframe past attractions as repulsions, this tendency might not show up for awhile. It takes time for break-up accounts to formulate and solidify, especially when the ending was unanticipated, and the timeframe used here was short. A study of accounts over an extended period of time following a breakup would be useful in determining the stages at which disenchantment emerges and to what extent these stages differ depending on if the individual was responsible for the relationship demise.

Attractions Based on Physical Attributes

In addition, the multivariate analyses reveal that physical attractions are less likely to be fatal than those based on personality characteristics. Part of the explanation for this finding is due to the fact that unlike personality characteristics, positive physical features often lack clear negative interpretations. One respondent, for example, said he was drawn to his girlfriend because, "She looked great in a bathing suit." In order for this case to be considered a fatal attraction, he had to interpret this quality negatively and to say that, in retrospect, "she looked too great in a bathing suit." Needless to say, he said nothing of the sort. Also, note that few words exist to describe an excessive amount of beauty. A person who is too nice is a wimp, one who is too assertive is pushy, one who is too laidback is lazy, and so forth, but what is someone who looks too good? A vain person? A beauty queen? There are several possible answers, but none are obvious, and this may be why fatal attractions are underrepresented in physical attractions. In addition, there were some physical attractions that were fatal, but these tended to be based on sexuality—something that has a clear negative cognitive reinterpretation, at least regarding females (i.e., slut).

This is not to say that attractions based only on the physical attributes of another are unproblematic. It was not uncommon, for example, for respondents involved in such relationships to complain that, in retrospect, they realized that their partner was lacking in "intellect" or in "personality." If the definitions used here were broader, these cases would be considered examples of fatal attractions as well. That is, in a certain sense the individuals in these romances got what they wanted—a beautiful partner—but nothing more. Thus, the corresponding dark side to being primarily drawn to the physical characteristics of a companion is that certain personality attributes in a partner (that are also salient to the individual, but that were ignored in the initial attraction) are absent.

Gender Differences

Another finding is that women are somewhat more likely than men to dislike a partner's quality that they once found attractive, that is, to have a fatal attraction. Part of the reason for this finding is a byproduct of the data collection process in that male participants were more apt than their female counterparts to use vague, general terms, such as "looks" and "personality," to describe the characteristics that attracted them to their partner. Nonspecific partner qualities, such as "personality," were uniformly coded as *nonfatal*, and thus, fewer men than women were at risk for being counted as experiencing a fatal attraction. This lack of precision in men's responses indicates less awareness on their part of the affection and disaffection processes inherent in their relationships or it means that they spend less time than do females in analyzing their relationships and in generating detailed breakup accounts.

The Over-Time Process

The findings in this chapter also speak to the over-time process of fatal attractions. Several possible hypotheses were outlined at the beginning of the chapter, including Time Will Tell (it takes time for a partner's liabilities to surface), Sour Grapes (a partner is evaluated negatively after a breakup), Rose-Colored Glasses (infatuation produces a positive assessment of a partner), People Pleasing (people change to please their partner), and Familiarity Breeds Contempt (traits lose their appeal with time). The findings presented here are used to evaluate these differing hypotheses.

First, if the Time-Will-Tell hypothesis is true, then we expect fatal attractions to be more probable as time progresses in a relationship and as the weaknesses of a partner begin to surface. Of course, the size of the interval that passes before imperfections in a loved one becomes evident varies from individual to individual and from characteristic to characteristic. Some partners are more adept than others at concealing their drawbacks; certain individuals also are quicker than some to recognize flaws in another, and certain qualities are more quick than others to manifest their duality. Nevertheless, it seems reasonable to assume that some amount of time is necessary before awareness occurs, and if this is the case, relationship duration should be associated with fatal attraction propensities in the aggregate. Yet, length of relationship is not significantly related to the likelihood of a fatal attraction, neither in a linear nor a curvilinear fashion. Short relationships are about ·as susceptible to this particular pattern of disillusionment as are medium-length and long relationships. Thus, these findings fail to provide support for the learning hypothesis (Time Will Tell).

Second, we expect the Sour Grapes hypothesis to be particularly applicable in cases in which someone is the unwilling victim of a breakup because cognitive dissonance is apt to be especially high when one is rejected by a desired partner. Nevertheless, fatal attractions were not more prevalent in relationships in which it was the other person's idea to breakup, according to the analyses reported herein. In fact, they were significantly less likely in these situations and more likely when individuals reported that the demise of the relationship was their own idea. It remains possible, of course, that some breakups, identified by the respondent as their idea were actually instigated by a partner and that fatal attractions in such cases were instances of sour grapes. Barring such misreports, however, these findings in general do not lend support to the Sour Grapes hypothesis.

If the Rose-Colored Glasses hypothesis is accurate, then we expect fatal attractions to be particularly frequent in cases in which individuals themselves initiate the ending of a relationship, rather than when they are at the receiving end of a breakup. Someone who terminates a romantic liason is likely to be uninfatuated and well aware of the downside of a partner's attractive characteristics, unlike one who is the breakup victim. Fatal attractions are significantly more likely when an individual reports having initiated the idea for a breakup rather than when the idea was mutual or when it was the other person's, thus supporting the Rose-Colored Glasses argument.

Other research also generates evidence for this third hypothesis. Experimental investigations reveal that those in a state of infatuation are able to correctly evaluate a potential partner, but this evaluation is more positive than that of those not infatuated (Gold, Ryckman, & Mosley, 1984; McClanahan, Gold, Lenney, Ryckman, & Kulberg, 1990). Similarly, Tennov (1979) found that a large majority of men and women were able to clearly identify the weaknesses of their partners while in a state of *limerence*, her term for infatuation. She argued that negative features of a love object are seen, but ignored, when experiencing limerence.

However, there is little information in this empirical work that can speak to the last two scenarios, People Pleasing and Familiarity Breeds Contempt. One cannot tell from the cross-sectional data presented here whether the former companions of these respondents modified their behavior over time, and thus, the People Pleasing argument receives neither confirmation nor disconfirmation on the basis of these analyses. One also cannot determine whether positive qualities of a partner lost their reinforcement value over time and therefore became irritating (i.e., Familiarity Breeds Contempt). Additional research is necessary to directly address these claims.

In sum, of all five possible explanations of the fatal attraction process, the one that receives some empirical support is the Rose-Colored Glasses argument. Yet, none of these hypothesis can be completely ruled out. Longitudinal studies are necessary to examine these various hypotheses more rigorously. Information on the positive and negative assessments of an intimate partner over time, for example, allows a more thorough examination of the question as to whether individuals are aware of a partner's shadow side from the very beginning and when, and if, they stop ignoring it.

IMPLICATIONS AND CONCLUSION

The findings discussed in this chapter have a number of important theoretical implications. First, they speak to the dark side of attraction. The process of interpersonal attraction is not always upbeat and straightforward, and people can have romantic inclinations toward others on the basis of characteristics they will later find repellant. This also suggests that stage theories of relationship development are irrelevant for some couples who are doomed from the very beginning because of a fatal partner selection process.

The results reported herein also inform the theoretical debate as to whether opposites attract (e.g., Winch, 1955). There are cases in which respondents report being attracted to a dissimilar, or different individual, but these instances are less common than those in which similarity is the basis of appeal. Furthermore, differences are much more apt than similarities to result in fatal attractions, and the dark side of differences typically reported by individuals in such attractions is "strange," which implies a lack of mutual understanding among members of a couple. Of course, we do not know the extent to which opposites may attract in ongoing, developing relationships, and perhaps certain types of appealing differences, such as those that are complementary, can be compatible for some couples. Nevertheless, the conclusion derived from the terminated relationships reported here is: Opposites may initially attract, but they later repel.

Research on relationship dissolution is yet another area for which these results have potential ramifications. Many accounts of breakups imply that these endings are circumstantial and are out of an individual's control. Yet, fatal attraction research indicates that for a substantial proportion of couples, individuals play an instigative role in the demise of their relationship by selecting (as a partner) someone whose strengths they will eventually find annoying. Such cases suggest that some couples are destined to breakup from the start of their relationhip, as implied by the *Pre-Existing Doom* model of relationship dissolution (Duck, 1982).

The potential battlegrounds for relationship endings are also evident in these findings. The dark sides of fatal attractions identified here indicate that common complaints about a mate—that are likely to appear in breakup accounts and in couples' disagreements—include, for example, lack of seriousness, domineering ways, or unpredictable and irresponsible behavior. The puzzle, of course, is that these types of grievances about a partner seem so closely related to the features initially found pleasing. The ideas discussed in this chapter, therefore, raise the intriguing possibility that such objections and related dyadic conflict, might have been predicted from the initial stages of the relationship.

Nonetheless, a partner's positive features may emerge as problematic only after some significant change in the situation facing the couple has occurred. For example, a person's hard-edged evaluativeness and decisiveness may be attractive early in a relationship, but once this relationship is in a situation of real value conflict (e.g., deciding to live with one's stepparents after becoming unemployed), it suddenly evokes this characteristic that only now serves to drive a wedge between the couple. In other words, some characteristics that are initially attractive for all the right reasons may become fatal when a particular context draws them forth as a basis for dissension.

Note that fatal attractions may not be limited to romantic breakups, but they can also appear in some ongoing, stable relationships. That is, certain couples may remain together despite the fact that both members, or only one, dislike aspects of the qualities that caused them to gravitate to each other. Attracting characteristics are still fatal in such cases, but the overall relationship is not. To the extent such instances occur, a question for future research is as follows: "How do some couples successfully negotiate an intimate relationship and, at the same time, remain cognizant of the negative dimensions of each other's attractive features?"

Finally, perhaps another type of contradiction occurs in romantic relationships, one that is in some sense the opposite of a fatal attraction. In such a situation people may find themselves drawn to qualities in a prospective partner that initially repelled them (i.e., a nonfatal repulsion). For example, someone's sense of humor could be interpreted as offensive at first glance, but after repeated exposure it is found to have an element of charm (e.g., see Sally's, Meg Ryan's, reaction to Harry, Billy Crystal, in the movie *When Harry Met Sally*). In many instances, an initial negative reaction to a prospective companion precludes this possibility because future interaction is terminated. Some potential relationships are doomed, thus, because the individuals never get to entertain the lighter side of the features in question. Yet, if repulsed partners can get past initial negative reactions, with time they may find that they begin to appreciate the positive dimensions of each other's faults.[4]

In conclusion, research on the dark side of interpersonal attraction has just begun to scratch the surface. Fatal attractions represent just one of the many contradictions or ambiguities inherent in close pairings. More indepth, interview studies of this and other attraction paradoxes are needed, using broader samples of married as well as nonmarried couples and over a long timeframe. Nevertheless, the arguments and findings in this chapter presented an initial glimpse into the ways in which the process of romantic attraction is more dark and contradictory than it may seem. These ways also imply that there is more than a grain of truth to the notion that what is appealing in a loved one can become appalling in the blink of an eye.

ACKNOWLEDGEMENTS

Thanks go to Larry Cohen, Bill Cupach, Scott Gartner, and Brian Spitzberg for their contributions to this chapter.

---

[4]On a more general vein, these ideas suggest that, in line with theories of emotion (Berscheid, 1983), things that are arousing are often negative in nature (socioevolution has developed us to view interruptions in routine as potentially threatening), but such arousal can be cognitively switched in valence.

REFERENCES

Altman, I., Vinsel, A., & Brown, B. B. (1981). Dialectic conceptions in social psychology: An application to social penetration and privacy regulation. In L. Berkowitz (Ed.), *Advances in experimental social psychology* (Vol. 14, pp. 107–160). New York: Academic Press.

Aron, A., & Aron, E. (1986). *Love and the expansion of self: Understanding attraction and satisfaction.* New York: Hemisphere.

Aronson, E., & Worchel, S. (1966). Similarity versus liking as determinants of interpersonal attractivenes. *Journal of Abnormal and Social Psychology, 59*, 177–181.

Baxter, L. A. (1986). Gender differences in the heterosexual relationship rules embedded in break-up accounts. *Journal of Social and Personal Relationships, 3*, 289–306.

Baxter, L. A., & Montgomery, B. M. (1996). *Relating: Dialogues and dialectics.* New York: Guilford.

Bell, R. A., Tremblay, S. W., & Buerkel-Rothfuss, N. L. (1987). Interpersonal attraction as a communication accomplishment: Development of a measure of affinity-seeking competence. *The Western Journal of Speech Communication, 51*, 1–18.

Berscheid, E. (1983). Emotion. In H. H. Kelley, E. Berscheid, A. Christensen, J. H. Harvey, T. L. Huston, G. Levinger, E. McClintock, L. A. Peplau, & D. R. Peterson (Eds.), *Close relationships* (pp. 110–168). Beverly Hills, CA: Sage.

Burleson, B. R., & Denton, W. H. (1992). A new look at similarity and attraction in marriage: Similarities in social–cognitive and communication skills as predictors of attraction and satisfaction. *Communication Monographs, 59*, 268–287.

Buss, D. M. (1994). *The evolution of desire.* New York: Basic Books.

Byrne, D. (1971). *The attraction paradigm.* New York: Academic Press.

Byrne, D., & Clore, G. L. (1970). A reinforcement model of evaluative processes. *Personality: An International Journal, 1*, 103–128.

Cupach, W. R., & Metts, S. (1986). Accounts of relational dissolution: A comparison of marital and non-marital relationships. *Communication Monographs, 53*, 311–334.

Duck, S. W. (1977). *The study of acquaintance.* Farnborough, UK: Saxon House.

Duck, S. W. (1982). A topography of relationship disengagement and dissolution. In S. Duck (Ed.), *Personal relationships. 4: Dissolving personal relationships* (pp. 1–30). New York: Academic Press.

Duck, S. W. (1994a). *Meaningful relationships: Talking, sense and relating.* Newbury Park, CA: Sage.

Duck, S. W. (1994b). Stratagems, spoils, and a serpent's tooth: On the delights and dilemmas of personal relationship. In B. H. Spitzberg & W. Cupach (Eds.) *The dark side of interpersonal communication* (pp. 3–24). Hillsdale, NJ: Lawrence Erlbaum Associates.

Eagly, A. H., Ashmore, R. D., Makhijani, M. G., & Longo, L. C. (1991). What is beautiful is good, but … : A meta-analytic review of research on the physical attractiveness stereotype. *Psychological Bulletin, 110;* 109–128.

Feingold, A. (1988). Matching for attractiveness in romantic partners and same-sex friends: A meta-analysis and theoretical critique. *Psychological Bulletin, 104*, 226–235.

Feingold, A. (1990). Gender differences in effect of physical attractiveness on romantic attraction: A comparison across five research paradigms. *Journal of Personality and Social Psychology, 59*, 981–993.

Feingold, A. (1992). Good-looking people are not we think. *Psychological Bulletin, 111*, 304–341.

Felmlee, D. H. (1995). Fatal attractions: Affection and disaffection in intimate relationships. *Journal of Social and Personal Relationships, 12*, 295–311.

Felmlee, D. H. (in press, a). "Be careful what you wish for … ": Determinants of fatal attractions. *Personal Relationships.*

Felmlee, D. H. (in press, b). Fatal attractions: Contradictions in Intimate Relationships. In J. Harvey (Ed.), *Perspectives on loss: A handbook.* Washington, DC: Taylor & Francis.

Felmlee, D. H., & Greenberg, D. F. (1996). *The couple as a dynamic system: A formal model.* Paper presented at the Annual Meetings of the American Sociological Association, New York, August.

Festinger, L. (1951). Architecture and group membership. *Journal of Social Issues, 7,* 152–163.

Festinger, L. (1957). *A theory of cognitive dissonance.* New York: Harper & Row.

Freeman, H. R. (1985). Somatic attractiveness: As in other things, moderation is best. *Psychology of Women Quarterly, 9,* 311–322.

Gold, J. A., Ryckman, R. M., & Mosley, N. R. (1984). Romantic mood induction and attraction to a dissimilar other: Is love blind? *Personality and Social Psychology Bulletin, 10,* 358–368.

Goldberg, J. G. (1993). *The dark side of love.* New York: Putnam.

Goode, W. J. (1956). *After divorce.* New York: The Free Press.

Harvey, J. H., Orbuch, T. L., & Weber, A. L. (1992). *Attributions, accounts, and close relationships.* New York: Springer-Verlag.

Hatfield, E., & Rapson, R. L. (1993). *Love, sex, and intimacy: Their psychology, biology, and history.* New York: HarperCollins.

Hatfield, E., & Sprecher, S. (1986). *Mirror, mirror ... The importance of looks in everyday life.* Albany: State University of New York Press.

Hill, C. T., Rubin, Z., & Peplau, L. A. (1976). Breakups before marriage: The end of 103 affairs. *Journal of Social Issues , 32,* 147–168.

Huston, T. L., McHale, S. M., & Crouter, A. C. (1986). When the honeymoon is over: Changes in the marriage relationship over the first year. In R. Gilmour & S. Duck (Eds.), *The emerging field of personal relationships.* Hillsdale, NJ: Lawrence Erlbaum Associates.

Jackson, L. A., Hunter, J. E., & Hodge, C. N. (1995). Physical attractiveness and intellectual competence: A meta-analytic review. *Social Psychology Quarterly, 58,* 108–122.

Jung, C. B. (1973). *Memories, dreams, reflections.* Edited by (A. Jaffe, Ed. & R. Winston and C. Winston, Trans.). New York: Pantheon.

Kerchoff, A. C. (1974). The social context of interpersonal attraction. In T. Huston (Ed.), *Foundations of interpersonal attraction* (pp. 61–78). New York: Academic Press.

Kerchoff, A. C., & Davis, K. E. (1962). Value consensus and need complementarity in mate selection. *American Sociological Review, 27,* 295–303.

Lewis, R. A. (1973). A longitudinal test of a developmental framework for premarital dyadic formation. *Journal of Marriage and the Family , 35,* 16–25.

Marshall, L. L. (1994). Physical and psychological abuse. In B. H. Spitzberg & W. Cupach (Eds.) *The dark side of interpersonal communication* (pp. 281–311). Hillsdale, NJ: Lawrence Erlbaum Associates.

McClanahan, K. K., Gold, J. A., Lenney, E., Ryckman, R. M., & Kulberg, G.E. (1990). Infatuation and attraction to a dissimilar other: Is love blind? *The Journal of Social Psychology, 130,* 433–445.

Moore, T. (1992). *Care of the soul: A guide for cultivating depth and sacredness in everyday life.* New York: Pantheon.

Murstein, B. I. (1970). Stimulus-value-role: A theory of marital choice. *Journal of Marriage and the Family, 32,* 465–481.

Neimeyer, G. J. (1984). Cognitive complexity and marital satisfaction. *Journal of Social and Clinical Psychology, 2,* 258–263.

Newcomb, T. M. (1961). *The acquaintance process.* New York: Holt, Rinehart & Winston.

Purdum, T. S. (1996, May 19). Facets of Clinton. *New York Times Magazine,* pp. 36–41, 62.

Rosenbaum, M. E. (1986). The repulsion hypothesis: On the nondevelopment of relationships. *Journal of Personality and Social Psychology , 51,* 1156–1166.

Smith, E. R., Byrne, D., & Fielding, D. (1995). Interpersonal attraction as a function of extreme gender role adherence. *Personal Relationships, 2,* 161–172.

Snyder, C. R., & Fromkin, H. L. (1980). *Uniqueness: The human pursuit of difference.* New York: Plenum.

Spanier, G., & Thompson, L. (1984). *Parting: The aftermath of separation and divorce.* Beverly Hills, CA: Sage.

Spitzberg, B. H. (1997). Intimate violence. In W. R. Cupach & D. J. Canary (Eds.), *Competence in interpersonal conflict.* New York: McGraw-Hill.

Sprecher, S. (1994). Two sides to the breakup of dating relationships. *Personal Relationships, 1,* 199–222.

Sprecher, S., Sullivan, Q., & Hatfield, E. (1994). Mate selection preferences: Gender differences examined in a national sample. *Journal of Personality and Social Psychology, 8,* 1074–1080.

Stephen, T. (1987). Attribution and adjustment to relationship termination. *Journal of Social and Personal Relationships, 4,* 47–61.

Sunnafrank, M. (1991). Interpersonal attraction and attitude similarity: A communication-based assessment. In J. A. Anderson (Ed.), *Communication yearbook 14* (pp. 451–483). Newbury Park, CA: Sage.

Surra, C. A. (1991). Mate selection and premarital relationships. In A. Booth (Ed.), *Contemporary families* (pp. 54–75). Minneapolis, MN: National Council on Family Relations.

Tennov, D. (1979). *Love and limerence: The experience of being in love.* New York: Stein & Day.

Tseëlon, E. (1992). What is beautiful is bad: Physical attractiveness as stigma. *Journal for the Theory of Social Behavior, 22,* 295–310.

Vaughan, C. (1986). *Uncoupling: How relationships come apart.* New York: Random House.

Whitehouse, J. (1981). The role of the initial attracting quality in marriage: Virtues and vices. *Journal of Marital and Family Therapy, 7,* 61–67.

Winch, R. F. (1955). The theory of complementary needs in mate selection: A test of one kind of complementariness. *American Sociological Review, 20,* 552–555.

Zajonc, R. B. (1968). The attitudinal effects of mere exposure. *Journal of Personality and Social Psychology (Monograph Supplement No. 2), 9,* 1–27.

2
The Dark Side of Jealousy and Envy: Desire, Delusion, Desperation, and Destructive Communication

Laura K. Guerrero
Arizona State University

Peter A. Andersen
San Diego State University

"Where there's no emotion, there's no motive for violence."

—Spock to Kirk on an episode of *Star Trek* (Wincelberg, 1966)

A *New York Times* headline screams: "Texas Executes Man who Killed his Ex-Girlfriend out of Jealousy" (August 15, 1995). For months, television news covered the O. J. Simpson trial, with all its implications for jealousy and domestic violence. Television docudramas have been made about a teenager (Amy Fischer) who maims her alleged lover's wife, a high school student who stabs and kills a popular girl that she idolizes (in *A Friend to Die For*), and a high society La Jolla, CA, wife (Betty Broderick) who kills her husband and his secretary/lover. Movies such as *Fatal Attraction*, which portrays a jealous, obsessive ex-lover's acts of violence, and *The Lion King*, which features Scar's envy of his brother, King Mufasa, and his nephew, Simba, earn millions of box office dollars. Indeed, if Spock had lived on

33

earth in the 20th century, the media accounts of emotion-laden crimes would have provided ample anecdotal evidence for the validity of his statement on the human condition. Moreover, Spock would likely have concluded that jealousy, and to a lesser extent, its sister construct, envy, are prime elicitors of violence.

Fortunately, emotions such as jealousy and envy do not always cumulate in violence, and they do not always have negative consequences for individuals and relationships. In fact, these emotions sometimes have positive effects. Jealousy can show love and affection. It can also help a person realize the extent to which he or she cares about another. As Salovey and Rodin (1985) stated, "jealousy can be a reasonable and healthy emotion. Sometimes the irrational feelings of jealousy can be taken as signs of caring and devotion, rather than as possessiveness and insecurity" (p. 29). Pines (1992) argued that jealousy can lead people to re-examine their relationships, to stop taking their partners for granted, to feel more passionate toward their partners, and to become more committed to their relationships. In addition, Pines noted that jealousy can function as a sign of commitment, an emotion intensifier, and a relationship protection device.

Like jealousy, envy has positive consequences, such as when it leads to self-improvement and accomplishment. Parrott (1991) distinguished between *malicious* and *nonmalicious* jealousy. He noted that Aristotle made a similar distinction between envy that motivates "people to take good things away from others" and envy that motivates "people to improve themselves" (p. 9). As Smith (1991) argued, "Understanding why some individuals can use unflattering social comparisons as a basis for more constructive, emulative impulses, whereas other[s] seem overcome by destructive, hateful feelings, is an important social–psychological problem" (p. 96).

Despite potential benefits of jealousy and envy, in most situations, these emotions have negative consequences for individuals and their relationships. Jealous or envious individuals typically feel negative emotions, such as fear and/or anger, and worry about the state of their relationships or accomplishments. In more rare cases, physical violence occurs. White and Mullen (1989) summarized the potential negative consequences of romantic jealousy: "Jealousy involves the outrage of an act of infidelity, of disloyalty; it threatens loss of the central relationship; it involves humiliation; it raises an intensely ambivalent eroticism; it escalates interpersonal conflict within the relationship; and it is accompanied by uncertainty, frustration, and helplessness" (p. 233).

In this chapter, we concentrate on the dark side of jealousy and envy by focusing on the negative impact that the experience and expression of these emotions can have on individuals and relationships. The chapter begins by distinguishing jealousy from envy and placing these two emotions in a historical and social context. Then we focus on some of the darker consequences of jealousy and envy. These include intrapersonal reactions, such as feeling anger, fear, or sadness; evaluating oneself as inferior to others; and experiencing lowered self-esteem, as well as interpersonal outcomes, such as loss of trust, competitiveness, aggressive communication, and violence. We also briefly discuss how communication is used to cope more effectively with jealousy and envy.

DISTINCTIONS BETWEEN JEALOUSY AND ENVY

Although jealousy and envy are generally considered to be related, they are distinctly different constructs. Research shows that people tend to view jealousy as the broader construct (see Smith, Kim, & Parrott, 1988) and readily use it to describe feelings that are truly jealous (e.g., feeling hurt that your current dating partner talks on the phone a lot with his ex-girlfriend or boyfriend) as well as those that are envious (e.g., feeling upset because someone at work always upstages you). People who feel jealous tend to experience a variety of emotions, including envy. In fact, Pines and Aronson (1983) asked people to rate how jealous they would feel in situations involving 9 potential rivals (e.g., a family member, someone they knew and found similar to them, or someone they disliked and knew little about). They found that people reported the most intense jealousy when the rival was someone they knew and envied.

Research also suggests that jealousy is a more prototypic emotion than is envy (Shaver, Schwartz, Kirson, & O'Connor, 1987). The words jealousy and zeal share a common etymology, suggesting that fervor and intensity are part of jealous emotion. Jealousy almost always involves emotional experiences such as anger, fear, and sadness. In contrast, envy is less passionate and more cognitive, such as when a person wishes he or he was as attractive as someone else, but does not feel resentment toward the beautiful person or sadness about one's own shortcomings. Given that jealousy is the broader term, it is not surprising that social scientists have focused more attention on jealousy than envy, especially in the last few decades (Parrott, 1991).

There are several other important distinctions between the sister constructs of jealousy and envy. The two emotions differ in terms of who possesses the desired person or trait, what other emotions and perceptions accompany them, and how society views their experience and expression.

Possession of the Desired Person or Trait

The concept of *relationship possession* helps distinguish jealousy and envy (Bryson, 1977; Salovey & Rodin, 1989). Generally, jealousy occurs when people feel they are in danger of losing a valued relationship that they already possess. In the case of romantic jealousy, lovers fear losing the love and/or exclusivity they share with their partners. Yet, jealousy is not limited to romantic relationships. Jealousy can occur between friends, coworkers, or family members (Parrott, 1991). Consider the following examples:

> Sarah and Teresa are best friends. They usually spend part of their weekend together going to the movies, to nightclubs, or just talking. Then Teresa meets Ron, falls head over heals in love with him, and starts spending more time with him and less time with Sarah, who fears that she is losing her relationship with Teresa.

> Steve is an associate producer at a large television station. He enjoys his work and is extremely proud of his position, especially because he is highly regarded by the executive producer who gives him full autonomy to make programming decisions. Then Rita comes along and impresses the executive producer with her programming expertise.

> Bob and Samantha have been married for 5 years when they have their first child. With the birth of their son, Bob begins to feel neglected because Samantha is so busy caring for their new son. It seems to him that all of Samantha's affections are now directed at the newborn.

All of these examples represent ordinary, potential jealousy situations. In each case, Sarah, Steve, and Bob are likely to feel threatened; something they value—whether it be the time they spend with their friend, the work they enjoy doing, or the attention they receive from their spouse—is in jeopardy of being taken away or changed. Notice that in each of these cases, the potentially jealous person perceives that he or she *possesses* a valued relationship, but is in danger of losing it or at least of having it altered in an undesirable manner. Thus, jealousy involves a threat to a desired, pre-existing relational state.

Envy, in contrast, occurs when a person does not possess a valued commodity, but wishes to possess it. The commodity could be a relationship with someone, a material possession, a position of power or status, or a personal characteristic such as intelligence, humor, or beauty. Parrott (1991) conceptualized envy as occurring "when a person lacks what another has and either desires it or wishes the other did not have it" (p. 4). Envy is strongest when it leads to a negative comparison between oneself and others in an area highly relevant to one's self-concept (Salovey & Rodin, 1989; Salovey & Rothman, 1991). Because envy is derived from the Latin *inuidre*, which translates as "to see intensively," envy always involves comparing one's own situation to that of a scrutinized other.

In many situations, our self-comparisons to others are negative, but we do not feel envy. For example, when we watch the Olympic games we admire the speed of the sprinters and the grace of the gymnasts, but we do not necessarily envy them. This is especially true if the skills they possess are not in an area that is personally relevant to us. In other words, most of us do not expect to be able to compete with world-class athletes, and we do not long to do so. Instead, we expect to enjoy their performances, to feel happiness at their successes, and disappointment at their defeats. If envy is felt, it is likely to be of the admiring or nonmalicious variety. In contrast, if you were a moderately successful professional golfer in your late 40s, you might be quite envious of younger players, such as Tiger Woods, who have already achieved high levels of success and international recognition. In this case, a comparison is likely to be drawn in a highly relevant area of self-identity.

The following examples further illustrate scenarios that are likely to produce negative self-to-other comparisons and envious feelings:

> Jim studies hard for all his classes. It is important for him to do well because he hopes to get into medical school. His roommate, Mark, however, rarely studies and gets better grades than he does.

> Christie is in love with Ryan, yet Ryan does not even notice her. He is too infatuated with Victoria, a beautiful, outgoing woman whom he recently started dating.

> Randy works extremely hard to keep a roof over his family and to provide them with life's necessities. He feels resentment toward John, who inherited money from his wealthy family and only has to work part-time.

Notice that in all these cases someone else possesses the commodity (whether it be intelligence, affection from a loved one, or a life of wealth and leisure) that the envious person wishes to possess. Such situations call forth an implicit negative comparison between the envious person and the rival.

Notice also that only two relations are necessary for envy to occur: An envious person who desires something and a rival who possesses the desired commodity. In the case of jealousy, however, there is always a "triangle of relations" (Parrott, 1991, p. 16; see also Farrell, 1980). This is not to say that envy cannot co-occur with jealousy within a triangle of relationships. Indeed, the previous example of Christie, Ryan, and Victoria illustrates that envy can occur within love triangles. In this case, however, Christie does not possess Ryan's affections and she is likely to envy Victoria's ability to attract him to her. In other words, Christie wishes she could trade places with Victoria—a common wish when one is envious. Similarly, people are likely to feel envious if their romantic partner mentions how good looking someone is, although there is no possibility for the partner to become involved with the third party. For instance, a wife may comment that a movie star is gorgeous. Her husband knows that she will almost certainly never meet the handsome actor, so he has no reason to fear losing the relationship to him. He is likely, however, to envy the actor's good looks. Thus, although jealousy and envy are separate phenomena, they can co-occur.

Related Emotions and Perceptions

Research demonstrates that jealousy and envy are qualitatively different emotional experiences. Most definitions of jealousy center on feelings of fear that result from threat. For example, White and Mullen (1989) conceptualized *romantic jealousy* as "A complex of thoughts, emotions, and actions that follows loss of or threat to self-esteem and/or the existence or quality of the romantic relationship" due to the actual or potential interference of a rival (p. 9). In contrast, most definitions of envy focus on feelings of longing and resentment. Smith, Parrott, and Diener (1990), for instance, demonstrated that feelings of inferiority and resentment are at the heart of the envious experience. Parrott (1991) argued that *envy* is typically composed of feelings of longing, inferiority, resentment, guilt, and admiration. Berke (1988) stated that "envy is a state of exquisite tension, torment, and ill will provoked by an overwhelming sense of inferiority, impotence, and worthlessness" (p. 19).

Two studies shed further light on these distinctions. Smith et al. (1988) examined people's everyday conceptions of both jealousy and envy. Their research illustrated that people associated jealousy with suspiciousness, rejection, hostility, fear of loss, and hurt. These jealous feelings and reactions involve a triangle of relations. The jealous person may be suspicious that a rival relationship exists, feel rejected in favor of the rival, and fear losing the partner to the rival. In contrast, Smith et al. found envy to associate more strongly with feelings of inferiority, dissatisfaction, self-criticism, and motivation to improve. Only a dyadic comparison is necessary for these reactions to occur.

Parrott and Smith (1993) further demonstrated the qualitative distinctions between jealousy and envy. In this study, self-reported responses (to recalled and hypothetical situations) were adjusted for intensity level because jealousy is typically experienced as a stronger emotion than is envy.

When intensity level was controlled, several substantial differences between jealousy and envy emerged. Jealousy was distinguished from envy by higher scores in four areas: (a) *distrust*, including feeling betrayed, rejected, and suspicious; (b) *fear*, including feeling worried, anxious, and threatened; (c) *uncertainty*, including feeling confused about the state of the relationship; and (d) *loneliness*, including feeling left out and abandoned. Four reactions also differentiated envy from jealousy. Specifically, envious individuals experienced more: (a) *disapproval* of their own feelings; (b) *longing* for what another person possesses; (c) *motivation* to improve oneself; and (d) *degradation*, which included feeling humiliated and inferior. Insecurity appears to be related to both jealousy and envy. However, the insecurity stemming from jealousy is more strongly focused on uncertainty about the status of one's relationship or position, whereas insecurity associated with envy centers more squarely on one's perceived inferiority to others.

Jealousy and envy may not only produce different emotional reactions and perceptions, but they may also originate in different emotions. Ciabattari (1988) proposed the interesting hypothesis that jealousy and envy originate in love and hate, respectively. According to this view, *jealousy* (though it may ultimately lead to hate) can only exist when a person loves someone and wants to protect the relationship. In contrast, envy stems from resenting or hating someone for having something you do not possess. If this is true, then the functions that jealousy and envy serve are very different. On the positive side, jealous individuals should strive to protect and maintain their relationships, whereas envious individuals should strive to improve themselves so they are competitive with the rival. On the negative side, jealous individuals may become overly possessive and demanding, whereas envious individuals may strike out against those people who make them feel inferior. Ciabattari's predictions, however, await scientific testing.

Historical Context and Social Significance

Jealousy and envy have different societal meanings, partially because of the historical contexts surrounding them as their meanings evolved. In the following section, we show that both jealousy and envy have social significance and can lead to aggression and violence. We also show that although jealousy and envy are both frequently condemned in our society, envy is generally seen as the more evil culprit, despite being felt with less intensity and leading less often to grave consequences. As Parrott (1991) stated:

"The hostility that accompanies envy is not socially sanctioned, whereas that accompanying jealousy often is" (p. 79).

The Paradoxical Societal View of Jealousy.   Jealousy and its paradoxes have intrigued writers for centuries, as plays such as Shakespeare's *Othello*, operas such as Bizet's *Carmen*, and novels such as Zola's *The Beast in Man* attest. These historic works, along with the media reports on violence resulting from jealousy, send our society a message that jealousy is a highly dangerous and uncontrollable emotion. Jealousy itself is personified as a "green-eyed monster." The perception that jealousy is an uncontrollable emotion is so powerful that in American courts people who kill their spouses out of jealousy can sometimes claim temporary insanity. In other cases, individuals who kill someone in the heat of jealous passion are convicted of manslaughter rather than second-degree murder (Delgado & Bond, 1993). Salovey and Rodin (1989) noted that the legal definition of *manslaughter* is as "any intentional killing committed under the influence of extreme mental or emotional disturbance for which there is a reasonable explanation or excuse" (pp. 239–240). Such is one paradox of jealousy: Jealousy-induced violence is reprehensible, but sometimes perceived as justifiable.

Jealousy has always been a two-edged sword—an expression of love on the one hand, of perceived paranoia on the other; positively valued in some relationships, but distressing in others. In *The Immortals*, Korda's (1992) fictional account about John Kennedy's (JFK) alleged affair with Marilyn Monroe, both JFK and Marilyn are portrayed as dealing with the jealousy and suspicion of their respective spouses, Jackie Kennedy and Joe Dimaggio. In one scene, JFK acts jealous when Marilyn mentions other men:

> "You're *jealous*!" She cried.
> "The hell I am."
> "You are … Oh, sweetheart, don't worry. I *like* a man to be jealous."
> "You *do*? What about Joe? You're always complaining about the fact that he's jealous."
> "Oh honey, he's my *husband*! A jealous *husband* is no fun at all. A jealous lover is a whole different story." (p. 65)

Like Marilyn, many people have ambivalent attitudes stemming from a paradox between autonomy and commitment (see Baxter, 1988). Jealousy in a committed relationship may be perceived as an unjustified and unnecessary constraint on individual autonomy. Jealousy in an uncommitted relationship may symbolize love and connection.

Societal attitudes about jealousy have been characterized by paradox, ambivalence, and dynamism. Clanton (1989) conducted an intriguing analysis of all magazine articles on jealousy indexed in *The Reader's Guide to Periodical Literature* from 1945 to 1985. He found two very different trends. From 1945 to 1965, jealousy was treated as "proof of love." As Clanton summarized, "virtually all of the articles in popular magazines said that a certain amount of jealousy was natural, proof of love, and good for marriage" (p. 182). Readers were cautioned, however, to avoid irrational displays of emotion. Women, in particular, were told to curb their own emotional expressions of jealousy but to interpret their husband's expression of jealousy as a sign of love and affection. This view is consistent with the idea that jealousy serves as a device to help people retain their mates and protect the relationship (see Buss, 1988). As Delgado and Bond (1993) claimed, "historically jealousy has been positively valued" (p. 1337).

From 1970 to 1980, jealousy was depicted in the popular press as a "personality defect" (Clanton, 1989). At this time, people began feeling guilty about being jealous. Jealousy was viewed as evidence that a person was distrustful, suspicious, and/or insecure, as well as unable to properly manage emotion (Stearns, 1989). Moreover, some articles "suggested that jealousy was becoming outdated as society moved into an era of 'liberated' relationships between men and women" (Clanton, 1989, p. 183). Within such a liberated society, jealousy was seen as abnormal, paranoid, and irrational and as having only negative effects on relationships. Stearns (1989) summarized the sentiments of this era by stating, "Though a few magazine articles found tiny windows of merit in jealousy, as against the unadulterated blasts, they were at best silver specks in a very dark cloud" (p. 121).

So where are we today? Contemporary attitudes remain ambivalent and paradoxical. We are repulsed and fascinated by jealousy. Jealousy is a more frequent topic of magazine articles today than ever before. Moreover, the 1990s explosion of television talk shows and docudramas revolving around jealousy has increased public awareness of this sometimes destructive emotion. Jealousy is still portrayed as a personality defect on many of these shows, possibly because this depiction highlights the dramatic, negative consequences of jealousy and makes a better story. Yet, in the 1990s age of AIDS awareness, monogamy is valued more than it was in the 1970s and 1980s (Brehm, 1992). The renewed emphasis on affectionate, committed relationships and safe sex suggests that jealousy is justified in many situations. Indeed, unsafe sex during an extradyadic affair can affect both the emotional and physical well-being of all three members of the romantic triangle.

Taken together, a sociological and historical perspective on jealousy suggests that paradox is operating. Jealousy is seen as a stronger, more potentially violent emotion than is envy, it is often seen as a personality defect, and yet there are still times when it is socially sanctioned. Aune and Comstock (1996; Comstock & Aune, 1995), for example, found that romantic partners saw jealousy experience and expression as unpleasant, but fairly acceptable in their relationships. Similarly, Fitness and Fletcher (1993) reported that most people generally "understand and forgive each other's occasional insecurity and jealousy, despite the widespread belief that jealousy is a destructive, unacceptable emotion in close relationships" (p. 957).

Jealousy is also paradoxical in that it creates a dilemma. As Stearns (1989) contended, people may "scorn jealousy, regarding it as an emotion at once juvenile and outdated," yet they may still feel "susceptible and even on occasion justify their [jealous] feeling" (p. 129). The experience and expression of jealousy by relational partners is quite natural. One of the reasons people tolerate jealous partners is that they have experienced jealous thoughts and feelings themselves. Indeed, jealousy of all types, particularly emotional and behavioral jealousy, is correlated within dyads, indicating that jealous people are attracted to one another or that jealousy is reciprocated by one's relational partner (Guerrero, Eloy, Jorgensen, & Andersen, 1993).

Perhaps unjustifiably, jealous individuals need reassurance and understanding from their partners rather than judgment. However, when jealousy becomes violent and/or obsessive, most people find it unacceptable. Indeed, Delgado and Bond (1993) found that most people do not view jealousy as a better justification for homicide than financial issues. Yet, our court system, as well as our conventional wisdom, provides some level of social acceptance and personal sympathy for the jealous lover who engages in destructive, seemingly uncontrollable behavior. Delgado and Bond labeled *jealousy* as the "oldest excuse for wrong doing" (p. 1338). White and Mullen (1989) noted that, "The so-called 'crime of passion' has always aroused both fascination and considerable sympathy for the offender" (p. 231). Whether it is a friend telling another friend, "I understand why you hit her; she really hurt you badly when she slept with him" or a jury acquitting an individual who injured another because she was "temporarily insane with jealousy," our society sends a dual message: Highly jealous individuals are insecure and volatile, but we should understand and sympathize with their pain. Such a message has dangerous implications for our personal relationships because we expect others to forgive our aggressive actions when we are jealous.

The Paradoxical Societal View of Envy.   Like jealousy, envy has fascinated writers for centuries. Aristotle (1886) stated:

Envy (is) defined as a species of pain felt at conspicuous prosperity on the part of persons like ourselves ... not with any view to our personal advantage but solely because they are prosperous. As regards the occasions of envy, the goods which provoke it have already been stated; for all achievements or possessions of which we covet the reputation or are ambitious, all things which arouse in us a longing for reputation, as well as all the various gifts of fortune are practically without exception natural objects of envy. (pp. 158–159)

In Shakespeare's *Julius Caesar*, envy permeates Roman politics. In the Bible, the book of Genesis contains several accounts of envy. For example, one passage describes how Jacob made one of his son's, Joseph, a long tunic. Joseph's brothers see the tunic, realize that their father loves Joseph best, and "hate him so much that they would not even greet him." (Gen. 37: 3, New American Bible). Later, the brothers' envious hatred leads them to sell Joseph to Midianite traders, who take him to Egypt to be sold as a slave.

The Bible also provides a foundation for the contemporary view of envy as morally wrong. Specifically, the 10th commandment dictates that a person shall not covet someone else's spouse or property. Envy is also considered one of the seven deadly sins. Parrott (1991) reported that envious individuals, as opposed to jealous individuals, are more likely to feel shame, embarrassment, guilt, "sinfulness," and worry about disapproval (see also Parrott & Smith, 1993). This modern day evidence suggests that envy is still viewed as a socially condemned, morally reprehensible emotion. This is at least partially due to the perception that envy stems from a deficit within oneself, whereas jealousy can stem from one's righteous indignation over another's indiscretions.

In individualistic, capitalistic countries like the United States or Great Britain, envy is particularly likely to flourish. Individualism naturally leads people to compare themselves to others. As Salovey and Rodin (1989) stated, "In a competitive culture, individualistic concerns for material possessions, status, and affection are often manifested as envy" (p. 241). Scholars (e.g., Burke, Genn-Bash, & Haines, 1988; Tracy, 1991) also argued that competitiveness is an integral part of North America's economy, politics, and social policies. Furthermore, capitalism allows people from widely different social stations to interact within the same society, making comparisons inevitable. Competition and envy then become mechanisms by which to better oneself and to try to move up the "social ladder" (Tracy, 1991). Indeed, during the 1980s era of the me generation, Ciabattari (1988) asked: "Will the '90s be the age of envy?" (p. 47)

The U.S. Declaration of Independence declares that all people are created equal, yet we know from experience that this is not the case. People inherit, acquire, and possess unique combinations of traits and talents. As Parrott (1991) stated:

> It is a fact of life that people are unequal. Certainly some inequalities stem from injustice, but even in a just world some people would be born with more beauty than others, some would receive more of a given talent than others, some would fairly come to acquire more possessions than others, and so forth. It is difficult to imagine that these differences among peers could be made not to matter. When one contemplates how common the situations promoting envy are, one appreciates envy's potential ubiquity and influence. (p. 8)

In most societies, laws and policies are erected to protect people from envy and to try to maintain some level of equality (see Schoeck, 1969). Of course, whether these laws and policies are fair depends on your perspective. Affirmative action is a case in point. Proponents of affirmative action claim that such a policy is necessary to ensure a fair system of equal access for all Americans, for without affirmative action, underrepresented groups would not be operating on a level playing field. Opponents of affirmative action contend that the policy is unjust because it gives some unqualified applicants an unfair advantage and causes reverse discrimination. Clearly, the issue at stake is how to provide people with equal, yet fair opportunity.

In interpersonal relationships, envy is often seen as selfish and petty. Our friends and loved ones expect us to be happy for them when they accomplish something. If we are envious, our negative emotion violates their expectations. Instead of being able to validate their happiness by sharing it with us, envy disconfirms their accomplishment and dampens their mood. Interestingly, envy and pride (two of the seven deadly sins) are probably associated with one another in some cases. Salovey and Rothman (1991) noted that often people have a hard time accepting compliments and become embarrassed when they receive excessive praise. Demure acceptance of compliments and embarrassed responses to praise may function to decrease the likelihood of envy. As noted previously, some scholars differentiated between malicious and admiring envy. A boastful individual is more likely to elicit malicious envy and hostility, whereas a modest individual is more likely to elicit admiring envy and liking.

Taken together, this evidence suggests that most people regard envy as a socially inappropriate emotion. Yet, modern society is likely to foster comparisons between people, making envy unavoidable. As with jealousy, envy can lead to violence, hostility, and political intrigue (Schoeck, 1969). Like jealousy, envy also presents people with a paradoxical situation: In many societies, people strive to be praiseworthy and to be compared favorably with their peers, yet when people appear too praiseworthy, they are likely to engender envy from others and to be resented and disliked.

Summary

Although jealousy and envy can be distinguished by who possesses the desired commodity, what the predominant accompanying emotions and perceptions are, and how society views them, they both have a similar quality at their core: Both revolve around desire. With jealousy, the desire focuses on preserving an existing relationship in the face of threats. With envy, the desire focuses on wanting something one does not have. In both cases, negative consequences can result.

THE DARK SIDE OF JEALOUSY AND ENVY

Jealousy and envy can result in numerous negative consequences for individuals and their relationships, notwithstanding the positive consequences mentioned earlier. In this section, we examine some of the most common negative consequences. These include the experience of a cluster of negative emotions and accompanying negative self-perceptions, negative relational outcomes, and destructive communicative behavior.

Intrapersonal Consequences: Negative Emotional Reactions and Self-Perceptions

Jealousy and envy are usually considered to be blended emotions because they are comprised of a number of distinct emotional experiences, such as anger and sadness. When these emotions are highly intense and negative, they may entrap jealous or envious individuals by making them increasingly fearful, suspicious, and insecure. Bryson (1991) discussed one common response to jealousy—*emotional devastation*, which includes feeling helpless, insecure, confused, inadequate, fearful, anxious, depressed, and exploited. Those experiencing emotional devastation report being unable to cope with other aspects of their lives and crying when they are alone. Thus, jealous emotional devastation encompasses the cognitive, emotional, and behavioral reactions that associate with "the serious negative emotional consequences of jealousy" (p. 180). When jealous individuals are so emotionally devastated that they doubt themselves and are unable to cope with other aspects of their lives, they are likely to dwell on their jealousy and to remain uncertain, suspicious, and irrational.

Envy can also be associated with emotional devastation, especially when envious individuals dwell on their shortcomings and their unfulfilled desires. Parrott's (1991) work shows that at least five different kinds of emotion may be a part of what we are terming envious emotional devastation: (a) frustrated desire; (b) sadness and distress over feelings of inferiority; (c) agent-focused resentment, which involves feeling anger and hatred toward "superior" others; (d) global resentment, which involves feeling a general resentment toward the injustice of circumstances or fate; and (e) guilt over wishing rivals ill will.

Blame is also an essential characteristic of envious emotional devastation, with the most emotionally devastated people blaming everyone, including themselves, for their problems. Statements such as "Nothing ever goes my way," "I can't do anything right," and "Everyone seems out to get me" are symptoms of envy proneness. Furthermore, both agent-focused and global resentment add to the perception that the envious person cannot achieve success in comparison to others. After all, if an envious person believes that others are naturally superior, that fate and circumstances are unjust, and that they just fail to measure up to other people, they are likely to see attempts at improving themselves as pointless. For these individuals, it is easier to give up and harbor resentment toward more fortunate others than to face more rejection and more negative self-to-other comparisons by trying to improve oneself.

Emotions associated with jealousy and envy are summarized in Table 2.1. Because the majority of these emotions are negatively valenced, the experience of jealousy and envy can be emotionally devastating. Although passion, love, pride, and appreciation are positive emotions that can accompany jealousy and admiration and liking can accompany envy, the emotions most central to both jealousy and envy are fear, anger, and sadness.

Fear. Both jealousy and envy are typically associated with feelings of fear, but the type of fear that accompanies these emotions is different. *Jealous fear*, which is more common than envious fear, stems from two interrelated sources—fear of abandonment and relational loss (White & Mullen, 1989) and uncertainty about the state of the relationship (Bringle, 1991). *Envious fear*, on the other hand, stems from fear of failure and/or rejection, and anxiety over "the prospect of undesirable future outcomes, and uncertainty about one's self" (Parrott, 1991, p. 13).

Fear emanates from humans' self-protection needs. The potential loss of a mate deprives an individual of biological resources (i.e., the ability to reproduce offspring), relational resources (i.e., a loving, nurturing compan-

TABLE 2.1

Emotional Reactions Most Commonly Associated With Jealousy and Envy

JEALOUSY	ENVY
1. Anger, rage, or hatred toward partner or rival (A, ASI, B2, KR, P1, P2, S2, SSK, TM, WM)	1. Anger, hatred, or resentment towards the rival (BS, CBL, P2, S1).
2. Fear, anxiety, or panic over possible abandonment or relationship change (A, ASI, B2, CS, P1, P3, SSK, TM, WM)	2. Distress and anxiety stemming from one's feelings of inferiority (CBL, P2, SI, SKP, SR2).
3. Sadness or grief over actual or potential relationship loss (WM)	3. Sadness, discontent, and hopelessness stemmin from one's own shortcomings (BS, CBL, P2, S1, SKP, SR1, SR2).
4. Hurt over being betrayed (B1, B3, SKP)	4. Guilt over harboring ill will toward others (BS, P2, PS, SR1)
5. Envy of the rival's relationship with the partner and/or the rival's positive characteristics (CS, WM).	5. Despair that you will never posses the valued commodity that the rival possesses.
6. Heightened sexual arousal or passion (B2, PA, WFR, WM)	6. Longing and/or frustrated desire (BS, P2)
7. Positive affect, including love, appreciation, and pride toward the partner (A, B1, GA).	7. Admiration and liking for the rival (P2).

Note: A= Arnold (1960); ASI= Ausubel, Sullivan & Ives (1980); B1= Baumgart, 1990; B2= Bohm (1961; B3= Bryson (1991); BS= Bers & Rodin (1984); CBL= Campos, Barrett, Lamb, Goldsmith, & Stenberg (1983); CS= Clanton & Smith (1977); GA= Guerrero & Andersen (in press); KR= Klein & Riviere (1964); P1= Panskeep (1982);P2= Parrott (1991); P3= Plutchik (1980); PS= Parrott & Smith (1993); PA= Pines & Aronson (1983); S1= Smith (1991); S2= Solomon (1976); SSK= Shaver, Schwartz, Kirson, & O'Connor (1987); SKP= Smith, Kim, & Parrott (1988); SR1= Salovey & Rodin (1984); SR2= Salovey & Rothman (1991); TM= Teismann & Mosher (1978); WFR= White, Fishbein, & Rutstein (1981); WM= White & Mullen (1989).

ion), and personal resources (i.e., less self-esteem or social status). Fear is typically communicated both verbally (Rimé, Mesquita, Philippot, & Boca, 1991) and nonverbally (Ekman, Friesen, & Ellsworth, 1972), probably to elicit comforting or sympathy. In the case of jealousy-induced fear, its experience and subsequent expression may elicit sympathy and relational repair, particularly if it accompanies integrative communication (Andersen, Eloy, Guerrero, & Spitzberg, 1995).

Of course, fear is often based on unrealistic or imagined threats that become phobic responses. White and Mullen (1989) provided recommendations for the treatment of infidelity delusions, a major and dark source of jealousy reactions. Their reviews of treatments include antipsychotic medication, electroconvulsive therapy, psychoanalytic approaches, and cognitive-behavior therapies. Of course, different remedies are necessary for treatment of jealousy stemming from actual jealousy, as opposed to delusional jealousy.

A prototype perspective also helps explain why jealousy and envy are associated with fear. Sharpsteen (1991) argued that many of the events that are seen as prototypical antecedents of fear are also likely to produce jealousy and envy. For example, Shaver et al. (1987) reported that the threat of social rejection, the possibility of loss or failure, and loss of control or competence are all situations that generally elicit fear. Perceived threats to self-esteem are at the heart of experiences of both jealousy and envy. Perceived threats to the relationship uniquely accompany the experience of jealousy. Thus, generalized threats produce fearful reactions, with more specialized forms of threats (i.e., those that focus on threatening one's relationship or one's self-esteem) producing not only fear, but also jealousy or envy.

Anger. Anger is such a powerful part of the jealousy experience that Bryson (1991) included it as a factor separate from emotional devastation. *Jealous anger* includes feeling angry at the partner and rival, feeling betrayed and disappointed in the partner, and feeling a need to get revenge.

Jealousy-related anger is highly associated with feelings of betrayal. For example, when romantic relationships end, people are particularly likely to be angry when they are replaced by a rival. Mathes, Adams, and Davies (1985) examined emotional reactions to four possible scenarios—losing a romantic relationship because of fate, destiny, rejection, or the inference of a romantic relationship. Anger was relatively high for both the rejection and interference situations, but particularly high for the latter. A cross-cultural study conducted by Bryson (1991) suggests that individuals who feel betrayed also tend to doubt their partners, feel angry toward their partners, give their partners the cold shoulder, end the relationship, or spy on their partners.

Research also indicates that jealous individuals are more likely to be angry at the partner than the rival (Mathes & Verstraete, 1993; Mullen & Maack, 1985; Paul, Foss, & Galloway, 1993), especially when the anger is intensely hostile or violent (White & Mullen, 1989). Daly and Wilson (1983), for example, found that jealous individuals are more likely to direct anger and violence toward spouses than rivals. Paul et al. (1993) explained that the partner is the more likely target of anger and aggression for at least four reasons:

1. The jealous individual typically has greater access to the partner.
2. It is the partner, not the rival, who is perceived as breaking a commitment and engaging in an act of betrayal.
3. The rival may not know the extent to which the partner is already committed, and, thus, the rival may be unknowingly engaging in a hurtful act.
4. It may be difficult for the jealous person to blame the rival for being attracted to the partner when he or she feels the same attraction.

Nonetheless, anger toward the rival appears to be likely if the rival is a close friend of the jealous person. Parker (1994) suggested that when the rival is someone who is not well-known to the jealous person, stress is generally confined to the romantic relationship. When the rival is a friend of the jealous person, stress pervades the entire social network. Indeed, Parker found that if the rival was a close friend, jealous individuals were unlikely to seek support from their social networks, perhaps because they felt betrayed and humiliated. As Parker summarized, feelings of betrayal and anger are likely "magnified when a close friend becomes a rival in a romantic relationship" (p. 26).

Taken together, these findings suggest that jealous individuals are most likely to experience anger when they feel betrayed by close relational partners. When the rival is unknown to them, anger is most likely directed at the partner. When the rival is a friend, anger is likely to be directed at both the partner and the rival and perhaps at the social network in general. Of course, some jealous individuals are also angry at themselves for acting in a way that they perceive pushed the partner away.

When envious individuals experience anger, it is usually rooted in resentment, hatred, and frustration rather than in betrayal. As Parrott and Smith (1993) noted, jealousy and envy can both produce hostility, but the type of hostility they produce is different: Jealous individuals tend to feel "anger over betrayal," whereas envious individuals tend to feel "resentment and rancor" (p. 907). Parrott (1991) also argued that, "It should be apparent that there are strong similarities between malicious envy and anger. In fact, the distinction between the two rests primarily on whether the hostility is justified" (p. 10).

Envious anger and resentment can be directed at a person, a group of people, or at the general state of affairs, but envy can also be experienced apart from any feelings of anger and hostility. As Parrott (1991) stated, "One may feel angry at the fates for making some people beautiful without feeling angry at beautiful people for being beautiful" (p. 11). In our close relationships with others, we expect some admiration, awe, or nonmalicious envy to exist, but not anger and resentment. For example, if we are bowling or playing tennis with friends, we label them as "bad sports" if they grow angry because they are losing.

Envious anger also stems from frustration. As Smith (1991) contended, envy can lead to anger because the envious person feels he or she cannot reach a goal or desired state that someone else has achieved. This frustration is often directed at the rival, who is seen as achieving success much too easily. As cognitive dissonance theory predicts, people find it difficult to reconcile the fact that they may work hard for something but not achieve it, whereas someone else appears to effortlessly obtain the same goal. To decrease dissonance (and the attendant frustration), envious individuals search for shortcomings in rivals. They also find reasons to dislike the rival in an effort to bolster their liking for themselves (e.g., "She might be a great tennis player, but she's not as smart or pretty as I am"). For example, Salovey and Rodin (1984) found that envious individuals reportedly felt anxious about interacting with rivals, did not want to pursue friendships with them, and disparaged them on various personal traits.

Sadness.   Similar to fear, sadness is a common affective response when people experience jealousy and envy, yet the type of sadness differs depending on whether the individual is jealous or envious. Jealous sadness stems from the potential loss of a valued relationship and the loneliness that accompanies such loss. Envious sadness stems from one's feelings of inferiority, hopelessness, and helplessness.

Some research suggests that sadness is more central to envy than jealousy. The logic behind this argument is that sadness follows, rather than accompanies, the jealousy experience. White and Mullen (1989) put it this way:

> Sadness is present in most experiences of jealousy. The fear of a future that is depleted and empty usually leads to sadness. Sadness may well be muted, because jealousy is a state in which loss is feared rather than accepted, and sadness is likely to predominate in jealousy only when hope is abandoned. Jealousy is primarily a state of excitement and activation that is directed at the future and at changing that future, rather than a state of passive and sad acceptance. (p. 180)

White and Mullen also noted that jealousy-related depression is associated with feelings of guilt and worthlessness, as well as anger and suspicion. These feelings of worthlessness can lead jealous individuals to believe they deserve betrayal.

Work by Sharpsteen (1991) also supports the argument that intense sadness is most likely to follow rather than accompany jealousy. Arguing from a prototype perspective, Sharpsteen asserted that although jealousy is "a singular blend of anger, sadness, and fear," sadness is probably the least central of these emotions to the jealousy experience (p. 36). According to Shaver et al.'s (1987) prototype analysis, common antecedents of sadness include the loss of a valued relationship and separation from a loved one, which supports the contention that sadness is most likely to occur after relationship loss.

Some measure of sadness still commonly accompanies jealousy. Bringle (1991), for example, argued that in jealousy situations, "sadness results from the combination of high levels of commitment and relational losses that are irretrievable or the *possibility* of relationship termination" (p. 111, emphasis added). Mathes et al. (1985) argued that the loss of relationship rewards is responsible for the feelings of sadness elicited in jealousy situations. Certainly, jealous individuals often feel that they have lost trust in their partners and that "things will never be the same" even if the relationship continues. Thus, some level of sadness is expected to accompany jealousy because of the potential for relationship loss and the diminished reward value of the relationship.

Sadness appears to be a central, vital part of the experience of envy. Shaver et al. (1987) found that the prototypical antecedents of sadness included undesirable outcomes; rejection or exclusion; not getting what one wants, wishes for, or strives for; and having reality fall short of expectations. Thus, situations such as failing at a particular task, being rejected in favor of another, and receiving less praise than expected would all be likely candidates to produce sadness. When a rival is also involved (i.e., as the person who succeeds, is accepted, or receives the praise), envy is also likely to surface. It appears, then, that there are many situations that call forth both sadness and envy. This is not surprising given that negative comparisons to others and the resultant focus on one's own shortcomings are at the heart of the envious experience. Moreover, the desperate desire to possess something, followed by the disappointment of not achieving one's goal, appears to be a ready-made recipe for promoting sadness and despair. In short, the self-reflective process that produces feelings of envy is also likely to elicit feelings of sadness and discontent.

Both jealousy and envy are most likely to be accompanied by feelings of sadness when the jealous or envious person engages in brooding behavior and harbors deep feelings of low self-worth. In his study on reactions to jealousy, Bryson (1976, 1991) found a jealousy factor labeled *intropunitiveness*. Individuals scoring highly on this factor tended to internalize their jealous feelings and blame themselves for potential relationship termination or de-escalation. These individuals reported punishing themselves for being jealous rather than directing any negative affect toward the partner or the rival. Such self-directed blame is likely to lead to brooding and intense feelings of sadness. In Fitness and Fletcher's (1993) study of prototypical responses to emotion, jealousy was associated with brooding and negative feelings toward the self.

Lowered self-esteem is also likely to contribute to the sadness experienced with jealousy and envy. According to a survey conducted by Salovey and Rodin (1985), jealous and envious individuals tend to have low opinions of themselves, to see their "actual" selves as inferior to their "ideal" selves, and to value visible accomplishments and status symbols such as popularity, fame, wealth, positions of authority, and beauty. Parrott and Smith (1993) noted that jealousy and envy are both associated with lowered self-esteem and feelings of sadness, hopelessness, and despair. However, the explanatory mechanism is different for the two emotions. For jealousy, lowered self-esteem is likely due to feelings of projected rejection and loss. For envy, lowered self-esteem is likely a function of feelings of inferiority and longing.

Summary. The experiences of jealousy and envy often produce negative emotional reactions and self-perceptions. In the case of jealousy, individuals are likely to feel fear due to possible abandonment and relational loss, anxiety related to relational uncertainty, anger in response to perceived betrayal, and sadness at the prospect of potentially losing a valued relationship. In the case of envy, individuals are likely to fear rejection, experience anxiety or despair due to their perceived inferiority, and feel sad and hopeless if they do not see a way of improving their situation. In both cases, lowered self-esteem is a likely outcome because a negative self-to-other comparison has been made. Jealous individuals generally believe that their partners compared them unfavorably to a rival. Envious individuals make the unfavorable self-to-other comparison themselves.

Despite the considerable inner turmoil that jealousy and envy often produce, these emotions are more than purely intrapersonal phenomena. Both emotions originate in social interaction and/or social comparison, both usually have consequences for relationships, and both are expressed in interpersonal communication. In the following section, we outline some negative interpersonal consequences of these emotions, including the destructive forms of communication that are used to express jealousy and envy. We begin by examining the relational outcomes and communicative behaviors that are associated with jealousy (see Table 2.2 for a listing of relevant communication strategies).

Interpersonal Consequences and Communication Related to Jealousy

Uncertainty, Suspicion, and Distrust. Romantic jealousy is associated with three interrelated intrapersonal experiences—uncertainty, suspicion, and distrust. When individuals suspect that their partners are involved with rivals or distrust their partners, they are likely to experience high levels of relational uncertainty. Likewise, when people are uncertain about the state of their relationships, they may feel there is greater potential for their partner to become involved with a rival. Suspicion and distrust are also likely to co-exist, although distrust is likely to be the most pervasive when uncertainty is reduced so that suspicions are confirmed. As White and

TABLE 2.2

Negatively Valenced Communicative Behaviors Associated With Uncertainty, Distrust, and Suspicion

Behaviors and Definition/Examples

Surveillance and Guarding

1. *Surveillance/vigilance.* Behaviors that function to verify the partner's actions and reduce uncertainty about the nature of the rival relationship, for example, spying on the partner or looking through the partner's personal belongings and calling the partner unexpectedly to verify her/his whereabouts.
2. *Concealment/restriction.* Behaviors that function to conceal the partner and/or to restrict the partner's access to potential rivals, for example, refusing to introduce the partner to potential rivals and refusing to take the partner to a party where rivals would be present.
3. *Monopolizing the partner's time.* Behaviors that function to maximize the time the partner spends with the jealous person and minimize the time the partner spends with potential rivals, for example, planning joint activities that take up all of the partner's time and insisting that the partner spends all her/his free time with you.

Communication With the Rival

1. *Information seeking.* Communicating with the rival in order to find out more about the rival and the rival relationship, for example, talking with the rival to determine what kind of a person he or she is and asking the rival questions about the relationship with the partner.
2. *Derogation of the mate to rivals.* Disclosing negative information (whether true or untrue) about the partner in an effort to discourage the rival from pursuing the partner, for example, telling the rival that the partner is not very bright and is irritable and telling the rival that having a relationship with her/him is a bad experience.
3. *Rival threats.* Threatening the rival through the use of aggressive communication, hostility, and warnings, for example, staring coldly at the rival, trying to intimidate the rival, or threatening to hit the rival.
4. *Violence Toward rivals.* Actually causing physical harm to the rival or the rival's property, for example, pushing the rival out of the way and vandalizing the rival's car.

Signs of Possession

1. *Verbal signs of possession.* Verbal communication that asserts the relationship between the jealous person and the partner, for example, introducing the partner as one's "husband, " "wife, " "girlfriend, " and so forth and bragging to rivals about how much she or he and the partner love one another.
2. *Physical signs of possession.* Nonverbal communication that functions as relationship displays, for example, holding the partner's hand when others are around and kissing the partner in front of potential rivals.
3. *Possessive ornamentation.* Utilizing objects to display the relationship, for example, asking the partner to wear a ring or letterman's jacket and hanging the partner's picture in prominent places.

Avoidance

1. *Physical and emotional withdrawal.* Withdrawing from the partner, for example, spending less time with the partner and withdrawing affection from the partner
2. *Situation avoidance.* Avoiding jealousy-provoking situations, for example, refusing to go places where jealousy could surface and avoiding situations where the rival might be present.
3. *Unwillingness to communicate.* Refusing to communicate with the partner, for example, becoming quiet around the partner and failing to call the partner on the telephone.

Note. Category labels and examples are adapted from Buss (1988) and Guerrero et al. (1995).

Mullen (1989) stated, "Sadly, trust is often abandoned when jealousy takes root. The past actions and future intentions of the partner are exactly what jealousy puts in question; the fidelity of the partner is at issue, and therefore he or she cannot be trusted" (p. 233). Similarly, Buunk (1991) noted that when jealousy is a reactive emotional response to a partner's infidelity, many people label their emotion as anger rather than jealous per se. This is because infidelity is usually perceived as a disloyal act of betrayal that diminishes relational trust.

Relational uncertainty, suspicion, and distrust prompt a number of communicative responses to jealousy that have the potential to be valenced negatively. Four such responses are surveillance and guarding, communication with the rival, possessiveness, and avoidance (see Table 2.2).

Surveillance behavior is typically used to reduce uncertainty and guard the relationship. Guerrero and Afifi (1997), for example, found that individuals who wanted to reduce uncertainty about the rival relationship reported engaging in surveillance behaviors and restricting the partner's access to potential rivals. Pfieffer and Wong (1989) described *cognitive jealousy* as a composite of suspicious thoughts and worries and *behavioral jealousy* as a group of surveillance behaviors, including actions such as questioning the partner about her or his whereabouts, paying a surprise visit to the partner to see who is with her or him, and looking through the partner's belongings for evidence of an affair. In this and many other conceptualizations of jealousy, cognitive suspicion and behavioral jealousy are inextricably linked. Buss (1988) discussed several guarding or mate retention behaviors, including vigilance, mate concealment, and monopolization of the mate's time. These guarding behaviors are most likely to be used when the jealous individual is suspicious or worried about the partner's potential involvement with others.

Communication with the rival is also associated with uncertainty reduction and mate guarding. Guerrero and Afifi (1997) found that jealous individuals who wanted to reduce uncertainty about the rival relationship were likely to communicate with the rival directly (e.g., ask them how long they have known their partner or tell them to keep away from the partner). Bryson (1976, 1991) reported that jealous individuals sometimes seek information by confronting the rival. Jealous individuals also denigrate their partners in front of others as a method of discouraging rivals from pursuing their partners. For instance, a male might tell a rival that his girlfriend is demanding, lazy, or even that she has a social disease (Buss, 1988). In more rare circumstances, jealous individuals threaten rivals through verbal aggression, intimidation, or physical violence.

Signs of possession are also used to ward off potential rivals. Interestingly, signs of possession also function to show how devoted and close a couple is. For example, tie signs (e.g., holding hands, or wearing a wedding ring) reflect affection and caring between relational partners. However, these signs also function as a public signal that the partner is "taken." Jealous individuals may publicly flaunt their relationship with the partner when they are suspicious and/or distrustful. In this case, signs of possession are designed to reduce the rival's uncertainty about the unavailability of the partner. Buss (1988) described three types of possessiveness cues—verbal, physical, and ornamentation (see Table 2.2). Pinto and Hollandsworth (1984) discussed several ways that people display possessiveness, including discouraging the partner from making new friends and spending excessive amounts of time with the partner. Possessive individuals feel lonely and worry when they are separated (even briefly) from their partners. Due to high levels of suspicion and distrust, possessive individuals also feel an insatiable need to keep the partner to themselves by isolating the partner from a broader social circle (Pinto & Hollandsworth, 1984).

Finally, uncertainty and suspicion sometimes lead individuals to avoid active communication with their partners. Schaap, Buunk, and Kerkstra (1988) found a small but significant association between jealousy and an avoidant conflict style. Specifically, jealous individuals became unwilling to discuss relational problems and retreated (both physically and emotionally) from conflict situations. Afifi and Reichert (1996) used an uncertainty reduction theory framework to explain the association between jealousy and avoidance. According to these authors, jealousy is a highly uncertainty-proking situation. Indeed, their research shows that jealousy increases motivation to decrease uncertainty. Afifi and Reichert also found a tendency for uncertain, jealous individuals to avoid communicating with their partners, presumably because they felt uncertain regarding the partner's reaction.

Retaliation, Conflict, and Violence. Because jealousy is such an intense emotion and because it can engender feelings of deep hurt and betrayal, jealous individuals sometimes engage in aggressive, manipulative, and/or violent behavior (see Table 2.3). Buunk (1991) discussed the link between intense jealous feelings and aggressive behavior. Specifically, he argued that:

> In a normal, satisfying relationship there will usually be a preference for problem solving and compromise, and for taking into account the interests of the other person. However, when the other shows a clear interest in someone else, the tendency to be cooperative will diminish ... and the [jealous] individual's attitude seems to become ... more competitive and aggressive. (p. 165)

Schaap, Buunk, and Kerkstra (1988) examined associations between five conflict styles and jealousy. They found that jealousy was most strongly associated with an aggressive conflict style ($r = .78$), although it also associated with compromise ($r = .42$), soothing ($r = .40$) and avoidance ($r = .27$). Jealousy was inversely related to problem solving ($r = -.21$), as Buunk (1991) argued.

Sometimes jealous individuals feel a strong desire to enact revenge against their partners. Bryson (1976, 1991) discussed the concept of *reactive retribution*, which involves active attempts to get back at the partner who provoked jealous feelings. Reactive retribution includes behavior such as counterjealousy inductions, becoming sexually aggressive with others, criticizing the partner in front of others, and dating others to get back at the partner. Guerrero and Afifi (1997) discussed retaliation as a potential goal in jealousy situations. According to these authors, retaliation functions to vent frustration, anger, and hurt, and also serves to restore equity by "evening the score" (p. 8).

TABLE 2.3
Negatively Valenced Communicative Behaviors Associated With Retaliation and Conflict

Behaviors and Definitions/Examples

Aggressive Communication

1. *Distributive communication.* Direct and aggressive communication with the partner, for example, yelling at and arguing with the partner and making accusations and criticizing the partner's actions.

2. *Active distancing.* Indirect modes of communicating aggression to the partner, for example, pointedly ignoring the partner and acting cold and distant; withdrawing affection.

Manipulation Attempts

1. *Counterjealousy inductions.* Attempts to make the offending partner feel jealous too, for example, threatening to date and/or have sex with other people and flirting with a third party to make the partner jealous.

2. *Guilt inductions.* Attempts to make the offending partner feel guilty about her/his actions, for example, crying and telling the partner how hurt you are and threatening to harm oneself if the partner leaves.

Violent Behaviors

1. *Violence toward the partner.* Actions that physically harm the partner in some way, for example, slapping the partner and cutting off the partner's hair so he or she looks "ugly."

2. *Violence Toward Objects.* Directing aggression toward physical objects, for example, slamming doors or throwing dishes and throwing the partner's possessions out of the house.

Note. Category labels and examples are adapted from Buss (1988) and Guerrero et al. (1995).

Common retaliation strategies include aggressive communication and manipulation. Guerrero and Afifi (1997) found that individuals who wanted to get even with their partners engaged in behaviors such as arguing with the partner, making accusations, giving the partner "the silent treatment, trying to make the partner feel guilty, and trying to induce counter-jealousy. Similarly, Buss (1988) forwarded a *punishment strategy*, which comprises tactics such as becoming angry, ignoring the partner, threatening to terminate the relationship, yelling at the partner, and breaking off communication.

Unfortunately, jealous individuals sometimes go beyond verbal aggression and manipulation and resort to violence. In the midst of an epidemic of interpersonal violence and the current publicity of sensational court cases, jealousy has been shown to be a major contributor to violence. Hansen's (1991) comprehensive review of literature concluded "that male sexual jealousy may be the major source of conflict in an overwhelming majority of spousal homicides in North America. Similarly, numerous studies have noted the prevalence of jealousy as a motive in non-fatal wife abuse" (p. 225). Considerable research has also shown that jealousy, money, and alcohol are the three key antecedents of violence in the United States and Great Britain (see Delgado & Bond, 1993, for a review). Stets and Pirog-Good (1987) found the jealousy variable to increase females' use of violence in dating relationships by 240%. Sugarman and Hotaling (1989), in their review of the literature on dating violence, came to the startling conclusion that "in every study in which a respondent had a chance to list jealousy as a cause, it was the most frequently mentioned reason" for violence in dating relationships (p. 12). Similarly, Laner (1990) found that jealousy was one of the top precipitators of violence among high school- and college-age dating couples. She further argued that couples often see jealousy "as the 'real' problem, and violence as merely an 'ordinary' or predictable response to the problem" (p. 320).

As discussed previously, violence has historically been a socially sanctioned course of action in jealousy situations, which makes it more difficult to stop and easier to excuse. This unfortunate state of affairs may explain why some people tolerate violent jealousy. Fortunately, however, there is reason to believe that the link between jealousy and violence is weakening. The percentage of jealousy-related murders in the United States has declined since the mid-1970s, dropping from 10.7% of all murders in 1964 to only 2% of all murders in 1987 (Delgado & Bond, 1993; Stearns, 1989). The largest drop occurred from 1975 to 1976, when the percentage decreased from 7.3% to 2.8%. From 1975 to 1987, the rate stayed under 3%, suggesting that jealousy is regarded as a less justifiable motivation for violence now than it was previously (Stearns, 1989).

Jealous violence stems from imagined, as well as real, extradyadic interaction. In his book on morbid jealousy that results from delusions of infidelity, Mowat (1966) described the history of murder at the British "lunatic asylum," Broadmoor: "Possessed of these delusions, the jealous man persistently accuses his wife or mistress of infidelity. Thirty of the male murderers and all six of the female murderers accused their partners of infidelity" (p. 92). White and Mullen (1989), who reviewed numerous studies on the association between jealousy and violence, concluded that pathologically jealous individuals are sensitive to "every nuance in [their] environment that may hint at unfaithfulness" (p. 226). They also describe how jealous violence is triggered by symbolic association. For example, in their case studies, White and Mullen reported that one woman attacked her husband when he asked for a beer because she believed that he had an affair with a bar maid. Another woman gripped hold of a rival's clothing and told her to stay away from her husband. The rival's throat constricted and she began making choking noises and trying to breathe. At this point, the jealous woman associated the heavy breathing with the sound the rival would make when having sex with her husband. The jealous woman then became even more violent.

Given these vivid examples, it might seem that jealousy biologically leads to inevitable violence (see Guerrero & Andersen, 1998 for a discussion of sociobiological forces contributing to jealousy). Such is not the case. Among the thousands of jealous episodes that occur each day, few result in violence. However, whereas violence is not a common consequence of jealousy, jealousy is a common antecedent of violence. As Hupka (1991) pointed out, 37% to 50% of the U.S. population has extramarital affairs, but less than .01% of the U.S. male population commits murder in response to jealousy. Guerrero, Andersen, Jorgensen, Spitzberg, and Eloy (1995) found violence to be a relatively infrequent response to jealousy. Nonetheless, a significant percentage of murders are jealousy induced. This is another paradox of jealousy. Few emotions create such a unique combination of fear, anger, and sadness. For a small percentage of the population, this emotional devastation leads to extreme violence.

In some cases, violence and/or verbal aggression is used as a form of guarding and protecting the relationship or manipulating the relational partner. Paul et al. (1993) argued that whether we like it or not, aggressive action can sometimes be functional. They contended that jealousy-induced aggression can lead people to feel guilty and rethink their actions. Moreover, if the offending partner does not show any regret, the jealous individual probably extrapolates that there is a high likelihood of similar transgressions occurring in the future and may thereby terminate the relationship. Despite the potential functions that aggression might serve,

Paul et al. cautioned that "physical aggression is unlikely to strengthen the relationship. Emotional hurt is more likely to do the job" (p. 403). In the long run, we believe that emotional hurt is damaging to the relationship as well.

Relational (Dis)Satisfaction. All of the communicative behaviors just discussed—ranging from active distancing, to distributive communication, manipulation and threats, avoidance, and violence—have been found to have some negative impact on relational satisfaction. Jealousy, in general, associates with relational dissatisfaction. For example, two recent studies (Andersen et al., 1995; Guerrero & Eloy, 1991) found that cognitive jealousy shares a robust negative association with relational satisfaction. The causal nature of this relationship has yet to be determined, but it is likely that individuals who are dissatisfied with their relationships are likely to think that their partners are also dissatisfied, and therefore, their partners may be involved with or interested in others. It is also likely that the jealousy experience itself can lead to relational dissatisfaction, particularly when negative emotional reactions and aggressive, manipulative behaviors occur. It is likely, then, that the association between jealousy and relational satisfaction operates as a bidirectional process.

However, jealousy is not always destructive. Research suggests that couples who use integrative communication methods often emerge from the jealousy situation feeling secure and gaining new insight into their relationships. *Integrative communication,* such as disclosing jealous feelings, questioning the partner in a nonaccusatory fashion, and discussing the future of the relationship often leads to open discussion and promotes relational satisfaction (Andersen et al., 1995). Expressing negative emotion also promotes relational happiness under certain circumstances. Andersen et al. found that when jealousy-related emotions such as anger, frustration, and sadness were communicated alone or alongside distributive communication, active distancing, and/or avoidance, the result was decreased relational satisfaction. However, when negative emotions were expressed in the midst of discussing the problem via integrative communication, satisfaction levels were at their peak. It may be that the expression of negative emotion, within the context of integrative communication, leads the partner to see the jealous person as open, sincere, and caring.

Other communicative responses to jealousy, collectively labeled *compensatory restoration behaviors* (see Guerrero, Andersen, Jorgensen, Spitzberg, & Eloy, 1995), may also be associated with relational satisfaction. *Compensatory restoration behaviors* encompass strategies designed to improve the self or the relationship in an effort to retain the partner. Guerrero et al. listed tactics such as trying to improve one's appearance and trying to be the best partner possible as compensatory restoration behaviors. Buss (1988) discussed similar tactics, including resource display (e.g., spending money on or buying gifts for the partner), sexual inducements (e.g., giving in to the partner's sexual requests), enhancing physical appearance (e.g., using make-up and/or wearing the latest fashions), and emphasizing love and caring (e.g., being especially complimentary, affectionate, and helpful). Because these behaviors demonstrate love, caring, and a concern for the relationship, they sometimes promote relational satisfaction. However, if these behaviors are seen as desperate attempts to win back the partner, they are actually counterproductive (Guerrero et al., 1995).

Another tactic listed by Buss (1988), labeled *submission and debasement*, is especially likely to be viewed as such a desperate ingratiation attempt. *Submission and debasement* involves engaging in behaviors such as promising to change in order to please the partner, going along with everything the partner says, giving in to the partner's wishes, and becoming the partner's "slave" (p. 299). Even if these behaviors are successful in preserving the relationship, they are likely to promote low self-esteem.

Interpersonal Consequences and Communication Related to Envy

Coping With Negative Self-Evaluation. Because envy is precipitated by some type of negative self-to-other comparison, our close relationships with friends, family, and romantic partners form fertile ground for promoting envy, rivalry, and competition. Two theoretical frameworks help explain this phenomenon—Social comparison theory and the self-evaluation maintenance view (Messman, 1995; Salovey & Rodin, 1989).

Festinger's (1954) social comparison theory is predicated on the principles that people are driven to evaluate themselves and people make self-evaluations by comparing themselves to others. Research and theory indicates that these self-to-other comparisons are most likely to be made in the context of our interpersonal networks. Festinger, for example, argued that people tend to compare themselves with similar others. A study by Dakin and Arrowood (1981) provides support for this principle by demonstrating that people were most likely to compare themselves to others who were relatively close to them in terms of ability. Because similarity is a cornerstone in many friendships, it is logical that self-to-other comparisons tend to occur within the confines of such relationships. In addition, people spend time with their friends making them proximal targets for competitive comparisons.

The self-evaluation maintenance view (Tesser & Campbell, 1982), which was built on some of the premises of social comparison theory, is grounded in the notion that positive self-evaluation is a primary motive behind the actions of most individuals, particularly in Western cultures. According to this theory, positive self-evaluation occurs through the process of self-reflection and comparison to others. Reflection is likely to occur under several conditions, such as when people fall short or exceed their own expectations for achieving goals. In addition to having an internal yardstick for evaluating ourselves, Tesser and Campbell (1982; Tesser, 1986) argue that we use other people's successes and failures as points of reference for reflection and comparison, especially when those people are close to us. For example, if a good friend suddenly achieves a high degree of financial success, you may question whether your own financial situation is acceptable.

In a test of the self-evaluation maintenance view, Salovey and Rodin (1984) tested and found support for the contention that envy is strongest under three eliciting conditions.

1. There must be a negative self-to-other comparison.
2. This comparison must be in an area that is highly self-relevant to the potentially envious person.
3. The envious person and the rival should be similar in abilities and/or share a close relationship.

When these conditions are present, envy is likely to be experienced and the envious person should engage in coping behaviors to help alleviate negative affect. Salovey and Rodin (1988, 1989) forwarded three such coping strategies: (a) *self-reliance*, which includes avoiding outward emotional expression, keeping busy, and refusing to ask others for help; (b) *self-bolstering*, which includes concentrating on one's positive qualities and doing nice things for oneself; and (c) *selective ignoring*, which includes re-evaluating the importance of a goal so that it is no longer highly self-relevant. Communicative behaviors associated with these coping strategies might include the following: avoiding communication with the rival, spending time with people who are positively reinforcing, engaging in activities in which one has exceptional ability, and talking about one's achievements with others.

Intense feelings of envy may also lead a person to behave negatively toward the rival. Based on Salovey and Rodin's (1984) findings, it appears that envious individuals not only avoid communicating with the rival, but also bad mouth them. For example, an envious person may point out a rival's negative characteristics to others. If others agree with these negative assessments and show liking for the envious person, the sting of the initial self-to-other comparison is diminished. Obviously, communicative behaviors such as these can have negative effects on the relationship between the envious person and the rival.

Competitive Behaviors.   New research on the link between competitive-ness and communication suggests that avoidance and bad mouthing the rival are only two of several strategies that envious individuals use to cope with their feelings (see Messman, 1995, 1996; Messman & Cupach, 1996). Messman (1995) argued that competitiveness occurs when people make social comparisons for purposes of self-evaluation. When the self-to-other comparison is negative, people are likely to experience envy. To examine the link between competitiveness and communication, Messman asked students to describe the types of behaviors that they typically view as competitive. Using a thematic content analysis to sort these behaviors, Messman found five overarching categories of themes—antagonistic be-haviors, success-oriented behaviors, comparative behaviors, antisocial be-haviors, and context-bound behaviors. Of these, antagonistic and antisocial behaviors appear to be particularly likely to produce negative relational consequences. Therefore, we discuss these two strategies in more detail (see Table 2.4).

Antagonistic behaviors promote self-to-other comparisons. Individuals who express superiority and/or brag are particularly likely to become targets of malicious envy. These individuals may possess low self-esteem and feel a strong need to present themselves as superior. As Salovey and Rodin (1988) found, individuals sometimes cope with envy by engaging in self-bolstering. Certainly, communicative behaviors, such as expressed superiority and bragging, are part of the self-bolstering process.

Envious individuals also make themselves feel better by belittling others. Rather than casting themselves as superior, individuals who belittle cast others as inferior. The result, however, is the same. The envious individual has bolstered her or his own self-image at the expense of another. Belittling may also accompany the cognitive strategy of *selective ignoring*, which involves reducing the importance of certain skills and abilities. As a case in point, imagine finding out that one of your close friends and colleagues received a prestigious award that you coveted. Rather than facing the idea that your friend is more worthy than you are, you might convince yourself that the award was not that important. Salovey and Rodin (1984) also provided a nice example of this. They described a situation in which a colleague informs them that his article on jealousy will be published as the lead article in a prestigious journal. Because the authors also publish research on jealousy, they speculate that this news would be likely to elicit envy. To maintain their positive definitions of self and reduce the threat that their colleague poses, Salovey and Rodin (1989) speculated that they might cognitively downgrade the journal or write the journal editor a letter describing the study's flaws. If the envious person went a step further and

TABLE 2.4

Competitive Behavior Likely to Be Associated with Negative Relational Outcomes

Behaviors and Definition/Example

ANTAGONISTIC BEHAVIORS:
Behaviors That Encourage Negative Self-to-Other Comparisons

Expressed superiority. Actions that cast oneself as superior to others, for example, correcting other people in front of others

Belittling. Actions that cast others as inferior to oneself, for example, downplaying, dismissing, or laughing at another person's ideas, telling the partner that s/he got "lucky" when he or she accomplished something, and saying that the partner's accomplishment is "not such a big deal."

Bragging. Actions that call undue attention to one's achievements, for example, telling others about one's achievements or showing people a big paycheck.

Aggressiveness. Verbal or nonverbal behaviors that challenge or intimidate others, for example, frequently disagreeing with someone and becoming argumentative, and giving people the "evil eye."

Insincerity/manipulation. Using manipulation to force a negative self-to-other comparison, for example, acting phony or condescending or forcing a compliment.

Subterfuge. Purposeful actions that are designed to diminish the rival's positive image, for example, making negative, untrue remarks about the rival to others, trying to make the rival lose concentration so he or she will perform poorly, and making it seem as though the rival cheated.

ANTISOCIAL BEHAVIORS:
Behaviors That Reflect Competitiveness and/or Envy-Proneness

Social distance. Behaviors directed at the rival that show disinterest and avoidance, for example, avoiding direct eye contact with the rival, not paying attention to what the rival is saying, and staying away from the rival in social situations.

General anxiety/defensiveness. Behaviors that show anxiety and/or defensiveness, for example, acting nervous when it is time to perform a task, becoming especially serious when engaging in a competitive task, and acting defensive when one does poorly.

Noncooperative efforts. Behaviors that indicate unwillingness to work with a group, for example, suddenly working harder when someone else in the group starts doing well, refusing to help others in the group do better, and working alone instead of with others.

Self-focus. Behaviors that demonstrate self-absorption, for example, using "I" rather than "we" when speaking about a joint project, insisting on doing things a certain way, and dominating discussions.

Note. This table is adapted from Messman's (1996) work on competitiveness.

verbalized these thoughts to the colleague (e.g., "That journal's not that great anyway" and "Did you consider correcting these flaws ... ?"), belittling would occur.

Another form of behavior that is often perceived as competitive is *subterfuge* (Messman, 1996). When people use this strategy, they are intentionally trying to prevent the rival from excelling or from maintaining a positive self-image within the social network. For example, an envious person might try to harm the rival's reputation. Strategies such as this are probably most likely to be used when individuals experience intense envy or rivalry. *Rivalry* is somewhat different from envy in that neither person possesses the valued commodity and both are actively seeking it (Bryson, 1977; Salovey & Rodin, 1989). Whether the situation involves envy or rivalry, *subterfuge* is likely to be used when people want others to evaluate them more positively than a rival and/or when people want to get revenge at the rival.

The final two forms of antagonistic behaviors—*aggressiveness* and *insecurity or manipulation*—involve communication styles that reflect a competitive orientation (Messman, 1996). Aggressive behaviors are viewed as personally challenging and often intimidating, and therefore, they likely lead to competition and self-to-other evaluations. *Insecurity or manipulation behaviors* appear to force others to either make a positive evaluation of the communicator or a negative evaluation of themselves. For example, people who fish for compliments are trying to bolster their positive images of themselves, whereas people who act condescending or stand offish imply that the sender's message is not worthwhile.

Messman (1996) also described four types of antisocial behaviors. The first of these—*social distance*—involves showing disinterest and avoiding interaction with the rival. This strategy corresponds with Salovey and Rodin's (1984) research, that found people want to avoid future interaction with rivals. When individuals are faced with a person who engenders a negative self-to-other comparison, a natural reaction is to avoid them and thus, to avoid feeling badly about themselves. The second antisocial behavior, *general anxiety or defensiveness*, is likely a symptom of envy proneness and competitiveness. Individuals who take competitive situations to heart are most likely to be nervous when performing important tasks and become defensive if the task is not performed well. The final two antisocial behaviors—*noncooperative efforts* and *self-focus*—represent an unwillingness to work with others and a need to be the best or the leader when conversing with others. These two objectives may appear contradictory on the surface, however, when you consider that competitive people want to stand apart from others (but also want to be recognized for their accomplishments), such actions make sense.

All of the antagonistic and antisocial behaviors just described lead to negative interpersonal consequences. Some behaviors falling under Messman's (1996) success-oriented theme also promote negative consequences. For example, Messman discussed behaviors such as making a bet with someone, openly challenging someone's position, and telling a group that the most important thing is to win. These behaviors increase the self-relevance of a skill or topic area, which can lead to envy. In addition, some people reported that they or their partners got upset when they lost. These types of success-oriented behaviors appear likely to promote conflict and separation rather than harmony and solidarity.

Relational (Dis)Satisfaction. Because envy and competitiveness are often found within the context of close relationships, it is natural to wonder how envious thoughts, emotions, and behaviors affect relational satisfaction. It appears obvious that many of the behaviors discussed are detrimental to relationships. Behaviors such as expressed superiority and bragging are likely to make others uncomfortable. Moreover, because envy and pride are popularly perceived as two of the seven deadly sins, individuals who verbally express their superiority are viewed as arrogant rather than self-confident. Behaviors such as belittling, aggressiveness, and insincerity or manipulation are also likely to promote relational dissatisfaction because they force others to take a defensive stance. Put simply, most people do not want to be around someone who is constantly disagreeing with or belittling them; although such a process may help one person bolster positive self-to-other evaluations, it causes the other person to see herself or himself more negatively.

Messman and Cupach (1996) confirmed the contention that many antagonistic and antisocial behaviors negatively affect relationships. In their study, friends completed questions regarding competitive communication, facework (i.e., how they present themselves to one another), and interpersonal solidarity. Results showed that across same-sex and cross-sex friendships, malevolent competitive behaviors were negatively associated with interpersonal solidarity. *Malevolent competition* was measured with items such as: "My friend tries to 'one-up' me," "My friend responds *unhappily* to something I did well," "My friend might make it seem like I am cheating when we play a game," and "My friend acts stand-offish when wishing me well."

Certain competitive behaviors, however, were positively related to interpersonal solidarity. Specifically, behaviors that reflected achievement competition appear to associate with positive relational outcomes (Messman & Cupach, 1996). These behaviors include saying that one wants to work hard and excel, sharing one's achievements with others without bragging, and asking about the friend's accomplishments. Interestingly, these behaviors are competitive in that they could call forth a self-to-other comparison; however, they are framed in a way that emphasizes accomplishments over defeats and solidarity over conflict.

Finally, it is noteworthy that nonmalicious or admiring envy leads to liking and relational satisfaction. Such envy is likely to occur when the ability, talent, or personal characteristic in question is only self-relevant for one of the relational partners. For example, a husband might be immensely proud of his wife's ability to understand finances and build them a sound investment portfolio because he is not good with numbers. Two friends may brag about one another's successes in two different areas such as academics and athletics. In these cases, people are likely to admire their partners for possessing desirable traits. In addition, they might bask in the reflected glory of their partner's accomplishments (see Salovey & Rodin, 1989). In such cases, the idea that your relational partner is a good, talented, and worthwhile person, coupled with the knowledge that your partner has chosen you as a companion, is likely to lead you to evaluate yourself positively. Similarly, to the extent that relational partners possess positive personal characteristics and abilities, they have the power to deposit rewards into the relationship, which ultimately makes the relationship more satisfying.

CONCLUSION

Although we primarily focused on the dark side of jealousy and envy, it should be evident that these emotions have a bright side as well. Jealousy and envy are related yet distinct constructs. Both experiences are accompanied by a similar constellation of emotion that includes anger, fear, and sadness. The cause of these emotions, however, differs. Jealousy, which is the broader of the two constructs, is associated with fear over the prospect of losing a valued relationship, anger over betrayal, and sadness over potential relationship loss. Envy, on the other hand, is rooted in anger at oneself and resentment toward others, fear stemming from perceptions of inferiority, and sadness regarding one's failures and shortcomings. Both jealousy and envy are associated with more negative than positive emotions, but the positive emotions should not be overlooked. Jealousy can show love and appreciation, add romance to a dull relationship, or help one realize the extent of care and commitment he or she feels for another. Envy can lead to admiration and self-improvement.

Similarly, although jealousy and envy sometimes lead to destructive forms of interpersonal communication and, ultimately, to relational dissatisfaction, at other times, these emotions lead to understanding and solidarity. Thus, it appears that the way jealousy and envy are expressed is a key determinant of relational satisfaction. Jealous individuals who show distrust by monitoring their partners' actions and becoming possessive, as well as those who show their anger through verbal or physical aggression, are likely to push their partners further away. Similarly, those who handle envy by engaging in negatively valenced, competitive behaviors, such as belittling, bragging, manipulation, and subterfuge, are likely to alienate others, which in turn, leads to even stronger feelings of resentment and inferiority. However, the picture is not as dark as it might at first seem. When jealous individuals approach the situation by discussing the problem with their partner in a calm and constructive manner, a new relational understanding may emerge. Jealousy sometimes serves a protective function by prompting the jealous individual to express love and affection when the relationship is in danger of going astray. Envy can also be functional, especially when it is used as a motivational tool to improve oneself. Thus, as with many human emotions, jealousy and envy have both a dark, dysfunctional side and a bright, functional side. Understanding both sides of these complex emotions is an important enterprise for scholars, clinicians, and all who value their relationships with others.

ACKNOWLEDGMENT

We thank Susan Messman for sharing her work on competitiveness with us and for her valuable comments on the competitiveness section of this chapter.

REFERENCES

Afifi, W. A., & Reichert, T. (1996). Understanding the role of uncertainty in jealousy experience and expression. *Communication Reports, 9*, 93–103.

Andersen, P. A., Eloy, S. V., Guerrero, L. K., & Spitzberg, B. H. (1995). Romantic jealousy and relational satisfaction: A look at the impact of jealousy experience and expression. *Communication Reports, 8*, 77–85.

Aristotle. (1886). *The Rhetoric* (J. E. C. Welldon, Trans.). London: Metheun (Original work published in 344 B.C.)

Arnold, M. B. (1960). *Emotion and personality.* New York: Columbia University Press.

Aune, K. S., & Comstock, J. (1996, May). *The effect of relationship length on the experience, expression, and perceived appropriateness of jealousy.* Paper presented at the annual meeting of the International Communication Association, Chicago.

Ausubel, D. P., Sullivan, E. V., & Ives, S. W. (1980). *Theory and problems of child development.* New York: Grune & Stratton.

Baumgart, H. (1990). *Jealousy.* Chicago: University of Chicago Press.

Baxter, L. A. (1988). A dialectical perspective on communication strategies in relational development. In S. W. Duck (Ed.), *Handbook of personal relationships: Theory, research, and interventions* (pp. 257–273). New York: Wiley.

Berke, J. H. (1988). *The tyranny of malice: Exploring the dark side of culture and character.* New York: Summit Books.

Bers, S. A., & Rodin, J. (1984). Social comparison jealousy: A developmental and motivational study. *Journal of Personality and Social Psychology, 47*, 766–769.

Bohm, E. (1961). Jealousy. In A. Ellis & A. Abarbanel (Eds.), *The encyclopedia of sexual behavior* (vol. 1, pp. 567–574). New York: Hawthorn Books.

Brehm, S. S. (1992). *Intimate relationships* (2nd ed.). New York: McGraw-Hill.

Bringle, R. G. (1991). Psychosocial aspects of jealousy: A transactional model. In P. Salovey (Ed.), *The psychology of jealousy and envy* (pp. 103–131). New York: Guilford.

Bryson, J. B. (1976, September). *The nature of sexual jealousy: An exploratory paper.* Paper presented at the annual meeting of the American Psychological Association, Washington, DC.

Bryson, J. B. (1977, September). *Situational determinants of the expression of jealousy.* Paper presented at the annual meeting of the American Psychological Association, San Francisco, CA.

Bryson, J. B. (1991). Modes of responses to jealousy-evoking situations. In P. Salovey (Ed.). *The psychology of envy and jealousy* (pp.1–45). New York: Guilford.

Burke, T., Genn-Bash, A., & Haines, B. (1988). *Competition in theory and practice.* London: Croom Helm.

Buss, D. M. (1988). From vigilance to violence: Tactics of mate retention in American undergraduates. *Ethology and Sociobiology, 9*, 291–317.

Buunk, B. P. (1991). Jealousy in close relationships: An exchange-theoretical perspective. In P. Salovey (Ed.), *The psychology of jealousy and envy* (pp. 148–177). New York: Guilford.

Campos, J. J., Barrett, K. C., Lamb, M. E., Goldsmith, H. H., & Stenberg, C. (1983). Socioemotional development. In M. M. Haith & J. J. Campos (Eds.), *Handbook of Child Psychology: Vol. 2. Infancy and developmental psychobiology* (4th ed., pp. 783–915). New York: Wiley.

Ciabattari, J. (1988, December). Will the '90s be the age of envy? *Psychology Today*, 47–50.

Clanton, G. (1989). Jealousy in American culture 1945–1985: Reflections from popular literature. In D. D. Franks & E. D. McCarthy (Eds.), *The sociology of emotions: Original essays and research papers* (pp. 179–193). Greenwich, CT: JAI.

Clanton, G., & Smith, L. G. (1977). *Jealousy.* Englewood Cliffs, NJ: Prentice-Hall.

Comstock, J., & Aune, K. S. (1995, May). *Is jealousy prescribed or against the rules: Comparisons among same-sex friends, cross-sex friends, and romantic partners.* Paper presented at the annual meeting of the International Communication Association, Albuquerque, NM.

Dakin, S., & Arrowood, A. J. (1981). The social comparison of ability. *Human Relations, 34*, 80–109.

Daly, M., & Wilson, M. (1983). *Sex, evolution, and behavior.* Boston, MA: Willard Grant Press.

Delgado, A. R., & Bond, R. A. (1993). Attenuating the attribution of responsibility: The lay perception of jealousy as a motive for wife battery. *Journal of Applied Social Psychology, 23*, 1337–1356.

Ekman, P., Friesen, W. V., & Ellsworth, P. (1972). *Emotions in the human face: Guidelines for research and integration of findings.* New York: Pergamon.

Farrell, D. M. (1980). Jealousy. *The Philosophical Review, 89* 527–529.

Festinger, L. (1954). A theory of social comparison processes. *Human Relations, 7*, 11–140.

Fitness, J., & Fletcher, G. J. O. (1993). Love, hate, anger, and jealousy in close relationships: A prototype and cognitive appraisal analysis. *Journal of Personality and Social Psychology, 65*, 942–958.

Guerrero, L. K., & Afifi, W. A. (1997, June). *Toward a functional approach to studying strategic communicative responses to jealousy.* Paper presented at the annual meeting of the International Network on Personal Relationships, Oxford, OH.

Guerrero, L. K., & Andersen, P. A. (1998). The experience and expression of romantic jealousy. In P. A. Andersen & L. K. Guerrero (Eds.), *The handbook of communication and emotion: Research, theory, applications, and contexts* (pp. 155–188). San Diego, CA: Academic Press.

Guerrero, L. K., Andersen, P. A., Jorgensen, P. F., Spitzberg, B. H., & Eloy, S. V. (1995). Coping with the green-eyed monster: Conceptualizing and measuring communicative responses to romantic jealousy. *Western Journal of Communication, 59*, 270–304.

Guerrero, L. K., & Eloy, S. V. (1991). Relational satisfaction and jealousy across marital types. *Communication Reports, 5*, 23–31.

Guerrero, L. K., Eloy, S. V., Jorgensen, P. F., & Andersen, P. A. (1993). Hers or his? Sex differences in the communication of jealousy in close relationships. In P. Kalbfleisch (Ed.), *Interpersonal communication: Evolving interpersonal relationships* (pp. 109–131). Hillsdale, NJ: Lawrence Erlbaum Associates.

Hansen, G. L. (1991). Jealousy: Its conceptualization, measurement, and integration with family stress theory. In P. Salovey (Ed.), *The psychology of jealousy and envy* (pp. 211–230). New York: Guilford.

Hupka, R. B. (1991). The motive for the arousal of romantic jealousy. In P. Salovey (Ed.), *The psychology of jealousy and envy* (pp. 252–270). New York: Guilford.

Klein, M., & Riviere, J. (1964). *Love, hate, and reparation.* New York: Norton.

Korda, M. (1992). *The immortals.* New York: Poseidon Press.

Laner, M. R. (1990). Violence or its precipitators: Which is more likely to be identified as a dating problems? *Deviant Behavior, 11,* 319–329.

Mathes, E. W., Adams, H. E., & Davies, R. M. (1985). Jealousy: Loss of relationship rewards, loss of self-esteem, depression, anxiety, and anger. *Journal of Personality and Social Psychology, 48,* 1552–1561.

Mathes, E. W., & Verstraete, C. (1993). Jealous aggression: Who is the target, the beloved or the rival? *Psychological Reports, 72,* 1071–1074.

Messman, S. J. (1995). *Competitiveness in close relationships: The role of communication competence.* Unpublished doctoral dissertation, Ohio University, Athens, OH.

Messman, S. J. (1996, February). *Competitiveness and communication: Conceptualization and operationalization.* Paper presented at the annual meeting of the Western States Communication Association, Pasadena, CA.

Messman, S. J., & Cupach, W. R. (1996, November). *Perceptions of competitive communication behavior in friendship: Associations with face predilections and solidarity.* Paper presented at the annual meeting of the Speech Communication Association, San Diego, CA.

Mowat, R. R. (1966). *Morbid jealousy and murder.* London: Tavistock.

Mullen, P. E., & Maack, L. H. (1985). Jealousy, pathological jealousy, and aggression. In D. P. Farrington & J. Gunn (Eds.), *Aggression and dangerousness* (pp. 103–126). New York: Wiley.

Panskeep, J. (1982). Towards a general psychobiological theory of emotions. *Behavioral and Brain Sciences, 5,* 407–467.

Parker, R. G. (1994, November). *An examination of the influence of situational determinants upon strategies for coping with romantic jealousy.* Paper presented at the annual meeting of the Speech Communication Association, New Orleans, LA.

Parrott, W. G. (1991). The emotional experiences of envy and jealousy. In P. Salovey (Ed.), *The psychology of jealousy and envy* (pp. 3–30). New York: Guilford.

Parrott, W. G., & Smith, R. H. (1993). Distinguishing the experiences of envy and jealousy. *Journal of Personality and Social Psychology, 64,* 906–920.

Paul, L., Foss, M. A., & Galloway, J. (1993). Sexual jealousy in young women and men: Aggressive responsiveness to partner and rival. *Aggressive Behavior, 19,* 401–420.

Pfeiffer, S. M., & Wong, P. T. (1989). Multidimensional jealousy. *Journal of Social and Personal Relationships, 6,* 181-196.

Pines, A. (1992). *Romantic jealousy: Understanding and conquering the shadow of love.* New York: St. Martin's Press.

Pines, A., & Aronson, E. (1983). Antecedents, correlates, and consequences of sexual jealousy. *Journal of Personality, 51,* 108-136.

Pinto, R. P., & Hollandsworth, J. G., Jr. (1984). A measure of possessiveness in intimate relationships. *Journal of Social and Clinical Psychology, 6,* 505–510.

Plutchik, R. (1980). *Emotion: A psychoevolutionary theory of emotion.* New York: Harper & Row.

Rimé, B., Mesquita, B., Philippot, P., & Boca, S. (1991). Beyond the emotional event: Six studies of the social sharing of emotion. *Cognition and Emotion, 5,* 435–465.

Salovey, P., & Rodin, J. (1984). Some antecedents and consequences of social-comparison jealousy. *Journal of Personality and Social Psychology, 47,* 780–792.

Salovey, P., & Rodin, J. (1985, September). The heart of jealousy. *Psychology Today,* 22–25, 28–29.

Salovey, P., & Rodin, J. (1988). Coping with envy and jealousy. *Journal of Social and Clinical Psychology, 7,* 15–33.

Salovey, P., & Rodin, J. (1989). Envy and jealousy in close relationships. In C. Hendrick (Ed.), *Close relationships* (pp. 221–246). Newbury Park: Sage.

Salovey, P., & Rothman, A. J. (1991). Envy and jealousy: Self and society. In P. Salovey (Ed.), *The psychology of jealousy and envy* (pp. 271–286). New York: Guilford.

Schaap, C., Buunk, B., & Kerkstra, A. (1988). Martial conflict resolution. In P. Noller & M. A. Fitzpatrick (Eds.), *Perspectives on marital interaction* (pp. 203–244). Philadelphia: Multilingual Matters.

Schoeck, H. (1969). *Envy: A theory of social behavior.* New York: Harcourt Brace.

Sharpsteen, D. J. (1991). The organization of jealousy knowledge: Romantic jealousy as a blended emotion. In P. Salovey (Ed.), *The psychology of jealousy and envy* (pp. 31–51). New York: Guilford.

Shaver, P. R., Schwartz, J., Kirson, D., & O'Connor, C. (1987). Emotion knowledge: Further explorations of a prototype approach. *Journal of Personality and Social Psychology, 52,* 1061–1086.

Sharpsteen, D. J. (1991). The organization of jealousy knowledge: Romantic jealousy as a blended emotion. In P. Salovey (Ed.), *The psychology of jealousy and envy* (pp. 31–51). New York: Guilford.

Smith, R. H. (1991). Envy and the sense of injustice. In P. Salovey (Ed.), *The psychology of jealousy and envy* (pp. 79–99). New York: Guilford.

Smith, R. H., Kim, S. H., & Parrott, W. G. (1988). Envy and jealousy: Semantic problems and experiential distinctions. *Personality and Social Psychology Bulletin, 14,* 401–409.

Smith, R. H., Parrott, W. G., & Diener, E. (1990). *The development and validation of a scale for measuring enviousness.* Unpublished manuscript.

Solomon, R. C. (1976). *The passions.* Garden City, NY: Doubleday.

Stearns, P. N. (1989). *Jealousy: The evolution of an emotion in American history.* New York: New York University Press.

Stets, J. E., & Pirog-Good, M. A. (1987). Violence in dating relationships. *Social Psychology Quarterly, 50,* 237-246.

Sugarman, D. B., & Hotaling, G. T. (1989). Dating violence: Prevalence, context, and risk markers. In M. A. Pirog-Good & J. E. Stets (Eds.), *Violence in dating relationships: Emerging social issues* (pp. 3–32). New York: Praeger.

Teismann, M. W., & Mosher, D. L. (1978). Jealous conflict in dating couples. *Psychological Reports, 42,* 1211–1216.

Tesser, A. (1986). Some effects of self-evaluation maintenance on cognition and action. In R. M. Sorrentino & E. T. Higgins (Eds.), *Handbook of motivation and cognition* (pp. 435–464). New York: Guilford.

Tesser, A., & Campbell, J. (1982). Self-evaluation maintenance and the perception of friends and strangers. *Journal of Personality, 50,* 261–279.

Texas executes man who killed his ex-girlfriend out of jealousy. (1995, August 15). *The New York Times,* p. A1.

Tracy, L. (1991). *The secret between us: Competition among women.* Boston, MA: Little, Brown.

White, G. L., Fishbein, S., & Rutstein, J. (1981). Passionate love and the misattribution of arousal. *Journal of Personality and Social Psychology, 41,* 56–62.

White, G. L., & Mullen, P. E. (1989). *Jealousy: Theory, research, and clinical strategies.* New York: Guilford.

II

CONFUSING

3

(Mis)Understanding

Alan L. Sillars
University of Montana

One day, I invited a colleague to eat dinner at my house after work. At the arranged time, I went to meet my friend at his office, however, he was not there. I returned to my office, made several phone calls, and waited for a further signal about what to do. Meanwhile, my colleague had gone to my home. Eventually, we connected and had dinner. This example is typical of what people mean when they refer to a "misunderstanding." However, there is also a second way in which people refer to "misunderstanding," which is suggested by the cliche, "my husband (or family, friends, parents, etc.) doesn't/don't understand me." For example, a married couple has a quarrel about whether to ask the wife's sister to watch their child. As the argument progresses, each person has a variety of thoughts. He thinks that the request is only fair because they helped her sister in the past. She thinks her daughter would not be welcome and in addition, she does not want her daughter exposed to the smoke at her sister's house. He thinks that she is just making excuses and that she does not care about spending time together as a couple. She thinks he is only concerned about himself. He feels frustrated and angry and thinks she is trying to evade the issue. She thinks that he is unwilling to compromise and will say anything to get his way.

In the first example given, misunderstanding might be the result of innocent assumptions, a lack of information, or a failure to communicate explicitly. Misunderstandings of this nature are mostly easy to correct and are not taken personally. The second example is more typical of misunder-

73

standing in relationship conflicts. In this case, misunderstanding mixes freely with disagreement (i.e., the disagreement about what to do is compounded by incongruous attributions about the thoughts, desires, and intentions of each person). This type of misunderstanding is not so easily dismissed as an error resulting from incomplete information. It often occurs despite the fact that the people are intimately familiar with the issue and each other.

As an observation about general trends, the idea that understanding increases with increased closeness in relationships (e.g., Colvin, Vogt, & Ickes, 1997; Planalp & Garvin-Doxas, 1994) seems irrefutable. This is, after all, what is meant when a relationship is described as "close"; the psychological gap between separate individuals has narrowed. At the same time, one of the ironies of close relationships is that they are often the source of the most persistent and troubling misunderstandings. The central issue of this chapter is how to best account for such cases of persistent misunderstanding. In essence, the answer I suggest is that closeness and efforts to communicate sometimes diminish rather than increase understanding.

The adopted perspective emphasizes the interaction of interpersonal perception, interpersonal communication, and interpersonal relationships. Perception, communication, and relationships are, in effect, the same phenomenon viewed from different angles, however, they are ususally ordered in a particular way. Whereas many authors have considered how the properties of perception and cognition affect communication, far fewer have considered how the characteristics of communication affect interpersonal perception. Reversing this emphasis provides some additional insight into the nature of understanding in long-term relationships. Understanding may be affected, for example, by the emotionality and interdependence of close relationships, by the inherent ambiguity and complexity of communication, and by communicative goals that influence the selectivity and structure of perception.

In the forthcoming chapter I first discuss general issues with regard to the meaning of understanding. Second, I consider how properties of communication and relationships might affect interpersonal perception and understanding. Third, I discuss probable sources of misunderstanding in relationship conflicts based on two recent studies in progress and related work.

THE NATURE OF UNDERSTANDING AND MISUNDERSTANDING

Following Laing, Phillipson, and Lee (1966), *understanding* is the congruence between one person's *meta-perspective* (i.e., his or her estimate of the partner's perspective) and the other person's *direct perspective* (i.e., what the other person actually thinks). The simplicity of this definition of understanding is deceiving. Understanding, because it describes a relationship between two intangibles (i.e., perspectives and metaperspectives), is highly abstract, subject to various interpretations, and difficult to operationalize. Any difficulties encountered in identifying a person's perspective are multiplied when considering mutual understanding.

Because perspectives are multifaceted, there are many areas in which understanding could be assessed. Understanding and related concepts have been investigated in the context of trait perceptions, attitudes, role expectations, relationship beliefs and patterns, self-concepts, conflict issues, communicative intentions, feelings, and immediate thoughts (see Ickes & Simpson, 1997; Sillars & Scott, 1983). The diversity of this research literature shows that understanding has many levels. Furthermore, relationships can (and generally do) reflect understanding in some areas and misunderstanding in others. Therefore, depending on what aspects of understanding are assessed, studies may suggest different conclusions about basic issues (e.g., the extent to which people understand or misunderstand one another or how understanding affects relationship adjustment, (Ickes & Simpson, 1997; Sillars, 1989).

Common use of the term *understanding* has a few misleading implications. One such implication is that misunderstanding is relatively simple and unmotivated, that is, some problems are "just misunderstandings." Misunderstanding results from a variety of sources, some of which are simple, whereas others are subtle and persistent. One sort of misunderstanding results from a lack of mutual knowledge or a shared communication code. These situations could be called *innocent misunderstandings* because the motivations of the parties have little to do with the source of misunderstanding. Innocent misunderstandings are generally simple and often trivial. When two people come to know one another better, innocent misunderstandings should decrease.

The complexity of interaction goals distinguishes innocent misunderstanding from other cases. In all instances of interpersonal communication, the parties have multiple goals, including identity and relationship goals as well as information goals. When multiple goals are in alignment (i.e., identity and relationship goals are also served by being clear and by understanding others), communication is straightforward and usually leads to greater understanding. However, there are other situations in which perception and communication reflect tangled motivations. Ickes and Simpson (1997) noted that both egocentric and altruistic goals influence how people attend to, process, and ignore information during interactions. For example, two people who are determined to assert themselves in an quarrel might structure their representations of one another in a way that supports self-justification and bolsters personal arguments. Alternatively, people might be motivated to misunderstand one another out of benevolent goals, such as a desire to mitigate a perceived threat to the relationship posed by an uncomfortable topic of conversation (Simpson, Ickes, & Blackstone, 1995). In addition, multiple goals affect the readability of the target. For example, people often equivocate to maintain privacy and avoid negative consequences that might result from being too clear (Bavelas, Black, Chovil, & Mullett, 1992; Chovil, 1994). Thus, both the production and interpretation of messages are affected by motives aside from the desire to understand and be understood.

Another common implication of the term *understanding* is that the accuracy of understanding is an individual process (as in "Joanne misunderstood Kevin," or "My husband doesn't understand me."). Although interpretation is an individual process, understanding is inherently relational. One problem with viewing understanding as an individual process rests with the equivocality of direct perspectives, which serve as the criteria for determining the accuracy of metaperspectives. Direct perspectives should not be regarded as a faithful representation of actual thoughts, feelings, attitudes, or communicative intentions (Thomas & Fletcher, 1997). Direct perspectives are filtered, distorted, strategically reported, and otherwise translated in much the same manner as metaperspectives as they are transformed from live experience to accounts of that experience.

By way of illustration, consider a case of misunderstanding between mother and daughter. In this instance, the mother states her concern about the way her daughter is dressed for school. The message is delivered with flat, neutral affect (as trained raters would verify if they could observe), however, the daughter finds the remark to be full of condescension and sarcasm. The mother believes, on the other hand, that she is merely trying to be helpful. Similar misunderstandings appear to be commonplace; for example, incongruous evaluations of communicative intent often occur among married couples, especially low adjustment couples (see Noller & Ruzzene, 1991). It may be tempting, in this example, to say that the daughter misunderstands her mother. However, the daughter might counter by citing a variety of contextualizing elements that enrich the meaning of the message (e.g., the mother always comments when the daughter wears a particular blouse, her mother did not want her to buy the blouse in the first place, and they had a fight about the same thing just 2 days earlier). Of course, this does not settle the matter, because the mother might counter with her own list of contextualizing factors. The correct interpretation could be argued indefinitely because the meaning of the mother's message is ultimately a matter of perspective and is not fixed by reference to any single source of translation. Understanding is, therefore, an act of collaboration, not individual insight alone.[1]

Yet another misleading implication is that understanding is a benchmark for good or effective communication. Spitzberg (1994) suggested that there is an ideology of accuracy in popular and academic circles that equates clarity and understanding with competence in communication. In contrast, Spitzberg noted that misunderstanding is often quite functional (see also Chovil, 1994; Eisenberg, 1984; Kursh, 1971). Of course, it would be easy to overstate this point. It is difficult to imagine how pervasive, chronic misunderstanding in relationships could be functional. Most studies that have considered the issue have found a positive association between understanding or congruence of perception and relationship satisfaction/adjustment (see Ickes & Simpson, 1997; Sillars & Scott, 1983). However, there are significant exceptions that beg explanation (Thomas & Fletcher, 1997), including a few studies that reported a negative association between understanding and satisfaction in marriage (Allen & Thompson, 1984; Sillars, Pike, Jones, & Murphy, 1984).

The relationship between understanding and satisfaction/adjustment is complicated by two basic considerations. First, as suggested earlier, there is a need to balance multiple, often conflicting goals in communication. Thus, although some understanding is probably inherent to effective communication, the effort to balance competing goals (e.g., intimacy/autonomy, politeness/assertiveness, communality/instrumentality) inevitably leads to a degree of censorship, obfuscation, selective interpretation, and limited understanding, even in well-adjusted relationships (Spitzberg, 1993).

The second complication is that there are many areas in which understanding could be assessed. Furthermore, the association between understanding and relationship satisfaction seems to rest on the context and domain of understanding. For example, the research by Sillars et al. (1984) looked at understanding marital conflict issues. In this case, less satisfied couples had more understanding about which issues were salient marital conflicts, presumably because they communicated irritations and complaints in an unequivocal manner. In support of this interpretation, the research found that the partner's negative and verbally competitive behavior during a structured discussion predicted understanding better than

---

[1]I do not mean to suggest that understanding is always negotiated. As Berger (1992) emphasized, understanding may result substantially from the fortuitous overlap of individual perspectives that people bring with them to relationships and indiscriminately project onto others. In addition, I do not mean to dismiss the potential importance of individual differences in empathic ability. There do seem to be consistent individual differences in the ability to form understanding relationships, although the traits that account for these differences remain a mystery (Colvin, Vogt, & Ickes, 1997; Marangoni, Garcia, Ickes, & Teng, 1995).

other aspects of communication. These results do not establish that couples were dissatisfied *because* they understood their partner's complaints, since causality can be reversed (i.e., couples had greater understanding because their dissatisfactions were expressed more freely). However, it seems likely that increased recognition of irreconcilable differences and unpleasant truths adds to dissatisfaction (Ickes & Simpson, 1997; Sillars, 1985).

There is also a counterpoint to the last observation, that is, fondness for the partner is often associated with an inflated expectation of agreement and unrealistically positive or optimistic perceptions (Hendrick & Hendrick, 1988; Ickes & Simpson, 1997; Murray & Holmes, 1996; Simpson et al., 1995; Thomas & Fletcher, 1997). Several authors have suggested that these positive illusions or "benevolent misconceptions" preserve and enhance relationship satisfaction (Ickes & Simpson, 1997) because "reality so often falls short of a person's hopes" (Murray & Holmes, 1996, p. 91). In contrast, Fletcher and Kininmonth (1991) noted the possibility that "those who are disillusioned or unhappy with their relationships may [in certain respects] perceive their relationships in a realistic, even-handed, and hence, pessimistic fashion (p. 243)." Thus, not only is misunderstanding a normal and expected consequence of communication, but there are also instances where misunderstanding might reduce irreconcilable conflict and preserve needed optimism in relationships.

INTERPERSONAL PROPERTIES OF PERCEPTION

Now, consider how characteristics of interpersonal relationships and interpersonal communication might contribute to the persistence of misunderstanding. Because interpersonal perceptions are formed and maintained in particular relationships, their structure is naturally affected by the key features of this context.

There are at least four such features that contribute to misunderstanding—the biasing effects of familiarity and intimacy, inherent and strategic ambiguity in communication, the tendency to regard ambiguous inferences with certainty, and narrative and rhetorical influences on interpersonal perceptions.

Familiarity and Bias

Some of the difficulties involved in understanding another person are situational, the most apparent difficulty being a lack of familiarity, mutual knowledge, experiential background, or shared vocabulary. Misunderstandings that result from a lack of familiarity are common with strangers, "out-group" members, members of different cultures, and so forth. With increased familiarity and closeness, there is an increase in the amount of information one has about another person, which should facilitate understanding in many respects. However, there is also a potential tradeoff between knowledge and objectivity (Sillars & Scott, 1983).

The first half of this tradeoff is illustrated by the greater use of mutual knowledge in conversations among friends versus those among strangers (Colvin et al., 1997; Planalp & Garvin-Doxas, 1994). Planalp and Garvin-Doxas (1994) noted that the use of mutual knowledge is an obvious feature of conversations, such that observers can easily tell whether two people are friends based on what they assume to know in common (i.e., what details are omitted in speech but assumed to be understood). Colvin et al. (1997) summarized several studies that show the impact of mutual knowledge on empathic accuracy during interactions. In these studies, people watched a videotape of an earlier conversation and tried to infer the thoughts that another person reported having during the conversation. In two studies, friends were 50% more accurate than strangers in judging the other person's thoughts (Graham, 1994; Stinson & Ickes, 1992). Stinson and Ickes (1992) found that the advantage of friends was greatest when inferring thoughts about events that occurred at another time or place, suggesting that greater mutual knowledge accounted for the greater empathic accuracy of friends. Furthermore, another study indicated that the degree of empathic accuracy among same-sex friends was predicted by the perceived closeness of the perceiver-target relationship (Gesn, 1995).

Colvin et al. (1997) interpreted these and other findings as indicating that friends develop an intersubjective meaning context, in which they draw on shared memories of previous events to anticipate the other's thoughts. Friends also develop more complex and integrated knowledge structures that facilitate retrieval and learning of information about the other (Planalp & Garvin-Doxas, 1994). According to Planalp and Garvin-Doxas, the difference between strangers and friends is analogous to the difference between novices and experts. That is, experts, as well as friends, remember complex and related patterns of information rather than isolated details.

Surra and Ridley (1991) advanced a similar argument regarding interpersonal perception in close relationships and families. These authors noted that insider reports of family interaction differ systematically from reports provided by observers. Furthermore, insiders may agree more with each other than with outsiders (Margolin, Hattem, John, & Yost, 1985). Surra and Ridley suggested that these trends reflect the development of private meaning systems within close relationships, based on relational knowl-edge that is specific, complex, and unique (see also Surra & Bohman, 1991).

On the other hand, there seems to be a point of diminishing returns where increased familiarity and closeness do not bring further under-standing. For example, couples who have been married longer do not necessarily have greater understanding. Sillars and Zietlow (1993) found no differences between younger and older couples in understanding, whereas Thomas, Fletcher, and Lange (1995; see also Fletcher & Thomas, 1996; Thomas & Fletcher, 1997) found lower empathic accuracy among couples who had been married longer. Furthermore, there are a number of systematic biases in interpersonal perception that occur at all stages of close relationships (see Sillars & Scott, 1983).

In contrast to acquaintances (where people are simply ignorant about one another), close relationships present a complex situation in which inferences about others may be equally well-informed and biased. There are two sources of bias in close relationships that are most relevant here. First, there is the flip side of the phenomena noted by Planalp and Garvin-Doxas (1994). Although becoming another person's expert allows one to make sophisticated and organized inferences, it also increases the tendency to view potential sources of information selectively and to make new inferences fit existing relationship theories (Fletcher & Thomas, 1996). Over time, frequently activated inferences become increasingly entrenched and monitoring the relationship for new information might decline as people listen more selectively and assume they "have heard it all before." Thomas and Fletcher (1997) speculated along similar lines that empathic accuracy peaks during early marriage when spouses are expend-ing more effort to understand one another; thereafter, complacency might diminish empathic accuracy. In the extreme, existing relationship schema can become rigid, absorbing, and impermeable structures that dictate the outcome of communication (Raush, Barry, Hertel, & Swain, 1974; Watzlawick, Beavin, & Jackson, 1967).

A second, broad influence on interpersonal perception is the greater degree of conflict and emotionality associated with intimate relationships (see Sillars & Scott, 1983). Strong emotions account for a number of specific biases in interpersonal perceptions, for example, mood-induced memory and cognition (Bradbury & Fincham, 1987; Forgas, 1996); selec-tive attention to vivid, negative behavior, particularly within conflictual relationships (Bradbury & Fincham, 1987); self-serving attributions for negative events in distressed relationships (Fincham, Bradbury, & Scott, 1990); decreased perspective-taking and complexity of thought during stressful conflicts (Sillars & Scott, 1983); and "motivated inaccuracy" in threatening situations (Ickes & Simpson, 1997). In addition to these cognitive effects of emotion, the disorderly structure of relationship conflicts also contributes to misunderstanding in close relationships, which is a point we return to later in the chapter (see *Relationship Conflicts*). The primary implication here is that understanding is most problematic in the context of emotional conflicts.

Ambiguity

Another factor contributing to misunderstanding in close relationships is the ambiguity of interpersonal communication. Misunderstanding is often attributed to a lack of communication, but this emphasis neglects the more subtle and difficult aspects of communication. Communication is sometimes viewed as a mechanical process of transplanting ideas from the head of one person to another using words (Berger, 1992). In contrast, Berger described communication as "an inferential game in which individuals do their best to make sense of sketchy patterns of sights, sounds, and markings on paper," a process that is "difficult and chancy" (p. 47). Even when accompanied by the best intentions, communication achieves only partial success and, in an occasional instance, drives perspectives further apart.

All instances of communication are potentially problematic because explicit codes, such as language, are incomplete; they symbolize some aspects of the speaker's "meaning" to the neglect of many others (e.g., Suzuki, 1978). Also, explicitly coded information is not, by itself, sufficient to distinguish between the possible meanings of a message. To resolve this ambiguity, it is necessary to infer the speaker's intent based on nonlinguistic, contextual information (Berger, 1992; Ritchie, 1991; Sperber & Wilson, 1995).

Naturally, different aspects of meaning are not equally problematic. Scott, Fuhrman, and Wyer (1991) noted that different levels of inference are involved in communication, ranging from low-level semantic concepts necessary to understand the literal meaning of a message to abstract inferences about the implications of encoded information (e.g., whether the husband's observation about Lyme disease at Yosemite is meant as an excuse for canceling a trip there; Scott et al., 1991, p. 41). Similarly, a number of authors distinguished between the literal or propositional content of a message and a second, pragmatic level of meaning that "defines the relationship" (Watzlawick et al., 1967). The second level of meaning, variously referred to as the *command* or *relationship* (Watzlawick et. al., 1967), *presentational* (Danziger, 1976), *illocutionary* (Searle, 1969), or *episodic* (Frentz & Farrell, 1976) aspect of meaning includes the type of action and expected response conveyed (e.g., a request for information, a plea for help, or a command) as well as the social or evaluative implications of the act (e.g., whether the act shows commitment, restraint, formality, independence, or antagonism).

At each level of meaning, inferences about the speaker's intent are constrained by formal or informal communication rules. However, the propositional content of a statement is determined to a much greater extent by the formal code, whereas relational or illocutionary meanings rely heavily on informal and tacit knowledge. The social conventions at this level are not always shared or consistently followed, so an act may variously be seen as an instance of advising versus needling, explaining versus lecturing, concern versus intrusion, and so forth. Several considerations further complicate interpretations:

- A great variety of linguistic expressions may perform a given illocutionary or relationship act. For example, a "promise" or "threat" can assume many linguistic forms.
- Speech acts are often expressed indirectly (Jacobs & Jackson, 1983).
- Relationship-level meaning is mostly implicit and analogic and is not readily translatable into words. Thus, it is difficult to clarify (Watzlawick et. al., 1967).

In addition to inherent ambiguity, there is also strategic ambiguity in communication, reflecting the multiple goals of individuals in interactions. That is, a speaker may, through obfuscation, attempt to preserve harmonious relations, prevent recriminations, maintain personal privacy, or avoid being pinned down in an argument. Ironically, intimacy often increases the intensity of equivocation strategies. Individuals escalate their efforts at obfuscation partly in response to the potential transparency of close relationships, as in the case of an adolescent who reveals much more to family outsiders than to insiders. This reaction represents a compensatory effort designed to maintain a comfortable level of integration versus autonomy, which is one of the main dialectic tensions in close relationships (see Bochner & Eisenberg, 1987).

There are a few further implications of inherent and strategic ambiguity in communication. First, ambiguity invites selectivity. The more ambiguous the message, the less constrained the listener is in furnishing an interpretation (Sanders, 1984). The second implication stems partly from the first. Specifically, the impact of explicit communication on understanding is complex and is mediated partly by the ambiguity of the referent. This is a point that my colleagues and I investigated in several studies of marital communication.

The first of these studies (Sillars et al., 1984) considered the association between observed communication patterns and understanding of marital conflicts based on structured discussions and questionnaires, that were administered to two samples of couples. There was no association between direct disclosure about conflict and understanding. Spouses largely projected their own views to the partner, although couples who were more negative had somewhat greater understanding. A second study (Zietlow, 1986, Sillars & Zietlow, 1993) used parallel methods to investigate communication and conflict patterns among young, midlife, and elderly married couples. This research indicated that elderly couples self-disclosed less, discussed conflict issues less directly, and projected their self-cognitions to the partner more than younger couples; however, their understanding of the partner's attitudes was about the same, even after controlling for the confounding influence of projection on understanding.

A third study (Sillars, Weisberg, Burggraf, & Zietlow, 1990) also used a structured discussion of marital issues, but here we distinguished between understanding of instrumental versus companionate attitudes. Companionate attitudes have to do with affective and expressive qualities of marriage, whereas instrumental attitudes have to do with activities and tasks. We also considered how closely and accurately spouses attended to their conversations, based on their recall of the conversations immediately afterward. We reasoned that the companionate items (e.g., "In a good marriage, people don't have secrets") were more abstract, relational, and ambiguous than the instrumental items (e.g., "A neat house is very important"), which referred to more concrete and stable aspects of married life. Therefore, we expected understanding of instrumental attitudes to exceed understanding of companionate attitudes. This prediction was confirmed. In addition, recall accuracy was related to understanding of instrumental attitudes but not understanding of companionate attitudes. This suggests that more attentive and accurate processing of conversation primarily affected understanding of less ambiguous (i.e., instrumental) perceptions.

Finally, some aspects of the previous research were replicated by Sillars, Folwell, Hill, Maki, Hurst, and Casano (1994). This time we relied on simple questionnaire measures of communication, that indicated how often couples discussed various instrumental and companionate topics. The husband's understanding of the wife was not related to this measure of communication; however, we found a positive association between communication frequency and the wife's understanding of the husband on instrumental items. In contrast, there was a *negative* association between communication frequency and the wife's understanding of the husband on companionate items. This research, along with the other studies, indicates that more frequent, open, or direct communication is not associated in any simple way with greater understanding in marriage. Furthermore, it appears that misunderstanding is most likely to persist, despite explicit communication, in areas that are more ambiguous due to their abstract and relational nature.

Certainty

The significance of ambiguity in communication is magnified by a companion phenomenon, which is the tendency of perceivers to give little self-reflective attention to sources of ambiguity and bias. People routinely make strong inferences about others in ambiguous circumstances, with little acknowledgment of their perceptions as inferences. This is not a new insight but a variation on the well-worn principle of fact–inference confusion, with additional implications for communication in close relationships. Inferences about communication are insulated from subsequent re-evaluation and they elicit stronger reactions, in part, because they are not seen as inferences at all, but as objective observations (Fincham et al., 1990). Furthermore, certainty, predictability, and understanding are expected in close relationships, so people are even more likely to regard their inferences with certainty in this context. Of course, these tendencies do not hold in all cases, as there are clearly times when people experience great uncertainty and subjective confusion in close relationships (e.g., Planalp & Honeycutt, 1985; Planalp & Rivers, 1996). However, episodes of uncertainty are striking precisely because they stand out against a backdrop of strong expectations.

I am not aware of any direct support for the argument that subjective certainty exceeds actual understanding; however, there are several indications of related insensitivity toward ambiguity and bias in interpersonal perception. For example, spouses generally assume that they agree more than they actually do (e.g., Acitelli, Douvan, & Veroff, 1993; Sillars & Scott, 1983). In some areas, spouses show so little awareness of differences in perception that understanding scores drop dramatically when the influence of agreement is factored out (Sillars, 1989; Sillars et al., 1994). Shapiro and Swensen (1969) also found that spouses overestimated how much they knew about their partners and, conversely, how much their partners knew about them. Finally, several studies support Icke's (1993) conclusion that people lack metaknowledge regarding their own empathic accuracy. For example, various measures of self-reported empathy did not predict empathic accuracy based on Icke's thought-recall procedure (Ickes, Stinson, Bissonnette, & Garcia, 1990). Furthermore, subjects' confidence in their empathic accuracy did not correlate with their actual empathic accuracy in simulated clinical interviews (Marangoni, Garcia, Ickes, & Teng, 1995) or in marital interactions (Thomas et al., 1995). Thomas et al. also found that less educated spouses were more confident but less accurate than more educated spouses when predicting their partner's thoughts. This may indicate that confidence impedes understanding. Noller and Venardos (1986) looked at a similar process, but from a reverse angle—that is, the confidence of spouses that their messages were being understood versus confidence in one's understanding of the other. This research showed that the sender's confidence predicted accuracy of encoding and decoding among high marital adjustment couples, but not among low adjustment couples.

The characteristics of interpersonal communication contribute to the insensitivity often shown toward ambiguity and bias. Even simple exchanges require numerous coordinated decisions in real time (Bavelas & Coates, 1992). The complexity of communication virtually requires an unquestioning stance toward routine inference, because it is not possible to consciously attend to more than a tiny percentage of the inferences and decisions involved in interpersonal communication without constant disruptions and digressions in the flow of conversation (Bavelas & Coates, 1992; Fletcher & Fincham, 1991; Kellerman, 1992). Thus, cognitive processing of communication is generally "geared to achieving the greatest possible cognitive effect for the smallest possible processing effort" (Sperber & Wilson, 1995, p. vii), as suggested by the "cognitive miser" metaphor for social cognition. In an occasional instance, people adopt a much more self-reflective and questioning stance toward communication. However, this primarily occurs during intervals between interactions, when the pace of activity has slowed. Furthermore, there is generally little chance that meanings are re-evaluated subsequent to interactions, once an interpretation has been supplied (Scott et al., 1991).

A second consideration is that all communication requires intentionality attributions because, as we have said, formal coding rules alone are not sufficient to determine a speaker's meaning. Intentionality attributions are made so routinely as a condition of all communication, that these attributions are largely experienced as unmediated observations. Thus, language use conditions individuals to make automatic intentionality attributions.

A third factor contributing to subjective certainty is a lack of feedback regarding the occurrence of misunderstanding. Misunderstanding is mostly benign and does not lead to any overt difficulty, therefore, it remains latent. Furthermore, the informal criteria used to assess understanding in communication are not exacting. People do not seek complete understanding of others; rather, they seek a partial understanding that is adequate for their own interaction goals. As has been said, there are even cases in which people are motivated to preserve misunderstanding, as in the case of positive illusions that are relationship-enhancing or negative perceptions that are self-serving (see Ickes & Simpson, 1997, Murray & Holmes, 1996, Thomas & Fletcher, 1997).

The tendency to regard communication with certainty is not problematic in and of itself, rather it becomes problematic in certain contexts, for example, when ambiguous, negative inferences about pragmatic intent are framed in the same unequivocal terms as routine, semantic inferences. In this respect, problems do not arise because of maladaptive processing strategies, but, because normative strategies are extended to inappropriate contexts. The same tendencies that generally provide a functional basis for managing the complexity of interaction most of the time become maladaptive at other times because they short circuit the formation of more flexible and reflective communication strategies.

Narrative and Rhetorical Properties of Perception

A final point about the interpersonal context of perception is that perceptions reflect the goals and requirements of particular communication episodes. Interpersonal perceptions are not passive, detached observations, but rather accounts that are constructed to manage and cope with a complex and involving stimulus. These accounts are constructed for the benefit of both self and others. Other people and their reactions influence accounts either tacitly, as in the case of imagined dialogues that go unexpressed, or directly in the event that accounts are actually expressed to the partner or to third parties. Thus, communication (whether imaginary or real) helps to shape interpersonal perception.

Taking this argument a step further, particular types of communication episodes are expected to encourage or inhibit understanding. Some communicative activities encourage "other-centeredness," for example, affinity-seeking, comforting, reminiscing, and playing. In these instances, goals are met through perspective taking and convergent thinking. However, different demands apply in contexts in which individualistic goals (e.g., self-justification or self-assertion) dominate. In such contexts, communication reinforces divergent thinking. Although this point is admittedly speculative, there seem to be at least two situations in which communication is expected to polarize interpersonal perceptions—individual storytelling and interpersonal argument.

The first case involves situations in which people develop stories about their relationships for the benefit of real or imagined third parties. This appears to be a recurring, involving, and psychologically significant context, as suggested by the considerable body of recent literature concerned with personal narratives about relationships (e.g., Burnett, McGhee, & Clarke, 1987; Coupland & Nussbaum, 1993; Harvey, Orbuch, & Weber, 1992). Furthermore, this literature generally affirms a long-standing observation that people mostly provide highly selective personal narratives, that are greatly simplified in the interests of maintaining consistency and coherence.

Although it is possible to explain how elements are selected for stories in mostly psychological terms (e.g., script-driven encoding or memory), it is likely that selectivity has a social basis as well. Because narratives are developed for the purpose of relating personal experiences to an audience, narratives show responsiveness to the requirements of effective storytelling (i.e., the implicit standards held about a good story). Furthermore, the requirements of the storytelling situation encourage individuals to embellish certain details at the expense of others. For example, in order to be understandable, a story should be *coherent*; that is, it should put events in sequence, define the principal characters clearly, and explain motives. Great selectivity is necessarily involved in organizing stories into an unbroken sequence of cause and effect, that sometimes extends over many separate acts and interaction episodes. In order to engage and hold the listener's attention, a story should be both *simple* (i.e., it should have an uncomplicated plot line, highlight important details, and avoid tangents) and *dramatic* (i.e., it should build suspense and emphasize extreme or surprising elements). Numerous details are dropped and other elements recruited to enhance the interest value of stories. In order to receive the listener's approval, a story should be *plausible*, (e.g., it should rely on a familiar plot structure and employ socially acceptable explanations).

Weiss' (1975) study of marital separation provides an illustration of how personal accounts of relationships are shaped by criteria similar to these. Weiss noted that the individuals he interviewed generally constructed simple, highly selective stories about their separation that provided a convenient and socially acceptable explanation. Development of a coherent account seemed to facilitate adaptation to separation and divorce partly by restoring a sense of predictability, but also by meeting the social demands of situations in which the account came into play. In such a case, personal narratives are probably tranformed over time, becoming streamlined with repeated tellings and increasingly capitalizing on the elements that affect listeners favorably. As a consequence, the independently developed narratives of two ex-spouses from the same marriage may tell entirely different, unrelated stories (Weiss, 1975). This difference reflects not only the psychological perspective of the individual telling the story, but also the relationship he or she forms with various audiences.

Although independent development of relationship narratives should exaggerate differences in interpersonal perception, Berger (1992) noted that the joint rendering of accounts increases the likelihood of mutual understanding by making the elements explicit. However, this principle does not apply in all cases. The difficulty is that individual narratives are often hard to reconcile, so jointly authored accounts can be fragmented and incoherent (Burnett, 1991, Gergen & Gergen, 1987). One study my colleagues and I conducted (Sillars, Burggraf, Yost, & Zietlow, 1992) revealed wide variation among married couples in the degree of integration and continuity of relationship themes from one speaker to the next during their conversations. Some highly interdependent couples (based on separate measures of marital ideology and satisfaction) offered completely integrated accounts in which they reiterated and elaborated on the same themes (even completing one another's speaking turns). However, other, more autonomous spouses mostly offered separate, fragmented accounts that were frequently interrupted and often unrelated to the previous speaker. In such cases, the joint rendering of stories simply motivates further development of separate narratives.

The second context in which communication is expected to contribute to misunderstanding is interpersonal argument. In some respects, arguments increase understanding in the same manner as joint storytelling, (e.g., by making perspectives explicit or by stimulating convergent, jointly constructed arguments; see Canary, Brossmann, Brossmann, & Weger, 1995). However, in some circumstances, construction and rehersal of arguments leads to a more extreme and one-sided perception of relationship issues (Cloven & Roloff, 1991). In part, this reflects the general tendency to make self-serving attributions when self-esteem is threatened (e.g., Bradley, 1978). In addition, there are rhetorical influences on interpersonal perception, which are cognitive and communicative demands of the interpersonal setting in which arguments occur.

Again, it is important to consider what people are doing in the situation—that is, developing, expressing, defending, supporting, and refuting arguments. These goals have a number of potential consequences, for example: (a) thoughts about the relationship might be dramatized and sharpened, reflecting a person's efforts to achieve maximum persuasive effect; (b) commitment and certainty may increase as a consequence of efforts to defend one's position; (c) ambiguous messages and other information might be selectively interpreted in a way that favors personal arguments; (d) evidence, in the form of past relationship events, might be selectively remembered, based on how the examples serve persuasive goals; and (e) metaperceptions about the partner's opinions and intentions might be represented in simplified or distorted terms (as in the "straw man" fallacy of argument), thereby, making it easier to refute or dismiss criticism. Thus, certain devious misunderstandings assist the maintenance of a particular line of argument.

Such egocentric thinking is not inherent to effective argument; in fact, perspective-taking ability may increase an individual's persuasive competence (e.g., O'Keefe & Sypher, 1981). However, the cognitive demands of communication during argument limit one's ability to take the perspective of others. Perspective taking requires temporary suppression of one's own perspective, which is especially difficult in a stressful and cognitively demanding environment (Ickes & Simpson, 1997). Interpersonal arguments impose complex cognitive demands on the individual, requiring simultaneous consideration of shifting issues, relationship concerns, and argument tactics, with no allowance for leisurely consideration of alternative perspectives. Thus, thought processes can be monopolized by the effort to bolster personal arguments.

One further consequence of rhetorical demands on perception is that considerable mulling often takes place as a carryover from previous arguments and as an effort to bolster one's position in anticipation of future episodes. As Cloven and Roloff (1991, 1993, 1995) showed in their research, mulling often has the effect of making perspectives on conflict more extreme, particularly when people anticipate a future interaction in which they primarily convey rather than receive information. Arguments sometimes erupt at the beginning of interaction episodes "for no apparent reason" because considerable priming has already taken place in the form of silent rehearsal (Berger, 1992, p. 44). When an argument ensues with little objective provocation and escalates rapidly, this is a sign that one or both parties have previously been carrying on the argument internally. Because this internal dialogue is apt to take place on very uneven terms, mulling can be a significant source of misunderstanding; for example, one person might be oblivious to the source of the partner's brooding and taken completely off guard by their sudden expression of strong feelings (Berger, 1992).

MISUNDERSTANDING RELATIONSHIP CONFLICTS

Although misunderstanding in human relationships is mostly covert and benign, there are clear exceptions to this trend in the case of relationship conflicts. Every mediator, councelor, or family therapist realizes, of course, that communication, interpersonal perception, and conflict management are interconnected. Conflicts are nearly always seen differently from the perspectives of different parties. In a bitter dispute, perceptions become so diametrically opposed that constructive communication is impossible without some initial softening of perceptions and reframing of the situation. Furthermore, perceptions of conflict are not merely opposed, but they often depict entirely different conflicts from the point of view of either party. In this sense, relationship conflicts are often one-sided affairs, in which the parties neither participate in the same issues nor observe the same sequence of events.

Again, characteristics of the communicative context help to account for misunderstanding and selectivity of interpersonal perception. In a previous publication, a colleague and I suggested that ambiguity, confusion, and disorganization are important, basic features of relationship conflicts (Sillars & Weisberg, 1987). For example, there is often considerable ambiguity regarding the source of conflict. Serious relationship conflicts are difficult to isolate or define objectively and they are multilayered, involving different issues at different levels of abstraction. A vague sense of dissatisfaction over core relationship issues (such as .affection, equity, or respect) may have a rippling effect, creating conflict on many specific topics (Morton, Alexander, & Altman, 1976). Characteristically, relationship conflicts are manifested through discussion of these symptomatic issues (Hocker & Wilmot, 1991), adding to further confusion about the source of difficulty. In addition, the process of communication during serious relationship conflicts often lacks coherence. For example, discussions may lose focus and ramble across a variety of issues, conventional rules of conversation are frequently violated, and the mixed motives of the parties (e.g., the simultaneous urge to maintain lash out and to maintain composure) sometimes leads to schizophrenic-like communication, such as alternation between confrontation and denial of conflict (Sillars & Weisberg, 1987). Thus, relationship conflicts present a confusing stimulus field, that further increases the likelihood that interpersonal perceptions reflect idiosyncratic and self-serving elements.

In the following section, I suggest some ways that individuals selectively monitor and interpret communication during family conflicts. This section is based on preliminary results from two recent studies, in which my colleagues and I analyzed online thoughts about communciation, which were elicited through video-assisted recall.

The Studies

In the first of these studies, married couples discussed a salient marital conflict and then individually viewed videotapes of the discussion. The spouses were prompted every 20 seconds to report whatever thoughts or feelings they recalled having during the discussion. Because the instructions were nondirective, these data reveal spontaneous attributions about communication. We coded the recall data using a detailed, inductively-derived set of categories that was designed to reveal the content of reported thoughts and feelings as descriptively as possible. Hereafter, I refer to this as the Marital Interaction Project (MIP) study, following the title of the larger project (Leonard & Roberts, 1996). The larger project was an experimental study of the effects of alcohol on marital communication in physically aggressive and nonaggressive marriages. I base my observations here on an analysis of 73 couples who were not affected by the alcohol treatment (Dun, Sillars, Roberts, & Leonard, 1996).

In the second study, my colleagues (Ascan Koerner, Mary Anne Fitzpatrick, and Amy Kampen) and I video taped 50 families (i.e., mother, father, and adolescent child) while they discussed parent–child conflicts. We again elicited video-assisted recall of the interactions from individual family members, but in this case, each person was prompted to report what s/he was thinking and what each of the other family members was thinking at regular intervals in the discussions. The methods were adapted from the protocol developed by Ickes and his colleagues (see Ickes & Tooke, 1988; Ickes, 1997). At the time of this writing, we have not completed formal coding of these data, but I comment here on some characteristics evident from a qualitative reading of the transcribed thoughts. I refer to these data as the Wisconsin study (after the location of the research).

There seem to be three main trends in the online perceptions of communication in these studies, which help to account for misunderstanding of relationship conflicts. These trends are: actor–partner differences in the way communicative intentions are assigned, selective monitoring of different elements of the communication process, and limited complexity of thoughts associated with communication.

Attributing Communicative Intentions

Previous research on cognition in relationship conflicts has given considerable attention to attributions about responsibility, causality, and personality (see Canary, Cupach & Messman, 1995; Fincham & Bradbury, 1991; Retzinger, 1991). The reasons for this emphasis are obvious. Blame and other attributions often inflame conflicts and become the explicit focus as conflicts evolve and digress. At the same time, abstract attributions are preceded by an intermediate level of inference, which has received much less attention. At a level below abstract attributions, interactions are understood in terms of pragmatic meanings, intentions, and strategies; for example, whether a person is presumed to be apologizing, accusing, avoiding, or lying.

The MIP data provide some indication of how often people spontaneously engage in both forms of attribution. Abstract attributional analysis was frequently evident in these reports; for example, the thoughts often revealed admission or denial of responsibility for problems as well as negative attributions about the causes of the partner's behavior. Still, these direct examples of attributional analysis collectively comprised only about 7% of the codable thoughts. More typically, attributions of blame or responsibility were implied by the disparaging tone of other inferences. Attributions about the communication process were quite common. Over one fourth (28%) of the codable thoughts referred to communicative intentions and strategies (i.e., what either person was seen as doing in the interaction), whereas another 10% of the thoughts were other appraisals of the communication process (such as thoughts about the progress or lack of progress being made in the discussion).

Just as other studies documented actor–partner differences in attributions of blame and responsibility for conflicts, the MIP data revealed strong differences in communicative intentions attributed to self (as actor) versus the partner. Spouses often reported thinking that the partner was being confrontive (e.g., by dominating the floor, being inflexible, and distorting and exaggerating to prove a point). Spouses were much less likely to think of their own behavior as confrontive and when they did it was mostly cast in positive or self-justifying language (e.g., "I was basically calling her bluff," or "This is when we really get into it … when she's not making sense and I tell her"). Similarly, spouses were twice as likely to think that the partner was avoiding the issue (e.g., through withdrawl, topic shifting, stonewalling, or lying) than they were to think that their own communication was evasive. Spouses frequently construed their own communication as a form of constructive engagement (i.e., as an effort to discuss issues in a collaborative and open fashion). They rarely described their partner's communication in these same terms, although they sometimes attributed collaboration to both people (e.g., "At that point … we were compromising").

Abusive marriages had a particularly slanted view of the communication process. The spouses in physically aggressive marriages attributed more avoidance to their partner, less avoidance to self, and more constructive engagement to self, when compared with the nonaggressive spouses. Both husbands and wives in physically aggressive marriages often saw themselves as making a frustrated effort to communicate constructively with an evasive partner. Ironically, observer coding of communication in aggressive marriages indicates that these relationships are characterized by high rates of negativity and negative reciprocity on the part of both spouses (Burman, Margolin, & John, 1993; Cordova, Jacobson, Gottman, Rushe, & Cox, 1993). An analysis of the MIP discussion data also supported this conclusion (Leonard & Roberts, 1996). Although this suggests a clear discrepancy between observer and insider coding of the interactions, there is probably a connection between these perspectives as well. That is, the incompatible images of communication held by different spouses probably contributes to the mutually escalatory behavior seen by observers. Of course, these data do not resolve complicated issues about the causes of marital violence; however, they partly account for the apparent communicative incompetence of aggressive relationships (see Feldman & Ridley, 1995; Sabourin & Stamp, 1995).

An additional feature of these reports about communication is their narrative structure. This aspect is not documented in any formal analysis that we have performed to date, but anecdotally, the construction of incompatible subjective narratives seems to underlie some cases of escalating conflict avoidance and confrontation. For example, in one case in which the couple discusses the husband's drinking, the wife has a series of related thoughts; the husband knows he has a problem, but he will not accept it. Until he accepts it, they cannot work it out; he never wants to talk about it. He is always changing the topic and making it into a joke; he needs to wake up, he will not look at her because he knows she is right; she is sick of his tactics and may move out to make him understand. At the same time, the husband constructs a different scene; he drinks because he wants to, not as an escape. He loves her, even though she is overly critical, insensitive, and needs to relax. He does not want to get into a deep argument and thinks that bickering is a waste of breath, she is getting offended for little reason and is trying to upset and intimidate him; she resorts to name calling because she knows that he is right. In a different discussion characterized by escalating confrontation, the husband thinks that his wife does not really care about the conversation, that she just wants to argue and verbally attack him, that she intentionally distorts and exaggerates, and that she knows he is right. The wife thinks that the husband gets angry for little reason, takes everything personally when she is just telling the truth, he does not like to hear the truth; and therefore, he will not listen and is trying to cut her off.

There are certain notable features in these examples. First, there is an overall coherence to each person's thoughts. Spouses seem to experience their own interactions, not in terms of isolated thoughts, but as a connected chain of events leading toward a particular outcome. In many cases, these outcomes are seen as highly predictable. In fact, the repetition of behavior is a prominent theme in the thoughts that we coded (e.g., "She gets like this at least every day," "He's like a never ending road," and "We can talk for hours like this and it never gets resolved"). Second, each person falsely assumes that the partner shares the same bedrock perceptions of reality (e.g., "She knows I am right") and attributes the difficulty to the partner's motivated distortions (e.g., "he does not like to hear the truth"). There seems to be a sense that the truth is so obvious, it cannot be constructed otherwise. Third, the narratives are both separate and interdependent. They are separate in the sense that the concurrent thought lines have very few overlapping elements (i.e., they tell different stories), but are interdependent in the sense that they are interactively cued and mutually reinforcing. For example, in the first couple, the wife's narrative provides a frame for assimilating and reacting to specific cues linked to the husband's withdrawal (e.g., the meaning of his jokes and topic shifts), whereas the husband's narrative likewise furnishes an interpretive frame for the wife's assertive behavior. The result is a mutually escalatory demand–withdraw sequence that further reinforces the original attributions of each person (see Watzlawick, Weakland, & Fisch, 1974).

Selective Monitoring of Communication

Misunderstanding in relationship conflicts often seems to result from differential monitoring of the stimulus field. In short, people are usually not thinking about the same thing at the same time, so they assign meaning to the behavioral stream using different constructs. This is quite evident from the Wisconsin study. There are numerous cases of misunderstanding in these data, but only an occasional instance in which the direct perspective reported by one family member actually contradicts the metaperspective of another (e.g., the wife thinks her husband is too critical with their son; according to the husband, they both agree that their son is too sensitive). More often, direct perspectives and metaperspectives are simply irrelevant to one another (e.g., the wife wants more help from her husband with housework; he assumes that she is thinking about their son's lack of responsibility). As suggested earlier, this sort of mutual irrelevance is encouraged by the complexity of issues in relationship conflicts and the different levels of analysis potentially employed.

A specific type of selectivity results from focusing attention on particular actors (i.e., on self, partner, or the relationship) during interactions. Results from the MIP study suggest that the degree of self-focus is gender related. In an interesting reversal, wives in this research were more likely to think about their partners rather than themselves, whereas husbands were more likely to think about themselves than about their partners. In effect, both husbands and wives were thinking about the husband most of the time. Wives were also much more likely to report thinking that their partner was not understanding them, which suggests that wives were more sensitized to the partner at the level of metaperspectives as well as direct perspectives.

Another form of selectivity results from differential monitoring of content and relationship aspects of communication. A frequent situation occurred in both studies in which one person was more sensitized to relationship-level meaning, whereas their partner attended primarily to the overt topic of discussion (e.g., the husband is thinking about band practice and the wife is thinking that he does not listen to her). Some authors propose that selective monitoring of content and relationship meaning is also gender-related. For example, Scott et al. (1991) suggested that women tend to store representations of conversations in a "relationship bin," whereas men may think about conversations more in terms of the issue being discussed. Acitelli and Young (1996) also suggested that women think more frequently about relationships than men.

An interesting question to consider at this point is how heightened monitoring of the relationship might affect mutual understanding. On the one hand, a certain sensitivity to the relationship is presumably necessary in order to sense impending difficulties, track areas of probable misunderstanding, and make adjustments in communication. On the other hand, an exaggerated state of relationship vigilance might cause individuals to assign additional, idiosyncratic meaning to ambiguous cues.

There are some indications from the literature on marital violence that abusive spouses might be hypervigilant toward relational meaning. For example, Sabourin and Stamp (1995) found that abusive couples engaged in frequent relational digressions when they were asked to describe a typical day, whereas nonabusive couples stuck to a more literal interpretation of the task. Other authors speculated that aggressive husbands are particularly sensitive to any affront to self-esteem (see Feldman & Ridley, 1995) and that they tend to view their interactions as a struggle for relational dominance (Dutton, 1988; Rouse, 1990). The MIP data did not show evidence of these tendencies, although this might be partly because the sample excluded severe cases of violence—where marital violence is more apt to be strategic (i.e., "instrumental" rather than "expressive"; see Feldman & Ridley, 1995). The spouses from aggressive marriages in the MIP study were actually less mindful of the communication process than nonaggressive spouses. That is, the aggressive couples had fewer thoughts about the progress of the discussion and about communicative strategies or intentions. Interestingly, the aggressive husbands also had fewer thoughts about the issue under discussion than the nonaggressive husbands, suggesting that they were less mindful about communication in general, including both content and relationship aspects. It may be that abusive husbands lack involvement in communication, or possibly, these individuals might alternate between cognitive withdrawal in some situations and extreme vigilance and reactivity in others. This matter deserves further study.

Complexity of Inferences About Communication

Although selective attention in communication is unavoidable, it is possible to calibrate and adjust for differences in perception by shifting to a higher metalevel, that is, by anticipating how the partner is processing the interaction. Yet, how frequently and deeply do people reflect on the perspectives of others during conflicts?

In the MIP study, we found very little indication of spontaneous, complex perspective taking. Inferences about the partner were often global and one-sided, showing little differentiation of perspectives, minimal documentation in terms of specific details, and a lack of hedging or qualification of inference even with strong, chancy attributions. These characteristics particularly described negative attributions about the partner (e.g., "I'm thinking he's just making a lot of excuses," "She was trying to push my buttons," "Lying, he's lying," "She's going to pick at anything she can to convince me," and "She ain't even paying attention to what I really said"), but many neutral and positive attributions also showed a lack of differentiation. Explicit metaperspectives (i.e., thoughts about how the partner was interpreting the situation) were rare. Furthermore, in the few explicit metaperspectives that we found, the perspectives attributed to the partner were sometimes undifferentiated and simplistic (e.g., "He knows that's a lie," "She knows I'm sick of talking about this," or "He thinks he's right and I'm wrong"). As suggested earlier, spontaneous interpersonal perceptions are often framed with certainty and show little self-reflective attention to potential sources of bias.

Although the MIP study showed little evidence of spontaneous perspective taking, most people do not seem to have great trouble providing metaperspectives on relationship conflicts when they are prompted to do so. In the Wisconsin study (where we directly asked family members to report what others were thinking), they generally provided metaperspectives without difficulty and only occasionally reported that they could not predict what others were thinking or feeling. The complexity of these reports is another matter, however, because metaperspectives reflect a variety of inferential processes, including reliance on self-knowledge and stereotypes rather than cognitive decentering (see Thomas & Fletcher, 1997).

There seem to be two trends with respect to the complexity of metaperspectives in the Wisconsin study. First, direct perspectives generally appeared more complex than metaperspectives. Even when there was understanding (i.e., a rough match between one person's direct perspective and another's metaperspective), metaperspectives were often stripped down by comparison with direct perspectives. A general explanation is that self schemata are, as a rule, more complex and accessible than partner-schemata (Scott et al., 1991). In addition, the greater elaboration of direct perspectives reflects the perceiver's efforts at encoding arguments. This is suggested by the manner in which metaperspectives tend to be stripped down. Metaperspectives often convey the general sentiments of others, but omit contextualizing information, such as the partner's rationale for his or her direct perspective (e.g., the father recognizes that his son does not want to spend time with the family but does not know why). The omitted information relates to the partner's self-justifications or persuasive arguments, but not to the perceiver's own goals. In some cases, omission of contextualizing information in metaperspectives represents hostile reframing of another's direct perspective, whereby the partner comes to appear simplistic, naive, or rigid (e.g., "He thinks that every time we do a favor for someone, they owe us a favor" or "He is wondering how much he can get away with"). In such cases, any overlap between direct perspectives and metaperspectives is superficial and masks a deeper discrepancy.

Although in most cases direct perspectives appear more complex than metaperspectives, there appear to be frequent exceptions in parent–adolescent relationships. Specifically, parental metaperspectives about their adolescent children were often overly rich and embellished by comparison with adolescent direct perspectives. This situation reflects heightened vigilance of parents due to the distancing behaviors of adolescents. In addition, children at this stage often vacillate between sophisticated, adult-like patterns of social reasoning and more concrete and egocentric patterns that typify earlier stages of development (Kidwell, Fischer, Dunham, & Baronowski, 1983). Because adolescent perspectives often present a confusing, moving target for parents, parents may in turn make overly rich assessments of some adolescent messages.

Another general trend evident in the Wisconsin study is that family members appear to use their own direct perspective as a basis for understanding the perspective of others, either by assimilation (i.e., projection of one's own perspective to others) or contrast. Furthermore, there may be a generational basis to projection and contrast tendencies in family interactions. Quite often, parents predicted that they shared the same thoughts as their spouses. Quite often, they were misled by this assumption. On the other hand, it was curious how frequently parents expected their children to express disagreement, resistance, and resentment, even in cases where children were privately agreeing with their parents (e.g., the daughter is thinking that she should have finished her work earlier; the father assumes that she is thinking up excuses). Despite being rather analytic about their children, it seems that parents may tend to overgeneralize differences based on episodic parent–adolescent conflicts. As much anecdotal experience also suggests, generational and developmental differences between parents and adolescents make this a particularly confusing and difficult context of interpersonal perception.

CONCLUSION

Every social situation involves many suppositions about what other people think, feel, know, expect, and intend. These suppositions are so commonplace that, as a practical matter, they are only occasionally questioned or tested. At the same time, our understanding of other people is tenuous, given the private nature of subjective experience and inherent limitations of human communication. There is an ironic contrast between the seeming transparency and great difficulty sometimes associated with communication, particularly in close relationships. As Retzinger (1991) noted: "Because language has a common surface and private base, it is both very easy and very difficult for people to understand one another" (p. 10).

We are used to thinking about misunderstanding in a certain way—as a temporary problem that occurs particularly in unfamiliar situations where we lack the basic implements of understanding, such as mutual knowledge, common background, or a shared code. However, misunderstanding is more appropriately seen as a normal state that occurs in varying ways and degrees in all communicative situations.

Several features of the interpersonal context of perception help to explain the persistence of misunderstanding in close relationships. First, familiarity increases knowledge of another person, but erodes objectivity. Second, communication is characterized by multiple goals and levels of meaning. These complexities account for the inherent and strategic ambiguity of communication, which is particularly felt in the case of relationship conflicts. The complexity of issues and confusing structure of relationship conflicts invite even greater selectivity of inference. This, in turn, is manifested in such areas as actor–partner differences in attributions for communication, differential monitoring of self versus partner, and varying degrees of relational vigilance. Third, the complexity of online communication requires an unquestioning stance toward most inferences. This normative tendency is frequently extended to contexts where it is nonadaptive. For example, online thoughts about the partner may be undifferentiated and show minimal perspective taking. Fourth, interpersonal perceptions are simplified and sharpened in response to narrative and rhetorical goals in communication. In relationship conflicts, individuals may interpret one another's communicative behavior based on separate but interdependent narratives. Metaperspectives are also stripped down in a manner that serves the perceiver's efforts at encoding arguments. In sum, the persistence of misunderstanding in close relationships relates to the complexity and ambiguity of interpersonal communication on the one hand, and, the certainty and simplicity of most interpersonal perception on the other.

REFERENCES

Acitelli, L. K., Douvan, E., & Veroff, J. (1993). Perceptions of conflict in the first year of marriage: How important are similarity and understanding? *Journal of Social and Personal Relationships, 10,* 5–19.

Acitelli, L. K., & Young, A. M. (1996). Gender and thought in relatiosnhips. In G. J. Fletcher & J. Fitness (Eds.), *Knowledge structures in close relationships: A social psychological approach* (pp. 147–168). Mahwah, NJ: Lawrence Erlbaum Associates.

Allen, A., & Thompson, T. (1984). Agreement, understanding, realization, and feeling understood as predictors of communicative satisfaction in marital dyads. *Journal of Marriage and the Family, 46,* 915–921.

Bavelas, J. B., Black, A., Chovil, N., & Mullett, J. (1992). *Equivocal communication.* Newbury Park, CA: Sage.

Bavelas, J. B., & Coates, L. (1992). How do we account for the mindfulness of face-to-face dialogue? *Communication Monographs, 59,* 301–305.

Berger, C. R. (1992). Goals, plans, and mutual understanding in relationships. In S. Duck (Ed.), *Understanding relationship processes, Vol. 1: Individuals and relationships* (pp. 30–59). Newbury Park, CA: Sage.

Bochner, A. P., & Eisenberg, E. M. (1987). Family process: Systems perspectives. In C. R. Berger & S. H. Chaffee (Eds.), *Handbook of communication science* (pp. 540–563). Beverly Hills, CA: Sage.

Bradbury, T. N., & Fincham, F. D. (1987). Affect and cognition in close relationships: Towards an integrative model. *Cognition and Emotion, 1,* 59–87.

Bradley, G. (1978). Self-serving biases in the attribution process: A reexamination of the fact or fiction question. *Journal of Personality and Social Psychology, 67,* 636–640.

Burman, B., Margolin, G., & John, R. S. (1993). America's angriest home videos: Behavioral contingencies observed in home reenactments of marital conflict. *Journal of Consulting and clinical psychology, 61,* 28–39.

Burnett, R. (1991). Accounts and narratives. In B. M. Montgomery & S. Duck (Eds.), *Studying interpersonal interaction* (pp. 121–140). New York: Guilford.

Burnett, R., McGhee, P., & Clarke, D. D. (Eds.) (1987). *Accounting for relationships: Explanation, representation and knowledge.* London: Methuen.

Canary, D. J., Brossmann, J. E., Brossmann, B. G., & Weger, H. (1995). Toward a theory of minimally rational argument: Analyses of episode-specific effects of argument structures. *Communication Monographs, 62,* 183–212.

Canary, D. J., Cupach, W. R., & Messman, S. J. (1995). *Relationship conflict.* Thousand Oaks, CA: Sage.

Chovil, N. (1994). Equivocation as an interactional event. In W. R. Cupach & B. H. Spitzberg (Eds.), *The dark side of interpersonal communication* (pp. 105–123). Hillsdale, NJ: Lawrence Erlbaum Associates.

Cloven, D. H., & Roloff, M. E. (1991). Sense-making activities and interpersonal conflict: Communicative cures for the mulling blues. *Western Journal of Speech Communication, 55,* 134–158.

Cloven, D. H., & Roloff, M. E. (1993). Sense-making activities and interpersonal conflict, II: The effects of communicative intentions on internal dialogue. *Western Journal of Communication, 57,* 309–329.

Cloven, D. H., & Roloff, M. E. (1995). Cognitive tuning effects of anticipating communication on thought about an interpersonal conflict. *Communication Reports, 8,* 1–9.

Colvin, C. R., Vogt, D. S., & Ickes, W. (1997). Why do friends understand each other better than strangers do? In W. Ickes (Ed.), *Empathic accuracy* (pp. 169–193). New York: Guilford.

Cordova, J. V., Jacobson, N. S., Gottman, J. M., Rushe, R., & Cox, G. (1993). Negative reciprocity and communication in couples with a violent husband. *Journal of Abnormal Psychology, 102,* 559–564.

Coupland, N., & Nussbaum, J. F. (Eds.). (1993). *Discourse and lifespan identity.* Newbury Park, CA: Sage.

Danziger, K. (1976). *Interpersonal communication.* New York: Pergamon.

Dun, T., Sillars, A., Roberts, L. J., & Leonard, K. E. (1996, June). *On-line thoughts about marital interaction within distressed, nondistressed, and aggressive couples.* Paper presented to the International Conference on Personal Relationships, Banff, Alberta.

Dutton, D. G. (1988). *The domestic assault of women.* Boston: Allyn & Bacon.

Eisenberg, E. M. (1984). Ambiguity as strategy in organizational communication. *Communication Monographs, 51,* 227–242.

Feldman, C. M., & Ridley, C. A. (1995). The etiology and treatment of domestic violence between adult partners. *Clinical psychology: Science and practice, 2,* 317–348.

Fincham, F. D., & Bradbury, T. N. (1991). Cognition in marriage: A program of research on attributions. In W. H. Jones & D. Perlman (Eds.), *Advances in personal relationships* (Vol. 2, pp. 159–203). London: Kingsley.

Fincham, F. D., Bradbury, T. N., & Scott, C. K. (1990). Cognition in marriage. In F. D. Fincham & T. N. Bradbury (Eds.), *The psychology of marriage* (pp. 118–149). New York: Guilford.

Fletcher, G. J. O., & Kininmonth, L. (1991). Interaction in close relationships and social cognition. In G. J. O. Fletcher & F. D. Fincham (Eds.), *Cognition in close relationships* (pp. 235–255). Hillsdale, NJ: Lawrence Erlbaum Associates.

Gletcher, G. J. O., & Thomas, G. (1996). Close relationship lay theories: Their structure and funciton. In G. J. O. Fletcher & J. Fitness (Eds.), *Knowledge structures in close relationships: A social psychological approach* (pp. 3–24). Hillsdale, NJ: Lawrence Erlbaum Associates.

Forgas, J. P. (1996). The role of emotion scripts and transient moods in relationships: Structural and function perspectives. In G. J. O. Fletcher & J. Fitness (Eds.), *Knowledge structures in close relationships: A social psychological approach* (pp. 275–296). Mahwah, NJ: Lawrence Erlbaum Associates.

Frentz, T. S., & Farrell, T. B. (1976). Language-action: A paradigm for communication. *Quarterly Journal of Speech, 62,* 333–349.

Gergen, K. J., & Gergen, M. M. (1987). Narratives of relationship. In R. Burnett, P. McGhee, & D. D. Clarke (Eds.), *Accounting for relationships: Explanation, representation and knowledge* (pp. 269–288). London: Methuen.

Gesn, P. R. (1995). *Shares knowledge between same-sex friends: Measurement and validation.* Unpublished master's thesis. University of Texas at Arlington.

Graham, R. (1994). Gender, relationship, and target differences in empathic accuracy. Unpublished master's thesis. University of Texas at Arlingtoon.

Harvey, J. H., Orbuch, T. L., & Weber, A. L. (Eds.) (1992). *Attributions, accounts, and close relationships.* New York: Springer-Verlag.

Hendrick, C., & Hendrick, S. S. (1988). Lovers wear rose colored glasses. *Journal of Social and Personal Relationships, 5,* 161–184.

Hocker, J. L., & Wilmot, W. W. (1991). *Interpersonal conflict* (3rd ed.). Dubuque, IA: William C. Brown.

Ickes, W. (1993). Empathic accuracy. *Journal of Personality, 61,* 587–610.

Ickes, W. (Ed.) (1997). *Empathic accuracy.* New York: Guilford.

Ickes, W., & Simpson, J. A. (1997). Managing empathic accuracy in close relationships. In W. Ickes (Ed.), *Empathic accuracy* (pp. 218–250). New York: Guilford.

Ickes, W., Stinson, L., Bissonnette, V., & Garcia, S. (1990). Naturalistic social cognition: Empathic accuracy in mixed-sex dyads. *Journal of Personality and Social Psychology, 59,* 730–742.

Ickes, W., & Tooke, W. (1988). The observational method: Studying the interaction of minds and bodies. In S. Duck, D. Hay, S. Hobfoll, W. Ickes, & B. Montgomery (Eds.), *The handbook of personal relationships: Theory, research, and interventions* (pp. 79–97). Chichester, England: Wiley.

Jacobs, S., & Jackson, S. (1983). Strategy and structure in conversational influence attempts. *Communication Monographs, 51,* 283–304.

Kellerman, K. (1992). Communication: Inherently strategic and primarily automatic. *Communication Monographs, 59,* 288–300.

Kidwell, J., Fischer, J. L., Dunham, R. M., & Baronowski, M. (1983). Parents and adolescents: Push and pull of change. In H. I. McCubbin & C. R. Figley (Eds.), *Stress and the family, Vol. 1: Coping with normative transitions* (pp. 74–89). New York: Brunner/Mazel.

Kursh, C. O. (1971). The benefits of poor communication. *Psychoanalytic Review, 58,* 189–208.

Laing, R. D., Phillipson, H., & Lee, A. R. (1966). *Interpersonal perception: A theory and a method of research.* New York: Springer-Verlag.

Leonard, K. E., & Roberts, L. J. (1996). *Marital interactions in aggressive and nonaggressive couples: Baseline differences and the effect of alcohol and placebo administration.* Unpublished manuscript, Research Institute on Additions, Buffalo, New York.

Marangoni, C., Garcia, S., Ickes, W., & Teng, G. (1995). Empathic accuracy in a clinically relevant setting. *Journal of Personality and Social Psychology, 68,* 854–869.

Margolin, G., Hattem, D., John, R. S., & Yost, K. (1985). Perceptual agreement between spouses and outside observers when coding themselves and a stranger dyad. *Behavioral Assessment, 7,* 235–247.

Morton, T. L., Alexander, J. F., & Altman, I. (1976). Communication and relationship definition. In G. R. Miller (Ed.), *Explorations in interpersonal communication* (pp. 105–125). Newbury Park, CA: Sage.

Murray, S. L., & Holmes, J. G. (1996). The construction of relationship realities. In G. J. O. Fletcher & J. Fitness (Eds.), *Knowledge structures in close relationships: A social psychological approach* (pp. 91–120). Mahwah, NJ: Lawrence Erlbaum Associates.

Noller, P., & Ruzzene, M. (1991). Communication in marriage: The influence of affect and cognition. In G. J. O. Fletcher & F. D. Fincham (Eds.), *Cognition in close relationships* (pp. 203–233). Hillsdale, NJ: Lawrence Erlbaum Associates.

Noller, P., & Venardos, C. (1986). Communication awareness in married couples. *Journal of Social and Personal Relationships, 3,* 31–42.

O'Keefe, D. J., & Sypher, H. E. (1981). Cognitive complexity measures and the relationship of cognitive complexity to communication. *Human Communication Research, 8,* 72–92.

Planalp, S., & Garvin-Doxas, K. (1994). Using mutual knowledge in conversation: Friends as experts on each other. In S. Duck (Ed.), *Dynamics of relationships* (pp. 1–26). Thousand Oaks, CA: Sage.

Planalp, S., & Honeycutt, J. M. (1985). Events that increase uncertainty in relationships. *Human Communication Research, 11,* 593–604.

Planalp, S., & Rivers, M. (1996). Changes in knowledge of personal relationships. In G. J. O. Fletcher & J. Fitness (Eds.), *Knowledge structures in close relationships: A social psychological approach* (pp. 299–324). Mahwah, NJ: Lawrence Erlbaum Associates.

Raush, H. L., Barry, W. A., Hertel, R. J., & Swain, M. A. (1974). *Communication, conflict, and marriage.* San Francisco: Jossey-Bass.

Retzinger, S. M. (1991). *Violent emotions: Shame and rage in marital quarrels.* Newbury Park, CA: Sage.

Ritchie, L. D. (1991). *Information.* Newbury Park, CA: Sage.

Rouse, L. P. (1990). The dominance motive in abusive partners: Identifying couples at risk. *Journal of College Student Development, 31,* 330–335.

Sabourin, T. C., & Stamp, G. H. (1995). Communication and the experience of dialectical tensions in family life: An examination of abusive and nonabusive families. *Communication Monographs, 62,* 213–242.

Sanders, R. E. (1984). Style, meaning, and message effects. *Communication Monographs, 51,* 154–167.

Scott, C. K., Fuhrman, R. W., & Wyer, R. S. (1991). Information processing in close relationships. In G. J. O. Fletcher & F. D. Fincham (Eds.), *Cognition in close relationships* (pp. 37–67). Hillsdale, NJ: Lawrence Erlbaum Associates.

Searle, J. R. (1969). *Speech acts.* London: Cambridge University Press.

Shapiro, A. L., & Swenson, C. (1969). Patterns of self-disclosure among married couples. *Journal of Consulting Psychology, 16,* 179–180.

Sillars, A. L. (1985). Interpersonal perception in relationships. In W. Ickes (Ed.), *Compatible and incompatible relationships* (pp. 277–305). New York: Springer-Verlag.

Sillars, A. L. (1989). Communication, uncertainty and understanding in marriage. In B. Derrin, L. Grossberg, B. O'Keefe, A. E. Wartella (Eds.), *Rethinking communication: Vol 2. Paradigm exemplars* (pp. 307–328).

Sillars, A. L., Burggraf, C. S., Yost, S., & Zietlow, P. H. (1992). Conversational themes and marital relationship definitions: Quantitative and qualitative investigations. *Human Communication Research, 19,* 124–154.

Sillars, A. L., Folwell, A. L., Hill, K. C., Maki, B. K., Hurst, A. P., & Casano, R. A. (1994). Marital communication and the persistence of misunderstanding. *Journal of Social and Personal Relationships, 11,* 611–617.

Sillars, A. L., Pike, G. R., Jones, T. S., & Murphy, M. A. (1984). Communication and understanding in marriage. *Human Communication Research, 10,* 317–350.

Sillars, A. L., & Scott, M. D. (1983). Interpersonal perception between intimates: An integrative review. *Human Communication Research, 10,* 153–176.

Sillars, A. L., & Weisberg, J. (1987). Conflict as a social skill. In M. E. Roloff & G. R. Miller (Eds.), *Interpersonal processes: New directions in communication research* (pp. 140–171). Newbury Park, CA: Sage.

Sillars, A. L., Weisberg, J., Burggraf, C. S., & Zietlow, P. H. (1990). Communication and understanding revisited: Married couples' understanding and recall of conversations. *Communication Research, 17,* 500–522.

Sillars, A. L., & Zietlow, P. H. (1993). Investigations of marital communication and lifespan development. In N. Coupland & J. F. Nussbaum (Eds.), *Discourse and lifespan identity* (pp. 237–261). Newbury Park, CA: Sage.

Simpson, J. A., Ickes, W., & Blackstone, T. (1995). When the head protects the heart: Empathic accuracy in dating relationships. *Journal of Personality and Social Psychology, 69,* 629–641.

Sperber, D., & Wilson, D. (1995). *Relevance: Communication and cognition* (2nd ed.). Cambridge, MA: Blackwell.

Spitzberg, B. H. (1993). The dialectics of (in)competence. *Journal of Social and Personal Relationships, 10,* 137–158.

Spitzberg, B. H. (1994). The dark side of (in)competence. In W. R. Cupach & B. H. Spitzberg (Eds.). *The dark side of interpersonal communication* (pp. 25–49). Hillsdale, NJ: Lawrence Erlbaum Associates.

Stinson, L., & Ickes, W. (1992). Empathic accuracy in the interactions of male friends versus male strangers. *Journal of Personality and Social Psychology, 62,* 787–797.

Surra, C. A., & Bohman, T. (1991). The development of close relationships: A cognitive perspective. In G. J. O. Fletcher & F. D. Fincham (Eds.), *Cognition in close relationships* (pp. 281–305). Hillsdale, NJ: Lawrence Erlbaum Associates.

Surra, C. A., & Ridley, C. A. (1991). Multiple perspectives on interaction: Participants, peers, and observers. In B. Montgomery & S. Duck (Eds.), *Studying interpersonal interaction* (pp. 35–55). New York: Guilford.

Suzuki, T. (1978). *Words in context: A Japanese perspective on language and culture.* Tokyo: Kodansha International.

Thomas, G., & Fletcher, G. J. O. (1997). In W. Ickes (Ed.), *Empathic accuracy* (pp. 194–217). New York: Guilford.

Thomas, G., Fletcher, G. J. O., & Lange, C. (1995). *On-line empathic accuracy and projection in marital interaction.* Unpublished manuscript, University of Canterbury, Christchurch, New Zealand.

Watzlawick, P., Beavin, J., & Jackson, D. D. (1967). *Pragmatics of human communication: A study of interactional patterns, pathologies, and paradoxes.* New York: Norton.

Watzlawick, P., Weakland, J. H., & Fisch, R. (1974). *Change: Principles of problem formation and problem resolution.* New York: Norton.

Weiss, R. S. (1975). *Marital separation.* New York: Basic Books.

Zietlow, P. H. (1986). *An analysis of the communication behaviors, understanding, self-disclosure, sex-roles, and marital satisfaction of elderly couples and couples in earlier life stages.* Unpublished doctoral dissertation, Ohio State University, Columbus.

4

Who's Up on the Low Down:
Gossip in Interpersonal
Relations

Marianne E. Jaeger
Temple University

Anne A. Skelder
Alvernia College

Ralph L. Rosnow
Temple University

Why is gossip like a three-pronged tongue? Because it destroys three people: the person who says it, the person who listens to it, and the person about whom it is told.

—The Babylonian Talmud

This proverb highlights the role of gossip in the dark side of relationships. Gossip has the potential to destroy reputations. What is more interesting is that it has the potential to destroy the relationships among the gossip producer, the recipient of gossip, and the target of gossip. Gossip's characterization as a moral problem received much attention from philosophers and theologians—both ancient and modern. Its characteristic as a social problem is inferred from the numerous treatises about decorum that condemn gossip as well as anthropological studies that document sanctions against the telling of unfounded stories about others. Its potential to destroy affords those with little power to wield a dangerous sword. In the words of Spacks (1985), "Like the notion that taking a photograph of someone endangers his spirit, the view that saying something bad has the force of *doing* something bad wells from pre-rational depths ... . Anyone can invoke the dangerous magic of language; a weapon for the otherwise powerless, a weapon (as many have noted) usable from dark corners" (p. 30).

GOSSIP'S NEGATIVE REPUTATION

The Middle Ages seemed a particularly gossipy time, and censure of gossip was equally rampant. According to Schein (1994), this censure was influenced by Biblical writings that warned against slander and revealing secrets through gossip as well as those writings in the New Testament that placed gossip among transgressions such as malice, envy, and deceit. Gossip's idle character aligned it with one of the seven deadly sins—sloth. Furthermore, gossip appeared as the enemy of love in the literature about courtly love; the ideal lover was discreet, did not gossip about his love to his friends, and even sought to protect his love from becoming the target of gossip by others. Gossip, in the form of an allegorical figure, the "evil tongue," aroused jealousy through the telling of false tales and hence, came between the lover and his beloved. The subject matters of gossip were diverse, but the most popular topic appeared to be love, especially extramarital love affairs. The structure of medieval society, with its dependence on oral communication for news and its strict codes of conduct, appeared to reinforce gossip's potency; "Gossip was often accepted as truth, and, given the strict codes of behavior, gossip could destroy people's reputations and their position in society" (p. 151). In these times, sanctions for gossiping were severe, ranging from dunking stools, stocks, and other forms of public shaming to masks of torture, which projected iron spikes into the wearer's mouth in order to stop her loose tongue (Emler, 1994).

Although legalized sanctions against gossip mercifully disappeared, some writers note that the moral prohibitions against gossip remain essentially intact. Some suggest that gossip as a moral problem derives from its unwarranted invasion of privacy, although as Thomas (1994) pointed out, gossip can be about information that is widely known. Bok (1984) noted that each of us develops standards, however inarticulate, for the type and amount of gossip we may find tolerable; thus, gossip becomes a moral problem for each of us when those boundaries are crossed. Bok singled out three categories of gossip that are particularly reprehensible: gossip that breaches confidences, gossip known to be false, and gossip that is unduly invasive. It is these three categories that define gossip and distinguish it from mere idle chatter. Bergmann (1993), for example, quoted a German definition of *gossip* that equates it with "nasty, deprecatory, ugly talk about one's neighbor" (p. 26).

English language definitions of gossip focus more on its idle or trivial nature. To *gossip* is "to talk idly, mostly about other people's affairs, to go about tattling" according to *The Oxford English Dictionary* (Simpson & Werner, 1989, p. 700). *The American Heritage Dictionary* defines gossip as "trifling, often groundless rumor, usually of a personal, sensational, or intimate nature; idle talk" (Morrs, 1981, p. 569). Some condemn gossip for its triviality. Heidegger (1962), for example, felt that gossip was far too trivial to help us to understand the profundities of human existence. What is more, he argued, it subverts such understanding by leading he or she to believe they already know it all. Bok (1984) noted that gossip is morally questionable because its trivial tone demeans the lives of its targets.

A gossip is stereotypically a woman, and it is a common perception that women gossip more maliciously than do men (Tebbutt, 1995). An historical analysis of changes in the meaning of gossip shows how its more pejorative connotations developed as gossip became identified as a largely female activity (e.g., Rysman, 1977; Tebbutt, 1995). Traditionally powerless in society, women were paradoxically feared because of their gossiping tendencies, as evidenced by the old Welsh saying "Be she old, or be she young, A woman's strength is in her tongue" (Tebbutt, 1995, p.19).

"TECHNIQUES OF REHABILITATION"

The previous phrase comes from Emler (1994), who is one of a number of philosophers, linguists, and social scientists who have attempted to address the question of whether gosssip's sullied reputation is warranted. Although their techniques differ, each attempts to attack one or more facets of gossip's negative connotations in order to repair the good name of gossip.

Ben-Ze'ev (1994) provided a philosophical analysis of the premise that gossip is an intrinsically valuable activity. Like intellectual thinking that is motivated by creativity or intellectual curiosity rather than by external rewards such as money or academic publications, gossip typically derives its value from the activity itself and not from achieving external ends. Ben-Ze'ev highlighted the role of gossip in satisfying certain basic human personal and intimate details of the lives of others so that we can better understand and control our own lives. Participation in gossip also satisfies a so-called *tribal need*—the need to be accepted by an exclusive group characterized by intimate and affective ties. Although he acknowledged that gossip is not always a virtuous activity, Ben-Ze'ev attempted to show that it is not a vicious activity either.

Sociolinguistic studies examining gender differences in speech and styles of conversation highlight positive dimensions of gossip. These studies serve to portray women's talk in a more favorable light as well as focus on the positive consequences of gossip. Some studies suggest that men tend to focus on the task at hand, whereas women pay more attention to relationships (cf. Eagly, 1987). Others characterize men's conversation as individualistic and competitive, whereas women's conversation is more cooperative and mutually supportive (e.g., Spender, 1980). Gossip, with its focus on personal details of individuals' lives, is seen as an essential component of communication style characterized by cooperation, mutual support, and collective activity and is used to establish and maintain friendships among its participants (Tannen, 1990).

Several authors provide sociopsychological analyses of gossip's functions and conclude that, far from being trivial, gossip serves useful functions interpersonally and intrapersonally. Gluckman (1963) suggested that gossip is a means of maintaining the unity of social groups. Gossip maintains group unity by discouraging individuals from violating group norms and standards through fear of public sanctions. Gossip unites a group against other groups or even the larger society in a number of ways. According to Gluckman, the right to gossip is a hallmark of group membership. Outsiders should not join in gossip, for to do so can result in rebuke. On the other hand, gossiping with an outsider is a sure sign that one has been accepted as a member with all the rights and privileges that membership entails.

Levin and Arluke (1987) suggested that gossip is used to enhance self-esteem or status in a group, to obtain information that serves our need to evaluate our opinions and beliefs through comparison with others in a reasonable and nonpainful way, to establish or maintain social cohesiveness within a group, to define ambiguous or anxiety-laden situations, or more simply, to entertain or relax. Rosnow and Georgoudi (1985) outlined three general (although not mutually exclusive) functions of gossip that operate at the individual and interpersonal level—to inform, to influence, and to entertain. Emler (1994) suggested that the reputational inquiry accomplished through gossip is a complex and sophisticated instrument of adaptation in our social world.

EMPIRICAL STUDIES OF GOSSIP

Researchers examined several aspects pertaining to gossip's negative reputation, but our knowledge about gossip and gossiping is still relatively
rudimentary. Researchers determined that we engage in gossip quite
frequently as adults (Emler, 1994; Levin & Arluke, 1985) and that gossip
is considered one of the most salient social processes among children and
adolescents (Gottman & Mettetal, 1986). The information conveyed in
gossip is rarely totally negative, although there may be times in our lives
when we focus more on the negative. In a study examining the quantity,
content and tone of instances of gossip overheard among college students,
Levin and Arluke (1987) found that negative and positive information were
equally likely to be discussed in gossip and that nearly half of the information was neither clearly negative nor positive. The evaluative tone of gossip
appears to change with age. Gottman and Mettetal (1986) found that
among 8- to 12-year-olds, gossip contained primarily negative evaluations,
whereas among adolescents, gossip contained both positive and negative
evaluations of the same person. Although gossiping is a frequent activity,
there are individual differences in the tendency to gossip. Nevo, Nevo, and
Derech-Zehavi (1994) found that the tendency to gossip was related to
social desirability, gender, and vocational choices. Individuals with a self-
reported tendency to gossip were lower in need for social approval, were
more likely to be women, and were more interested in people-oriented
professions.

The paucity of empirical research on gossip may be due in part to its
secretive nature. According to Sabini and Silver (1982), we all gossip, but
feel that we should not; therefore, we gossip discreetly. Rosnow and
Georgoudi (1985) pointed out that feelings of privacy and protection are
necessary preconditions of gossip. The empirical investigator faces the
difficult task, then, of finding ways of sampling gossip or finding individuals
who are willing to talk about their gossip or the gossip of others. Levin and
his associates accomplished the former by systematic eavesdropping of
conversations overheard on a college campus or by sampling newspaper
gossip columns (Levin & Arluke, 1987). Emler (1994), using a diary record
approach, collected information about who talks to whom and about what.
Nevo et al. (1994) developed a Tendency to Gossip measure by which
individuals indicate the frequency with which they engage in gossip-like
behaviors, such as talking to friends about other people's successes, their
love affairs, and so forth. Each of these methods deals with the discreet
nature of gossip in different ways, but vary in the extent to which they can

reflect other essential preconditions for gossip, namely the broader context in which gossip can flourish.

Sociability is another precondition of gossip (Rosnow & Georgoudi, 1985). Gossip rarely occurs among strangers or among acquaintances whose relationship is characterized by aloofness. Thus, methods for studying gossip should be usable in situations characterized by a level of amiable familiarity among potential gossipers and gossipees. A third precondition for gossip is a common frame of reference (Rosnow & Georgoudi, 1985). This shared frame of reference includes shared values and attitudes as well as access to background knowledge in which a particular piece of gossip is understood.

In our research, we sought to examine characteristics of gossipers and the people about whom they gossip because of the conflicting portraits of the gossipmonger that exist in the literature. We chose to study gossiping within a college sorority because many of the characteristics of sororities provide the preconditions for gossip to occur. Sororities are exclusive groups of young women—situated within the wider university population—that are characterized by a sense of community and communality. A shared frame of reference is virtually assured because women are likely to choose a sorority with goals and values similar to their own and because the process of pledging further socializes them in its prevailing values and goals. Sororities are usually small enough that everyone knows everyone else, and their relative exclusivity provides privacy and protection from the hurly-burly of life in a large urban university.

Who Gossips About Whom?

Attempts in the literature to describe the typical gossiper result in seemingly conflicting portraits. For example, there is the social isolate, the least popular in a group, who suffers from feelings of worthlessness, social anxiety, and need for esteem from others and who gossips in an attempt to make friends or to gain attention or esteem from others (cf. Ben-Ze'ev, 1994; Levin & Arluke, 1987). Conversely, gossipers have been characterized as sensitive, curious, and social-minded, whereas it is the nongossiper who is uninterested in the affairs of others and who has no friends to gossip with or about (Levin & Arluke, 1987). Thus, on the one hand, the gossiper has few or no relationships and may pass on malicious information about others to raise his or her own worth in the eyes of others. On the other hand, the gossiper is social-minded and involved in the lives of others—one hardly likely to take joy in destroying the reputations of others. Although these disparate claims seem intuitively correct, there is, unfortunately, no direct evidence to support them.

Who are the targets of gossip? The subjects of gossip columns, talk shows, or "people in the news" features on television and in print concern either the everyday aspects of the lives of famous people or extraordinary events in the lives of ordinary people (cf. Levin & Arluke, 1987). Ben Ze'ev (1994) suggested that the targets of gossip are the subjects of envy. It is almost a given that the target of gossiping is someone familiar to its participants, but little else is known about the person others are discussing behind his or her back.

The goals of this research were to examine empirically the characteristics of gossipers and of their targets. Are they people for whom relationships may be problematic and who gossip in order to gain entry to the possibility of relationships or are they individuals who enjoy the company of others and for whom gossip might be an integral part of their sociability? Both of these views seem intuitively correct and by examining their characteristics empirically, we confirm or modify these seemingly disparate portraits.

Method

After making an initial contact with a service sorority at a large public university, we received permission from the membership to conduct a study of "communication networks." The 36 members served as participant informants; they provided information about each other and about themselves by means of confidential or anonymous questionnaires in two phases. They were of traditional college age (from 18 to 22 years old), and many of them lived on campus, either in the sorority house or in campus dormitories, whereas others lived off campus.

Phase 1. The first questionnaire, which was filled out anonymously, asked the participants a number of questions about others in the sorority. The goals in this first phase were (a) to identify who gossiped about whom and thus, to determine which individuals most frequently engaged in gossip and who was frequently targeted in gossip by others; (b) to explore the cliques or friendship patterns in the sorority and thereby, determine the relative popularity of each person in the sorority; and (c) to determine the extent to which each person was viewed as likable or not. The 15 individuals who returned the first questionnaire were considered anonymous participant informants to help us determine the extent of gossiping in the sorority.

The respondents were first presented with a list of 143 adjectives and a list of all members of the sorority. They were asked to indicate next to the name of each person, those adjectives that best described that person.

No minimum or maximum number was suggested. Next, respondents were asked to indicate others in the sorority that each member tended to gossip about; they were instructed to say "no one" if they felt a particular person did not engage in gossip about others. As a check on the extent to which each person gossiped, respondents were also asked to indicate each person's general gossiping tendencies on a scale from 0 (*never*, or *hardly ever, gossiped*) to 100 (*all of the time*). Then respondents were asked to name, for each member, her closest friends in the sorority. In general, respondents were instructed to make a best guess in the case of uncertainty or to indicate if they were clearly uncertain about a particular member's gossip target(s) and/or closest friends. In the final portion of the question- naire, respondents were asked to define gossip in their own words, being as thorough or brief as they wished. The latter part of the questionnaire was designed to tap commonsense understandings of the nature of gossip and its potential for enhancing or destroying relationships.

The first questionnaire was distributed at a monthly meeting of the sorority after one of the authors introduced the study as an investigation of "communication networks" and obtained the necessary informed con- sent from the participants. They were instructed to complete the ques- tionnaire later in the privacy of their own rooms and then to return the questionnaire, sealed in the envelope provided, to an enclosed box located in the sorority house within 2 weeks. When respondents dropped off the first questionnaire, they collected the second questionnaire, which was to be mailed to the investigator in the stamped, addressed envelope enclosed.

Phase 2.   The second questionnaire consisted of measures of various personality traits that were thought to characterize gossipers. Need for approval by others was measured by the Marlowe-Crowne Social Desir- ability scale. The higher the score, the more strongly motivated the respondent is to seek the approval of important others, and it follows that a person's behavior should be directed toward that aim (Crowne & Marlowe, 1964, p.39). Self-esteem was measured by Rosenberg's (1965) Self-Esteem scale. Rosenberg's validation of the scale suggested that individuals with low self-esteem were characterized by self-rejection, self-dissatisfaction, and self-contempt, and they were more likely to be on the periphery of a social group, a portrait similar to the nature of the gossiper as hypothesized by others. The Taylor Manifest Anxiety scale (MAS) was used to measure trait or chronic anxiety (Taylor, 1953).

Rosnow (1991) and his colleagues demonstrated a consistent relation- ship between anxiety and awareness of a rumor (Anthony, 1973) or propensity to transmit a rumor (Jaeger, Anthony, & Rosnow, 1980). Rumor is a phenomenon that shares some features in common with gossip, although it is problematic whether results pertaining to rumormongering also apply to gossip. Respondents were asked to identify themselves on the second questionnaire so that their responses could be related to information obtained in the first phase. However, they were assured that their responses would remain completely confidential.

Participants were sent reminder letters 2 weeks after the second questionnaire. In addition, one of the investigators attended the next monthly meeting to ask all the members to complete the second questionnaire even if they had not completed the first one. Thirty-one members returned the second questionnaire for a return rate of 86%.

Derived Measures. Various measures were derived from the initial questionnaire, most of which involved obtaining scores for each member by taking the mean ratings provided by the 15 informants. Specific details of these derived scores are given in Jaeger, Skleder, Rind, and Rosnow (1994), so only brief descriptions are given as follows:

Likability. The 143 adjectives used to describe each member were personality-trait words that were given likableness ratings in a previous study (Rosnow, Wainer, & Arms, 1969). Likability scores for each sorority member were determined by obtaining the mean of likability ratings of the words used to describe each member by the anonymous informants; these obtained means ranged from –6.9 (*most unlikable*) to 26.0 (*most likable*).

Gossipers. A gossiping tendency score for each member was derived from the informants' reports about who gossiped about whom. This involved obtaining the mean number of other people (averaged across the informants) each person was reported to have gossiped about in the sorority. The distribution of gossiping tendency scores was then divided into terciles in order to categorize members as *high, moderate,* or *low gossipers*; cut points were slightly adjusted in order to ensure that persons in a group were more similar to other group members than to persons in neighboring groups. As a consequence, 14 people were classified as *low gossipers*, 13 as *moderate gossipers*, and 9 as *high gossipers*.

Gossip targets. From the same information just discussed, another score was derived to reflect the propensity for each member to be the target of gossip. This reflected the mean number of times (averaged across informants) each person was named as a target of gossip. Each member was classified into a *high, moderate, or low target group*, using close approximations of tercile points; again, these cut points were adjusted slightly to ensure that persons in a group were more similar to each other than to those in neighboring groups.

Popularity. Based on reports from the informants on who was friendly with whom, it was possible to determine how many members each person chose as a close friend and how many times each member was chosen as a close friend by others. These data also formed the basis of a sociogram that allowed us to determine the cliques or smaller friendship groupings in the sorority.

Results

The following describes the characteristics of the gossip and of the targets of gossip. Next, a fine-grained analysis of who gossips about whom is provided. In the Discussion section, we touch on certain themes about gossip in the context of interpersonal relations, as raised by the sorority members.

Gossipers. We explored differences among high, moderate and low gossipers on the basis of personality characteristics, such as need for social approval, self-esteem, and anxiety, and on indicators of popularity, such as perceived likability, number of close friends, and number of times one was chosen as a close friend. In some cases, specific linear relationships were hypothesized. For example, inasmuch as gossip has a perjorative connotation, we expected the inveterate gossiper to be lower in social desirability as well as a less likable individual. We also expected the gossiper to be more anxious in view of such results in earlier studies of rumormongers.

A simple way to test such hypotheses is to compute contrasts using t or F; the specific linear predictions are represented by lambda weights of 1, 0, −1 or −1, 0, 1. A convenient method for evaluating the success of such contrasts relative to the sum of squares (SS) for the noncontrast between-groups effect is simply to square the correlation between the group means and their respective lambdas, which gives the proportion of between-groups SS explained by a given contrast (Rosnow & Rosenthal, 1996a, 1996b). We get an intuitive idea of how well each contrast did by comparing this value with that theoretically associated with any randomly chosen contrast. In the case of three levels (*low, moderate,* and *high anxiety*, for example), the expected value is 1/2 *df* or 50% of the between-groups SS would be accounted for by a randomly chosen contrast.

The expected negative linear relationship between gossiping and social approval accounted for 84% of the between-groups SS. However, a much better prediction (accounting for virtually all the between-groups SS) would have been that low gossipers were higher in need for social approval ($M = 19.67$) than moderate ($M = 14.91$) or high gossipers ($M = 14.29$), with $F(1,29) = 5.74$, and $p = .02$, and approximate effect size $r = .41$. The effect size of the comparison between scores of low and high gossipers was $r = .36$ with $t(27) = 2.01$, and p .03 (one-tailed).

None of the comparisons on self-esteem was revealing (all $Fs < .25$), and the linear contrast accounted for merely 7% of the SS between groups. The mean self-esteem scores for the high, moderate, and low gossipers were 31.00, 31.64, and 30.75, respectively. Anxiety as a linear predictor of amount of gossiping accounted for 71% of the between-groups SS. Virtually all the variability (99%) between groups could be accounted for by the difference between high gossipers (M = 17.14) and the low (M = 12.33) and moderate (M = 12.09) ones, with $F(1,27)$ = 5.16, and p = .03, effect size r = .40.

Those who gossiped least were rated more likable (M = 18.76) than moderate (M = 12.75) or high gossipers (M = 10.25), with $F(1,33)$ = 6.85, and p = .01, accounting for 95% of between groups SS. None of the groups was rated negatively, however. Moderate gossipers appeared more popular than high or low gossipers. Those who engaged in gossip to a moderate degree were reported as having more close friends (M = 3.08) than high (M = 2.11) or low gossipers (M = 1.64), with $F(1,33)$ = 8.24, and p = .007, accounting for 95% of the between-groups SS.

Targets of Gossip.   In this group there was a strong correlation between the tendency to gossip and the frequency with which an individual was named as a target of gossip (r = .76). Because of this high correlation, we expected relationships similar to those previously discussed between the tendency to be named as a target of gossip and the various personality and popularity measures.

Those least frequently named as targets of gossip were also higher in need for social approval (M = 19.73) than moderate (M = 15.63) or frequent targets (M = 14.36). This linear relation, with $F(1,27)$ = 4.85, and p = .04, accounted for 92% of the between-groups SS. There were virtually no differences in self-esteem among the three groups (M = 31.64, 30.38, 31.18 for low, moderate, and high targets, respectively). Contrary to the findings when levels of gossiping were compared, the tendency to be a target of gossip was unrelated to anxiety (M = 13.09, 13.88, 13.27 for high, moderate, and low target groups, respectively).

Those most frequently targeted were perceived as less likable (M = 8.90) than moderate (M = 15.68) or low targets of gossip (M = 19.37), with $F(1,33)$ = 10.80, and p = .002, accounting for 97% of the between-groups SS (approximate effect size r = .50). Being targeted by others was related to the number of close friends: those most frequently targeted by others had more close friends (M = 2.85) than moderate (M = 2.64) or infrequent targets (M = 1.33), with $F(1,33)$ = 4.52, and p = .04, accounting for 85% of the between-groups SS.

Gossiping and Friendship.   Even though a sorority shares common goals and values, smaller groups or cliques of friends are likely to occur. From a sociometric matrix, which reflects who chooses whom as a friend, we were able to discern a number of more-or-less interconnected clusters of friends or cliques—defined as *groups* where three or more individuals mutually choose each other as friends (cf. Festinger, Schachter, & Back, 1950)—and a variety of friendship pairs. Two of the cliques stand out in sharp contrast when the members' gossiping tendencies are taken into account. One group is not connected with others in the sorority, and members of this clique rarely gossiped or were named as targets of gossip. A second group is connected to at least two other identifiable cliques in the sorority, and persons in this group were among the most gossiping and gossiped about members of the sorority.

We wanted to determine whether members gossiped about close friends, women who were not friends, or both. To determine who gossiped about whom, specific targets of gossip for each person were identified based on the informants' responses on the phase 1 questionnaire. Gossipers and their targets who could be reliably identified are indicated in Fig. 4.1, which superimposes people's gossiping patterns on their friendship choices. It appears that individuals were as likely to gossip about their close friends as about other members of the sorority.

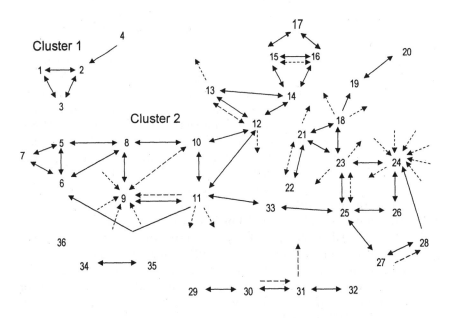

Fig. 4.1. Gossipers and their targets of gossip in relationship to friendship choices. *Note.* Dashed lines indicate gossip targeted at close friends, short outward arrows indicate gossip targeted at non-friends, and short inward arrows indicate members targeted by nonfriends.

Discussion

In our initial attempt to study gossip, we chose to study a sorority, because such a setting appeared to provide the necessary conditions for gossip to flourish. We recognized that we had to tread carefully, as we were entering a closed system of ongoing relationships and we did not want to disturb their sense of community and communality. As a result, there were questions about their gossiping that we did not ask. Our attempts to respect the members' sense of privacy prevented us from finding out some of the "juicier" aspects of their gossiping, and our choice of setting limited the generalizability of our findings. Nonetheless, we believe our findings shed some light on the seemingly disparate portraits of the gossiper found in the literature.

We found that frequent gossipers were not as likable as those who rarely gossiped or whose gossiping tendencies fell somewhere in between. We asked informants to provide likability ratings before they reported on others' gossiping tendencies, so it is unlikely that these less favorable ratings resulted from being labeled as a gossip. Although those who frequently gossiped were also perceived less favorably, it is not the case that they suffered from a lowered self-esteem. Indeed, the self-esteem of members in this sorority was uniformly high. Contrary to the conjecture that individuals gossip to gain favor from others, the frequent gossipers in this study had less of a need for social approval than others who gossiped less frequently. Frequent gossipers were more anxious than their other members; this finding is reminiscent of research indicating that anxious individuals were more likely to pass on rumors about unknown others (Jaeger et al., 1980).

This research seems to suggest that relationships are fundamental for gossiping activity. People need people to gossip with and about. Our sociometric analysis suggested that gossiping activity largely emanated from a clique of the most popular (but not necessarily the most likable) members of this sorority. This clique appeared to contain the movers and shakers, that is, the more active and influential members of the sorority. These individuals were among the most active gossipers and the most frequently gossiped about. In general, however, moderate gossipers had the most close friends, whereas infrequent gossipers had the fewest. In this sorority, gossipers were also more likely to be targets of gossip. In general, therefore, characteristics of the targets of gossip were similar to those of gossipers. Women who were frequent targets of gossip were somewhat less likeable than those less frequently targeted, but their self-esteem was not any lower than others and their need for social approval was less than that of others. Frequent targets seemed to have more close friends in the sorority and were also more frequently chosen as close friends by other members.

At the end of the questionnaire, we asked our respondents to describe what gossip meant to them. Although only 9 of the respondents provided an answer, their responses reflect the complex and often contradictory nature of gossip and its role in interpersonal relationships. About half of the comments reflected the negative side of gossip, either explicitly or implicitly. For example, *gossip*, as explicitly negative, is "when someone talks about another person in a negative way" or when it is defined as "catty remarks." *Gossip* is implicitly negative because it involves talk about others "behind their backs." The remaining comments reflected gossip as basically a harmless activity that could sometimes "get out of hand"; for example, "some people definitely come close to the line between innocent gossip and malicious intent to destroy a reputation." Gossip is a kind of social glue, something that can be used to establish and maintain close personal relationships. For example, it is "hanging out and talking." In the words of one respondent, "What else do you call it when a group of friends get together and talk about what happened that day or a funny story?"

Our theoretical and empirical analyses suggest that the nature of gossip is complex. Like any action directed toward another, it has the potential to hurt its target and thereby, disrupt close personal relationships. Furthermore, the reputation of its source is questioned and further upsets interpersonal relationships. Nonetheless, gossiping is a common activity—one that appears to be enjoyed by its participants. In addition, it serves useful functions for the individual and the establishment and maintenance of close personal relationships. Although gossip is an element of the dark side of relationships, it also plays a positive role in the establishment and maintenance of close personal ties.

REFERENCES

Anthony, S. (1973). Anxiety and rumor. *Journal of Social Psychology, 89*, 91–98.

Ben-Ze'ev, A. (1994). The vindication of gossip. In R. F. Goodman & A. Ben-Ze'ev (Eds.), *Good gossip* (pp. 11–14). Lawrence: University of Kansas Press.

Bergmann, J. R. (1993). *Discreet indiscretions: The social organization of gossip.* New York: Aldine DeGruyter.

Bok, S. (1984). *Secrets: On the ethics of concealment and revelation.* New York: Vintage.

Crowne, D. P., & Marlowe, D. (1964). *The approval motive: Studies in evaluative dependence.* New York: Wiley.

Eagly, A. H. (1987). *Sex differences in social behavior: A social-role interpretation.* Hillsdale, NJ: Lawrence Erlbaum Associates.

Emler, N. (1994). Gossip, reputation, and social adaptation. In R. F. Goodman, & A. Ben-Ze'ev (Eds.), *Good gossip*, (pp. 117–138). Lawrence: University of Kansas Press.

Festinger, L., Schachter, S., & Back, K. (1950). *Social pressures in informal groups*. New York: Harper & Row.

Gluckman, M. (1963). Gossip and scandal. *Current Anthropology, 4*, 307–316.

Gottman, J., & Mettetal, G. (1986). Speculations about social and affective development: Friendship and acquaintance through adolescence. In J. Gottman, & J. Parker (Eds.), *Conversations of friends: Speculations on affective development* (pp. 192–237). New York: Cambridge University Press.

Heidegger, M. (1962). *Being and time*. New York: Harper & Row.

Jaeger, M. E., Anthony, S., & Rosnow R. L. (1980). Who hears what from whom and with what effect: A study of rumor. *Personality and Social Psychology Bulletin, 6*, 473–478.

Jaeger, M. E., Skleder, A. A., Rind, B., & Rosnow, R. L. (1994). Gossip, gossipers, gossipees. In R. F. Goodman & A. Ben-Ze'ev (Eds.), *Good gossip* (pp. 154–168). Lawrence, KS: University of Kansas Press.

Levin, J., & Arluke, A. (1985). An exploratory analysis of sex differences in gossip. *Sex Roles, 12*, 281–286.

Levin, J., & Arluke, A. (1987). *Gossip: The inside scoop*. New York: Plenum.

Morris, W. (Ed.). (1981). *American heritage dictionary of the English language*. Boston, MA: Houghton Mifflin Company.

Nevo, O., Nevo, B., & Derech-Zehavi, A. (1994). The tendency to gossip as a psychological disposition: Constructing a measure and validating it. In R. F. Goodman, & A. N. Ben-Ze'ev (Eds.), *Good gossip* (pp. 180–189). Lawrence: University of Kansas Press.

Rosenberg, M. J. (1965). *Society and the adolescent self-image*. Princeton, NJ: Princeton University Press.

Rosnow, R. L. (1991). Inside rumor: A personal journey. *American Psychologist, 46*, 484–496.

Rosnow, R. L., & Georgoudi, M. (1985). Killed by idle gossip: The psychology of small talk. In B. Rubin (Ed.), *When information counts* (pp. 59–73). Lexington, MA: Heath.

Rosnow, R. L., & Rosenthal, R. (1996a). Computing contrasts, effect sizes, and counternulls on other people's published data: General procedures for research consumers. *Psychological Methods, 1*, 331–340.

Rosnow, R. L., & Rosenthal, R. (1996b). Contrasts and interactions redux: Five easy pieces. *Psychological Science, 7*, 253–257.

Rosnow, R. L., Wainer, H., & Arms, R. L. (1969). Anderson's personality trait-words rated by mean and women as a function of stimulus sex. *Psychological Reports, 24*, 787–790.

Rysman, A. R. (1977). How gossip became a woman. *Journal of Communication, 27*, 176–180.

Sabini, J., & Silver, M. (1982). *Moralities of everyday life*. Oxford, England: Oxford University Press.

Schein, S. (1994). Used and abused: Gossip in medieval society. In R. F. Goodman, & A. Ben-Ze'ev (Eds.), *Good gossip*, (pp. 139–153). Lawrence: University of Kansas Press.

Simpson, J. A., & Weiner, E. S. C. [prepared by]. (1989). *The Oxford English dictionary* (2nd ed., Vol. 6). Oxford, UK: Clarendon Press.

Spacks, P. M. (1985). *Gossip*. New York: Knopf.

Spender, D. (1980). *Man made language*. London: Routledge & Kegan Paul.

Tannen, D. (1990). *You just don't understand: Women and men in conversation*. New York: Morrow.

Taylor, J. A. (1953). A personality scale of manifest anxiety. *Journal of Abnormal and Social Psychology, 48*, 285–290.

Tebbutt, M. (1995). *Women's talk? A social history of 'gossip' in working-class neighbourhoods, 1880–1960*. Aldershot, UK: Scolar Press.

Thomas, L. (1994). The logic of gossip. In R. F. Goodman, & A. Ben-Ze'ev (Eds.), *Good gossip*, (pp. 47–55). Lawrence: University of Kansas Press.

III

BRUISING

5

Patterns of Conflict in Personal Relationships

Susan J. Messman
Daniel J. Canary
Pennsylvania State University

Therefore, there are five traits that are dangerous in generals. Those who are ready to die can be killed; those who are intent on living can be captured; those who are quick to anger can be shamed; those who are puritanical can be disgraced; those who love people can be troubled.

—Sun Tzu, *The Art of War*, 1991

Written approximately 2,000 years ago, *The Art of War* presents principles of conflict that are profitably applied to personal relationships as well as international wars (Sun Tzu, 1991, p. viii). A primary presumption of *The Art of War* is that war should be waged in cool detachment of one's emotions. Accordingly, the above traits found to be dangerous in generals cannot be found in good generals: "Good generals are otherwise: they are not committed to death yet do not expect to live; they act in accord with events, not quick to anger, not subject to embarrassment. ... Their action and inaction are matters of strategy, and they cannot be pleased or annoyed" (p. 66).

This chapter suggests that everyday social actors resemble bad generals when it comes to managing interpersonal conflicts. By focusing on patterns of conflict interaction, we see that people often respond to each other in ways that reflect anything but cool, detached, strategic orientations. Instead, conflict behaviors more frequently reflect emotional responses sometimes designed for self-defeat.

We examine patterns of conflict-interaction behavior that represent the research in close, personal relationships. In particular, we emphasize normative patterns of conflict that were found in family and romantic relationships. This focus is mandated by the research that has, in the past 30 years, paid the most attention to romantic couple conflicts, followed by family conflict interactions (e.g., Raush, Barry, Hertel, & Swain, 1974). We mostly rely on quantitative analyses, although we realize that several good efforts were offered that delineate conflict patterns with conversational and discourse-analytic techniques (e.g., Alberts & Driscoll, 1992; Grimshaw, 1990). We do not review some of the intriguing and important work concerning violence, paradoxes, or codependence. Instead, we seek to uncover the everyday and sometimes subtle interactions that occur in conflict episodes (Canary, Cupach, & Messman, 1995).

Before we review the research findings, however, we attempt to clarify the nature of conflict patterns and how they are studied (see also Watt & Van Lear, 1996). Using this discussion of conflict patterns, we then review the literature on conflict patterns in families and romantic relationships. Finally, we conclude by summarizing the implications of the literature regarding the dark side of interaction in close relationships.

DEFINING AND DETECTING CONFLICT PATTERNS

Defining Conflict Patterns

In accordance with most of the empirical literature, we define *patterns* as recurring act-to-act sequences of interaction behaviors (Raush, 1965; see also Street & Cappella, 1985). Most of the research on conflict patterns relies on the act-to-act behavioral sequence (also called lag one, first-ordered lags, or the interact, these simply refer to two consecutive behaviors or turns). In our view, a first-order sequence represents a fundamental, sufficient, and elegant unit for depicting patterns. Researchers often operationalize *recurring* as a minimum of 5% of the first-ordered sequences observed (Gottman, 1979). As the literature review that follows shows, first-ordered lags provide a powerful quantitative means to represent patterns of conflict behavior that demarcate satisfactory from unsatisfactory relationships. Indeed, some studies found that first-ordered patterns are more predictive than higher ordered sequences of relational quality (e.g., Margolin & Wampold, 1981). Although conflict patterns entail more complexity than first-ordered sequences detect, it is not necessary to go beyond first-ordered lags to remain in the province of patterned communication. Moreover, some scholars identified very complex derivations of first-ordered sequences to describe higher ordered patterns (e.g., Gottman, 1979; Revenstorf, Hahlweg, Schindler, & Vogel, 1984).

In addition, researchers frequently use the term *reciprocity* when discussing conflict sequences and patterns. Schaap (1984) proposed three types of reciprocity: (a) *simultaneity-based reciprocity* refers to partners' immediate reciprocation of behaviors (e.g., partners frowning at each other); (b) *baserate-based reciprocity* refers to each party's frequency of behavior in a given interaction (e.g., sums of husband's and wife's cooperative behaviors in a 15-minute discussion); and (c) *contingency-based reciprocity* concerns how one person's behavior follows the partner's preceding behavior. Naturally, a person can respond to the partner without acting in like manner, thus creating different types of message exchanges. As Rogers (1981) stated, *reciprocity* refers to the way that people communicate with each other in terms of *symmetrical* and *complementary* exchanges. According to Rogers, symmetrical and complementary response types were first used by Bateson (1935) to describe how group members mirror each other's behavior in a symmetrical fashion (e.g., proposal–counterproposal) or to provide the implied preferred (complementary) response (e.g., proposal–agreement to the proposal). In this manner, when we speak of patterns and sequences, we do not presume reciprocation of behavior, although many sequences are symmetrical.

Detecting Conflict Patterns

Baserate-based analyses—such as frequencies or correlations—only provide indirect glimpses of conflict patterns. For example, Birchler, Vincent, and Weiss (1975) showed how positive and negative behaviors surface within an overall picture one obtains from the frequencies of pleasant or unpleasant activities. Likewise, correlations provide some sense of the degree to which couples engage in patterns of responses. However, a problem emerges when studies that employ baserate-based analyses are based on self-report data. Self-reports of conflict behaviors offer biased estimates of interaction baserates to the extent that people's perceptions distort their interaction behaviors (Canary et al., 1995). Observational studies are preferred in examinations of conflict patterns, even for baserate-based studies.

Baserate-based measures do not fully represent interaction patterns (Cappella, 1987). The reciprocation of behavior in sequence differs from the general give and take that people sometimes reference in discussions of reciprocity (Gottman, 1979). In addition, correlations of frequencies do not reveal the emergence of behavior in real time; the emergence of one's conflict behavior, in light of the partner's behavior, contains information beyond the mere occurrence of behavior, as most information and systems theorists argued (e.g., Bateson, 1979; Gottman, 1979). Likewise, Vuchinich (1984) argued that "linguistic and sequential organization are central in determining the social constitution and impact of utterances" (p. 217; see also Circourel, 1980; Goffman, 1981; Labov & Fanshel, 1977).

In addition, accounting for sequences of interaction adds explained variance beyond baserate-based measures. For instance, in a comparison of adjusted and maladjusted children, Raush (1965) reported that approximately 30% of conversational variance between children was accounted for by the partner's preceding behavior. In a study of marital interaction, Margolin and Wampold (1981) found that sequential data added substantially more explained variance in relational quality beyond that accounted for by frequencies alone—8% for marital adjustment, 15% for desired areas of change, 8% for items assessing pleasing spousal behavior, and 15% for items assessing displeasing spousal behavior. The fact that the sequences were added after the variance due to the baserates (using the same behavioral categories) was accounted for indicates impressive gains in predictive power. Moreover, to the extent that one conceptually defines patterns as sequences of behavior, then act-to-act behaviors appear fundamental as well as predictive, even in light of other predictors (e.g., Billings, 1979). Given the integral nature of act-to-act behaviors to relating, the next two sections review the conflict literature that focuses on such sequences of behavior in families and romantic relationships.

CONFLICT PATTERNS IN FAMILY INTERACTION RESEARCH

TV families in the past, such as the Cleavers and the Bradys, were characterized as perfectly happy, interacting in ways that display love, respect, and support. Certainly, such interactions can be common in families. However, as more recent television families illustrate, not all family interaction reflects such positivity. The ever-present dark side of family interaction includes conflict in the form of hostile, aggressive, argumentative, and/or antagonizing behaviors. Indeed, families probably have more conflict than other social groups (Shantz & Hobart, 1989). Family contexts provide more frequent opportunities for interpersonal boundary violations than do other personal relationship contexts (Petronio, 1994; Vuchinich, 1984). Merely living with family members increases the opportunity for all types of interaction, especially conflict.

People's first experiences with conflict occur with family members. *Conflict-interaction behavior* represents social behavior that is learned in the individual's first interactions with parents and siblings and is developed throughout childhood (Dunn, 1983). Conflict experiences in childhood contribute to the individual's personal and social development (Shantz & Hobart, 1989). Based on this developmental argument, one particularly dark outcome of conflict in families occurs when children learn ineffective, inappropriate, dysfunctional, and even violent conflict-interaction behaviors as part of normal conflict patterns and perpetuate such behaviors in later relationships.

How families manage conflict appears to differentiate healthy families from dysfunctional families. Research supports the conclusion that dysfunctional families are typified by their relatively rigid patterns of conflict (Doane, 1975). As Courtright, Millar, and Rogers (1980) noted, research efforts "have seemingly confirmed the notion that normal families are more flexible in their communication patterns than are abnormal families" (p. 199). In addition, Bochner and Eisenberg (1987) noted that "healthy families are able to find solutions to their problems that do not escalate the severity of the problem" (p. 557). Collectively, family interaction provides a rich context for the exploration of the dark side of relationships (Stafford & Dainton, 1994). Research on patterns of conflict behaviors specifically illustrates the dark nature of family life.

Although a great deal of research on family conflict exists, Dunn (1983) noted that observational studies of family conflict interactions are relatively rare and studies of interaction patterns and consequences of patterns are especially rare. In addition, Shantz and Hobart (1989), in discussing sibling conflict strategies, observed that "few studies to date have focused on the process by which the siblings themselves resolve their conflicts" (p. 83). Nonetheless, several observational studies of sibling and parent–child conflict reveal some insight into the nature of conflict patterns in families. The findings of these studies are reviewed in the following paragraphs. However, two limitations of these studies require mention. First, the studies are predominantly descriptive and rarely link the interaction patterns to outcome variables. Second, *conflict* is broadly defined to include agonistic (i.e., negative) interaction behaviors—attempts to gain compliance, arguments, oppositional interactions, quarrels, and so forth.

Conflict Patterns Among Siblings

Interactions with siblings constitute at least half of children's family interactions in families with children (Bank & Kahn, 1975; Lawson & Ingleby, 1974). Dunn (1983) observed that 80% of children in the United States and

Great Britain have siblings and that "sibling behavior is of prime importance in the elicitation and maintenance of aggressive behavior" (p. 799; see also Patterson, 1975; Wiehe, 1990). Dunn and McGuire (1992) cited Rafaelli in noting that sibling relationships are typified as being more tolerant to conflict yet containing more anger and aggression than relationships with peers. Vuchinich (1984) found that in conflicts during family dinnertime, siblings did not restrain their hostility when opposing each other and were likely to be direct versus indirect in their oppositions with each other.

The research on sibling conflict-interaction behaviors appears to support the argument that older children decide what is done to whom in conflicts with their younger siblings (Shantz & Hobart, 1989). For example, Abramovitch, Corter, and Pepler (1980) observed 36 pairs of preschool siblings in their homes (see also Abramovitch, Corter, Lando, 1979; Pepler, Abramovitch, & Corter, 1981). Children's behaviors were coded as *agonistic*, *prosocial*, or *imitative*, and their responses were coded as well (see Table 5.1). The findings revealed that older children initiated more agonistic behavior. Moreover, the pattern of responses to agonistic behaviors revealed that older children were more likely to respond to younger children with a counterattack rather than a submission. Complementing this pattern, younger siblings more likely responded to agonistic, negative behavior by submitting rather than engaging in a counterattack. Apparently, older siblings in the preschool age group exert control over their younger siblings by being the primary instigators of conflicts and by responding more powerfully to agonistic behaviors. The patterns of conflict in these studies revealed that, at least for preschool children, interactions with siblings reflect unfair complementarity versus symmetry (see Dunn, 1983).

Older children also appear to have the advantage of more sophisticated communication behaviors in conflicts with their younger siblings. For example, Dunn and Munn (1987) found that older siblings were able to use justifications in their disputes with their younger siblings, who eventually learned to use justifications as well. Phinney (1986) examined 5-year-olds' conflict patterns involving a sibling (either older—age 6 to 9—(or younger—age 2 to 4) and a peer. The researcher coded the verbal moves of each speaker following an assertion as either *simple moves* (counterassertions that simply rejected, denied, or contradicted the assertion) or *elaborated moves* (those that provided reasons, explanations, or justifications for a counterassertion, queried a preceding counterassertion, or in some other way verbally altered the simple repetitive pattern; p. 50). Consistent with Dunn and Munn (1987), Phinney (1986) found that instances of elaborated moves increased with the child's age. In addition, 5-year-olds were more likely not to reply to a simple counterassertion from a younger sibling and not to reply to an elaborated counterassertion from

TABLE 5.1

Behavioral Coding Scheme for Preschool Siblings

Category	Definition
Agonistic Behaviors	

Physical

Physical aggression	Assertive physical contact, specifically, hit, push, pull, shove, kick, bite, pinch, or pull hair.

Object Related

Object struggle	A fight over an object.

Verbal

Command	An order or demand stated with authority in a loud tone of voice, may be accompanied by threatening facial expressions or gestures.
Insult–disapproval	Teasing, name calling, unfavorable judgments.
Threat	Statements of intent to harm, take toys away.
Tattle–tell	Telling the mother about the other sibling's wrong doing.

Prosocial Behaviors	
Give or share an object	Give an object spontaneously or on request; let other sibling share an object with which child is already playing—spontaneously or on request.
Cooperate or help	Engaging in behaviors that require two individuals; explanations or physical aid.
Request	Asking for something (e.g., a toy)
Praise or approval	Verbal statements of approval or admiration of sibling or his behavior.
Comfort or reassurance	Verbal or physical consolation when sibling is in some way distressed.
Physical affection	Positive physical contact, specifically
Laugh or smile	Facial expression of laughter or smiling directed at the sibling.
Approach	Moving to within .5 m of sibling with no evidence of agonistic intent.

Imitation	
	Following sibling to another room or another area in room; performing the same behavior as sibling within 10 sec (imitation was not recorded if an act was apparently elicited by the environment—e.g., bouncing a ball); that is, only instances of imitating relatively novel behaviors were recorded.

Responses	

To Agonism

Submit	Cry, scream, whine, withdraw, request cessation, give up object, or obey.
Counterattack	Any direct physical or verbal agonism (following the agonism categories above).
No response	No change occurs in ongoing behavior as a result of agonistic act.

To Prosocial

Positive	Positive acceptance (following prosocial categories above).
Negative	Physical or verbal rejection—hit, push, etc.; "no," "go away," etc. (following agonistic categories above).
No response	No change occurs in ongoing behavior as a result of prosocial act.

Note: From "Sibling interaction in the home," by R. Abramovitch, C. Corter, and B. Lando, 1979, *Child Development, 50*, p. 1000. Copyright © 1979 by The Society for Research in Child Development Inc. Reprinted with permission.

an older sibling. Phinney suggested that with a younger sibling, the 5-year-olds did not feel compelled to respond to an unjustified move, whereas with an older sibling, the 5-year-olds felt intimidated by the older child's knowledge level. Clearly, age differences among siblings play an important role in the imbalanced enactment of conflict-interaction patterns. The following sample dialogue provided by Phinney illustrates an apparent power imbalance in a dispute between an older child (David, age 6 years, 8 months) with his 5-year-old sister, labeled with the codes assigned by the researcher (*A* = Assertion, *E* = Elaborated Move, and *S* = Simple Move):

(*A*) David: Remember, this is my tent, isn't it?
(*E*) Judith: And mine. (Considered elaborated because it does not contradict the preceding utterance, but rather qualifies it.)
(*E*) David: No, I just let you have it, don't I, to share.
(*S*) Judith: It's mine too.
(*S*) David: No, I just share it with you.
(*E*) Judith: Yes, and when you share it, it's mine with yours. Both together, it's ours.
(*E*) David: Yes, but I'm in charge here 'cause it was mine.
(*E*) Judith: I helped Mummy put it up. Does that matter to you?
(*S*) David: No. (p. 55)

The preceding dialogue reveals another pattern characteristic of sibling conflict interactions among children. Elaborated moves were most often followed with elaborated moves by the other child; similarly, simple moves were followed by simple moves (Phinney, 1986). Apparently, preceding moves greatly influenced how the sibling responded. This finding coincides with other research indicating that one communicator's verbal behavior limits and, to some degree, determines the options of another in family conflict situations (Vuchinich, 1984). Vuchinich argued that in conflicts involving the family unit as a whole, the unmitigated linguistic structure of "No" is frequently followed with a similarly unmitigated response. Such connections between interactants' conversational moves were observed in studies focused specifically on dyadic conflicts between parents and children.

Conflict Patterns Between Parents and Children

In addition to interactions with siblings, interactions with parents often involve conflict. However, much of the research literature on parent–child interaction focuses on two particular types of conflict. Eisenberg (1992) noted that "traditional emphases in research on child development ... define conflict as 'parental discipline' or 'child non-compliance'" (p. 21).

For example, Rocissano, Slade, and Lynch (1987) examined the synchrony of talk turns between mothers and toddlers (16- to 20-month-olds) in episodes where mothers were attempting to gain toddler compliance. Rocissano et al. found that conflict talk turns were connected and patterned in mother–child interactions (see also Phinney, 1986). More specifically, Rocissano et al. asked mothers to teach their toddlers a tea-party script during a videotaped play session in the lab. Talk turns were coded as either *synchronous* (staying on topic with partner's immediately preceding turn) or *asynchronous* (initiating a new topic with no mention of partner's topic). The researchers also recorded whether the child complied with maternal instructions. Rocissano et al. held that compliance was a special case of synchrony. These authors used the following dialogue to illustrate that the child's turn may be synchronous but not compliant:

Mother: Can you give Mommy some tea?
Child: [Stirring in cream pitcher and holding spoon to mother.]
Mother: No, Mommy doesn't want cream, Mommy wants tea.
Child: [Stirring in cream pitcher and holding spoon to mother] No, Mommy eat cream! (p. 700)

Using sequential analysis, Rocissano et al. (1987) found that children were more likely to engage in asynchronous turns. When mothers' turns were synchronous, children were more likely to follow with synchronous turns. Moreover, children were more likely to comply following a mother's synchronous versus asynchronous turn. Rocissano et al. observed that "children whose mothers were most flexible in following their children's changing attentional focus were both more likely to comply with instructions and to maintain dialogic exchange" (p. 702). Flexibility (as illustrated in the following dialogue) in interaction behaviors is strongly linked to effective conflict management with toddlers. In addition, successful interactions in terms of compliance are marked by mothers following their child's lead.

Mother: Pour some tea.
Child: [Puts spoon in teapot; holds it there.]
Mother: OK, let's mix the tea. [Demonstrates stirring motion.]
Child: [Stirs in pot with spoon.] (p. 703)

Other research similarly supported the existence of a first-order dependency between child compliance or noncompliance and the type of parent's verbal control attempt: Positive actions on the part of parents more likely facilitate child compliance, whereas negative actions more likely facilitate noncompliance (Lytton, 1979; see also Lytton & Zwirner, 1975). Lytton also argued that the parent's behavior in the interaction preceding the verbal control interaction was likely to influence the child's response. Lytton (1979) observed disciplinary encounters between parents and 2- and 3-year-old boys to discover connections between such second-order antecedents and child compliance or noncompliance. The researcher observed the families in their homes and coded both the interact in which the parent attempts to verbally control the child and the parent's actions in the preceding interact (see Table 5.2). The child's behavior was coded as *compliant, noncompliant,* or *neither.*

Lytton (1979) found that the second-order antecedents combined with the verbal control in the first-order antecedents were associated with the child's likelihood to comply. Specifically, the use of physical control in a preceding interact reduced the likelihood that a child would respond to a command or prohibition with compliance. In addition, positive action in the preceding interact "boosts the facilitating effect of command-prohibition on compliance but lowers it for noncompliance" (p. 261). Lytton's findings illustrate that in some cases, a research focus on Lag 1 only causes one to overlook other aspects of interaction patterns in conflict situations. Nonetheless, in other cases, only the two behaviors that comprise Lag 1 appear to be connected, and second-order dependencies were not found to be significant.

For instance, Fletcher, Fischer, Barkley, and Smallish (1996) observed neutral and conflict discussions between a mother and her teenager. Utterances were coded as *negative* (commands or put downs and defends or complains), *positive* (problem solution, facilitates, and defines or evalu-

TABLE 5.2

Summary of Lytton's Coding Scheme for Parent Behaviors in Disciplinary Encounters

Category	Examples/Description
Verbal Control Types	
Command/prohibition	A direct imperative, positive or negative.
Suggestion	"Would you like to...?"
Control with reasoning	Giving a justification for the command or prohibition.
Actions Preceding the Verbal Control Interact	
Physical control	A slap or physically restraining or restricting.
Negative action	Expression of displeasure, criticism, threat, or a refusal of the child's request.
Positive action	Expression of love or approval, hugging, smiling, playing with the child, or complying with the child's request.
Neutral action	Less emotionally loaded kinds of behavior (e.g., neutral speech, handing something other than food to the child, and caretaking activities).

Note. From "Disciplinary encounters between young boys and their mothers and fathers: Is there a contingency system?" by H. Lytton, 1979, *Developmental Psychology, 15,* p. 257. Copyright 1979 by American Psychological Association. Reprinted with permission.

ates), or *neutral talk*. Using Markov analyses, the researchers examined both first-order and second-order dependencies. Only the Lag 1 exchanges were significant. Fletcher et al. explained that "these parent-teen interactions seemed highly flexible in the course they took over the longer sequence of exchanges, yet they revealed a closely linked contingent relationship at each exchange in the sequence" (p. 293). Additionally, mothers' behaviors were flexible and positive compared to teenagers' behaviors. For example, regardless of the teen's comment, mothers were less likely than teens to make negative comments; Fletcher et al. observed that "a mother was most likely to respond with a positive comment, whereas the teen's response tended to parallel the mother's comment, negative following a negative, neutral following a neutral, and positive following a positive" (p. 284). Although when in conflict, both mother and teen made negative comments more often and positive comments less often, "mothers were still most likely to make positive comments, teens were most likely to make negative comments" (p. 285).

These findings, combined with those reviewed earlier in this section, indicate that flexibility in conflict situations is developed as people mature. Although by adolescence individuals mature in many aspects of their interaction behaviors, conflict-management interactions appear to require still more maturity (see also Selman, 1980). For example, Vuchinich (1984) observed that "the older generation transfers more mitigated hostility with vague boundary information. This pattern describes the relatively primitive social control efforts of children compared with more subtle social control efforts by the parents, who avoid unmitigated hostility" (p. 231). In addition, the findings of these parent–child studies illustrate that positivity in conflict situations leads to parent effectiveness in conflicts over compliance and the negativity of one partner leads to negativity in the other partner. However, a few studies examine parent–child conflict in broader terms than child compliance or noncompliance.

Eisenberg (1992) argued that child noncompliance is only one type of parent–child conflict and that "children may learn more about negotiation when mothers are noncompliant than when they themselves fail to comply" (p. 25). The researcher had mothers audiotape conversations between themselves and their 4-year-olds in natural settings. The transcribed conversations were coded for spontaneous conflicts (defined as oppositional moves) and the interaction that immediately followed (see Table 5.3). Eisenberg's findings revealed that disagreements about child compliance constituted a small portion of mother–child conflict and that mothers both opposed the children more and were more noncompliant to the child than the reverse.

Similar to other studies of parent–child conflict, Eisenberg (1992) found connections among the utterances and interaction strategies of participants.

TABLE 5.3

Eisenberg's Coding Categories for Mother–Child Conflict Behaviors

Type of Speech Act of the Opposed Utterance	
Request for action	Included direct and indirect requests and prohibitions (e.g., mother says, "Why don't you come in and hold my hand?").
Requests for permission	Beginning with "Can I..." or "Can we..."
Statements of intent	Utterance stated a plan to perform some action (e.g., child says, "I'm gonna make some more").
Statements of fact	Utterance that asserted a proposition (e.g., mother says, "That's a firefly").
The Topic of the Conflict	
Caretaking	Disputes focused on eating, bathing, and spilling.
Possession/rights	Conflicts involved touching objects, possession, and turn taking.
Destructive/hurtful	Disputes focused on hurtful or unkind actions and offensive behaviors such as making noise, making a mess, or disgusting behaviors.
Rules and manners	Disputes centered on rules about dangerous behavior, politeness routines, rudeness, not talking baby talk, and references to family rules.
Assistance	Conflicts involved demands for aid or independence.
Other	Conflicts that did not fall into other categories.

Note. From "*Conflicts between mothers and their young children,*" by A. R. Eisenberg, 1992 by Wayne State University Press.

Specifically, participants were more likely to use reasoning in conflicts with negative affect and in response to a partner's use of reasoning. Eisenberg surmised that "supplying a reason leads the opponent to take one's position into account" (p. 38). Moreover, the patterns of opposition appeared to indicate that mothers and children were sensitive to the relational messages implied by utterances. For example, Eisenberg observed that "Opposition to requests for permission and assertions were least likely to lead to mutual opposition, followed by opposition to requests for action, and finally to statements of intent" (p. 39). Eisenberg reasoned that certain utterances relegate more power or choice to the partner and that mothers and children communicated as if they realized such relegations. Specifically, mothers and children tended not to oppose their partner when the partner opposed a *request for permission* (an utterance that relegates power to the partner). On the other hand, the speakers tended to follow the partner's opposition with opposition when the speaker's original utterance was a *statement of intent* (an utterance that relegates no power to the partner).

Eisenberg's (1992) findings also illustrate power differences in conflicts between mothers and their young children. For example, in conflicts where the mother was noncompliant (versus conflicts where the child was noncompliant), the interaction was less likely to entail mutual opposition. In addition, when the child was noncompliant, the conflict was less likely to end in a standoff. Eisenberg also observed that "maternal opposition affected the course of the conflict differently than did child opposition" (p. 32). When the mother opposed the child, conflict was less likely to ensue than when the child opposed the mother. Moreover, when the mother's opposition contained an explicit negative, the child was less likely to oppose the mother in response. Not surprisingly, mothers' behaviors can be characterized as more powerful than children's behaviors.

Yet, a mother's power is not absolute. Children were more likely to follow the mother's opposition with opposition when the mother did not provide a justification or alternative. Eisenberg (1992) explained that children's sensitivity to reasoned argument illustrated that the children recognized the social rule that "one cannot 'just say no'" in conflict situations with others (p. 37). Children also appeared empowered in factual disputes; mothers tended to submit to the child. In a line of research based on social learning principles, Patterson (1979) showed that a mother's punishment of her child's coercion (e.g., yelling, hitting, or arguing) increases the likelihood that the child will continue using coercion. Ironically, children using some types of coercion (e.g., showing disapproval and ignoring the parent) eliminated the parent's negative behaviors more than 50% of the time.

Studies involving the family unit as a whole further illustrate the nature of power in family conflict situations. Vuchinich (1984) examined Lag 1 sequences of conflict among family members having dinner in their homes. He found that children did not oppose parents as frequently as parents opposed parents. In addition, children opposed mothers more often than they opposed fathers. Vuchinich reported that family members rarely followed a father's simple negation opposition with a similarly unmitigated opposition, whereas they did so more frequently with the mother. The sex difference in oppositions to parents is found elsewhere. In their review, Paikoff and Brooks-Gunn (1991) noted that sons increase their forceful behaviors during adolescence and mothers often complement their sons' assertions by acting less dominant, whereas fathers become more dominant with their sons. One other difference that Vuchinich labeled as a *power difference* was that sons tended to oppose parents more often than daughters opposed parents. Clearly, when the number of participants in the conflict interaction increases, the web of power differences increases in complexity.

Family conflict interaction also increases in complexity in nonpower related aspects when the focus is the entire family rather than selected dyads (e.g., mother–child). For example, Vuchinich, Emery, and Cassidy (1988) videotaped family dinner conversations and coded the verbal conflict defined as oppositional moves (see Table 5.4). The findings illustrate that third parties affect the conflicts between family members. For example, Vuchinich et al. found that when third parties first intervened in conflicts with a conflict continuation move, the conflicts were longer than when third parties used other moves first. In addition, the final outcome of family conflicts varied based upon whether or not a third party intervened such that submission was less likely and withdrawal was more likely when a third party intervened.

Vuchinich et al. (1988) also found patterns of reciprocity in family conflict. Specifically, when one fighter used a conflict move, the second fighter tended to respond with a conflict move. Similarly, when a nonconflict strategy was used, the response was most likely to be a nonconflict move. This latter tendency was also found for third-party responses to nonconflict moves. However, Vuchinich et al. observed that "third parties tended not to reciprocate conflict moves" (p. 1300).

Moreover, the patterns of reciprocation, combined with the outcomes of such conflicts, illustrate how normal families diffuse routine and frequent conflicts with flexibility. For example, none of the episodes of reciprocated conflict moves were very long. Conflicts without third-party intervention contained an average of 3.7 turns. In addition, Vuchinich et al. (1988) observed that most conflict (64.5%) ended in stand-offs. Hence, although conflict moves tended to be reciprocated by fighters, such episodes were short-lived and ended with an avoidance strategy. Vuchinich (1987) concluded that successful conflict management in families entails such strategies as stand-offs to diffuse family disputes. Although regular use of conflict avoidance tactics is often decried as "unhealthy" by textbooks, avoidance nonetheless represents a norm of family conflict management. Avoidance also appears to be a popularly used response in romantic relationships.

CONFLICT PATTERNS IN RESEARCH ON ROMANTIC INVOLVEMENTS

At this juncture, we examine conflict patterns germane to romantic involvements. We use the term *romantic involvements* to reference personal relationships that involve sexual bonds. Accordingly, we examine partners who are married, as well as those who are dating, engaged, or living together to locate conflict and argument patterns. Similar to families, couples experience conflict as a routine aspect of relational life. However,

TABLE 5.4

Summary and Example of Third-Party Intervention Coding Categories

Categoy	Codes
Sides-against	(1) identity of opponent; (2) no sides
Sides-with	(1) identity of ally; (2) no sides
Role	(1) fighter (always two); (2) third party
Fighter move	(1) conflict continuation; (2) give in; compromise; (3) withdrawal; (4) other/neutral
Third-party move	(1) conflict continuation; (2) authority (3) mediation/information; (4) distraction; (5) noninvention
Outcome	(1) compromise; (2) submission; (3) stand-off; (withdrawal)

Example

The following conflict begins when the mother opposes the daughter's plans for Saturday. Sue and Rita are friends of the daughter who are not present at the dinner. Column 1 gives the "sides-against" code, column 2 gives the "sides-with" code, column 3 gives the role, and column 4 gives the move type.

1	2	3	4		
D		f	c	M (to D):	There you go again, looking for trouble. You know we're going to Grandma's Saturday.
M		f	c	D (to M):	You didn't say I had to go.
D		f	c	M (to D):	You know what I meant.
D	M	t	c	F (to D):	Don't argue with your mother. You're going.
M		f	c	D (to M):	But I've been planning this for weeks.
No	No	t	m	S (to F):	Why couldn't she have them over in the morning, then we could go to Grandma's in the afternoon?
S		f	c	D (to S):	You stay outa this. You're just makin' trouble.
D		f	c	S (to D):	I was trying to help, you jerk …
No	No	t	a	F:	I don't want to listen to this. You two button it. [2.3 second silence]
No		t	d	M (to F):	Did Mr. Baxter show you that big tomato?
				F (to S)	Yeah, wasn't that something?

(This episode is a standoff)

Note. From "Family Members As Third Parties in Dyadic Family Conflict: Strategies, Alliances, and Outcomes," by S. Vuchinich, R. E. Emery, and J. Cassidy, 1988, *Child Development, 59,* p. 1296. Copyright 1988 by The Society for Research in Child Development. Reprinted with permission. In the example, M = mother, F = father, S = son, D = daughter, f = fighter, t = third party, c = conflict continuation, a = authority, m = mediation/information, d = distraction, No = no sides taken.

the routine nature of conflict renders fights, arguments, and confrontations no less hurtful to partners.

Reciprocation of Negative Affect

Although it may appear self-evident, researchers found that dissatisfied partners engage in more negative behaviors relative to satisfied couples (Gottman, 1979; Schaap, 1984). In terms of behavioral patterns, the research also reveals that dissatisfied couples reciprocate negative behaviors (Gottman, 1994; Schaap, 1984). Such reciprocation reflects symmetrical exchanges. For example, the husband's statement, "Now don't say anything to Jack," is symmetrically reciprocated in the wife's reply, "You just don't say anything to Jill." Such a reciprocation epitomizes *transactional redundancy*—the extent to which couples find themselves in a conversational rut (Courtright et al., 1980).

Reciprocation of behavior does not necessarily reflect a clear contingency (Sillars & Weisberg, 1987). Reciprocation of negative behavior is also reflected in *negative reactivity* (Margolin & Wampold, 1981, p. 555)—or instances where a negative comment is met with an asymmetrical negative response, as in attack–defend sequences (Ting-Toomey, 1983). The following example illustrates negative reactivity (lines 94–103) as well as behaviors that appear unrelated to each other (lines 103–108; data described in Mikesell, 1996).

(Couple #17)

94	Husband	Well, look at what you did. Look at the scene you made!
95	Wife	Yeah, well you deserved it.
96	Husband	No, I didn't ...
97	Wife	Everybody fights.
98	Husband	deserve that.
99	Wife	So ...
100	Husband	No, everybody ...
101	Wife	Yeah, everybody fights dear. 'cause if they don't ...
102	Husband	Yeah, but not in the presence of company. Not when, honey, we had 15 people.
103	Wife	See, I'm a very prompt [sic] person. I don't care.
104	Husband	But I do.
105	Wife	I knew everybody there.
106	Husband	Yes, but I DO.
107	Wife	And most of them was [sic] your family, and I couldn't care what they think anyway.
108	Husband	Well, I do.
109	Wife	Well, I don't!
110	Husband	Well, then I shouldn't care what your family thinks.

In an important study of couple interaction, Billings (1979) compared act-to-act sequences of 12 maritally dissatisfied couples with 12 maritally satisfied couples. Billings categorized behaviors into one of four types: friendly-dominant; friendly–submissive; hostile–dominant; and hostile–submissive. Given his initial finding that the effective, friendly–dominant dimension was more powerful than the dominant–submissive dimension, Billings calculated the ratio of hostile sequences for both partners from each couple as they enacted two role plays (i.e., one where the spouse acts distant and one where self acts distant). Results indicated that the dissatisfied couples "make more negative and fewer positive statements [versus satisfied couples]. ... Sequential analyses suggest that distressed couples exhibited greater, whereas nondistressed couples exhibited lesser, reciprocity of negative acts than statistically expected" (p. 374). Also, dissatisfied couples escalated their sequences of hostility. Billings (1979) reported these findings in point graphs, with each point indicating the ratio of hostility. This graphic method of representing the progression of act-to-act conflict sequences remains a popular one (e.g., Gottman, 1994, p. 159). Figure 5.1 represents Billings' comparison of satisfied versus dissatisfied couples.

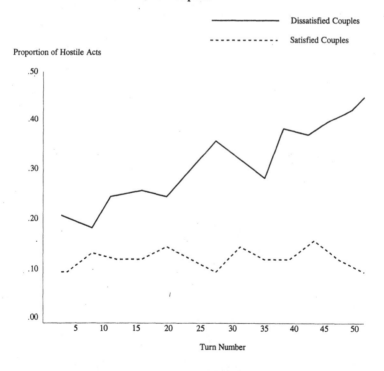

FIG. 5.1 Comparison of satisfied and dissatisfied couple conversations in the proportion of hostile messages enacted over time. Adapted from Billings (1979, p. 374).

Following a review of similar research and forecasting his own findings, Gottman (1979) concluded that the reciprocation of negative behaviors, such as criticism, complaints, defensiveness, and stonewalling, works against relational satisfaction and stability. However, according to Gottman (1979, 1994), the reciprocation of positive conflict behaviors, such as agreement and problem solving with positive affect, does not consistently correspond to relational satisfaction. Likewise, Schaap's (1984) review indicated that people in dissatisfied couples (vs. satisfied couples) were more likely to reciprocate negative behaviors. In addition, Schaap found that dissatisfied couples were more likely than satisfied couples to engage in reciprocations of positive behaviors.

Gottman's Phases of Patterns

As indicated previously, Gottman identified several conflict patterns. He did so by first coding couples' problem-solving interaction with the Couples Interaction Scoring system (CISS), which is partly derived from The Marital Interaction Coding system (MICS); for a review of observational coding systems, see Markman & Notarius, 1987. The CISS is summarized in Table 5.5. The patterns that Gottman identified occur in one of three phases—*agenda building*, *arguing*, and *negotiating*—wherein couples are

TABLE 5.5
Summary of the Couples Interaction Scoring System

AG	*Agreement*. Agreement involves direct agreement, acceptance of responsibility, compliance, assent, and change of opinion.
DG	*Disagreement*. Disagreement can be explicit, involve "yes-but" answers (i.e., initial agreement stating why one disagrees), be offered with a rationale, or be stated in the form of a command or explicit non-compliance.
CT	*Communication talk*. CT concerns communication about communication as well as statements directing the discussion to the task or seeking clarification.
MR	*Mindreading* concerns one's beliefs about the partner's internal states—beliefs, emotions, attitudes, and the like—as well as explaining or predicting behaviors.
PS	*Problem Solving/information exchange* refers to instances where one offers some kind of specific or nonspecific) solution is offered or one provides information about one's beliefs or relational activities.
SS	*Summarizing self*, which includes statements about one's expressed opinions.
SO	*Summarizing other*, which includes summaries of the partner or both parties' behavior.
PF	*Expressing feelings about a problem* involves one talking about a general personal issue or the relationship in particular.

Note: Adapted from Gottman (1979), pp. 82–86, and Notarius and Markman (1981), pp. 114–119.

said to state an opinion, state their agreement or disagreement, and then offer reasons for their positions.

Agenda Building. The agenda building phase contains three act-to-act patterns: *Validation,* wherein one finds partner agreement; *cross-complaining,* which entails the spouse mirroring a complaint; and *feeling probe,* which involves one mind reading the partner (i.e., saying what the partner thinks or feels) and the partner agrees or disagrees. As one might anticipate, validation was more likely in nonclinic couples, whereas crosscomplaining was more likely in clinic couples. These findings contextualize Alberts' (1988) more specific analysis of complaints. She found that dissatisfied (vs. satisfied) cohabiting couples more frequently enacted complaints about personal features of the partner, whereas satisfied couples complained more about behavior. Alberts also reported that satisfied couples (vs. dissatisfied couples) responded to the partner with agreement (a form of validation). In addition, disagreement following a mind read was more likely in distressed, clinical couples (Gottman, 1979, p. 115)—for example, "You appear really tense and stressed out," to which the partner responds with, "Well, I'm not—I've just had a tough day" (vs. the response, "Well, you may be right—I've had a tough day").

The arguing phase contains several responses to disagreements, the two most prevalent being disagreement and statements of one's own feelings. According to Gottman (1979), the primary discriminator of satisfied from dissatisfied couples in this phase resides in the manner in which metacommunication (i.e., talk about talk) is offered. If said with positive affect, metacommunication functions to promote satisfaction; conversely, if said with negative affect, metacommunication appears to frustrate partners (Gottman, 1982).

Finally, the negotiation phase involves *contracting sequences,* which are terminated by agreement, and *counterproposal sequences,* which involve spouses exchanging proposals or solutions. According to Gottman (1979), satisfied couples are more likely to reach consensus on what to do, whereas dissatisfied couples disagree with each other's suggestions for solutions and offer counterproposals:

> Whereas clinic couples are likely to *mirror* one another's codes, for example, PF PF and PS PS sequences, nonclinic couples intersperse agreement and negative affect chains by some editing process that intercedes between nonverbal behaviors while listening and nonverbal behaviors during message delivery. Whereas the behavior of clinic couples is more linked and contingent, nonclinic couples operate well at each stage of the discussion by *unlatching* their interaction patterns. (p. 122)

Gottman (1980) indicated that the critical factor separating clinical from nonclincal couples' conflict patterns appears to be agreement; "In these results describing the differences in how satisfied and dissatisfied couples attempt to resolve a marital issue, a critical role is played by *agreement codes*. In effect, satisfied couples continually intersperse various subcodes of agreement into their sequences" (p. 957). This interpretation suggests that if one could demarcate sequences involving couples agreeing with each other's ideas as they are presented during discussion, then one could target how couples' joint idea development associates with relational satisfaction as well as assessments of the partner's competence during the conflict.

Couple Types

Fitzpatrick and colleagues (e.g., Fitzpatrick, 1988a, 1988b; Witteman & Fitzpatrick, 1986) showed that modern marriage is composed of different types. *Traditionals* hold conventional sex role beliefs, have high interdependence, and value relational welfare over individual wants. *Independents* adopt egalitarian beliefs, want interdependence as well as autonomy, and negotiate almost everything to further their personal goals. *Separates* enter marriage to maintain a traditional ideology without affective interdependence or conflict. *Mixed* couples occur when partners adopt different marriage models, and approximately 40% of couples fit this description (Fitzpatrick, 1988a). The most common mixed type is the separate husband and traditional wife. Table 5.6 presents the most significant findings for each type of conflict pattern according to couple type.[1]

Traditional couple patterns, as presented in Table 5.6, included solution-based (not agreement-based) validation and contracting sequences in addition to metacommunication and feeling probes. Traditional husbands and wives reciprocated their partners' disagreements. As Fitzpatrick (1988a) summarized, "Complementary in neutral discussions, Traditionals refuse to relinquish control in conflict. ... During conflict, Traditionals tend to use less agreement than the other couples but more information seeking" (pp. 129–130). This image slightly differs from that found in Burggraf and

---

[1]Similarly, but based on observations of couples' conflict behaviors (vs. questionnaire responses), Gottman (1994) identified three functional and two dysfunctional couple types. According to Gottman, the three functional types resemble Fitzpatrick's pure types. *Validating couples* resemble traditional couples in their interdependence and neutral affect in managing conflict. Next, *volatile couples* emulate independents in their conflict engagement tendencies. *Conflict minimizers* resemble Separates in their maintenance of distance through avoidance. Gottman indicated that two other marital types exist, but appear dysfunctional in their reliance on defensiveness, withdrawal, and contempt.

TABLE 5.6

Patterns Used By Different Couple Types

Patterns

Validation	Contracting	Metacomm	Cross-Comp	Disagreement	Feeling Probe
Traditional					
HPF*WPS (.387)	HPS*WPS (.298)	HCT*WCT (.089)		HDIS*WDIS (.155)	HMR*WAG (.184)
WPF*HPS (.381)	WPS*HPS (.352)		WDIS*HDIS (.188)	HMR*WDG (.184)	
Independent					
WPF*HAG* WPF (.120, .170)	WPS*HAG (.075)		HPF*WPF (.122)		
Separate					
WPF*HPS (−.143)	WPS*HAG (.075)		HPF*WPF (.208)		HMR*WAG (.080)
			WPF*HPS (−.143)		WMR*HAG (.092)
Separate/ Traditional					
WPF*HAG* WPF (.244, .311)	WPS*HAG (.145)				
		HPS*WPS (-.065)			

Note. H = husband; W = wife; PF = statement of feeling about a problem; AG = argument; PS = problem-solving/information exchange; CT = communication talk; DIS = disagreement; MR= Mind reading. Metacomm = metacommunication; Cross-Comp = Cross-complaining. Adapted from Fitzpatrick (1988b), p. 251.

Sillars (1987, Study 1), wherein traditionals used avoidance behaviors to initiate conflict discussion and preferred conciliatory messages.

Independents also enacted validation sequences, as indicated by the husband's agreement; however, Gottman (1979) found that wife agreement was the key in validation sequences. Fitzpatrick (1988b) also reported that independents used *cross complaining sequences* (where the wife reciprocates negative feelings about the conflict issue). These results complement those of Burggraf and Sillars (1987), who found that independent partners engaged in rational, analytic forms of conflict management and followed an avoidance act with a confrontational one. This last finding comports with the view that independents prefer direct assessment of issues and respond negatively to avoidance.

According to Table 5.6, separate husbands were less likely than expected by chance to respond to their wives' statements of problems with a solution, either as a validation or as a crosscomplaining response. Separate husbands and wives engaged in more agreements, although these probabilities are not very large. Interestingly perhaps, the strongest pattern was found for an exchange of negative feelings (crosscomplaining). Apparently, the relatively benign conversation of separates heats when one partner complains. This finding was twice replicated in Burggraf and Sillars (1987, Studies 1 and 2); that is, separates appeared to reciprocate confrontational conflict behaviors and rely less on rational, analytic comments (unlike independents).

Finally, mixed couple types appear to rely on both validation and contracting sequences, when the husband agrees with the wife. Burggraf and Sillars (1987) similarly reported that mixed couples used analytic behaviors and infrequently resorted to distributive, confrontational acts. In brief, these findings indicate support for the contention that couple type affects conflict interaction, although the tendency for all couples is to reciprocate behavior; that is, avoidance is met with avoidance, analysis is met with analysis, and fire is met with more of the same.

More Complex Conflict Patterns

As mentioned earlier, act-to-act sequences are combined to form more elaborate patterns of conflict interaction. As Gottman (1980) indicated, "The probabilistic approach to the detection of temporal form may begin by identifying small chains of interaction and then build to longer chains as the data becomes available ... or as new and longer coding units are employed" (p. 952).

Researchers found complex patterns using Lag 1 sequences by replicating the same Lag 1 sequences over several turns, by identifying other chains of act-to-act sequences that follow the original Lag 1 sequence, and/or by including more than one lag in the sequence (i.e., by simultaneously analyzing more than two consecutive behaviors). Each approach offers insight about the emergence of behavior in real time, although each approach has its drawbacks as well. For example, simply repeating the initial act-to-act sequence may underrepresent the complexity inherent in conflict (Sillars & Wesiberg, 1987). Yet, connecting sequences in chains of lag 1 (as Gottman did) violates assumptions critical to lag sequential analysis (Poole, Folger, Ghewes, 1987; Revenstorf et al., 1984). In addition, the use of more than two consecutive behaviors reduces the size of the observational pool. Perhaps more critically the research reporting complex sequences remains a highly specialized venture with little to no history. Although largely speculative, initial research investments in quantified examinations of complex conflict patterns promises an enviable return in the near future.

As just indicated, act-to-act sequences reveal redundancy in couples' conflict communication. For instance, Ting-Toomey (1983) found that for dissatisfied couples, "the long strings of reciprocal interacts of confront-confront, confront-defend, complain-defend, and defend-complain acts were identified as the key sequential patterns that characterized this system" (p. 305). In terms of the probability estimates, for example, the criterion behavior of confrontion predicting defense at .33 or confrontion at .16 (Lag 1), then confrontion at .27 (Lag 2), then defense at .28 (Lag 3), and then confrontion at .15 (Lag 4). Incredibly, Ting-Toomey found 11 significant behavior strings for complain–defend act-to-act sequences (i.e., complain–defend–complain–defend–complain, etc.), with each probability estimate between behaviors as significant (z 1.96). However, satisfied couples did not engage in these long chains of negative behavior (evidence for Gottman's "unlatching" metaphor), and they enacted briefer, and more positive, act-to-act sequences.

Act-to-act sequences also expand to complex derivations. Figure 5.2 illustrates some differences between satisfied and dissatisfied couples' conflict interaction patterns during Gottman's negotiation phase. This example, taken from Gottman (1979), depicts a metamorphosis of actions when the wife (not the husband) presents a solution. First, note the pattern

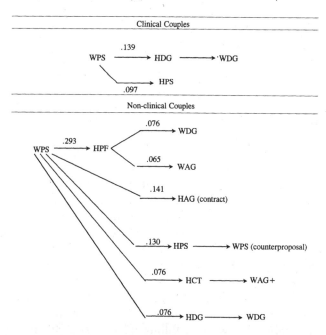

FIG 5.2. Patterns of responses to wife offering a solution. From Marital interactions, experimental investigations, by J. M. Gottman (1979, p. 117). Copyright 1979 by Academic Press. Reprinted with permission.

for the clinical couples in the top portion of Fig. 5.2: After the wife presents the solution, the husband either disagrees (to which the wife disagrees) or he presents his own proposed solution (forming a counterproposal).

The bottom portion of Fig. 5.2 shows the patterns for nonclinical couples (Gottman, 1979). Sequences for the nonclinical couple are more varied, although two of the five resemble responses for the clinical couple. Following the wife's solution proposal, the husband offers a statement of his feelings about the problem (to which the wife agrees or disagrees); he agrees (and thereby forms a contract), offers a proposal of his own (thereby forming a counterproposal), engages in metacommunication (to which the wife agrees); or disagrees (to which the wife disagrees). This example of what happens when the wife initiates a proposal reflects only one of several complex patterns of conflict reported in Gottman.

Likewise, in charting the chains of lag-to-lag sequences, Revenstorf et al. (1984) devised a probability tree for tracing the act-to-act probabilities that link three to five sequential behaviors. Revenstorf et al.'s probability tree shows how pretreatment clinical couples differ from postclinical couples in their patterns of responses following a wife's statement of a problem.

For instance, two paths appear more likely, given a wife's initial statement of a problem. These paths involve MICS derived codes of positive (+) and negative (-) statements of problem (P), and filler (v). The most probable paths for pretreatment distressed couples involve a positive statement or a negative statement, and the negative statement is more likely followed by a filler and two negative statements. In addition, posttreatment therapy couples were more likely to have positive statements or fillers than negative statements following the wife's initial problem statement. In addition, both initial responses (positive or filler) led to a higher probability of problem statement elaborations and positive responses.

Revenstorf et al. (1984) did not appear to hold much faith in their probability tree analysis because the outcomes do not reflect Lag N analysis as much as they do a series of Lag 1 analyses. As Revenstorf et al. noted, although other authors infer complex patterns as being reliable, "the present authors hesitate to do so, since it is unclear from these data what is happening in the time between the antecedent and the lagged response. The consecutive conditional distributions do not constitute a chain of behavior; instead, in each case they refer back to the antecedent rather than to the preceding lagged distributions" (p. 174). Instead, Revenstorf et al. resorted to "generalized interaction patterns" of escalation and de-escalation to characterize complex conflict patterns (pp. 174–180). This move resembles the work of Billings (1979) and Gottman (1994) in charting the ratios of negative to positive conflict statements over time.

Finally, researchers can simply combine more than one lag. Revenstorf et al. (1984) examined three, four, and five combinations of consecutive conflict behaviors. These authors found that certain combinations were very rare. For instance, two negative responses followed by a positive response was very infrequent in their three subsamples of pretreatment distressed couples, posttreatment distressed couples, and nondistressed couples. Common complex behavioral responses included strings of negative responses (e.g., - - - - -), the "yes, but" response sequence (i.e.., + v -). Moreover some sequences were common in pretreatment couples but not posttreatment or nonclinic couples (e.g., P - v +, where an initial negative reaction met with a filler becomes a positive reaction).

CONCLUSION: THE DARK SIDE OF CONFLICT PATTERNS

Conflict patterns reflect the dark side of interaction in relationships in part because the existence of patterns of interactions suggest that in conflict situations, relational partners relinquish their personal control over the situation and blindly follow the course of the conflict. For example, relational partners get caught in spirals of negativity if both interactants reciprocate the partner's preceding negative comment. However, becoming aware of the properties and characteristics of conflict patterns helps partners control their conflict patterns instead of vice versa (Gottman, 1980). For instance, Sillars and Wilmot (1994) noted that satisfied (more than dissatisfied) couples balance the extent to which their conflict patterns vary in terms of *behavioral fluctuation* (i.e., variety), *topical continuity* (i.e., the number of topics discussed), *symmetry* (i.e., reciprocation of like behavior vs. asymmetrical responses), *stationarity* (i.e., phases of patterns over time), and *spontaneity* (i.e., reactive vs. strategized responses). In other words, properties that characterize conflict patterns help partners gauge how their conflict discussions help them keep their romantic system up and running. Sillars and Wilmot suggested that moderate amounts of variety, continuity, symmetry, stationarity, and spontaneity in the enactment of conflict patterns promote relational welfare. Similarly, the family-conflict research illustrates that flexibility promotes healthy family functioning (e.g., Fletcher, et al., 1996; Rocissano et al., 1987).

Lest we offer the impression that all negative conflict behaviors occur in dysfunctional families or relationships, we emphasize the following: Several patterns often appear in adjusted families and romantic relationships (see also Millar, Rogers, & Bavelas, 1984; Sillars & Weisberg, 1987). Based on our review, several patterns tend to be darker than others.

First, children with more development appear to control their siblings through interaction behaviors. For example, Abramovitch and colleagues (i.e., Abramovitch et al., 1979; Abramovitch et al., 1980) observed that older siblings at the preschool-age group antagonized their younger siblings more than the reverse and older siblings did not yield to younger siblings in conflict situations. In addition, Dunn and Munn's (1987) observation that older children are more capable of using justifications in disputes than are younger children implies that older siblings could take advantage of younger siblings based on their argument abilities. Phinney (1986) suggested that 5-year-olds cannot assert themselves in conflicts with older siblings because the 5-year-olds felt intimidated by their more knowledgeable and skilled older siblings. The power imbalance created by the developmental differences between the children sets the stage for abuses of power. Although such examples of manipulation are considered to be unethical interpersonal communication for adults, manipulation appears to be considered normal sibling interaction behavior.

Another characteristic of sibling patterns is that conflict between young children consists of aggressive and violent behaviors. Abramovitch and colleagues (i.e., Abramovitch et al., 1979; Abramovitch et al., 1980) observed that children engage in physical aggression, object struggles, insults, and threats with their siblings. Corsaro (1981) noted that what is common conflict-interaction behavior for young children is perceived as cruel or combative by adults. Hay and Ross (1982) found that in response to an antagonist, toddlers used one word commands, such as "mine" or "no," 53% of the time, used forcible contact 17% of the time, and used more positive responses, such as gentle touch or offering of the object, only 23% of the time. Similarly, Abramovitch and colleagues found that responses to conflict initiated by a sibling included crying, whining, relinquishing object, obeying, physical or verbal agonism, and avoidance. Note that none of these response behaviors appear positive or prosocial. In addition, some violent behaviors commonly employed against siblings, such as physical aggression, are taboo behaviors for adults. For example, whereas an older brother can knock his sister's tooth loose as a child, such behavior in adulthood results in assault charges.

A dark pattern that emerges in normal parent–child conflict interactions is that parents' greater sophistication in communication skills allows for strategic and manipulative conflict management. The authors of the parent–child studies reviewed herein did not examine whether parents consciously selected the interaction behaviors used to gain compliance from their children. Undoubtedly, parents vary in how strategically they manage conflicts with their children. However, strategies are easily inferred from studies reviewed. For example, Rocissano et al. (1987) implied that parents manipulate young children into compliance by using synchrony of talk turns. In addition, Lytton (1979) indicated that using positive interaction behaviors in the interact preceding the attempt at verbal control tended to meet with child compliance. Fletcher et al.'s (1996) observations revealed that a strategy of positivity on the part of mothers is a strategy to elicit positivity from an adolescent. Although strategic interaction behaviors are not necessarily dark, when strategies are used to manipulate others, they become open to ethical criticism. Also, if a parent is highly strategic even without a manipulative intent, a child might begin to feel manipulated and perhaps become distrustful of parents or others. Children who are not ever allowed to win arguments with parents develop difficulties learning how to negotiate with others (Eisenberg, 1992) and experience lower self-esteem.

A clearly dark conflict pattern that appears in family relationships, as well as romantic relationships, concerns how relational partners tend to reciprocate negative behaviors. Although those in dysfunctional relationships reciprocate negative affect for longer periods of time, the tendency to reciprocate negative affect occurs in all types of relationships (Dunn, 1983; Fletcher et al., 1996; Gottman, 1979; Schaap, 1984). For instance, Kiecolt-Glaser et al. (1993) found that negative behaviors were highly reciprocated in highly satisfied, newly married couples ($r = .74$).

Several scholars explained that the reciprocation of negativity over the course of time erodes the relationship, largely in terms of how systems self-regulate to prevent decay. For instance, Wilmot (1988) discussed such patterns as spirals of escalation and de-escalation; that is, Wilmot argued that dysfunctional couple communication radically fluctuates about a baseline of behavior, and the interactions become more negative over time at the expense of the partners. Likewise, Rogers, Courtright, and Millar (1980) observed that satisfied couples establish and fluctuate about a "homeostatic set-point" that helps the parties coordinate the rise and fall of conversational intensity (p. 208). Similarly, Gottman (1994) argued that couples must maintain a balance of positive to negative statements, and dysfunctional, unhappy marriages engage in an equal amount of positive and negative conflict behaviors. Yet, happy couples engage in five positive conflict behaviors for each negative behavior. Bochner and Eisenberg (1987), in reviewing the family interaction literature, observed that unhealthy families not only fall into spirals of reciprocated negativity, but they also tend to be paranoid and look for ways to blame each other as well as look for hidden motivations in their partners' utterances. However, we stress that even satisfied partners are not immune from the urge to reciprocate the other person's negative behaviors.

A common conflict pattern that appears to invoke a rather rigid asymmetrical sequence is the demand–withdrawal pattern in romantic involvements. The *demand–withdrawal pattern* refers to how one partner wants to discuss a topic of conflict, but his or her partner reacts with a tendency to avoid the issue. This inclination to withdraw in the face of the partner's confrontation appears uniform.

One group of researchers (Christensen & Heavey, 1990; Heavey, Layne, & Christensen, 1993; Sagrestano, Heavey, & Christensen, 1988) tested alternative explanations for the demand–withdrawal pattern using both self-report and observational data. The *individual difference* view adopts the stereotypes of women as communal and of men as instrumental. Ostensibly due to a communal, relational orientation, women approach men, and men (who are instrumental in orientation) avoid discussions about relational matters. The *structural* explanation concerns the inequity regarding the topic in question. That is, the person who wants the partner's compliance in order to restore a fair exchange of effort is more likely to confront the partner (e.g., regarding help with household tasks or raising children, Christensen & Heavey, 1990). Yet, the partner who does not want to change the current situation is more likely to withdraw, regardless of the person's sex. Because they tend to experience greater benefits in marriage, men might avoid their partner to maintain those benefits (e.g., meals, a clean home, affection; Sagrestano et al., in press).

The results from this program of research are very consistent: The partner who seeks change from the other person is more likely to confront that person, regardless of sex. The change of demand–withdrawal roles between spouses suggests one general tendency—withdrawal in the face of partner demand for change. If Sillars and Wilmot (1994) were correct in their assessment, then a constant replication of the (asymmetrical) demand–withdrawal pattern leads to relational dysfunction. Not only does the relational system remain inequitable, but the perpetuation of the asymmetrical pattern prevents the couple's adaptation to future challenges.

The previous observations indicate the normality and the prevalence of a dark side of interaction in close relationships. One additional (and perhaps most egregious) facet of conflict patterns concerns their sometimes subtle but significant influence on partners. For instance, as Gottman's (1979) and Revenstorf et al.'s (1984) research illustrates, the likelihood of any one behavior leading to the consequent behavior tends to be rather small in magnitude. When one combines that observation with the realization that we are sometimes only discussing about 5% of interaction behavior, it is very probable that couples in the midst of responding to each other are often unaware of the small but significant influence that some conflict patterns have over them as individuals attempting to live happy lives. In addition, as Sillars and Weisberg (1987) noted, conflict behaviors often objectively appear disorderly and without a recognizable structure. For social actors caught in the emotions of the moment, conflict patterns probably fall outside their ability to make much sense of the conflict episode. Accordingly, and to revisit our earlier discussion of Sun Tzu's *The Art of War*, everyday social actors are most often poor generals in the theater of personal conflict.

An additional concluding metaphor further develops how we see the dark side of conflict patterns that emerge in personal realtionships: In a very real sense, conflict patterns—and all communication patterns for that matter—resemble dancing (Frank Millar, personal communication, November 17, 1984). More precisely, knowing how two people dance requires a careful examination of how the dance partners coordinate steps, move closer or farther apart, and repeat themselves in time to the music. Of course, a person can learn how to dance by himself or herself, but that person will never quite know whether the steps are good unless the partner makes similar and complementary moves. Unfortunately, the problem with conflict is that people seldom rehearse for it—the music can be loud and the rhythm frenetic—and those who are really bad at it tend to repeat the same stupid steps over and over.

REFERENCES

Abramovitch, R., Corter, C., & Lando, B. (1979). Sibling interaction in the home. *Child Development, 50,* 997–1003.

Abramovitch, R., Corter, C., & Pepler, D. J. (1980). Observations of mixed-sex sibling dyads. *Child Development, 51,* 1268–1271.

Alberts, J. K. (1988). An analysis of couples' conversational complaints. *Communication Monographs, 55,* 184–197.

Alberts, J. K., & Driscoll, G. (1992). Containment versus escalation: The trajectory of couples' conversational complaints. *Western Journal of Communication, 56,* 394–412.

Bank, S., & Kahn, M. D. (1975). Sisterhood-brotherhood is powerful: Sibling subsystems and family therapy. *Family Process, 14,* 311–337.

Bateson, G. (1935). Culture contact and schismogenesis. *Man, 35,* 178–183.

Bateson, G. (1979). *Mind and nature: A necessary unity.* New York: Dutton.

Billings, A. (1979). Conflict resolution in distressed and nondistressed married couples. *Journal of Consulting and Clinical Psychology, 47,* 368–376.

Birchler, G. R., Weiss, R. L., & Vincent, J. P. (1975). Multimethod analysis of social reinforcement exchange between maritally distressed and nondistressed spouse and stranger dyads. *Journal of Personality and Social Psychology, 31,* 349–360.

Bochner, A. P., & Eisenberg, E. M. (1987). Family process: Systems perspectives. In C. R. Berger & S. H. Chaffee (Eds.), *Handbook of communication science* (pp. 540–563). Newbury Park, CA: Sage.

Burggraf, C. S., & Sillars, A. L. (1987). A critical examination of sex differences in marital communication. *Communication Monographs, 54,* 276–294.

Canary, D. J., Cupach, W. R., & Messman, S. J. (1995). *Relationship conflict: Conflict in parent–child, friendship, and romantic relationships*. Thousand Oaks, CA: Sage.

Cappella, J. N. (1987). Interpersonal communication: Fundamental questions and issues. In C. R. Berger & S. H. Chaffee (Eds.), *Handbook of communication science* (pp. 184–238). Newbury Park, CA: Sage.

Christensen, A., & Heavey, C. L. (1990). Gender and social structure in the demand/withdrawal pattern of marital conflict. *Journal of Personality and Social Psychology, 59*, 73–81.

Circourel, A. V. (1980). Three models of discourse analysis: The role of social structure. *Discourse Processes, 3*, 101–132.

Corsaro, W. A. (1981). Friendship in the nursery school: Social organization in a peer environment. In S. R. Asher & J. M. Gottman (Eds.), *The development of children's friendships* (pp. 207–241). London, England: Cambridge University Press.

Courtright, J. A., Millar, F. E., & Rogers, L. E. (1980). Message control intensity as a predictor of transactional redundancy. In D. Nimmo (Ed.), *Communication yearbook* (pp. 199–216). New Brunswick, NJ: Transaction Books.

Doane, J. A. (1978). Family interaction and communication deviance in disturbed and normal families: A review of research. *Family Process, 17*, 357–376.

Dunn, J. (1983). Sibling relationships in early childhood. *Child Development, 54*, 787–811.

Dunn, J., & McGuire, S. (1992). Sibling and peer relationships in childhood. *Journal of Child Psychology and Psychiatry, 33*, 67–105.

Dunn, J., & Munn, P. (1987). Development of justification in disputes with mother and sibling. *Developmental Psychology, 23*, 791–798.

Eisenberg, A. R. (1992). Conflicts between mothers and their young children. *Merrill-Palmer Quarterly, 38*, 21–43.

Fitzpatrick, M. A. (1988a). *Between husbands and wives: Communication in marriage*. Thousand Oaks, CA: Sage.

Fitzpatrick, M. A. (1988b). Negotiation, problem solving and conflict in various types of marriages. In P. Noller & M. A. Fitzpatrick (Eds.), *Perspectives on marital interaction* (pp. 245–270). Philadelphia: Multilingual Matters.

Fletcher, K. E., Fischer, M., Barkley, R. A., & Smallish, L. (1996). A sequential analysis of the mother–adolescent interactions of ADHD, ADHD/ODD, and normal teenagers during neutral and conflict discussions. *Journal of Abnormal Child Psychology, 24*, 271–297.

Goffman, E. (1981). *Forms of talk*. Philadelphia: University of Pennsylvania Press.

Gottman, J. M. (1979). *Marital interaction: Experimental investigations*. New York: Academic Press.

Gottman, J. M. (1980). Temporal form: Toward a new language for describing relationships. *Journal of Marriage and the Family, 44*, 943–962.

Gottman, J. M. (1982). Emotional responsiveness in marital conversations. *Journal of Communication, 32*, 108–120.

Gottman, J. M. (1983). How children become friends. *Monographs of the Society for Research in Child Development, 48*, (2, Serial No. 201).

Gottman, J. M. (1994). *What predicts divorce? The relationship between marital processes and marital outcomes*. Hillsdale, NJ: Lawrence Erlbaum Associates.

Grimshaw, A. D. (Ed.). (1990). *Conflict talk*. Cambridge, England: Cambridge University Press.

Hay, D. F., & Ross, H. S. (1982). The social nature of early conflict. *Child Development, 53*, 105–113.

Heavey, C. L., Layne, C., & Christensen, A. (1993). Gender and conflict structure in marital interaction: A replication and extension. *Journal of Consulting and Clinical Psychology, 61*, 16–27.

Kiecolt-Glaser, J. K., Malarkey, W. B., Chee, M. A., Newton, T., Cacioppo, J. T., Mao, H. Y., & Glaser, R. (1993). Negative behavior during marital conflict is associated with immunological down-regulation. *Psychosomatic Medicine, 55*, 395–409.

Labov, W., & Fanshel, D. (1977). *Therapeutic discourse: Psychotherapy as conversation*. New York: Academic Press.

Lawson, A., & Ingleby, J. D. (1974). Daily routines of pre-school children: Effects of age, birth order, sex and social class, and developmental correlates. *Psychological Medicine, 4*, 399–415.

Lytton, H. (1979). Disciplinary encounters between young boys and their mothers and fathers: Is there a contingency system? *Developmental Psychology, 15,* 256–268.

Lytton, H., & Zwirner, W. (1975). Compliance and its controlling stimuli observed in a natural setting. *Developmental Psychology, 11,* 769–779.

Margolin, G., & Wampold, B. E. (1981). Sequential analysis of conflict and accord in distressed and nondistressed marital partners. *Journal of Consulting and Clinical Psychology, 49,* 554–567.

Markman, H. J., & Notarius, C. L. (1987). Coding marital and family interaction: Current status. In T. Jacob (Ed.), *Family interaction and psychopathology: Theories, methods, and findings* (pp. 329–390). New York: Plenum.

Mikesell, R. (1996). *The use of humor in couple's conflict management.* Doctoral dissertation, School of Interpersonal Communication, Ohio University, Athens.

Millar, F. E., Rogers, L. E., & Bavelas, J. B. (1984). Identifying patterns of verbal conflict in interpersonal dynamics. *Western Journal of Speech Communication, 48,* 231–246.

Notarius, C., & Markman, H. (1981). Couples interaction scoring system. In E. E. Filsinger & R. A. Lewis (Eds.), *Assessing marriage: New behavioral approaches* (pp. 112–127). Beverly Hills, CA: Sage.

Paikoff, R. L., & Brooks-Gunn, J. (1991). Do parent–child relationships change during puberty? *Psychological Bulletin, 110,* 47–66.

Patterson, G. R., (1975). The aggressive child: Victim and architect of a coercive system. In L. A. Hamerlynck, E. J. Marsh, & L. C. Handy (Eds.), *Behavior modification and families* (pp. 260–301). New York: Brunner/Mazel.

Patterson, G. R. (1979). A performance theory for coercive family interaction. In R. B. Cairns (Ed.), *The analysis of social interactions* (pp. 119–162). Hillsdale, NJ: Lawrence Erlbaum Associates.

Pepler, D. J., Abramovitch, R., & Corter, C. (1981). Sibling interaction in the home: A longitudinal study. *Child Development, 52,* 1344–1347.

Petronio, S. (1994). Privacy binds in family interactions: The case of parental privacy invasion. In W. R. Cupach & B. H. Spitzberg (Eds.), *The dark side of interpersonal communication* (pp. 241–258). Hillsdale, NJ: Lawrence Erlbaum Associates.

Phinney, J. S. (1986). The structure of 5-year-olds' verbal quarrels with peers and siblings. *The Journal of Genetic Psychology, 147,* 47–60.

Poole, M. S., Folger, J. P., & Hewes, D. E. (1987). Analyzing interpersonal interaction. In M. E. Roloff & G. R. Miller.(Eds.), *Interpersonal processes: New directions in communication research* (pp. 220–256). Newbury Park, CA: Sage.

Raush, H. L. (1965). Interaction sequences. *Journal of Personality and Social Psychology, 2,* 487–499.

Raush, H. L., Barry, W. A., Hertel, R. J., & Swain, M. A. (1974). *Communication, conflict, and marriage.* San Francisco: Jossey-Bass.

Revenstorf, D., Hahlweg, K., Schindler, L., & Vogel, B. (1984). Interaction analysis of marital conflict. In K. Hahlweg & N. S. Jacobson (Eds.), *Marital interaction: Analysis and modification* (pp. 159–181). New York: Guilford.

Rocissano, L., Slade, A., & Lynch. (1987). Dyadic synchrony and toddler compliance. *Developmental Psychology, 23,* 698–704.

Rogers, L. E. (1981). Symmetry and complementarity: Evolution and evaluation of an idea. In C. Wilder-Mott & J. H. Weakland (Eds.), *Rigor and imagination: Essays from the legacy of Gregory Bateson* (pp. 231–251). New York: Praeger.

Rogers, L. E., Courtright, J. A., & Millar, F. E. (1980). Message control intensity: Rationale and preliminary findings. *Communication Monographs, 47,* 201–219.

Sagestrano, L. M., Heavey, C. L., & Christensen, A. (1998). Theoretical approaches to understanding sex differences and similarities in conflict behavior. In D. J. Canary & K. Dindia (Eds.), *Sex differences and similarities in communication.* Mahwah, NJ: Lawrence Erlbaum Associates.

Schaap, C. (1984). A comparison of the interaction of distressed and nondistressed married couples in a laboratory situation: Literature survey, methodological issues, and an empirical investigation. In K. Hahlweg & N. S. Jacobson (Eds.), *Marital interaction: Analysis and modification* (pp. 133–158). New York: Guilford.

Selman, R. L. (1980). *The growth of interpersonal understanding: Developmental and clinical analyses*. New York: Academic Press.

Shantz, C. U., & Hobart, C. J. (1989). Social conflict and development: Peers and siblings. In T. J. Berndt & G. W. Ladd (Eds.), *Peer relationships in child development* (pp. 71–94). New York: Wiley.

Sillars, A. L. (1980a). The sequential and distributional structure of conflict interactions as a function of attributions concerning the locus of responsibility and stability of conflicts. In D. Nimmo (Ed.), *Communication Yearbook 4* (pp. 217–235). New Brunswick, NJ: Transaction.

Sillars, A. L. (1980b). The sequential and distributional structure of conflict interactions as a function of attributions concerning the locus of responsibility and stability of conflicts. In D. Nimmo (Ed.), *Communication Yearbook 4* (pp. 217–235. New Brunswick, NJ: Transaction Books.

Sillars, A. L., & Weisberg, J. (1987). Conflict as a social skill. In M. E. Roloff & G. R. Miller (Eds.), *Interpersonal processes: New directions in communication research* (pp. 140–171). Newbury Park, CA: Sage.

Sillars, A. L., & Wilmot, W. W. (1994). Communication strategies in conflict and mediation. In J. A. Daly & J. M. Wiemann (Eds.), *Strategic interpersonal communication* (pp. 163–190). Hillsdale, NJ: Lawrence Erlbaum Associates.

Stafford, L., & Dainton, M. (1994). The dark side of "normal" family interaction. In W. R. Cupach & B. H. Spitzberg (Eds.), *The dark side of interpersonal communication* (pp. 259–280). Hillsdale, NJ: Lawrence Erlbaum Associates.

Street, R. L., & Cappella, J. N. (Eds.). (1995). *Sequence and pattern in communicative behavior*. London, UK: Edward Arnold.

Sun Tzu, (1991). *The art of war* (T. Cleary, Trans.). Boston: Shambhala.

Ting-Toomey, S. (1983). An analysis of verbal communication patterns in high and low marital adjustment groups. *Human Communication Research, 9*, 306–319.

Vuchinich, S. (1984). Sequencing and social structure in family conflict. *Social Psychology Quarterly, 47*, 217–234.

Vuchinich, S. (1987). Starting and stopping spontaneous family conflicts. *Journal of Marriage and the Family, 49*, 591–601.

Vuchinich, S., Emery, R. E., & Cassidy, J. (1988). Family members as third parties in dyadic family conflict: Strategies, alliances, and outcomes. *Child Development, 59*, 1293–1302.

Watt, J. H., & Van Lear (Eds.) (1996). *Dynamic patterns in communication processes*. Thousand Oaks, CA: Sage.

Wiehe, V. R. (1990). *Sibling abuse: Hidden physical, emotional, and sexual trauma*. New York: Lexington.

Wilmot, W. W. (1988). *Dyadic communication* (2nd ed.). New York: Random House.

Witteman, H., & Fitzpatrick, M. A. (1986). Compliance-gaining in marital interaction: Power bases, processes, and outcomes. *Communication Monographs, 53*, 130–143.

6

Codependence: The Paradoxical Nature of the Functional-Afflicted Relationship

Beth A. Le Poire
Jennifer S. Hallett
Howard Giles
University of California, Santa Barbara

Consider a typical couple including an alcoholic or drug-addicted member. Like many nonaddicted partners we interviewed, Jill did many supportive, inadvertently reinforcing, things surrounding Jack's drinking when they were first living together and even after they got married. Given that she did not suspect Jack had a problem with alcohol, it is not surprising that she often drank with him, sacrificed things that she needed so that he could have the extra money he asked for, and picked him up after he had been drinking heavily.

After a time, Jill began to notice that things were not quite as they seemed and she began to allude to others that she thought Jack's drinking was problematic. Yet, she still refused to believe that her husband was an alcoholic—for all of the stigmatizing reasons that any of us would not want to admit that our partner was an alcoholic. Eventually, something critical happened that forced Jill to accept Jack's alcoholism. Often the Jacks we encounter have horrific car accidents, become violent or verbally abusive toward their Jills or their children, get put in jail for one reason or another, or receive a drunk driving citation.

After the critical incident, Jill's denial crumbles and she consistently punishes Jack's drinking behavior by verbally confronting him, withdrawing her affection, refusing to sleep with or share the same room with Jack, and threatening to leave or asking him to move out. This consistency is maintained for a while because Jill can no longer endure his behavior. Then after a while, she begins to realize that there is absolutely nothing she can do to affect Jack's drinking behavior and begins to mix reinforcing and punishing behaviors associated with Jack's drinking. Sometimes she keeps the children out of his way and takes over household chores and responsibilities that were once his. At the same time, she withdraws affection, calls an advice bureau about getting a divorce, and actually becomes physically abusive with him as well. This mix of reinforcing, punishing, then intermittent reinforcing and punishing behavior is at the crux of Inconsistent Nurturing as Control (INC) theory. Although Jill is doing the best that she can (in an extremely difficult situation) to try to get Jack to stop ruining both their lives, by applying learning theory principles, it becomes evident that she is inadvertently strengthening the very behavior that she is attempting to extinguish through intermittent reinforcement and intermittent punishment.

Although current statistics indicate that 80% of the patients presenting themselves for drug abuse treatment are male, codependents may also be male (A. Brumbaugh, personal communication, November 3, 1996). Although our own research shows that it is difficult to find couples in which the female is addicted and the male is not, consider the following couple—heroin-addicted Jane and her alcoholic partner Dick—that we also interviewed. The only difference with (heroin-addicted relations) is that the stakes are higher and the intermittent nature of the reinforcement and punishment is more apparent. Jane has been a hardcore heroin addict since she was 15 years old. She often spent the rent money that Dick gave her on the drug. Although he gave her a hard time about it, Dick replaced the rent money for several months in a row. Dick also brought Jane fixes of heroin at work so she could function and bring home a paycheck. He also encouraged Jane to use heroin at various times so she would have sex with him or so he could avoid being with her when she became sick and mean from withdrawal. This mix of reinforcement and punishment is not uncommon in the codependent-afflicted relationship; this is the point of exploration herein.

Although the dark side of relationships is socially ubiquitous, as evident in this volume (e.g, fatal attractions, jealousy, betrayal, and sexual coercion), this chapter discusses the nature of *codependency*—those relationships that include stigmatized individuals (e.g., alcoholics, drug addicts or sex addicts, gamblers, mentally ill individuals) who usually extend their stigma to their significant others. The partners are known to be strong and caring individuals who nurture their partners through difficult periods, while simultaneously attempting to control, or reduce, their partners' tendency to engage in some undesirable behavior or another. These partners are often referred to as *codependents*, and our objective here is to explore the dynamics of the relationship (as we view codependency as a relational phenomenon) and the communication between codependents and their partners.

In understanding the dark side of this relationship, we invoke INC theory to argue that contrary to the codependent's goals, it is likely that their attempts to control the undesirable behavior of the afflicted (e.g., drug addict) may have opposite effects than they intend and could actually exacerbate the very behavior they are trying to eradicate (Le Poire, 1992, 1995). INC theory contends that the power structure in distressed relationships is paradoxical and limits the strategies that codependents can use in their attempts to control their partners' undesirable behaviors.

In this vein, the chapter begins with a brief discussion of the nature of codependency in terms of the definitions, characteristics, and psychological disorders associated with codependence. Most of this work is clinical in nature, but it helps inform the nature of the relationship and aid in exploration of the interactional implications of the dynamics of the codependent-afflicted relationship. Given current problems with the conceptualizations of codependency, INC theory offers useful definitions to study codependents as functional individuals, whereas their partners are differentiated as afflicted individuals. Beside these definitions, this theory also proffers predictions regarding the potential ineffectiveness of the functional's controlling attempts of the afflicted's behavior. Finally, initial research on the theory with alcoholics and drug addicts is reviewed, and implications for future research and intervention are explored.

CONCEPTUALIZING CODEPENDENCY

Although the term *codependency* is widely used in both professional and popular press, its precise meaning has not been firmly established. Notwithstanding, there is even greater variability in the characteristics said to describe those who are codependent (albeit with surprising agreement between authors). To put these characteristics in high relief, Table 6.1 presents seven categories of characteristics of codependents: socialization–development, psychological–relational, emotional, cognitive, com-

TABLE 6.1

Some Characteristics of Codependency

Category	Characteristic	Recent Citation
Socialization/ Development	Dysfunctional family, unaccepting family	Carson & Baker, 1994; Cowan & Warren, 1994
	Felt invisible as a child	Mellody, Miller, & Miller, 1989
Psychological/ Relational	Difficulty in acknowledging impact of behavior on other	Mellody, Miller, & Miller, 1989
	Fear of abandonment	Carson & Baker, 1994
	Self-esteem comes from controlling other	Cowan & Warren, 1994; Cermak, 1986
	Become dependent on other	Beattie, 1987
Emotional	Have difficulty feeling appropriate emotions	Becker, 1989
	Anxiety or nervousness	Hawks, Bahr, & Wang, 1994
	Low self-esteem, self-condemning	Cowan & Warren, 1994
Cognitive	"All or nothing" mentality	Mellody, Miller, & Miller, 1994
	Inflexibility or rigidity	Cowan & Warren, 1994
	Obsessive or compulsive	Peterson & Seligson, 1992; Phillips, 1988
Communicative	Protects other through lying, denying, or rationalizing	Hawks, Bahr, & Wang, 1994; Koffinke, 1991
	Become resentful when their needs are not met by other	Phillips, 1988
	Unable to ask for what they want and need from other	Peterson & Seligson, 1992
Behavioral	Focus on other, deny own needs	Carson & Baker, 1994
	Make themselves "indispensable" to other	Phillips, 1988; Schaef, 1986
Consequences upon "failure"	Feelings of inadequacy, incompetency, guilt, or shame	Carson & Baker, 1994
	Become critical of, or blame other	Robinson, 1990

municative, behavioral, and consequences of so-called "failure." This table is a summary and is not exhaustive, but it is a fair representation of those qualities most commonly associated with codependent individuals. It also serves to illustrate that most of the characteristics attributed to codependents are negative and serves to fuel the criticism that current conceptualizations of codependency include so many common characteristics that they have become virtually fruitless with regard to treatment or clear diagnosis.

In an attempt to obviate the current confusion surrounding definitions of codependency in the literature, the following section distinguishes an operationalism of codependency useful to the INC theory. A brief review of this literature points out that definitions of *codependency* focus on control (e.g., Beattie, 1987; Cermak, 1984; Schaef, 1986), nurturing (e.g., Friel & Friel, 1987; Gordon & Barrett, 1993; Kasl, 1989), and maintenance of relationships with chemically dependent individuals (e.g., Phillips, 1988; Wegscheider-Cruse, 1985; Whitfield, 1987), or individuals who engage in undesirable behavior, including alcoholism or drug dependence (e.g., Becker, 1989; Cermak, 1986; DuPont & McGovern, 1991).

Although views of codependency vary, a commonly accepted definition that points to the central nature of control in this relationship is "one who has let another person's behavior affect him or her, and who is obsessed with controlling that person's behavior" (Beattie, 1987, p. 31; see also Schaef, 1992). Whereas such a definition allows that this reaction to the out-of-control behavior of one's partner is normal, still others argue that codependents unconsciously perpetuate the unhealthy behavior of family members. Dupont and McGovern (1991) went so far as to argue that codependent individuals "share the responsibility for the unhealthy behavior, primarily by focusing their lives on the sick or the bad behavior and by making their own self-esteem and well-being contingent on the behavior of the unhealthy family member" (p. 316).

Such a critical focus led to the argument that codependency is a psychological disorder capable of a Diagnostic and Statistical Manual of Mental Disorders (DSM) diagnosis (e.g., Nathans, 1981). Cermak (1986) defined *codependence* as "a recognizable pattern of personality traits, predictably found within most members of chemically dependent families, which are capable of creating sufficient dysfunction to warrant diagnosis of Mixed Personality Disorder in DSM III" (p. 1). He argued that the diagnosis of Codependent Personality Disorder can be made through the following five diagnostic criteria:

1. Investment of self-esteem in the ability to control oneself and others in adverse situations.
2. Assumption of responsibility for meeting others' needs to the exclusion of one's own.
3. Anxiety and boundary distortions around intimacy and separation.
4. Enmeshment in relationships with personality disordered, chemically dependent, other codependent, and/or impulse-disordered individuals.
5. Three or more of the following: excessive denial, constricted emotions, depression, hypervigilance, compulsions, anxiety, substance abuse, sexual or physical abuse victim, stress-related illness, or maintenance of a primary relationship with an active substance abuser for two or more years.

Although certainly useful in terms of operationalizing codependence in terms of nurturing, control, and relationship maintenance, diagnosing codependence as a psychiatric disorder is consistent with theorizing that wives unconsciously encourage substance-dependent behavior due to their own pathological problems of martyrdom or desire for domination over their husbands (e.g., Paige, La Pointe, & Krueger, 1971; Rae & Drewery, 1972; Whalen, 1953). Whereas this perspective is often discounted as overly blaming of the spouse, and particularly female spouses (e.g., Anderson, 1994; Haaken, 1990), the more current theorizing of family systems is also consonant with this line of reasoning (Kaufman, 1985a; Kaufman & Kaufmann, 1979; Steinglass, 1976). Ewing and Fox (1968) argued that *homeostasis*—the principle of balance within the system—is used in the alcoholic family to resist change, and alterations by one spouse (e.g., reduction in drinking behavior) prompts the other to attempt to maintain the status quo. In other words, these theorists argue that spouses of newly sober alcoholics may be uncomfortable with losing their role behavior and may unconsciously encourage their spouses' relapse. Fundamentally, the systems approach discounts the disease model of alcoholism and proffers instead that the sickness of the family (vs. the individual) may be causing and/or maintaining the drinking.

Contrary to this thinking, much work that focused on wives of alcoholics indicated that they cannot be consistently characterized in terms of mental health disorders. Using Cermak's (1986) diagnostic criteria, Martin and Piazza (1995) found that codependency is not a separate personality disorder in women, but is indicative of women presenting combined personality disorders or situationally adaptive response mechanisms. Similarly, Chiauzzi and Liljegren (1993) noted the lack of empirical support for the disease conceptualization of codependency.

Ballard (1959) found that wives of alcoholics did not score higher on maladjustment than a comparable control group. Kogan, Jackson, and Fordyce (1963) found that although many wives of alcoholics exhibited some personality dysfunction, just as many did not. This equal split is consistent with the more recent findings of Walfish, Stenmark, Shealy, and Krone (1992) who studied the Minnesota Multiphasic Personality Inventory (MMPI) of 73 women presenting themselves as codependents (via self-identification). Additionally, O'Brien and Gaborit (1992) found that codependent people were no more depressed than noncodependent people. Furthermore, Corder, Hendricks, and Corder's (1964) results caused them to question the widely accepted caricature of wives of alcoholics as neurotic, disturbed, and poorly integrated. Edwards, Harvey, and Whitehead (1973) argued that any dysfunction a wife of an alcoholic may experience is situationally dependent on their spouses' drinking. In other words, mental health dysfunction of wives is higher when their spouse drinks and lower when their spouse is abstinent.

Similar to the previously reviewed literature, INC theory (Le Poire, 1992, 1995) views codependent partners in terms of their interactive communication environment, which is difficult and out-of-control. With more sympathy for the codependent partner, it is very possible that they are doing the best they can to try to alleviate the pressures of addiction or the other's out-of-control behavior. At the same time, it is also possible that what they are doing is not only ineffective, but may also inadvertently contribute further to the problem.

This contribution to the problem is likely the result of the two competing goals of the typical codependent—nurturing and controlling. In INC theory, this partner is referred to as the *functional partner*. Although some might argue that this partner is also dysfunctional in some ways, the term was utilized to recognize that this partner has no unique problem (other than being in a relationship with an out-of-control partner) that interferes with his or her day-to-day functioning. The partner identified as having a problem (e.g., drinker, smoker, overeater, under eater, gambler, depressed person) is referred to as the *afflicted partner*, as he or she is afflicted with some form of behavioral compulsion. Finally, the compulsive behavior of the afflicted partner is referred to as *undesirable behavior* (e.g., drinking, smoking, overeating, anorexia, gambling addiction, violence, depressive behavior), as this behavior is typically the focus of extinguishing attempts. This delineation allows us to discuss these individuals and behaviors in general terms that allows the theory to generalize across several types of caregiver–caregivee relationships.

INCONSISTENT NURTURING AS CONTROL AND OTHER RELEVANT THEORIES

In line with the arguments of Jacob and Leonard (1988), Jacobson (Jacobson, Holtzworth-Munroe, & Schmaling, 1989), and Kaufman (1984, 1985b; Kaufman & Kaufmann, 1979), Stanton (1986), INC theory stresses that family involvement is crucial for all types of substance-dependence intervention. In comparison to studies of the characteristics of the wife of the alcoholic (e.g., Bailey, 1961), very little research made attempts to examine directly the communication patterns that exist in this marital relationship (e.g., Jacob & Leonard, 1988). The unique focus of INC theory, then, is its attempts to examine the communication patterns in relationships with substance-dependent or otherwise afflicted individuals, with an emphasis on the dynamics of the relationship rather than focusing on the identified-patient or the pathological wife.

Le Poire (1992, 1995) argued that functional partners act as naive learning theorists (Skinner, 1953), using both reinforcements (nurturance) and punishments (control attempts) to attempt to diminish the undesirable behavior of afflicted partners. Specifically, learning theorists posit that behavioral tendencies are strengthened by the consequences that follow them (i.e., reinforcers; Skinner, 1974). Additionally, reinforcers are positive (pleasant and rewarding) or negative (removal of some unpleasant or aversive outcome) and are continuous (with reinforcement following each behavior), or intermittent (with some behaviors reinforced, whereas other like behaviors are not). Intermittent reinforcement results in greater recurrence of behavior than does continuous reinforcement (e.g., Burgoon, Burgoon, Miller, & Sunnafrank, 1981). Punishment, on the other hand, involves presenting an aversive stimulus in an effort to extinguish undesirable behavior.

Le Poire (1992) argued that if the functional partner nurtures the afflicted partner when he or she is exhibiting undesirable behavior, this caretaking behavior ultimately becomes pleasant (i.e., comforting, understanding, etc.) to the afflicted and thus (at least partially), reinforces the behavior. Eventually, caregivers begin to resent the demands placed on them by the afflicted (Asher, 1992; Steiner, 1974; Wiseman, 1991), and they may stop nurturing (and inadvertently reinforcing) undesirable behavior. This inconsistent nurturing (nurturing, then lack of nurturing, and often punishment) behavior is at the heart of INC theory. The inconsistency of this behavior approximates intermittent reinforcement and ultimately strengthens the undesirable behavior of the afflicted person. What is clear is that this lack of nurturing behavior is most likely an attempt to extinguish the afflicted behavior. In learning theory terms, inconsistent nurturing is an attempt to punish the afflicted or remove the undesirable behavior from the partner's repertoire. Unfortunately, the intermittent nature of punishing behavior actually increases the likelihood of the undesirable behavior. Specifically, in studies of battered women, Long and McNamara (1989) found that punishment serves as a discriminative stimulus for immediate or eventual reinforcement; speeds up responding and prolongs extinction; and enhances responsiveness by increasing the motivation for obtaining positive reinforcement. Thus, the inconsistent nurturing behavior of the functional partner actually strengthens the undesirable behavior in two independent yet related ways. First, it promotes undesirable behavior through intermittent reinforcement (nurturing followed by lack of nurturing). Second, it increases the likelihood for undesirable behavior through intermittent punishment (lack of nurturing, followed by nurturing, followed by lack of nurturing, etc.). Given these arguments, it is possible to contend that most functional partners are inconsistent in their use of reinforcement and punishment over the long term in a relationship and during the micromanagement of interactions between partners.

Another useful perspective undergirding INC theory's understanding of the functional person's use of nonverbal approach and avoidance is provided through the frame of *social exchange theory*. Briefly, social exchange theory seeks to explain the development, maintenance, and decay of social relationships by focusing on the balance of rewards and costs (e.g., Blau, 1964; Brinberg & Castell, 1982; Thibaut & Kelley, 1959). In terms of power, the partner controlling the most rewards, which builds the partner's power base, is assumed to be the powerful one and the other is indebted to him or her. In terms of the functional–afflicted relationship, the functional partner typically maintains his or her power base through caretaking behavior (Beattie, 1987). Thus, behaviors associated with caretaking, namely, immediacy and altercentrism, are of focus for consideration of the functional person's power base.

In consonance with Thibaut and Kelley's (1959) discussion of comparison level of alternative relationships, Blau (1964) discussed conditions that predict social independence and less subjection to another's power. Most pertinent to the codependent relationship is that the more alternative sources of supply persons have, the more likely they are to be socially independent. As previously noted, family units with drug or alcohol abusers are socially isolated (Beattie, 1987, 1989; Gorski & Miller, 1988; Whitfield, 1987), thus reducing the opportunity for alternate sources of relational rewards. Additionally, drug or alcohol abusers, and their respective spouses, typically have low self-esteem (e.g., Carson & Baker, 1994; Cowan & Warren, 1994; Shulman, 1988), thus devaluing their resources and underestimating their potential reward level in alternative relationships and in the present relationship. This has two implications. First, it is unlikely that either partner perceives that he or she has the ability to leave the relationship, thereby increasing dependence. Second, it is probable that each perceives the partner's resources as much more rewarding than anything he or she has to offer. Thus, it is very likely that both partners are highly dependent on the relationship and experience subjective powerlessness in the situation. This powerlessness, in turn, leads to a greater desire to exercise control.

Because of the predicted greater reliance on nonverbal communication to control, functional–afflicted relationships cycle more dramatically between approach and avoidance behaviors, as the functional partner tends to use both nonverbal approach behaviors (i.e., altercentrism or immediacy) and avoidance behaviors (i.e., withdrawal) in order to gain control in the relationship. Additionally, there is an overreliance on these latter avoidant punishing mechanisms because the codependent partner is not allowed to reference past giving behavior during times of crisis, as it calls the unwritten rule system into jeopardy. Thus, whereas more traditional relationships are able to call forward personal commitment, or obligation due from past rewarding behavior, the functional partner is most likely restricted to the more passive removal of previous rewarding behavior in an attempt to indirectly reference past rewarding behavior.

One of the primary resources in the functional person's power base is the ability to be immediate (i.e., communicatively indicating psychological closeness) and altercentered (i.e., other-focused and self-sacrificing) toward the afflicted person during times of crisis (e.g., providing messages of affection and services). The primary assumption underlying this argument is that the afflicted person has a high need for nurturing and the functional person possesses the ability to fulfill this need by being aware of the afflicted person's need and by focusing on that individual.

Immediacy and its expression were studied by many researchers. *Immediacy* is defined by Mehrabian (1969) as "the extent to which communication behaviors enhance closeness to or nonverbal interaction with another" (p. 203) and includes such behaviors as interpersonal distance, gaze, posturing, touch, body and facial orientation, body lean, and vocalic cues (Coker & Burgoon, 1987). These nonverbal behaviors, although typically seen as serving the instrumental function of expressing immediacy and affection, ultimately act as rewards in the functional–afflicted relationship and reinforce subsequent controlling behavior of the functional partner.

Burgoon and Hale (1984, 1987) argued for, and revealed, several interrelated themes in the expression of immediacy, such that immediacy and/or intimacy consists of affection, similarity or depth, receptivity, and trust. Thus, in the functional–afflicted relationship, behaviors communicating these messages are considered to be rewarding and part of the functional person's power base, whereas withholding these behaviors is considered punishing and has the potential to act as control strategies. More specifically, control strategies consist of messages of lack of affection, lack of similarity (supported by Burgoon & Hale's measure of dominance), and lack of receptivity.

In an attempt to study nonverbal behaviors associated with these relational themes, Burgoon, Buller, Hale, and deTurk (1984) found that greater intimacy and trust were conveyed by increased eye contact, close proximity, forward body lean, and smiling. Detachment, conversely, was associated with decreased eye contact, distal position, backward body lean, and absence of smiling and touch. According to the argument that behaviors associated with immediacy operate from the functional partner's power base, these latter behaviors are considered to be punishing and should operate as (or facilitate) control mechanisms in the functional–afflicted relationship.

Additionally, Andersen, Andersen, and Jensen (1979) provided a comprehensive synthesis of studies examining behaviors associated with immediacy. These include: reduced proxemic distance, increased touch, increased eye contact or gazing, positive facial expressions (smiling), positive head nods, increased gesturing, bodily relaxation, increased time with the interactant, direct head and body orientation, and vocal expressiveness. Again, given the argument that these behaviors should be rewarding to the afflicted partner, the opposites of these behaviors should be considered to be punishing and function as control mechanisms in the functional–afflicted relationship.

Coker and Burgoon (1987) argued that the broader construct of involvement (the degree to which participants are cognitively and behaviorally engaged in a topic) consists of immediacy, expressiveness, interaction management, altercentrism, and social anxiety. Narrowing our focus to remain consistent with the functional–afflicted relationship, attention is given to immediacy and altercentrism expression. Although behaviors associated with immediacy include those previously mentioned by Andersen et al. (1979), they also distinguish behaviors associated with altercentrism. Behaviors associated with altercentrism include: kinesic and proxemic attentiveness (i.e., involved, interested, attentive, focused, and alert behaviors), and vocal warmth and interest (i.e., warm, interested, involved, pleasant, friendly, and appealing behaviors). Keeping in line with the argument that lack of altercentrism is punishing to the functional–afflicted relationship, and thus act as control mechanisms, lack of altercentrism is communicated through (a) lack of kinesic and proxemic attentiveness (i.e., uninvolved, uninterested, inattentive, unfocused, and unalert behaviors), and lack of vocal warmth and interest (i.e., cool, uninterested, uninvolved, unpleasant, unfriendly, and unappealing behaviors).

Other types of communication behavior that function to communicate messages of immediacy and altercentrism, and ultimately affect messages of relational control, include synchrony (e.g., Als, Tronick, & Brazelton, 1979; Bernieri, Reznick, & Rosenthal, 1988; Brazelton, Tronick, Adamson, Als, & Wise, 1975), reciprocity or compensation (e.g., Andersen, 1984; Burgoon & Hale, 1988; Cappella & Greene, 1982; Patterson, 1983, Street & Cappella, 1985), and communication accommodation (e.g., Giles, Mulac, Bradac, & Johnson, 1987). Communication accommodation, for example, includes both convergence and divergence of speech patterns. *Convergence*, or movement toward similarity in speech behavior, expresses a speaker's desire for social integration, seeking or showing approval, identification, or communicative effectiveness with another. *Divergence*, conversely, is movement toward dissimilarity in speech behavior and is deliberately used to maintain a definite social distance between interactants. Because convergence is expressive of similarity or immediacy, it should be rewarding to dependent partners, whereas maintenance (i.e., nonaccommodation) or divergence should be punishing and should act as, or emphasize control strategies in the functional–afflicted relationship. Specific behaviors on which individuals were found to converge or diverge include accent, language choice, speech rate, response latency, turn duration, and content (for review, see Giles, Coupland, & Coupland, 1991). Thus, convergence on these behaviors should be a part of the functional partner's power base, whereas divergence should be punishing and should potentially act as control strategies in functional–afflicted relationships.

The theory also invokes three other strategies of accommodation that are distinct from interpersonal matching, of which two are particularly relevant here (see Giles, Coupland, & Coupland, 1991). The first is so-called, "interpretability strategies," where individuals attune (or not) to their partners' communicative competence. For instance, individuals accommodate others who are under the influence—or reviving from being in that state—by modifying the complexity of their speech (e.g., decreasing the diversity of the vocabulary, simplifying syntax, or slowing down rate). Of course, such modifications might be attributed to be overaccommodating by the afflicted, who is more alert than anticipated. Of course, such attuning is not forthcoming from the functional partner and/or is perceived by the recipient to be underaccommodating. Another relevant attuning strategy is *discourse management*, whereby the functional partner facilitates the afflicted's problematic sequences and generally works to redress positive or negative face threats to a recipient. Such strategies are paralleled (or not, of course) by what we might call here "affective accommodation," which takes into account the emotional state of the afflicted at the time—or in recent times—by empathic words, verbalized support, and comforting nonverbals (Williams, Giles, Coupland, Dalby, & Manasse, 1990).

In sum, afflicted partners should find behaviors associated with immediacy and altercentrism to be rewarding. These behaviors, in turn, help to develop or maintain the functional partner's power base. Because functional partners are restricted from calling on the obligation that these behaviors have incurred, they must rely on more subtle methods of control.

Thus, removal of the power bases actually reference the past rewarding behavior and act to induce afflicted partners to action.

CORE PARADOXES OF CODEPENDENCY
(AS CONCEPTUALIZED BY INC)

In order to most fully explore the unique dynamics of the functional–afflicted relationship, it is important to consider the paradoxes that exist in that relationship. A *paradox* is "a contradiction that follows correct deduction from consistent premises" (Watzlawick, Beavin, & Jackson, 1967, p. 188; see also Weeks & L'Abate, 1982; Wilder & Collins, 1994). Pragmatic paradoxes (as separate from logicomathematical and semantic paradoxes) are interactional in nature and are of most interest because of their behavioral implications. An example of a pragmatic paradox evidenced in schizophrenic families is the maxim "you can only help me by not being what you are" (Palazzoli, Boscolo, Cecchin, & Prata, 1978, p. 157). The paradox exists in its impossibility of execution. This paradox has direct implications for families that include functional and afflicted members.

The first paradox is the most crucial to the propositional delineation of INC theory (Le Poire, 1995). The first assumption is that functional partners are dependent on, and desire maintenance of, relationships with afflicteds (e.g., Cermak, 1986; Friel & Friel, 1987; Kasl, 1989; Phillips, 1988; Wegscheider-Cruse, 1985). Because a majority of functional partners are female, this assumption is consistent with theorizing that battered wives stay with their husbands because of the value of being a good wife and mother, the secondary status of women in our society, and the economic conditions that encourage dependency of women on men (Ferraro & Johnson, 1983). In seeming contradiction, the second assumption is that functional partners are obsessed with controlling the afflicteds' behavior and attempt to extinguish the undesirable behavior of the afflicted person (e.g., Beattie, 1987; Cermak, 1986; Schaef, 1986). For example, previous research showed that wives of alcoholics often attempt to control substance availability, hide car keys, and withhold sexual activity (James & Goldman, 1971; Orford et al., 1975). Notwithstanding these control attempts (which may not be perceived positively by the afflicted individual for much of the time), other theorists argue that one of the reasons the afflicted person maintains the relationship with the functional partner is because the functional is especially rewarding for him or her during times of crises.

Given these assumptions, it is possible to conclude that functionals actually destroy the relationship if they are successful at extinguishing the undesirable behavior. Ironically, functional partners ultimately need the existence of the undesirable behavior they are trying to extinguish in order to maintain the relationship. This paradox is central to INC theory, especially with regard to the use of nurturing and controlling behavior in attempts to control. Even though the functional partner fervently desires amelioration of disruptive behavior, he or she may ultimately be driven by the fear that stopping the undesirable behavior lessens the afflicted's dependency on him or her (although it might be argued that length of valued relationship lessens this fear). Thus, functional partners ultimately have competing intentions: They want to diminish the out-of-control behavior of the afflicted that is disrupting their lives, and they are afraid that being successful at extinguishing the undesirable behavior might actually destroy the relationship, which gives them their sense of identity and well-being (Kasl, 1989). These competing intentions serve as an explanatory function for the realization that the control attempts made by functional partners are often not that effective in diminishing undesired behavior.

Another paradox in the functional–afflicted relationship is illustrated by inferring both the premises and the conclusion from Beattie's (1987) definition. The first premise is that functionals believe they are more in control in the relationship than afflicteds. The second premise is consistent with the first in that afflicteds are out of control in some aspect of their lives. However, using alternative punctuation of the events sure to exist in this relationship, it is possible to conclude that the afflicteds are ultimately in control of the relationship because it is their behavior that precedes and causes the controlling behavior of the functional partner. This conclusion directly contradicts the first premise by negating the functional partners' ability to be in control, as they are responding to the afflicteds rather than actively taking control.

The final paradox that Le Poire (1992) laid out also has implications for dominance and control in the functional–afflicted relationship. Consistent with the earlier paradox, it was argued that two of the primary characteristics of the codependent partner are caretaking and controlling (Beattie, 1987; Carson & Baker, 1994; Peterson & Seligson, 1992). This complies with the argument that functionals subordinate their needs to those of the afflicteds during times of crises (e.g., rather than getting groceries, they give their partners money). Another argument is that this self-sacrificing behavior earns credit in future bargaining situations with the afflicted partner. Following this thinking, if afflicteds alter their undesirable behavior, it can be concluded that this is in order to return the obligation incurred by the self-sacrificing behavior of the functional partner (cf., norm of reciprocity, Gouldner, 1960). This conclusion contradicts the first premise in that the functionals' "one down" behavior actually placed them "one up" in terms of control. Thus, once again, it becomes unclear who is actually in control in the functional–afflicted relationship. The paradoxical nature of this relationship serves as an explanation for restricted forms of control attempts in the functional–afflicted relationship.

Le Poire (1992) argued that the most relevant outcome of interactional paradoxes for communication researchers is that individuals are unable to metacommunicate, or talk openly, about the contradiction or paradox (whether or not they know of its existence). Watzlawick et al. (1967) asserted that the existence of paradoxes in interactions affects both behavior and sanity—by challenging a belief in consistency. This is based, in part, on work by Bateson, Jackson, Haley, and Weakland (1956), who argued that persons caught in paradoxical injunctions, or double binds, develop schizophrenic symptoms. They claimed that one of the outcomes of the paradox is that individuals are involved in an intense relationship and in that relationship, they are unable to metacommunicate concerning the contradiction or paradox. This helps to explain why functional partners are often enmeshed in relationships with afflicted partners, as proposed by Cermak (1986). The most important implication for individuals in codependent relationships is that they are unable to discuss openly the nature of control within their relationship because this is where the paradoxes exist.

Codependent relationships, especially those that include excessive alcohol or drug use, often encourage social isolation of the couple or family unit (e.g., Beattie, 1987, 1989; Gorski & Miller, 1988; Jacob & Seilhamer, 1982; Koffinke, 1991; Moos & Moos, 1984), which fosters the development of solidarity. This solidarity, in combination with restricted metacommunication due to paradoxical relations, induces reliance on restricted linguistic codes (Steinglass, 1982a) that should be apparent during any discussion in which control is at stake. Thus, as alluded to earlier, it would be possible for researchers to examine the contention that relational partners in substance-dependent relationships rely most heavily on nonverbal strategies of influence over the more direct verbal strategies.

Family members in codependent relationships adapt to their family system by protecting and enabling the dysfunctional family secret (e.g., addiction, mental illness, etc.) through the maintenance of certain unwritten, unspoken rules (Greenleaf, 1988; Mason, 1988; Shulman, 1988). These unwritten, restrictive rules include inappropriateness of discussion of problems, lack of open emotional expression, encouragement of indirect communication, lack of selfishness, and abstinence from "rocking the boat" (Subby & Friel, 1988); they should be especially apparent during expressions of control due to the paradoxical nature of the power structure in the codependent relationship. In other words, codependent or functional partners are less free to reference verbally their past rewarding (e.g., enabling or immediate) behavior as an inducement for the dependent partners' compliance. It is highly unlikely, for instance, for the functional partner to say, "After all I've done for you when you were puking your guts out on the floor," because it violates the unspoken rule system and directly addresses the nature of the undesirable behavior. In turn, greater reliance on restricted linguistic codes should foster an even greater reliance on nonverbal strategies of control, as functional partners rely on strategies that do not make direct reference to the undesirable behavior. However, it is quite possible that past giving or enabling behavior lends reinforcement to these nonverbal strategies of influence.

STUDIES IN SUPPORT OF INCONSISTENT NURTURING AS CONTROL THEORY

Initial tests of INC theory from a macro-overtime perspective were consistent with expectations (Le Poire, Hallett, & Erlandson, 1996). Twenty-five couples—in which one member was substance-dependent or abusive—were interviewed in their homes. Members of the couple were assessed for qualification of the study with the chemical use, abuse, and dependency scale (CUAD; McGovern & Morrison, 1992), which provides a DSM–III diagnosis of severity, dependence, and abusiveness of substances. Additionally, they were separated and both asked individually what the nonaddicted, functional partner did around the drug use (a) prior to it being labeled problematic, (b) after it was labeled problematic, and (c) subsequent to frustration with influence attempts. The expectation was that partners would reinforce the behavior more before the drug use was labeled problematic, punish the behavior more after the labeling, and revert to a mix of reinforcement and punishment after they experienced frustration with the lack of success of their persuasive attempts. After coding the strategies as reinforcing or punishing of addictive behavior or reinforcing or punishing of alternative behavior, consistency of the attempts was calculated. It was expected that greater consistency would result in less relapse and greater persuasive effectiveness on the part of the functional partner as perceived by the addicted partner.

The results of this first study of INC theory with substance abusers and their partners indicates that functional partners are inconsistent in their use of punishment and reinforcement of substance use. They reported the greatest reinforcement and the least punishment before the drug abuse was labeled problematic and reported the greatest amount of punishment and the least amount of reinforcement after the drug abuse was labeled problematic. Additionally, the results of this same study indicate that partners are fairly inconsistent (around 67% of the behaviors used by functional partners were inconsistent with the behavior they followed) throughout all three time periods (prelabeling, postlabeling, and postfrustration) and present their afflicted partners with a mix of reinforcing and punishing communication behavior following a frustration period. This inconsistency, as predicted, had serious consequences on the afflicted partners' reported relapse (or continued drug use) and perceptions of the functionals' persuasive effectiveness. Specifically, functional partners who reported consistent reinforcement of substance abuse during the postlabeling and postfrustration periods had partners who reported greater relapse (accounting for 44% of the variance). Hence, the overall findings of this initial study support the INC contention that inconsistent nurturing is implicated in the recidivism among a drug-using sample. Interestingly, drug abusers did not perceive their functional partners to be less persuasively effective when they consistently reinforced substance-abusive behavior.

An earlier pilot investigation also revealed that homogamy of the couple in terms of drug abuse or dependence made a difference in terms of strategies used to alter the drug abuse of one partner (Le Poire, O'Sullivan, & Hallett, 1996). Persuading partners differed based on drug dependence, with functional (i.e., nonusing) partners doing more favors (i.e., indirect reinforcement) and afflicted partners using more assertion (i.e., direct punishment). Most important, a test of the effectiveness of strategy type revealed that increased use of avoidance, which is a strategy composed of a mix of reinforcing and punishing strategies (e.g., hitting, paying bills, arguing while under the influence, making partner comfortable while using, or giving food while using), actually led to greater rates of recidivism. This finding supports INC theory in that inconsistency led to greater recidivism.

SUMMARY AND DARK SIDE IMPLICATIONS

At a time when recovery programs are burgeoning, much time and effort is devoted to altering behaviors that are considered to be deviant, undesirable, or negative. For example, countless recovery programs and research protocols are devoted to substance abuse recovery (e.g., Jacob, Favorini, Meisel, & Anderson, 1978; Jacobson, Holtzworth-Munroe, & Schmaling, 1989; Kaufman & Kaufmann, 1979), the reduction of aggressive behavior in children (Patterson & Reid, 1970), the reduction of depression (Biglan et al., 1985; Hops et al., 1987), and lessening interpersonal conflicts in distressed couples (Patterson, Hops, & Weiss, 1975). Although these problems are varied, one consistency among them is a life partner who often shares the pain of the problem and the gain of recovery.

Although it should be obvious that codependent relationships offer many benefits to both partners, it seems that those advantages are actually at the heart of the paradoxical nature of the relationship, as they are often double-edged swords. For example, focusing all of their time and attention on afflicted partners allows the functional to avoid too much self-focus and thereby self-criticism. Alternatively, this other focus is also the cause of much suffering for functionals. Furthermore, the functional partners are also allowed the luxury of feeling a greater sense of emotional and physical health by comparison to afflicted partners. Alternatively, this ill health on the part of afflicted partners requires much caregiving behavior, which breeds great resentments. Finally, afflicteds greatly benefit from functionals' caregiving behavior and simultaneously have someone to blame for their undesirable behavior when functionals attempt to control it (i.e., "I wouldn't have to get drunk if you would just quit nagging me about it!"). Ultimately, however, this rewarding behavior, on the part of functionals, only serves to strengthen or enable the undesirable behavior. Any way you look at it, the benefits of the relationship ultimately are seen as costs from another vantage point.

Given these paradoxical contradictions, functional partners deserve attention in the healing and recovery process as well. Current treatment options for codependents include support groups, seminars, and workshops, as well as family, individual, and group therapies (for review, see Riordan & Simone, 1993). Whereas many recommend group approaches (e.g., Bogdaniak & Piercy, 1987; Cutter & Cutter, 1987; Downing & Walker, 1987), others focus treatment on the family (e.g., Newton, 1992). With regard to the paradoxical nature of the power structure in the functional–afflicted relationship, Palazzoli et al. (1978) and Weeks and L'Abate (1982) encouraged undermining paradoxical requests with counterparadoxes. The counterparadox, or therapeutic double-bind, forces the client into a no-lose situation. With this method, the therapist prescribes the very behavior that the client is trying to eradicate. This entails that the client either gains control over the symptom by giving it up or by enacting it intentionally and voluntarily. Either way, the client learns control. Given the success of such methods, it would be interesting to test whether the use of counterparadoxes by functional partners empowers the afflicted in a similar manner. Several functional partners we interviewed reported such counterparadoxes in their seemingly facetious requests that their partner continue to self-destruct (i.e., "Go ahead then, go out and get drunk—see if I care"). Future research on the effectiveness of such counterparadoxes could prove fruitful in understanding behavioral eradication in the family.

Family treatment is consistent with an INC theory approach, emphasizing that the patterns of inconsistent nurturing and control, and the functional's success or lack thereof, has implications for the mental health of the functional partner. Spouses continuing to live with a partner who alternates between sobriety and drunkenness experience substantial anxiety (e.g., Archer, 1979; Conway, 1981; Howard & Howard, 1985). Additionally, other research found that the stress effects of living with an alcoholic partner diminish when the partner makes attempts to control his or her excessive drinking (Edwards et al., 1973; Paolino & McCrady, 1977). Additionally, satisfying family relationships leads to greater well-being (e.g., Coombs, 1991; Gove, Briggs Style, & Hughes, 1990). Finally, partners whose attempts are rewarded by cessation of drinking (or otherwise undesirable behavior) should feel more in control. This greater feeling of control translates into greater mental health.

Thus, focus of treatment should also be on functional partners, not only because they aid in the reduction of undesirable behavior, but also because they aid in the increase of their own mental well-being. Utilizing INC theory and related research, a communication program aimed at training families to assist with the recovery of substance-dependent (or otherwise afflicted) members could be developed. If INC theory predictions are correct, functional partners should be assisted in learning to diminish inconsistent control attempts directed at afflicted partners. Functional partners should also be trained concerning which communication behaviors are likely to be experienced as rewarding and punishing, as reported by individuals in such situations. Additionally, future research is necessary to examine such a program's effectiveness in reducing drug recidivism as well as other undesirable behaviors. If the theory holds, this communication training program could be based on the fully cataloged range of reinforcing and punishing macrononverbal, macroverbal, micrononverbal, and microverbal strategies discovered in INC theory research.

For such a training program to be complete, future research efforts should endeavor to examine the micro-aspects of control attempts in the functional–afflicted relationship. This could be accomplished through examination of both microverbal and micrononverbal influence strategies. These strategies could be organized in reinforcing and punishing categories

to determine whether intermittent reinforcement and punishment manifest themselves during conversations between functionals and afflicteds,
in which the functionals are trying to alter the afflicteds' deviant behaviors.
Given the large impact that functional partners have been shown to have
on drug-addicted partners' recidivism, it is time for communication to be
utilized as an aid in the reduction of undesirable behavior.

REFERENCES

Als, H., Tronick, E., & Brazelton, T. B. (1979). Analysis of face-to-face interaction in infant–adult
    dyads. In M. E. Lamb, S. J. Suomi, & G. R. Stephanson (Eds.), *Social interaction analysis* (pp.
    33–76). Madison: University of Wisconsin Press.
Andersen, J. F., Andersen, P. A., & Jensen, A. D. (1979). The measurement of nonverbal
    immediacy. *Journal of Applied Communication Research, 7*, 153–180.
Andersen, P. A. (1984). Nonverbal immediacy in interpersonal communication. In A. W. Siegman
    & S. Feldstein (Eds.), *Multichannel integrations of nonverbal behavior* (pp. 1–36). Hillsdale,
    NJ: Lawrence Erlbaum Associates.
Anderson, S. C. (1994). A critical analysis of the concept of codependency. *Social Work, 39*,
    677–685.
Archer, N. S. (1979). Perceptions and attitudes of family members (codependents): Pre- and
    post-treatment. *Labor-Management Alcoholism: Clinic and Journal, 9*, 75–80.
Asher, R. M. (1992). *Women with alcoholic husbands.* Chapel Hill: University of North Carolina
    Press.
Bailey, M. (1961). Alcoholism and marriage: A review of research and professional litera-
    ture.*Quarterly Journal of Studies on Alcohol, 22*, 81–97.
Ballard, R. G. (1959). The interaction between marital conflict and alcoholism as seen through
    MMPIs of marriage partners. *American Journal of Orthopsychiatry, 29*, 528–546.
Bateson, G., Jackson, D. D., Haley, J., & Weakland, J. (1956). Toward a theory of schizophrenia.
    Behavioral Science, 1, 251–264.
Beattie, M. (1987). *Codependent no more: How to stop controlling others and start caring for
    yourself.* New York: Harper & Row.
Beattie, M. (1989). *Beyond Codependency.* New York: Harper & Row.
Becker, R. (1989). *Addicted to misery: The other side of co-dependency.* Deerfield Beach, FL:
    Health Communications, Inc.
Bernieri, F. J., Reznick, J. S., & Rosenthal, R. (1988). Synchrony, pseudosynchrony, and dissyn-
    chrony: Measuring the entrainment process in mother–infant interactions. *Journal of Person-
    ality and Social Psychology, 54*, 243–253.
Biglan, A., Hops, H., Sherman, L., Friedman, L. S., Arthur, J., & Osteen, V. (1985). Problem-solv-
    ing interactions of depressed women and their husbands. *Behavior therapy, 16*, 431–451.
Blau, P. M. (1964). *Exchange and power in social life.* New York: Wiley.
Bogdaniak, R. C., & Piercy, F. P. (1987). Therapeutic issues of adolescent children of alcoholics
    (AdCA) groups. *International Journal of Group Psychotherapy, 37*, 569–587.
Brazelton, T. B., Tronick, E., Adamson, L., Als, H., & Wise, S. (1975). Early mother–infant
    reciprocity. In M. A. Hofer (Ed.), *Parent–infant interaction, Ciba Foundation Symposium 33*
    (pp. 137–168). Amsterdam: Elsevier.
Brinberg, D., & Castell, P. (1982). A resource exchange theory approach to interpersonal
    interactions: A test of Foa's theory. *Journal of Personality and Social Psychology, 43*, 260–269.
Burgoon, J. K., Buller, D. B., Hale, J. L., & de Turk, M. A. (1984). Relational messages associated
    with nonverbal behaviors. *Human Communication Research, 10*, 351–378.
Burgoon, J. K., Burgoon, M., Miller, G. R., & Sunnafrank, M. (1981). Learning theory approaches
    to persuasion. *Human Communication Research, 7*, 161–179.

Burgoon, J. K., & Hale, J. L. (1984). The fundamental *topoi* of relational communication. *Communication Monographs, 51*, 19–41.

Burgoon, J. K., & Hale, J. L. (1987). Validation and measurement of the fundamental themes of relational communication. *Communication Monographs, 54*, 19–41.

Burgoon, J. K., & Hale, J. L. (1988). Nonverbal expectancy violations: Model elaboration and application to immediacy behaviors. *Communication Monographs, 55*, 58–79.

Cappella, J. N., & Greene, J. O. (1982). A discrepancy-arousal explanation of mutual influence in expressive behavior for adult and infant–adult interactions. *Communication Monographs, 49*, 89–114.

Carson, A. T., & Baker, R. C. (1994). Psychological correlates of codependency in women. *International Journal of the Addictions, 29*, 395–407.

Cermak, T. L . (1984). Children of alcoholics and the case for a new diagnostic category of codependency. *Alcohol Health and Research World, 3*, 38–42.

Cermak, T. L. (1986). *Diagnosing and treating co-dependence: A guide for professionals who work with chemical dependents, their spouses and children.* Minneapolis: Johnson Institute books.

Chiauzzi, E. J., & Liljegren, S. (1993). Taboo topics in addiction treatment: An empirical review of clinical folklore. *Journal of Substance Abuse Prevention, 10*, 303–316.

Coker, D. A., & Burgoon, J. K. (1987). The nature of conversational involvement and nonverbal encoding patterns. *Human Communication Research, 13*, 463–494.

Conway, J. (1981). Significant others need help too: Alcoholism treatment as important to rest of family. *Focus on Alcohol and Drug Issues, 4*, 17–19.

Coombs, R. H. (1991). Marital status and personal well-being: A literature review. *Family Relations, 40*, 97–102.

Corder, B. F., Hendricks, A., & Corder, R. F. (1964). An MMPI study of a group of wives of alcoholics. *Quarterly Journal of Studies on Alcohol, 25*, 551–554.

Cowan, G., & Warren, L. W. (1994). Codependency and gender-stereotyped traits. *Sex Roles, 30*, 631–645.

Cutter, C. G., & Cutter, H. S. G. (1987). Experience and change in Al-anon family groups: Adult children of alcoholics. *Journal of Studies on Alcohol, 48*, 29–32.

Downing, N. E., & Walker, M. E. (1987). A psychoeducational group for adult children of alcoholics. *Journal of Counseling and Development, 65*, 440–442.

DuPont, R. L., & McGovern, J. P. (1991). The growing impact of the children-of-alcoholics movement on medicine: A revolution in our midst. In T. M. Rivinus (Ed.), *Children of chemically dependent parents: Multiperspectives from the cutting edge* (pp. 313–329). New York: Brunner/Mazel.

Edwards, P., Harvey, C., & Whitehead, P. (1973). Wives of alcoholics, a critical review and analysis. *Quarterly Journal of Studies on Alcohol, 34*, 112–132.

Ewing, J. A., & Fox, R. E. (1968). Family therapy of alcoholism. In J. Masserman (Ed.), *Current Psychiatric Therapies*, (Vol. 18, pp. 86–91), New York: Grune & Stratton.

Ferraro, K. J., & Johnson, J. M. (1983). How women experience battering: The process of victimization. *Social Problems, 30*, 325–339.

Friel, J. C., & Friel, L. D. (1987). Uncovering our frozen feelings: The iceberg model of co-dependency. *Focus on the Family and Chemical Dependency, 46*, 10–12.

Giles, H., Coupland, J., & Coupland, N. (Eds.). (1991). *Contexts of accommodation.* Developments in applied sociolinguistics. New York: Cambridge University Press.

Giles, H., Mulac, A., Bradac, J. J., & Johnson, P. (1987). Speech accommodation theory: the first decade and beyond. In M. L. McLaughlin (Ed.), *Communication Yearbook 10* (pp. 13–48). Beverly Hills, CA: Sage.

Gordon, J. R., & Barrett, K. (1993). The codependency movement: Issues of context and differentiation. In J, S. Baer, G. A. Marlatt, & R. J. McMahon (Eds.), *Addictive behaviors across the life span: Prevention, treatment, and policy issues* (pp. 307–339). Newbury Park, CA: Sage.

Gorski, T. T., & Miller, M. (1988). Family factors and warning signs. *Codependency*, 81–88. .

Gouldner, A. W. (1960). The norm of reciprocity: A preliminary statement. *American Sociological Review, 25*, 161–178.

Gove, W. R., Briggs Style, C., & Hughes, M. (1990). The effects of marriage on the well-being of adults. *Journal of Family Issues, 11*, 4–35.

Greenleaf, J. (1988). Co-alcoholic/Para-alcoholic: Who's who? In *Codependency*, (pp. 5–18). Deerfield Beach, FL 33442.

Haaken, J. (1990). A critical analysis of the co-dependence construct. *Psychiatry, 53*, 396–406.

Hawks, R. D., Bahr, S. J., & Wang, G. (1994). Adolescent substance use and codependence. *Journal of Studies on Alcohol, 55*, 261–268.

Hops, H., Biglan, A., Sherman, L., Arthur, J., Friedman, L. S., & Osteen, V. (1987) Home observations of family interactions of depressed woman. *Journal of Consulting and Clinical Psychology, 55*, 341–346.

Howard, D., & Howard, N. (1985). Treatment of the significant other. In S. Zimberg, J. Wallace, & S. Blume (Eds.), *Practical approaches to alcoholism psychotherapy* (pp. 137–162). New York: Plenum.

Jacob, T., Favorini, A., Meisel, S. S., & Anderson, C. M. (1978). The alcoholics' spouse, children, and family interactions: Substantive findings and methodological issues. *Journal of Studies on Alcohol, 39*, 1231–1251.

Jacob, T., & Leonard, K. E. (1988). Alcoholic–spouse interaction as a function of alcoholism subtype and alcohol consumption interaction. *Journal of Abnormal Psychology, 97*, 231–237.

Jacob, T., & Seilhamer, R. A. (1982). The impact on spouses and how they cope. In J. Orford & J. Harwin (Eds.), *Alcohol and the family* (pp. 114–126). London: Croom Helm.

Jacobson, N. S., Holtzworth-Munroe, A., & Schmaling, K. B. (1989). Marital therapy and spouse involvement in the treatment of depression, agoraphobia, and alcoholism. *Journal of Consulting and Clinical Psychology, 57*, 5–10.

James, J. E, & Goldman, M. (1971). Behavior trends of wives of alcoholics. *Quarterly Journal of Studies on Alcoholism, 32*, 3773–3781.

Kasl, C. D. (1989). *Women, sex, and addiction: A search for love and power.* New York: Ticknor and Fields.

Kaufman, E. (1984). *Power to change: Family case studies in the treatment of alcoholism.* New York: Gardner Press.

Kaufman, E. (1985a). Family systems and family therapy of substance abuse: An overview of two decades of research and clinical experience. *The International Journal of the Addictions, 20*, 897–916.

Kaufman, E. (1985b). *Substance abuse and family therapy.* Orlando, FL: Grune & Stratton.

Kaufman, E., & Kaufmann, P. (1979). *Family therapy of drug and alcohol abuse.* New York: Gardner Press.

Koffinke, C. (1991). Family recovery issues and treatment resources. In D. C. Daley & M. S. Raskin (Eds.), *Treating the chemically dependent and their families* (pp. 195–216). Newbury Park, CA: Sage.

Kogan, K. L., Jackson, J. K., & Fordyce, W. E. (1963). Personality disturbance in wives of alcoholics. *Quarterly Journal of Studies of Alcohol, 24*, 227–238.

Le Poire, B. A. (1992). Does the codependent encourage substance-dependent behavior? Paradoxical injunctions in the codependent relationship. *The International Journal of the Addictions, 27*, 1465–1474.

Le Poire, B. A. (1995). Inconsistent nurturing as control theory: Implications for communication-based research and treatment programs. *Journal of Applied Communication Research, 22*, 60–74.

Le Poire, B. A., Hallett, J. S., & Erlandson, K. T. (1996, November). *An initial test of inconsistent nurturing as control theory: How partners of drug abusers help their partners 'kick.'* A paper presented at the Interpersonal and Small Group Division of the Speech Communication Association, San Diego.

Le Poire, B. A., O'Sullivan, P., & Hallett, J. S. (1996, May). *Punishing versus reinforcing strategies of drug discontinuance within primary relationships: A pilot study of functional–afflicted and dual-drug using couples.* A paper presented at the Health Communication Division of the International Communication Association, Chicago.

Long, G. M., & McNamara, J. R. (1989). Paradoxical punishment as it relates to the battered woman syndrome. *Behavior Modification, 13*, 192–205.

Martin, A. L., & Piazza, N. J. (1995). Codependency in women: Personality disorder or popular descriptive term? *Journal of Mental Health Counseling, 17*, 428–440.

Mason, M. (1988). Sexuality issues during recovery. *Codependency*, 65–70. Deerfield Beach, FL 33442.

McGovern, M. P., & Morrison, D. H. (1992). The chemical use, abuse, and dependence scale (CUAD): Rationale, reliability, and validity. *Journal of Substance Abuse Treatment, 9*, 27–38.

Mehrabian, A. (1969). Some referents and measures of nonverbal behavior. *Behavioral Research Methods & Instrumentation, 1*, 203–207.

Mellody, P., Miller, A. W., & Miller, J. K. (1989). *Facing Codependence: What it is, where it comes from, how it sabotages our lives*. San Francisco: Harper & Row.

Moos, R. H., & Moos, B. S. (1984). The process of recovery from alcoholism: III. Comparing functioning in families of alcoholics and matched control families. *Journal of Studies of Alcohol, 45*, 111–118.

Nathans, J. A. (1981, March). *Borderline personality: A new psychiatric syndrome or another example of male disapproval or female behavior?* Paper presented at the Symposium, Eighth Annual Conference, for the Association for Women in Psychology, Boston.

Newton, M. (1992). Living again: Family treatment at KIDS of North Jersey. *Journal of Substance Abuse Treatment, 9*, 71–80.

O'Brien, P. E., & Gaborit, M. (1992). Codependency: A disorder separate from chemical dependency. *Journal of Clinical Psychology, 48*, 129–136.

Orford, J., Guthrie, S., Nicholls, P., Oppenheimer, E., Egert, S., & Hensman, C. (1975). Self-reported coping behavior of wives of alcoholics and its association with drinking outcome. *Journal of Studies on Alcohol, 36*, 1254–1267.

Paige, P. E., La Pointe, W., & Krueger, A. (1971). The marital dyad as a diagnostic treatment variable in alcohol addiction. *Psychology Savannah, 8*, 64–73.

Palazzoli, M. S., Boscolo, L., Cecchin, G., & Prata, G. (1978). *Paradox and counterparadox*. New York: Aronson.

Paolino, T. J., & McCrady, B. S. (1977). *The alcoholic marriage: Alternative perspectives*, New York: Grune & Stratton.

Patterson, G. R., Hops, H., & Weiss, R. L. (1975). Interpersonal skill training for couples in early stages of conflict. *Journal of Marriage and the Family, 37*, 295–303.

Patterson, G. R., & Reid, J. B. (1970). Reciprocity and coercion: Two facets of social systems. In C. Neuringer and J. Michael (Eds.), *Behavior modification in clinical psychology* (pp. 133–177). New York: Appleton-Century-Crofts.

Patterson, M. L. (1983). *Nonverbal behavior: A functional perspective*. New York: Springer-Verlag.

Peterson, K. E., & Seligson, M. R. (1992). Workshop on codependency and AIDS. In M. Ross Seligson & K. E. Peterson (Eds.), *AIDS prevention and treatment: Hope, humor, and healing* (pp. 225–227). London: Hemisphere Publishing.

Phillips, B. (1988). Codependency: A real problem. In F. Duckman, B. R. Challenger, W. G. Emener, & W. S. Hutchinson, Jr. (Eds.), *Employee assistance programs: A basic text* (pp. 194–203). Springfield, IL: Thomas.

Rae, J. B., & Drewery, J. (1972). Interpersonal patterns in alcoholic marriages. *British Journal of Psychiatry, 120*, 615–621.

Riordan, R. J., & Simone, D. (1993). Codependent christians: Some issues for church-based recovery groups. *Journal of Psychology and Theology, 21*, 158–164.

Robinson, J. (1990). Unhooking: Codependence, substance abuse, and countertransference. In B. Genevay & R. Katz (Eds.), *Countertransference and older clients*. Newbury Park, CA: Sage.

Schaef, A. W. (1986). *Co-dependence: Misunderstood-mistreated*. San Francisco: Harper & Row.

Shulman, G. (1988). Sexuality and recovery. *Codependency*, 75–80.

Skinner, B. F. (1953). *Science and human behavior*. New York: Macmillan.

Skinner, B. F. (1974). *About behaviorism*. New York: Knopf.

Stanton, G. W. (1986). Preventive intervention with step families. *Social Work, 31*, 201–206.

Steiner, C. M. (1974). *Scripts people live: Transactional analysis of life scripts*. New York: Bantam.

Steinglass, P. (1976). Experimenting with family treatment approaches to alcoholism, 1950–1975, a review. *Family Process, 15*, 97–123.

Steinglass, P. (1982). The roles of alcohol in family systems. In J. Orford & J. Harwin (Eds.), *Alcohol and the family* (pp. 127–150). London: Croom Helm.

Street, R. L., & Cappella, J. N. (Eds.). (1985). *Sequence and pattern in communicative behavior: A model and commentary* (pp. 243–276). London: Edward Arnold.

Subby, R., & Friel, J. (1988). Codependency. *Codependency*, 31–45. Deerfield Beach, FL 33442.

Thibaut, J. W., & Kelley, H. H. (1959). *The social psychology of groups*. New York: Wiley.

Walfish, S., Stenmark, D. E., Shealy, S. E., & Krone, A. M. (1992). MMPI profiles of women in codependency treatment. *Journal of Personality Assessment, 58*, 211–214.

Watzlawick, P., Beavin, J., & Jackson, D. D. (1967). *Pragmatics of human communication*. New York: Norton.

Weeks, G. R., & L'Abate, L. (1982). *Paradoxical psychotherapy: Theory and practice with individuals, couples, and families*. New York: Brunner/Mazel.

Wegscheider-Cruse, S. (1985). *Choicemaking: For co-dependents, adult children, and spirituality seekers*. Pompano Beach, FL: Health Communications.

Whalen, T. (1953). Wives of alcoholics: Four types observed in a family service agency. *Quarterly Journal of Studies of Alcohol, 14*, 632–641.

Whitfield, C. L. (1987). *Healing the child within*. Deerfield Beach, FL: Health Communications, Inc.

Wilder, C., & Collins, S. (1994). Patterns of interactional paradoxes. In W. R. Cupach & B. H. Spitzberg, (Eds.), *The dark side of interpersonal communication* (pp. 83–103). Hillsdale, NJ: Lawrence Erlbaum Associates.

Williams, A., Giles, H., Coupland, N., Dalby, M., & Manasse, H. (1990). The communicative contexts of elderly social support and health: A theoretical model. *Health Communication, 2*, 123–143.

Wiseman, J. P. (1991). *The other half: Wives of alcoholics and their social–psychological situation*. New York: Aldine de Gruyter.

IV

ABUSING

7

Sexual Coercion in Courtship Relations

Brian H. Spitzberg
San Diego State University

COMMUNICATION AND CONSENT

In response to a more politically correct social environment, media reports of widespread sexual coercion and violence, and a long overdue redress of a gender disparate system of courtship relations, Antioch College in 1993 instituted a bold policy of communication regulation (Glazer, 1994). Students were instructed to make explicit the requests to increase each behavioral level of intimacy with a partner. If a person wanted to escalate intimacy from holding hands to kissing, it should be requested overtly. If the desire were to move from kissing to petting underneath the clothes, again this should be prefaced with a specific request to that effect. At each stage, a confirmation of the partner's affirmation is sought. The advantages and disadvantages of such policies have been the subject of vigorous debate (e.g., Abrams & Herman, 1994; Schwartz, 1994).

Sex, it seems, is a touchy subject. Western society increasingly came to grips with it as a biological phenomenon, but as a social phenomenon it remains controversial and conceptually evasive. This chapter attempts to synthesize the ever expanding scholarly literature (e.g., Allgeier, 1987; Burkhart, & Bourg, 1991; Belknap & Erez, 1995; Benson, Charlton, & Goodhart, 1992; Berkowitz, 1994; Burkhart & Stanton, 1988; Craig, 1990;

179

Hall, 1990; Lloyd, 1991; Lottes, 1988; Lundberg-Love & Geffner, 1989; Marshall, 1993; Muehlenhard, Harney, & Jones, 1991; Muehlenhard et al., 1992; Prentky & Knight, 1991; Thiessen & Young, 1994) regarding one of the dark sides of sexuality: coercion. Before attempting this conceptual synthesis, it is necessary to narrow the focus of review by first identifying a number of assumptions and qualifications for review, and second, by defining the concepts of interest.

NEGOTIATING THE BOUNDARIES OF THE PHENOMENON

Assumptions

There are several assumptions and limitations that affect this review. Some of these parameters reflect the nature of the literature on sexual coercion. Others are selected to make the review more manageable. In some cases, they reveal areas in need of further study. In all cases, it is important to recognize them as boundaries on the phenomenon under examination.

First, with the noted exceptions, the vast majority of research to be reviewed emphasized White (cf., Belknap, 1989; Broude & Greene, 1976; Burnam et al., 1988; Fischer, 1987; Giacopassi & Dull, 1986; Moore, Nord, & Peterson,, 1989; Sorenson & Siegel, 1992; South & Felson, 1990; Zimmerman, Sprecher, Langer, & Holloway,, 1995), North American (cf., Foo & Margolin, 1995; Gavey, 1991; Koss, Heise, & Russo, 1994; Rozée, 1993; Tang, Critelli, & Porter, 1993; Yoshihama & Sorenson, 1994), upper middle class (cf., Alder, 1985; Belknap, 1989; Hall & Flannery, 1984), heterosexual (cf., Baier, Rosenzweig, & Whipple, 1991; Brand & Kidd, 1986; Comstock, 1991; Kalichman & Rompa, 1995; Renzetti, 1988, 1992), adolescent and young adult (cf., Best, Resnick, Saunders, & Lipovsky, 1992; DiVasto et al., 1984; George, Winfield, & Blazer, 1992; Kilpatrick, Saunders, Veronen, Best & Von, 1987; Koss, Woodruff, & Koss, 1991; Laumannn, Gagnon, Michael, & Michaels, 1994; Moore et al., 1989; Sorenson, Stein, Siegel, Golding, & Gurnam, 1987; Winfield et al., 1990) subjects. This is perhaps not surprising, given the convenience and natural relevance of college students to the study of dating, courtship, and sexual relations. However, it places considerable restrictions on the types of generalizations that can be drawn from the research.

Second, partly as a consequence of this first restriction and partly because of the potential differences in motives, power, and cultural norms associated with other contexts, this review primarily focuses on dating and courtship contexts. This excludes at least two important domains of research: stranger rape (e.g., Amir, 1971; Bart & O'Brien, 1985; Ellis, 1989; Katz & Mazur, 1979; Macdonald, 1971; Marshall, Laws, & Barbaree, 1990; and McCahill, Meyer & Fischman, 1979) and marital rape (e.g., Allison & Wrightsman, 1993; Peacock, 1995; Russell, 1982b, 1991; Yllö & Finkelhor, 1985). The issue of acquaintance rape (Parrot & Bechhofer, 1991) is an ambiguous category. Acquaintance rape is often equated with date rape, although they are clearly distinguishable in many cases. A platonic friend is an acquaintance, but not a courtship partner. A friend of a courtship partner is a potential rapist, but may not be an intended lover. Family members and relatives are generally acquaintances as well as potential rapists. *Acquaintance* merely concerns whether the perpetrator is known to the victim. *Courtship* and *dating* imply a context in which the person who is known is an object of attraction and a potentially intimate and romantic relationship. Although the primary interest of this review is sexual coercion occurring in courtship contexts, research will be drawn from the larger acquaintance and even stranger rape literature wherever it is considered relevant.

The fact that coercion and rape occur in the context of courtship leads to one of the most vexing difficulties of reasonably objective study in this area. In the context of dating and courtship, sexual relations are normatively considered to be one of the many natural possible outcomes. Thus, the problem is the form of the act of sexual pursuit rather than the fact of sexual intercourse itself. Unlike relations among strangers, courtship is a context in which sexual pursuit and consent are normatively and bilaterally often expected, produced, and enjoyed. Courtship is also a context in which sexual pursuit is often coercive and forceful. It is important, therefore, to be very careful in defining what is meant by such terms as *rape, coercion, consent* and related concepts.

Frameworks for Definition

There are several different perspectives from which to conceptualize these terms, and there are social and political implications to each (Muehlenhard, Powch, Phelps, & Guisti, 1992; Reinholtz, Muehlenhard, Phelps, & Satterfield, 1995). There are legal (see Bechhofer & Parrot, 1991; Bohmer, 1991; Dixon, 1991; Paquin, 1995), social (e.g., Cook, 1995; Cowen & Campbell, 1995; Hall, Howard, & Boezio, 1986), relational (e.g., Gavey, 1992; Metts & Spitzberg, 1996), and individual (e.g., Cahoon & Edmonds, 1992; Klemmack & Klemmack, 1976; Koss, 1988; McLendon et al., 1994; Remer & Witten, 1988; Sugarman, 1994) frames for defining *rape, coercion,* and *consent,* and these frames often reveal significantly divergent constructions of the terms.

At the legal level, although there has been extensive revision of state statutes in recent years to accommodate more sexually egalitarian values, most statutes require the fulfillment of three criteria for an act to constitute *rape*: sexual intercourse (penile penetration of the vagina), lack of consent, and force or threat of force. *Sexual assault*, often carrying lesser penalties, generally applies if instead of sexual intercourse some other form of sexual contact occurs. Although lack of consent might, under ideal societal circumstances, be equated with a lack of verbal or nonverbal confirmation of agreement, case law and jury decision making define it in terms of force, and force, in turn, is determined by degree of resistance (Muehlenhard & Schrag, 1991). Thus, lack of consent is not often defined in actual trials as a lack of verbal acquiescence or agreement, but in terms of whether verbal and physical resistance is offered and when it is offered. This appears to be both a legal presumption (Bohmer, 1991) as well as a societal presumption (Langley et al., 1991; Shotland & Goodstein, 1983). Regardless, despite the need for precision in legal contexts, "the legal definition of consent is usually not very helpful, because it is spare enough to require fleshing out in each individual case" (Bohmer, 1991, p. 321).

At the societal–individual level, the perceptions and definitions of *rape* and *consent* are influenced by the cultural script surrounding courtship. In an extensive review of survey and experimental research on attitudes toward rape, Ward (1995) drew the following conclusions:

1. More than 10% of people (and sometimes much higher percentages) surveyed believe that women can provoke rape by their appearance or behavior; women who go out alone at night put themselves in a position to be raped; all rapists are mentally sick and normal men do not commit rape; a woman should be responsible for preventing her victimization; a woman cannot be forced to have intercourse against her will; and women often falsely accuse men of rape.
2. As the perpetrator's use of force increases, the more the episode is perceived to be rape (Murnen, Perot, & Byrne 1989; Stacy, Prisbell, & Tallefsrud, 1992).
3. As the victim's use of both verbal and nonverbal resistance increases, and the earlier resistance occurs in the episode, the more the event is perceived to be rape, both by self (Koss, 1985) and third party judges (Shotland & Goodstein, 1992).
4. The more injured the victim, physically and psychologically, the more the episode is perceived to be rape.
5. The use of alcohol by either party diminishes the attribution of rape.
6. Episodes are less likely to be labeled as "rape" if the perpetrator is a friend or date (Bell, Kuriloff, & Lottes, 1994; Klemmack & Klemmack, 1976; Shotland & Goodstein, 1992).
7. The more provocatively dressed, the less attractive, the greater the sexual experience, the less cautious, and the more emotionally expressive victims (i.e., women) are, the more responsibility (i.e., blame) they are attributed with in the episode.

In general, when sex differences are found, relative to females, males tend to view responsibility as being more shared rather than exclusively the perpetrator's fault; males are also less prone to label coercive events as "rape" (Bell et al., 1994; Calhoun, Selby, Cann, & Keller, 1978; Gerdes, Dammann, & Heilig, 1988; Jacobson; 1981; Kanekar, Shaherwalla, Franco, Kumbu, & Pinto, 1991; cf. Cahoon & Edmonds, 1992; McLendon et al., 1994).

An important and often overlooked qualification to such claims is that most people—male and female—comply when sexual advances are rejected (Byers, 1988; Byers & Lewis, 1988; O'Sullivan & Byers, 1993), reject the legitimacy of rape, and blame the perpetrator (almost always depicted as male) in coercive vignettes (Fischer, 1986; Gerdes et al., 1988), especially as coerciveness of the perpetrator increases (Goodchilds, Zellman, Johnson, & Giarrusso, 1988; Harris & Weiss, 1995). For whatever set of reasons, "as many as 40–60% of attempts at sexual aggression in courtship are unsuccessful" (Metts & Spitzberg, 1996, p. 73). Although the vast majority of people view rape as wrong under "any circumstances" (Cook, 1995; Goodchilds et al., 1988), when specific conditions are specified (e.g., "He spends a lot of money on her," "He's so turned on he can't stop," "She says she's going to have sex with him then changes her mind," "She's led him on," etc.), the percentages of respondents categorically rejecting forcible sex decreases among both males and females (Cook, 1995; Goodchilds et al., 1988). Such beliefs are closely related to rape myths, and some evidence indicates that females overestimate the extent to which males hold such beliefs (Cahoon & Edmonds, 1992; Cahoon, Edmonds, Spaulding, & Dickens, 1995; Edmonds & Cahoon, 1993).

At the relational level, it is particularly difficult to circumscribe the boundaries of courtship rape. For example, a large percentage of victims do not attribute the label of "rape" to what otherwise meets the legal or behavioral definition of rape (see Koss, 1988; Layman, Gidycz, & Lynn, 1996; Murnen et al., 1989), and the vast majority of males do not consider their own such actions to be rape (Koss, 1988). Sizable percentages also continue dating (Johnson & Sigler, 1996; Murnen et al., 1989) and having sex with (Koss, 1988; Koss, Dinero, Seibel, & Cox, 1988; Layman et al., 1996) the perpetrator of courtship rape. In one study, although subjects on average perceived coercive episodes to be rape, the more prior sex the woman was described as having with the male, the less prone it was to be defined as rape (Shotland & Goodstein, 1992).

Defining the Coerciveness Continuum

If the perception of coercion depends substantially on one's attitudinal and cultural frame of reference, then it is important to attempt a set of conceptual definitions to provide touchstones for comparison and synthesis of findings. This is not a simple task (see, e.g., Muehlenhard et al., "Definitions ... " 1992). For the purposes of this review, coerciveness is aligned along a continuum from rape to sexual aggression or contact, to sexual coercion, to unwanted sex, and to consensual sex. To a large extent, this continuum is one that ranges from degree of force and violation, on one end, to degree of choice and legitimacy on the other. It is, in short, intended primarily as a continuum of coerciveness.

What Is Consent?

The concept of consent has been problematic for centuries (Brundage, 1993) and continues to be a central fulcrum on which sexual relations are balanced (Adams, 1996; Harris, 1996; Pineau, 1996; Wells, 1996). Muehlenhard (1996), in reviewing such domains as commitment of the mentally ill and participation of experimental subjects, concluded that there are at least two conditions to consent: It requires knowledge and free choice. *Knowledge* implies that the consenting party knows what is being consented to and has all relevant information. Thus, deception, selective disclosure, or pursuit of compliance beyond that which is implied by previous messages suggest nonconsensual intercourse. *Free choice* implies a true ability to decide whether to participate, free of undue influence. Thus, a subordinate or student may not be entirely free to choose when the pursuer is a boss or professor. Obviously, being under the influence of alcohol, rohypnol, or other mind-altering substances to the extent that persons are no longer in control of their decision-making faculties constitutes a condition in which full knowledge and free choice are significantly impaired and cannot be assumed.

In addition, Muehlenhard (1996) pointed out that consent differs from acquiescence. Factors such as the value of preserving one's standard of living, maintaining one's interpersonal status, the value of being in a relationship, the cultural value of heterosexuality, and the available societal discourses of legitimate options influence a person's perceived freedom of choice. People may give in to sex rather than freely engage in it because of numerous forces such as these, real or perceived. True consent, therefore, is by this conceptualization, a very reflective, conscious act, whether that reflection occurs well before what later becomes spontaneous during the episode itself.

This perspective seems rooted in the mental aspect of consent. Sex and consent, however, are also interactional phenomena (see Adams, 1996; Harris, 1996; Pineau, 1996). People search for interactional cues of consent, and often, offering no resistance, or even such behaviors as french kissing and genital fondling, constitute evidence of consent in people's eyes

(Schultz & DeSavage, 1975). People also use a variety of cues to indicate a lack of consent, from explicit refusals to subtle nonverbal distancing behaviors (Byers & Lewis, 1988; O'Sullivan & Byers, 1992, 1993). Thus, although explicit verbal consent may not always be offered (Greer & Buss, 1994; Jesser, 1978) and may seem awkward in the context of romance, it still appears to be the best evidence of consent. As Haffner (1996) enjoined, "The essence of consent for sexual relationships is communication—honest, open, direct communication—about interests, expectations, hopes, desires, and consequences" (p. 2).

A Continuum of Coerciveness

"Sexual activity has been construed along a continuum of coerciveness ranging from voluntary, to altruistic, to verbally coerced, to physically coerced" (Muehlenhard & Cook, 1988, p. 58). This continuum is reflected in intuitive senses of the severity of coercion employed and is reflected in the most common measure of sexual victimization (Koss & Oros, 1982). However, there is surprisingly little effort to validate this continuum (Porter & Critelli, 1992) or to explore the implicit and explicit characteristics of its underlying conceptual dimension (cf. Christopher, 1988; Kelly, 1987, 1988). Part of the problem is the variance in the ways labels and terms have been used. *Unwanted sex* means sexual coercion in one project (e.g., Lewin, 1985) and merely sex that was not wanted in another (e.g., Muehlenhard & Cook, 1988). An attempt is made to provide a conceptual continuum of coercion and to explicate briefly its underlying dimension (see Fig. 7.1). It should be noted that the categories are not intended to be mutually exclusive and in many instances, a given experience seems to straddle several categories. The continuum is presented to suggest the breadth of strategies involved in sexual violence and to presage the estimation of sexual coercion in society.

Violated Nonconsent. Several strategies of consent violation are represented in the literature. *Rape* is defined here as sexual intercourse (vaginal or anal penetration) without consent and with force or threat of force.

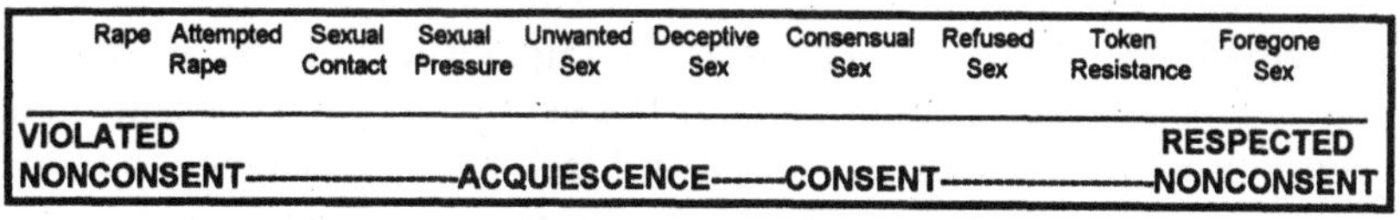

Rape	Attempted Rape	Sexual Contact	Sexual Pressure	Unwanted Sex	Deceptive Sex	Consensual Sex	Refused Sex	Token Resistance	Foregone Sex
VIOLATED NONCONSENT———————ACQUIESCENCE———CONSENT———————RESPECTED NONCONSENT									

FIG. 7.1. A continuum of sexual compliance types.

Attempted rape is an unsuccessful attempt at rape. *Sexual contact* is applied here to forms of sexual activity other than intercourse (i.e., penetration) that occur without consent and with force or threat of force (e.g., petting, fondling, disrobing, kissing, etc.). *Sexual pressure*, often referred to as sexual coercion, consists of dispreferred sex in the context of implicit or explicit messages that the person should have sex. These messages may be cultural and societal, but to be considered coercive, they must have specific communicative manifestations in the form of peer pressure, persistent arguments or nonverbal passes from one's partner, or symbolic or face-impairing contingent threats (Tedeschi & Felson, 1994). Sexual pressure includes actions such as continual arguments, getting a partner to drink alcohol, threatening to end the relationship, and threatening to leave the person stranded without a ride.

Acquiescence.   The dividing line between giving in to pressure and acquiescing to sexual invitation may be diaphinous. Nevertheless, *unwanted sex* occurs when someone decides to engage in sexual relations without persistent or obvious resistance despite a concomitant conscious preference to avoid having sex (see Muehlenhard & Cook, 1988; Murnen et al., 1989; cf. Lewin, 1985). A person may engage in unwanted sex for any number of social, cultural, or relational reasons (see Muehlenhard & Cook, 1988) and specific coercive messages need not be manifest. Presumably, the reasons for having sex (despite a dispreference for having it) are motivated by both egocentric and altercentric reasons. A person may want to please the other person (or avoid their anger or disappointment) or may merely desire to avoid the hassle of an argument that may ensue. *Deceptive sex* occurs when a person voluntarily has sex with an actor because the actor has portrayed himself, herself, or the situation in a false or misleading manner. For example, promising to marry someone or falsely professing love are sometimes strategies for obtaining sex; yet if the truth were known, sex would not occur.

Consent.   Consensual sex consists of consciously and mutually agreed on sexual relations in the context of reasonably accurate mutual understanding of intentions. The assumption is that the parties voluntarily and consciously engaged in "negotiated sexual involvement" (Metts & Spitzberg, 1996, p. 60), regardless of the implicitness of this negotiation. It is not clear to experts or interactants the extent to which consent should be considered in an affirmative sense or if lack of any resistance to pursuit can reasonably be taken as evidence of consent (e.g., Schultz & DeSavage, 1975). For example, in Canada (Altman, cited in Gilbert, 1995, p. xii), and presumably at Antioch college, rape is considered intercourse without "affirmative consent."

Respected Nonconsent. · *Refused sex* here refers to the situation in which a person turns down an offer or pursuit of sex and this refusal is respected. Relatedly, *accepted token resistance* occurs when sex is offered or pursued, desired by both parties, but quashed by an insincere message of verbal and/or nonverbal refusal. Sex could have occurred, but the script being followed by the pursued is not recognized as only a script by the pursuer (Metts & Spitzberg, 1996). Interestingly, accepted token resistance is a conceptual opposite of deceptive sex, in that a deceptive message is accepted as truthful and consequently sex does not occur. In contrast, although not apparent in the literature, the hypothetical entity of *foregone sex* is employed here to represent situations in which sex is clearly offered or pursued, and due to ambigous comprehension or diversion of the actors, does not occur. It is a missed opportunity for sexual relations that is missed for reasons that are probably not even apparent to the actors themselves.

Some of these definitions are heavily influenced by a common measurement schema (Koss & Oros, 1982; Koss, Gidycz, & Wisniewski, 1987). However, several of these terms are also defined more in terms of an assumption of a hypothetical underlying continuum of (non)consent, and thus, a continuum of coerciveness (see Fig. 7.1). The assumption is that the continuum of foregone sex to rape is a continuum of respected consent to violated nonconsent. In some cases, sex ought to occur and does not, and in others, sex ought not to occur and does. Wedged obscurely in the relative middle is the idealized consensual sex, in which the participants feel comfortable that they know what they need to know about the other(s) and their intentions, and all parties concur that sex is a desired activity. It is important to note that no assumption is made that seriousness, severity, or psychological harm are aligned in the same way as the coerciveness. A person may experience just as much trauma from deceptive sex as from attempted rape. Whether there is any correlation between coerciveness and personal effects of the sexual act is an empirical question that has yet to be studied adequately, although one review indicates that increasing coerciveness is associated with increased trauma (Wyatt, Newcomb, & Riederle, 1993).

An attempt has been made in these working definitions to avoid obvious gendering (i.e., viewing sex as only heterosexual or as only being with female victims) or traditionalizing (i.e., presuming only two people are having sex) of the act. Males are clearly capable of being victimized as well as females (e.g., Groth & Burgess, 1980; Kalichman & Rompa, 1995; Letellier, 1994; Mezey & King, 1989; Sarrel & Masters, 1982; Struckman-Johnson, 1988; Struckman-Johnson, Rucker, Bumby, & Donaldson, 1996; Waterman, Dawson, & Bologha, 1989), and not all rape occurs as a one-on-one situation (e.g., gang rape, see Amir, 1971; O'Sullivan, 1991).

What Is Coercion?

Coercion itself, despite its centrality to many writings on sexual court-ship and violence (e.g., Grauerholz & Koralewski, 1991) has not been clearly defined (Craig, 1990). According to the *Compact Oxford English Dictionary (OED)*, coercion refers to "constraint, restraint, compulsion; the application of force to control the action of a voluntary agent." "In everyday language, to be coerced is to be compelled under duress or threat to do something 'against our will'" (Sidman, 1989, p.31). Because physical force is viewed as one of many forms of duress or negative sanction (Roloff, 1996), rape through physical force is a subset of the coerciveness contin-uum. Certain feminist treatments make expansive statements about physi-cal coercion (e.g., Clark & Lewis, 1977), but generally make few explicit claims about its interactional forms (cf., Gavey, 1992). Others define it very expansively—"any sexual behavior that is forced upon an unwilling victim" (Baron & Richardson, 1994, p. 282). An extensive review of conceptual and methodological treatments of coercion reveals vast diver-sity (Craig, 1990).

One of the more extensive treatments is offered by Tedeschi and Felson (1994), who defined *coercion* as an action "taken with the intent of imposing harm on another person or forcing compliance. Threats, bodily force, and punishments are the three types of coercive actions" (p. 348). The gray area of "threats" and "punishments" expand beyond brute physical force and into the realm of symbolic inducements. Tedeschi and Felson identified three possible areas of harm that may be threatened or inflicted: physical (direct physical or biological damage), deprivation (re-striction of valued opportunities available to the victim), and social (im-pairment of the actor's desired face or social identity).

Muehlenhard and Schrag's (1991) analysis of coercion identified two basic forms—indirect and direct. *Indirect* includes all those pressures and inducements towards an implicit or explicit mandate of heterosexuality and of having sex. Thus, the degree to which society monolithically defines monogamy, heterosexuality, and sex as the primary ends of courtship is viewed as a strong cultural imperative that coerces people into having sex, forms of sex, or sex with certain types of partners. Furthermore, forms of inducement, such as fear of male reprisal, loss of status, economic loss, and so forth, also form indirect forms of coercion. Unfortunately, these forms represent widely discrepant modes of influence. A person who engages in sex because society produces a climate that reinforces heterosexual sex as a natural phase of a dating relationship is in a radically different situation than when a boss engages in implicit quid pro quo sexual harassment. In the former, society is partially (but still ambiguously) held to account, whereas in the latter, a particular person is influencing the victim and has particular punishments to employ in an implicitly contingent manner in the process of influence.

According to Muehlenhard and Schrag (1991), *direct* coercion occurs through verbal, chemical, or spontaneous means. Verbal coercion involves such things as threats to end the relationship, persistent arguments, making the victim feel guilty, questioning the person's sexual orientation, claiming biological necessity, and threatening to do self-harm. Coercion can also involve the use of alcohol or other drugs to diminish a person's ability to make decisions. The third form of direct coercion is labeled "rape without force," and involves a person spontaneously engaging in sexual activity, despite the victim's expression of dispreference. In essence, the perpetrator simply starts doing it copulating against the victim's explicit protest.

These varied conceptualizations of coercion identify at least two dimensions of coercion that frequently and ambiguously intertwine—intention and behavior. On the *intention* continuum, *coercion* is defined by the extent to which the victim's expressed preferences are ignored, disregarded, or simply violated. On the *behavioral* continuum, tactics are viewed as coercive to the extent that they are deceptive, exploitative, unilateral, or forceful. In all cases, the presumption is that the outcome of sex is a dispreferred alternative of the victim and a preferred outcome of the perpetrator. Interestingly, none of these dimensions alone are satisfactory as a definition of coercion. Force alone can be a preferred feature of sexual encounters (e.g., sadomasochism), and pursuer's preferences are often violated through simple refusal that is respected by the participants. Thus, sexual coercion is the expressed dispreferred inducement of sexual relations through force, threat of force, deceit, or the practical removal of choice from the victim. Rape, sexual aggression, and some unwanted sex represent subsets of the coercion continuum, which ranges, hypothetically, from mild dispreference and minor inducement to extreme dispreference and severe inducement. Behaviors cannot be aligned to permanent points along this continuum because preference and severity are subjective. For example, Struckman-Johnson and Struckman-Johnson (1991) found that although all five coercive strategies they studied (i.e., verbal, stimulation, mock force, intoxication, and physical force) tended to be viewed as unacceptable, there were significant differences due to tactic type, gender of rater, gender of tactic initiator and interaction effects with level of sexual precedence in the relationship.

THE SCOPE AND SIGNIFICANCE OF THE PROBLEM

If it seems laborious to identify the nature of sexual coercion, it is even more fraught with difficulty to estimate the true magnitude of the problem in society. One approach is to trust certain methods, instruments, and studies. Another is to trust the law of large numbers. The attempt is made here to trust the latter more. The following sections are interpretations made on the basis of summarizing 95 studies offering empirical estimates of the incidence of various forms of sexual coercion, inclusively covering over 80,000 subjects.

Incidence of Sexual Coercion

Given the many problems identified in defining coercion, it is understandably difficult to estimate the extent of coercion in society (Koss, 1996). "In viewing sexual violence as a continuum ... research on incidence becomes both a wider and a more complex area of investigation" (Kelly, 1987, p. 52). An attempt by Spitzberg (1997a) was made to provide the most reliable base for estimation. Over 95 studies that provided some form of comparable empirical estimate of sexual coercion were summarized in tabular form. The definitions and statistical reporting practices varied widely, requiring extensive interpretation and interpolation. The category of sexual coercion itself is distinct from the definition previously offered because the literature heavily relies on the nomenclature of the Sexual Experiences Survey. Furthermore, summary estimates (see Table 7.1) are generalized across time periods (e.g., "since the age of 16," "since high school," "during your lifetime," etc.), age of subject samples (e.g., adolescents, college, adults), and other sample characteristics (e.g., ethnicity, gender orientation, etc.). Consequently, it is still premature to place great confidence in these extrapolations. However, collectively, this summary represents a much larger sample of persons (over 83,000) and studies (over 95) than previous attempts at estimation. In addition, initial analyses reveal surprisingly few statistical differences based on such categories as date of study, duration since victimization, and type of sample (e.g., college vs. adult). To the extent that the numbers are reasonably accurate and classified appropriately, the summary statistics offer several intriguing conclusions.

First, by virtue of the research design and priority, it is obvious that the prevailing zeitgeist of sexual coercion is strongly gender asymmetric. Specifically, males are rarely viewed as victims relative to females, and females are virtually inconceivable as perpetrators. Judging strictly from this pattern, one would expect, and one does indeed find, that females report rates of victimization much higher than males.

Second, average female rape victimization is over 13%, and male victimization is close to 4% (Table 7.1). This does not represent the occurrence of repeated incidents of victimization for a given person, which may

TABLE 7.1

Statistical Summary Data Derived from Previous Studies (N=99 samples).

	Female Victimization	Female Perpetration	Male Victimization	Male Perpetration	General Victimization
	Mean Std. Dev. (Study N)	Mean Std. Dev. (Study N)	Mean Std. Dev. (Study N)	Mean Std. Dev. (Study N)	Mean Std. Dev. (Study N)
Rape	13.33 7.39 (48)	NA	3.58 3.70 (12)	4.73 5.14 (11)	8.80 5.31 (5)
Attempted Rape	18.40 12.81 (30)	NA	5.67 7.01 (6)	11.33 8.74 (3)	NA
Sexual Assault	22.24 18.59 (17)	3.67 3.06 (3)	8.00 2.71 (4)	10.67 8.82 (6)	8.50 6.36 (2)
Sexual Contact	23.57 20.72 (21)	8.75 9.67 (4)	6.17 4.71 (6)	13.40 16.26 (10)	9.00 1.41 (2)
Sexual Coercion	25.00 17.99 (27)	29.00 0.00 (1)	23.18 23.57 (11)	24.30 17.76 (10)	29.00 0.00 (1)

Source: Adapted from Spitzberg (1997a).

be substantial (Sorenson, Siegel, Golding, & Stein, 1991). The female-to-male victimization ratios of sexual assault (22.24/8.0 = 2.78) and attempted rape (18.40/5.67 = 3.25) are somewhat similar to that of rape (13.33/3.58=3.72). The ratio is highest for sexual contact (23.57/6.17 = 3.82), perhaps suggesting that males often make "moves" in courtship that make sexual contact, but stop short of rape or assault, presumably because of female resistance. The ratio (25.00/23.18=1.08) is actually close to unity for sexual coercion (typically defined as sex through persistence of arguments, intoxication, or use of authority). Thus, although the rates are generally gender asymmetric, they do not appear so divergent as to exclude the importance of studying male victims and female perpetrators.

Third, the ratios of female victimization to incidence of male perpetration for rape (13.33/4.73 = 2.82), attempted rape (18.40/11.33 = 1.62), and sexual contact (23.57/13.40 = 1.76), are high but are virtually isomorphic for sexual coercion (25.00/24.50 = 1.03). If these findings continue to be replicated, it is highly suggestive that the traditional assumption of strong self-report biases operating to underestimate male perpetration may need to be specified more rigorously.

In a relevant aside, several authors alarmingly viewed the findings that large percentages (27%–60%) of males indicate some "likelihood of raping" if they were assured of anonymity (e.g., Briere & Malamuth, 1983; Malamuth, 1981, 1989; Petty & Dawson, 1989; Tieger, 1981). However, other studies indicate that males overwhelmingly reject the legitimacy of rape (Cook, 1995; Mills & Granoff, 1992; Szymanski, Devlin, Chrisler, & Byse, 1993). Furthermore, likelihood of raping measures may correlate to acceptance of rape myths, but not to actual reported sexually coercive behavior (Greendlinger & Byrne, 1987). Indeed, in their nationally representative survey, Laumann et al. (1994) found that less than 0.5% of males and females "found either forcing another or being forced to have sex very appealing ... " (p. 160). The data in Table 7.1 are suggestive that "the use of coercive strategies by men is more the exception than the rule" (Quinn, Sanchez-Hucles, Coates, & Gillen, 1991, p. 25), and perhaps, by extension, that "most discrepancies in the desired levels of sexual intimacy do not result in the use of coercion" (O'Sullivan & Byers, 1996, p.64).

Fourth, the estimate of the percentage of all rapes that occur on dates reported by Spitzberg (1997a) is 14%. If the population estimate of female rape victimization is close to 13%, and 14% of this occurs in dating contexts, then it gives what is probably a reasonable estimate of the extent of courtship rape. The population estimate for experience of date rape would be around 1.5%. However, it should also be noted that some studies differentiate "date" from "lover," "spouse," and "good friend" perpetrators, any of which may involve courtship.

Fifth, the variances across studies are generally large, and for certain categories, they are huge. This suggests that type of sample, design, year of study, and perhaps regional characteristics mediate estimates of incidence. Several statistical tests were attempted relating year or decade of study on female rape victimization and no significant relationships emerged, suggesting that there is no consistent trend in this statistic over time. However, a more complete analysis of this data is beyond the scope of this chapter.

Sixth, the variances across studies also represent conceptual problems with the operationalization of the categories. The modal measure is clearly some version of Koss' Sexual Experiences Survey (SES), which has been the basis of extensive debate (e.g., Gilbert, 1991, 1993, 1995; Gylys &

McNamara, 1996; Koss, 1992a, 1992b, 1993; Porter & Critelli, 1992; Ross & Allgeier, 1996). Other analyses identified the considerable extent to which definitions affect estimates (e.g., Muehlenhard, Sympson, Phelps, & Highby, 1994) and understanding (e.g., Craig, 1990). The SES avoids some demand effects by avoiding the terms *rape, attempted rape*, and so forth. Instead, it provides 10 to 12 behavioral descriptions (e.g., "Have you ever had sexual intercourse with a man [woman] when you [she] didn't really want to because you [she] felt pressured by his [your] continual arguments?") and subjects who answer "yes" to any of certain groups of these descriptions constitute victims of one of the four basic categories (i.e., rape, attempted rape, sexual contact, sexual coercion). Given this type of measure, subjects who answer "yes" to certain of these descriptions were compared to subjects who self-attribute the label of having been raped. These latter victims are referred to as "unacknowledged victims" (e.g., Koss, 1985, 1988, 1989). Unacknowledged victims have reported less forceful encounters, less resolute refusal, and lower trauma (Layman et al., 1996).

Effects of Sexual Coercion

Most research on effects has emphasized rape and attempted rape, with strangers or acquaintances. Far less research investigated the effects of other forms of sexual coercion in courtship contexts. Sexual experiences in general, whether coercive or noncoercive, can have ambivalent effects, both when experienced in childhood and in adolescence (Kilpatrick, 1992; Wyatt et al., 1993). Furthermore, most effects research has been cross-sectional in design. There is the possibility that people who are anxious, fearful, depressed, psychotic, distrusting, and so forth put themselves at greater risk of sexual coercion in various ways. However, conceptually, there is strong reason to expect the causal order of sexual violation leading to trauma. The weight of the evidence, especially the longitudinal research, has largely been supportive of this causal order.

Rape trauma has been studied across a vast array of somatic, sociobehavioral, psychological, and affective realms. More recently, these various traumas were viewed as manifestations of a posttraumatic stress disorder related specifically to rape (Burgess & Holmstrom, 1974; Gidycz & Koss, 1991a, 1991b; Kilpatrick, Edmunds, & Seymour, 1992; Kilpatrick, Veronen, et al., 1987). Among the somatic symptoms studied include physical injury, stomach irritability, genito-urinary disturbance (e.g., vaginal discharge, burning with urination, etc.), sleep disorders, and loss of appetite (Burgess & Holmstrom, 1974). Among the affective symptoms noted are fear and anxiety (Gidycz, Coble, Latham, & Layman, 1993; Kelly & DeKeseredy, 1994; Kilpatrick, Resick, & Veronen, 1981), depression (Gidycz et al., 1993; Kilpatrick et al., 1992), anger, phobias (e.g., agoraphobia, fear of being alone, fear of sex, etc.), panic disorders, and obsessive–compulsive disorders. Among the psychological symptoms are included lower self-esteem, suspicion, distrust, confusion, guilt, desire for revenge, suicide ideation (Gidycz & Koss, 1989, 1991a; Kilpatrick et al., 1985; Mezey & King, 1989; Resick, 1993), and generally lowered psychological adjustment (Roth, Wayland, & Woolsey, 1990; Santello & Leitenberg, 1993). Among the sociobehavioral symptoms are changing one's daily routine and movements, changing one's telephone number and address, suicide attempts, and alcohol and drug abuse (Kilpatrick et al., 1992; Mezey & King, 1989).

Some research indicates that many victims experience a significant decrease in symptomology within months of the episode, but compared to nonvictims, generally remain at elevated levels for long periods of time (George, Veronen, & Resick, 1992; Kilpatrick et al., 1981; Kilpatrick et al., 1979; McCahill et al., 1979; Resick, 1993; Valentiner, Foa, Riggs, & Gershuny, 1996). In one of the few studies of male victims, it was found that males perceive far less negative short-term impact of unwanted sex than do females, and they are less likely to report long-term impacts (Struckman-Johnson, 1988). Male victims may view coercion as both highly unpleasant and inappropriate, but not necessarily traumatic (Struckman-Johnson & Struckman-Johnson, 1996). This is likely to be highly contextual, however, as other studies of male victims of sexual coercion find that large percentages report experiencing very negative effects (Hillman, O'Mara, Raylor-Robinson, & Harris, 1990; Struckman-Johnson et al., 1996) and a small study of male rape victims found "a wide range of distressing and disabling symptoms often experienced for years afterwards" (Mezey & King, 1989, p. 207). Some research also indicates that experience of sexual coercion in childhood (see Kendall-Tackett, Williams, & Finkelhor, 1993) is more traumatic than experience as an adult (e.g., Burnham et al., 1988). Finally, what little research explored the relationship generally found minor or no differences in the trauma experienced by stranger rape victims compared to acquaintance or date rape victims (e.g., Koss et al., 1988; Roth et al., 1990; cf. Katz, 1991).

Another intriguing and poorly understood finding is that the experience of sexual victimization appears to be a risk factor for future sexual victimization. In one study, Gidycz, Hanson, & Layman, (1995) observed:

"Women who had a history of victimization were 1.5–2 times more likely to be victimized during their first quarter of participation than those women without a history of victimization. Furthermore, women who were victimized during their initial quarter of participation were approximately three times as likely as those not victimized during that time to be revictimized during their second quarter of participation. (p. 24)

Other studies reveal that victimization is often not a one-time occurrence (Kelly & DeKeseredy, 1994; Koss et al., 1991; Russell, 1982a; Sorenson et al., 1991).

Excellent reviews are available on the effects of rape and sexual coercion (Koss & Harvey, 1991; Resick, 1993). The conclusions of these reviews, and of the vast majority of the studies performed, is that rape has significant and often devastating effects on female victims. These effects are most serious shortly after the victimization, but continue for extended periods of time. Importantly, acquaintance rape may have effects as serious as stranger rape, at least psychologically (Wiehe & Richards, 1995); attempted rape and sexual coercion can be equally traumatic as rape itself (Arata & Burkhart, 1996). Finally, it is significant that in addition to the impact that coercion has on its direct victims, nonvictims, especially women, often live in a more fearful and constrained world because of the possibility of sexual violence (Bohmer & Schwarz, 1996; Cook, 1995; Kelly & DeKeseredy, 1994; Stanko, 1990).

Sexual coercion is obviously a significant problem that adversely affects a significant number of people. Yet, the problem is still not well-understood in terms of its causes. Several theories have been developed to account for sexual coercion. These theories are not necessarily mutually exclusive and may even be complementary. Strangely, few studies of sexual coercion explicitly claim to be testing theories.

THEORIES OF SEXUAL COERCION

"Most sexual coercion research has been conducted atheoretically" (Byers & O'Sullivan, 1996, p. 3). However, in what work has been done, theories of sexual coercion can be roughly aligned along a continuum of determinism, from dispositional theories that seek the cause in distant evolutionary processes genetically reinforced over millenia through selective courtship processes to episodic theories that locate the cause of the sexual coercion purely in the dynamics of the coercive context itself (see Fig. 7.2). These characterizations are somewhat oversimplified for the purpose of review, but also represent basic themes common to the theories identified. A thorough examination of theories of sexual coercion is beyond the scope of this review (see Allgeier, 1987; Baron & Straus, 1989; Burkhart & Fromuth, 1991; Craig, 1990; Ellis, 1989; Muehlenhard et al., 1992; Nurius & Norris, 1996; Stock, 1991).

Biological Theories

Biological theories generally presume the relevance of natural selection on reinforcing adaptive mating strategies over time (Buss, 1994; Malamuth,

DISPOSITIONAL				EPISODIC
←---→				
Biological	**Socio-Cultural**	**Intra-psychic**	**Contextual**	**Interactional**
Socioevolutionary (Buss, 1994)	Feminism (Brownmiller, 1975; Russell, 1984)	Attitudes & Beliefs (e.g., Rape Myths) (Burt, 1980;	Opportunism (e.g., Alcohol, situation, etc.) (Abbey, 1991a)	Negotiation (Metts & Spitzberg, 1996)
Adaptationism (Ellis, 1989; Thornhill, 1996)	Sex Role Socialization (Mosher (& Anderson, 1986)	Personality & Psycho-pathology (e.g., Dominance) (Malamuth, 1989)	(Mis)Communication (Muehlenhard, 1988)	Coercion & Manipulation (Muehlenhard & Linton, 1987)
		Psychoanalytic		

<-----------------Social Learning---------------------->
(Scripts, Behavioral Modeling, Social SkillsDeficits,
Suspicion Schemata, Developmental Trauma, etc.)
(Byers, 1996; Metts & Spitzberg, 1996, Muehlenhard
& Falcon, 1990)

FIG. 7.2. Explanatory loci and exemplars of sexual coercion theories.

1996; Smuts, 1996; Thornhill, 1996; Thornhill & Thornhill, 1992). Given the asymmetric nature of pregnancy, gestation, and childrearing, and the evolutionary premium on knowing the genetic parentage of offspring, it is reasoned that males adopted rape as a strategy in their repertoire of mating techniques. Because the male's required investment in parenting is relatively brief, there is advantage to the male mating often and with multiple partners to assure the continuance of his genetic lineage. Because the primary criterion is successful mating, males tend to pursue females who will become pregnant and carry to term. This leads to a male preference for females with physical characteristics indicative of physical health and child-bearing potential. Females, in contrast, have extensive investments in parenting and therefore, look for signs of commitment, status, physical strength, and ability to provide. It follows that females become specialists in *gate keeping*, or regulating the selectivity component of sexual pursuit, in complement to males' specialization in the tactics of sexual pursuit—among them rape.

According to Ellis (1989), several basic hypotheses derive from evolutionary theory, including the following:

1. The tendency to rape is genetically influenced.
2. Rapes must lead to pregnancy sufficiently to outweigh the risks of punishment involved.
3. Rape victims tend to be younger (or revealing of childbearing characteristics).
4. Rapes tend to be resisted by the victim, especially when the perpetrator is sexually unattractive to the female.
5. Rapists tend to be less able to attract voluntary sexual partners.

Sociocultural and Intrapsychic Theories

These categories include theories positing a crucial role of culture and socialization in the reinforcement of rape (Warshaw & Parrot, 1991). Other theories in these categories focus on the products of these socialization practices in the forms of values, beliefs, and personality proclivities leading to rape (e.g., Marshall, Hudson, Jones, & Fernandez, 1995; Sarwer, Kalichman, Johnson, Early, & Akram, 1993). References to a "rape culture" are often indicative of these theoretical orientations. These two categories blend together in many cases because society and culture are often viewed as the source of people's attitudes, beliefs, and cognitive processing tendencies. The theoretical framework most common to these categories is some variation on social learning theory.

Social learning theory posits that a large component of social behavior is learned through direct observation and internalization of the behavior of models. These models are often those significant others in a person's developmental periods, but can also be imaginative (e.g., movie or comic book characters) or somewhat peripheral (e.g., social network or peers). To the extent that a person grows up in a context of violence, that violence becomes a normal part of that person's repertoire for coping with the environment. To the extent that violence and coercion are revealed as fundamentally, exclusively, or even intermittently effective tactics for coping with the social environment and are positively reinforced (e.g., by peer group pressure or success in valued courtship outcomes such as sex), the strategies of violence and coercion become preferred modes of interaction with the social environment. To the extent that culture represents violence as a male tactic for dealing with females, this asymmetry continues to be reinforced in behavior.

Over time, people are socialized into appropriate role behavior, as depicted in both actual (e.g., family, peers, and society) and imaginative (e.g., pornography, cartoons, etc.) interaction. This socialization leads (over time) to selective cognitive organization of information in accord with the broader patterns of society. Thus, if females are primarily depicted and reinforced for being the sexual gatekeepers and males reinforced for being the sexual pursuers, then mental representations of these roles, and their associated plans of action appropriate to relevant goals, are abstracted to provide efficient cognitive structures for organizing relevant social information. Such relatively stable organizations are known as scripts and exist at personal, interpersonal and cultural levels (Gagnon, 1990).

According to Ellis (1989), social learning theory leads to several basic predictions, including: (a) rapists adhere to rape-favorable attitudes more than nonrapists; (b) rapists reveal greater arousal to depictions of sexual violence or coercion; (c) exposure to violent pornography increases the tendency of males to rape; and (c) the greater the exposure to pornography that is demeaning or derogating to women, the more males adhere to similar attitudes and beliefs. Furthermore, researchers often assumed that people who do not learn appropriate models for their sexual and communicative behavior are deficient in social skills and thereby engage in sexual coercion for lack of more appropriate or competent tactics of courtship. Thus, (e) rapists tend to be less socially skilled than nonrapists.

Feminism also offers a socialization theory of sexual coercion, but one sufficiently distinct from social learning to merit attention. Although there are several versions of feminism, most assume that longstanding social and cultural traditions were established by men to subordinate women in ways favorable to men (Brownmiller, 1975). This results in women being deprived of their own voices through the exclusion of female access to positions of power, competence, and status beyond those favorable to men's positions. This pattern of subordination is reflected in various forms of male exploitation of females, including pornography, prostitution, and coercive sexuality.

Among the common types of empirical claims a feminist theory of rape would claim include (Ellis, 1989):

1. Rape is almost exclusively male-perpetrated against female victims.
2. Rape is related to status and power disparities.
3. Rape is motivated more by power than by sex.
4. Exposure to pornography and prostitution increase proclivity to rape
5. As societal sexual egalitarianism increases, rape incidence should decrease.
6. Rapists should adhere more to traditional sex-asymmetric attitudes than nonrapists.

Contextual Theories

Contextual theories are in fact rarely complete theories. Instead, they represent a complex of research investigations into the "opportunism" of sexual coercion. Specifically, many studies and investigators hypothesize that sexual coercion and rape are highly situational. The suggestion is that sex is a desired outcome (especially for males) and is pursued opportunistically. The factors that affect opportunity, relative to risk, include such characteristics as: who pays for the dating expense (Bostwick & DeLucia, 1992; Emmers & Allen, 1995b; Muehlenhard, Friedman, & Thomas, 1985; Muehlenhard & Linton, 1987;); what kind of date it was and whose place the partners go to after the date (Copenhaver & Grauerholz, 1991; Emmers & Allen, 1995b; Goodchilds et al., 1988; Koss, 1988; Muehlenhard et al., 1985); the sexual suggestiveness of the female's dress (Abbey, Cozzarelli, McLaughlin, & Harnish, 1987; Goodchilds et al., 1988; Muehlenhard & Linton, 1987); the consumption of alcohol or other psychoactive or debilitating drugs (Abbey, 1991a, Abbey, Ross, McDuffie, & McAusian, 1996b; Ageton, 1988; Alzenman & Kelley, 1988; Amir, 1971; Boeringer, Shehan, & Akers, 1991; Canterbury et al, 1993; Carter, Prentky, & Burgess, 1988; Copenhaver & Grauerholz, 1991; Gidycz et al., 1995; Harrington & Leitenberg, 1994; Himelein, 1995; Koss, 1988; Koss et al., 1988; Koss & Dinero, 1989; Muehlenhard & Linton, 1987; Norris & Cubbins, 1992; Seto & Barbaree, 1995; Small & Kerns, 1993; Ward, Chapman, Cohn, White, Williams, 1991); the privacy or relative seclusion of the physical environment (Copenhaver & Grauerholz, 1991; Emmers & Allen, 1995b; Koss, 1988; Muehlenhard & Linton, 1987; Murnen et al., 1989; O'Sullivan & Byers, 1993; Ward et al., 1991); the day of the week (Meilman & Haygood-Jackson, 1996); and the experience of foreplay (Kanin, 1957, 196,; 1984; Kanin & Parcell, 1977).

All of these factors were found in at least one study to increase the risk of sexual coercion. The implication is that virtually all people (especially males) are motivated to have sex and are capable of engaging in, and being victimized by, sexual coercion when the opportunity presents itself. Presumably the opportunity would need to be perceived as one in which the desirability of sex offsets the potential social (e.g., spoiled reputation, or loss of friends), physical (e.g., resistance with mace, or physical injury from resistance), and personal (e.g., being kicked out of school or work) risks involved. Finally, from this perspective, the experience of sexual coercion (both perpetration and victimization) is likely to be related to the amount of sexual experience and number of sexual partners (i.e., an opportunity effect). Indeed, studies indicate that number of previous sexual partners and experiences (Koss, 1985; Malamuth, Heavey, & Linz, 1993), as well as previous coercion victimization (Himelein, 1995) are predictive of sexual-coercion victimization risk.

Interactional Theories

There are surprisingly few theoretical endeavors in the realm of sexual coercion that could be considered truly interactional. The assumption of such a theory is that coercion results from the interaction, both nonverbal and discursive (Metts & Spitzberg, 1996; Muehlenhard, 1988). In essence, biology, culture, society, cognition, and context become relevant only through interpersonal interaction, and it is the interaction that determines the outcome. Coercion is not the inevitable product of pre-existing forces, but of the indeterminate ebb and flow of relational and sexual negotiation.

Although there is a dearth of actual theories in this domain, the presumption of interactional influence is commonly revealed in studies of strategies, tactics, the influence of nonverbal cues and courtship discourse. The study of sexual initiation moves, rejection moves, deception, threats, promises, sexual talk, persistent arguments, invocation of relational debts, and evocation of social or personal guilt all reflect the game of courtship. In this sometimes fun and sometimes dangerous game, rape is still viewed as one of the most powerful moves available, a move that carries risks, but that may be played none the less. Core predictions from this perspective might include the following:

- Sexually coercive persons hold more exploitative and game-like beliefs about gender relations than noncoercive persons.
- Socially underskilled persons are more likely to employ physical coercion, whereas socially hyperskilled persons are more likely to employ discursive and nonviolent tactics of coercion (Muehlenhard & Falcon, 1990).
- The mutual tactics employed account for more variance in the outcome of coercive encounters than do individual difference variables.
- The sequential coproduction of sexual pursuit and coercion is at least as important as each individual's frequency of tactic use in predicting sexual outcome.
- Most sexual coercion encounters (short of strong physical force) in courtship are interpreted by participants as acts of miscommunication, ambiguous resistance, overattribution of sexual interest, and mutual blame, rather than as strictly some person's fault.

Miscommunication, typically in the forms of discounting or clarity of resistance (Koss, 1985, 1988; Koss et al., 1988), the use of actual token resistance (Holcomb, Holcomb, Sondag, & Williams, 1991; Mills & Granoff, 1992), and misreading of cues of sexual consent (Abbey, 1982, 1987; Abbey & Melby, 1986; Abbey et al., 1987; Baier et al., 1991; Bridges, 1991; Byers & Lewis, 1988; Goodchilds et al., 1988; Kanin, 1957, 1969; Koeppel, Montague-Miller, O'Hair, & Cody, 1993; Koss, 1985, 1988, Koss et al., 1988; Kowalski, 1993; Malamuth & Brown, 1994; Malamuth et al., 1993; Muehlenhard & Andrews, 1985; Muehlenhard & Linton, 1987; Muehlenhard & MacNaughton, 1988; Muehlenhard & McCoy, 1991; O'Sullivan & Byers, 1992; Saal, Johnson, & Weber, 1989; Shea, 1993; Shotland & Craig, 1988), are implicated as a risk factor and a plausible causal factor in many studies. In addition, empathy (Christopher, Owens, & Stecker, 1993; Deitz, Blackwell, Daley, & Bentley, 1982) and knowledge of victim trauma (Hamilton & Yee, 1990) appear to diminish the likelihood of coercing another person, suggesting that interactionally oriented skills, such as affective understanding, may be important. If sexual coercion is interactionally produced, then the communicative nature of sexual pursuit needs elaboration.

AN INTERACTIONAL APPROACH

Most of these theories were elaborated and studied, as theories, for some time. However, although strategies and tactics are commonly studied, the assumption that the causal nature of sexual coercion is interactional in nature has seldom been considered appropriate for scholarly effort, much less formally articulated. Research and theory in violence and aggression is increasingly positing interactional and impression-management theories (e.g., Tedeschi & Felson, 1994). Considerable research indicates that the strategies and tactics of sexual compliance gaining significantly influence outcomes of courtship encounters. In addition, research on attributions of sexual coercion often reveal (mis)communication problems as likely candidates. Finally, research on individual difference variables, although generally revealing significant effects, also tend to reveal relatively small to moderate effects. It follows that it is time to pursue research and theory relevant to the co-construction of sexual coercion. This may not be a very politically correct pursuit, but to the extent that risk factors can be identified in people's behavior patterns, these risk markers will be far more visible than psychological traits and far more precedent to the actual violence of rape and rape resistance than mace and stun guns.

The Tactical Face of Coercion

Given the ethical constraints on studying such sensitive events as sexual coercion, most research is understandably self-report and retrospective or imaginative in nature. With this limitation in mind, the behavior of sexual compliance gaining is examined. The literature is disparate in measurement schemata and research intentions. Consequently, many of the categories employed to represent sexual compliance-gaining behavior are relatively uninformative. For example, *intimidation* is understood easily enough as a term, but what it looks like in terms of actual behaviors is not likely to produce much consensus. *Verbal manipulation* seems an apropos summary of something many people do, yet there seem to be so many techniques of verbal manipulation that perhaps the category does a disservice to an understanding of the process. As a result of such divergent terminologies, it is difficult to compare findings across studies.

One way of summarizing studies is to make a general distinction between strategies and tactics. Strategies are viewed as functional game plans or goals, with tactics as the plays and techniques by which the strategies are pursued. Thus, studies examined the use of tactical instantiations of many strategies, including enticement or temptation (e.g., Amir, 1971; Muehlenhard & Cook, 1988; Struckman-Johnson & Struckman-Johnson, 1994: "bribe"), persuasion (e.g., Christopher & Frandsen, 1990: "logic and reason;" Koss, 1988: "reason;" Murnen et al., 1989; Ward et al., 1991: "verbal"; Struckman-Johnson & Struckman-Johnson, 1994; Yegidis, 1986), punishment (e.g., Christopher & Frandsen, 1990: "antisocial;" Struckman-Johnson & Struckman-Johnson, 1994: "love withdrawal"); verbal or psychological pressure (e.g., Christopher & Frandsen, 1990; Koss et al., 1987; Struckman-Johnson, 1988; Struckman-Johnson & Struckman-Johnson, 1991), threats (e.g., Christopher, 1988; Copenhaver & Grauerholz, 1991; Kanin, 1984, 1985, Koss et al., 1988; Mahoney, Shively, & Traw, 1986; Mosher & Anderson, 1986; Murnen et al., 1989; Struckman-Johnson & Struckman-Johnson, 1994; Yegidis, 1986), intimidation (e.g., Amir, 1971; Yegidis, 1986), intoxication (e.g., Boeringer et al., 1991; Kanin, 1985; Mosher & Anderson, 1986; Muehlenhard & Cook, 1988; Struckman-Johnson, 1988; Struckman-Johnson & Struckman-Johnson, 1991, 1994; Yegidis, 1986), deception (e.g., Cochran & Mays, 1990; Fischer, 1992; Kanin, 1985; McCormick, 1979; Miller & Marshall, 1987; Muehlenhard & Falcon, 1990; Poppen & Segal, 1988; Spitzberg, Marshall, & Cupach, 1996; Struckman-Johnson & Struckman-Johnson, 1991: "mock force;" Knox, Schact, Holt, & Turner, 1993; Tooke & Camire, 1991), persistence (e.g., Christopher, 1988; Koss et al., 1987; Mahoney et al., 1986: "ignore protests;" Ward et al., 1991: "just did it"), physical restraint (e.g., Copenhaver & Grauerholz, 1991: "pin down;" Kanin, 1984: "physical strength;" Koss, 1988: "held down;" Koss et al., 1988: "holding/twisting;" Mahoney et al., 1986: "physically restraining;" Spitzberg et al., 1996; Struckman-Johnson, 1988; Struckman-Johnson & Struckman-Johnson, 1994), and force (e.g., Christopher, 1988; Copenhaver & Grauerholz, 1991; Kanin, 1984; Koss, 1988; Koss et al., 1988; Mahoney et al., 1986; Mosher & Anderson, 1986; Muehlenhard & Cook, 1988; Murnen et al., 1989; Spitzberg et al., 1996; Struckman-Johnson, 1988; Struckman-Johnson & Struckman-Johnson, 1994; Ullman & Knight, 1992; Ward et al., 1991; Yegidis, 1986). Finally, rape itself may be viewed as an extreme form of sexual compliance-gaining strategy (Buss, 1996; Buss & Schmitt, 1993; Thornhill, 1996). A somewhat simpler a priori typology is in Table 7.2.

Some studies attempted, through various means, to identify reasonable typologies of strategies. McCormick (1979; see also LaPlante, McCormick, & Brannigan, 1980) developed an a priori set of sexual pursuit and resistance strategies consisting of reward, coercion, logic, information, manipulation, body language, deception, moralizing, relationship conceptualizing, and seduction. Perper and Weis (1987) coded seduction essays

TABLE 7.2.

A Priori Classification of Sexual Coercion Tactics Identified in the Literature

PRESSURE & PERSISTENCE

Other person was too aroused to stop (Anderson & Cummings, 1993; Byers & Eno, 1991; Miller & Marshall, 1987; Mills & Granoff, 1992; Struckman-Johnson & Struckman-Johnson, 1991)

Verbal persuasion (George et al., 1992; Murnen et al., 1989; Sorenson et al., 1987; Yegidis, 1986)

Bribe (Sorenson et al., 1987)

Made to feel inadequate (Poppen & Segal, 1988)

Psychological or verbal pressure (Sorenson et al., 1987; Struckman-Johnson, 1988; Struckman-Johnson & Struckman-Johnson, 1991)

Said things to make me feel guilty

Verbal coercion (Byers & Eno, 1991)

Continual arguments (Anderson & Cummings, 1993; Miller & Marshall, 1987; Poppen & Segal, 1988; Ward et al., 1991)

DECEPTION

Surprise

Saying things the other person doesn't mean (Anderson & Cummings, 1993)

Said things that later proved to be untrue (e.g., I love you) (Waldner-Haugrud & Magruder, 1995)

Falsely profess love (Kanin, 1985; Kirkendall, 1961)

Falsely promise pinning, engagement, or marriage (Kanin, 1985)

Mock force (Struckman-Johnson & Struckman-Johnson, 1991)

Lies (Poppen & Segal, 1988)

Tricked (Mills & Granoff, 1992)

THREAT

Threaten to terminate relationship (love withdrawal) (Anderson & Cummings, 1993; Kanin, 1985; Miller & Marshall, 1987; Sorenson et al., 1987)

Threaten to leave person stranded (Kanin, 1985)

Verbal threats (or blackmail) (George et al., 1992; Murnen et al., 1989; Ward et al., 1991; Yegidis, 1986)

Threaten/intimidate by size or strength (physical intimidation) (George et al., 1992; Mills & Granoff, 1992; Sorenson et al., 1987; Yegidis, 1986)

Threats of bodily harm or force (Anderson & Cummings, 1993; Copanhaver & Grauerholz, 1991; George et al., 1992; Koss et al., 1988; Sorenson et al., 1987; Ward et al., 1991)

Weapon (displayed/threatened) (Copenhaver & Grauerholz, 1991; George et al., 1992; Koss et al., 1988; Sorenson et al., 1987)

PHYSICAL RESTRAINT

Just did it (Ward et al., 1991)

Mild physical (Murnen et al., 1989)

Intoxication (George et al., 1992; Kanin, 1985; Mills & Granoff, 1992; Sorenson et al., 1987; Struckman-Johnson, 1988; Struckman-Johnson & Struckman-Johnson, 1991; Yegidis, 1986)

Physical force or restraint (Anderson & Cummings, 1993; Byers & Eno, 1991; Poppen & Segal, 1988; Sorenson et al., 1987; Struckman-Johnson, 1988; Ward et al., 1991)

Twisting arm, holding down (Koss et al., 1988; Copenhaver & Grauerholz, 1991)

Pin down (Copenhaver & Grauerholz, 1991; Koss, 1988)

PHYSICAL FORCE/INJURY

Strong physical force (Murnen et al., 1989)

Physical harm (George et al., 1992; Sorenson et al., 1987)

Hitting, slapping, pushing (Copenhaver & Grauerholz, 1991; Koss, 1988; Koss et al., 1988; Yegidis, 1986)

Choking, beating (Koss et al., 1988; Yegidis, 1986)

Weapon (used) (Ageton, 1983; Copenhaver & Grauerholz, 1991; Koss, 1988; Koss et al., 1988; Sorenson et al., 1987; Yegidis, 1986)

Injury from a weapon

into an eight strategy scheme: environmental or situational strategies (e.g., dress, drink, etc.), verbal strategies (e.g., sexy romantic talk, compliments, etc.), nonverbal strategies (e.g., eye contact, touch, etc.), contingency strategies (e.g., recalcitrant male, "if–then," etc.), masculine sexual initiative (e.g., man takes over), nonproceptive themes without masculine sexual assertion (e.g., happens naturally), sexual limitation, and experience. Hirsch and Paul (1996) categorized mating tactics into the three broad functional strategic categories of quality (e.g., interacting with friends and family; discussions of values and goals; and expending resources of time, effort, and money), quantity (e.g., threats, sexual talk, physical contact, and getting her alone), and shared (e.g., flattery and promises). Quality tactics are oriented toward long-term mate bonding, quantity tactics are oriented toward multiple short-term matings, and shared tactics are a hybrid between these orientations. The tactics in these strategies were further coded into an ordinal continuum of categorically honest, relatively honest, relatively exploitative, and categorically exploitative. Buss (1988) categorized 104 mating tactics into two broad categories—intersexual, consisting of direct guarding tactics (e.g., vigilance, concealment of mate, monopolization of mate's time, etc.), negative inducements (e.g., infidelity threat, emotional manipulation, derogation of competitors, etc.), and positive inducements (e.g., resource display, sexual inducements, enhancement of physical appearance, etc.), and intrasexual, including public signals of possession (e.g., verbal signals, physical signals, ornamentation, etc.) and negative inducements (e.g., derogation of mate to competitors, threats, violence, etc.).

Several other studies attempted more dimensional approaches to strategy identification. Christopher and Frandsen (1990) factor analyzed sexual compliance-gaining tactics and found five dimensions: antisocial (covert) antisocial (overt), emotional and physical closeness, logic and persuasion, and pressure and manipulation. Mosher and Anderson (1986) factor analyzed coercive tactics and derived a six-factor solution: sexual force, drugs and alcohol, verbal manipulation, angry rejection, anger expression, and threat. Muehlenhard and Cook (1988) factor analyzed reasons for people engaging in unwanted sex, and found many of the same types of strategies: enticement, physical coercion, intoxication, altruism, inexperience, peer pressure, termination of relationship (threats), popularity, partner's verbal coercion, sex-role concerns, reluctance, partner's threat of self-harm, and family pressure.

In regard to three of the strategies, there is considerable differentiation of specific tactics across studies. Deception was studied under several guises, including falsely professing love (Kanin, 1985), making false promises (Kanin, 1985), and mock force (e.g., Struckman-Johnson & Struckman-Johnson, 1991). Tooke and Camire (1991) inductively developed an extensive listing of deceptive tactics, which they categorized into two broad categories: intrasexual tactics (e.g., sexual promiscuity, indifference, appearance alteration, exaggerated superiority, etc.) and intersexual tactics (e.g., dominance or resources, enhanced appearance or body, sexual intentions, deception involving third parties, etc.). Threats also seem to come in many guises, including verbal threats (e.g., Kanin, 1984; Murnen et al., 1989), threats to terminate the relationship (Muehlenhard & Cook, 1988), threats to leave the person stranded (e.g., Kanin, 1985), threats of force (e.g., Christopher, 1988; Mosher & Anderson, 1986), threats with weapons (Amir, 1971; Copenhaver & Grauerholz, 1991; Mahoney et al., 1986; Struckman-Johnson & Struckman-Johnson, 1994; Yegidis, 1986) and threats of bodily harm (Copenhaver & Grauerholz, 1991; Koss et al., 1988). Force is also a highly differentiated category. In addition to types of physical restraint, it includes such tactics as arm twisting (Copenhaver & Grauerholz, 1991; Koss et al., 1988), slapping (Koss et al., 1988), physical roughness (Yegidis, 1986), use of fists (Kanin, 1984), hitting (Koss, 1988; Koss et al., 1988), and the use of weapons (Belknap, 1989; Copenhaver & Grauerholz, 1991; Koss, 1988; Mahoney et al., 1986; Yegidis, 1986).

As might be implied by the diversity of tactics and strategies, generalizations are rather difficult. Nevertheless, it appears reasonable to conclude from these studies that strictly in regard to courtship sexual coercion, persistence is probably the most common strategy. The most common forceful tactic appears to be holding the person down, relying on superior weight, and strength (Copenhaver & Grauerholz, 1991), and perhaps the implicit threat of escalating force or the apparent uselessness of resistance. Most research in the area of courtship and date rape suggests that the use of weapons is rare (Belknap, 1989; Copenhaver & Grauerholz, 1991; Kilpatrick, 1992; Laumann et al., 1994; Mahoney et al., 1986; Yegidis, 1986; cf. Amir, 1971). Furthermore, injury, beatings, and severe physical nonsexual aggression are similarly rare (Hannan & Burkhart, 1993; Kanin, 1984; Koss, 1988; Koss et al., 1988; Muehlenhard & Linton, 1987; cf. Belknap, 1989). Kanin's (1984) retrospective interview study of date rapists indicated that males' use of pinning the woman down was the maximum level of violence they would have employed.

Finally, despite the considerable effort at getting subjects to report what strategies and tactics they experienced or used, little is known about the evaluations of these behaviors. Hirsch and Paul (1996) found that subjects tend to view quantity oriented strategies as exploitative, and quality strategies as honest. Buss (1988; Greer & Buss, 1994) found that the tactics of being nice, kind, considerate, affectionate, and complimentary were viewed as most effective, the tactics of violence and snooping through mate's possessions were viewed as relatively ineffective, and males and females had strikingly similar ratings of effectiveness of mating tactics.

Struckman-Johnson and Struckman-Johnson (1991) had subjects rate the acceptability of five coercive strategies as displayed in vignettes. None of the strategies were perceived over the midpoint in acceptability, ranging on a 7-point scale from verbal pressure ($\overline{X}$ = 3.30), stimulation ($\overline{X}$ = 3.03), mock force ($\overline{X}$ = 2.30), intoxication ($\overline{X}$ = 1.46), to physical force ($\overline{X}$ = 1.41), although women were less accepting of all strategies than men. Rape itself is strongly rejected by members of both sexes in terms of its acceptability (Cook, 1995), although this attitude was found to be very sensitive to conditions, such as the extent of previous sex in the relationship, intoxication level, amount of money and/or time invested in the relationship, clothing, foreplay, arousal (Byers, 1988; Goodchilds et al., 1988; Hall et al., 1986), ethnicity (Fischer, 1987), attitudes about gender relations (Hall et al., 1986), and prior sexual aggression (Kanin, 1985).

The tactical face of coercion in courtship encounters is generally one of persistence, physical mismatch, physical restraint, and implied threat. The tactical face of responses to coercion appear at least as diverse. Verbal refusal, pleading, physical struggle and resistance, turning cold, running away or fleeing the scene, crying, and screaming are common responses (e.g., Copenhaver & Grauerholz, 1991; Kanin, 1969; Koss, 1985; Koss et al., 1988; Murnen et al., 1989), although a far greater variety of tactics are available (Carter et al., 1988; Furby, Fischhoff, & Morgan, 1992). Certainly, it appears that some form of obvious resistance is offered in the vast majority of instances (e.g., Sorenson et al., 1987), although in one study, "nothing" is noted as a response to unwanted sex in a third of the instances (Murnen et al., 1989). In addition, in courtship contexts, resistance may be initially offered but not persistently (Kanin, 1984). It is difficult to know if this is due to the perceived threat of resistance, the perceived uselessness of resistance, the perceived relational costs of resistance, or some combination of these concerns.

Several binds appear to be at work in courtship encounters. People tend to go out with people to whom they are attracted and with whom an ongoing relationship is often desired. Resistance is viewed as a threat to the pursuer's face, and yet, without that resistance, a person becomes a victim. In general, the more direct (Metts, Cupach, & Imahori, 1992) and distributive (Burgoyne & Spitzberg, 1992) the resistance, the more incompetent the resistance is perceived to be. Men and women also seem to differ in their perceptions of resistance effectiveness (Brady, Chrisler, Hosdale, Osowiechi, & Veal, 1991) and the relational implications of resistance (Motley & Reeder, 1995), although there do not appear to be substantial sex differences in the usage of resistance tactics (Emmers & Allen, 1995a; Rosenthal & Peart, 1996). The effectiveness of resistance tactics is unclear. Some research suggests that physical resistance is effective in avoiding sexual attack and injury (Bart, 1981), but other studies indicate that physical resistance is associated with increased injury (Atkeson, Calhoun, & Morris, 1989), even when the coercer is an intimate (Bachman & Carmody, 1994). Active avoidance strategies (e.g., running away or screaming) appear to be reasonably effective in acquaintance rapes (Levine-MacCombie & Koss, 1986), although ironically, acquaintance rapes may be harder to avoid in general than stranger rapes (Bart, 1981). Thus, women tend to view resistance as threatening to the relationship, and this risk is often viewed with considerable ambivalence, despite the alternative of sexual victimization and the finding that most men tend not to find sexual resistance by females very disconfirming (Motley & Reeder, 1994, 1995).

Sexual compliance-gaining and sexual compliance-resisting tactics do not occur in abstract space. They are produced and coproduced in contexts. To the extent that people attend to contextual features in their interaction, it is assumed in the interactional approach that contexts play a significant role in mediating the use and influence of sexual compliance-gaining tactics. To the extent that features of the coercive interaction tend to co-occur with certain features of the context, it evidences such a potential mediating role.

The Contextuality of Coercion

Sexual coercion is often a premeditated, willful activity. Yet, it reflects considerable contextual opportunism. The confluence of contextual factors seems at least as important as other psychological (e.g., rape myth acceptance) and societal factors (e.g., status incongruity) in predicting sexual coercion in courtship relations. Several contextual factors have been identified, some rather obvious (e.g., coercion tends to occur in relatively private or secluded environments, such as his or her place or the car; Copenhaver & Grauerholz, 1991; Emmers & Allen, 1995b; Goodchilds et al., 1988; Koss, 1988; Muehlenhard & Linton, 1987; Murnen et al., 1989; O'Sullivan & Byers, 1993; Ward et al., 1991) and others rather subtle (e.g., who paid for, the date, who drove, or who asked for the date; Bostwick & DeLucia, 1992; Emmers & Allen, 1995b; Muehlenhard & Linton, 1987; Muehlenhard et al., 1985). Less formal, party-oriented dates appear to be riskier than more formal dates (e.g., going to a theater or to dinner; Muehlenhard et al., 1985). In addition, the stage of the dating relationship may influence the occurrence of sexual coercion, which appears more likely in early rather than later stages of dating (Kanin & Parcell, 1977, 1984; Muehlenhard & Linton, 1987; Quinn et al., 1991). This reflects continuing findings that males tend to expect sexual intercourse to occur sooner in relationships (Knox & Wilson, 1981; McCabe & Collins, 1984), are more accepting of casual sex (Oliver & Hyde, 1993), and expect greater levels of sexual involvement than do females (Mongeau & Johnson, 1995).

Alcohol was implicated as a strong risk factor in regard to sexual coercion (see Abbey, 1991a; Abbey et al., 1996a, 1996b). Several studies found at least some significant effect on the risk of sexual coercion based on reports of one or both of the parties drinking (e.g., Ageton, 1988; Alzenman & Kelley, 1988; Amir, 1971; Boeringer et al., 1991; Canterbury et al., 1993; Copenhaver & Grauerholz, 1991; Harrington & Leitenberg, 1994; Himelein, 1995; Koss, 1988; Koss et al., 1988; Koss & Dinero, 1989; Muehlenhard & Linton, 1987; Norris & Cubbins, 1992; Small & Kerns, 1993; Ward et al., 1991). However, in the only prospective study, alcohol was found to be a risk factor at Time 1, but not at Time 2 or 3 (Gidycz et al., 1995). That is, re-victimization was not affected by alcohol use, but its use did affect the first instance of sexual aggression in the study. This suggests that alcohol plays a complex and very episodic role in sexual aggression. It is difficult to ascertain the extent to which intoxication is a strategically conscious action, or more a common activity that happens to co-occur or contribute to the efficacy of other concurrent strategies.

In adolescence, reinforcement from a person's social network and peers has a significant influence on sexual coercion. A person's friends and peer group can reinforce the appropriateness of coercive behavior by modelling it, and talking about it as a normatively accepted practice (e.g., Ageton, 1988; Alder, 1985; Drout, Becker, Bukkosy, & Mansell, 1994; Hall & Flannery, 1984). In addition, a person's reputation with a given peer group may be facilitated by the number of "notches on the bedpost" scored by the person (Kanin, 1985). A person may also simply feel a conformity effect that leads to engaging in unwanted sex (Small & Kerns, 1993). The effects of peer pressure can operate among college-age students as well, such as with the fraternity or male athletic cultures of sexual pursuit (Boeringer et al., 1991; Kalof, 1993; Melnick, 1992). However, some research indicates that relatively few adolescents feel pressured by their peers in regard to sexual behavior (Sexuality Information and Education Council of the United States, 1994).

The role of context does not carry necessary implications for the "power versus sex" interpretations of sexual coercion. People planning to coerce may strategically manipulate contextual events. However, what little research exists suggests that courtship sexual coercion is not highly planned (Baier et al., 1991; Johnson & Sigler, 1996; cf. Amir, 1971). Instead, some evidence indicates that date rapists plan on seduction, but not rape (Kanin, 1984). In characterizing the contextuality of date rape, Kanin (1984) concluded that "A strong fortuitous element seems to be involved here. Put simply, a substantial number of these rapes occurred because the 'right man' (sexually aggressive and determined) did the 'right thing' (presented a level of force not usually encountered in dating) to the 'right girl' (easily frightened or inebriated)" (p. 102).

Factors of Miscommunication

An interactional approach depends on the assumption that many factors work to put people's tactical accomplishments at odds with one another in sexually coercive contexts. Such an approach assumes that sexual compliance gaining is problematic in terms of the meanings attributed to tactics and the contextual motives of the interactants. If courtship is often oriented toward opposing or incompatible objectives and if various factors conspire to problematize sexual compliance interactions, then sexual coercion becomes a more probable outcome. The reasoning is that coercion is used to compensate for the lack of efficacy of more noncoercive means, and it will be less certain that coercion has occurred, less obvious what people's reactions should be, and less obvious whose fault it is. Several such factors were evidenced in the literature on motives and scripts surrounding the sexual aspect of courtship.

Differences in Motive

Whether accounted for by socioevolutionary (e.g., Buss & Schmitt, 1993; Palmer, 1991; Thornhill, 1996) or sociocultural (e.g., MacKinnon, 1989) forces, it is widely accepted that males and females generally pursue distinct mating strategies for distinct reasons. According to socioevolutionary theory, females, given their need for long-term partner investment, are attracted to signs of status, willingness and ability to invest (time, effort, money, etc.), ambition, dependability and reliability, intelligence, size and strength, and commitment (Brigman & Knox, 1992; Buss, 1988, 1994). Women are more likely to pursue sex with men who show signs of investing in long-term, enduring, monogamous relationships. Men, given the potential genetic success of mating often and with many different partners, are instead attracted to signs of fertility, such as youth, physical attractiveness, physical health, and fidelity (Buss, 1988, 1994). Cultural factors, including divergent sex-role socialization, status disparities between males and females, and media messages reinforce similar patterns of behavior (Clark & Lewis, 1977; Russell, 1984; Stock, 1991). Some authors even attempted to locate such gender-based differences in the actual biology of the sexes (e.g., Kemper, 1990).

The result of such divergent motives is a divergence in mating strategies. Males, more than females, engage in quantity strategies, focusing "on short-term matings with little or no paternal investment" (Hirsch & Paul, 1996, p. 56). Females, more than males, engage in quality strategies, seeking long-term paternal investment. A result of such strategy differences is that males are more likely to specialize in and employ a wider variety of sexual compliance-gaining tactics, including coercive tactics, and females specialize in and employ a wider variety of sexual compliance-resisting tactics (Buss & Schmitt, 1993; Grauerholz & Serpe, 1985; Hirsch & Paul, 1996; LaPlante et al., 1980; McCormick, 1979; O'Sullivan & Byers, 1992; Paul & Hirsch, 1996; Perper & Weis, 1987).

Perceptual Differences.   Another manifestation of these differences in motive is that men experience a more sexualized world than women. Men, compared to women, engage in more autoerotic activity, display preferences for more sexual partners, use a more diverse set of sexual techniques, and have more elaborate sexual scripts (Laumann et al., 1994; Oliver & Hyde, 1993). Men think about, are aroused by, and fantasize about sex more than women (Greendlinger & Byrne, 1987; Knoth, Boyd, & Singer, 1988; Leitenberg & Henning, 1995; Loren & Weeks, 1986). Men expect sex earlier in relationships (Knox & Wilson, 1981; McCabe & Collins, 1984; Mongeau & Johnson, 1995), initiate and consider initiating sex more often (Byers & Heinlein, 1989), and are far more accepting and desirous of casual or anonymous sex (Clark, 1990; Clark & Hatfield, 1989; Hendrick & Hendrick, 1995; Oliver & Hyde, 1993; Symons & Ellis, 1989). Finally, men attribute more sexual intention and seductiveness to women's behavior than women intend (Abbey, 1991b; Bostwick & DeLucia, 1992; Harnish, Abbey, & DeBono, 1990; Johnson, Stockdale, & Saal, 1991; Koeppel et al., 1993; Kowalski, 1993; Saal et al., 1989; Shotland & Craig, 1988; cf. McCornack, Avery, & Bidol, 1995; Shea, 1993; Sigal, Gibbs, Adams, & Derfler, 1988).

The evidence seems clear that males and females differ in sexual motives, tactics, and perceived roles in regard to each other (Sigler & Curry, 1995). One approach to integrating many of these differences into an interactional framework is script theory (Gagnon, 1990; Laumann & Gagnon, 1995). Scripts are cognitive structures that organize information on plans, actions, and episodes. To the extent that socioevolutionary and sociocultural patterns of gendered behavior re-occur over time, it is reasonable to expect that people will incorporate these patterns into their cognition as sets of categorical and normative expectancies (cf. Kemper,

1990). However, to the extent that these scripts specify incompatible roles, role conflict and communication problems become more likely. There are several sources in the traditional courtship script of North American culture that increase the likelihood of miscommunication and communication difficulties (see Metts & Spitzberg, 1996, for review).

Distortions of Overreliance on Scripts

If scripts are relatively stable cognitive structures relied on for guiding action alternatives in courtship and sexual encounters, then they are likely to enhance cognitive efficiency, but may also increase the likelihood of miscommunication and sexual conflict. If males and females tend to operate by somewhat incompatible scripts and if they follow these scripts too rigidly, then the scripts may guide the interactants into divergent paths of behavior. There are several reasons to expect that scripts facilitate miscommunication-based sexual coercion.

First, to the extent that scripts are stable and enduring over time, both for individuals and for society, it follows that when a person deviates from the traditional script it may be difficult for the other person to understand and cope with such deviations. Furthermore, the potential rigidity of such scripts make it difficult to adapt new behavioral routines to such deviations. Abbey's (1987) work indicates that misperceptions of friendly behavior occur often. People may be unclear how to navigate the waters of platonic cross sex friendships when flirtatious and immediacy behaviors are displayed (Egland, Spitzberg, & Zormeier, 1996).

Second, a particular set of script elements that were found in large numbers of people is rape myth acceptance (RMA) and the associated complex of attitudes, including adversarial sex-attitudes, sexual conservatism, sex role stereotyping, and acceptance of interpersonal violence (Burt, 1980). Rape myths include beliefs such as "women who get raped while hitchhiking get what they deserve," and "a woman who goes to the home or apartment of a man on their first date implies that she is willing to have sex." Newman and Colon (1994) found four relatively self-explanatory factors of rape myths: rape only happens to women who provoke it, disbeliefs of rape claims, victim responsible for rape, and rape reports as manipulation. This complex of attitudes and beliefs carries obvious implications for the interpretation of courtship scripts. Despite extensive research (Lonsway & Fitzgerald, 1994; Malamuth, 1981), several studies find no or only relatively small effects of the RMA complex of attitudes on coercive experiences (e.g., Anderson & Cummings, 1993; Briere & Malamuth, 1983; Burke, Stets, & Pirog-Good, 1988; Byers & Eno, 1991; Christopher, London, & Owens, 1990; Greendlinger & Byrne, 1987; Himelein, 1995; Koss, 1985; Koss, Leonard, Beezley, & Oros, 1985; Koss

& Dinero, 1989; Malamuth, Linz, Heavey, Barnes, & Acker, 1995; Margolin et al., 1989; Muehlenhard & Linton, 1987; Murphy, Coleman, & Hayes, 1986; Struckman-Johnson & Struckman-Johnson, 1992; Vogel & Himelein, 1995; cf. Malamuth, Sockioskie, Koss, & Tanaka, 1991; Malamueth et al., 1993). The possibility of very subtle influences of these beliefs, however, is suggested by several findings. Marx and Gross (1995) found adherence to such myths related ($r = -.22$) to response latency in reacting to token resistance messages. Murphy et al. (1986) found small but statistically significant correlations ($r = -.15$ to $-.20$) between rape-supportive beliefs and ability to discriminate friendly from seductive female cues. Males high in such beliefs tend to overattribute sexual interest to female behavior (Kowalski, 1993). Although males tend to adhere to such beliefs more than females (Holcomb et al., 1991; Szymanski et al., 1993), females significantly overattribute such beliefs to males (Edmonds & Cahoon, 1993), who, as with females, tend overwhelmingly to reject such beliefs (Giacopassi & Dull, 1986; Gilmartin-Zena, 1987). Women victims of nonconsenual intercourse, who possess more stereotyped rape scripts (i.e., violent stranger perpetrator), are less likely to label their experience as rape (Kahn, Mathie, & Torgler, 1994). Such miscues, attributions, and misattributions may substantially increase the risks of misinterpretation of interpersonal behavior.

Third, the double standard is still alive and well in much of society. The double standard is an attitude complex that considers it acceptable for males to pursue sex qua sex, without implications for commitment, whereas females are supposed to pursue sex qua relationship (Krueger, 1996; Muehlenhard, 1988; Muehlenhard & McCoy, 1991). Such a double standard has numerous script implications, including that males, compared to females, are permitted to lose their virginity earlier, engage in more infidelity, and pursue sex with forceful persistence and relative singlemindedness. However, they also simultaneously make the appropriateness and legitimacy of resistance ambiguous.

Fourth, courtship and flirtation, in general, and sexual compliance gaining, in particular, rely heavily on nonverbal communication (Abbey & Melby, 1986; Abbey et al., 1987; Egland et al., 1996; Fichten, Tagalakis, Judd, Wright, & Ansel, 1992; Garcia & Derfel, 1983; Givens, 1978; Kirkendall, 1961; cf. Goodchilds et al., 1988; Kowalski, 1993; McCormick & Jones, 1989; Muehlenhard, Danoff-Burg, & Powch, 1986). Nonverbal behavior is more iconic, but less capable of metacommunicative clarification than verbal communication. To the extent that explicit verbal communication may be viewed as diminishing the romance of the context, people may rely extensively on reading between the lines in attributing sexual intentions. Furthermore, males appear to attribute considerable importance to the woman's clothing in determining sexual intentions (Abbey & Melby, 1986; Abbey et al., 1987; Muehlenhard & Linton, 1987). Add to this that males tend to be less nonverbally sensitive than females (Hall, 1984) and the possibilities for operating according to divergent scripts appear manifold.

Fifth, arousal, a surprisingly overlooked feature of sexual encounters, can lead to distortions of cognitive processing. Several studies (Bajracharya, Sarvela, & Isberner, 1995; Kanin, 1957, 1969; Kanin & Parcell, 1977) indicate that foreplay is a frequent precursor of sexual coercion. The suggestion that arousal is a strong influence was particularly noted in Kanin's (1984) interviews of self-admitted date rapists. Not one of the interviewees claimed any planning of the rape, although virtually all planned for seduction. In accounting for their rape, "of paramount impor-tance, over 90 percent dwelled upon their perception of their compan-ions' extreme sexual arousal, which, in turn, intensified their own sexual arousal to the extent that they experienced a rather exaggerated selective perception of the females' receptivity" (p. 100). Byers' (1988) role-play study found complex interconnections among RMA, intimacy, and sexual arousal. Surprisingly, in several conditions, men viewing a sexually erotic video were more compliant with women's refusals, although high RMA women viewing the arousing video provided less resolute verbal refusals. If alcohol is also consumed in the context of sexual arousal, then the potential for arousal-based distortion of cues, and sexual coercion (Cue, George, & Norris, 1996), would seem to be magnified considerably.

Sixth, token resistance is a behavior people are likely to experience at some point in their courtship journeys. *Token resistance* is the offering of a sexual resistance message (e.g., "No," "I don't want to"), when in fact the person intends or is willing to have sex (see Metts & Spitzberg, 1996, for a review). Across many studies spanning time, region, and culture, approximately 40% or more of people claim to have used token resistance (e.g., Johnson et al., 1991; Marx & Gross, 1995; Mills & Granoff, 1992; Muehlenhard & Rodgers, 1993; Muehlenhard, Giusti, & Rodgers, 1993; Sprecher, Hatfield, Cortese, Potapova, & Levitskaya, 1994). A small percentage of people even claim to be initially coerced and then to enjoy the sexual activity (McConaghy & Zamir, 1995). Although the motives behind the use of token resistance vary and it may be employed more in established relationships than in the early stages of courtship (Muehlen-hard & Hollabaugh, 1988; O'Sullivan & Allgeier, 1994; Shotland & Hunter, 1995), the existence of the "no that doesn't mean no" permits the perpetuation of potential misunderstandings in the courtship context.

Seventh, Malamuth and Brown (1994) tested three models of men's perception of women's communication in sexual compliance-gaining situations. The first hypothesized that sexual aggression is due to male overattribution of seductiveness and/or lack of discrimination of women's hostility from assertiveness. The assumption is that sexual aggression results when the male fails to recognize when the woman is only being friendly and when she is extreme in her rejection. The second model represents a general disregard for negative cues, suggesting that sexual aggression occurs when males inaccurately decode rejection behaviors. The third model predicts that sexual aggression results when males are overly suspicious of the veracity of women's sexual communication, generally, and their rejection cues, specifically. Although the effect sizes were relatively small, the results generally supported the role of suspiciousness schemata in predicting sexual aggression. The authors concluded that such a schema may facilitate sexual aggression not only by creating miscommunication of intentions, but also by priming the male to pursue sex exploitatively or coercively even in the face of apparently favorable cues (such as on a first date). The male may distrust the favorable cues, and thereby use coercion for fear that the relationship may not last long enough to obtain sex through more cooperative means.

Collectively, there are manifold sources of misperception, misattribution, and miscommunication in the sexual compliance-gaining context. Surprisingly, however, explicit communication does not appear to be commonly practiced in these contexts. In a detailed analysis of sexual encounter narratives, Kirkendall (1961) found that many encounters occur with little or no verbal communication about sex at all. People simply made the moves that seemed appropriate at the time. There may be implicit rules in the courtship script that sex should not be explicitly and directly discussed in terms of intentions and the process of pursuit (Metts & Spitzberg, 1996).

The argument here is that the interaction and context play significant roles in the production of sexual coercion. It is clear that many instances of sexual coercion are attributed by the victims and perpetrators to "miscommunication," being "led on," ambiguity of cues (Abbey, 1982, 1987; Baier et al., 1991; Bridges, 1991; Kanin, 1957, 1969, Muehlenhard, 1988; Muehlenhard & McNaughton, 1988; O'Sullivan & Byers, 1992), or lack of clarity in nonconsent (Koss, 1985, 1988, Koss et al., 1988). This position seems to diminish the culpability of the perpetrators of violence. However, from another perspective, it offers one of the most productive views for intervention. A person on a date cannot open up the other person's mind and peer inside for evidence of his or her childhood, previous sexual experiences, or sexual belief systems. However, a person can immediately see, hear, and experience a threat, a roving hand, or a bodily restraint of movement. Developing a more precise understanding of the sequelae of interactional moves in sexual compliance gaining offers a potentially invaluable source of risk prevention and avoidance information.

A final concern of communication in sexual coercion is the role of interpersonal incompetence. Numerous studies attempted to identify a role for deficient social skills in accounting for sexual coercion and rape. A common approach is to study the social skills of incarcerated rapists and sometimes, to compare such groups to subjects imprisoned for nonsexual crimes and to matched samples of nonincarcerated normals (e.g., Lipton, McDorel, & McFall, 1987; Overholser & Beck, 1986; Prentky & Knight, 1991; Segal & Marshall, 1985; Stahl & Sacco, 1995; Stermac & Quinsey, 1986). Although the results vary somewhat, in general, rapists do not consistently differ from other prisoners in their social skills, but are lower than nonincarcerated people in a variety of measured skills. Knight, Prentky, Schneider, and Rosenberg (1983) found no significant multivariate effect for interpersonal competence in differentiating types of rapists, although Prentky and Knight (1991) still suggested the possibility of a moderating role.

Results are similarly mixed in nonincarcerated groups. Murphy et al. (1986) found no significant correlation between social perception indexes and likelihood of raping, although there were small effects in predicting arousal to rape stimuli. In an extensive test using multiple methods of social skills assessment, Koralewski and Conger (1992) found virtually no social skill differences among low, medium, and high sexual coercion groups. In one of the few studies that proposed the possibility that the victim's interpersonal competence may influence victimization, Gidycz et al. (1995) found no effect of interpersonal problem solving on subsequent victimization.

Perhaps the most intriguing potential resolution of the role of interpersonal competence was suggested by Muehlenhard and Falcon (1990), who proposed that competence is curvilinear to coercion. Specifically, interpersonally incompetent persons are more likely to use physical coercion, and interpersonally hypercompetent persons are more likely to employ verbal and psychological coercion. Carter et al. (1988) discussed a category of rapist labeled "exploitative," which they indicated may "appear highly socialized, or at least of high social competence" (p. 112). Partial support was found in their study, in which high and moderate socially skilled persons reported obtaining more sexual intercourse, in general, and by arguing, lying, and intoxication, compared to low-skilled persons. However, physical coercion was not differentiated by social skill level. Spitzberg's (1995) study revealed only small, negative correlations between ratings of male interpersonal competence and extent of sexual coerciveness. This hypothesis also received indirect support from Kanin's

(1984, 1985) interview and study of self-admitted date rapists, which indicated that they lead a very active sexual and social life, even compared to controls, although Smithyman's (1979) study of self-admitted rapists found that they viewed themselves as generally no more or no less popular than their immediate social group. Thus far, there does not appear to be any research on the role of interpersonal competence in avoiding sexual coercion. It seems clear that more research is needed in the role of communication and interpersonal competence in facilitating sexual coercion and its avoidance, especially given that at the most basic level, more direct communication appears to be both effective and appropriate in diminishing the risk of date rape (Muehlenhard, Andrews, & Beal, 1996).

COERCING TRUTH OUT OF COERCION

Sexual coercion is a widespread problem in our society. Women are victimized more than men and experience greater trauma as a result of this victimization. Regardless of whether coercion results from culture, biology, personal dispositions, or the ephemeral nature of situated action, it is a problem that cries out for better scholarly understanding and societal prevention. At the same time, any claims that courtship and intercourse themselves are forms of rape and that gender relations are inherently status asymmetric in favor of men seem wildly overstated beyond the bounds of responsible scholarly evidence. There are powerful forces—both scholarly and political—at work to position the claiming of sexual coercion. Fortunately, extensive scholarly work has been conducted that provides useful glimpses into the nature of sexual coercion and the factors that influence this complex form of human interaction.

One of the most enduring debates in the scholarly rendering and rending of rape is whether rape and sexual coercion are motivated by power or by sex (Craig, Kalichman, & Follingstad, 1989; Emery & Lloyd, 1994; Felson, 1993; Felson & Krohn, 1990; Gregor, 1990; Groth & Burgess, 1980; Groth, Burgess, & Holmstrom, 1977; Hall, 1987; Hamilton & Yee, 1990; Kellett, 1995; Lisak & Roth, 1988; Muehlenhard et al., 1996 "Sex or violence"; Palmer, 1988; Plummer, 1984; Szymanski et al., 1993; Tang et al., 1993; Tedeschi & Felson, 1994). More recently, however, feminist and traditional researchers alike argued that either the dichotomy is an oversimplification (e.g., Muehlenhard et al., 1992) or that date rape (vs. stranger rape) is best viewed as the use of power to get sex, rather than the use of sex to get power (e.g., Bechhofer & Parrot, 1991; Kanin, 1984; Spitzberg, 1997b). The empirical data are beginning to reveal multiple paths to sexual aggression, consisting of both sexual- and power-oriented (e.g. hostility) factors (e.g., Malamuth et al., 1995). A more differentiated model than dominance and power is needed to account for sexual coercion in courtship contexts.

However else theorists may need to conceptualize the macrolevel societal and cultural factors framing the issue of sexual coercion in court- ship, coercion itself is ultimately enacted at the microlevel in specific contexts through a process of interaction. One episode at a time, people are drawn into, eniticed, persuaded, cajoled, manipulated, deceived, and sometimes forced to enage in unwanted and nonconsentual sexual acts. Such acts violate one of the most personal psychological and physical boundaries any human possesses. Such acts also ironically mimic one of the potentially most enjoyable activities available to humans. Until our society learns to differentiate coercion from consent, and rids itself of the former, the latter will continue to be an intrinsically problematic concern in courtship encounters.

ACKNOWLEDGMENTS

My sincere thanks go to Amber Cousins, William Cupach, Alana Nicastro, and John Theid, who offered useful feedback on this chapter. Any mistakes or misjudgments remain, of course, my own.

REFERENCES

Abbey, A. (1982). Sex differences in attributions for friendly behavior: Do males misperceive females' friendliness? *Journal of Personality and Social Psychology, 42,* 830–838.

Abbey, A. (1987). Misperceptions of friendly behavior as sexual interest: A survey of naturally occurring incidents. *Psychology of Women Quarterly, 11,* 173–194.

Abbey, A. (1991a). Acquaintance rape and alcohol consumption on college campuses: How are they linked? *Journal of American College Health, 39,* 165–169.

Abbey, A. (1991b). Misperceptions as an antecedent of acquaintance rape: A consequence of ambiguity in communication between men and women. In A. Parrot & L. Bechhofer (Eds.), *Acquaintance rape: The hidden crime* (pp. 96–112). New York: Wiley.

Abbey, A., Cozzarelli, C., McLaughlin, K., & Harnish, R. J. (1987). The effects of clothing and dyad sex composition on perceptions of sexual intent: Do women and men evaluate these cues differently. *Journal of Applied Social Psychology, 17,* 108–126.

Abbey, A., & Melby, C. (1986). The effects of nonverbal cues on gender differences in perceptions of sexual intent. *Sex Roles, 15,* 283–298.

Abbey, A., Ross, L. T., McDuffie, D., & McAuslan, P. (1996a). Alcohol and dating risk factors for sexual assault among college women. *Psychology of Women Quarterly, 20,* 147–169.

Abbey, A., Ross, L.T., McDuffie, D., & McAuslan P. (1996b). Alcohol, misperception, and sexual assault: How and why are they linked? In D.M. Buss & N.M. Malamuth (Eds.), *Sex, power,* conflict: Evolutionary and feminist perspectives (pp. 138–161). New York: Oxford University Press.

Abrams, A., & Herman, K. (1994, January 26). Antioch is not legislating 'sexual correctness.' Chronicle of Higher Education, p. B3.

Adams, D. M. (1996). Date rape and erotic discourse. In L. Francis (Ed.), Date rape: Feminism, philosophy, and the law (pp. 27–40). University Park: Pennsylvania State University.

Ageton, S. S. (1988). Vulnerability to sexual assault. In A. W. Burgess (Ed.), Rape and sexual assault II (pp. 221–243). New York: Garland.

Ageton, S. S. (1983). Sexual assault among adolescents. Lexington, MA: Lexington Books

Alder, C. (1985). An exploration of self-reported sexually aggressive behavior. Crime and Delinquency, 31, 306–331.

Allgeier, E. R. (1987). Coercive versus consensual sexual interactions. In V.P. Makoski (Ed.), The G. Stanley Hall Lecture Series (Vol. 7, pp. 9–63). Washington, DC: American Psychological Association.

Allison, J. A., & Wrightsman, L. S. (1993). Rape: The misunderstood crime. Newbury Park, CA: Sage.

Alzenman, M., & Kelley, G. (1988). The incidence of violence and acquaintance rape in dating relationships among college men and women. Journal of College Student Development, 29, 305–311.

Amir, M. (1971). Patterns in forcible rape. Chicago: University of Chicago.

Anderson, W. P., & Cummings, K. (1993). Women's acceptance of rape myths and their sexual experiences. Journal of College Student Development, 34, 53–57.

Arata, C. M., & Burkhart, B. R. (1996). Post-traumatic stress disorder among college student victims of acquaintance assault. In E. S. Byers & L. F. O'Sullivan (Eds.), Sexual coercion in dating relationships (pp. 79–92). New York: Haworth.

Atkeson, B. M., Calhoun, K. S., & Morris, K. T. (1989). Victim resistance to rape: The relationship of previous victimization, demographics, and situational factors. Archives of Sexual Behavior, 18, 497–507.

Bachman, R., & Carmody, D. C. (1994). Fighting fire with fire: The effects of victim resistance in intimate versus stranger perpetrated assaults against females. Journal of Family Violence, 9, 317–331.

Baier, J. L., Rosenzweig, M. G., & Whipple, E. G. (1991). Patterns of sexual behavior, coercion, and victimization of university students. Journal of College Student Development, 32, 310–322.

Bajracharya, S. M., Sarvela, P. D., & Isberner, F. R. (1995). A retrospective study of first sexual intercourse experiences among undergraduates. Journal of American College Health, 43, 169–177.

Baron, L., & Straus, M. A. (1989). Four theories of rape in American society: A state-level analysis. New Haven, CT: Yale University Press.

Baron, R. A., & Richardson, D. R. (1994). Human aggression (2nd ed.). New York: Plenum.

Bart, P. B. (1981). A study of women who both were raped and avoided rape. Journal of Social Issues, 37, 123–137.

Bart, P. B., & O'Brien, P. H. (1985). Stopping rape: Successful survival strategies. New York: Pergamon.

Bechhofer, L., & Parrot, A. (1991). What is acquaintance rape? In A. Parrot & L. Bechhofer (Eds.), Acquaintance rape: The hidden crime (pp. 9–25). New York: Wiley.

Belknap, J. (1989). The sexual victimization of unmarried women by nonrelative acquaintances. In M. A. Pirog-Good & J. E. Stets (Eds.), Violence in dating relationships: Emerging social issues (pp. 205–218). New York: Praeger.

Belknap, J., & Erez, E. (1995). The victimization of women on college campuses: Courtship violence, date rape, and sexual harassment. In B.S. Fisher & J.J. Sloan (Eds.), Campus crime: Legal, social, and policy perspectives (pp. 156–178). Springfield, IL: Thomas.

Bell, S. T., Kuriloff, P. J., & Lottes, I. (1994). Understanding attributions of blame in stranger rape and date rape situations: An examination of gender, race, identification, and students' social perceptions of rape. Journal of Applied Social Psychology, 24, 1719–1734.

Benson, D., Charlton, C., & Goodhart, F. (1992). Acquaintance rape on campus: A literature review. Journal of American College Health, 40, 157–165.

Berkowitz, A. D., Burkhart, B. R., & Bourg, S. E. (1994). Research on college men and rape. In A. D. Berkowitz (Ed.), *Men and rape: Theory, research, and prevention programs in higher education* (pp. 3–19). San Francisco: Jossey-Bass.

Best, C., Resnick, H., Saunders, B. E., & Lipovsky, J. (1992). *Rape in America: A report to the nation.* Arlington VA: National Victim Center/Charleston, SC: Crime Victims Research and Treatment Center.

Boeringer, S. B., Shehan, C. L., & Akers, R. L. (1991). Social contexts and social learning in sexual coercion and aggression: Assessing the contribution of fraternity membership. *Family Relations, 40,* 58–64.

Bohmer, C. (1991). Acquaintance rape and the law. In A. Parrot & L. Bechhofer (Eds.), *Acquaintance rape: The hidden crime* (pp. 317–333). New York: Wiley.

Bohmer, G., & Schwarz, N. (1996). The threat of rape: Its psychological impact on nonvictimized women. In D. M. Buss & N. M. Malamuth (Eds.), *Sex, power, conflict: Evolutionary and feminist perspectives* (pp. 162–177). New York: Oxford University Press.

Bostwick, T. D., & DeLucia, J. L. (1992). Effects of gender and specific dating behaviors on perceptions of sex willingness and date rape. *Journal of Social and Clinical Psychology, 11,* 14–25.

Brady, E. C., Chrisler, J. C., Hosdale, D. C., Osowiecki, D. M., & Veal, T. A. (1991). Date rape: Expectations, avoidance strategies, and attitudes toward victims. *Journal of Social Psychology, 131,* 427–429.

Brand, P. A., & Kidd, A. H. (1986). Frequency of physical aggression in heterosexual and female homosexual dyads. *Psychological Reports, 59,* 1307–1313.

Briere, J., & Malamuth, N. M. (1983). Self-reported likelihood of sexually aggressive behavior: Attitudinal versus sexual explanations. *Journal of Research in Personality, 17,* 315–323.

Bridges, J. S. (1991). Perceptions of date and stranger rape: A difference in sex role expectations and rape-supportive beliefs. *Sex Roles, 24,* 291–307.

Brigman, B., & Knox, D. (1992). University students' motivations to have intercourse. *College Student Journal, 26,* 406–408.

Broude, G. J., & Greene, S. J. (1976). Cross-cultural codes on twenty sexual attitudes and practices. *Ethnology, 15,* 409–429.

Brownmiller, S. (1975). *Against our will: Men, women and rape.* New York: Simon & Schuster.

Brundage, J. A. (1993). Implied consent to intercourse. In A. E. Laiou (Ed.), *Consent and coercion to sex and marriage in ancient and medieval societies* (pp. 245–256). Washington, DC: Dumbarton Oaks Research Library and Collection.

Burgess, A. W., & Holmstrom, L. L. (1974). Rape trauma syndrome. *American Journal of Psychiatry, 131,* 981–986.

Burgoyne, S. G., & Spitzberg, B. (1992, July). *An examination of communication strategies and tactics used in potential date rape episodes.* Paper presented at the International Society for the Study of Personal Relationships Conference, Orono, ME.

Burke, P. J., Stets, J. E., & Pirog-Good, M. A. (1988). Gender identity, self-esteem, and physical and sexual abuse in dating relationships. *Social Psychology Quarterly, 51,* 272–285.

Burkhart, B., & Fromuth, M. E. (1991). Individual psychological and social psychological understandings of sexual coercion. In E. Grauerholz & M. A. Koralewski (Eds.), *Sexual coercion: A sourcebook on its nature, causes, and prevention* (pp. 75–90). Lexington, MA: Lexington Books.

Burkhart, B. R., & Stanton, A. L. (1988). Sexual aggression in acquaintance relationships. In G. W. Russell (Ed.), *Violence in intimate relationships* (pp. 43–65). New York: PMA Publishing.

Burnam, M. A., Stein, J. A., Golding, J. M., Siegel, J. M., Sorenson, S. B., Forsythe, A. B., & Telles, C. A. (1988). Sexual assault and mental disorders in a community population. *Journal of Consulting and Clinical Psychology, 56,* 843–850.

Burt, M. R. (1980). Cultural myths and supports for rape. *Journal of Personality and Social Psychology, 38,* 217–230.

Buss, D. M. (1988). The evolution of human intrasexual competition: Tactics of mate attraction. *Journal of Personality and Social Psychology, 54,* 616–628.

Buss, D. M. (1994). *The evolution of desire: Strategies in dating relationships.* New York: Basic Books.

Buss, D. M. (1996). Sexual conflict: Evolutionary insights into feminism and the "battle of the sexes." In D. M. Buss & N. M. Malamuth (Eds.), *Sex, power, conflict: Evolutionary and feminist perspectives* (pp. 296–318). New York: Oxford University Press.

Buss, D. M., & Schmitt, D. P. (1993). Sexual strategies theory: An evolutionary perspective on human mating. *Psychological Bulletin, 100,* 204–232.

Byers, E. S. (1988). Effects of sexual arousal on men's and women's behavior in sexual disagreement situations. *Journal of Sex Research, 25,* 235–254.

Byers, E. S. (1996). How well does the traditional sexual script explain sexual coercion? Review of a program of research. In E. S. Byers & L. F. O'Sullivan (Eds.), *Sexual coercion in dating relationships* (pp. 7–26). New York: Haworth.

Byers, E. S., & Eno, R. J. (1991). Predicting men's sexual coercion and aggression from attitudes, dating history, and sexual response. *Journal of Psychology and Human Sexuality, 4,* 55–70.

Byers, E. S., & Heinlein, L. (1989). Predicting initiations and refusals of sexual activities in married and cohabiting heterosexual couples. *Journal of Sex Research, 26,* 210–231.

Byers, E. S., & Lewis, K. (1988). Dating couples' disagreements over the desired level of sexual intimacy. *Journal of Sex Research, 24,* 15–29.

Byers, E. S., & O'Sullivan, L. F. (1996). Introduction. In E. S. Byers & L. F. O'Sullivan (Eds.), *Sexual coercion in dating relationships* (pp. 1–6). New York: Haworth.

Cahoon, D. D., & Edmonds, E. M. (1992). Did rape occur? A comparison of male and female opinions concerning the definition of rape. *Contemporary Social Psychology, 16,* 60–63.

Cahoon, D. D., Edmonds, E. M., Spaulding, R. M., & Dickens, J. C. (1995). A comparison of the opinions of black and white males and females concerning the occurrence of rape. *Journal of Social Behavior and Personality, 10,* 91–100.

Calhoun, L. G., Selby, J. W., Cann, A., & Keller, G. T. (1978). The effects of victim physical attractiveness and sex of respondent on social reactions to victims of rape. *British Journal of Social and Clinical Psychology, 17,* 191–192.

Canterbury, R. J., Grossman, S. J., & Lloyd, E. (1993). Drinking behaviors and lifetime incidents of date rape among high school graduates upon entering college. *College Student Journal, 27,* 75–84.

Carter, D. L., Prentky, R. A., & Burgess, A. W. (1988). Victim response strategies in sexual assault. In A. W. Burgess (Ed.), *Rape and sexual assault II* (pp. 105–132). New York: Garland.

Christopher, F. S. (1988). An initial investigation into a continuum of premarital sexual pressure. *Journal of Sex Research, 25,* 255–266.

Christopher, F. S., & Frandsen, M. M. (1990). Strategies of influence in sex and dating. *Journal of Social and Personal Relationships, 7,* 89–105.

Christopher, F. S., Londen, H. L., & Owens, L. A. (1990, June). *Individual and relational correlates of premarital sexual aggression.* Paper presented at the International Network on Personal Relationships, Normal, IL.

Christopher, F. S., Owens, L. A., & Stecker, H. L. (1993). Exploring the dark side of courtship: A test of a model of male premarital sexual aggressiveness. *Journal of Marriage and the Family, 55,* 469–479.

Clark, L., & Lewis, D. (1977). *Rape: The price of coercive sexuality.* Toronto: Women's Press.

Clark, R. D., III. (1990). The impact of AIDS on gender differences in willingness to engage in casual sex. *Journal of Applied Social Psychology, 20,* 771–781.

Clark, R. D., III., & Hatfield, E. (1989). Gender differences in receptivity to sexual offers. *Journal of Psychology and Human Sexuality, 2,* 39–55.

Cochran, S. D., & Mays, V. M. (1990). Sex, lies, and HIV. *New England Journal of Medicine, 322,* 774–775.

Comstock, G. D. (1991). *Violence against lesbians and gay men.* New York: Columbia University Press.

Cook, S. L. (1995). Acceptance and expectation of sexual aggression in college students. *Psychology of Women Quarterly, 19,* 181–194.

Copenhaver, S., & Grauerholz, E. (1991). Sexual victimization among sorority women: Exploring the link between sexual violence and institutional practices. *Sex Roles, 24,* 31–41.

Cowen, G., & Campbell, R. R. (1995). Rape causal attitudes among adolescents. *Journal of Sex Research, 32,* 145–153.

Craig, M. E. (1990). Coercive sexuality in dating relationships: A situational model. *Clinical Psychology Review, 10,* 395–423.

Craig, M. E., Kalichman, S. C., & Follingstad, D. R. (1989). Verbal coercive sexual behavior among college students. *Archives of Sexual Behavior, 18,* 421–434.

Cue, K. L., George, W. H., & Norris, J. (1996). Women's appraisals of sexual-assault risk in dating situations. *Psychology of Women Quarterly, 20,* 487–504.

Deitz, S. R., Blackwell, K. T., Daley, P. C., & Bentley, B. J. (1982). Measurement of empathy toward rape victims and rapists. *Journal of Personality and Social Psychology, 43,* 372–384.

DiVasto, P. V., Kaufman, A., Rosner, L., Jackson, R., Christy, J., Pearson, S., & Burgett, T. (1984). The prevalence of sexually stressful events among females in the general population. *Archives of Sexual Behavior, 13,* 59–67.

Dixon, J. (1991). Feminist reforms of sexual coercion laws. In E. Grauerholz & M. A. Koralewski (Eds.), *Sexual coercion: A sourcebook on its nature, causes, and prevention* (pp. 161–172). Lexington, MA: Lexington.

Drout, C., Becker, T., Bukkosy, S., & Mansell, M. (1994). Does social influence mitigate or exacerbate responsibility for rape? *Journal of Social Behavior and Personality, 9,* 409–420.

Edmonds, E. M., & Cahoon, D. D. (1993). The "new" sexism: Females' negativism toward males. *Journal of Social Behavior and Personality, 8,* 481–487.

Egland, K. L., Spitzberg, B. H., & Zormeier, M. M. (1996). Flirtation and conversational competence in cross-sex platonic and romantic relationships. *Communication Reports, 9,* 105–118.

Ellis, L. (1989). *Theories of rape: Inquiries into the causes of sexual aggression.* New York: Hemisphere.

Emery, B. C., & Lloyd, S. A. (1994). Women who use aggression in close relationships. In D. L. Sollie & L. A. Leslie (Eds.), *Gender, families, and close relationships: Feminist research journeys* (pp. 237–262). Thousand Oaks, CA: Sage.

Emmers, T. M., & Allen, M. (1995a, February). *Resistance to sexual coercion behaviors: A meta-analysis.* Paper presented at the Western States Communication Association Conference, Portland, OR.

Emmers, T. M., & Allen, M. (1995b, November). *Factors contributing to sexually coercive behaviors: A meta-analysis.* Paper presented at the Speech Communication Association Conference, San Antonio, TX.

Felson, R. B. (1993). Motives for sexual coercion. In R. B. Felson & J. T. Tedeschi (Eds.), *Aggression and violence: Social interactionist perspectives* (pp. 233–253). Washington, DC: American Psychological Association.

Felson, R. B., & Krohn, M. (1990). Motives for rape. *Journal of Research in Crime and Delinquency, 27,* 222–242.

Fichten, C. S., Tagalakis, V., Judd, D., Wright, J., & Amsel, R. (1992). Verbal and nonverbal communication cues in daily conversations and dating. *Journal of Social Psychology, 132,* 751–769.

Fischer, G. J. (1986). College student attitudes toward forcible date rape: I. Cognitive predictors. *Archives of Sexual Behavior, 15,* 457–466.

Fischer, G. J. (1987). Hispanic and majority student attitudes toward forcible date rape as a function of differences in attitudes toward women. *Sex Roles, 17,* 93–101.

Fischer, G. J. (1992). Sex attitudes and prior victimization as predictors of college student sex offenses. *Annals of Sex Research, 5,* 53–60.

Foo, L., & Margolin, G. (1995). A multivariate investigation of dating aggression. *Journal of Family Violence, 10,* 351–377.

Furby, L., Fischhoff, B., & Morgan, M. (1992). Preventing rape: How people perceive the options of defending oneself during an assault. In E. C. Viano (Ed.), *Critical issues in victimology: International perspectives* (pp. 174–189). New York: Springer-Verlag.

Gagnon, J. H. (1990). The explicit and implicit use of the scripting perspective in sex research. In J. Bancroft (Ed.), *Annual review of sex research* (Vol. 1, pp. 1–44). Lake Mills, IA: Society for the Scientific Study of Sex.

Garcia, L. T., & Derfel, B. (1983). Perception of sexual experience: The impact of nonverbal behavior. *Sex Roles, 9,* 871–878.

Gavey, N. (1991). Sexual victimization prevalence among New Zealand University students. *Journal of Consulting and Clinical Psychology, 59*, 464–466.

Gavey, N. (1992). Technologies and effects of heterosexual coercion. *Feminism & Psychology, 2*, 325–351.

George, L. K., Winfield, I., & Blazer, D. G. (1992). Sociocultural factors in sexual assault: Comparison of two representative samples of women. *Journal of Social Issues, 48*, 105–125.

Gerdes, E. P., Dammann, E. J., & Heilig, K. E. (1988). Perceptions of rape victims and assailants: Effects of physical attractiveness, acquaintance, and subject gender. *Sex Roles, 19*, 141–152.

Giacopassi, D. J., & Dull, R. T. (1986). Gender and racial differences in the acceptance of rape myths within a college population. *Sex Roles, 15*, 63–76.

Gidycz, C. A., Coble, C. N., Latham, L., & Layman, M. J. (1993). Sexual assault experience in adulthood and prior victimization experiences. *Psychology of Women Quarterly, 17*, 151–168.

Gidycz, C. A., Hanson, K., & Layman, M. J. (1995). A prospective analysis of the relationships among sexual assault experiences. *Psychology of Women Quarterly, 19*, 5–29.

Gidycz, C. A., & Koss, M. P. (1989). The impact of adolescent sexual victimization: Standardized measures of anxiety, depression, and behavioral deviancy. *Violence and Victims, 4*, 139–149

Gidycz, C. A., & Koss, M. P. (1991a). The effects of acquaintance rape on the female victim. In A. Parrot & L. Bechhofer (Eds.), *Acquaintance rape: The hidden crime* (pp. 270–283). New York: Wiley.

Gidycz, C. A., & Koss, M. P. (1991b). Predictors of long-term sexual assault trauma among a national sample of victimized college women. *Violence and Victims, 6*, 175–190.

Gilbert, N. (1991). The phantom epidemic of sexual assault. *Public Interest, 103*, 54–65.

Gilbert, N. (1993). Examining the facts: Advocacy research overstates the incidence of date and acquaintance rape. In R. J. Gelles & D. R. Loseke (Eds.), *Current controversies on family violence* (pp. 120–132). Newbury Park, CA: Sage.

Gilbert, N. (1995). *Was it rape? An examination of sexual assault statistics*. Menlo Park, CA: Henry J. Kaiser Family Foundation.

Gilmartin-Zena, P. (1987). Attitudes toward rape: Student characteristics as predictors. *Free Inquiry in Creative Sociology, 15*, 175–182.

Givens, D. B. (1978). The nonverbal basis of attraction: Flirtation, courtship, and seduction. *Psychiatry, 41*, 346–359.

Glazer, S. (1994). Sex on campus. *CQ Researcher, 4*(41), 961–984.

Goodchilds, J. D., Zellman, G. L., Johnson, P. B., & Giarrusso, R. (1988). Adolescents and their perceptions of sexual interactions. In A. W. Burgess (Ed.), *Rape and sexual assault II* (pp. 245–270). New York: Garland.

Grauerholz, E., & Koralewski, M. A. (1991). What is known and not known about sexual coercion. In E. Grauerholz & M. A. Koralewski (Eds.), *Sexual coercion: A sourcebook on its nature, causes, and prevention* (pp. 187–198). Lexington, MA: Lexington.

Grauerholz, E., & Serpe, R. T. (1985). Initiation and response: The dynamics of sexual interaction. *Sex Roles, 12*, 1041–1058.

Greendlinger, V., & Byrne, D. (1987). Coercive sexual fantasies of college men as predictors of self-reported likelihood to rape and overt sexual aggression. *Journal of Sex Research, 23*, 1–11.

Greer, A. E., & Buss, D. M. (1994). Tactics for promoting sexual encounters. *Journal of Sex Research, 31*, 185–201.

Gregor, T. (1990). Male dominance and sexual coercion. In J. W. Stigler, R. A. Shweder, & G. Herdt (Eds.), *Cultural psychology: Essays on comparative human development* (pp. 477–495). Cambridge, England: Cambridge University Press.

Groth, N., & Burgess, A. W. (1980). Male rape: Offenders and victims. *American Journal of Psychiatry, 137*, 806–810.

Groth, N., Burgess, A. W., & Holmstrom, L. L. (1977). Rape: Power, anger, and sexuality. *American Journal of Psychiatry, 134*, 1239–1243.

Gylys, J. A., & McNamara, J. R. (1996). A further examination of validity for the sexual experiences survey. *Behavioral Sciences and the Law, 14*, 245–260.

Haffner, D. W. (1996). The essence of "consent" is communication. *SIECUS Report, 24*, 2–3.

Hall, E. R. (1987). Adolescents' perceptions of sexual assault. *Journal of Sex Education and Therapy, 13*, 37–42.

Hall, E. R., & Flannery, P. J. (1984). Prevalence and correlates of sexual assault experiences in adolescents. *Victimology: An International Journal, 9,* 398–406.

Hall, E. R., Howard, J. A., & Boezio, S. L. (1986). Tolerance of rape: A sexist or antisocial attitude? *Psychology of Women Quarterly, 10,* 101–118.

Hall, G. C. N. (1990). Prediction of sexual aggression. *Clinical Psychology Review, 10,* 229–245.

Hall, J. A. (1984). *Nonverbal sex differences: Communication accuracy and expressive style.* Baltimore: Johns Hopkins University Press.

Hamilton, M., & Yee, J. (1990). Rape knowledge and propensity to rape. *Journal of Research in Personality, 24,* 111–122.

Hannan, K. E., & Burkhart, B. (1993). The topography of violence in college men: Frequency and comorbidity of sexual and physical aggression. *Journal of College Student Psychotherapy, 8,* 219–237.

Harnish, R. J., Abbey, A., & DeBono, K. G. (1990). Toward an understanding of "the sex game": The effects of gender and self-monitoring on perceptions of sexuality and likability in initial interactions. *Journal of Applied Social Psychology, 10,* 1333–1344.

Harrington, N. T., & Leitenberg, H. (1994). Relationship between alcohol consumption and victim behaviors immediately preceding sexual aggression by an acquaintance. *Violence and Victims, 9,* 315–324.

Harris, A. R. (1996). Forcible rape, date rape, and communicative sexuality: A legal perspective. In L. Francis (Ed.), *Date rape: Feminism, philosophy, and the law* (pp. 51–62). University Park: Pennsylvania State University.

Harris, L. R., & Weiss, D. J. (1995). Judgments of consent in simulated rape cases. *Journal of Social Behavior and Personality, 10,* 79–90.

Hendrick, S. S., & Hendrick, C. (1995). Gender differences and similarities in sex and love. *Personal Relationships, 2,* 55–65.

Hillman, R. J., O'Mara, N., Taylor-Robinson, D., & Harris, J. R. W. (1990). Medical and social aspects of sexual assault of males: A survey of 100 victims. *British Journal of General Practice, 40,* 502–504.

Himelein, M. J. (1995). Risk factors for sexual victimization in dating. *Psychology of Women Quarterly, 19,* 31–48.

Hirsch, L. R., & Paul, L. (1996). Human male mating strategies: I. Courtship tactics of the "quality" and "quantity" alternatives. *Ethology and Sociobiology, 17,* 55–70.

Holcomb, D. R., Holcomb, L. C., Sondag, K. A., & Williams, N. (1991). Attitudes about date rape: Gender differences among college students. *College Student Journal, 25,* 434–439.

Jacobson, M. B. (1981). Effects of victim's and defendant's physical attractiveness on subjects' judgments in a rape case. *Sex Roles, 7,* 247–255.

Jesser, C. J. (1978). Male responses to direct verbal sexual initiatives of females. *Journal of Sex Research, 14,* 118–128.

Johnson, C. B., Stockdale, M. S., & Saal, F. E. (1991). Persistence of men's misperceptions of friendly cues across a variety of interpersonal encounters. *Psychology of Women Quarterly, 15,* 463–475.

Johnson, I. M., & Sigler, R. T. (1996). Forced sexual intercourse on campus: Crime or offensive behavior? *Journal of Contemporary Criminal Justice, 12,* 54–68.

Kahn, A. S., Mathie, V. A., & Torgler, C. (1994). Rape scripts and rape acknowledgement. *Psychology of Women Quarterly, 18,* 53–66.

Kalichman, S. C., & Rompa, D. (1995). Sexually coerced and noncoerced gay and bisexual men: Factors relevant to risk for human immunodeficiency virus (HIV) infection. *Journal of Sex Research, 32,* 45–50.

Kalof, L. (1993). Rape-supportive attitudes and sexual victimization experiences of sorority and nonsorority women. *Sex Roles, 29,* 767–780.

Kanekar, S., Shaherwalla, A., Franco, B., Kunju, T., & Pinto, A. J. (1991). The acquaintance predictament of a rape victim. *Journal of Applied Social Psychology, 21,* 1524–1544.

Kanin, E. J. (1957). Male aggression in dating-courtship relations. *American Journal of Sociology, 63,* 197–204.

Kanin, E. J. (1969). Selected dyadic aspects of male sex aggression. *Journal of Sex Research, 5,* 12–28.

Kanin, E. J. (1984). Date rape: Unofficial criminals and victims. *Victimology: An International Journal, 9*, 95–108.

Kanin, E. J. (1985). Date rapists: Differential sexual socialization and relative deprivation. *Archives of Sexual Behavior, 14*, 219–231.

Kanin, E. J., & Parcell, S. R. (1977). Sexual aggression: A second look at the offended female. *Archives of Sexual Behavior, 6*, 67–76.

Katz, B. L. (1991). The psychological impact of stranger versus nonstranger rape on victims' recovery. In A. Parrot & L. Bechhofer (Eds.), *Acquaintance rape: The hidden crime* (pp. 251–269). New York: Wiley.

Katz, S., & Mazur, M. A. (1979). *Understanding the rape victim: A synthesis of research findings.* New York: Wiley.

Kellett, P. M. (1995). Acts of power, control, and resistance. In R. K. Whillock & D. Slayden (Ed.), *Hate speech* (pp. 142–162). Thousand Oaks, CA: Sage.

Kelly, K. D., & DeKeseredy, W. S. (1994). Women's fear of crime and abuse in college and university dating relationships. *Violence and Victims, 9*, 17–30.

Kelly, L. (1987). The continuum of sexual violence. In J. Hanmer & M. Maynard (Eds.), *Women, violence and social control* (pp. 46–60). Atlantic Highlands, NJ: Humanities Press.

Kelly, L. (1988). *Surviving sexual violence.* Minneapolis: University of Minnesota Press.

Kemper, T. D. (1990). *Social structure and testosterone: Explorations of the socio-bio-social chain.* New Brunswick, NJ: Rutgers University Press.

Kendall-Tackett, K. A., Williams, L. M., & Finkelhor, D. (1993). Impact of sexual abuse on children: A review and synthesis of recent empirical studies. *Psychological Bulletin, 113*, 164–180.

Kilpatrick, A. C. (1992). *Long-range effects of child and adolescent sexual experiences.* Hillsdale, NJ: Lawrence Erlbaum Associates.

Kilpatrick, D. G., Best, C. L., Veronen, L. J., Amick, A. E., Villeponteaux, L. A., & Ruff, G. A. (1985). Mental health correlates of criminal victimization: A random community survey. *Journal of Consulting and Clinical Psychology, 53*, 866–873.

Kilpatrick, D. G., Edmunds, C. N., & Seymour, A. (1992). *Rape in America: A report to the nation.* Arlington, VA: National Victim Center/Charleston, SC: Crime Victims Research and Treatment Center.

Kilpatrick, D. G., Resick, P. A., & Veronen, L. J. (1981). Effects of a rape experience: A longitudinal study. *Journal of Social Issues, 37*, 105–122.

Kilpatrick, D. G., Saunders, B. E., Veronen, L. J., Best, C. L., & Von, J. N. (1987). Criminal victimization: Lifetime prevalence, reporting to police, and psychological impact. *Crime and Delinquency, 33*, 479–489.

Kilpatrick, D. G., Veronen, L. J., & Resick, P. A. (1979). The aftermath of rape: Recent empirical findings. *American Journal of Orthopsychiatry, 49*, 658–669.

Kilpatrick, D. G., Veronen, L. J., Saunders, B. E., Best, C. L., Amick-McMullan, A., & Paduhovich, J. (1987). *The psychological impact of crime: A study of randomly surveyed crime victims.* Washington, DC: National Institute of Justice.

Kirkendall, L. A. (1961). *Premarital intercourse and interpersonal relationships.* New York: Julian Press.

Klemmack, S. H., & Klemmack, D. L. (1976). The social definition of rape. In M. J. Walker & S. L. Brodsky (Eds.), *Sexual assault: The victim and the rapist* (pp. 135–147). Lexington, MA: Lexington.

Knight, R., Prentky, R., Schneider, B., & Rosenberg, R. (1983). Linear causal modeling of adaptation and criminal history in sexual offenders. In K. T. Van Dusen & S. A. Mednick (Eds.), *Prospective studies of crime and delinquency* (pp. 303–341). Boston: Kluwer-Nijoff.

Knoth, R., Boyd, K., & Singer, B. (1988). Empirical tests of sexual selection theory: Predictions of sex differences in onset, intensity, and time course of sexual arousal. *Journal of Sex Research, 24*, 73–89.

Knox, D., Schact, C., Holt, J., & Turner, J. (1993). Sexual lies among university students. *College Student Journal, 27*, 269–272.

Knox, D., & Wilson, K. (1981). Dating behaviors of university students. *Family Relations, 30*, 255–258.

Koeppel, L. B., Montagne-Miller, Y., O'Hair, D., & Cody, M. J. (1993). Friendly? Flirting? Wrong? In P. J. Kalbfleisch (Ed.), *Interpersonal communication: Evolving interpersonal relationships* (pp. 13–32). Hillsdale, NJ: Lawrence Erlbaum Associates.

Koralewski, M. A., & Conger, J. C. (1992). The assessment of social skills among sexually coercive college males. *Journal of Sex Research, 29,* 169–188.

Koss, M. P. (1985). The hidden rape victim: Personality, attitudinal, and situational characteristics. *Psychology of Women Quarterly, 9,* 193–212.

Koss, M. P. (1988). Hidden rape: Sexual aggression and victimization in a national sample of students in higher education. In A. W. Burgess (Ed.), *Rape and sexual assault II* (pp. 3–25). New York: Garland.

Koss, M. P. (1989). Hidden rape: Sexual aggression and victimization in a national sample of students in higher education. In M. A. Pirog-Good & J. E. Stets (Eds.), *Violence in dating relationships: Emerging social issues* (pp. 145–168). New York: Praeger.

Koss, M. P. (1992a). Defending date rape. *Journal of Interpersonal Violence, 7,* 122–1126.

Koss, M. P. (1992b). The underdetection of rape: Methodological choices influence incidence estimates. *Journal of Social Issues, 48,* 61–75.

Koss, M. P. (1993). Detecting the scope of rape: A review of prevalence research methods. *Journal of Interpersonal Violence, 8,* 198–222.

Koss, M. P. (1996). The measurement of rape victimization in crime surveys. *Criminal Justice and Behavior, 23,* 55–69.

Koss, M. P., & Dinero, T. E. (1989). Discriminant analysis of risk factors for sexual victimization among a national sample of college women. *Journal of Consulting and Clinical Psychology, 57,* 242–250.

Koss, M. P., Dinero, T. E., Seibel, C. A., & Cox, S. L. (1988). Stranger and acquaintance rape: Are there differences in the victim's experience? *Psychology of Women Quarterly, 12,* 1–24.

Koss, M. P., Gidycz, C. A., & Wisniewski, N. (1987). The scope of rape: Incidence and prevalence of sexual aggression and victimization in a national sample of higher education students. *Journal of Consulting and Clinical Psychology, 55,* 162–170.

Koss, M. P., & Harvey, M. R. (1991). *The rape victim: Clinical and community interventions* (2nd ed.). Newbury Park, CA: Sage.

Koss, M. P., Heise, L., & Russo, N. F. (1994). The global health burden of rape. *Psychology of Women Quarterly, 18,* 509–537.

Koss, M. P., Leonard, K. E., Beezley, D. A. & Oros, C. J. (1985). Nonstranger sexual aggression: A discriminant analysis of the psychological characteristics of undetected offenders. *Sex Roles, 12,* 981–992.

Koss, M. P., & Oros, C. J. (1982). Sexual experiences survey: A research instrument investigating sexual aggression and victimization. *Journal of Consulting and Clinical Psychology, 50,* 455–457.

Koss, M. P., Woodruff, W. J., & Koss, P. G. (1991). Criminal victimization among primary care medical patients: Prevalence, incidence, and physician usage. *Behavioral Sciences and the Law, 9,* 85–96.

Kowalski, R. M. (1993). Inferring sexual interest from behavioral cues: Effects of gender and sexually relevant attitudes. *Sex Roles, 29,* 13–36.

Krueger, M. (1996). Sexism, erotophobia, and the illusory "no": Implications for acquaintance rape awareness. In E. S. Byers & L. F. O'Sullivan (Eds.), *Sexual coercion in dating relationships* (pp. 107–116). New York: Haworth.

Langley, T., Beatty, G., Yost, E., O'Neal, E. C., Faucett, J. M., Taylor, S. L., Frankel, P., & Craig, K. (1991). How behavioral cues in a date rape scenario influence judgments regarding victim and perpetrator. *Forensic Reports, 4,* 355–358.

LaPlante, M. N., McCormick, N., & Brannigan, G. G. (1980). Living the sexual script: College students' views of influence in sexual encounters. *Journal of Sex Research, 16,* 338–355.

Laumann, E. O., & Gagnon, J. H. (1995). A sociological perspective on sexual action. In R. G. Parker & J. H. Gagnon (Eds.), *Conceiving sexuality: Approaches to sex research in a postmodern world* (pp. 183–213). New York: Routledge.

Laumann, E. O., Gagnon, J. H., Michael, R. T., & Michaels, S. (1994). *The social organization of sexuality: Sexual practices in the United States.* Chicago: University of Chicago.

Layman, M. J., Gidycz, C. A., & Lynn, S. J. (1996). Unacknowledged versus acknowledged rape victims: Situational factors and posttraumatic stress. *Journal of Abnormal Psychology, 105,* 124–131.

Leitenberg, H., & Henning, K. (1995). Sexual fantasy. *Psychological Bulletin, 117,* 469–496.

Letellier, P. (1994). Gay and bisexual male domestic violence victimization: Challenges to feminist theory and responses to violence. *Violence and Victims, 9,* 95–106.

Levine-MacCombie, J., & Koss, M. P. (1986). Acquaintance rape: Effective avoidance strategies. *Psychology of Women Quarterly, 10,* 311–320.

Lewin, M. (1985). Unwanted intercourse: The difficulty of saying no. *Psychology of Women Quarterly, 9,* 184–192.

Lipton, D. N., McDonel, E. C., & McFall, R. M. (1987). Heterosocial perception in rapists. *Journal of Consulting and Clinical Psychology, 55,* 17–21.

Lisak, D., & Roth, S. (1988). Motivational factors in nonincarcerated sexually aggressive men. *Journal of Personality and Social Psychology, 55,* 795–802.

Lloyd, S. A. (1991). The darkside of courtship: Violence and sexual exploitation. *Family Relations, 40,* 14–20.

Lonsway, K. A., & Fitzgerald, L. F. (1994). Rape myths. *Psychology of Women Quarterly, 18,* 133–164.

Loren, R. E. A., & Weeks, G. R. (1986). Sexual fantasies of undergraduates and their perceptions of the sexual fantasies of the opposite sex. *Journal of Sex Education and Therapy, 12,* 31–36.

Lottes, I. L. (1988). Sexual socialization and attitudes toward rape. In A. W. Burgess (Ed.), *Rape and sexual assault II* (pp. 193–220). New York: Garland.

Lundberg-Love, P., & Geffner, R. (1989). Date rape: Prevalence, risk factors, and a proposed model. In M. A. Pirog-Good & J. E. Stets (Eds.), *Violence in dating relationships: Emerging social issues* (pp. 169–185). New York: Praeger.

Macdonald, J. M. (1971). *Rape: Offenders and their victims.* Springfield, IL: Thomas.

MacKinnon, K. (1989). *Toward a feminist theory of the state.* Cambridge, MA: Harvard University Press.

Mahoney, E. R., Shively, M. D., & Traw, M. (1986). Sexual coercion & assault: Male socialization and female risk. *Sexual Coercion & Assault, 1,* 2–8.

Malamuth, N. M. (1981). Rape proclivity among males. *Journal of Social Issues, 37,* 138–157.

Malamuth, N. M. (1989). Predictors of naturalistic sexual aggression. In M. A. Pirog-Good & J. E. Stets (Eds.), *Violence in dating relationships: Emerging social issues* (pp. 219–240). New York: Praeger.

Malamuth, N. M. (1996). The confluence model of sexual aggression: Feminist and evolutionary perspectives. In D. M. Buss & N. M. Malamuth (Eds.), *Sex, power, conflict: Evolutionary and feminist perspectives* (pp. 269–295). New York: Oxford University Press.

Malamuth, N. M., & Brown, L. M. (1994). Sexually aggressive men's perceptions of women's communications: Testing three explanations. *Journal of Personality and Social Psychology, 67,* 699–712.

Malamuth, N. M., Heavey, C. L., & Linz, D. (1993). Predicting men's antisocial behavior against women: The interaction model of sexual aggression. In G. C. N. Hall, R. Hirschman, J. R. Graham, & M. S. Zaragoza (Eds.), *Sexual aggression: Issues in etiology, assessment, and treatment* (pp. 63–97). Washington, DC: Taylor & Francis.

Malamuth, N. M., Linz, D., Heavey, C. L., Barnes, G., & Acker, M. (1995). Using the confluence model of sexual aggresion to predict men's conflict with women: A 10–year follow-up study. *Journal of Personality and Social Psychology, 69,* 353–369.

Malamuth, N. M., Sockloskie, R. J., Koss, M. P., & Tanaka, J. S. (1991). Characteristics of aggressors against women: Testing a model using a national sample of college students. *Journal of Consulting and Clinical Psychology, 59,* 670–681.

Margolin, L., Miller, M., & Moran, P. B. (1989). When a kiss is not just a kiss: Relating violations of consent in kissing to rape myth acceptance. *Sex Roles, 20,* 231–243.

Marshall, D. L. (1993). Violence and the male gender role. *Journal of College Student Psychotherapy, 8,* 203–218.

Marshall, W. L., Hudson, S. M., Jones, R., & Fernandez, Y. M. (1995). Empathy in sex offenders. *Clinical Psychology Review, 15,* 99–113.

Marshall, W. L., Laws, D. R., & Barbaree, H. E. (Eds.). (1990). *Handbook of sexual assault: Issues, theories, and treatment of the offender.* New York: Plenum.

Marx, B. P., & Gross, A. M. (1995). Date rape: An analysis of two contextual variables. *Behavior Modification, 19,* 451–463.

McCabe, M. P., & Collins, J. K. (1984). Measurement of depth of desired and experienced sexual involvement at different stages of dating. *Journal of Sex Research, 20,* 377–390.

McCahill, T. W., Meyer, L. C., & Fischman, A. M. (1979). *The aftermath of rape.* Lexington, MA: Lexington.

McConaghy, N., & Zamir, R. (1995). Heterosexual and homosexual coercion, sexual orientation and sexual roles in medical students. *Archives of Sexual Behavior, 24,* 489–502.

McCormick, N. B. (1979). Come-ons and put-offs: Unmarried students' strategies for having and avoiding sexual intercourse. *Psychology of Women Quarterly, 4,* 194–211.

McCormick, N. B., & Jones, A. J. (1989). Gender differences in nonverbal flirtation. *Journal of Sex Education and Therapy, 15,* 271–282.

McCornack, S. A., Avery, P. B., & Bidol, H. F. (1995, November). *Perceptions of female sexual resistance cues: The male misperception myth.* Paper presented at the Speech Communication Association Conference, San Antonio, TX.

McLendon, K., Foley, L. A., Hall, J., Slooan, L., Wesley, A., & Perry, L. (1994). Male and female perceptions of date rape. *Journal of Social Behavior and Personality, 9,* 421–428.

Meilman, P. W., & Haygood-Jackson, D. (1996). Data on sexual assault from the first 2 years of a comprehensive campus prevention program. *Journal of American College Health, 44,* 157–165.

Melnick, M. (1992). Male athletes and sexual assault. *Journal of Physical Education, Recreation, and Dance, 63,* 32–35.

Metts, S., Cupach, W. R., & Imahori, T. T. (1992). Perceptions of sexual compliance-resisting messages in three types of cross-sex relationships. *Western Journal of Communication, 56,* 1–17.

Metts, S., & Spitzberg, B. H. (1996). Sexual communication in interpersonal contexts: A script-based approach. In B. R. Burleson (Ed.), *Communication yearbook 19* (pp. 49–91). Thousand Oaks, CA: Sage.

Mezey, G., & King, M. (1989). The effects of sexual assault on men: A survey of 22 victims. *Psychological Medicine, 19,* 205–209.

Miller, B., & Marshall, J. C. (1987). Coercive sex on the university campus. *Journal of College Student Personnel, 28,* 38–47.

Mills, C. S., & Granoff, B. J. (1992). Date and acquaintance rape among a sample of college students. *Social Work, 37,* 504–509.

Mongeau, P. A., & Johnson, K. L. (1995). Predicting cross-sex first-date sexual expectations and involvement: Contextual and individual difference factors. *Personal Relationships, 2,* 301–312.

Moore, K. A., Nord, C. W., & Peterson, J. L. (1989). Nonvoluntary sexual activity among adolescents. *Family Planning Perspectives, 21,* 110–114.

Mosher, D. L., & Anderson, R. D. (1986). Macho personality, sexaul aggression, and reactions to guided imagery of realistic rape. *Journal of Research in Personality, 20,* 77–94.

Motley, M. T., & Reeder, H. M. (1994, November). *Messages used by women to thwart male escalation of sexual intimacy: One more instance of male/female misunderstandings.* Paper presented to the Speech Communication Association Conference, New Orleans.

Motley, M. T., & Reeder, H. M. (1995). Unwanted escalation of sexual intimacy: Male and female perceptions of connotations and relational consequences of resistance messages. *Communication Monographs, 62,* 355–382.

Muehlenhard, C. L. (1988). "Nice women" don't say yes and "real men" don't say no: How miscommunication and the double standard can cause sexual problems. *Women and Therapy, 7,* 95–108.

Muehlenhard, C. L. (1996). The complexities of sexual consent. *SIECUS Report, 24,* 4–7.

Muehlenhard, C. L., & Andrews, S. L. (1985, November). *Open communication about sex: Will it reduce risk factors related to date rape?* Paper presented at the Association for Advancement of Behavior Therapy Conference, Houston, TX.

Muehlenhard, C. L., Andrews, S. L., & Beal, G. K. (1996). Beyond "just saying no": Dealing with men's unwanted sexual advances in heterosexual dating contexts. In E. S. Byers & L. F. O'Sullivan (Eds.), *Sexual coercion in dating relationships* (pp. 141–168). New York: Haworth.

Muehlenhard, C. L., & Cook, S. W. (1988). Men's self-reports of unwanted sexual activity. *Journal of Sex Research, 24*, 58–72.

Muehlenhard, C. L., Danoff-Burg, S., & Powch, I. G. (1996). Is rape sex or violence? Conceptual issues and implications. In D. M. Buss & N. M. Malamuth (Eds.), *Sex, power, conflict: Evolutionary and feminist perspectives* (pp. 119–137). New York: Oxford University Press.

Muehlenhard, C. L., & Falcon, P. L. (1990). Men's heterosocial skill and attitudes toward women as predictors of verbal sexual coercion and forceful rape. *Sex Roles, 23*, 241–259.

Muehlenhard, C. L., Friedman, D. E., & Thomas, C. M. (1985). Is date rape justifiable? The effects of dating activity, who initiated, who paid, and men's attitudes toward women. *Psychology of Women Quarterly, 9*, 297–310.

Muehlenhard, C. L., Guisti, L. M., & Rodgers, C. S. (1993, November). *The social construction of "token resistance to sex": The nature and function of the myth.* Paper presented at the Society for the Scientific Study of Sex, Chicago.

Muehlenhard, C. L., Harney, P. A., & Jones, J. M. (1992). From "victim-precipitated rape" to "date rape": How far have we come? *Annual Review of Sex Research* (Vol. 3, pp. 219–253). Mt. Vernon, IA: Society for the Scientific Study of Sex.

Muehlenhard, C. L., & Hollabaugh, L. C. (1988). Do women sometimes say no when they mean yes? The prevalence and correlates of women's token resistance to sex. *Journal of Personality and Social Psychology, 54*, 872–879.

Muehlenhard, C. L., & Linton, M. A. (1987). Date rape and sexual aggression in dating situations: Incidence and risk factors. *Journal of Personality and Social Psychology, 34*, 186–196.

Muehlenhard, C. L., & MacNaughton, J. S. (1988). Women's beliefs about women who "lead men on." *Journal of Social and Clinical Psychology, 7*, 65–79.

Muehlenhard, C. L., & McCoy, M. L. (1991). Double standard/double bind: The sexual double standard and women's communication about sex. *Psychology of Women Quarterly, 15*, 447–461.

Muehlenhard, C. L., Powch, I. G., Phelps, J. L., & Giusti, L. M. (1992). Definitions of rape: Scientific and political implications. *Journal of Social Issues, 48*, 23–44.

Muehlenhard, C. L., & Rodgers, C. S. (1993, August). *Narrative descriptions of "token resistance" to sex.* Paper presented at the American Psychological Association, Toronto.

Muehlenhard, C. L., & Schrag, J. L. (1991). Nonviolent sexual coercion. In A. Parrot & L. Bechhofer (Eds.), *Acquaintance rape: The hidden crime* (pp. 115–128). New York: Wiley.

Muehlenhard, C. L., Sympson, S. C., Phelps, J. L., & Highby, B. J. (1994). Are rape statistics exaggerated? A response to criticism of contemporary rape research. *Journal of Sex Research, 31*, 144–145.

Murnen, S. K., Perot, A., & Byrne, D. (1989). Coping with unwanted sexual activity: Normative responses, situational determinants, and individual differences. *Journal of Sex Research, 26*, 85–106.

Murphy, W. D., Coleman, E. M., & Haynes, M. R. (1986). Factors related to coercive sexual behavior in a nonclinical sample of males. *Violence and Victims, 1*, 255–278.

Newman, B. S., & Colon, I. (1994). Beliefs about rape among college males: A revision of the rape myth acceptance scale. *College Student Journal, 28*, 10–17.

Norris, J., & Cubbins, L. A. (1992). Dating, drinking, and rape: Effects of victim's and assailant's alcohol consumption on judgments of their behavior and traits. *Psychology of Women Quarterly, 16*, 179–191.

Nurius, P. S., & Norris, J. (1996). A cognitive ecological model of women's response to male sexual coercion in dating. In E. S. Byers & L. F. O'Sullivan (Eds.), *Sexual coercion in dating relationships* (pp. 117–140). New York: Haworth.

Oliver, M. B., & Hyde, J. S. (1993). Gender differences in sexuality: A meta-analysis. *Psychological Bulletin, 114*, 29–51.

O'Sullivan, C. S. (1991). Acquaintance gang rape on campus. In A. Parrot & L. Bechhofer (Eds.), *Acquaintance rape: The hidden crime* (pp. 140–156). New York: Wiley.

O'Sullivan, L. F., & Allgeier, E. R. (1994). Disassembling a stereotype: Gender differences in the use of token resistance. *Journal of Applied Social Psychology, 24*, 1035–1055.

O'Sullivan, L. F., & Byers, E. S. (1992). College students' incorporation of initiator and restrictor roles in sexual dating interactions. *Journal of Sex Research, 29*, 435–446.

O'Sullivan, L. F., & Byers, E. S. (1993). Eroding stereotypes: College women's attempts to influence reluctant male sexual partners. *Journal of Sex Research, 30*, 270–282.

O'Sullivan, L. F., & Byers, E. S. (1996). Gender differences in responses to discrepancies in desired level of sexual intimacy. In E. S. Byers & L. F. O'Sullivan (Eds.), *Sexual coercion in dating relationships* (pp. 49–68). New York: Haworth.

Overholser, J. C., & Beck, S. (1986). Multimethod assessment of rapists, child molesters, and three control groups on behavioral and psychological measures. *Journal of Consulting and Clinical Psychology, 54*, 682–687.

Oxford University Press. (1971). *The compact edition of the Oxford English dictionary* (Vol. I, A-O). Oxford: Oxford University Press.

Palmer, C. T. (1988). Twelve reasons why rape is not sexually motivated: A skeptical examination. *Journal of Sex Research, 25*, 512–530.

Palmer, C. T. (1991). Human rape: Adaptation or by-product? *Journal of Sex Research, 28*, 365–386.

Paquin, G. W. (1995). The legal aspects of acquaintance rape. In V. R. Wiehe & A. L. Richards (Eds.), *Intimate betrayal: Understanding and responding to the trauma of acquaintance rape* (pp. 88–107). Thousand Oaks, CA: Sage.

Parrot, A., & Bechhofer, L. (Eds.). (1991). *Acquaintance rape: The hidden crime.* New York: Wiley.

Paul, L., & Hirsch, L. R. (1996). Human male mating strategies: II. Moral codes of "quality" and "quantity" strategists. *Ethology and Sociobiology, 17*, 71–86.

Peacock, P. L. (1995). Marital rape. In V. R. Wiehe & A. L. Richards (Eds.), *Intimate betrayal: Understanding and responding to the trauma of acquaintance rape* (pp. 57–73). Thousand Oaks, CA: Sage.

Perper, T., & Weis, D. L. (1987). Proceptive and rejective strategies of U. S. and Canadian college women. *Journal of Sex Research, 23*, 455–480.

Petty, G. M., Jr., & Dawson, B. (1989). Sexual aggression in normal men: Incidence, beliefs, and personality characteristics. *Personality and Individual Differences, 10*, 355–362.

Pineau, L. (1996). Date rape: A feminist analysis. In L. Francis (Ed.), *Date rape: Feminism, philosophy, and the law* (pp. 1–26). University Park: Pennsylvania State University.

Plummer, K. (1984). The social uses of sexuality: Symbolic interaction, power and rape. In J. Hopkins (Ed.), *Perspectives on rape and sexual assault* (pp. 37–55). London: Harper & Row.

Poppen, P. J., & Segal, N. J. (1988). The influence of sex and sex role orientation on sexual coercion. *Sex Roles, 19*, 689–701.

Porter, J. F., & Critelli, J. W. (1992). Measurement of sexual aggression in college men: A methodological analysis. *Archives of Sexual Behavior, 21*, 525–542.

Prentky, R. A., & Knight, R. A. (1991). Identifying critical dimensions for discriminating among rapists. *Journal of Consulting and Clinical Psychology, 59*, 643–661.

Quinn, K., Sanchez-Hucles, J., Coates, G., & Gillen, B. (1991). Men's compliance with a woman's resistance to unwanted sexual advances. *Journal of Offender Rehabilitation, 17*, 13–31.

Reinholtz, R. K., Muehlenhard, C. L., Phelps, J. L., & Satterfield, A. T. (1995). Sexual discourse and sexual intercourse: How the way we communicate affects the way we think about sexual coercion. In P. J. Kalbfleisch & M. J. Cody (Eds.), *Gender, power, and communication in human relationships* (pp. 141–162). Hillsdale, NJ: Lawrence Erlbaum Associates.

Remer, R., & Witten, B. J. (1988). Conceptions of rape. *Violence and Victims, 3*, 217–232.

Renzetti, C. M. (1988). Violence in lesbian relationships: A preliminary analysis of causal factors. *Journal of Interpersonal Violence, 3*, 381–399.

Renzetti, C. M. (1992). *Violent betrayal: Partner abuse in lesbian relationships.* Newbury Park, CA: Sage.

Resick, P. A. (1993). The psychological impact of rape. *Journal of Interpersonal Violence, 8*, 223–255.

Roloff, M. E. (1996). The catalyst hypothesis: Conditions under which coercive communication leads to physical aggression. In D. D. Cahn & S. A. Lloyd (Eds.), *Family violence from a communication perspective* (pp. 20–36). Thousand Oaks, CA: Sage.

Rosenthal, D., & Peart, R. (1996). The rules of the game: Teenagers communicating about sex. *Journal of Adolescence, 19*, 321–332.

Ross, R. R., & Allgeier, E. R. (1996). Behind the pencil/paper measurement of sexual coercion: Interview-based clarification of men's interpretations of sexual experiences survey items. *Journal of Applied Social Psychology, 26,* 1587–1616.

Roth, S., Wayland, K., & Woolsey, M. (1990). Victimization history and victim-assailant relationship as factors in recovery from sexual assault. *Journal of Traumatic Stress, 3,* 169–180.

Rozee, P. D. (1993). Forbidden or forgiven? Rape in cross-cultural perspective. *Psychology of Women Quarterly, 17,* 499–514.

Russell, D. E. H. (1982a). The prevalence and incidence of forcible rape and attempted rape of females. *Victimology: An International Journal, 7,* 81–93.

Russell, D. E. H. (1982b). *Rape in marriage.* New York: Collier.

Russell, D. E. H. (1984). *Sexual exploitation: Rape, child sexual abuse, and workplace harassment.* Beverly Hills, CA: Sage.

Russell, D. E. H. (1991). Wife rape. In A. Parrot & L. Bechhofer (Eds.), *Acquaintance rape: The hidden crime* (pp. 129–139). New York: Wiley.

Saal, F. E., Johnson, C. B., & Weber, N. (1989). Friendly or sexy? It may depend on whom you ask. *Psychology of Women Quarterly, 13,* 263–276.

Santello, M. D., & Leitenberg, H. (1993). Sexual aggression by an acquaintance: Methods of coping and later psychological adjustment. *Violence and Victims, 8,* 91–104.

Sarrel, P. M., & Masters, W. H. (1982). Sexual molestation of men by women. *Archives of Sexual Behavior, 11,* 117–131.

Sarwer, D. B., Kalichman, S. C., Johnson, J. R., Early, J., & Akram, S. (1993). Sexual aggression and love styles: An exploratory study. *Archives of Sexual Behavior, 22,* 265–275.

Schultz, L. G., & DeSavage, J. (1975). Rape and rape attitudes on a college campus. In L. G. Schultz (Ed.), *Rape victimology* (pp. 77–90). Springfield, IL: Thomas.

Schwartz, P. (1994). The politics of desire. *SIECUS Report, 22,* 7–9.

Segal, Z. V., & Marshall, W. L. (1985). Heterosexual social skills in a population of rapists and child molesters. *Journal of Consulting and Clinical Psychology, 53,* 55–63.

Seto, M. C., & Barbaree, H. E. (1995). The role of alcohol in sexual aggression. *Clinical Psychology Review, 15,* 545–566.

Shea, M. E. C. (1993). The effects of selective evaluation on the perception of female cues in sexually coercive and noncoercive males. *Archives of Sexual Behavior, 22,* 415–433.

Shotland, R. L., & Craig, J. M. (1988). Can men and women differentiate between friendly and sexually interested behavior? *Social Psychology Quarterly, 51,* 66–73.

Shotland, R. L., & Goodstein, L. (1983). Just because she doesn't want to doesn't mean it's rape: An experimentally based causal model of the perception of rape in a dating situation. *Social Psychology Quarterly, 46,* 220–232.

Shotland, R. L., & Goodstein, L. (1992). Sexual precedence reduces the perceived legitimacy of sexual refusal: An examination of attributions concerning date rape and consensual sex. *Personality and Social Psychology Bulletin, 18,* 756–764.

Shotland, R. L., & Hunter, B. A. (1995). Women's "token resistant" and compliant sexual behaviors are related to uncertain sexual intentions and rape. *Personality and Social Psychology Bulletin, 21,* 226–236.

Sidman, M. (1989). *Coercion and its fallout.* Boston: Authors Cooperative, Inc.

Sexuality Information and Education Council of the United States. (1994). *Teens talk about sex: Adolescent sexuality in the 90s.* New York: SIECUS/Roper Starch.

Sigal, J., Gibbs, M., Adams, B., & Derfler, R. (1988). The effect of romantic and nonromantic films on perception of female friendly and seductive behavior. *Sex Roles, 19,* 545–554.

Sigler, R. T., & Curry, B. S. (1995). Perceptions of offender motivation in unwanted aggressive sexual advances. *International Review of Victimology, 4,* 1–14.

Small, S. A., & Kerns, D. (1993). Unwanted sexual activity among peers during early and middle adolescence: Incidence and risk factors. *Journal of Marriage and the Family, 55,* 941–952.

Smithyman, S. D. (1979). Characteristics of "undetected" rapists. In W. H. Parsonage (Ed.), *Perspectives on victimology* (pp. 99–120). Beverly Hills, CA: Sage.

Smuts, B. (1996). Male aggression against women: An evolutionary perspective. In D. M. Buss & N. M. Malamuth (Eds.), *Sex, power, conflict: Evolutionary and feminist perspectives* (pp. 231–268). New York: Oxford University Press.

Sorenson, S. B., & Siegel, J. M. (1992). Gender, ethnicity, and sexual assault: Findings from a Los Angeles Study. *Journal of Social Issues, 48*, 93–104.

Sorenson, S. B., Siegel, J. M., Golding, J. M., & Stein, J. A. (1991). Repeated sexual victimization. *Violence and Victims, 6*, 299–308.

Sorenson, S. B., Stein, J. A., Siegel, J. M., Golding, J. M., & Burnam, M. A. (1987). The prevalence of adult sexual assault: The Los Angeles epidemiologic catchment area project. *American Journal of Epidemiology, 126*, 1154–1164.

South, S. J., & Felson, R. B. (1990). The racial patterning of rape. *Social Forces, 69*, 71–93.

Spitzberg, B. H. (1995, November). *Communication predictors of sexual coercion.* Paper presented at the Speech Communication Association Conference, San Antonio, TX.

Spitzberg, B. H. (1997a, November). *An analysis of empirical estimates of rape and sexual coercion.* Paper presented at the National Communication Association Conference, Chicago.

Spitzberg, B. H. (1997b). Intimate violence. In W. R. Cupach & D. J. Canary (Eds.), *Competence in interpersonal conflict* (pp. 174–201). New York: McGraw-Hill.

Spitzberg, B. H., Marshall, L. L., & Cupach, W. R. (1996). *Obsessive relational intrusion and sexual coercion victimization.* Unpublished manuscript, San Diego State University, San Diego, CA.

Sprecher, S., Hatfield, E., Cortese, A., Potapova, E., & Levitskaya, A. (1994). Token reistance to sexual intercourse and consent to unwanted sexual intercourse: College students' dating experiences in three countries. *Journal of Sex Research, 31*, 125–132.

Stacy, R. D., Prisbell, M., & Tollefsrud, K. (1992). A comparison of attitudes among college students toward sexual violence committed by strangers and by acquaintances: A research report. *Journal of Sex Education and Therapy, 18*, 257–263.

Stahl, S. S., & Sacco, W. P. (1995). Heterosocial perception in child molesters and rapists. *Cognitive Therapy and Research, 19*, 695–706.

Stanko, E. (1990). *Everyday violence: How women and men experience sexual and physical danger.* San Francisco: HarperCollins.

Stermac, L. E., & Quinsey, V. L. (1986). Social competence among rapists. *Behavioral Assessment, 8*, 171–185.

Stock, W. E. (1991). Feminist explanations: Male power, hostility, and sexual coercion. In E. Grauerholz & M. A. Koralewski (Eds.), *Sexual coercion: A sourcebook on its nature, causes, and prevention* (pp. 61–74). Lexington, MA: Lexington.

Struckman-Johnson, C. (1988). Forced sex on dates: It happens to men, too. *Journal of Sex Research, 24*, 234–241.

Struckman-Johnson, C. (1991). Male victims of acquaintance rape. In A. Parrot & L. Bechhofer (Eds.), *Acquaintance rape: The hidden crime* (pp. 192–213). New York: Wiley.

Struckman-Johnson, C., & Struckman-Johnson, D. (1991). Men and women's acceptance of coercive sexual strategies varied by initiator gender and couple intimacy. *Sex Roles, 25*, 661–676.

Struckman-Johnson, C., & Struckman-Johnson, D. (1992). Acceptance of male rape myths among college men and women. *Sex Roles, 27*, 85–100.

Struckman-Johnson, C., & Struckman-Johnson, D. (1994). Men pressured and forced into sexual experience. *Archives of Sexual Behavior, 23*, 93–114.

Struckman-Johnson, C., Struckman-Johnson, D., Rucker, L., Bumby, K., & Donaldson, S. (1996). Sexual coercion reported by men and women in prison. *Journal of Sex Research, 33*, 67–76.

Struckman-Johnson, D., & Struckman-Johnson, C. (1996). College men's reactions to hypothetical forceful sexual advances from women. In E. S. Byers & L. F. O'Sullivan (Eds.), *Sexual coercion in dating relationships* (pp. 93–106). New York: Haworth.

Sugarman, D. B. (1994). The conception of rape: A multidimensional scaling approach. *Journal of Social Behavior and Personality, 9*, 389–408.

Symons, D., & Ellis, B. (1989). Human male–female differences in sexual desire. In A. E. Rasa, C. Vogel, & E. Voland (Eds.), *The sociobiology of sexual and reproductive strategies* (pp. 131–146). New York: Chapman & Hall.

Szymanski, L. A., Devlin, A. S., Chrisler, J. C., & Vyse, S. A. (1993). Gender role and attitudes toward rape in male and female college students. *Sex Roles, 29*, 37–57.

Tang, C.S-K., Critelli, J. W., & Porter, J. F. (1993). Motives in sexual aggression: The Chinese context. *Journal of Interpersonal Violence, 8*, 435–445.

Tedeschi, J. T., & Felson, R. B. (1994). *Violence, aggression, and coercive actions.* Washington, DC: American Psychological Association.

Thiessen, D., & Young, R. K. (1994). Investigating sexual coercion. *Society, 31,* 60–63.

Thornhill, N. W. (1996). Psychological adaptation to sexual coercion in victims and offenders. In D. M. Buss & N. M. Malamuth (Eds.), *Sex, power, conflict: Evolutionary and feminist perspectives* (pp. 90–105). New York: Oxford University Press.

Thornhill, R., & Thornhill, N. W. (1992). The evolutionary psychology of men's coercive sexuality. *Behavioral and Brain Sciences, 15,* 363–421.

Tieger, T. (1981). Self-rated likelihood of raping and the social perception of rape. *Journal of Research in Personality, 15,* 147–158.

Tooke, W., & Camire, L. (1991). Patterns of deception in intersexual and intrasexual mating strategies. *Ethology and Sociobiology, 12,* 345–364.

Ullman, S. E., & Knight, R. A. (1992). Fighting back: Women's resistance to rape. *Journal of Interpersonal Violence, 7,* 31–43.

Valentiner, D. P., Foa, E. B., Riggs, D. S., & Gershuny, B. S. (1996). Coping strategies and posttraumatic stress disorder in female victims of sexual and nonsexual assault. *Journal of Abnormal Psychology, 105,* 455–458.

Vogel, R. E., & Himelein, M. J. (1995). Dating and sexual victimization: An analysis of risk factors among precollege women. *Journal of Criminal Justice, 23,* 153–162.

Waldner-Haugrud, L. K., & Magruder, B. (1995). Male and female sexual victimization in dating relationships: Gender differences in coercion techniques and outcomes. *Violence and Victims, 10,* 203–215.

Ward, C. A. (1995). *Attitudes toward rape: Feminist and social psychological perspectives.* Thousand Oaks, CA: Sage.

Ward, S. K., Chapman, K., Cohn, E., White, S., & Williams, K. (1991). Acquaintance rape and the college social scene. *Family Relations, 40,* 65–71.

Warshaw, R., & Parrot, A. (1991). The contributions of sex-role socialization to acquaintance rape. In A. Parrot & L. Bechhofer (Eds.), *Acquaintance rape: The hidden crime* (pp. 73–82). New York: Wiley.

Waterman, C. K., Dawson, L. J., & Bologna, M. J. (1989). Sexual coercion in gay male and lesbian relationships: Predictors and implications for support services. *Journal of Sex Research, 26,* 118–124.

Wells, C. P. (1996). Date rape and the law: Another feminist view. In L. Francis (Ed.), *Date rape: Feminism, philosophy, and the law* (pp. 41–50). University Park: Pennsylvania State University Press.

Wiehe, V. R., & Richards, A. L. (1995). *Intimate betrayal: Understanding and responding to the trauma of acquaintance rape.* Thousand Oaks, CA: Sage.

Winfield, I., George, L. K., Swartz, M., & Blazer, D. G. (1990). Sexual assault and psychiatric disorders among a community sample of women. *American Journal of Psychiatry, 147,* 335–341.

Wyatt, G. E., Newcomb, M. D., & Riederle, M. H. (1993). *Sexual abuse and consensual sex.* Newbury Park, CA: Sage.

Yegidis, B. L. (1986). Date rape and other forced sexual encounters among college students. *Journal of Sex Education and Therapy, 12,* 51–54.

Yllö, K., & Finkelhor, D. (1985). Marital rape. In A. W. Burgess (Ed.), *Rape and sexual assault: A research handbook* (pp. 146–158). New York: Garland.

Yoshihama, M., & Sorenson, S. B. (1994). Physical, sexual, and emotional abuse by male intimates: Experiences of women in Japan. *Violence and Victims, 9,* 63–77.

Zimmerman, R. S., Sprecher, S., Langer, L. M., & Holloway, C. D. (1995). Adolescents' perceived ability to say "No" to unwanted sex. *Journal of Adolescent Research, 10,* 383–399.

Obsessive Relational Intrusion and Stalking

William R. Cupach
Illinois State University

Brian H. Spitzberg
San Diego State University

Violent behavior toward self or others as the denouement *of unrequited love is as old as antiquity.*

—Meloy, 1992, p. 19

He began calling me at home approximately 3 weeks after the break up of the relationship. We dated for 4 years; he went out with someone else behind my back (for the third time), and I decided to end the relationship for good. At first, his phone calls were occurring about once every couple of weeks, and although the calls were friendly in nature, they were painful to me. He called because he said he "cared about me" and was concerned because I was taking the break up so hard. He continued to date others and continued to call me once or twice every couple of weeks. Then he started to drive by my home. He came to the door probably four or five times. Now, 14 months later, he has a steady girlfriend of 8 months, but he continues to call me and drive by my home. The calls range anywhere from once a week to five or six times per week and several times each night. I usually see him driving by my home once every couple of weeks. I have not been answering his calls for several weeks now. I have my answering machine answer the calls; I also have caller ID on my phone and can tell when the phone calls are from him. Often when the phone calls begin in the evening, I will turn out the lights and pretend I'm not home—and he usually drives by. It's getting

233

to be a very predictable pattern. Over the last 14 months, I repeatedly asked him to leave me alone. I have been civil to him—I have been mean to him. Nothing seems to deter him. So now, I just ignore the calls and don't speak to him. I feel very threatened by his behavior. I am a little scared of him because his obsessive behavior doesn't stop. Yet, I am also angry that I have to deal with this type of behavior on a daily basis. Unfortunately, this person has become head of the company that I work for. He threatened to terminate my job only once, but he knows he has the power to ruin this part of my life also. This is why I feel I have no recourse but to ignore his calls. Any course of action against him would probably result in worse consequences for me than what is occurring now (loss of job, bad publicity for my reputation, etc.). I have gone to the extent of changing positions within the company so I can be in a different office building. I did this to minimize daily contact.

This story was told to us by a 38-year-old woman who continues to be harassed by a former dating partner. It is just one of many diverse accounts we heard from individuals who are pestered, badgered, harassed, intimidated, and even stalked by a person desiring relational contact, which is unwanted by the object of pursuit. We discovered, in our preliminary research, that unwanted pursuit is both more pervasive and threatening than we imagined. Sensational cases of celebrities being stalked appear in the media, and increasing attention to the problem of domestic violence recently raised public consciousness about crimes of passion (see Lowney & Best, 1995). Popular books (Gross, 1994; Lardner, 1995; Markman & LaBrecque, 1994; Olsen, 1991; Orion, 1997; Schaum & Parrish, 1995) now offer gruesome and horrifying accounts of murderous obsessions. Yet, these severe and publicized cases of relational harassment represent only the tip of a large iceberg. Unwanted relationship pursuit manifests itself in complex and subtle ways, owing to such commonplace experiences as jealousy, unrequited love, and divorce.

In this chapter, we attempt to lay the groundwork for studying the phenomenon of *obsessive relational intrusion* (ORI). We begin with a conceptualization of the phenomenon and its cousin—stalking. We describe four general profiles of individuals who exhibit ORI and describe the behavioral manifestations of unwanted pursuit. The consequences for, and reactions of, individuals who are the object of unwanted pursuit are then considered. Finally, we conclude the chapter with an agenda to guide a program of research designed to shed light on the sequelae of ORI and on the efficacy of strategies for managing it.

CONCEPTUALIZING ORI AND STALKING

We define (ORI) as repeated and unwanted pursuit and invasion of one's sense of physical or symbolic privacy by another person, either stranger or acquaintance, who desires and/or presumes an intimate relationship. There are several key components of this conceptualization. First, ORI grows out of nonmutuality of relationship definition (see Morton, Alexander, & Altman, 1976). The pursuer and the object of pursuit are at odds over the fundamental relationship dialectic of autonomy versus connection (Baxter, 1990; Goldsmith, 1990). The pursuer presses his or her need for more connection, intimacy, and interdependence with the object of pursuit, whereas the victim simultaneously desires autonomy and freedom from imposition, at least with respect to the pursuer. This dialectical tension is endemic to the formation and ongoing construction of all interpersonal relationships (see Baxter & Montgomery, 1996, for a review). Mismanagement of this dialectic is central to the problem of unwanted pursuit, particularly when pursuit is obsessive.

Second, ORI is not commonly associated with a single event. Rather, obsessive intrusion is repeated over several occasions. Isolated, individual acts of harassment or imposition are not by themselves obsessive. Obsessiveness is reflected in the fact that the intruder is fixated on the target of attention; the intruder's thoughts and behaviors are persistent, preoccupying, and often morbid. Pursuit is persistent despite the absence of reciprocity by the obsessional object and despite resistance by the object. Consequently, episodes of intrusion tend to escalate in intensity over time as the pursuer exerts greater and greater effort to capture the attention and affection of the object. It is such intrusive relationships that concern us in this chapter, rather than the odd moment of revenge or starstruck passion. It is partly in the relationship that the dynamics of unwanted intrusion are found, as much as in the recesses of individual psychopathology. Thus, a complete understanding of ORI necessitates an examination of the various contingent actions of pursuer and pursued over time.

Third, intrusion can also be psychological and symbolic as well as physical. Imposition on one's autonomy and invasion of one's privacy are meaningful manifestations of intrusion and are even associated with forms of psychological abuse (Follingstad & DeHart, 1997). Assaults on and threats to a person and property are overt forms of harassment. However, unwanted intrusion on psychological or symbolic space can be accomplished without overt threat and can be just as debilitating for the victim of intrusion. Importantly, however, intrusion necessarily implies a form of behavior on the part of the intruder, and the behavioral topography of obsessive relational intrusion and stalking is extensive (see, Table 8.1, later in this chapter; Coleman, 1997; Lindsey, 1993; Wright et al., 1996).

Stalking typically represents a severe form of ORI. *Stalking* is commonly defined as "the willful, malicious, and repeated following and harassing of another person that threatens his or her safety" (Meloy & Gothard, 1995,

p. 258). Although extreme episodes of ORI include stalking behaviors, there are forms of harassment and intrusion that would not legally constitute stalking. (For a discussion of issues regarding the legal definition of stalking and the efficacy of anti-stalking statutes, see Anderson, 1993; Bureau of Justice Assistance, 1996; Diacovo, 1995; Hueter, 1994; Jordan, 1995; Morin, 1993; Moses-Zirkes, 1992; National Institute of Justice, 1993; Perez, 1993; Strikis, 1993; and Welch, 1995). ORI entails a broader domain of intrusive activity than does stalking. As stated in a report by the National Institute of Justice (1996):

> Stalking is a distinctive form of criminal activity composed of a series of actions (rather than a single act) that taken individually might constitute legal behavior. For example, sending flowers, writing love notes, and waiting for someone outside her place of work are actions that, on their own, are not criminal. When these actions are coupled with an intent to instill fear or injury, however, they may constitute a pattern of behavior that is illegal. (p. 1)

Stalking is a pattern of behavior that stems from various underlying motives. When it is motivated by a desire on the part of the pursuer to increase intimacy with the object, it is a manifestation of ORI. In some cases, however, the stalker pursues a victim because the stalker perceives (accurately or not) that the victim has perpetrated some transgression against the stalker. In such cases, the stalker's attachment to the victim is more persecutory or angry as opposed to affectionate or amorous (Harmon, Rosner, & Owens, 1995). Such a motive suggests investigation of the broader issue of revenge (Stuckless & Goranson, 1992). Some stalkers stalk exclusively intending to do harm to their object of pursuit (e.g., assassins; Holmes, 1993). Sociopathic stalkers are not interested in cultivating a relationship with their victims; they pursue individuals who happen to meet their assault criteria (Evans, 1994). We do not focus in this chapter on harassment that is strictly sociopathic or persecutory in nature. Instead, we specifically concentrate on obsessive intrusion that seeks relational connection. We recognize, however, that the distinction between affectionate and persecutory motives can become blurred. Amorous intent can lead to rejection, which in turn, can result in feelings of persecution and deep-seated anger.

INCIDENCE AND MANIFESTATIONS OF ORI

The essence of ORI is one person attempting to establish an interpersonal relationship with another person who does not want this relationship. By definition, a *relationship* requires contact between individuals. When the pursuer encounters barriers to normal face-to-face interaction with an intended relational partner, then he or she considers employing all of the other available means of communication. Pursuers use a number of mediums to connect with their objects, including the telephone (Katz, 1994; Leets, de Becker, & Giles, 1995; Murray, 1967; Murray & Beran, 1968; Savitz, 1986; Sheffield, 1989; Smith & Morra, 1994; Warner, 1988), letters (Dietz, Matthews, Martell, et al., 1991; Dietz, Matthews, Van Duyne, Martell, et al., 1991), and now, e-mail (Ross, 1995). Pursuers show up unexpectedly at the home or workplace of their objects and often engage in clandestine surveillance.

As the most blatant form of ORI, stalking received the most research attention. Yet surprisingly, although 50 states passed some form of anti-stalking legislation in less than 10 years, there is a paucity of trustworthy data on the extent of victimization. Several expert opinions emerge with minimal foundation offered for the bases of these estimates. For example, numerous authors repeat the estimate that "There are approximately 200,000 people in this country who are currently stalking someone"[1] (Cohen, 1993, p. 5). The source of this estimate appears to be stalking expert and forensic psychiatrist Park Dietz, who also claims that 5% of women will be stalked at some time in their lives (Puente, 1992). The exact nature of the evidence for such estimates, however, remains a mystery. Similarly, Landau (1996) boldly claimed that "In 1992, 1,500 women were stalked and murdered by former husbands or boyfriends" (p. 14). This unattributed statistic was obtained from a transcript of the *Oprah Winfrey Show*. Clearly, a need exists for reliable and scientifically based estimates of stalking and obsessive relational intrusion.

The most important descriptive research thus far was sponsored recently by the National Institute of Justice (NIJ) and the Centers for Disease Control (CDC). On behalf of the NIJ and CDC, the Center for Policy Research conducted a telephone survey of a national probability sample of 8,000 women and 8,000 men regarding stalking experiences (Tjaden & Thoennes, 1997). Results showed that stalking is far more ubiquitous than previously assumed. Among adult Americans, 8% of

---

[1] A report published by the National Institute of Justice (1996) indicated that "Estimates of the number of stalkers in the United States vary from 20,000 to 200,000" (p. 4). The report contends that "The 200,000 figure includes the broadest spectrum of stalkers, including those who send threatening mail to public figures, such as Hollywood celebrities and members of Congress. If incidents involving public figures are excluded from this count, the estimate of stalkers' numbers declines significantly" (p. 15). Contrarily, we believe that the 200,000 figure may seriously underestimate the problem because many forms of obsessive intrusion are not included in the somewhat narrow legal parameters of stalking. The more recent national study conducted by the Center for Policy Research (and cosponsored by the NIJ) suggests that stalking is much more pervasive (Tjaden & Thoennes, 1997).

women and 2% of men have been stalked at some time in their lives. Annually, an estimated 1.7 million persons are the victims of stalking in the United States. The vast majority of stalking victims are female (78%) and the vast majority of stalking perpetrators are male (87%). In general, women tend to be stalked by former intimate partners, whereas men tend to be stalked by male strangers or male acquaintances. Some unknown number of children are also the objects of stalking (McCann, 1995).

Additional data on the pervasiveness of stalking are provided by studies of college samples. For example, Gallagher, Harmon, and Lingenfelter (1994) surveyed 1,100 member institutions of the National Association of Student Personnel Administrators in the United States and Canada. Data from the Chief Student Affairs Officers (CSAOs) representing 504 4-year institutions indicated that 34.5% of CSAOs "had to intervene in one or more stalking cases during the past year" (p. 42). In 15% of these cases, a warning to the pursuer was sufficient. However, stronger sanctions were required in many cases. "Eighteen percent ... were denied access to residence halls, 31% were brought before judicial boards for sanctions short of suspension or dismissal, and 15% were suspended or dismissed from school after other interventions failed" (p. 42). "CSAOs reported that during the 1991–92 academic year, 57 students were injured by their pursuers, one female pursuer 'torched' a church after leaving a fatal attraction note, and five students were killed by obsessive pursuers" (p. 43). In a study of college students specifically, McCreedy and Dennis (1996) received responses from 760 undergraduates at an eastern university, indicating that just over 6% of the students claimed to have been stalked at some time. However, two studies of college samples on opposite sides of the continent, when asking students directly whether they had ever been stalked, found that 27% answered "yes" (Fremouw, Westrup, & Pennypacker, 1997; Nicastro, Cousins, & Spitzberg, 1997).

An investigation by Hall (1996) revealed the obsessive nature of stalking behaviors. In her study of more than 100 adult victims, she discovered that 17% were stalked between 1 and 6 months, 23% for 6 months to 1 year, 29% for 1 to 3 years, and 13% for more than 5 years. The national survey conducted by the Center for Policy Research found that the average duration of stalking was 1.8 years, which was longer for victims of intimate or formerly intimate partners (2.2 years) than for victims of stranger stalking (1.1 years).

According to Kurt (1995), "there is no doubt that some stalking behavior represents a form of domestic violence and can be construed, at the very least, as a type of interpersonal coercion" (p. 221; see also Coleman, 1997). According to a recent report by the National Institute of Justice (1996), "Some advocates of battered women believe that up to 80% of stalking cases occur in a domestic context. Currently, there is little hard data, however, on how many stalkers and victims are former intimates, how many murdered were stalked beforehand, or how many stalking incidents overlap with domestic violence" (p. 3). Nevertheless, the most dramatic picture of stalking behavior is suggested by the statistics regarding domestic violence. In the United States alone, there are more than 400,000 protective orders issued annually. Most often they are requested by victims of domestic violence (Biden, 1993). The importance, and impotence of these restraining orders is suggested by the FBI estimate that "30% of all women murdered in 1990 were killed by their husbands or boyfriends in domestic violence incidents" (Cohen, 1993, p. 10; also cited in Flowers, 1994). Moreover, 90% of women murdered by their partners were stalked before the attack, according to one estimate (Beck et al., 1992).[2] Studies done in Detroit and Kansas City reportedly indicate that "some 90% of all those who are murdered by their intimate partners called the police at least once, and more than half have called five times or more" (Cohen, 1993, p. 8).[3] According to Bradburn (1992), "Approximately 50% of all females who leave their husbands for reasons of physical abuse are followed, harassed, or further attacked by their former spouses" (p. 271). Harrell and Smith (1996), in a study of 355 women who obtained temporary restraining orders against their spouse or lover, found that 21% reported "tracking or stalking" within the first 3 months of the order. This rate remained stable over a period of 1 year.

Reliable evidence regarding the propensity for violence in stalking cases is generally scant. Samples in reported research were extremely small and unrepresentative, making it risky to draw any firm conclusions. Moreover, the underlying motives for stalking considerably vary. Preliminary data is offered by Meloy (1996b), who systematically reviewed clinical studies of obsessional followers reported over the past 10 years. Inspection of the largest studies (Harmon et al., 1995; Meloy & Gothard, 1995; Zona, Sharma, & Lane, 1993; total N = 142) reporting statistics regarding incidence of threats and incidence of actual subsequent violence revealed the following: About one half of obsessional followers threatened a person, property, or both, and 75% of those who threatened were not subsequently violent. These findings comport with those of the Center for Policy Research that found, in a national probability sample, that less than

---

[2]We unsuccessfully attempted to locate the original study or studies on which this "90% of women murdered by their partners were stalked" estimate was based. Given the tendency in the stalking literature for the careless repetition of estimates regardless of their methodology, this estimate should be read with caution.

[3] We unsuccessfully attempted to locate the original study or studies on which this "90% of all those who are murdered by their intimate partners called the police" estimate was based. Consequently, this estimate should be read with caution.

one half of all stalking victims are overtly threatened by their assailant (Tjaden & Thoennes, 1997). Meloy (1996b) noted that threats are probably underreported, which tends to inflate the 75%. Naturally, it is possible for a pursuer who has not made a threat to become unexpectedly violent, but this seems to be rare in the reported literature. It is also possible that some murder victims were obsessively pursued prior to the attack, but the stalking was never reported. Furthermore, although violence as part of or a result of stalking is not yet well-demonstrated, there is clear evidence of an association. The Center for Policy Research study found that for women stalked by husbands or cohabiting partners, 81% were also physically assaulted and 31% were sexually assaulted by this partner. These rates are significantly higher than those for women who do not report stalking victimization (Tjaden & Thoennes, 1997).

Other small scale studies on forms of harassment and intrusion that do not necessarily qualify as stalking clarify the nature and scope of unwanted pursuit. Some research indicates that many obscene telephone calls are targeted toward a particular recipient (Savitz, 1986). Studies reach widely varied estimates of the percentage of people who received such calls, ranging from 8% to 90% (DiVasto et al., 1984; Herold, Mantle, & Zemitis, 1979; Katz, 1994; Murray, 1967; Murray & Beran, 1968; Savitz, 1986; Sheffield, 1989; Smith & Morra, 1994). As many as 30% of people experienced someone exposing himself or herself to them (DiVasto et al., 1984; Herold et al., 1979), some instances of which could be directed to the target or based on some degree of pursuit. One study found that 10% of college students reported having received "unwanted personal attention" in the forms of "unwanted letters, calls, visits, pressure for meetings, dates, etc., where personal or romantic interest in you was implied, but no sexual expectations were stated" (Leonard et al., 1993, p. 176). In the same vein, Herold et al. (1979) found that 24% of college students reported being followed for the purpose of harassment. Providing a little more detail, a study by Roscoe, Strouse, and Goodwin (1994) found that many adolescents experience unwanted telephone calls (20.7%), unwanted letters or notes (19.1%), unwanted pressure for dates (18.9%), and unwanted sexual advances (16.6%).

Even in intact relationships, individuals engage in intrusive behaviors. Larkin and Popaleni (1994) found, for example, in their focus groups and interviews, that:

> Young men intimidate their girlfriends by using surveillance tactics to closely monitor their girlfriends' behavior, activities, and access to other friends. Young women disclosed experiences of being spied on through windows, having their diaries, address books and mail read without permission, being telephoned countless times to verify their whereabouts and being visited unexpectedly at different events or in different places. (p. 221)

Similarly, Guerrero, Andersen, Jorgensen, Spitzberg, & Eloy (1995) discovered that surveillance tactics represented one common type of response to feeling jealousy in a relationship.

The surveillance and relational harassment that occur in existing relationships (Guerrero et al., 1995; Patterson & Kim, 1991) seem to foreshadow what can occur when the relationship breaks up. In a dating survey of 48 undergraduate women, Jason, Reichler, Easton, Neal, and Wilson (1984) found that 56% reported being "harassed by a male for at least a month after indicating a desire not to date" (p. 265). In a separate network and convenience sample, Jason et al. conducted structured interviews with 50 women who were harassed for at least 1 month subsequent to terminating a dating relationship with a male partner. Results indicated that "On the average the harassment occurred for 13 months (range 1–120 months), and harassment episodes occurred on an average of 6.5 per week (range 0.1-49)" (Jason et al., 1984, p. 263). The harassing behaviors reported by the women included phone calls (92%), visits at home or work (48%), verbal or physical threats or assaults (30%), being followed or watched (26%), and being sent flowers, letters, or notes (6%).

Spitzberg and colleagues investigated the incidence of a broad range of ORI behaviors among undergraduate men and women sampled from three universities—one in Illinois, Texas, and California (Cupach & Spitzberg, 1997a; Spitzberg & Cupach, 1996; Spitzberg, Marshall, & Cupach, 1997). A list of 63 behaviors was developed based on prior literature and consultation with professionals (i.e., a psychologist, a security consultant, and a city attorney specializing in stalking). Table 8.1 shows the average percentage of respondents reporting that they were the recipients of each harassing behavior at least once. This list of behaviors is not exhaustive, although it depicts the wide diversity of actions that can be perceived as intrusive. Not surprisingly, behaviors that are relatively less intrusive and less threatening are reported more frequently.

THE DYNAMIC NATURE OF ORI

We clarify three important points about the occurrence of ORI in general. First, it should be apparent that ORI is composed of behaviors that can be arrayed on a continuum of severity (see Fig. 8.1). Some behaviors are mildly intrusive, some moderately so, and some intensely invasive (Cupach & Spitzberg, 1997a). Mildly intrusive behaviors amount to pestering and importunity; they are annoying, but not particularly threatening. Receiving unwanted gifts or favors, being pestered for a date, being begged for forgiveness, or getting numerous nonthreatening calls or messages are

TABLE 8.1

Average Percentage of Respondents Reporting Being the Target of ORI Behaviors Across Three Samples

(Total N = 876)	%
Called and argued with you	73
Asked if you were seeing someone	72
Would call and hang up without answering	70
Constantly asked for another chance	64
Watched or stared at you from a distance	62
Made exaggerated claims about his or her affection for you	61
Refused to take hints that he or she was not welcome	61
Gossiped or bragged about your relationship to others	61
Checked up on you through mutual acquaintances	58
Drove by your house or work	57
Constantly apologized for past wrongs or transgressions	57
Told you to stop doing certain things	56
Argued with you about your relationships with other people	55
Used third parties to spy or keep tabs on you	55
Engaged in excessive self-disclosure	54
Accused you of being unfaithful	53
Performed large favors for you without your permission	52
Told others you were more intimate than you currently were	51
Tried to argue with you in public places	50
Called at all times of the day to check up on you	50
Spread false rumors about you to your friends	49
Visited you at work	48
Used profanity and/or obscenities in reference to you	47
Showed up before or after work	47
Spied on you	46
Left notes on your car windshield	45
Complained to you how you ruined his or her life	45
Accused you of sleeping around	44
Made up things about your past relationship	43
Sent you unwanted cards or letters	42
Joined you uninvited while you were conversing with others	42
Called you while you were working	41
Waited around near your conversation with another person	40
Left you written messages in or at your residence	38
Increased contact with your family members to stay involved	37
Waited outside your place	36
Described acts of sex to you	36
Inappropriately touched you in an intimate way	35
Waited in a car near where you were	35
Left frequent messages on your answering machine	34
Sent you unwanted gifts	34
Went through your private things in your room	34
Made vague warnings that bad things will happen to you	34
Showed up before or after classes	34
Claimed to still be in a relationship with you	34
Physically shoved, slapped, or hit you	32

242

TABLE 8.1 (continued)

Threatened you with physical harm	30
Followed you in a walking conversation	30
Made obscene phone calls to you	30
Warned that bad things would or might happen to you	29
Followed you from place to place	27
Damaged property or possessions of yours	26
Exposed himself or herself to you	26
Knocked on your window unexpectedly	25
Mailed or left gifts you previously gave	16
Sent threatening notes/letters/messages to you	16
Forced sexual behavior	16
Called radio station and devoted songs to you	15
Took photos of you without your knowledge or consent	11
Cluttered your e-mail with messages	11
Recorded conversations without your knowledge	8
Broke into your home or apartment	8
Sent you offensive photographs	5

inconveniencing and intrusive to a degree, but they tend not to be threatening or highly upsetting (Cupach & Spitzberg, 1997a). Using a 100-point scale, Lees-Haley, Price, and Williams (1994) reported that the following experiences appear to be only moderately emotionally distressing: repeatedly receiving love letters from a coworker after asking him or her to stop ($M = 26$), repeatedly being asked for a date by a supervisor after initially saying no ($M = 28$), repeatedly receiving obscene notes from a coworker after asking him or her to stop ($M = 30$), and repeatedly being asked out by one's teacher after initially saying "no" ($M = 34$). Highly distressing experiences ($M > 80$) included death of a child or spouse and rape.

Behaviors that invade privacy but pose little threat, such as being spied on or having false rumors spread about you to your friends, are relatively more aggravating. They are more than merely annoying; they are moderately severe. Most upsetting of all are behaviors that are perceived to be threatening such as being the victim of stalking, home invasion, verbal threats, physical assault, or property damage. Thus, behaviors are interpreted by objects of pursuit as being more or less intrusive, more or less invasive of privacy, and more or less threatening.

Second, the continuum of intrusiveness implies that the boundary between reasonable and obsessive is fuzzy. Some behaviors that are seen as modestly intrusive in one context are construed as appropriate intimacy in another context (e.g., leaving notes on a car window, sending gifts, making frequent calls, etc.). A degree of persistence in relational pursuit is sometimes expected and rewarded. It is unclear at what point persist-

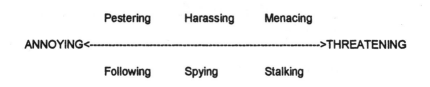

FIG. 8.1. Continuum of ORI severity.

ence in pursuit becomes excessive. There is a gray area between persever-ance and obsession. It is precisely this aspect of pursuit—when intrusion becomes both unwanted and obsessive—that renders interaction between pursuer and object problematic.

Third, intrusive behavior occurs in a relational (or perhaps sometimes quasirelational) context. Intrusion has a serial quality, consisting of sequen-tial and cumulative actions and reactions. A specific instance of intrusion (e.g., discovering a note on your car windshield) represents one event at one point in time. ORI entails multiple events between pursuer and target over time. Thus, ORI is not only characterized by specific types of behavior, but also temporal patterns of behavior. For example, the intensity and threatening nature of intrusiveness tend to escalate over time. A report issued by the National Institute of Justice (1996) indicated that "over time a stalker's behavior typically becomes more and more threatening, serious and violent. The stalking activity generally escalates from what initially may be bothersome and annoying but legal behavior to the level of obsessive, dangerous, violent, and potentially fatal acts" (p. 5). Further-more, the behaviors of both pursuers and targets are likely to be contingent. The target's response to an intrusive event influences the pursuer's sub-sequent actions, which in turn affect the victim's subsequent actions, and so on. At present, our knowledge about ORI is primarily at the level of particular actions and events that are construed as intrusive. A more complete understanding of the dynamics of ORI requires investigations of the temporal and interactive facets of pursuer and target behaviors.

PROFILES OF PURSUERS

Types of Pursuers

Pigeonholing types of obsessional pursuers is tricky business. Perhaps contrary to common belief, pursuers are a heterogeneous lot (see Meloy, 1996a; Meloy & Gothard, 1995). As Meloy (1996b) remarked, "What obsessional followers do is less varied [and less complicated] than who they are" (p. 161). Different types of pursuers have been variously labeled *stalkers, obsessional followers, love addicts,* and *erotomanics.* There are different types of obsessional intruders and they show different profiles. Researchers distinguished among different groups of intruders based on criteria such as: the presence of certain psychiatric disorders, the motive of the pursuer, the type of victim (e.g., public figures versus ordinary citizens), and the nature of the relationship between the pursuer and the victim (e.g., stranger, coworker, or former spouse; Geberth, 1992; Holmes, 1993; Kurt, 1995; McAnaney, Curliss, & Abeyta-Price, 1993; Wallace, 1995; Wright et al., 1996; Wright, Burgess, Burgess, McCrary, & Douglas, 1995; Zona et al., 1993). Using some of these distinctions, we offer our own tentative typology of obsessive relational pursuers consisting of four broad categories—erotomanics, borderline erotomanics, obsessional acquaintances, and obsessional estranged lovers.

Erotomanics. The mental condition of *"psychose passionelle"* described by French psychiatrist de Clérambault (1942) is known by a number of labels, including *de Clérambault's syndrome* (Leong, 1994; Leong & Silva, 1991), *old maid's insanity, delusional loving* (Seeman, 1978), and *pathologies of love* (Mullen & Pathé, 1994b). The most common name is *erotomania*, which refers to the clinical diagnosis of delusional disorder, erotomanic being the subtype (American Psychiatric Association, 1994). Erotomanics hold the delusional belief that they are loved by another individual. The erotomanic exhibits a morbid infatuation with the object, and commonly, the affection is more idealized and spiritual, rather than sexual. In fact, erotomanics typically have little or no contact with the object of affection, except through media exposure (in the case of celebrities) or fleeting, nominal interaction, such as an exchanged glance. Often the object of affection is someone of a higher social or financial status.

Erotomania is a chronic condition, resistant to legal and psychiatric remedies. In Zona et al.'s (1993) study of seven individuals diagnosed as erotomanic, the average duration of obsession was 125 months. The erotomanic's delusion is persistent and perpetuated by rationalization. The rejecting behaviors of the ostensible lover are interpreted as evidence of the lover's reciprocation.

Erotomania is infrequently diagnosed in its pure form. It usually co-occurs with the diagnosis of other conditions, such as paranoid schizophrenia or organic mental disorders (e.g., El Gaddal, 1989; Mullen & Pathé, 1994a, 1994b). In addition, many cases reported as erotomania do not provide sufficient information for a definitive diagnosis (Gillett, Eminson, & Hassanyeh, 1990).

Early clinical reports suggest that erotomanic patients are more often women than men, and their victims are men. However, there is no definitive evidence that this is generally the case. Male erotomanics are now commonly reported in the clinical literature as are cases in which the erotomanic and the object of affection are the same sex (Dunlop, 1988; Goldstein, 1987; Harmon et al., 1995; Meloy, 1992; Taylor, Mahendra, & Gunn, 1983; Signer, 1989; Zona et al., 1993).

Explanations for the occurrence of erotomania range from psychological to organic. Among the more prominent factors are low self-esteem (Mullen & Pathé, 1994a, 1994b; Segal, 1989) and pathological mourning (Evans, Jeckel, & Slott, 1982; Raskin & Sullivan, 1974). Organic factors that were implicated include dementia, right temporal lobe epileptic focus, and use of alcohol, cortisone, or birth control pills (Carrier, 1990; Doust & Christie, 1978; Drevets & Rubin, 1987; El Gaddal, 1989; Signer & Cummings, 1987).

Although they stalk their objects and occasionally become violent toward them, "the risk and extent of actual physical harm posed by erotomanic subjects may be less than by other categories of stalker" (Menzies, Fedoroff, Green, & Isaacson, 1995, p. 535). Meloy (1992) concluded that "The best estimate is that less than 5% of individuals with the erotomanic subtype of Delusional (Paranoid) Disorder will be violent" (p. 38).

Menzies et al. (1995) conducted a study to discern predictors of dangerousness among a group of male erotomanics. They examined the files of 13 psychiatric patients diagnosed with erotomania and an additional 16 cases reported in the psychiatric literature. The cases were classified into dangerous and benign groups based on the presence or absence of at least one of five types of serious antisocial behavior related to the erotomanic delusions (e.g., physical harm or threats of physical harm). Dangerousness was significantly predicted by two factors: The patient had multiple delusional objects and the patient exhibited a history of serious antisocial behavior unrelated to the delusion. Classification into benign and dangerous groups based on these two factors showed 88.9% accuracy (hit rate).

Borderline Erotomanics.   Meloy (1989) proposed a distinction between pure erotomanics, as just described, and borderline erotomanics, who do not possess the delusion that the object of their desire loves them. *Borderline erotomania* "indicates a gross disturbance of attachment or bonding, but not necessarily a loss of reality testing" (p. 480). Although Meloy seemed to employ the term *borderline erotomanic* to cover a broad spectrum of obsessional followers, we prefer to circumscribe its application to pursuers whose victims are virtual strangers. Zona et al. (1993) referred to this group as "love obsessionals."

Borderline erotomanics are similar to their pure erotomanic counterparts; however, instead of showing a primary diagnosis of delusion (erotomanic subtype), they exhibit other primary psychiatric diagnoses, such as personality disorders, schizophrenia, or organic mental disorder. Similar to erotomanics, borderline erotomanics know their objects only through the media or casual contact. Thus, a prototypical victim in Zona et al.'s (1993) study of love obsessionals "was one possessing the entertainment/movie industry image of a sexy actress, or 'bombshell'" (p. 901). Perhaps the most publicized case of borderline erotomania is that of John Hinckley, Jr., whose obsessive infatuation with the actress Jodie Foster lead him to shoot (then president) Ronald Reagan.

Borderline erotomanics are just as obsessed with their objects as are pure erotomanics, even though they do not perceive the affection to be requited. The average duration of obsession reported by Zona et al. (1993) was 146 months.

Obsessional Acquaintances. Although relational intrusion can be perpetrated by strangers, it often grows out of an existing (or previous) social or professional relationship between the pursuer and the pursued. Romans, Hays, and White (1996), for example, explored the incidence of stalking and other forms of harassment experienced by university counseling center staff members. Based on a random sample of counseling centers, the authors found that 64% of respondents were harassed in some way by a current or former client, 5.6% of staff members reported being stalked by a client, 8% had a family member who was stalked, and 10% reported that a supervisee was stalked.

Other researchers reported obsessional following by clients of lawyers, physicians, psychiatrists, social workers, and professors. Harmon et al. (1995) reported a fascinating example:

> A 41-year-old woman was referred for evaluation seven times between 1985 and 1994 subsequent to four arrests on the same charge. The defendant had worked at a hospital and [had] been harassing a doctor who also worked there for approximately ten years, believing that they had an affair. By the time of her most recent referral, this college educated women was working as a go-go dancer, and harassing the doctor, his wife and the Assistant District Attorney handling the case. At least 20 individuals connected with the case have taken out orders of protection against her (including four judges who have removed themselves from her case because of harassment or inappropriate behavior on her part). (pp. 194–195)

Objects of pursuit can also be friends, acquaintances, or coworkers of the pursuer. In a sample of 59 university students reporting on specific occurrences of ORI, 34% reported being harassed by an acquaintance, 19%

by a friend, and 9% by a co-worker; most of the rest were former dating partners (Cupach & Spitzberg, 1997b). According to Hall's (1996) study of stalking victims, 30% of the stalkers were prior acquaintances, but not sexual intimates.

Obsessional Estranged Lovers. Perhaps the largest category of pursuers consists of former relational partners who cannot let go of a terminated (or redefined) romantic relationship. In Hall's (1996) study, for example, 53% of stalkers were prior sexual intimates of the victims. Although biased by the fact that the cases were in the domestic violence unit of the city attorney's office in San Diego, a study of 50 stalking case files revealed that 96% of victims had prior relationships with their pursuer, most of which were a dating partner (60%), spouse (22%), or separated or divorced partner (6%; Cousins, 1997; Nicastro, 1997). The most commonly mentioned motive for pursuit in these cases was attributed as "reconciliation." In Tjaden and Thoennes' (1997) study, women tended to be stalked by former husbands and intimate partners. In these cases the lover or spouse is estranged; that is, love is unrequited or the once-intact relationship has gone sour. The pursuer's behavior is intended to restore or maintain the now unreciprocated relationship. When attempts to pursue a terminated romantic relationship become obsessive, they are said to represent *love addiction* (e.g., Nelson, Hill-Barlow, & Benedict, 1994; Peele, 1981; Timmreck, 1990). Whereas erotomanics are considered psychotic, obsessed estranged lovers are more often psychopathic (Geberth, 1992). It is important to note, however, that in the Center for Policy Research study, about one fifth of stalking incidents occurred before the relationship ended, whereas over 40% occurred after the relationship ended, and the remainder occurred both before and after the relationship ended (Tjaden & Thoennes, 1997). It is not known, in this study, to what extent some of the stalking in intact relationships occurred in the context of relationships transitioning to separation or dissolution.

The emotional distress attendant on relational termination is associated with a host of powerful feelings, including diminished self-esteem, hurt, humiliation, anger, and depression (e.g., Baumeister, Wotman, & Stillwell, 1993; Timmreck, 1990). Intrusion begins with protestations of love and attempts to interact with the former partner. After repeated rejection and the realization that the former relationship cannot be restored or reconciled, the jilted lover may seek retribution and threaten or harm the former partner. This is evidenced, in part, in the statistics on domestic violence presented earlier.

Of all the types of pursuers, obsessed estranged lovers (as a group) may be the most dangerous. Some evidence suggests that the propensity for violence is greatest in cases where the pursuer and victim were previously involved romantically. Meloy and Gothard (1995) found that obsessional followers were significantly more likely to threaten a prior spouse or intimate partner than to threaten a stranger.

Characteristics of Pursuers

A "consistent finding ... suggests that chronic failures in social or sexual relationships through young adulthood may be a necessary predisposing experience for some obsessional followers. In fact, failed relationships appear to be the rule among these individuals" (Meloy, 1996b, p. 151). Research on erotomanics painted a picture of lonely and socially isolated individuals, often unmarried (Raskin & Sullivan, 1974; Segal, 1989; Zona et al., 1993). Although the evidence is limited thus far, this pattern apparently extends to pursuers without a diagnosis of erotomania. In their investigation of obsessional followers, Meloy and Gothard (1995) found that, whether or not the pursuers were erotomanic, they tended to "have a history of impaired or conflicted relationships. Many ... whose victims were strangers never had a significant intimate relationship and consistently failed in their courtship attempts. This appeared to heighten their social isolation" (p. 261).

According to McReynolds (1996), "A 1993 district attorney's office survey of roughly 80 men convicted of stalking found that most were not only narcissistic, but egocentric. Half had previous criminal histories, many involving drugs and alcohol" (p. 41). Substantial percentages of stalking victims in Hall's (1996) study claimed to know that their pursuer had a violent family background (27%), had a history of violence or physical abuse (46%), and stalked another person or persons (30%). A large majority (72%) reported being threatened.

One interpretation contends that obsessional pursuit reflects "a pathology of attachment for some individuals" (Meloy, 1996b, p. 159; see Dutton, 1995). Dutton and colleagues demonstrated that an insecure attachment style is associated with jealousy and with domestic assault (Dutton, Saunders, Starzomski, & Bartholomew, 1994; Dutton, van Ginkel, & Landolt, 1996). They speculated that insecurely attached and jealous individuals are hypersensitive to abandonment. In a study of 30 wives separated from their husbands, Dutton et al. (1996) found that husbands' self-reported jealousy and fearful attachment style (a type of insecure attachment) significantly predicted wives' reports of their husbands' intrusiveness. Frequency of intrusiveness was measured by items such as "My partner followed me from place to place," "My partner engaged in threatening behavior directed at me," and "My partner has forced his way into my home against my will."

Data obtained by Levitt, Silver, and Franco (1996) also suggests the potential relevance of attachment styles. These researchers surveyed individuals who were involved in "troubled" relationships, including some relationships where the partner engaged in harassment, threats, and intrusive following. Although effects were small, they found that insecure attachment styles were significantly associated with involvement in troubled relationships. Because respondents reported the troublesome behaviors of their partners, the attachment style of victims may be implicated as much as that of pursuers.

Other studies of love and attachment suggest a link to pursuit. Williams and Schill (1994) describe people with a self-defeating personality as high in a mania love style, which is possessive, dependent, and jealous. "Once in a relationship, they appear to strive constantly to attract a partner's attention and are intensely jealous" (p. 33). Sperling and Berman (1991) also described people with a style of "desperate love" as people who have:

> experiences such as a feeling of fusion with the lover, a sense of urgency about the relationship, an overwhelming desire for and anxiety concerning reciprocation, idealization of the lover, feelings of insecurity outside the relationship, difficulty with interpersonal reality testing in the relationship, anxiety at separations, and extremes of happiness and sadness. (pp. 47–48)

Not surprisingly, they found that such people could be characterized by more dependent attachment styles.

In Meloy's (1996b) account of obsessional following, the factors of relational incompetence and narcissism are also prominent:

> The psychopathology of obsessional following appears to be, in part, a maladaptive response to social incompetence, social isolation, and loneliness. What differentiates these individuals from others, however, appears to be their aggression and pathological narcissism. The acting out of their obsession in pursuit, and in a few cases eventual violence, is likely due to a disturbance in their narcissistic economy. A real event, such as acute or chronic rejection, challenges the compensatory narcissistic fantasy that the obsessional follower is special, idealized, admired, superior to, in some way linked, or destined to be with the object of pursuit. Disturbance of this narcissistic fantasy, imbued with both a sense of grandiosity and a feeling of pride, triggers feelings of shame or humiliation that are defended against with rage. Such intense anger also fends off any feeling of sadness because the capacity to grieve the loss of a whole, real, and meaningful person is not available to the obsessional follower. (pp. 159–160)

Despite psychological disturbances, pursuers often exhibit cunning in their pursuit and are highly motivated by their obsession. Meloy and Gothard (1995) found that obsessional followers were more intelligent and educated than a comparison group of criminal offenders exhibiting mental disorders. They suggested that pursuers are especially resourceful and manipulative:

> obsessional followers would go to great lengths to find the residences and phone numbers of their victims. One posed as a police officer to get an address from the department of motor vehicles. Another used alligator clips and installation information to trace and decode the unlisted telephone number of the victim each time she had it changed. (p. 261)

Although pursuers sometimes intend to inflict terror on their victims, such as when revenge is a motivating factor, they often fail to realize the extent of distress they are causing. There are several contributing factors. First, because they are obsessed with the object of pursuit, obsessional pursuers tend to be egocentric, focusing more on their own feelings than on the feelings of the pursued.

Second, the pursuer rationalizes the appropriateness of his or her behavior. In their research on unrequited love, for example, Baumeister et al. (1993) suggested that the actions of a would-be (rejected) lover may be seen by that person as justified in the name of love. "The would-be lovers's blameworthiness for relentlessly pursuing the rejector despite his or her objections becomes mitigated by the would-be lover's honorable intentions" (chap. 10, this volume, p. 317).

Third, pursuers are guided by a cultural script that promotes persistence. Bratslavsky et al. (chap 10, this volume) argued:

> Movies, books, and songs often portray the would-be lover's persistence as paying off when the rejector comes to his or her senses and recognizes the would-be lover for the wonderful person he or she is. The presence of this script for the would-be lovers makes it easy to understand why an unrequited lover persists in the face of rejection. (p. 318)

In Jason et al.'s (1984) study, men, whose female dating partners had broke up with them, did not perceive persistence in contacting the women beyond a month as harassment. Nine of their 23 male participants "indicated there needed to be either physical abuse or threats (verbal abuse) for it to be harassment" (p. 266). Indeed, Stith, Jester, and Bird (1992) found that a major cluster of college students who used violence in their dating relationships were described as "hostile pursuers." These people expended great "energy pursuing their partner and attempting to maintain their relationships during frequent periods of conflict, while also expressing high levels of emotional abuse towards their partner" (p.417). Some degree of persistence apparently is viewed by rejected suitors as socially competent.

CHARACTERISTICS OF VICTIMS

Effects of ORI on Victims

We typically refer to the object of pursuit as a "victim" because intrusion is unwanted and persistent, and it adversely imposes on the object. Regardless of the severity of the intrusion, the object is a victim of at least mild harassment and invasion of symbolic privacy. In the most severe cases, of course, the object is the victim of physical violence. Most of the time, when pursuers commit violence in connection with their obsessional pursuit, it is perpetrated against the object of affection (about 80% of the time, by Meloy's, 1996b, reckoning). Less often, however, third parties blocking access to the pursuit object, innocent bystanders, and pursuers themselves can experience violence as well (Mullen & Pathé, 1994b).

Although firm data are not available on the incidence of violence linked to ORI, the consequences of physical assault are patently obvious. What is less obvious (and even less documented) are the psychological effects on victims of ORI. Mullen and Pathé, (1994b) indicate that " It is difficult to overstate the fear produced in most victims of stalkers simply by the repeated and intrusive contacts. Victims curtail their lives, giving up social and sometimes work activities. They change address, town and sometimes even country in the hope of evading the stalker's attentions" (p. 475).

In Hall's (1996) study, 83% of stalking victims reported that their personality had changed as a result of the stalking. This change consisted of considering themselves as less outgoing, more frightened, more paranoid, and/or more aggressive. In the Center for Policy Research study, 30% of women and 20% of men who were victims of stalking considered seeking counseling as a result. Victims of stalking were also more concerned for their safety than nonvictims (Tjaden & Thoennes, 1997). Indeed, Wallace and Silverman (1996) argued for viewing stalking victimization as a source of posttraumatic stress disorder, although they noted that "there have been no scientific studies of the long-term effects that stalking has on victims" (p. 204).

Even when pursuers do not technically stalk their objects, the psychological cost can be great. To assume that milder forms of relational intrusion are not serious because they occur in dating and casual relationships or because they do not involve overt physical threat would be a mistake. Victims of less severe forms of intrusion report various reactions, including annoyance, upset, stress, anxiety, depression, fear, shock, violation, self-blame, and a loss of trust in people (Cousins, 1997; Cupach & Spitzberg,

1997a; DiVasto et al., 1984; Herold et al., 1979; Nicastro, 1997; Nicastro et al., 1997; Savitz, 1986; Smith & Morra, 1994).

Victim Responses to ORI

Very little is known currently about how victims of ORI cope. Clearly, those who are pursued respond in a variety of ways that are likely to be adaptive or maladaptive, depending on the nature of the intruder and the unique circumstances of the prior relationship between the intruder and the victim.

In one study (Jason et al., 1984), 50 females who reported being harassed for over 1 month by a former dating partner after terminating the relationship responded in a number of ways. These included doing nothing (32%), talking to a friend, family member, or therapist (54%), making an environmental change, such as moving (19%), and becoming mean and distant with respect to the harasser (8%). Similarly, the literature on sexual harassment suggests that responses directed at a harasser can be arrayed on a continuum of assertiveness, ranging from avoidance to direct and forceful confrontation (e.g., Clair, McGoun, & Spirek, 1993; Gruber, 1989; Maypole, 1986).

Studies on coping with phenomena that are conceptually related to ORI can offer some insight into the various ways in which victims deal with intrusion. Burgoon et al. (1989; see also Hosman & Siltanen, 1995), for example, investigated privacy invasions and the tactics individuals employed to restore privacy. Respondents reported a broad repertoire of responses, including *interaction control* (e.g., stop talking or be silent, decrease involvement in the conversation, or pretend to be preoccupied to avoid interaction), *dyadic intimacy strategies* (e.g., hit or push the other person, or threaten the person with violence), *expressions of negative arousal* (e.g., yell at the person, stare at the person, or become irritated and angry and show it), *blocking and avoidance* (e.g., avoid eye contact or erect physical barriers), *distancing* (e.g., put back to the door, increase distance between self and other, or do not show any reaction), and *confrontation* (e.g., tell person you do not like his or her behavior, leave the situation, or tell the person to go away).

According to Burgoon et al. (1989), "It is noteworthy that no restoration behavior shows a particularly high propensity of use, implying a fundamental timidity on the part of victims to restore privacy" (p. 155). They argued that "In a culture as obsessed with good interpersonal relations as it is individual rights, it is likely that people in actual privacy-invading situations rely far more on passive and subtle strategies than on direct (and potentially more efficacious) ones" (p. 155). This conclusion is corroborated by

Werner and Haggard (1992) who found that individuals dealing with unwanted intrusions at the office indicated a preference for indirect forms of avoidance and rejection.

The tendency for victims of intrusion to respond relatively passively comports with the research on unrequited love. Individuals who are obsessionally pursued are cast into the role of rejector, to the extent that the pursuer desires a greater level of intimacy or contact than the victim permits. Based on their analysis of accounts regarding unrequited love, Baumeister and colleagues (Baumeister et al., 1993; Bratslavsky et al., chap. 10, this volume) suggested that rejectors' messages of disinterest were often inconsistent and ambiguous. They contended that unlike pursuers, rejectors lack a clear script to guide behavior.

> Even the few media treatments of unrequited love that focus on the rejector's viewpoints (such as the movies *Fatal Attraction* or *Play Misty for Me*) fail to feature effective means of handling the problem but rather dwell on the mystified futility of the protagonist in attempting to discourage unwanted romantic attentions from an increasingly intrusive, maniacal pursuer. These are hardly helpful guides. (Baumeister et al., 1993, p. 379)

Furthermore, evidence from several studies of social rejection indicate that rejectors try to soften messages of interpersonal resistance in an effort to save the rejected person's face and minimize the hurt inflicted (e.g., Folkes, 1982; Metts, Cupach, & Imahori, 1992; Snow, Robinson, & McCall, 1991). In their study of unrequited love, Bratslavsky et al. (chap. 10, this volume) indicated that "rejectors' accounts indicated that their unwillingness to hurt another person led them to behave in a considerate and warm manner, and this in turn was probably taken as a sign of encouragement by the would-be lovers" (p. 321). Similarly, de Becker (1997) contended that the politeness or indirectness of relational rejection is interpreted as a sign of affection.

In an effort to capture a broader range of victim responses to ORI, we developed a list of 50 potential coping behaviors (Spitzberg & Cupach, 1996; Spitzberg et al., 1997). Two surveys of college students ($N = 300$, $N = 366$, respectively) were conducted to assess the frequency with which targets exhibited each of the behaviors in response to an incident of relational intrusion. Factor analysis resulted in five distinct groupings of the response items. These were labeled *direct interaction* (e.g., yell at the person, have a serious talk with the person, or telling the person he or she was wrong), *protection* (e.g., obtaining a restraining order, calling the police, or changing jobs), *avoidance* (e.g., ignoring the person, avoiding common activities, or avoiding eye contact), *retaliation* (e.g., hitting the pursuer, trying to shame the person, or ridiculing the person), and *technology* (obtaining caller ID, obtaining telephone call-back feature, or pursuing telephone annoyance laws). These categories were replicated in open-ended descriptions of victim responses as well (Cupach & Spitzberg, 1997b). In response to stalkings, Fremouw et al. (1997) found that the most common coping strategies for both males and females was to either confront the stalker (i.e., direct interaction) or to ignore or hang up phone calls from the stalker (i.e., avoidance). Over 50% of the victims of stalking in the Center for Policy Research study claimed to have taken protective measures, including 17% who said they got a gun (Tjaden & Thoennes, 1997).

If we know little about how victims behaviorally respond to episodes of relational intrusion, we know even less about the relative efficacy of behavioral responses that victims enact in an effort to stifle intrusive behavior. In a study of women who were harassed after terminating a heterosexual relationship, Jason et al. (1984) found that assertive responses by women were no more effective than nonassertive, passive responses in stemming the harassment. Research on sexual harassment also suggests that relatively assertive and confrontive responses are perceived to be effective by some victims and counterproductive by other victims (e.g., Livingston, 1982). Clearly, we need to investigate how various factors modify the efficacy of coping responses. Such factors include the nature of the relationship between the victim and the pursuer prior to the onset of harassment and psychosocial characteristics of the pursuer and the target of pursuit.

One of the most formal and serious coping responses is legal action. Despite extensive legal reforms in antistalking legislation, the efficacy of current laws is suspect in a variety of regards (Sohn, 1994). The most likely legal response begins with the request for protective orders. The first such request is for a temporary restraining order (TRO), which later can be made permanent (in actuality, usually only for a period of months to three years) based on a hearing in front of a judge at which time the intruder can defend his or her actions.

Research recently began to examine the effectiveness of such protective orders, almost exclusively in domestic violence cases (e.g., Fisher & Rose, 1995; Gondolf, McWilliams, Hart, & Stuehling, 1994; Horton, Simonidis & Simonidis, 1987; Kaci, 1994). Unfortunately, the data thus far are not encouraging. Evidence from clinical studies of erotomanics (e.g., Harmon et al., 1995; Mullen & Pathé, 1994b), as well as the data regarding domestic violence previously presented, suggests that such orders are routinely ignored. Perhaps the first empirical warning was a study of 262 domestic violence incidents by Berk, Berk, Loseke, and Rauma (1983), who found that for the few couples with restraining orders, the existence of the order did not appear to have any effect on preventing future abuse (p. 207). They cautioned that their data are limited in various ways, but their finding of no deterrent effect has since been supported in several subsequent studies of domestic violence cases. Chaudhuri and Daly (1992), in a study of 30 TRO cases, found 11 men violated the order, 7 through forcible entry, 2 by deceit, and 1 was let in by a child. The paradoxical nature of such violations is illustrated by one man who "came to a woman's house four times, trying to convince her to take him back; he came with a dozen roses and chocolates in hand each time. At first she wanted to believe that he had changed, but he became violent during each visit" (p. 239). Perhaps the most disconcerting finding of this study was "that one in ten women in [the] study was beaten or threatened by men because the woman obtained a TRO" (p. 245).

The most extensive studies of restraining orders report similarly discouraging data (e.g., Harrell, Smith, & Newmark, 1993; Tjaden & Thoennes, 1997). Klein's (1996) study of 663 restraining order cases over a period of 2 years found that "Almost half of the abusers (48.8%) re-abused their victims within 2 years" of the restraining order (p. 199), although it is important to point out that this sample had an unusually high proportion of abusers with prior criminal histories (80%). Harrell and Smith (1996) conducted interviews with 35 women who filed petitions for TROs for abuse and 142 men named in consecutive complaints. They found that "Unwanted contacts in the first 3 months after the first order were reported by over half of all the women who obtained temporary orders. These contacts involved unwanted telephone calls (reported by 52%); tracking or stalking (21%); and visits to the home (21%)" (p. 222). Overall, 77% of the women and 71% of the men reported contacts after the restraining order, 57% of the women reported psychological abuse, and almost one third (29%) of the women reported at least one act of abuse (i.e., kicking, strangling, beating, forcing sex, or threatening with a weapon) within 3 months of the order. Tjaden and Thoennes (1997) found that 28% of women and 10% of men victimized by stalking obtained a protective order, but that 69% of the women and 81% of the men claimed their stalker violated the order.

Still, formal legal intervention sometimes is effective in stopping the stalking (Williams, Lane, & Zona, 1996). The question remains: "Under what circumstances?" In the case of temporary restraining orders, for instance, mutually served papers are more effective than nonmutually served papers (Meloy, Cowett, Parker, Hofland, & Friedland, 1996). De Becker (1997) argued that "court orders that are introduced early carry less risk than those introduced after the stalker has made a significant emotional investment or introduced threats and other sinister behavior" (p 205). Thus, restraining orders typically deter stalking by a rejected dating partner, but may be less effective in cases where the victim repeatedly was abused by the stalker and threats were escalated. In each case, there needs to be a careful assessment of whether a court order is likely to deter further intrusion. As de Becker (1997) said, "If a victim or professional in the system gets a restraining order to stop someone from committing murder, they have probably applied the wrong strategy" (p. 190).

MAPPING UNCHARTED TERRITORY

Obsessional relational intrusion is fairly common and it produces a number of undesirable consequences. Yet, we know very little about the dynamics of ORI. Preliminary research began to provide tentative and preliminary answers to such fundamental questions as: "What is the incidence of a broad range of relationally intrusive behaviors?" The answers open the door to additional questions that require serious scholarly attention, such as: "When do intrusive behaviors become threatening, rather than merely annoying?" "Under what circumstances, and why?" "What turning points characterize serial episodes of ORI?" "What symptoms (physical and psychological) are associated with ORI victimization?" "What are the precipitants of violent versus nonviolent pursuit?" "What are the profiles and correlates of ORI perpetration (e.g., jealousy, possessiveness, or inse- cure attachment)?" "What is the incidence of ORI among domestic violence perpetrators?" And perhaps most importantly "what is the relative effectiveness of victim responses designed to avoid ORI and/or to minimize its negative consequences?" "What types of responses are adaptive, what types are maladaptive, and under what circumstances?"

Investigating ORI represents our desire to shed some light on the dark side of interpersonal relationships. ORI reflects interactions in which relational goals are severely mismatched. It is one of the many ways in which interpersonal interactions derail and ultimately create distress for people. Understanding how and why such derailment occurs, and what is required to successfully manage such derailment, is integral to a complete understanding of social and relational competence, which inherently en- tails the successful management of problematic interpersonal encounters.

As in all phenomena of the dark side, stalking and obsessive relational intrusion reveal and produce paradoxes in human relationships. Often, persons only desiring love unknowingly terrorize the object of their affec- tions. Others methodically attempt to create a sense of fear and helpless- ness in the very person they once loved. The victims of such attentions often face the bind of action and inaction. Assertive or aggressive attempts to deter a pursuer may in fact trigger counterattacks of revenge or even be interpreted by a delusional pursuer as evidence of love, masked in the guise of the object's public face. However, inaction can reinforce the pursuer through its ambiguity.

An additional irony was noted by one of our associates, herself a victim of stalking by a former acquaintance. After obtaining a permanent protective order against her pursuer, she experienced a heightened sense of apprehension because she no longer could keep tabs on him because he was no longer keeping tabs on her—at least not overtly. In essence, it seemed just as scary not having any idea of his activities as it was when he was showing up in her life all the time; at least she had a sense of his whereabouts and the routine points and types of contact.

The paradoxes of obsessive relational pursuit and intrusion provide a rich nexus of dialectical forces at work in relationships. The pursuer desires intimacy, the target desires autonomy. The pursuer invades privacy, whereas the target attempts to secure privacy. The target often is debilitated by indecision regarding courses of action, whereas the pursuer is focused and clearly directed toward a specific goal. The pursuer thrives on the element of surprise and novelty of contact, whereas the target generally longs for a more ordered and predictable life. Just possibly, although not yet evidenced in the research, some relationships involve targets of pursuit who long for the friend they feel they lost, and the pursuers long for the romance their friendship never permitted. Such are some of the ironies implicit in stalking and obsessive relational intrusion.

REFERENCES

American Psychiatric Association. (1994). *Diagnostic and statistical manual of mental disorders* (4th ed.). Washington, DC: Author.

Anderson, S. C. (1993). Anti-stalking laws: Will they curb the erotomanic's obsessive pursuit? *Law and Psychology Review, 17*, 171–191.

Baumeister, R. F., Wotman, S. R., & Stillwell, A. M. (1993). Unrequited love: On heartbreak, anger, guilt, scriptlessness, and humiliation. *Journal of Personality and Social Psychology, 64*, 377–394.

Baxter, L. A. (1990). Dialectical contradictions in relationship development. *Journal of Social and Personal Relationships, 7*, 69–88.

Baxter, L. A., & Montgomery, B. M. (1996). *Relating: Dialogues & dialectics*. New York: Guilford.

Beck, M., Rosenberg, D., Chideya, F., Miller, S., Foote, D., Manly, H., & Katel, P. (1992, July 13). Murderous obsession. *Newsweek*, 60–62.

Berk, R. A., Berk, S. F., Loseke, D. R., & Rauma, D. (1983). Mutual combat and other family violence myths. In D. Finkelhor, R. J. Gelles, G. T. Hotaling, & M. A. Straus (Eds.), *The dark side of families: Current family violence research* (pp. 197–212). Newbury Park, CA: Sage.

Biden, J. R. (1993). *Antistalking proposals* (Hearing before the Committee on the Judiciary, United States Senate, Publication No. J–103–5). Washington, DC: U.S. Government Printing Office.

Bradburn, W. E., Jr. (1992). Stalking statutes. *Ohio Northern University Law Review, 19*, 271–288.

Bureau of Justice Assistance. (1996). *Regional seminar series on developing and implementing antistalking codes* (Monograph, Publication No. NCJ 156836). Washington, DC: U.S. Department of Justice.

Burgoon, J. K., Parrott, R., LePoire, B. A., Kelley, D. L., Walther, J. B., & Parry, D. (1989). Maintaining and restoring privacy through communication in different types of relationships. *Journal of Social and Personal Relationships, 6*, 131–158.

Carrier, L. (1990). Erotomania and senile dementia. *American Journal of Psychiatry, 147*, 1092.

Chaudhuri, M., & Daly, K. (1992). Do restraining orders help? Battered women's experience with male violence and legal process. In E. S. Buzawa & C. G. Buzawa (Eds.), *Domestic violence: The changing criminal justice response* (pp. 227–252). Westport, CT: Greenwood.

Clair, R. P., McGoun, M. J., & Spirek, M. M. (1993). Sexual harassment responses of working women: An assessment of current communication-oriented typologies and perceived effectiveness of the response. In G. L. Kreps (Ed.), *Sexual harassment: Communication implications* (pp. 209–233). Cresskill, NJ: Hampton Press.

Cohen, W. S. (1993). *Antistalking proposals* (Hearing before the Committee on the Judiciary, United States Senate Publication No. J-103-5). Washington, DC: U.S. Government Printing Office.

Coleman, F. L. (1997). Stalking behavior and the cycle of domestic violence. *Journal of Interpersonal Violence, 12*, 420–432.

Cousins, A. V. (1997). *Profiles of stalking perpetrators.* Unpublished masters thesis, San Diego State University, San Diego, CA.

Cupach, W. R., & Spitzberg, B. H. (1997a, February). *The incidence and perceived severity of obsessive relational intrusion behaviors.* Paper presented at the Western States Communication Association convention, Monterey, CA.

Cupach, W. R., & Spitzberg, B. H. (1997b). *Profiles of obsessive relational intrusion.* Unpublished data, Illinois State University, Normal, IL.

de Becker, G. (1997). *The gift of fear.* Boston: Little, Brown.

De Clérambault, C. G. (1942). Les psychoses passionelles. In *Oeuvres psychiatriques* (pp. 315–322). Paris: Presses Universitaires.

Diacovo, N. (1995). California's anti-stalking statute: Deterrent or false sense of security? *Southwestern University Law Review, 24*, 389–421.

Dietz, P., Matthews, D., Martell, D., Stewart, T., Hrouda, D., & Warren, J. (1991). Threatening and otherwise inappropriate letters to members of the United States Congress. *Journal of Forensic Sciences, 36*, 1445–1468.

Dietz, P., Matthews, D., Van Duyne, C., Martell, D., Parry, C., Stewart, T., Warren, J., & Crowder, J. (1991). Threatening and otherwise inappropriate letters to Hollywood celebrities. *Journal of Forensic Sciences, 36*, 185–209.

DiVasto, P. V., Kaufman, A., Rosner, L., Jackson, R., Christy, L., Pearson, S., & Burgett, T. (1984). The prevalence of sexually stressful events among females in the general population. *Archives of Sexual Behavior, 13*, 59–67.

Doust, J. W. L., & Christie, H. (1978). The pathology of love: Some clinical variants of de Clerambault's syndrome. *Social Science Medicine, 12*, 99–106.

Drevets, W. C., & Rubin, E. H. (1987). Erotomania and senile dementia of Alzheimer type. *British Journal of Psychiatry, 151*, 400–402.

Dunlop, J. L. (1988). Does erotomania exist between women? *British Journal of Psychiatry, 153*, 830–833.

Dutton, D. G. (1995). *The batterer: A psychological profile.* New York: Basic Books.

Dutton, D. G., Saunders, K., Starzomski, A., & Bartholomew, K. (1994). Intimacy anger and insecure attachment as precursors of abuse in intimate relationships. *Journal of Applied Social Psychology, 24*, 1367–1386.

Dutton, D. G., van Ginkel, C., & Landolt, M. A. (1996). Jealousy, intimate abusiveness, and intrusiveness. *Journal of Family Violence, 11*, 411–423.

El Gaddal, Y. Y. (1989). de Clérambault's Syndrome (erotomania) in organic delusional syndrome. *British Journal of Psychiatry, 154*, 714–716.

Evans, D. L., Jeckel, L. L., & Slott, N. E. (1982). Erotomania: A variant of pathological mourning. *Bulletin of the Menninger Clinic, 46,* 507–520.

Evans, R. (1994). Every step you take: The strange and subtle crime of stalking. *Law Institute Journal, 68,* 1021–1023.

Fisher, K., & Rose, M. (1995). When "enough is enough": Battered women's decision making around court orders of protection. *Crime and Delinquency, 41,* 414–429.

Flowers, R. B. (1994). *The victimization and exploitation of women and children: A study of physical, mental and sexual maltreatment in the United States.* Jefferson, NC: McFarland & Company.

Folkes, V. S. (1982). Communicating the causes of social rejection. *Journal of Experimental Social Psychology, 18,* 235–252.

Follingstad, D. R., & DeHart, D. D. (1997, July). *Defining psychological abuse: Contexts, behaviors, and typologies.* Paper presented at the International Network on Personal Relationships Conference, Oxford, OH.

Fremouw, W. J., Westrup, D., & Pennypacker, J. (1997). Stalking on campus: The prevalence and strategies for coping with stalking. *Journal of Forensic Sciences, 42,* 664–667.

Gallagher, R. P., Harmon, W. W., & Lingenfelter, C. O. (1994). CSAOs perceptions of the changing incidence of problematic college student behavior. *NASPA Journal, 32*(1), 37–45.

Geberth, V. J. (1992). Stalkers. *Law and Order, 40,* 138–143.

Gillett, T., Eminson, S. R., & Hassanyeh, F. (1990). Primary and secondary erotomania: Clinical characteristics and follow-up. *Acta Psychiatrica Scandinavia, 82,* 65–69.

Goldsmith, D. (1990). A dialectic perspective on the expression of autonomy and connection in romantic relationships. *Western Journal of Speech Communication, 54,* 537–556.

Goldstein, R. L. (1987). More forensic romances: De Clérambault's syndrome in men. *Bulletin of the American Academy of Psychiatry and the Law, 15,* 267–274.

Gondolf, E. W., McWilliams, J., Hart, B., & Stuehling, J. (1994). Court response to petitions for civil protection orders. *Journal of Interpersonal Violence, 9,* 503–517.

Gross, L. (1994). *To have or to harm: From infatuation to fatal attraction.* New York: Warner Books.

Gruber, J. E. (1989). How women handle sexual harassment: A literature review. *Sociology and Social Research, 74,* 3–7.

Guerrero, L. K., Andersen, P. A., Jorgensen, P. F., Spitzberg, B. H., & Eloy, S. V. (1995). Coping with the green-eyed monster: Conceptualizing and measuring communicative responses to romantic jealousy. *Western Journal of Communication, 59,* 270–304.

Hall, D. (1996, March). *Outside looking in: Stalkers and their victims.* Paper presented to the Academy of Criminal Justice Sciences Conference, San Francisco, CA.

Harmon, R. B., Rosner, R., & Owens, H. (1995). Obsessional harassment and erotomania in a criminal court population. *Journal of Forensic Sciences, 40,* 188–196.

Harrell, A., Smith, B., & Newmark, L. (1993). *Court processing and the effects of restraining orders for domestic violence victims* (Executive summary). Washington, DC: Urban Institute.

Harrell, A., & Smith, B. E. (1996). Effects of restraining orders on domestic violence victims. In E. S. Buzawa & C. G. Buzawa (Eds.), *Do arrests and restraining orders work?* (pp. 212–242). Thousand Oaks, CA: Sage.

Herold, E. S., Mantle, D., & Zemitis, O. (1979). A study of sexual offenses against females. *Adolescence, 14,* 65–72.

Holmes, R. M. (1993). Stalking in America: Types and methods of criminal stalkers. *Journal of Contemporary Criminal Justice, 9,* 317–327.

Horton, A. L., Simonidis, K. M., & Simonidis, L. L. (1987). Legal remedies for spouse abuse: Victim characteristics, expectations, and satisfaction. *Journal of Family Violence, 2,* 265–279.

Hosman, L. A., & Siltanen, S. A. (1995). Relationship intimacy, need for privacy, and privacy-restoration behaviors. *Communication Quarterly, 43,* 64–74.

Hueter, J. A. (1994). Lifesaving legislation: But will the Washington stalking law survive constitutional scrutiny? *Washington Law Review, 72,* 213–240.

Jason, L. A., Reichler, A., Easton, J., Neal, A., & Wilson, M. (1984). Female harassment after ending a relationship: A preliminary study. *Alternative Lifestyles, 6,* 259–269.

Jordan, T. (1995). The efficacy of the California stalking law: Surveying its evolution, extracting insights from domestic violence cases. *Hastings Women's Law Journal, 6,* 363–383.

Kaci, J. H. (1994). Aftermath of seeking domestic violence protective orders: The victim's perspective. *Journal of Contemporary Criminal Justice, 10,* 204–219.

Katz, J. E. (1994). Empirical and theoretical dimensions of obscene phone calls to women in the United States. *Human Communication Research, 21,* 155–182.

Klein, A. R. (1996). Re-abuse in a population of court-restrained batterers: Why restraining orders don't work. In E. S. Buzawa & C. G. Buzawa (Eds.), *Do arrests and restraining orders work?* (pp. 192–213). Thousand Oaks, CA: Sage.

Kurt, J. L. (1995). Stalking as a variant of domestic violence. *Bulletin of the Academy of Psychiatry and the Law, 23,* 219–223.

Landau, E. (1996). *Stalking.* New York: Grolier.

Lardner, G., Jr. (1995). *The stalking of Kristin.* New York: Atlantic Monthly Press.

Larkin, J., & Popaleni, K. (1994). Heterosexual courtship violence and sexual harassment: The private and public control of young women. *Feminism and Psychology, 4,* 213–227.

Lees-Haley, P. R., Lees-Haley, C. E., Price, J. R., & Williams, C. W. (1994). A sexual harassment–emotional distress rating scale. *American Journal of Forensic Psychology, 12,* 39–54.

Leets, L., de Becker, G., & Giles, H. (1995). Fans: Exploring expressed motivations for contacting celebrities. *Journal of Language and Social Psychology, 14,* 102–123.

Leonard, R., Ling, L. C., Hankins, G. A., Maidon, C. H., Potorti, P. F., & Rogers, J. M. (1993). Sexual harassment at North Carolina State University. In G. L. Kreps (Ed.), *Sexual harassment: Communication implications* (pp. 170–194). Cresskill, NJ: Hampton Press.

Leong, G. B. (1994). De Clérambault syndrome (erotomania) in the criminal justice system: Another look at this recurring problem. *Journal of Forensic Sciences, 39,* 378–385.

Leong, G. B., & Silva, J. A. (1991, May). Lovesick: The erotomania syndrome. *VA Practitioner,* 39–43.

Levitt, M. J., Silver, M. E., & Franco, N. (1996). Troublesome relationships: A part of human experience. *Journal of Social and Personal Relationships, 13,* 523–536.

Lindsey, M. (1993). *The terror of batterer stalking: A guideline for intervention.* Gylantic Publishing.

Livingston, J. A. (1982). Responses to sexual harassment on the job: Legal, organizational and individual actions. *Journal of Social Issues, 38*(4), 5–22.

Lowney, K. S., & Best, J. (1995). Stalking strangers and lovers: Changing media typifications of a new crime problem. In J. Best (Ed.), *Images of issues: Typifying contemporary social problems* (2nd ed., pp. 33–57). New York: Aldine de Gruyter.

Markman, R., & LaBrecque, R. (1994). *Obsessed: The anatomy of a stalker.* New York: Avon Books.

Maypole, D. (1986). Sexual harassment of social workers at work: Injustice within? *Social Work, 31,* 29–34.

McAnaney, K. G., Curliss, L., & Abeyta-Price, C. (1993). From imprudence to crime: Anti-stalking laws. *Notre Dame Law Review, 68,* 819–909.

McCann, J. T. (1995). Obsessive attachment and the victimization of children: Can antistalking legislation provide protection? *Law and Psychology Review, 19,* 93–112.

McCreedy, K. R., & Dennis, B. G. (1996). Sex-related offenses and fear of crime on campus. *Journal of Contemporary Criminal Justice, 12,* 69–80.

McReynolds, G. (1996, January–February). The enemy you know. *Sacramento Magazine, 22*(1), 39–42, 84.

Meloy, J. R. (1989). Unrequited love and the wish to kill: Diagnosis and treatment of borderline erotomania. *Bulletin of the Menninger Clinic, 53,* 477–492.

Meloy, J. R. (1992). *Violent attachments.* Northvale, NJ: Aronson.

Meloy, J. R. (1996a). A clinical investigation of the obsessional follower: "She loves me, she loves me not" In L. Schlesinger (Ed.), *Explorations in criminal psychopathology* (pp. 9–32). Springfield, IL: Thomas.

Meloy, J. R. (1996b). Stalking (obsessional following): A review of some preliminary studies. *Aggression and Violent Behavior, 1,* 147–162.

Meloy, J. R., Cowett, P. Y., Parker, S. B., Hofland, B., & Friedland, A. (1996, August). *Civil protection orders and the prediction of subsequent criminality and violence toward protectees.* Paper presented at the Threat Management Conference, Los Angeles, CA.

Meloy, J. R., & Gothard, S. (1995). Demographic and clinical comparison of obsessional followers and offenders with mental disorders. *American Journal of Psychiatry, 152,* 258–263.

Menzies, R. P. D., Fedoroff, J. P., Green, C. M., & Isaacson, K. (1995). Prediction of dangerous behavior in male erotomania. *British Journal of Psychiatry, 166,* 529–536.

Metts, S., Cupach, W. R., & Imahori, T. T. (1992). Perceptions of sexual compliance-resisting messages in three types of cross-sex relationships. *Western Journal of Communication, 56,* 1–17.

Morin, K. S. (1993). The phenomenon of stalking: Do existing state statutes provide adequate protection? *San Diego Justice Journal, 1,* 123–162.

Morton, T. L., Alexander, J. F., & Altman, I. (1976). Communication and relationship definition. In G. R. Miller (Ed.), *Explorations in interpersonal communication* (pp. 105–125). Beverly Hills, CA: Sage.

Moses-Zirkes, S. (1992). Psychologists question anti-stalking laws' utility. *APA Monitor, 23,* 53.

Mullen, P. E., & Pathé, M. (1994a). The pathological extensions love. *British Journal of Psychiatry, 165,* 614–623.

Mullen, P. E., & Pathé, M. (1994b). Stalking and the pathologies of love. *Australian and New Zealand Journal of Psychiatry, 28,* 469–477.

Murray, F. S. (1967). A preliminary investigation of anonymous nuisance telephone calls to females. *Psychological Record, 17,* 395–400.

Murray, F. S., & Beran, L. C. (1968). A survey of nuisance telephone calls received by males and females. *Psychological Record, 18,* 107–109.

National Institute of Justice. (1993). *Project to develop a model anti-stalking code for states* (Publication No. NCJ 144477). Washington, DC: U.S. Department of Justice.

National Institute of Justice. (1996). *Domestic violence, stalking, and anti-stalking legislation* (Annual Report to Congress under the Violence Against Women Act, Publication No. NCJ 160943). Washington, DC: U.S. Department of Justice.

Nelson, E. S., Hill-Barlow, D., & Benedict, J. O. (1994). Addiction versus intimacy as related to sexual involvement in a relationship. *Journal of Sex and Marital Therapy, 20,* 35–45.

Nicastro, A. M. (1997). *The communicative phenomenon of stalking victimology: Exploring a practical application of coping responses and preventative measures.* Unpublished masters thesis, San Diego State University, San Diego, CA.

Nicastro, A. M., Cousins, A. V., & Spitzberg, B. H. (1997, November). *Validation of stalking and obsessive relational intrusion: Exploring the communicative phenomenon of stalking victimology.* Paper presented at the Speech Communication Association convention, Chicago, IL.

Olsen, J. (1991). *Predator: Rape, madness, and injustice in Seattle.* New York: Delacorte Press.

Orion, D. (1997). *I know you really love me: A psychiatrist's journal of erotomania, stalking, and obsessive love.* New York: Macmillan.

Patterson, J., & Kim, P. (1991). *The day America told the truth.* New York: Prentice-Hall.

Peele, S. (1981). *Love and addiction.* New York: Signet Books.

Perez, C. (1993). Stalking: When does obsession become a crime. *American Journal of Criminal Law, 20*(2), 263–280.

Puente, M. (1992, Tuesday, July 21). Legislators tackling the terror of stalking, but some experts say measures are vague. *USA Today,* p. 9A.

Raskin, D. E., & Sullivan, K. E. (1974). Erotomania. *American Journal of Psychiatry, 131,* 1033–1035.

Romans, J. S. C., Hays, J. R., & White, T. K. (1996). Stalking and related behaviors experienced by counseling center staff members from current or former clients. *Professional Psychology: Research and Practice, 27,* 595–599.

Roscoe, B., Strouse, J. S., & Goodwin, M. P. (1994). Sexual harassment: Early adolescent self-reports of experiences and acceptance. *Adolescence, 29,* 515–523.

Ross, E. S. (1995). E-mail stalking: Is adequate legal protection available? *Journal of Computer and Information Law, 13,* 405–432.

Savitz, L. (1986). Obscene phone calls. In T. F. Hartnagel & R. A. Silvermamn (Eds.), *Critique and explanation: Essays in honor of Gwynne Nettler* (pp. 149–158). New Brunswick, NJ: Transaction.

Schaum, M., & Parrish, K. (1995). *Stalked: Breaking the silence on the crime of stalking in America.* New York: Pocket Books.

Seeman, M. (1978). Delusional loving. *Archives of General Psychiatry, 35,* 1265–1267.

Segal, J. H. (1989). Erotomania revisited: From Kraepelin to DSM–III–R. *American Journal of Psychiatry, 146,* 1261–1266.

Sheffield, C. J. (1989). The invisible intruder: Women's experiences of obscene phone calls. *Gender and Society, 3,* 483–488.

Signer, S. (1989). Homo-erotomania. *British Journal of Psychiatry, 154,* 729.

Signer, S. F., & Cummings, J. L. (1987). De Clerambault's syndrome in organic affective disorder: Two cases. *British Journal of Psychiatry, 151,* 404–407.

Smith, M. D., & Morra, N. N. (1994). Obscene and threatening telephone calls to women: Data from a Canadian national survey. *Gender and Society, 8,* 584–596.

Snow, D. A., Robinson, C., & McCall, P. L. (1991). "Cooling out" men in singles bars and nightclubs: Observations on the interpersonal survival strategies of women in public places. *Journal of Contemporary Ethnography, 19,* 423–449.

Sohn, E. F. (1994, May–June). Antistalking statutes: Do they actually protect victims? *Criminal Law Bulletin,* 203–241.

Sperling, M. B., & Berman, W. H. (1991). An attachment classification of desperate love. *Journal of Personality Assessment, 56,* 45–55.

Spitzberg, B. H., & Cupach, W. R. (1996, July). *Obsessive relational intrusion: Victimization and coping.* Paper presented at the International Society for the Study of Personal Relationships conference, Banff, Canada.

Spitzberg, B. H., Marshall, L., & Cupach, W. R. (1997). *Obsessive relational intrusion and sexual coercion victimization.* Unpublished manuscript, San Diego State University, San Diego, CA.

Stith, S. M., Jester, S. B., & Bird, G. W. (1992). A typology of college students who use violence in their dating relationships. *Journal of College Student Development, 33,* 411–421.

Strikis, S. A. (1993). Stopping stalking. *Georgetown Law Journal, 81,* 2771–2813.

Stuckless, N., & Goranson, R. (1992). The vengeance scale: Development of a measure of attitudes toward revenge. *Journal of Social Behavior and Personality, 7,* 25–42.

Taylor, P., Mahendra, B., & Gunn, J. (1983). Erotomania in males. *Psychological Medicine, 13,* 645–650.

Timmreck, T. C. (1990). Overcoming the loss of a love: Preventing love addiction and promoting positive emotional health. *Psychological Reports, 66,* 515–528.

Tjaden, P., & Thoennes, N. (1997). *Stalking in America: Findings from the National Violence Against Women survey.* Report to the National Institute of Justice and Centers for Disease Control and Prevention. Denver, CO: Center for Policy Research.

Wallace, H. (1995). A prosecutor's guide to stalking. *The Prosecutor, 29*(1), 26–30.

Wallace, H., & Silverman, J. (1996). Stalking and post traumatic stress syndrome. *Police Journal, 69,* 203–206.

Warner, P. K. (1988). Aural assault: Obscene telephone calls. *Qualitative Sociology, 11,* 302–318.

Welch, J. M. (1995). Stalking and anti-stalking legislation: A guide to the literature of a new legal concept. *Reference Services Review, 23,* 53–58, 68.

Werner, C. M., & Haggard, L. M. (1992). Avoiding intrusions at the office: Privacy regulation on typical and high solitude days. *Basic and Applied Social Psychology, 13,* 181–193.

Williams, D., & Schill, T. (1994). Adult attachment, love styles, and self-defeating personality characteristics. *Psychological Reports, 75,* 31–34.

Williams, W. L., Lane, J., & Zona, M. A. (1996, February). Stalking: Successful intervention strategies. *The Police Chief,* 24–26.

Wright, J. A., Burgess, A. G., Burgess, A. W., Laszlo, A. T., McCrary, G. O., & Douglas, J. E. (1996). A typology of interpersonal stalking. *Journal of Interpersonal Violence, 11,* 487–502.

Wright, J. A., Burgess, A. G., Burgess, A. W., McCrary, G. O., & Douglas, J. E. (1995). Investigating stalking crimes. *Journal of Psychosocial Nursing, 33,* 38–43.

Zona, M. A., Sharma, K. K., & Lane, J. (1993). A comparative study of erotomanic and obsessional subjects in a forensic sample. *Journal of Forensic Sciences, 38,* 894–903.

V

LOSING

Losing, Leaving, and Letting Go: Coping With Nonmarital Breakups

Ann L. Weber
University of North Carolina at Asheville

Undo it, take it back, make every day the previous one until I am returned to the day before the one that made you gone.

—Rapoport, 1994, p. 24

WHY STUDY NONMARITAL BREAKUPS?

"If you ever become a psychologist, I hope you write a book, and explain why someone would just break your heart." I vividly remember this plea from a high school classmate, almost three decades ago. I never forgot it, mainly because I heard it—and variations of the same need—many more times from my friends and colleagues. Sometimes it came from friends wryly laughing about their latest failures, other times it was more poignant and sincere: "Please find out, and help me—or help someone!" The subject of love, especially of love gone wrong, always ran through the conversations of friends. It never really seemed like a scholarly topic—if it had been, there surely would have been a plethora of books or theories about love and loss, wouldn't there? So we sought advice from each other, and I even

267

promised "someday" I would see what I could learn about heartbreak—what caused it, how it might be predicted, even prevented.

A SOCIAL–PSYCHOLOGICAL PERSPECTIVE

Rejection, false starts, failed loves—these make for great conversations and ennobling diary entries. They testify to people's warring impulses to live in hope—"Maybe this will be the brass ring," "Maybe this time we'll make it"—and, after such hope has died, they testify to the urge to commemorate the pain, or the ennobled feeling for at least having tried. Have *you*, the reader, "been there"? Have you wondered if someone else, someone once close to you, has been there *because of you*? The sad little story of failed love is so commonplace it barely seems noteworthy; operas, movies, and even melodramatic television miniseries normally seek something with true drama and real sensation. Yet, breakups happen every day; they are hardly the stuff of great art or literature, not without a tragic element, like Flaubert's stunning, maniacal, and self-dooming *Madame Bovary* or Wagner's plaintive, searing leitmotif as Isolde cries about loss and bliss over the mortally wounded Tristan. Heartfelt we may be, but artful we are not when we whine, "He broke it off, without any warning!" or "She just threw me over for that guy. I should've seen it coming, I guess, but I just can't believe it."

Conclusions

Writing about writing, Lamott (1994) advised, "If you don't believe in what you are saying, there is no point in your saying it. You might as well call it a day and go bowling" (p. 106). So why did I agree to assemble some of my thoughts and ideas into this chapter for *The Dark Side?* What do I think I have to say—what do I believe in—that warrants this effort instead of bowling, reading a murder mystery, or playing with my cats? As it happens, once I read Lamott's advice, I realized I could readily crystallize my feelings on the subject of nonmarital breakups and why they deserve special study. Here are my points—my conclusions, in fact. Starting with these, the remaining pages attempt to lead up to them:

1. Nonmarital breakups are different from marital breakups and other losses in ways that have important consequences for how they are experienced, how they must be studied, and how they might be survived.

2. Nonmarital breakups are also similar to other types of relationship losses in ways that help us to understand the nature of the issues involved, and the patterns of grief experienced.
3. Nonmarital breakups are meaningful to both persons, creating crises in intimacy, personal and social development, and expectations about future commitment.
4. Surviving a nonmarital breakup provides the opportunity for self-discovery, generosity, the dignity and nobility of grief, and the promise of recovery.

I have been collecting breakup stories, formally and informally, for almost 20 years. My interest in nonmarital breakups led to the exploration of grief in general, especially grief at interpersonal loss. Two discoveries repeatedly arose while venturing into this unfamiliar territory: First, people really want to know about breakups and how to cope with relationship loss, despite a wealth of information and common sense out there; second, solid information is hard to come by! Eventually, I resigned myself to accepting that, given my own limits and my day job, I will not be the one to collect the truly useful database on nonmarital breakups. Yet, I had local success in collecting and getting some respect for individuals' particular stories of their experiences. I branched out, from respondents' stories, with the support of my longtime colleagues John Harvey and Terri Orbuch, to examine stories of loss and recovery in other sources—including published fiction and nonfiction, poetry, news accounts, and personal communications.

Meaning and Value

In this chapter, the experience of nonmarital breakups is portrayed as a familiar yet distinct type of relationship loss, one that has meaning in itself and deserves the respectful interest of relationships scholars. Along the way, I summarize some key studies, weave in relevant theories, toss in some favorite quotes, and indulge in a few inappropriate self-disclosures. Breakups are sad, confusing, and enraging; they are also ironic, tragicomic, and poignant. The study of nonmarital breakups reveals much of what is funny and heart-rending about human feeling and action. A friendly warning to the reader: I am not writing dispassionately, but from the heart, with irony and flippancy, as well as sincerity, on behalf of myself and my respondents—those who loved, lost, let go, and moved on. Do not take my informality for irreverence—I am humbled to be in the presence of the other chapters and authors in this volume. I make my best contribution here by writing in my real voice and setting out for you some of the ideas and images—from literature, movies, and real people—that inspired me to focus on the experience of relationship loss.

DEFINING NONMARITAL BREAKUPS

Everything reminds me of you. I try to read, but four times on a single page some word begins the lightning chain of associations that summons my mind away from my work, and I must struggle to return my attention to the task at hand. [M]y imagination constructs long and involved and plausible reasons to believe that you love me. ... You said you loved me ...

—Tennov, 1979, p. viii

The end of something—even something barely known—represents the beginning of something unknown, a realization that threatens and even traumatizes our human longing for predictability, for knowing our place. In previous work, Harvey, Orbuch, and I posited that the loss of a close relationship, like any major stressor or trauma, initiates a long (even lifelong) process of coping (Harvey, 1996; Harvey, Orbuch, & Weber, 1990; Harvey, Weber, & Orbuch, 1990). After the outcry ("No, you can't mean it!," "This is so weird, so unreal," or "You want to *what?*") comes denial ("She'll be back"or "We agreed we need some time apart"), but reality intrudes in the form of lucid moments ("I thought he would call by now") and the painful sympathy of well-intentioned friends ("I'm sure you'll feel lonely, so call if you want company"). Ultimately, through a process of confronting the reality of the loss, through confiding and hearing oneself think, despite vacillating between muzzy-headed lethargy and anguished misery, one emerges a different person. We contend that the major outcome of this process of coping with loss is a new identity—altered self-realizations, new skills, refined goals, and certainly, a new social context.

This model of response to loss is based on a stress–response sequence originally developed by Horowitz (1986), in which coping is triggered by a trauma or stressor and culminates in a new approach to similar stressors—after all, one now has experience in this particular class of life challenges. Similar problems may erupt in the future, but never again "for the first time." Although it is helpful to see relationship dissolution as a type of trauma or stressor and to understand it in that context, it is also important to respect the qualities and issues that make breakups unique among traumas, different from other losses. This is the focus of this chapter.

I concentrated much of my interest and research on the distinctions of *nonmarital breakups*, the dissolution of relationships that were not (or not yet) publicly committed or contracted in the manner of most marital relationships and many formalized cohabitations and partnerships. Nonmarital does not refer here to relationships that simply do not involve legal, heterosexual marriage. Long-time cohabitating couples, whether gay or straight, have a commitment either implicit in their time together or explicit in the way they arrange their social and financial affairs. Noncommitted or nonmarital relationships, however, are more than interactions, affairs, or attractions, but less than commitments in terms of the stability and security they promise for the future. A *commitment* is a pledge to future action; whatever else nonmarital relationships have, they do not yet have such a pledge. One or both partners may privately feel or wish for a future, or for the prospect of a future ("Maybe this one *could* work out"). Yet, as long as the pledge or wish remains unspoken or not seriously developed, the relationship is not committed. It is the endings of such relationships—liaisons that range from budding romances to almost committed—that are explored in this chapter.

WHAT'S YOUR STORY? ACCOUNTS OF RELATIONSHIP LOSS

Vera said: "Why do you feel you have to turn everything into a story?"
So I told her why:
Because if I tell the story, I control the version.
Because if I tell the story, I can make you laugh, and I would rather have you laugh at me than feel sorry for me.
Because if I tell the story, it doesn't hurt so much.
Because if I tell the story, I can get on with it.

—Ephron, (*Heartburn*, 1983, pp. 176–177)

What do we know about nonmarital breakups? Even less than we know about intact nonmarital relationships—which is not much, for the simple reason that such alliances defy archival study. People do not register dating relationships or steady relationships in the way that they become a matter of public record once they announce an engagement, register a domestic partnership in the few municipalities that recognize gay or lesbian commitments, or obtain marriage licenses. Nonmarital relationships are invisible in the sense that they leave no trace for the unobtrusive researcher to detect. We can only know a nonmarital relationship *is* a relationship according to the testimony of the partners. This subjects research on nonmarital breakups to all the vicissitudes of the self-report technique reviewed elsewhere (e.g., see Ickes, 1994). Indeed, one of the first things you are told (warned) in many scholarly articles on nonmarital breakups is that "relatively little has been accomplished in the scientific portrayal of the ending of [nonmarital] romance" (Loren, 1984, p. 49).

Breakin' Up Is Hard to Study

Breakups researchers seldom have the luxury of accessing both sides of the story. As noted by Sprecher (1994), because most studies of marital and nonmarital breakup only examined one ex-partner's perspective, our understanding of whether people perceive and adjust to such losses is incomplete. Sprecher herself succeeded in collecting data from both partners of 47 heterosexual dating couples after they experienced a breakup and was able to confirm some agreement between former partners about issues such as control over and responsibility for the breakups and even some specific reasons for the breakup. Some gender differences were also found (e.g., women enumerate more possible reasons for a breakup than do men), but Sprecher found fewer gender differences than in earlier studies (e.g., Hill, Rubin, & Peplau, 1976). Sprecher's study of the two sides of breakup was part of an ongoing longitudinal study of dating relationships, but many researchers find longitudinal research dauntingly complex, expensive, and difficult to finish (see Ickes, 1994). Thus, most relationship scholars rationalize or content themselves with one-sided accounts of relationship loss.

Narratives or versions of only one partner who agrees to respond to an interview or survey questions gain procedural convenience at the expense of balance and even fairness. Such one-sided samples are highly self-selected and may have multiple motives for participation: presenting themselves in a good light (and their ex in a bad light); disclosing to someone—anyone, even a stranger; wheedling therapy or advice; or the very self-analysis and disclosure that is predicted by the Harvey et al. model of response to relationship loss.

Thus, nonmarital breakups are hard to study because nonmarital relationships are difficult to identify and confirm. Indeed, one partner's "breakup" is the other partner's dead end: The latter may reasonably claim that, in his or her mind, there was no "breakup" because there was no relationship to breakups! Some relationships never develop, at least not adequately in (at least) one member's mind; these nonstarters die before they are born. The other person may feel left and bereft not because explicit promises were broken or shared dreams were destroyed, but because unrequited wishes and hopes were never reciprocated (Baumeister & Wotman, 1992).

Are Nonmarital Relationships Real?

In early 1981, John Hinckley, Jr., attempted to assassinate president Ronald Reagan, shooting and wounding both Reagan and his press secretary,

James Brady. Investigations soon showed that Hinckley was a rabid fan of the young film actress Jodie Foster and his motive was to impress the celebrity he loved from afar. Foster took the stand at Hinckley's trial, and responded to the attorney's request that she describe her relationship with the defendant by insisting that she had no relationship with John Hinckley. Hinckley was observed weeping at this irrefutable denial of his love—the only emotional reaction he had been seen to display through the long legal proceedings that culminated in his commitment to a psychiatric hospital. Hinckley had no relationship with Foster, he merely had a fantasy about her (see discussion of erotomania in Cupach and Spitzberg, chap. 8, this volume). Yet, his dream had nothing to do with either the real John Hinckley or the real Jodie Foster—or reality itself, for that matter. Unrequited love, like real love before it, has been publicly committed and announced, and is so subjective that it defies proof (however, see Bratslavsky, Baumeister, & Sommer, chap. 10, this volume). Thus, a major challenge to studying nonmarital breakups is confirming whether there ever was a nonmarital relationship—a two-sided one—in the first place! Perhaps we must concede that it is impossible to study relating in a totally objective way. Ultimately, we must take—and only have—the participant's word for it.

The Value of Accounts

If we are not sure a real relationship ever existed between two given people, if they have different ideas about what they have and expect, if they never go on record in any measurable way, and if the termination of their relationship is a matter of debate between them, what exactly do we have? What we have are stories, or *accounts*—people's oral or written narratives explaining their experiences and actions, describing characters and events, and inferring meaning and motives in the course of retelling and reviewing their stories (Harvey, Weber, & Orbuch, 1990). In the sense of "data," accounts are at best, extremely qualititative; creative research can conduct headcounts of gender, age range, or content analyses of themes and images as a way of quantifying some of what respondents offer. However, such techniques miss the point of studying accounts. A compelling argument for this claim is that accounts are not artifactual, created only by the respondent's desire to meet the researcher's request for a story. Rather, accounts of relationship loss seem almost embarrassingly accessible, just below the surface of many people's overt behavior.

Ask a friend, acquaintance, or friendly stranger, "Have you ever lost a relationship? Do you have a story you could tell me about it?" and you might be startled at the ease, even the urgency, with which many people rattle off their narratives. Some have a rehearsed quality, and probably for a good, obvious reason: They have told these stories before, but have not necessarily finished their own internal editing and analysis. Some stories are wrought and presented in soap-opera format, clearly intended to entertain, as well as instruct, an audience. Screenwriter and director Nora Ephron offers an excellent example of this in *Heartburn* (1983), the thinly-disguised autobiographical account of the end of her marriage to journalist Carl Bernstein. The novel is entertaining, as well as poignant; it is about a woman who copes with painful betrayal and loss by focusing on the absurdity of her situation and relating her story as a series of funny observations: "'The most unfair thing ... ,' I said, 'is that I can't even date.' ... I was seven months pregnant" (p. 3).

Still other accounts are offered in the form of an epic narrative, personal yet fraught with moral conclusions and advice. As bereaved survivors struggle to make sense of their losses, they occasionally find themselves almost detached, watching their own anguish as if from a dispassionate place, observing how clichéd or melodramatic their own actions seem to be. Literary allusions are almost irresistible, as people who have never written a word feel an urgent need to compose poetry or songs, and normally soft-spoken writers now feel compelled to speak out. After novelist David Morrell's teenage son Matthew died from complications of treatment for a rare form of cancer, Morrell wrote *Fireflies* (1988) to describe the hallucinatory hysteria and life crisis he experienced in his grief:

> The worst thing that's ever happened to me? The most dreadful thing? I can tell you that with absolute certainty. Indeed, with terrible compulsion, I find myself driven to describe that ordeal. My effort isn't voluntary. It comes in torturous rushes. Distraught, I remind myself of Coleridge's *Ancient Mariner*, in a frenzy stopping friends and strangers to tell of my woe, as if by describing it often enough, I can numb myself and blunt the words—and in so doing heal myself of the cause behind the words. (p. 4)

A less literary version of the epic account is one that concludes with a moral lesson, advice the account-maker offers to anyone who might listen. One young woman, a 21-year-old college senior responding to an open-ended questionnaire on breakups that I advertised on my campus, related a tormented tale of teenage love gone horribly bad. Discovering she was pregnant at 15 years old, she gave in to her boyfriend's insistence that she have an abortion, later describing it as a painful and frightening experience. Months later, she found her boyfriend in bed with "another woman," a girl of 14 years old, and that was it—except that "it" took another two years to break off because she herself felt unwilling to have "Sam" out of her life. Ultimately, the time between contacts grew longer, until at last, she knew it was over. What haunted her long afterward, and still distressed her at the time of writing her account, was that she had kept the details of her ordeal a secret, even from her mother, with whom she had otherwise been so close:

> I wanted everyone to think everything was great. I regret that. I wish I could've talked to my parents, especially my mom whom I hurt lot during this time by not confiding in her. My friends were supportive, although I didn't talk to them about my problems either ... Looking back on my relationship with "Sam," there are many things I would do differently ... . [M]ost importantly, I would have confronted my parents with the pregnancy and based a decision on knowledge and understanding. ...To anyone going through a similar breakup today, be strong. Don't give up on yourself. Don't give up on life . ... [T]alk to someone. Anyone. Your parents really can handle just about anything you do because no matter what you are still their child.

An important lesson we learned in collecting people's accounts of loss and breakups is that these stories are not mere data (though they certainly may contain information, that might be discerned and analyzed) and they are not related or presented as such. The very process of writing or telling one's breakup account is meaningful to the respondent, now a storyteller, a participant in a shared confidence, even if the listener or reader is a stranger. To the account maker, the narration is no less an act of disclosure than if it were to a friend, perhaps more poignant because the confidant's motives are unknown.

The symbolic interaction between the narrator and his or her idea of the audience requires the accounts researcher to respect and honor these stories as gifts, personal offerings in their own right. They permit a glimpse into the narrator's phenomenological world; it matters less whether the story is correct or verifiable than that it is offered as part of the storyteller's own search for meaning in understanding what the loss has meant to him or her (Weber, 1992a). The survivor of a breakup tells a very subjective story; instead of trying to decode it or cut through that subjectivity, it can be appreciated in the context of the storyteller's life and quest for meaning.

THIS IS PERSONAL: GOOD REASONS TO STUDY BREAKUPS

Sorrow is better than laughter: for by the sadness of the countenance the heart is made better. The heart of the wise is in the house of mourning; but the heart of fools is in the house of mirth.

—Ecclesiastes, Chapter 7, verses 3–4; King James Version

My students sometimes ask whether it "does any good" to learn about close relationships, whether having information and an intellectual grasp of relationship processes can substitute for common sense, the school of hard knocks, or pure misery. My answer is "yes." Knowing about relationships in general can improve your specific experiences. In accounts work alone, for example, we found that breakup stories often generate lessons and these, in turn, influence future expectations and plans to choose and act differently next time (Harvey, Agostinelli, & Weber, 1989). Taking a broader view, understanding at least a few of the patterns in relationship development and demise reduces the isolation and hopelessness in our grief when love ends. "We read books in order to know we're not alone," remarks a character in the film *Shadowlands*, a movie about C. S. Lewis' grief at the death of his wife. Grief remains painful and each griever's circumstances are unique, but the trauma of loss is itself not new. We learn from each other, we forge better futures, and we use our minds as well as our hearts in resolving to be smarter and stronger in intimacy.

Breakup Accounts

Throughout this chapter, I quote excerpts from breakup accounts I collected. In a 2-year period I collected 100 accounts of nonmarital breakups that occurred sometime during the previous 2 years. Most of the accounts are from college students and most involve heterosexual relationships. Yet, by soliciting accounts from local gay and lesbian support groups and other community groups, I also managed to collect quite a few stories of same-sex relationships, older adult couples, and other liaisons. All these accounts are one-sided, providing only one respondent's view of the relationship and the breakup process, without the other ex-partner's input or counterpoint.

For this chapter, only a few accounts are cited to illustrate specific points about breaking up and coping. All names have been changed, though ages and gender, where known, are provided accurately. The reader is encouraged to find ways of collecting your own accounts of loss and carry on the work a few of us are only beginning.

THE BREAKUP PROCESS

In my personal and professional commiserations over breakups, I was struck by the familiarity of the scripts and plots people say they were forced to play out when their relationships ended. Almost no romance is entered with a realistic expectation that it will end any time soon. Whenever I ask my classes how many of my students expect to marry or find true love some day, almost all hands go up; when I then ask how many expect to divorce or part forever from that partner, virtually none go up. Yet, almost all are aware of the grim statistics—that about one half of all marriages end in divorce. It is impossible to measure precisely, but surely far more than half of nonmarital relationships change by ending, not by becoming more committed. Yet, the prospect of loss is painful, regardless of whether it is culturally expected or if one has been there before. Before looking at the stages and processes of breakup, we consider the risks involved in intimacy, and the incentives that make it worthwhile nonetheless.

Intimacy: A Cost–Benefit Analysis

Jones (Jones & Burdette, 1994) and others pointed out that, social creatures though we may be, we face two daunting risks when we pursue intimacy with another: rejection and betrayal. *Rejection* can occur when the hoped-for relationship never develops, is cut short, or fails or when the other expresses dissatisfaction. Betrayal is insidious, a threat that emerges only if intimacy succeeds—for a time. The other, having the advantage of special information, having gained our trust, turns around and turns on us, revealing our vulnerabilities, badmouthing us, teasing us with impunity, broadcasting our secrets, lying, cheating, or playing us for fools. Such painful experiences, although familiar to many of us, may actually be so unpleasant that we resist remembering them. We can barely bring ourselves—if we are not already steeped in clinical depression—to think about such real losses. How then, and why, do most of us sneer at the consequences and, as it were, leap into the fray? Why do we willingly hand that very risky unknown person our phone number? Why do we take that heartbreaker back one more time? Why do we pour out our hearts, desperate soul mates that we would be, knowing full well we might just be giving ammunition to an opportunist undeserving of our trust?

The Need to Belong. We are social creatures; we need each other, our presence, the possibility of closeness. Relationships confer unique benefits on individuals, the promise of which can outweigh the liabilities of even risky liaisons. So it is summed up by Alvie Singer, the character played by Woody Allen in *Annie Hall* the 1977 film about the ups and downs of a relationship that finally has finally ended:

> I thought of that old joke, you know, this guy goes to a psychiatrist and says, "Doc, uh, my brother's crazy. He thinks he's a chicken." And, uh, the doctor says, "Well, why don't you turn him in?" And the guy says, "I would, but I need the eggs." Well, I guess that's pretty much how I feel about relationships. You know, they're totally irrational and crazy and absurd ... but, uh, I guess we keep goin' through it because, uh, most of us need the eggs. (Allen, 1982, p. 105)

Intimacy is a test, and being rejected is failing that test. Failure is aversive even in trivial or purely symbolic ventures. In the life-central endeavor to belong, to be close to others, to be included, failure is devastating. So why court disaster, why set ourselves up for rejection, especially if we had past experience with heartbreak and have reason to suspect it might not work out? The short answer is that "hope springs eternal in the human heart": Most of us persist in seeking intimacy with others because we have a fundamental need to belong (Baumeister & Leary, 1995).

Decades of research in social psychology confirm that the presence of others lessens one's social anxiety, provides a model for social comparison, and yields valuable information in ambiguous situations. Self-disclosure to trusted others is essential to relationship development (Altman & Taylor, 1973; Derlega, 1997; Jourard, 1971). Opening up to confidants facilitates healing after physical or emotional trauma (Pennebaker, 1990). Friendship provides social support and validation, and romance further provides the legendary benefits of affection and the bliss of sexual union. In short, there may be more good reasons to hope for relationship success than to fear the consequences of yet another failure. Not taking a chance on love may be safe in terms of avoiding heartbreak, but it also guarantees one will forgo the benefits of intimacy. Then again, *this* time, it just *might* work out.

Phases and Stages of Breakup: Weiss's Study of Marital Separation

Much of what we know about nonmarital breakups derives from work on either marital breakups or the study of relationships that were intact when first studied. I often joked with classes who ask exactly how one studies "breakups"; I tell them, "First, find a happy couple ... then *wait*." (This is usually greeted with grim laughter—it hits close to home in some cases, although it does sum up the principle of longitudinal research!)

The sociologist Robert S. Weiss documented cases of fresh heartbreak by conducting a series of seminars for the separated in the Boston area, summarizing themes and experiences of the participants in his 1975 work *Marital Separation*. Early in the book, Weiss acknowledged the value of collecting and sifting through people's accounts in search of patterns:

> The account is of major psychological importance to the separated, not only because it settles the issue of who was responsible for what, but also because it imposes on the confused marital events that preceded the separation a plot structure with a beginning, middle, and end and so organizes the events into a conceptually manageable unity. (p. 15)

In reviewing the accounts of maritally separated persons, Weiss identified several issues and concerns that help explain some of what transpires during nonmarital breakups as well. I highlight three of those issues here: obsessive review, loneliness, and the persistence of attachment.

Obsessive Review. Obsessive review involves a mental search for explanations, driven to some extent by "if only's" and regrets. In Weiss' (1975) words, it is "a constant, absorbing, sometimes maddening preoccupation that refuses to accept any conclusion" (p. 79). For the leaver, as well as the leavee, the end of the relationship is painful, even traumatic, and it triggers a self-protective review of possible reasons and signs, which, if comprehended, one might use to predict and prevent future losses. You learn from your mistakes only if you understand why you made them. Even if termination made logical sense and you were the one who initiated the final break, this is not a scene you want to relive. Who, then, is to blame? If not who, then what? Could you have prevented this by paying better attention? You may find it difficult to sleep, as if nighttime vigilance could protect you from being victimized again—as if your heart had been burglarized by some nocturnal intruder.

Social psychologists recognize this flurry of attributional activity that a breakups triggers—self or other? stable or changeable? save face or save us? Holtzworth-Munroe and Jacobson (1985) observed that people are most likely to engage in attributional activity—asking "Why?" and seeking, or even making up, likely answers—under two conditions: when something *unexpected* has occurred and when something *unpleasant* has happened. The experience of a breakup, whether caused by your partner's sudden departure or as the culmination of terminal conflict, meets both these criteria. After a breakups, the survivor's mind, whether breaker or breakee, is likely to become an attributional Disneyland (or more aptly a house of horrors). Regardless of who left whom, both parties to relationship termination wonder, perhaps obsessively, "What did I do wrong?" "When did it begin?" "What signs did I miss? Is this really the end?" "Is there any way to keep from repeating this pain?"

Loneliness. In addition to this cognitive preoccupation that besets the newly separated, Weiss (1975) also found that seminar participants complained of two distinct types of loneliness: *emotional loneliness* or isolation, focused on missing one's intimate partner and losing the unique comforts of that relationship, and *social loneliness*, the disorientation and excommunication one feels when one has lost one's place and marital status. Unquestionably, many nonmarital breakups involve emotional loneliness just as intense as those who lost legal spouses. Social loneliness, however, may depend more on the degree to which one's social network was dependent on, or infiltrated by, one's former partner. Longer lasting relationships tend to have more overlap in their shared social networks; it may not be clear to the partners—or to the friends themselves—who gets custody of the friends after a breakup. Formerly shared friends divide up camps, each taking the other side as if in a war. Friends of both partners may feel awkward, caught in the middle, forced to take sides or betray confidences. Some acquaintances (or two-faced friends) may even seize on the breakups as an opportunity to impugn or wield power over the survivor. Consider the dilemma of this respondent, a woman who had a long-term lesbian affair with a still-married woman whose husband approved—what she described in her account as a "somewhat sick affair." The respondent was rebuffed after the husband divorced his wife, and the ex-wife blamed her lesbian lover for all the problems that led to the divorce:

> I was financially insecure, isolated ... I tried to make other friends ... My family was not involved. The people that I associated with, for the most part, did not discourage my isolation. I spoke with a couple of people about the breakup and they were just as dysfunctional as me, therefore it didn't help. Sometimes I'd just allow people to make snide remarks to me and I wouldn't try to defend myself or explain. (49-year-old counselor)

Sociologists have a term, *dyadic crystallization*, for the process in which two people are perceived as close enough for a long enough period of time to be considered a "couple" by both themselves as well as others. From this point, much of their social identity is construed in the context of their relationship. Thus, the breakup destroys part of each partner's social identity, leaving him or her to wonder, "Who are my friends? What is my life now? Where do I fit in?"

> I went into the supermarket—I go into the supermarket almost every day because I have three kids—and everything looked different. The people looked different. I looked at their faces and I wondered what their lives were like. (Woman, early thirties, newly separated; in Weiss, 1975, pp. 75–76)

> The breakup was difficult for me because from the time I was 15 to the time I was 19 I didn't know what it was like to be alone. It took me a long while to figure out that being alone doesn't always mean being lonely ... Unfortunately I was the type of person who didn't like to discuss my problems with others ... My friends were supportive, although I didn't talk to them about my problems either. They took me out, though, and got me circulating. When Sam would try to get in touch with me again, as he often did, they would stand by me and tell me how I deserved better. (21-year-old female college student)

The Persistence of Attachment.   Finally, a part of the continued disorientation of those who have survived both marital and nonmarital breakups is that one's former partner is still out there, living evidence of the failure of the relationship. This is a key distinction between the grief caused by a breakup and that caused by the death of one's partner. After a breakups, the visibility and social activity of one's ex exaggerates the individual's plight. If you have been left, his or her presence in your social network suggests that you are easily rejectable. If you are the one who left, he or she may offer testimony to all who would listen to your guilt and betrayal. Either way, post-breakup adjustment is stressful as well as mournful. You must try to find a way to save face and construct a convincing version of events before you can continue your social life.

The former partner's "thereness" is even more poignant in one's private life. In the accounts I collected, few respondents tell stories of a clean break; most breakups are lingering, vacillating processes—on again and off again. These stories describe repeated phone calls by both parties, running into each other, fantasizing about revenge or reconciliation, and feeling self-conscious about whether they will meet and how they will appear to each other. Weiss explained this among separated couples in terms of the *persistence of attachment*—a long-established need for each other's presence that is not severed by simple changes of heart, geography, or social status. Things the two had in common may still be important to each of them, such as music, sports events, or vacation destinations. This can make awkward post-breakup encounters inevitable, unless one or the other surrenders the passion.

Some years ago, I had a close friendship with a married couple, call them "Joe" and "Elaine," who split up after a few years when Joe suddenly left, complaining that he had been unhappy. Once divorced, Joe briefly dated different women for a while and then attended his high school reunion in another state, where he met an old sweetheart, "Sally," also recently divorced. Falling in love all over again, Joe and Sally soon married. Meanwhile, Elaine, who had always shared Joe's enthusiasm for local basketball, faithfully attended the games, both alone and with friends. Once, after Joe and Sally had been married about 1 year, Sally complained to me that she wished she could accompany Joe to the games, but felt uncomfortable doing so because they usually saw Elaine among the fans in attendance. "Why doesn't she just let go?" Sally whined. I wondered aloud whether Elaine even wanted to run into Joe, especially now that Joe had a new spouse and new life. Elaine already gave up Joe; why should she also give up basketball?

Sally had a point about the persistence of attachment. Elaine probably did look for Joe at these events, at least in the first months after their separation. Later, Sally may have picked up on some residual longing or attachment or even felt resentment or jealousy about the life that Elaine, unlike herself, had with Joe for so many years. (Seeing your partner's ex also reminds you that you, too, are not irreplaceable.) The intimacy once shared by former partners ends when they part, and becomes history—but history is not nothing. One's memories of what once existed, of shared experiences and passions, continues to be a source of pleasure and pain, a focus of wonder and resignation, for the remainder of life, irrespective of new life choices and partners. Thus, attachment to one's ex can persist and continue to shape thought, feeling, and behavior.

The End of 103 Affairs

Although work on relationship dissolution was primarily focused on marital relationships until well into the 1980s, a breakup breakthrough occurred in 1976 when Hill, Rubin, and Peplau accomplished the kind of work most of us only dream: From an enormous sample of 2,520 college students in the Boston area, they solicited 231 heterosexual dating couples in which both partners agreed to complete questionnaires about their relationship over a period of 2 years. At the end of 2 years, 103 of the couples had broken up, but material collected during the initial questionnaire (completed by intact couples) provided some clues about possible predictor variables for an eventual breakups outcome. In other words, Hill et al. were able, once they knew which couples had broken up, to go back and examine their data on the broken and unbroken couples; they were able to discern any fatal flaws that may have been there from the start. The researchers also asked, during their follow-up interviews, about some aspects and attitudes of the process of breakup. What they found was extremely interesting and is worth knowing before any of us breakups aficionados goes out to reinvent the wheel.

Predictors of Breakups.   What caused the breakups? Although Hill et al. (1976) did not specifically inquire about conflict issues or communication problems, they asked respondents for many self-descriptions and were later able to conclude that certain kinds of dissimilarity among the then dating couples were related to later breakup risk: dissimilarities in age, highest degree planned, math and verbal SAT scores, and physical attractiveness. The better the match between partners, the better their prospects for staying together. Ultimately, Hill et al. favored the theoretical view that filters continually operate throughout selection and relationship development, but did not favor that such filters kicked in at specific points in a fixed sequence. Once two people were paired, the fate of their relationship depended, to some extent on how they felt about each other and the degree of that feeling. Those who "loved" each other—felt both attached and intimate—were more like to stay together than those who "liked" each other (evaluated each other favorably, but without implications of need or closeness; Rubin, 1973). Living together or having sex were unrelated to eventual breakup, presumably because while both deepen intimacy, they also introduce new possibilities for conflict and inequity.

The Breakup Process. For this chapter, the most interesting findings in the 103 affairs study related to the process of breaking up—timing, initiation, and gender differences. Hill et al. (1976) found that, not surprisingly, the peak seasons for breakup coincided with changes in the academic year: Respondents were most likely to break up over the winter semester break, at the beginning of the summer break, and at the end of summer when classes began again. In other words, changes already occurring in people's lives bring home issues such as housing, travel, work, and play so that the future of the relationship must be carefully evaluated, as well as decisions made about whether to remain together or part ways. Furthermore, although Hill et al. pointed out that "there are two sides to every breakup" (p. 158), very few such partings are truly mutual. Their data showed that women were more likely to be the actual initiators of the breakup than were men, but respondents showed a "systematic self-bias" in explaining whose actions or needs had precipitated the breakup, seeing themselves, rather than their partners, as the agents of change.

Impact. Finally, what was the impact of breakup on these couples? Unfortunately, Hill et al. (1976) were able to obtain 1-year-later data from only 15 couples who had broken up. Among these, however, they confirmed that the men had been hit harder by the breakup than the women had been. The men described feeling more depressed, lonely, unhappy, less free—but also less guilty. "Some men found it extremely difficult to reconcile themselves to the fact that they were no longer loved and that the relationship was over" (p. 163). To summarize, Hill et al. found that women were less sentimental and clingy (than many popular stereotypes of the time) as well as more pragmatic about the future of their relationships and the consequences of commitment for their own lives. In terms of simple economics, having less social status and power in general, women could less afford to make a bad choice or invest in a risky or unpromising relationship than could men.

Hill et al. (1976) did their research on nonmarital breakups in the context of studying marital planning; the authors quoted the avuncular advice, "The best divorce is the one you get before you get married" (p. 147). Non- or premarital breakups may be seen as a type of filtering (a rather harsh type) or a trial-and-error experience one endures in order to find out what works. "Marriages seldom end so casually" as do nonmarital breakups, they pointed out (p. 164). There is an important clue here to the irony of such loss: Nonmarital breakups do not entail the baggage—literal, personal, or social—of divorce. They are inevitably easier and less costly; this very ease and economy may make breaking up a pattern, whereas commitment remains an elusive, ever idealized "brass ring," a prize for which one reaches, to no avail. If nonmarital breakups were not so easy or casual, more of us would be stuck in limbo longer not quite sure if we are on or off, whether this is it, or that this latest quarrel is just another in a continuing miserable series of arguments (Colgrove, Bloomfield & McWilliams, 1991). Hill et al. (1976) pointed out that breakups are especially difficult for those who resist self-examination and confrontation. Thus, nonmarital relationship loss, a process rather than an event, can be consciously experienced, something one learns from, if only it can be faced and acknowledged.

The Two Sides of a Breakup.   Hill et al. (1976) expanded on the differences between the one who really initiated the breakup versus the one who is broken up with. Weiss (1975) similarly distinguished between the rejection suffered by the leavee and the guilt (even during relief) experienced by the leaver.

In their eloquent study of unrequited love, Baumeister and Wotman (1992) went further, suggesting that in cases of unrequited love—if not in breakup—it is the one who does not reciprocate or does not wish to continue the relationship who really finds himself or herself in the more miserable role. Consider this: If you love someone in vain, you might at least comfort yourself with the idea that at least you tried, "'tis better to have loved and lost," or that there is nobility in offering your heart to another, especially without thought of the outcome or hope of success. In contrast, if someone loves you, but you no longer feel that way—or perhaps never did!—"you are damned if you do *and* damned if you don't." If you honestly and clearly reject the other, you are the worst sort of heartbreaker, but if you try to be kind with indirectness or platonic consideration, you are leading him or her on. The target of unwanted love is in an existentially odd spot: Who would not want love? Yet, Baumeister and Wotman found many respondents with stories about being the unwilling recipients of others' affections and most of those agreed theirs was an awful experience, personally and socially (see chap. 10, this volume). The giver of love, if it is likely to be unrequited, might fail to consider the negative impact of these unwanted attentions. If this were really love—including affection and concern for the other's welfare as well as attraction and need—then the unrequited lover ought to try sympathizing, realistically, with the recipient. Judy Collins sang, "I've looked at love from both sides now." If each party to conflict or breakup considered the other side, conflict might not become terminal, communication might improve, and grieving might be lessened when things do not work out.

Duck's Topographical Model

The fact that breaking up is a process and not a state or event is central to Duck's (1982) proposed topographical model of relationship disengagement and dissolution. After reviewing the literature on dissolved or terminated relationships (somewhat irrespective of marital status), Duck identified four latent models of dissolution: pre-existing doom, mechanical failure, process loss, and sudden death. *Pre-existing doom* describes the fate of those couples who, among Hill, Rubin, and Peplau's (1976) respondents, were badly matched from the start, so that whatever their attraction might be, it could not overcome inevitable clashes of background, goals, and values. *Mechanical failure* occurs when things break—when communication is poor, or interactions go badly. Some mechanical failures may be the result of unique, *emergent properties* of the relationship—qualities and processes produced by the partners' distinctive blend of styles and motives. Other mechanical failures, however, harken back to pre-dooming problems and mismatches, the symptoms of which only showed up after some wear and tear and time. *Process loss* refers to the slow death some relationships die when they never reach their potential—for example, their potential satisfaction or pleasure for both partners—because of fault and poor productivity on the part of one or both members of the dyad. Process loss leads to dissatisfaction in at least one partner's estimation—the first step, as we see in the next section, that sets in motion the four phases of dissolution.

Finally, Duck (1982) described how new information about one partner—proof of deception or betrayal, for example—can produce the *sudden death* of the developing relationship. Trust is slow-growing but fragile and easily broken. Davis (1973) also used this term and described three conditions that produce what he called "sudden death": *two-sided subsidence*, in which both partners maintain, for diverse reasons, a formal association that is no longer truly intimate; *one-sided subsidence*, in which one partner hangs on, dependently, while the other actively seeks to end the relationship; and *zero-sided subsidence*—an abrupt ending caused primarily by outside factors, such as an out-of-control argument that ends in an ultimatum or a rash choice in speech or action (uttering an insult or being unfaithful) that goes too far and makes retreat or repair impossible.

In contrast with Davis, Duck (1982) proposed that despite vicious or extreme circumstances, "there is no *psychological* necessity that such things do indeed cause the sudden death of the relationship: if they do, then they have to be allowed to do so, or identified as causes; but they may simply cause the intimacy or relationship level to be cranked back a notch, as when partners remain friends after divorce." (p. 7).

Duck also pointed out that not all rash acts precede dissolution, but sometimes follow it in fatalistic response to a *fait accompli* or in a wrong-headed scheme to redress imagined wrongs that have driven him or her to this pass. For example, if your partner believes that you cheated and has been punishing you for this until now imaginary infraction, perhaps you might as well pursue that affair you have been fantasizing about—right?

Phases of Dissolution.   Most interesting in Duck's (1982) description of the breakup process is his proposed topographical model or map of the phases of dissolution. The reference to topography is especially apt considering that, in several respondents' accounts, references are made to feeling "lost" and trying to "find their way" from the beginning to the end of some fixed space. Any discussion of loss lends itself to map-like metaphors of place: Heartbreak Hotel, the land of the living dead, graveyards, bleak terrain and wasteland, swamps and quagmires, and murky and bog-like conditions—even "Been there, done that," and "I've been through that myself" both allude to a "thereness" of loss. The walking wounded and other veterans of relationship loss are essentially travelers without a clear destination—wander in the dark, adrift in the cosmos, lost and abandoned, keenly aware of being in transition in a way their stable (stationary) acquaintances are not. We did not see the signs, never saw what hit us, and cannot find the light at the end of the tunnel ... (excuse me while I extricate myself from this appealing but murky metaphor and return to dry land and dry humor).

Duck (1982) identified four phases of relationship dissolution, each entered after one or both partners cross a cognitive threshold, each with distinctive tasks and possibilities:

1. The *intrapsychic phase* begins when one partner, feeling dissatisfied, realizes, "I can't stand this any more." A secret search is begun to understand what is wrong with the partner, whether and how, it can be fixed, and what it would take to feel satisfied. Vaughan (1986) began her book *Uncoupling* with the assertion that "Uncoupling begins with a secret" (p. 11). In Duck's model, this secret is "I am unhappy" or some variation thereon, festering and intensifying as it is kept secret throughout one's intrapsychic ruminations.

2.. A threshold—"I'd be justified in withdrawing"—is crossed when the dissatisfied partner resolves to confront the other person, beginning the *dyadic phase*. This takes one into dreaded and uncharted territory: How will the other react? What if we can still work it out—do I want that? Issues may be negotiated, the relationship itself redefined and even repaired. There may be fights, certainly arguments—this will not be a fun time for either partner. No wonder the intrapsychic partner may put off confrontation, even put off privately acknowledging critical dissatisfaction. Thus, misery can be tolerated and the intrapsychic phase drags on and on. Even the *dyadic phase* is only concluded when both partners resolve either to dissolve or repair the relationship. With two ambivalent people and the distractions of modern life, a couple might conceivably exist in this struggle indefinitely. If one of them gets so fed up as to conclude "I mean it" and determine to depart, he or she enters the next phase.

3. If the resolution is reached to dissolve the relationship, both soon-to-be-ex-partners enter the *social phase*, in which they figure out what happened, how to explain it to their respective social circles (including placing blame and saving face), and what to do next. For these many tasks, they rely on account making, mourning, gossip mongering, and even oscillating between reconciliation and total withdrawal. Yet, if "It's now inevitable," they both cross the threshold into the last phase of relationship dissolution.

4. The picturesquely-named *grave-dressing* phase captures the deceptively simple business of trying "To get over it all and put it behind one" (Duck, 1982, p. 25, Figure 5). Much must be done, and it can take a lifetime (Harvey et al., 1990). Yet, the immediate, pragmatic focus of now ex-partners is to create an acceptable story about their love and loss, to tidy up their memories, and to do whatever cognitive work is necessary—reflection, attribution, rationalization, reassessment of Self and Other—in order to get over the now deceased relationship. The relationship is dead and buried, but the grave marker can still be carved, and revised, and the whole legend prettified in order to glean some personal and/or social value from the loss.

In our work with accounts of loss (Harvey, 1996; Harvey et al., 1989; Harvey, Weber, & Orbuck 1990), we found that, over time, accounts of past relationships are modified, both in the mind and the delivery of the account maker. This modification is not unlike what happens when a rumor is repeated and reiterated. First, the version related (both to others and to oneself) is shortened and condensed ("Basically there were just a couple of things wrong with my last relationship ... "); the highlights are exaggerated, while contextual detail is omitted ("My partner was basically very self-centered, and I was too eager to please"); and finally, the story is adapted to assimilate the storyteller's own value system or self-biases ("We finally agreed to part amicably rather than continue to struggle with something that wasn't meant to be"). When relating the account to a confidant, or to one's social audience for social or entertainment value, the account maker also adjusts the rendition, á la self-monitoring, to suit the listener's preferences or status. For example, if your boyfriend dumps you, you might whine to your girlfriend "He just dropped this bombshell on me, at the worst possible time, and I'm a basket case!" whereas, in the same evening, you confide to your mother by phone that "He and I have agreed to see other people for a while, and I think it's really for the best."

Experiencing Grief

In late October, Roddy was lying on the table in the finch room. His eyes were open, and he was looking at a half-opened window in the skylight. A bird flew across it. He heard the door open, but didn't look up ... Mary walked into the finch room, and Roddy sat up on the table. He looked at her through an opening in the cages, and she stared back like a startled animal. He could not imagine what she was reading on his face, but when he focused he could see what was on hers. It was pure grief ...

—Laurie Colwin, "Animal Behavior," in *Passion and Affect*, (1976), p. 33

The legacies of Weiss, Hill et al., and Duck all provide a growing precision and confidence about examining breakups through the eyes of the broken; developing sound strategies for collecting data on breakup processes, difficult as it is to document the events; and a theoretical logic for assembling different levels and genres of experiences into a discernible road map of relationship dissolution. A somewhat different—but still complementary—tactic is taken by scholars who focus more on tasks than on their predictable order or sequence. Here, three task-oriented perspectives are reviewed: a general discussion of the *tasks of grief*, especially from the point of view of counselors; a focus on how partners *communicate* about disengagement; and a *script* of common, even essential, disengagement interactions.

The Tasks of Grief

Two Danish practitioners, Leick and Davidsen-Nielsen (1991), synthesized their findings in their clinical work with bereaved clients in *Healing pain: Attachment, Loss and Grief Therapy*. For Leick and Davidsen-Nielsen, grieving could not be described by any sequential or linear model. They found that grieving persons often cycled and recycled—some in seemingly endless loops—through once-covered terrain, until at last they accomplished some task necessary for psychological recovery. In interviews and in content-analyses of clients' accounts, Leick and Davidsen-Nielsen identified the tasks central to this process:

1. The individual must *recognize* the fact of the loss.
2. He or she must *release the emotions* of grief.
3. The bereaved person must not only pick up the pieces and develop face-saving attributions, but must *develop new skills* for the new life that lies ahead.
4. Finally, he or she must cease expectations of reconciliation or relinquish fantasies that block realistic thinking, and instead *reinvest emotional energy* in new interactions and relationships.

This task model of grieving honors the process-orientation of reacting to loss, as opposed to the state or event characterization. Furthermore, Leick and Davidsen-Nielsen focused on grief not only attendant to death or relationship dissolution, but also other kinds of losses such as depression, developmental crises (such as retirement), physical handicap, trauma, and illness. This model does not try to be an "all-purpose theory of grief," but rather a review of what grieving individuals must accomplish in order to deal with their losses and move on.

Applying the task model to nonmarital breakups, we encourage our clients, students, respondents, and ourselves to recognize that, after a loss, subjective as it may be in its import and impact, we must consider how and when we are to accomplish these tasks. We must expect them to interweave and we must tolerate some "unfinishedness" at any given point in the process. According to Leick and Davidsen-Nielson, the order of processes is not as important as the completion of the tasks.

Communicating and Disengagement

Duck (1982) and Vaughan (1986) both acknowledged that a breakup begins in the mind of one dissatisfied partner, who must determine whether and how to proceed. Yet, both also agreed that proceeding absolutely requires communicating with the other person. The longer the unhappy partner postpones the confrontation, the more matters between the two are likely to deteriorate—unless he or she has a change of heart. Yet, in this case, silence on the part of the dissatisfied and intrapsychically consternated partner creates not only exclusion (leaving the other out of decisions that are highly consequential for both) but also illusion (allowing the other to go on believing that things, however imperfect, are fine between them).

The departing partner's silence, prior to entering the sudden death phase, causes the shock and dismay that many of my respondents reported when they were the breakees because they did not see it coming:

> I was destroyed. I did not expect a breakup at all. She broke up with me the day after Christmas. I was in literal shock for a week. I couldn't eat, sleep, or function normally in school. My grades dropped a little ... I never found out why we broke up. I was left to only guess ... . I was devastated. I couldn't let her go. I never accepted for a long while [afterward] that she was gone, never to be in my arms again. (18-year-old heterosexual male)

As important as it is to both parties' mental health to experience clarity and honesty about the end of their relationship, such discourse is oddly easier said than done. No one wants to be the bad guy by admitting his or her loss of interest; we further tell ourselves it would be cruel to reject the other outright and much kinder to let things drift, or even to provoke the other person into being the rejector: "I knew that if I told her that I did not want to continue the relationship it would really hurt her, so I thought I would be an 'asshole' for a while to make her like me less and then I would tell her" (Baxter, 1984, p. 37).

Trajectories of Disengagement. Communication scholars contributed a unique perspective to the literature on breakups by examining the ways partners do—or do not—talk to each other about their dissatisfaction or intentions to leave. Baxter (1984) analyzed 97 heterosexual breakup accounts, identifying six distinctive features of the breakup process that might be traced through a flowchart, a series of choices or trajectories in discourse between parting partners.

1. Gradual versus sudden onset of relationship problems.
2. Unilateral versus bilateral desire to exit the relationship.
3. Direct versus indirect actions used to effect dissolution.
4. Rapid versus protracted negotiation of the breakup.
5. Presence or absence of efforts to repair the relationship.
6. Termination versus continuation as the final outcome.

Most germane to this discussion is Baxter's (1984) finding that most decisions to exit a relationship were unilateral, and most unilateral disengagement talk is *indirect*, consisting of hints or general complaints rather than a direct expression of a desire to breakup. By withholding any clear, explicit declaration of intention to leave—whether out of scriptlessness, confusion, or a concern that the left partner "can't take it"—the leaver allows the left partner to wallow in ambiguity, unsure whether the relationship is on or off, and what his or her response options might be. It is then that we are most likely to make fools of ourselves (or most fearful of doing so). The solution to this misery cannot lie in making dissatisfied partners stay, but rather equipping both partners with strategies to communicate information *and* feelings assertively and clearly. It is not enough to "just say 'go'"; we need scripts.

Separation Scripts. Did someone say we needed a script? Lee (1984) proposed five possible stages in dissolution: discovery of dissatisfaction, *exposure* (bringing the problem out into the open), *negotiation* (serious discussion about what to do), *resolution* (a decision by one or both partners), and, *transformation* (an actual change in the nature of the relationship). Lee argued that either partner can be the agent of change (or operator) at various stages of the breakup. Breakups vary in the content of the issues that have brought them into conflict or dissatisfaction, and in the latency or duration of each of the stages. Finally, Lee pointed out that not every breakup explicitly cover all five stages; breakups with missing stages are described as *omission formats*. Other formats extend the ordeal or mix the formats, combining and re-ordering tasks to produce convoluted termination scenarios. Thus, Lee suggested, we have scripts of a sort—or perhaps cognitive scenes and vignettes—for possible confrontations, dialogues, and outcomes in our breakups. It is easy to see how popular culture, song lyrics, and film and video images contribute to a rich lore of such script elements without sufficient connective logic or reality to make them work. However, ideas and ideals are no substitute for practiced, careful communication.

"Tell Me Something"

If we are lucky enough to have communication, even during otherwise painful disengagement, we might at least piece together the nature and meaning of the loss, and the moral of the story for our own lives and futures. If we were "taken in, we can resolve to be more cautious next time; if we were betrayed, perhaps we can learn to recognize the signs so that future deceptions are less life-disrupting and recovering is easier.

How awful will it be after a breakup? Clearly, it depends—but depends on what? Simpson (1987) surveyed over 200 undergraduates involved in a steady dating relationship, but who were not engaged or married. Three months after the initial survey, almost 95% of the original respondents completed follow-up measures of their relationships' status, intensity, and duration. Among 10 predictor variables, Simpson found three in particular that predicted the intensity and duration of emotional distress in the case of breakup: (a) how close the dating partners were reported to have been, (b) how long the pair had been dating at the time of the initial survey, and (c) respondents' expected ease of finding an alternative partner. Applying these findings to breakups in general, we conclude that we are more likely to suffer and grieve if we were close to the lost partner (Weiss' concept of emotional loneliness), if we were a couple for a relatively long time (dyadic crystallization, as well as integration of couplehood into one's social identity), and if postbreakup social prospects are bleak or difficult (social isolation, bruised esteem, and loss of hope).

If these circumstances—closeness, duration, and belief in available alternatives—are predictors of post-breakup distress, why do we not take preventive measures? For one thing, preventing distress would also prevent commitment, which is arguably a major goal of many nonmarital relationships. In other words, applying Simpson's conclusions, we might anticipate and prevent post-breakup distress by reducing closeness—by keeping our partner at arm's length, at least psychologically. Furthermore, keep it short—do not see each other too long, or you'll get hung up and expect too much. Finally, keep your options open, diversify your relationship investment portfolio, and you will not be disproportionately wounded when any one partner leaves. So what have you got when you are not close to your partner, have been seeing this person only briefly, and see other people? Well, it is not intimacy. Simpson's ingenious survey highlights the chicken-and-egg problem or more specifically, the "we-need-the-eggs" problem. The very qualities and experiences we seek from another are at risk as intimacy develops. We can only protect ourselves from loss by doing without them in the first place.

Left Hanging.   When I was a sophomore in college, I met and fell for "Geoff," a Big Man on Campus who was popular, attractive, an officer in the "best" fraternity, and a known heartbreaker. Despite warnings from friends not to get "hung up," I found him engaging and easy to like. I looked forward to our times together, and saw no dark clouds in our future. Geoff, a senior, graduated at the end of the semester and went to work in a town some distance away, but I lived only 1 hour away and we continued to date during the summer. We wrote almost daily (this was long before e-mail and long-distance calls were prohibitively expensive for us). Although we were not emotionally close, we dated steadily and, I believed, exclusively; I thought our best days lay ahead. One weekday, Geoff called me at my job from his, to tell me excitedly that he had just been notified of acceptance for postgraduate study. He promised before he hung up, "I'll drive home on Saturday and call you from my Mom's. We'll go out and celebrate on Saturday night." Happy for him, and excited about our weekend, I waited for his call, but I never heard from Geoff again.

Thus, began one of the most anguishing and baffling periods of post-breakup grief in my life. For weeks, I did not know what happened. Had he deliberately lied before disappearing from my life or was he in some sort of trouble? His mother never returned my calls, and our few mutual friends did not know or were not talking. I felt anguished, was an insomniac, and became obsessed. I pretended all was well, continued to write letters with carefully worded "curiosity" about what became of him. I suspected the worst—"dumped again"—but could not understand why it had hap-pened or why he would not just level with me. Did he fear a scene, or dread having to account for his actions? The rest of the summer I won-dered, pined, wrote (less and less often), and finally resigned myself to being a victim of the very "hung-upness" I'd been warned about. Summer ended, I wrapped up work at my job, and returned to the campus that had been the scene of so many good times. I played and replayed albums of maudlin love and heartbreak.

I had dreams—of running into him, or finding he had returned with apologies or explanations. Yet, Geoff, the one person who could give me actual information, never showed up or even bothered to write me a Dear Jane letter—not during the time I was dealing with my confusion and bereavement. (A few years later, I actually did run into him at an alumni affair. We had a pleasant conversation, chatted about our lives since graduation, and I met his new wife. A model of restraint, I never once said, "So what the hell happened that summer?!")

During the autumn of my Geoff grief, my old friend Kathy helped get me through the craziness with humor and perspective. A rueful, funny veteran of such kiss-offs, she grasped my need to understand, to label this disappointment as a "noncatastrophe," in order to get over it. Kathy reminded me of humor, of relevant lyrics in favorite songs from our high school years, and gently suggested that my disappointment in this deception was sad but not tragic. I would not only get over it, but I would learn from it. Together we speculated on what really happened, finally agreeing it was most likely not a bang, but a whimper: Geoff had probably met someone, put off telling me, and found it harder with every passing day to do the right thing, especially as I kept writing letters full of confusion and forgiveness. We were apart anyway, so we were not likely to run into each other and have awkward moments. We only dated a few months, so our circle of mutual friends was small and not much affected by whether or not we broke up. Perhaps he did not mean to break off all contact with me, but doing so certainly put off an unpleasant chore. We just were not that close after all, so it was not that hard for him to rationalize the breakup. End of story—probably.

Eventually I forgot my pain, healed, and moved on—with social support from Kathy and the involvement of work once my college studies resumed. Yet, I never forgot the strange obsession and sorrow that were caused more by not knowing than by the loss of a relationship, which had, after all, been neither central nor close. What I had lost was potential, the promise of a better relationship to come, and the sense that I had some control over my social fate, an equal contribution to make in a romantic partnership. Geoff's silence, which to this day I have never been able to explain, left me with a hole in my social confidence and self-esteem. Bad news would have been welcome—I expected it. Yet, endlessly not knowing, despite good guesses about why he disappeared, left me confused, hurt, and mistrustful.

The Need for Meaning. Cognitively and emotionally, one of the most painful consequences of a breakup is the confusion and doubt it creates, especially if one was clearly rejected or abandoned. Several years ago, I surveyed my classes about various reasons for breakups and assembled their offerings into a checklist: note enough in common; frequent arguments; partner cheats; intolerable jealousy, and so on. I then asked all my students to rank the "top five worst reasons" for a breakup, and scanned their results to discern a pattern. I found no obvious gender or other effects (this was a class exercise, not a formal analysis), but I discovered a consistent, glaring trend: The number one "worst reason" was *partner leaves without expla-nation* (or, as I still thought of it, the Geoff effect). In class discussions, students agreed that this scenario was the most painful, even among other reasons (such as being cheated on or left for a former love) that entailed considerable humiliation and anguish. What makes no explanation so horrible?

Humans need input, information, explanations, sometimes so desper-ately that we settle for rumor or fantasy in the absence of empirical data. Thus, we might happily accept bad news rather than no news at all: Your ex-partner is not sparing your feelings by avoiding contact and refusing to tell you directly that the relationship is over, but rather initiating a frustrating and tenacious search for meaning. How can you move on, if you do not know where you have been or how exactly you ended up there?

The Need for Closure.   In the event of a breakup, one is not satisfied with information, one also needs justification and closure. If you are lucky enough to get reasons from your ex, are those reasons good enough in your opinion? Do they justify the expense to you in pain, sorrow, and social discomfort? An ample literature on self-justification and cognitive disso-nance attests to our desire for getting things right, or at least making them look or feel right. Furthermore, do the reasons offered by your former partner make sense—are they valid explanations or excuses for the trauma that ended your relationship with the other? This need for closure is a conscious desire to save face and repair damaged pride and self-esteem: "At least she admitted she took the coward's way out, leaving me like that with a note and some lame complaint about having to 'find herself,'" one friend told me.

Our need for closure also comes from a less conscious, more basic cognitive agenda (Weber, 1992b). In 1938, Kurt Lewin's student Bluma Zeigarnik published a now classic study showing that subjects who were interrupted and prevented from finishing various tasks (such as reading short selections or working puzzles) retained more details of the unfinished tasks in memory than did subjects who were permitted to complete (and presumably, file away) the same tasks. In short, unfinished business is likely to nag us, whether it be the suspended farewell address that would finally terminate the relationship (Davis, 1973), an accounting of the dissatisfied partner's arguments (Duck, 1982), or the opportunity for the wronged party to make some sort of response or rebuttal. Without a final act or interaction, the relationship lacks finishedness; it may even seem to continue in some eerie, surreal sense as long as the leavee remains loyal to the memory of the other or holds on to the hope that he or she will return. In Thomas Hardy's *Far from the Maddening Crowd*, Bathsheba gets as far as her wedding day before her long-lost legal husband suddenly returns—with tragic consequences. The effect of such stories, fictional or true, on those who are left and bereft can only be to support continued wonder and confusion: "Is it really over? I haven't heard anything. For all I know, everything is fine ... " except the mail (or whatever is preventing the other person from getting in touch). Without receiving word, one cannot begin to comprehend what happened or even to rationalize it convincingly to oneself.

Comprehension and Control

> *"Geese mate for life," my mother said, just out of the blue, as we were driving.*
> *"I hope you know that. They're special birds."*
> *"I know that," Glen said in the front seat. "I have every respect for them."*
> *"So where were you for three months?" she said. "I'm only curious."*
>
> —Ford, 1987, p. 219

In Ford's short story "Communist," the narrator, Les, remembers a day when he was 16-years-old and his mother's ex-boyfriend showed up to take him geese hunting. When Glen first arrives, Les's mother Aileen displays pent-up anger and bitterness, and initially refuses to accompany them. Yet, her curiosity about why Glen disappeared for some time and what the day together might be like leads her to join the excursion. Despite her silence and disapproval, she manages to ask the question many abandoned lovers anguish over: Where were you? Why did you leave? For that matter, why have you come back?

Ford's story is compelling and complex, but it is fiction, and therefore, Aileen gets the chance, rare in real life, not only to ask her question (and get a predictably unsatisfying reply), but also to confront something about Glen and herself that makes it easier to let go of her ideals about that relationship. In real life, such confrontations are dreamed of—they would answer so much—but they are difficult to engineer. When someone does not call you, you may not have the social power to initiate the call. You may fear losing face or overreacting and ruining a fragile connection. To this day, I think of the Geoff period I described earlier as a time of odd sadness, nagging insecurity, and important lessons. Part of its poignancy for me is that I was young then and things hit me harder. Yet, I still wish I knew why Geoff disappeared. I had been through what Harvey (1996) called a *haunting loss*, one that caused distress that lingered over time. Typical of losses that haunt are feelings of regret, plaguing bouts of "what ifs" and other obsessive thoughts, and memories that recur in ways that seem beyond one's control. To be sure, Harvey described haunting mainly in the context of loss caused by the death of loved ones. To apply it to nonmarital breakups, seems to trivialize or diminish the real anguish suffered by the survivors of trauma.

My point is really to reflect on the niggling, demoralizing effects of any failure or rejection that seems inexplicable. If we do not know what happened, we do not know how to prevent it from happening again. We may be tempted to blame ourselves for the sheer sense of familiarity that comes from self-accusation. If I think it was my fault he left me, then even if it was not, at least I can make plans—including paying more attention to the "telltale signs" of my partner's dissatisfaction or to being less of a chump and demanding to know what happened—next time around.

Confrontation.   Armed with past self-blame and the resolution to find out reasons if I ever got the chance, years ago I finally confronted one man, call him "Mark," and demanded an explanation for his disappearance. Months earlier we dated exclusively and happily. One day, he returned from a weekend trip out of town and was different. He did not call for days, he was icily remote on the phone when I finally called him, and by now, I knew the drill: He changed his mind about us somehow during the 48 hours he visited old friends and it was clearly over. I recovered fairly quickly but was sad and baffled; why, I asked my close friends, didn't he just 'fess up and tell me it was over, and explain why? Why seemed to be so elusive to so many breakup veterans, it became the Holy Grail of the dating game—a noble but vain quest. The change in Mark was so sudden and complete, I likened it to what the aliens did to their victims in the 1956 film *Invasion of the Body Snatchers*: "The pods got him," I concluded to one friend. For all intents and purposes, the Mark I knew and cared for no longer existed—though a shell of his appearance was still to be seen out and about.

One evening our paths crossed in a restaurant where I had dinner with some coworkers. I greeted Mark and, ever polite, he invited me to join his safely crowded table. Then, a weird thing happened: All his friends finished their drinks and "had to go," not all at once, but very soon he and I were *alone* (in public) together for the first time in 1 year. I was very nice, but I seized my knightly opportunity: "So what happened to you that weekend?" I asked, still smiling. To his credit, he did not feign ignorance about "happened" or ask, "weekend?," but did hem and haw. I played a sort of 20 Questions and eventually extracted enough data to confirm the hypothesis I formulated long before: Call it commitment-phobia, or fear of intimacy, paranoia, or a healthy cynicism about entrapment, but he just did not want to be in a twosome. While he was away, his out-of-town friends asked about me, and his realization that others saw us as a couple made him uncomfortable. When he returned, he postponed seeing me until he knew what to say, allowing the days to drag on while he said nothing at all. Unavailable and remote, he believed he allowed our relationship to pass away (Davis, 1973), although for me the breakup was obvious and abrupt, just what Davis described as *sudden death*. After we talked, we parted on friendly terms, he was surprised, I think, that I did not argue with him or assail him, although I explained how angry I was, and how stupid it was to keep avoiding each other. A whimper instead of a bang, his confession nonetheless, gave me closure, and something more: the comfort of knowing that, because we talked, it was not necessary to wonder how he might react if and when we next ran into each other. Even though I had to drag it out of him, his explanation was a gift, and it made life easier for me afterward.

STRATEGIES FOR HEALING

A major challenge to recovering after a nonmarital breakup is the prior relationship's lack of definition or public commitment. The survivor of such breakup may find that he or she is not taken seriously by friends, who point out that "At least you weren't married!"—as though the bereft person should be relieved, even happy, that it never got that far. Orbuch (1988) put nonmarital breakups in the category of *disenfranchised grief*, a mourning process that is psychologically real but not socially validated. Harvey (1996) explained: "As a society, we do not typically provide the same types of social supports for people who experience dissolution [of a nonmarital relationship] .... In a certain sense, loss is loss, and each loss deserves due consideration of its meaning in the life of the survivor and requires a time for healing" (p. 40).

Dealing With Disenfranchisement

The hard lesson of this for the survivor of a nonmarital breakup is that he or she cannot expect to find ready understanding, sympathy, or practical support during grief. When marriages break up, entire social and professional networks seem to be activated by the event: friends console; former in-laws choose sides; and lawyers open files, list assets, and make adversarial plans for the passive victims to follow. My lawyer, for example, did so much domestic and divorce work that he finally had his business cards printed up on black stock: "I want prospective clients to know," he explained to me, "just how dark this business is likely to get if they want me to proceed as their advocate in a divorce" (Marvin Pope, personal communication).

The nonmarital breakee may indeed be relieved not to be caught up in the divorce industry or railroaded by a plot to make an enemy of someone whom he or she once loved. Yet, the other extreme—feeling clueless, abandoned by society, embarrassed by failure or betrayal, perhaps guilty about breaking another's heart—leaves one in a bleak, queasy limbo, unsure what to do, aware that everyone says "you'll get over it," but painfully unaware of how to accomplish just that.

We must take matters into our own hands. Because we are disenfranchised, we must chart our own course. Ironically, the pathways open to nonmarital breakees are well-worn, though they may not be the superhighways of divorce proceedings. There have been so many nonmarital breakups in almost any culture studied that we should not find a lack of advice and road maps for this experience. How, then, do we face nonmarital relationship loss, grieve through it, ultimately, to reach—and actively construct—the new sense of self at the end of the healing process?

Retrospection, Remembering—and Being Remembered

So much of the cognitive work of the breakup process is focused on obsession, attribution, and explanation of what happened that it seems clear we must establish some sense of meaning in order to grieve and move on. I essentially began this chapter by arguing for our need for meaning, and now come full circle. Meaning can be constructed, but such fabrications cannot provide the closure and consolation of the "real thing." For example, I wish I had the truth from old Geoff, my college boyfriend, rather than having to wonder and speculate for months after he ended all contact between us. I figured it out and am 99% sure today that he met someone else and found it more difficult over time to level with me. So I was able to garner meaning in that loss, but not with any expedience or dignity. In contrast, my confrontation years later with Mark, the man who seemed to have been snatched by the Pod people one weekend before breaking off our relationship, had a much more satisfying result emotionally, although the information I collected in that conversation was minimal. The difference was that I got meaningful closure and conclusion. I felt he, however reluctantly, leveled with me; this enabled me to regard myself as someone worth leveling with, and it genuinely eased my sadness over the lost relationship and my transition into a new social life.

Is the missing element dignity or honor? It certainly seems that, in interpersonal relations as well as international ones, a fair policy is to allow your opponent the opportunity to save face after defeat. When one partner leaves the other, does not the leaver owe the leavee an explanation, literally, an accounting? As suggested earlier, even bad news is better than no news at all. Furthermore, if the leaver lacks finesse and cannot depart without a few shots or insults, the pain this causes can eventually lead the rejected person to conclude, "Well, would I really want this person after all, knowing that?" (Work on unrequited love and limerence suggests that there are a few souls out there who say they do still want the abusive, uncaring ex-partner back, (Baumeister & Wotman, 1992; Tennov, 1979). However, I leave discussions of such dynamics to the authors of works on disordered personalities and dysfunctional relationships. For my part here, I am interested in the normal nonmarital breakup and what might be done to better understand it and cope.

Remember Me. A central part of accepting defeat with dignity is understanding whether and how the relationship is viewed and remembered by one's former partner. To be forgotten would mean my own memories were false and my value nill. At least acknowledge that it was once mutual or that I had some reason to be happy, even hopeful, when we were together. Mourning rituals are cultural universals; all humans engage in some act or construction of memorializing those who were dear to them. No nonmarital breakup warrants a notation in a county clerk's office, much less a tombstone or official monument. Yet, we keep souvenirs—or perhaps we dramatically destroy them, ripping up photographs, tossing letters on the fire. (One reason to mourn the passing of the fireplace as a form of central heating, frankly, is that now it is impossible to make a symbolic gesture by dropping love letters on a non-incendiary heating vent). We buy books, write poems, play sad songs; some people send dead flowers or spread rumors of social disease as a type of revenge against a former lover. All these acts, whether nostalgic or retaliatory, are types of mental and emotional remembrance. What we seek in return—in some form we can hardly request—is to know we too are remembered, whether as a great love or a bad time, as being real. The first step toward establishing one's new identity is learning about one's old identity, as seen and remembered by those most important to us.

Humor and Hope

As indicated earlier, Harvey, Orbuch, and I (1990) proposed that the goal of account making in the wake of loss is ultimately to forge a new identity. This sense of self, figuratively baptized by the fire or blood of loss and pain, must be firmly planted in the new reality of life after the loss, a different world from that which one originally inhabited or wished for. We approach this identity—itself, like breaking up, a process or work in progress rather than a finished state—with a number of resources, despite our bleak beginnings. We take stock of our material resources—the income we might still spend on rent if we must now find a new home or school if the partner who once promised to support us is now gone. We also call on social support, friends who stick by us and survive the odd custodial dispute with our ex-partner and strangers—new friends?—with whom we feel safe disclosing some of the humiliation attendant on our failure or rejection.

In the course of grieving, we also discover inner resources, including strength and endurance, even optimism and hope. Cartoonist Matt Groening (1984), creator of *The Simpsons* and the *Life in Hell* cartoon series, offered his own view of the stages of heartbreak: After the worst times (including "pain" and "pain pain pain"), eventually Binky the heartbroken rabbit experiences "occasional perkiness" and is, at last, "ready for further punishment" (p. 12). This readiness is not a replay of the neediness that preceded the now broken relationship, but rather a sadder but wiser version, a recognition that we need inclusion and desire intimacy, but are not infinitely self-sacrificing or telepathically gifted. We learn, in short, that it takes work, we are not good at all types of work but can do many things, it is reasonable to seek a partner to complement us in this noble work, and we will survive and even thrive. It may be a long journey to this point, but we can get there.

Strategies for Getting Over Breakup Grief

> *I am missing you*
> *far better than*
> *I ever loved you.*
>
> —Colgrove et al., 1991, p. 121

How do we get there? Pop psychology and self-help books, as well as regular magazine articles (often timed for publication around Valentine's Day), offer ample relationship and breakup advice, some of it sound. As the short poem above hints, reflection during grief can sometimes lead us to realize that the loss and its attendant grief are far more central to us emotionally than the relationship ever was. Some years ago, after being left by a man I dated only a few months, I expressed both misery to my friends and bafflement about just why I should be so miserable. We had not been that close, really, and I was surprised by how hard it hit me when he told me (yes, he told me, so that was some improvement) that he had fallen in love with someone else I did not even know he had been seeing. My friend Diane responded by asking me what I would most miss now that "Ralph" was out of my life. "The fun we had," I replied, "and the intelligent conversations and laughs we shared, among other things." "Well," replied Diane (too wisely, but she was right), "those are things you still have. You haven't lost them! You're still fun, you offer everyone you know intelligence and a sense of humor. Ralph had nothing to do with those qualities. So don't worry about losing something he never gave you."

Coping with grief involves taking stock, making a sort of inventory of one's assets in the wake of loss or trauma. Recall Harvey's (1996) earlier definition of *loss* as a depletion of resources; when you suffer loss, you may have to take some time to sort out what you had to start with, what was sacrificed in the breakup, and what remains for you to cherish, use, or depend on. In addition to these products, coping also requires that we respect the process of loss and grief. Neeld (1990) argued that grief after loss is not a passive experience of suffering setbacks and disappointments in the wake of tragedy, but rather a series of active choices the grieving person must confront and resolve, either in the direction of healing or prolonged suffering. Like many impassioned scholars of loss, Neeld herself was inspired by a terrible tragedy: Her husband died while jogging during a visit to a vacation cabin in Tennessee. With no warning about heart condition and no expectation that their life together could be cut short, Neeld found herself living in and observing her own shock and agony. In later analyzing her own experience and interviewing other survivors of all types of loss, she identified seven choices mourners must face and the many forms these crises can take. In her prologue, Neeld concluded that "those of us who have experienced traumatic loss do not have to be doomed" to pain, passivity, and hopelessness (p. 8). In this spirit, then, here is some of the wisdom I culled from writers who sought to speak to those whose hearts were broken but are determined to grieve actively, to learn from loss, and to get on with it.

Express Your Emotions. As Leick & Davidsen-Nielsen (1990) emphasize, expressing sorrow and rage is one of the four central tasks of grief. Perhaps you can vent your emotions at your ex-partner, but chances are he or she will not be available to "receive" this message. In that case, a confidant will do, a sympathetic listener who lets you think out loud without offering clichés or advice. But, when even a friend cannot be found, how do you express your grief? Work by James Pennebaker (1990) indicates that an audience might not be required for effective expressing and confiding. Instead of talking to someone, keeping a journal or writing out your thoughts and feelings can bring long-term benefits, such as greater physical well-being and emotional recovery.

Figure Out What Happened.   In *Coming Apart*, Kingma (1987) urged the survivor of a broken relationship to formulate his or her story—what we would call the account—and write it down. This provides some emotional release as well as a record, perhaps an ongoing diary, of one's memories and progress in coping. Do the cognitive work of assembling the souvenirs and reviewing the memories, as well as accepting the reasons. Identify what you need for closure and figure out how to get it on your own if necessary.

Realize, Don't Idealize.   In *How to Fall Out of Love* (1978), Phillips and Judd recommended several strategies to lessen the pain of a failed or impossible love. One strategy is *silent ridicule*, in which the client mentally pictures some real flaw in the former lover and then mentally exaggerates it in a humorous way. For example, I was once dumped by a man who had a fastidious streak; for example, he would overreact with dismay to a food stain on his tie, to the point of ruining the evening by obsessing about how to get it cleaned. In applying Phillips' advice to my own post-breakup disappointment, I readily conjured up an image of neatly attired "Ralph" with potato salad dumped on his head. It was a bit vengeful, but mainly I knew his reaction to such a silly experience would be self-imposed misery rather than annoyance. (Those of us who have survived food spills know the difference between real tragedy and mere embarrassed annoyance). By vividly imagining Ralph's neurotic neatnik fetish, I was able to chip away at my ideal image of him and so, miss him a bit less. Once I got him back down to human proportions in my mind, I was able to deal with realistic sadness rather than the death of a dream. The real is more mundane than the ideal and much easier to get over.

Prepare to Feel Better.   In his work with the recently separated, Weiss found that many survivors of breakup are surprised to feel euphoric, even a little embarrassed that they are not prostrate with grief or guilt. Yet, relief and even joy can make sense, especially if you are the leaver or if you have been waiting for the other shoe to drop for some time. This positive feeling may overtake you rather abruptly. In *The Heartbreak Handbook*, Frankel and Tien (1993) told the story of a woman who suddenly snapped out of her post breakup malaise one day in the middle of an aerobics class workout: "I was in full swing, ... when it suddenly popped into my head: 'I'm fine! I'm really doing okay. I have things to do; I can enjoy myself—I don't want to stay mired in the past. I want to go on with my life.' It was weird; it was kind of like an epiphany or something ... " (p. 187). A common theme in respondents' reports is that they feel like laughing or experience the epiphany while talking and joking with friends. Humor breaks the bonds of misery; it is incompatible with self-imposed mourning. By considering the possibility of healing and looking for what is funny—or at least ironic—in your experience, you may find you are better able to process the feelings and lessons of grief.

Expect to Heal. How is it possible to recover after going through a period of intense pain and despair? A break is an injury, and most injuries heal. Spontaneous-healing expert Weil (1997) advised, as a key step in self-promotion of health, make a list of all past illnesses and injuries from which you healed. The point of the listing is to recognize that you normally heal after you are hurt—your mind and body work together to restore you to health. This is true even when some changes have to be made, in order to get well. In the wake of loss and pain, we can change, adapt, and grow. To do this, it helps to remember that we have done so many times before.

Talk to Others. Tell those close to you about your situation, and be honest with them about what they can and cannot expect from you in days and weeks to come. If you do not know what they can expect, tell them that! Seek out those who have been there, not only to pour out your own tale to sympathetic ears, but also to listen to theirs and look for common themes. Resist the temptation to shut yourself away from others. This is one of those awful periods when you will not be charming or socially skilled but you will need and will appreciate the company of others. In *Love Stinks*, Overbeck (1990) warned that different people react differently—and not always constructively—to your loss. Some say, "I told you so," "I never liked her," or "Too bad, he seemed like a great guy," when it should seem obvious that these are not consoling responses, and may not even be true. Anticipate diversity, make bets with yourself about how others might react, and set yourself the reasonable goal of communicating with others and asking reasonably for what you need. Do not expect others to read your mind or just know how you feel, even those who have been through breakups themselves. Help those closest to you to stay that way—give them hints, even instructions, and encourage new bonds (not rebounds) with a few people you have not really connected with until now.

Get Some Perspective. With loss comes change, and life is so different it may as well be seen as a new start. Prepare yourself as you would for a major wilderness hiking excursion or a new business venture. Learn all you can about this new terrain, become an expert on where you have been and where you might go next. Education can be combined with entertainment. Ask friends to recommend perfect movies to rent or their favorite music to weep to and broaden your cultural horizons with these images and sounds. For example, Sumrall (1994) edited a collection of stories and poems by women, *Breaking Up is Hard to Do*, inspired by her own experience grieving over a breakup. Read poetry, especially if you never tried it before. Years ago, when grieving over yet another breakup, I traveled to visit an old girlfriend who was stationed in the air force in Ohio. We sat in the officer's club as she first listened to my latest tale of woe and then announced, "Ann, I think you are finally ready for country music." Pushing back her chair, she rose and strode over to the juke box in the bar, ceremoniously punching in several tunes selected to be depressing, plaintive, self-pitying, and simply wonderful to hear. To this day, I cannot imagine my life without Willie Nelson's voice in it occasionally, even on very happy days. The art and ideas you are ready for only after a breakup are gifts you have earned by your suffering. They can be lifelong sources of comfort and joy.

Ready for Further Punishment, or Maybe Reward. And so, we take our lessons to heart. We take this heart, this new heart and self, full of hope, humor, and irony, and we face the world—a new world with uncharted possibilities and dangers. Perhaps we try once again, explore a new love, although it will not be the same. Then again, the pain reminds us we do not want it to be exactly the same. We have some memories and fantasies to cherish, some sense of hard-won meaning, the moral of the story. Together these help to forge a sense of promise. Thus, silly to risk it, but crazy not to, we try again, and we take heart.

ACKNOWLEDGMENTS

I gratefully acknowledge the help of the following individuals, without whose assistance, inspiration, and information, I could not have produced a work of value on the subject of coping with the loss of nonmarital breakups: Cynthia Picklesimer of UNC-Asheville, for data collection; Laura Jenkins, of Western Carolina University, for content analysis; the staff of Accent on Books, Asheville, NC, for books and information; John

Harvey, Terri Orbuch, and Beverley Fehr, for thoughts and collaboration on the subject of breakups; and, John Quigley, my partner, for listening to all my stories, and for helping me to see breakup experience as part of my expertise—and my *past*.

REFERENCES

Allen, W. (1982). *Four films of Woody Allen*. New York: Random House.

Altman, I., & Taylor, D. (1973). *Social penetration: The development of interpersonal relationships*. New York: Holt, Rinehart & Winston.

Baumeister, R. F., & Leary, M. R. (1995). The need to belong: Desire for interpersonal attachment as a fundamental human motivation. *Psychological Bulletin, 117,* 497–529.

Baumeister, R. F., & Wotman, S. R. (1992). *Breaking hearts: The two side of unrequited love*. New York: Guilford.

Baxter, L. A. (1984). Trajectories of relationship disengagement. *Journal of Social and Personal Relationships, 1,* 29–48.

Colgrove, M., Bloomfield, H. H., & McWilliams, P. (1991). *How to survive the loss of a love*. Los Angeles: Prelude Press.

Colwin, L. (1976). *Passion and affect*. New York: Avon Books.

Davis, M. S. (1973). *Intimate relations*. New York: The Free Press.

Derlega, V. J. (1997). Creating a "big picture" of personal relationships: Lessons we can learn from 1970s-era theories. *Contemporary Psychology, 42,* 101–105.

Duck, S. (Ed.). (1982). *Personal relationships 4: Dissolving personal relationships*. New York: Academic Press.

Ephron, N. (1983). *Heartburn*. New York: Knopf.

Ford, R. (1987). *Rock springs*. New York: Vintage Books.

Frankel, V., & Tien, E. (1993). *The heartbreak handbook*. New York: Fawcett/Columbine.

Greene-Pepper, D. (1980). *Hate poems for ex-lovers, or how to breakup laughing*. Secaucus, NJ: Citadel Press.

Groening, M. (1984). Love is hell. New York: Random House.

Harvey, J. H. (1996). *Embracing their memory*. Boston: Allyn & Bacon.

Harvey, J. H., Agostinelli, G., & Weber, A. L. (1989). Account-making and the formation of expectations about close relationships. *Review of Personality and Social Psychology, 10,* 39–62.

Harvey, J. H., Orbuch, T. L., & Weber, A. L. (1990). A social psychological model of account–making in response to severe stress. *Journal of Language and Social Psychology, 9,* 191–207.

Harvey, J. H., Weber, A. L., & Orbuch, T. L. (1990). *Interpersonal accounts: A social-psychological perspective*. Oxford, England: Basil Blackwell.

Harvey, J. H., Wells, G. H., & Alvarez, M. D. (1978). Attribution in the context of conflict and separation in close relationships. In J. H. Harvey, W. Ickes, & R. F. Kidd (Eds.), *New directions in attribution research* (Vol. 2, pp. 235–259). Hillsdale, NJ: Lawrence Erlbaum Associates.

Heider, F. (1958). *The psychology of interpersonal relations*. New York: Wiley.

Hill, T., Rubin, Z., & Pepln, L. A. (1976). Breakups before marriage: The end of 103 affairs. *Journal of Social Issues, 33,* 197–168.

Holtzworth-Munroe, A., & Jacobson, N. J. (1985). Causal attributions of married couples. *Journal of Personality and Social Psychology, 48,* 1399–1412.

Horowitz, M. J. (1986). *Stress response syndromes* (2nd ed.). Northvale, NJ: Aronson.

Ickes, W. (1994). Methods of studying close relationships. In A. L. Weber & J. H. Harvey (Eds.), *Perspectives on close relationships* (pp. 18–44). Boston: Allyn & Bacon.

Jones, W. H., & Burdette, M. P. (1994). Betrayal in relationships. In A. L. Weber & J. H. Harvey (Eds.), *Perspectives on close relationships* (pp. 243–262). Boston: Allyn & Bacon.

Jourard, S. M. (1971). *The transparent self* (2nd ed.). New York: Van Nostrand.

Kelley, H. H. (1972). *Attribution: Perceiving the causes of behavior.* New York: General Learning Press.

Kingma, D. R. (1987). *Coming apart: Why relationships end and how to live through the ending of yours.* Berkeley, CA: Conari Press.

Lamott, A. (1994). *Bird by bird.* New York: Pantheon Books.

Lee, L. (1984). Sequences in separation: A framework for investigating endings of the personal (romantic) relationship. *Journal of Social and Personal Relationships, 1,* 99–73.

Leick, N., & Davidsen-Nielsen, M. (1991). *Healing pain: Attachment, loss, and grief therapy.* (David Stoner, Trans.). New York: Tavistock/Routledge.

Loren, L. (1984). Sequences in separation: A framework for investigating endings of the personal (romantic) relationship. *Journal of Social and Personal Relationships, 1,* 49–73.

Morrell, D. (1988). *Fireflies.* New York: Dutton.

Neeld, E. H. (1990). *Seven choices: Taking the steps to new life after losing someone you love.* New York: Dell Publishing.

Orbuch, T. L. (1988). *Responses to and coping with nonmarital relationship terminations.* (Doctoral) dissertation, University of Wisconsin, Madison.

Overbeck, J. (1990). *Love stinks: The romantic's guide to breaking up without breaking down.* New York: Pocket Books.

Pennebaker, J. (1990). *Opening up: The healing power of confiding to others.* New York: Avon Books.

Phillips, D., & Judd, R. (1978). *How to fall out of love.* New York: Fawcett Popular Library.

Rapoport, N. (1994). *A woman's book of grieving.* New York: Morrow.

Rubin, Z. (1973). Liking and loving: An invitation to social psychology. New York: Holt, Rienhart & Winston.

Shadowlands. (1993–British). Video, color, 130 min. Richard Ottenborough, director.

Simpson, J. A. (1987). The dissolution of romantic relationships: Factors involved in relationship stability and emotional distress. *Journal of Personality and Social Psychology, 53,* 684–692.

Sprecher, S. (1994). Two sides to the breakup of dating relationships. *Personal Relationships, 1,* 199–222.

Sumrall, A. C. (1994). *Breaking up is hard to do: Stories by women.* Freedom, CA: The Crossing Press.

Tennov, D. (1979). *Love and limerence: The experience of being in love.* New York: Stein and Day.

Vaughan, D. (1986). *Uncoupling: Turning points in intimate relationships.* New York: Oxford University Press.

Weber, A. L. (1992a). The account-making process: A phenomenological approach. In T. L. Orbuch (Ed.), *Close relationship loss: Theoretical approaches* (pp. 174–191). New York: Springer-Verlag.

Weber, A. L. (1992b). A meta-account. In J. H. Harvey, T. L. Orbuch, & A. L. Weber (Eds.), *Attribution, accounts, and close relationships* (pp. 280–287). New York: Springer-Verlag.

Weil, A. (1997). *Eight weeks to optimum health.* New York: Knopf.

Weiss, R. S. (1975). *Marital separation.* New York: Basic Books.

Zeigarnik, B. (1938). On finished and unfinished tasks. In W. D. Ellis (Ed.), *A sourcebook of Gestalt psychology.* London: Routledge & Kegan Paul.

10

To Love or Be Loved in Vain: The Trials and Tribulations of Unrequited Love

Ellen Bratslavsky
Roy F. Baumeister
Kristin L. Sommer
Case Western Reserve University

Love is regarded as one of the most exciting and pleasant experiences in life. Love is thought to fill one's life with purpose and meaning, and American society embraced love as one of its core values. A study of love and relationships expanded greatly in the last decade. Despite some difficulty in studying these phenomena, researchers are emphasizing the importance of understanding and studying love and relationships. However, relationships that fail to form is a category that can easily get lost. Most of the literature on love focuses on the individual in love and on cognitions, emotions, and behaviors that go along with love. This emphasis misses the interpersonal context of love that comes into focus in times when only one person is in love, as in unrequited love. Thus, studying unrequited love means overcoming a limitation of taking only the individual approach to love.

Ideally, passionate or romantic love progresses something like this: Two people meet and eventually develop a strong attraction to one another. They experience a sudden rush of positive emotion and sexual desire in each other's presence, and their overwhelming need for the relationship causes them to spend increasingly more time together while neglecting other people and concerns. The levels of emotional intimacy and commitment steadily escalate and finally culminate in a mutual state of ecstasy. To fall in love is to be fulfilled and to discover a degree of happiness that transcends ordinary experiences.

Unfortunately, love does not always progress this smoothly. Often, intense romantic love is experienced by only one person, and the target of that person's affections is left in the uncomfortable position of having to reject that love. Passionate love felt by one person toward another person who does not desire romantic involvement with the would-be lover is referred to as *unrequited love*. When one's love is not returned, when emotions, feelings, and longings are not mutual, the consequences for the would-be lover may be devastating. Not only does unrequited love fail to bring long-awaited happiness, but it can elicit pain and suffering.

Thus, to love in vain diminishes the joy and ecstasy normally associated with passionate love. Yet, what is it like to be loved in vain? There are two dark sides of unrequited love, but only one is made familiar by our culture. Movies, books, and songs explore the tragedy of unrequited love from the eyes of the would-be lover, yet the feelings and perspectives of the rejector remain largely ignored. Not only is the depiction of the rejector's experience incomplete, but it is often inaccurate. The rejector is often portrayed as a cold-hearted, unempathic individual who is either indifferent to the other's pain and suffering or who exploits the would-be lover for personal gain. Yet, this is a clear distortion of the prototypical unrequited love experience for the rejector. The findings presented in this chapter show how unrequited love usually ends with immense dissatisfaction and distress for both parties.

In our analysis, then, we give attention to the experiences of both would-be lovers and rejectors. Because the rejector's perceptions and emotions remain somewhat of a mystery in our culture, we view this side of unrequited love as particularly deserving of attention. Throughout our discussion, we emphasize the experiences of the rejector and the disparity between these experiences and stereotypes or misconceptions of the rejector's role.

The data on which the following conclusions are based are reported in detail in two recent publications by Baumeister and Wotman (1992) and Baumeister, Wotman, and Stillwell (1993). In these studies, participants were mostly young, unmarried adults who typically recently had unrequited-love experiences, both as would-be lovers and as rejectors. Participants were asked to write two stories—one about an important experience in which they loved someone who did not return their feelings and one about an experience in which someone loved them, but whose feelings they did not reciprocate. Because each participant related two accounts, one experience as a would-be lover and one as a rejector, the comparisons reflected meaningful differences between situational roles rather than between types of people. Thus, the experiences related by these participants may be assumed to represent those of most people who find themselves either in the position of loving another who does not love them back or of being the recipient of another's unwanted love.

We begin our chapter with a prototypical unrequited love story that highlights the experiences of both the would-be lover and the rejector. We follow with a discussion of the situations that give rise to unrequited love and provide a theoretical framework for understanding the experiences associated with each role. Then, we describe the primary emotional outcomes of the would-be lover and rejector, both during and following the unrequited-love experience. We conclude with a summary of what individuals claimed to learn from their unrequited-love experiences.

AN UNREQUITED LOVE SCENARIO

Mary and Paul were best friends in college. They carried the same major and therefore spent a lot of time studying as well as socializing together. After some time passed, Paul noticed that his feelings for Mary were changing. He started to become physically attracted to her and developed deep feelings for her. Initially, Paul remained silent, not sure of how to proceed, yet his desire for her became overwhelming and after struggling with his emotions for some time, Paul eventually confessed his love to Mary. Mary was surprised and flattered by Paul's love, but knew that she would never be able to reciprocate his feelings. Still, Mary cared about Paul and was concerned about hurting him. She tried to gently discourage Paul. She told him that she thought very highly of him and cherished their time together, but she wanted to remain "just friends."

Obviously, Paul was disappointed, but not willing to give up. Paul was convinced that he and Mary had something special and if he just persisted, she would come to realize her feelings for him. Paul continued to pursue Mary, expressing his longing for her and expressing his affection through letters and gifts. Mary became very confused; she felt guilty for hurting Paul, but simultaneously, felt frustrated by his incessant and futile pursuit of her. She was no longer flattered by his love, but instead, became desperate to end the situation. Mary began to withdraw physically and emotionally, figuring Paul would get the message and leave her alone.

Mary's plan backfired. Her ostracism of Paul made him even more diligent in his efforts to secure her love. Finally, at the end of her rope, Mary confronted Paul and clearly and explicitly told him that she did not love him and she never wanted to see him again. Paul felt Mary was breaking his heart, but finally desisted in his attempts to secure her love. Looking back, Paul confessed that he was devastated by Mary's rejection, but claimed that he would always have a soft spot in his heart for her. In contrast, Mary could not understand how she ever could have been friends with a person who could not accept her feelings. Mary felt guilty for hurting Paul, but also resented him for destroying their friendship. In short, she wished desperately that the whole incident never happened.

This scenario portrays a typical experience of unrequited love by would-be lovers and rejectors. It also vividly demonstrates the importance of reciprocity in the joy of love. Because unrequited love involves both a person who is in love and a person who is receiving love, one examines the hypothesis that it is the combination of loving and being loved that is necessary for happiness. Fromm (1956) emphasized the giving of love and proposed that the art of loving was the essential requirement for happiness, satisfaction, and fulfillment. In contrast, Rogers (1959) argued that it is the receiving of unconditional positive regard and love that carries the most weight. Unrequited love experiences such as those of Paul and Mary, however, strongly support a third alternative. To love or to be loved is necessary, but not sufficient for happiness. Rather, happiness seems to require mutual, reciprocated love.

WHY AND WHEN DOES UNREQUITED LOVE OCCUR?

Why exactly does unrequited love occur? One popular theory of relationship formation is equity theory (e.g., Walster, Berscheid, & Walster, 1976), which holds that people tend to match up with others similar to themselves. In order to explain why unrequited love occurs, however, it is important to understand that people initially are not attracted to those who are similar to themselves. Instead, people tend to prefer the most desirable partners (Walster, Aronson, Abrahams, & Rottman, 1966). Even though people end up marrying someone similar to themselves, they tend to initially fall in love with the best person they can find. One person may therefore become attracted to someone more desirable, but that someone is unlikely to reciprocate the romantic interest—or fall for a person less alluring. Baumeister and Wotman (1992) termed this *falling upward*, which refers generally to the act of falling in love with someone more attractive than the self.

Another source of unrequited love is platonic friendships. Friends who spend a lot of time together usually develop strong feelings of closeness and intimacy. Intimacy has been called the common core of all love relationships (Sternberg, 1986; Sternberg & Grajek, 1984). In this way, platonic friendships provide a fertile soil for unrequited love. One person's feelings may blossom, whereas the other's remain stagnant. In the previous scenario, a close friendship gave rise to unrequited love. Paul's feelings grew more intense over time, whereas Mary's feelings of friendship remained constant. Despite Paul's urgent wish to increase Mary's level of involvement in the relationship, Mary was simply incapable of seeing Paul in a more romantic light.

A third instance in which one witnesses unrequited love is in the early stages of a romantic relationship. Two people may form a mutual attraction and decide that they want to get to know each other better. They begin dating, and after a few interactions, one person's feelings diminish, whereas the other's flourish. It is under these circumstances that unrequited love should have the greatest impact on the emotions of both would-be lovers and rejectors. This is because early on, there exists the potential for the formation of a reciprocal, loving relationship. At the point at which one person begins to withdraw, the would-be lover already received some reinforcement and has good reason to believe that the partner will change his or her mind and decide to continue the romance. If the rejector fails to demonstrate this longed for change of heart, the final rejection is all the more painful to the would-be lover. To be rejected after allowing someone to get to know you poses a major threat to your self-esteem. It is as if the rejector is saying, "I liked you at first, but now that I know you better, I'm no longer interested."

This situation is distressing for the rejector, as well. The rejector finds it extremely difficult to try to break off a relationship that he or she willingly participated in creating. This includes trying to explain to the would-be lover—without inducing pain or misery—why exactly one's feelings took a turn for the worse. Rejectors may become frustrated and confused during this process because, often, they have little insight into their own reasons for losing interest. Baumeister and Wotman (1992) found that rejectors frequently reported feelings of respect, admiration, and liking for their admirers, but they failed to experience the requisite sexual attraction or desire. Sometimes, rejectors wanted to love their admirers and reported that the would-be lover would make someone an excellent partner. In the end, rejectors were left boggled by their own inexplicable lack of desire and felt extremely guilty for failing to return the other's affections.

We return to the experiences of would-be lovers and rejectors later in this chapter. Now, we explore the emotional outcomes available to each role and use this as a framework for understanding how would-be lovers and rejectors form different assessments of the situation and how these appraisals, in turn, determine the actions that they take.

INTERDEPENDENCE THEORY OF UNREQUITED LOVE

When trying to understand the behaviors of would-be lovers and rejectors, it is necessary to consider the options available to each. The situation is one paradigm of interdependence, in that each person's outcomes depend on what both people do (Kelley & Thibaut, 1978). Considering the structure of interdependence helps clarify the different situations and contingencies that confront the two roles.

Suppose you love someone who is reluctant or unable to return your love. You have two options available to you. First, you may actively try to win your rejector's heart. If you pursue your rejector despite his or her reluctance, you may eventually convince your rejector that you are worthy of his or her love and thus, succeed in securing the bond that you so desperately desire. Of course, your rejector may also continue to reject you and then you must deal with the ensuing feelings of rejection and despair. Your second option is thus to give up passively, which leaves no chance for happiness. An objective appraisal of the situation therefore, pushes you toward the active option. By persisting, you have at least one chance to win your rejector's love.

Suppose now that you are the object of another's unwanted affections. You also have two options available to you. The first, active option is to reject the other's love. This naturally brings suffering to your would-be lover, and actively inflicting suffering on another individual (especially one who thinks so highly of you) leads you to feel morally repugnant and guilty. Your second, passive option, then, is to play along with the would-be lover and hope that you can muster up some deep feelings for him or her. This passive option may be less painful in the short run because it prevents you from having to communicate those dreaded words of rejection. However, in the event that you cannot form an attraction to your partner, it only postpones the inevitable heartbreak. Because your chances of falling in love are low, if nonexistent, your most attractive option is the active one—that is, to reject your partner.

Thus, this interdependence analysis reveals that the would-be lover's situation is, seemingly ironically, more appealing than the rejector's. The would-be lover's potential outcomes span the spectrum from elation to despair. In contrast, the rejector's potential outcomes are nearly all bad. The would-be lover thus, sees the situation as a high-risk gamble, with at least a chance for happiness, whereas the rejector sees a no-win situation with almost nothing to gain. Hence, even though the would-be lover may suffer more acutely (on average) during the worst moments, would-be lovers in general are more interested in the experience, pursue it more eagerly, and regret it less afterward than the rejector.

PROLONGING THE AGONY THROUGH A CONSPIRACY OF SILENCE

Baumeister and Wotman (1992) found that both would-be lovers and rejectors often cooperated in avoiding the painful rejection through a conspiracy of silence. The rejector did not want to speak the message, and the would-be lover did not want to hear it. In the previous example, Paul dismissed Mary's initial rejection, and indeed, Mary demonstrated a reluctance to communicate directly and clearly her lack of interest in a romantic relationship. To accept another's rejection is to admit defeat and accept one's inferiority, and thus it is easy to see why someone such as Paul would downplay the significance of another's refusal. Yet, it is also difficult to refuse another's love bluntly. First, this behavior goes against a fundamental and pervasive motivation to form and sustain interpersonal attachments (Baumeister & Leary, 1995). Second, as noted earlier, love is highly valued in our society and to reject another's offering of love is to thwart something highly important to an individual. Thus even though the rejector wants to communicate the message of rejection clearly to the would-be lover, he or she tends not to do it very effectively. Indeed, to make the rejection more culturally acceptable, the rejector often attempts to soften it with warm words or compliments. Also, the rejector often bases the rejection on temporary and vague reasons, which give the would-be lover more hope for reciprocation.

The unrequited love experience is thus perpetuated by a conspiracy of silence. The would-be lover is motivated to avoid the painful message and therefore, is unlikely to perceive the refusal as a true rejection. Because the message of rejection is rarely made explicit by the rejector, the would-be lover continues to pursue the object of his or her love. This, in turn, leads the rejector to become more frustrated and annoyed with the situation.

EMOTIONAL OUTCOMES OF UNREQUITED LOVE

Interdependence theory predicts that one's emotional outcomes of the unrequited love experience depends on what the prospective partner does. Analysis of the autobiographical accounts of would-be lovers and rejectors revealed two primary (albeit different) emotions that were affected by the other's actions. For the would-be lover, this emotion was self-esteem or global feelings about the self. For the rejector, it was guilt. Unrequited love experiences usually led to a drop in self-esteem for the would-be lover and an increase in guilt for the rejector. We consider each of these in turn.

Self-Esteem

The need to protect and enhance one's self-esteem is regarded as one of the most basic and powerful human motivations (Baumeister, 1997; Greenberg, Pyszczynski, & Solomon, 1986). Self-esteem is a central concern for the would-be lover. As mentioned earlier in this chapter, people tend to initially fall in love with those who are more desirable than themselves. Because individuals' own views of their attractiveness are often exaggerated (Taylor & Brown, 1988), would-be lovers often consider themselves equal in attractiveness to the objects of their love. The rejectors also see themselves in a positive and distorted fashion, but see their admirers accurately. People are generally not attracted to less desirable others and hence, are unmotivated to form a romantic relationship with them.

As a would-be lover, you may begin to devalue yourself when you find you are being rejected by someone ostensibly equal in attractiveness. Rejection carries the implicit negative message of unequal attractiveness and inferiority. If the desired person does not love you, you must not be worth loving. This drop in self-esteem should be most significant when you feel your rejector knows you well. On the one hand, being rejected by an acquaintance is attributed to the fact that he or she simply does not know you well enough. On the other hand, being rejected by a close other carries a powerful humiliating message (Aronson & Linder, 1965). The later in a relationship the rejection comes, the greater the negative impact on your self-esteem.

Indeed, loss of self-esteem was far more commonly mentioned in the would-be lovers' accounts than in the rejectors' accounts. Would-be lovers were more likely to mention feeling silly, foolish, stupid, and embarrassed. For would-be lovers, recovery from the unrequited love experience often involved trying to repair the damage done to their self-esteem. Various strategies were used. First, would-be lovers tried to reaffirm their esteem directly. Nearly one half of would-be lovers mentioned made references to their positive traits or attractiveness to others, and they often noted that they deserved someone better than their rejector. In a related vein, would-be lovers sometimes derogated or devalued the object of their love.

This strategy of demeaning the rejector was relatively infrequent, how-ever, because derogating the rejector held negative implications for the self. (After all, if you have fallen for a person you consider repulsive and despicable, then presumably you are equally, if not more, repulsive and despicable) A popular option among would-be lovers was to instead derogate their rival or person who stole their beloved's heart. As one jilted woman wrote of her rejector and his new girlfriend, "Every time I see her or both of them together I keep asking myself what he sees in her ... .the strangest thing is, I'm not even jealous of her because I know that I am much better than she is" (Baumeister & Wotman, 1992, p. 94). A final effective strategy for boosting self-esteem was to find someone desirable and attractive who would reciprocate the would-be lover's affections. One rejected lover noted in her story, "I have a boyfriend whom I've been seeing for one year and he treats me so much better than Peter ever did, and he adores me to death" (p. 95).

Ideally, the best way for the would-be lover to regain self-esteem is to see the rejector come back and profess his or her love. Most often, though, rejectors do not come back wanting forgiveness and love. Would-be lovers may be willing to sacrifice some esteem in the beginning stages of unre-quited love. Persisting in the face of rejection is humiliating, but it may pay off in the end. The threat to self-esteem, however, becomes compounded by each additional rejection. Eventually, the would-be lovers must give up and try to salvage any self-esteem they have left. Thus, even though the would-be lovers' self-esteem is not initially an important aspect of their experience, it gradually becomes more important.

The opposite pattern is found among rejectors. The rejector may experience a temporary boost to self-esteem, but this experience is often short-lived. Simply knowing that someone has deemed you worthy enough to fall in love with you is bound to make you feel good. It is especially flattering when you know that you have done nothing to encourage that love, but rather that someone loves you just because he or she finds you so extremely desirable. The boost to self-esteem quickly wears off, how-ever, as the rejector becomes annoyed and frustrated by the would-be lover's futile persistence or even just because the admiration of an unde-sirable partner is regarded as worthless.

Thus, would-be lovers experienced a drop in self-esteem as the inter-personal rejection became more frequent and the prospects for forming the desired relationship grew increasingly bleak. To replenish their self-worth, would-be lovers invoked a variety of tactics, including derogating the rival lover and emphasizing the desirability of their new lovers. These tactics allowed would-be lovers to reaffirm their own attractiveness and value to others.

Guilt and Justification

Whereas the loss of self-esteem was a primary emotional experience of the would-be lovers, a strong sense of guilt was a central problem for the rejectors. Guilt is an interpersonal emotion that people experience on learning that they inflicted suffering on a person for whom they have affection or feelings of concern (Baumeister, Stillwell, & Heatherton, 1994; Tangney, 1995). The guilt experienced by the rejectors likely stems from two sources: First, most rejectors, at some point, found themselves on the other side of unrequited love and thus, empathize with the would-be lover's distress (Baumeister & Wotman, 1992). Second, rejecting another's love is difficult and runs contrary to the seemingly innate human desire for belongingness (Baumeister & Leary, 1995). Empathy and anxiety over loss of attachments are theorized to be the two main origins of guilt (Baumeister et al., 1994) and both are evident in unrequited love.

The intensity of guilt varies decisively with the closeness of the relationship (Baumeister, Reis, & Delespaul, 1995). As the rejector, you therefore suffer the most guilt, remorse, and regret after inflicting distress on another with whom you already formed some attachment. As was the case with Paul and Mary, many unrequited love experiences typically evolve from platonic friendships or even dating relationships—contexts in which some degree of intimacy has already been established. If you have an emotional investment in your would-be lover's suffering and are further concerned about maintaining a connection with him or her, your level of guilt is quite high.

Although one might expect the would-be lover to feel guilty for bringing guilt and frustration to the rejector, references to guilt feelings were far more common in the rejectors' accounts than in those of the would-be lovers. Despite their involuntary involvement, rejectors often felt a sense of obligation toward the would-be lover. People tend to feel a great deal of guilt over harm that was caused unintentionally (McGraw, 1987). Thus, although rejectors were unwillingly brought to the situation and did nothing to create the other's distress, they ended up experiencing much more guilt than the would-be lovers who were primarily responsible for the situation.

There are two explanations for the absence of guilty feelings in the would-be lovers' accounts. First, would-be lovers are usually lost in their own feelings of love and hope, and they are largely oblivious to the distress they are causing the rejectors. Would-be lovers focus on their own feelings, whereas rejectors primarily attend to the emotions of their would-be lovers. Second, because love is a powerful and pervasive value in our society, many things done in the name of love are considered to be justified

(Baumeister, 1991). The would-be lover's blameworthiness for relentlessly pursuing the rejector despite his or her objections becomes mitigated by the would-be lover's honorable intentions. The would-be lover is inflicting something negative (e.g., frustration and annoyance), but it is in the service of something highly desirable and good (i.e., mutual love and happiness). The rejector, conversely, cannot use love to justify the infliction of heartbreak on the would-be lover. From the rejector's perspective, the primary positive outcome is that of selfish escape. The rejector must therefore find other ways of justifying the rejection in order to escape the guilt.

Indeed, rejectors' intense feelings of guilt made justification more central to their experiences than to the would-be lovers' experiences. Rejectors displayed a number of justification strategies. As noted earlier, the magnitude of guilt increases with the strength of the interpersonal bond. One way that rejectors could escape their guilt, then, was to derogate the would-be lover and thereby lower the perceived importance of the attachment. The less they cared about the victims of their rejection, the easier it was to avoid feeling guilty. One rejector described her admirer in these terms: "This is rude, but Albert is a total turnoff-loser, not extremely well liked outside his circle, not exactly good looking either, personality not wonderful ... " (Baumeister & Wotman, 1992, p. 85).

A second strategy for escaping guilt was to absolve the self of responsibility for the would-be lover's turmoil. Indeed, rejectors often did nothing to encourage their admirers and reminded themselves of this fact when trying to alleviate their guilt. In fact, rejectors who thought highly of their admirers sometimes tried to fall in love with them. Rejectors reported wanting to reciprocate the love and became confused and frustrated by their inability to do so. Their lack of ability to control their feelings provided a third source of justification for the rejection. Rejectors reported a need to be true to themselves: This need is a common source of justification (Baumeister, 1991; Bellah, Madsen, Sullivan, Swidler, & Tipton, 1985; Vaughan, 1986).

Some rejectors justified their actions on the basis of what was best for the would-be lovers. This method reaffirms the rejector's caring and concern for the admirer, while allowing him or her to escape the aversive situation. Finally, some rejectors went so far as to present themselves as victims. They claimed that the would-be lovers' improper behaviors left them no choice but to sternly reject their admirers. Improper behaviors by the would-be lovers included boasting to others about their ostensible relationship with the rejector or relentlessly calling or coming to the rejector's house. The victim role may be especially important in unrequited love because rejectors can make themselves feel better by presenting themselves as deserving of sympathy rather than criticism.

The would-be lovers' improper behaviors were indicated in many rejectors' accounts, whereas none of the would-be lovers' accounts presented their own behaviors in a negative light. Instead, the would-be lovers' accounts portrayed their actions to be proper and acceptable. People's tendencies to see their own behavior in a positive light and others' behavior in a negative light explains an obvious contradiction among the stories (Baumeister, Stillwell, & Wotman, 1990; Taylor, 1989; Taylor & Brown, 1988). The rejectors' feelings of frustration and annoyance were often exaggerated by some questionable actions by the would-be lovers. Rejectors reported feeling pushed and bothered by the would-be lovers' hypocrisy, indecent actions, lack of consideration, and sometimes even threats to commit suicide.

Although improper acts by the would-be lovers were mentioned more often by the rejectors, it should be noted that the rejectors also participated in some objectionable actions. As noted earlier, would-be lovers and rejectors cooperated in a conspiracy of silence. Rejectors often opted to deal with the unpleasant situation by avoiding contact with the would-be lovers. This included fabricating other commitments when propositioned for a date and asking roommates to lie about the rejector's absence when the would-be lovers telephoned. These tactics offered temporary solutions and thus were only partially effective. Hiding or masking the inevitable rejection only postponed the hurt and despair for the would-be lover and prolonged the guilt and frustration for the rejector.

There is one final difference between the two roles that is relevant to the experience of guilt and therefore deserves mention. Unlike would-be lovers, rejectors suffered from a sense of scriptlessness. We noted earlier that modern American culture provides would-be lovers with clear and detailed scripts to follow. Movies, books, and songs often portray the would-be lover's persistence as paying off when the rejector comes to his or her senses and recognizes the would-be lover for the wonderful person he or she is. The presence of this script for the would-be lovers makes it easy to understand why an unrequited lover persists in the face of rejection. The rejectors, on the other hand, find themselves without an adequate script. There are very few literary or media sources where the perspectives and behaviors of the rejectors are found. The absence of firm standards or guidelines for what constitutes appropriate and inappropriate reactions to the rejection side of unrequited love leaves rejectors in a heightened state of frustration, uncertainty, and guilt. Due to the ambiguity about what exactly is "the right thing to do," rejectors fear doing the wrong thing. Also, because the would-be lovers are caught up in their own feelings and needs, they may be insensitive to rejector's scriptlessness and not realize what the rejector is going through.

Collectively, these findings challenge the myth of the cold-hearted rejector as someone who maliciously thwarts another's love and dispassionately induces mental anguish and heartbreak in the would-be lover. Instead, the evidence paints a much different, more sympathetic picture of the rejector. The rejector is often troubled by guilt for having inflicted harm on the would-be lover, but is simultaneously left with few avenues for escaping such guilt. Whereas the would-be lover easily justifies any perceptibly inappropriate actions by claiming an innocent and understandable need for love and companionship, the rejector finds it difficult to rationalize his or her rejection of the admirer and lack of interest in the relationship. The additional problem of scriptlessness among rejectors results in a perpetual state of confusion and uncertainty; it leaves open the possibility that any actions taken by the rejector may be reflected as having been wrong or inappropriate.

LOOKING BACK

We now turn to the perspectives and conclusions of would-be lovers and their rejectors after some time has passed. How do they label or define their unrequited love experiences?

The Irony of Retrospect

When examining the patterns of would-be lovers' and rejectors' emotions during and following the unrequited love experience, we witness what is called the *irony of retrospect* (Baumeister & Wotman, 1992). The would-be lover overall has a more humiliating and embarrassing experience, yet remembers it in much more pleasant colors. The rejector starts out having a pleasant, flattering experience and ends up wishing it was all a bad dream.

The stories of would-be lovers revealed that these individuals looked back on the whole incident with quite fond memories, despite their initial disappointment, pain, and heartbreak. Many of the would-be lovers' memories were bittersweet and warm. In retrospect, would-be lovers experienced significantly more positive affect than their rejectors. Almost none of the would-be lovers' accounts mentioned wishing that the whole thing never happened.

Most rejectors, conversely, had very negative recollections and feelings about the entire episode. Some rejectors searched for any positive aspects of the experience, and most failed to find anything remotely good. Rejectors were frustrated and annoyed by the unsolicited attention and were often left riddled with guilt after being forced to inflict emotional suffering on their admirers. Even though some rejectors and would-be lovers managed to remain friends, the rejectors' accounts repeatedly indicated the aversiveness of their experiences.

The research evidence on emotional experiences in unrequited love thus suggests an unexpected conclusion. Contrary to the popular stereotype, the heartbreaker experiences a great deal of emotional distress. Would-be lovers were distressed, disappointed, and ashamed of their behaviors, but they also experienced the rush of excitement and hope that normally comes with falling in love. Rejectors, conversely, ended up with a great amount of negative affect. It is interesting to note the imbalance in the degree to which would-be lovers and rejectors attended to the other's emotional outcomes. Comparison of the accounts revealed that rejectors were sensitive to the would-be lovers' suffering and distress, whereas would-be lovers had almost no awareness of the rejectors' emotional distress. This is consistent with the earlier finding that rejectors focused on alleviating their guilt, whereas would-be lovers focused on regulating their own self-esteem.

Interdependence theory once again is adopted as a framework for understanding the emotional outcomes of each role long after the unrequited love episode ended. Looking back, the would-be lover realizes both positive and negative outcomes as a result of knowing and interacting with the rejector, whereas the rejector perceives almost nothing positive from having been pursued by the would-be lover. The would-be lover ends up with something to appreciate, something to remember and learn from, despite his or her unsuccessful efforts to win the rejector's heart. In contrast, the rejector has a difficult time appreciating any aspects of his or her experience. The rejector remembers a situation he or she never wanted and did nothing to create. In fact, in many cases, the rejector loses a special friendship.

Interpretations of the Episode.

In hindsight, would-be lovers and rejectors perceived the pattern of events surrounding the unrequited love experience differently. Perusal of the autobiographical narratives (Baumeister & Wotman, 1992) revealed stark differences in the degree to which the rejection was perceived as clear and unambiguous. Whereas would-be lovers recalled receiving vague and confusing messages by the rejectors, the rejectors often argued that they clearly communicated their disinterest in the romantic relationship. Would-be lovers often felt that their rejectors initially reciprocated their love and led them on, whereas the rejectors almost never mentioned leading their admirers on. These findings were confirmed in a follow-up study, in which people were asked to make their own ratings of their experiences (Baumeister et al., 1993). When asked whether the rejector led them on, almost all of would-be lovers responded in the affirmative. The rejectors, however, denied that they ever encouraged the would-be lovers or led them on.

What accounts for these divergent perspectives? First, recall that would-be lovers wanted to protect their self-esteem and rejectors wanted to maintain a sense of morality. Looking back, the would-be lover loses pride and feels somewhat foolish for behaving in such a desperate fashion, whereas the rejector feels frustrated and guilty for hurting another's feelings. When trying to explain why they persisted and made fools of themselves, the would-be lovers point to the encouragement they received and hence, their ensuing optimism about the desired relationship. When trying to rationalize the pain they caused, rejectors referred to their obvious words of discouragement and thus their blamelessness. Both would-be lovers and rejectors were motivated to escape any residual, negative emotions from the unrequited love experience; forming biased memories for the clarity of the initial rejection may have helped them to do this.

Second, there is good reason to believe that the rejectors' messages of disinterest were in fact mixed and inconsistent. As previously noted, some rejectors initially reciprocated the attraction and then later lost interest in the relationship. The would-be lovers, convinced of the mutuality of their partners' affections, attributed this disinterest to transient or temporary reasons. However, even rejectors who were not romantically attracted to their admirers enjoyed the attention and flattery. As one rejector wrote of this problem in her account, "I'm sure the fact that I was flattered but not attracted gave him a mixed message" (Baumeister & Wotman, 1992, p. 147). Also, lack of a script among rejectors left them uncertain about the proper way to behave, and this uncertainty may have led to inconsistencies in their explanations and behaviors toward their would-be lovers. In fact, rejectors' accounts indicated that their unwillingness to hurt another person led them to behave in a considerate and warm manner, and this in turn was probably taken as a sign of encouragement by the would-be lovers.

This brings us back to our earlier discussion about the conspiracy of silence in unrequited love. Rejectors are reluctant to send a hurtful rejection message, and would-be lovers are reluctant to receive it. The obvious consequence is that the would-be lover continues to persist in winning the rejector's heart.

Even if the rejector sent a clear and explicit rejection message, it is highly plausible that the would-be lover did not interpret it as such. Tennov (1979) argued that, as a result of prevailing beliefs about the reciprocity of love, lovers often ignore what they do not wish to see. Thus, although rejectors may be blunt about their disinterest, wishful thinking and self-deception on the part of the would-be lovers can prevent the message from coming through loud and clear. Finding the courage to reject an admirer outright does not necessarily guarantee that the problem will be solved because that carefully rehearsed rejection message may fall on selectively deaf ears.

Once again, we see a no-win situation for the rejector. Even if the rejector behaves in an angry or cruel fashion, the would-be lover may keep trying, sometimes even harder than before. Research findings from studies on long-term relationships indicate that when one person expresses anger or discontent, the other may try even harder to fix the relationship (Levenson & Gottman, 1985; Vaughan, 1986). This pattern of behavior partly stems from modern media sources that portray would-be lovers as persistent, stubborn, and tenacious.

Last, it is interesting to note that rejectors seem to be more aware of the would-be lovers' persistence than the would-be lovers themselves. The difference was replicated in a follow-up study, in which people were asked to make their own ratings of their experiences (Baumeister et al., 1993). This inconsistency in perceived persistence comes from two sources. One is the almost nonexistent communication between the two parties—and thus the absence of any discussion or agreement about the appropriateness of the would-be lover's behaviors. The second source involves the script of the would-be lovers. To the would-be lover, persistence is the only way to win the other person's heart. To the rejector, persistence is unnecessary, annoying, and a waste of time.

In all, would-be lovers and rejectors differed in their perceptions of the episode. Would-be lovers maintained that their rejectors gave them reason for hope, whereas the rejectors claimed to have been unequivocal in their disinterest. Rejectors' uncertainty about how to respond may have led them to send mixed messages about their intentions and desires. At the point at which rejectors become severe or strict in their rejection, however, would-be lovers sometimes continue to persist. Persistence in the face of rejection is attributed, in part, to cultural stereotypes of the persistent and eventually gratified lover.

Confusion, Mystery, and Self-Knowledge

Did the experience of unrequited love lead individuals to discover something new or profound about themselves? Many stories made mention of such discoveries. In general, people found themselves acting in ways that were inconsistent with normal, established patterns of behavior. Cultural scripts or models led would-be lovers to act in an overly persistent and pushy manner. Some would-be lovers' accounts indicated surprise and disappointment in their behavior. As we might expect, many would-be lovers were very unhappy to discover these new and unusual aspects of themselves. Likewise, rejectors mentioned acting in ways that were out of character. They worried that their behaviors during the unrequited love experience violated their own standards for being kind, friendly, and considerate to other people. Overall, it appears that unrequited love often makes people act in strange or unexpected ways.

Additionally, both parties indicated that the episode led them to experience confusion and puzzlement. However, these experiences were greatest among would-be lovers. Would-be lovers felt lost, confused, and unable to understand the rejector. The main source of confusion was the rejectors' refusal of their love. Would-be lovers searched for a logical explanation of their rejectors' feelings or lack thereof. Some would-be lovers resolved their confusion by derogating their rejectors, others attributed the unreturned feeling to their own lack of desirable traits or characteristics. The rejectors' primary source of puzzlement was their would-be lovers' unsolicited attraction to them.

Did people report learning any lessons from their unrequited love experiences? Some people realized their need to change. However, others indicated that they already changed. Whereas some would-be lovers reported that they learned to be more cautious of love and relationships, others said that the experience helped them to form new relationships. Rejectors and would-be lovers reported newly gained understanding about intimate relationships and love. As one man noted in his story, "I believe that one cannot truly love someone unless there is a reciprocation of feelings … Love will fade if it is not returned" (Baumeister & Wotman, 1992, p. 188). Both the heartbreakers and the heartbroken claim to have learned a great deal about themselves following their experiences of unrequited love. The content of their claims suggest, however, that there were not many highly personal or deep lessons to be learned, apart from the broad futility of one-sided passion.

CONCLUSION

Unrequited love reveals a dark side of interpersonal relationships. When there exists an imbalance in the degree of need or desire for a relationship, the consequences can be destructive both to the emotional well-being of the players in the unrequited love experience and to the stability of any pre-existing interpersonal bond. Sometimes, people fall in love with someone objectively more attractive than themselves and thus, stand little chance of seeing their love returned. Other times, unrequited love results when one person develops a burgeoning attraction to a friend or romantic partner whose feelings remain platonic. The experience may be most painful for both parties when some intimacy has been established and affections have been reciprocated.

The evidence provides some support for the cliché "It is better to have loved in vain than never to have loved at all." Would-be lovers' failures to form the desired, romantic attachment were unanticipated and thus disappointing, but in retrospect they viewed their experiences as positive. Their self-esteem took some ups and downs and rebuilding self-esteem became an important part of the recovery process. In time, most would-be lovers got over their heartbreak and were able to look back with some happy feelings.

Can we also conclude that it is better to have been loved in vain than never to have been loved at all? To be accepted and cared for is a fundamental motivation among humans (McClelland, 1987), thus it is likely that people prefer to be loved by someone as opposed to no one. Assuming the pre-existence of some feelings of love and happiness, however, people faced with additional, unsolicited and unwanted love should find their predicament upsetting and aversive. The findings indicated that rejectors suffered from feelings of frustration, uncertainty, and guilt and tended to look back on their experiences with regret and a desire to erase it from their memories.

Contrary to cultural stereotypes of the rejector as a contemptible or base character, most rejectors emerged as innocent, well-meaning people whose primary motivation was to avoid bringing harm to others. Rejectors ended up feeling torn between their obligations to others and their obligations to their true feelings. Scriptlessness left the rejectors confused and constantly concerned about the morality of their actions and their occasional desire to return their admirers' affections left them confused and guilty.

The emotional outcomes of each person in unrequited love are dependent on other's behaviors. One implication of this interdependency is that both people can make each other miserable. In fact, in unrequited love, both the rejector and the would-be lover often end up feeling like victims. One is a victim of constant, persistent pursuit, whereas the other is a victim of rejection and heartbreak. Interdependence theory also suggests that in unrequited love, the would-be lover faces a high-stakes gamble with a lot to win or lose, whereas the rejector faces a no-win situation with almost nothing to gain and much to lose. This explains why rejectors' accounts were so negative about the entire episode.

Our description of unrequited love is only a first step toward a better understanding of this interpersonal phenomenon. Many questions about unrequited love still remain to be answered. The sample used by Baumeister and Wotman (1992) consisted primarily of young, unmarried, White, American, heterosexual, middle-class adults. It would be interesting to examine these conclusions with different samples, such as non-Western cultures and homosexual populations. Because we did not look directly at gender and personality differences in unrequited love, further studies may find it necessary to develop and test hypothesis regarding those differences. Finally, principles and issues important in unrequited love may also be applicable in other research areas, such as stalking and obsessive-relational intrusion.

The idea of love as an ultimate good has been embraced by many cultures throughout centuries. To be in love is to experience the kind of happiness and satisfaction that cannot be created by other emotions or situations. The research suggests, however, that in unrequited love, neither the would-be lovers nor their rejectors are very satisfied. Unrequited love, thus, shows a limitation of taking only the individual approach to love and a necessity of looking at love in an interpersonal context. Would-be lovers have to face the hurtful rejection from the loved one and the heartbreakers carry the enormously painful task of rejecting another person's love. The trials and tribulations of unrequited love show how it is the mutuality of love, not the giving or receiving of love, that is necessary for happiness and fulfillment.

REFERENCES

Aronson, E., & Linder, D. (1965). Gain and loss of esteem as determinants of interpersonal attractiveness. *Journal of Experimental Social Psychology, 1*, 156–171.

Baumeister, R. F. (1991). *Meanings of life.* New York: Guilford.

Baumeister, R. F. (1997). The self. In D. T. Gilbert, S. T. Fiske, & G. Lindzey (Eds.), *Handbook of Social Psychology* (4th ed.). New York: McGraw-Hill.

Baumeister, R. F., & Leary, M. R. (1995). The need to belong: Desire for interpersonal attachment as a fundamental human motivation. *Psychological Bulletin, 117*, 497–529.

Baumeister, R. F., Reis, H. T., & Delespaul, P. A. E. G. (1995). Subjective and experiential correlates of guilt in daily life. *Personality and Social Psychology Bulletin, 21*, 1256–1268.

Baumeister, R. F., Stillwell, A., & Wotman, S. R. (1990). Victim and perpetrator accounts of interpersonal conflict: Autobiographical narratives about anger. *Journal of Personality and Social Psychology, 59*, 994–1005.

Baumeister, R. F., Stillwell, A. M., & Heatherton, T. F. (1994). Guilt: An interpersonal approach. *Psychological Bulletin, 115*, 243–267.

Baumeister, R. F., & Wotman, S. R. (1992). *Breaking hearts: The two sides of unrequited love.* New York: Guilford.

Baumeister, R. F., Wotman, S. R., & Stillwell, A. M. (1993). Unrequited love: On heartbreak, anger, guilt, scriptlessness, and humiliation. *Journal of Personality and Social Psychology, 64,* 377–394.

Bellah, R. N., Madsen, R., Sullivan, W. M., Swidler, A., & Tipton, S. M. (1985). *Habits of the heart: Individualism and commitment in American life.* Berkeley, CA: University of California Press.

Fromm, E. (1956). *The art of loving.* New York: Harper & Row.

Greenberg, J., Pyszczynski, T., & Solomon, S. (1986). The causes and consequences of self-esteem: A terror management theory. In R. Baumeister (Ed.), *Public self and private self* (pp. 189–212). New York: Springer-Verlag.

Kelley, H. H., & Thibaut, J. W. (1978). Interpersonal relations: A theory of interdependence. New York: Wiley.

Levenson, R. W., & Gottman, J. M. (1985). Physiological and affective predictors of change in relationship satisfaction. *Journal of Personality and Social Psychology, 49,* 85–94.

McClelland, D. C. (1987). Human motivation. Cambridge, England: Cambridge University Press.

McGraw, K. M. (1987). Guilt following transgression: An attribution of responsibility approach. *Journal of Personality and Social Psychology, 53,* 247–256.

Rogers, C. R. (1959). A theory of therapy, personality, and interpersonal relationships, as developed in the client-centered framework. In S. Koch (Ed.), *Psychology: A study of science* (Vol. 3, pp. 184–256). New York: McGraw-Hill.

Sternberg, R. J. (1986). *A triangular theory of love.* Psychological Review, 93, 119–135.

Sternberg, R. J., & Grajek, S. (1984). The nature of love. *Journal of Personality and Social Psychology, 47,* 312–329.

Tangney, J. P. (1995). Shame and guilt in interpersonal relationships. In J. P. Tangney & K. W. Fischer (Eds.), *Self-conscious emotions: The psychology of shame, guilt, embarrassment, and pride* (pp. 114–142). New York: Guilford.

Taylor, S. E. (1989). *Positive illusions: Creative self-deception and the healthy mind.* New York: Basic Books.

Taylor, S. E., & Brown, J. D. (1988). Illusion and well-being: A social psychological perspective on mental health. *Psychological Bulletin, 103,* 193–210.

Tennov, D. (1979). *Love and limerence: The experience of being in love.* New York: Stein and Day.

Vaughan, D. (1986). *Uncoupling.* New York: Oxford University Press.

Walster, E., Aronson, V., Abrahams, D., & Rottman, L. (1966). Importance of physical attractiveness in dating behavior. *Journal of Personality and Social Psychology, 4,* 508–516.

Walster, E., Berscheid, E., & Walster, G.W. (1976). New directions in equity research. In L. Berkowitz (Ed.), *Advances in experimental social psychology* (Vol. 9, pp. 1–42). New York: Academic Press.

11

Disrupted Interpersonal Relationships and Mental Health Problems

Chris Segrin
University of Arizona

Every year hundreds of thousands of Americans suffer from mental health problems. Disorders such as depression, alcoholism, anxiety, and schizophrenia collectively afflict more individuals than certain health problems that captivated far more public attention, such as cancer and AIDS, for example. A recent prospective epidemiological investigation found that 9% of the male population and 25% of the female population were treated for depression *by 30 years old* (Angst, 1992). In Roscoe and Skomski's (1989) survey of over 1,600 adolescents, approximately 20% were classified as *lonely*. Among college freshmen, the point prevalence of bulimia is 4% (Pyle, Neuman, Halvorson, & Mitchell, 1991), a figure that may be an underestimate as rates of eating disorders are higher among those who choose not to participate in surveys (Beglin & Fairburn, 1992). Lifetime prevalence estimates of alcoholism in the United States range from 9% to 14% (Anthony, Warner, & Kessler, 1994; Helzer et al., 1990). Given the pervasiveness of mental health problems in society, it is likely that most people at some point in their lives, will have a relationship—be it romantic, family, occupational, or professional—with someone suffering from a mental health problem (and/or suffer from a mental health problem themselves).

Findings reviewed in this chapter show that many mental health problems are as much relationship communication problems as they are psychological problems. This is why depression, alcoholism, loneliness, and so forth are often characterized as being psychosocial problems. Empirical evidence indicates that some mental health problems are actually precipitated by disrupted and distressed interpersonal relationships. In other cases, mental health problems have a corrosive and deteriorating effect on close interpersonal relationships. In still other cases, mental health problems and distressed interpersonal relationships appear to be in a vicious cycle, whereby one perpetuates the other. In such instances, where depression, alcoholism, or schizophrenia are involved, the consequences can be disastrous, both psychologically and socially.

In the social and behavioral sciences, close relationships are typically characterized in positive terms. As is the case, however, *close* does not always imply *good*. A close relationship with an overprotective, intrusive, yet emotionally distant parent has been implicated in serious mental health problems. Being in a marital relationship that is dissatisfying can easily lead to episodes of depression (Beach, Jouriles, & O'Leary, 1985). To fully understand their form and function, students of close relationships must consider some of the potentially negative aspects of such relationships and their tremendous power to inflict serious psychological damage and impede the recovery process in some instances.

HISTORY OF INTERPERSONAL APPROACHES TO MENTAL HEALTH PROBLEMS

The idea that mental health problems and interpersonal relationships are meaningfully connected is indeed quite old. Eighty years ago, Freud spoke of the "determinants of falling ill as well as all the factors that come into effect *after* the patient has fallen ill," by referencing "the misfortunes of life from which arise deprivation of love, poverty, family quarrels, ill-judged choice of a partner in marriage, (and) unfavorable social circumstances" (Freud, 1917/1966, pp. 431–432). The sharp focus on problems that are interpersonal in nature is quite evident. Later, Sullivan (1953) more strongly emphasized the role of interpersonal and social forces in the development of self and disruption of mental health. One of his more notable contributions involved focusing attention on the importance of same-sex, adolescent, peer relationships in the developmental process. Sullivan unquestionably endorsed the proposition set forth by Freud that the architecture of our early interpersonal relationships can lead to later mental health problems. Conceptualizations of mental illness embedded in the milieu of the patient's interpersonal relationships are also evident in the writings of Sullivan's associates and contemporaries (e.g., Fromm-Reichmann, 1960; Meyer, 1957). Another significant development to emerge during this era was the publication of Leary's (1957) *Interpersonal Diagnosis of Personality*. With an obvious lineage traceable to Sullivan, Leary described his well-known *interpersonal circle* as a method of defining a range of interpersonal behavior that included abnormal or disturbed extremes.

These seeds of the interpersonal approaches to understanding mental illness have grown into what has been described as the "social-interactional viewpoint" (Carson, 1983) and the "interpersonal school" (Klerman, 1986). Carson (1983) eloquently summarized the foundation of this paradigm by stating that:

> symptoms presented by psychotherapy clients (e.g., "depression") actually tell us very little until they are decomposed into specific components, which vary from one client to another presenting a particular symptom. The symptom is, therefore, a prototype of a given class of problems, and the underlying problems usually turn out to be interpersonal in nature—frequently having the form, "I can't (do something interpersonal)." (p. 147)

Modern day instantiations of this perspective developed rapidly in the 1960s and 1970s by those who stressed the importance of concurrent, as opposed to early childhood, interpersonal relationships and mental health problems. In departing from some of the tenets of Sullivan's interpersonal theory and expanding the focus to a wider variety of interpersonal relationships, modern interpersonal approaches to psychopathology bear less resemblance to their originators. This era was launched by works such as the family communication and double-bind theory of schizophrenia by Bateson and associates in the 1960s, Coyne's interactional theory of depression, Lewinsohn's behavioral theory of depression, and the family systems model of alcoholism by Steinglass, all from the 1970s, each of which is discussed later in this chapter. These theories, models, and hypotheses have been developed to explain a wide range of disorders; yet, each shares the postulate that distressed and dysfunctional interpersonal relations are inextricably entwined with psychological distress. The dozens, and in some cases hundreds, of studies that have spawned these pioneering works are testimony to their heuristic value.

In the pages that follow, research findings on the interpersonal and social aspects of schizophrenia, depression, loneliness, alcoholism, and eating disorders are examined. Although conceptually and empirically distinct, each of these disorders has a common correlate: disturbed and dysfunctional relationships with other people. Notwithstanding the various cognitive, neurochemical, life-stress, genetic, and behavioral theories that provide valid accounts of the etiology of these disorders, this review shows that problematic interpersonal relationships also play a contributory causal role in the development and/or course of these disorders. As such, they are rightfully characterized as psychosocial disorders.

SCHIZOPHRENIA

Schizophrenia is a formal thought disorder (actually a family of disorders) characterized by symptoms such as delusions, hallucinations, disorganized speech, grossly disorganized or catatonic behavior, inability to initiate and persist in goal-directed activity, affective flattening, and impoverished thinking evident in speech and language behavior (DSM–IV; American Psychiatric Association, 1994). An additional diagnostic criterion is social–occupational dysfunction. Consequently, it is virtually true, by definition, that people afflicted with schizophrenia experience problems in their interpersonal relationships.

Schizophrenia was one of the first psychological disorders to be associated with intensive theorizing and research on its connection with interpersonal relationships. The majority of such energies were directed toward explaining and understanding the role of family interaction in the disorder. Although early theories probably overemphasized the role of family relationships in contributing to the disorder, family perspectives on schizophrenia remain prominent in the literature today (e.g., Anderson, Reiss, & Hogarty, 1986; McFarlane & Beels, 1988; Miklowitz, Goldstein, & Neuchterlein, 1995).

Early Family Approaches to Schizophrenia

One of the initial forays to family relationships and schizophrenia was headed by Bateson and his colleagues at the Palo Alto VA Hospital (e.g., Bateson, Jackson, Haley, & Weakland, 1956; Watzlawick, Bavelas, & Jackson, 1967). Out of this work emerged the well-known *double-bind theory*. According to this position, communication has multiple levels of meaning that include a literal content and a metamessage at a higher level that provides information about the interpretation of the message content and/or relationship between the sender and receiver. Observations of schizophrenic family interactions revealed paradoxical and contradictory communications in which the content of verbal messages was often contradicted by the metamessages that were typically, nonverbally communicated. Growing up in such families was thought to make logical communication impossible. Thus, the illogical and severely disturbed communication of the schizophrenic patient was thought to be the net result of growing up in a family plagued by such dysfunctional interactions.

Another early family process phenomenon to appear in the literature was *mystification* (Laing, 1965). *Mystified communication* involves ambiguities, misunderstandings, and misidentification of issues and topics. *Mystification* is commonly evident in a process whereby a person responds to the other in terms of his or her own needs, but at the same time behaves as if he or she is really responding to the needs of the other. So, for example, an aging mother might respond to her son's nutritional needs by giving him a lot of calcium-rich foods, when in fact, it is the mother who is in need of additional calcium in her diet. Such parent–child interactions are thought to have teleological significance in the development of dysfunctionally symbolic relationships that ultimately produce symptoms of the disorder. Laing's thesis was that schizophrenia was a logical reaction to an illogical family environment. As an unfortunate aside, Laing, like Leary, departed from the scientific milieu prior to seeing his innovative ideas come to their full fruition.

The family processes of *schism* and *skew* also figured prominently in early family approaches to schizophrenia (Lidz, Cornelison, Fleck, & Terry, 1957). The *schismatic pattern* of family interaction entailed open and hostile conflict. Schismatic parents continually attempt to undermine the standing of the other in the eyes of the child. In this sense their interactions are typically characterized as battles for the loyalty of the child. Lidz (et al.) highlighted the ineffectiveness, insecurity, and paranoia among the parents that drove this family process.

A skewed pattern of family interaction involves an extremely overintrusive mother who is apparently impervious to the needs of other family members. Fathers in such families are unable to control or counterbalance the deviant parenting of the mother. These fathers tend to be passive and are often themselves disturbed by addictions, psychosis, or other psychosocial problems. Children in such families are forced to accept a bizarre worldview that is skewed toward that of an overintrusive parent whose mental health could, itself, be questioned.

Hopes for explaining the etiology of schizophrenia with these family process variables were ultimately met with disappointment. McFarlane and Beels (1988) appropriately noted that concepts such as double-bind communication, schism, and skew are no longer considered to be causal agents in the disorder. Most of these early family constructs and hypotheses were defined on the basis of small-sample, clinical investigations, without matched control groups, random-sampling methods, or attention to the reliability of the clinical observations (Shean, 1978).

Contemporary Family Approaches to Schizophrenia

Contemporary investigations of family relationships and schizophrenia center more on explaining the course than the cause of the disorder. Two family variables that have been, and continue to be, particularly influential in this area are *expressed emotion* and *communication deviance* (Wynne, 1981).

Early investigations of family expressed emotion (EE; Brown, Monck, Carstairs, & Wing, 1962; Vaughn & Leff, 1976) identified a pattern of criticism, overinvolvement, overprotectiveness, excessive attention, and emotional reactivity that appeared to create a vulnerability to relapse and poor social adjustment among schizophrenic patients (see Hooley, 1985, for a review). Patients who returned to a home with high EE relatives exhibited a 9-month relapse rate of 51%, whereas only 13% of those who returned to a low EE family relapsed (Vaughn & Leff, 1976).

Vaughn and Leff (1981) specified four behavioral characteristics of EE: intrusiveness, anger and/or acute distress and anxiety, overt blame and criticism of the patient, and an intolerance of the patient's symptoms. Family therapy programs that improve communication and problem solving, thus lowering EE, significantly lower relapse rates (e.g., Doane, Goldstein, Miklowitz, & Falloon, 1986).

Recently, Rosenfarb and his colleagues examined the functioning of a sample of young and recently discharged schizophrenia patients who returned to either high or low expressed emotion families (Rosenfarb, Goldstein, Mintz, & Nuechterlein, 1995). Patients from high EE families exhibited more odd and disruptive behavior during a family interaction approximately 6 weeks after hospital discharge than did patients from low EE households. Relatives in the high EE households were more critical of the patients when they verbalized unusual thoughts than were low EE family members. Studies such as these clearly paint a picture of a vicious circle in high EE family relations: These parents respond to the patient with a lot of criticism because patients from these households appear to exhibit more bizarre and disruptive behavior than patients from low EE homes. It is likely that the negative reactions they receive from their families further contribute to the potential for relapse among the patients.

Research on family expressed emotion continues to flourish (e.g., Cole, Grolnick, Kane, Zastowney, & Lehman, 1993; Docherty, 1995; Mueser et al., 1993). In addition to being a useful and reliable predictor of relapse, EE may also be fruitfully understood as a familial risk indicator for schizophrenia (Miklowitz, 1994) as well as a family response to dealing with a schizophrenic member.

A considerable body of evidence indicates that families with a schizophrenic member communicate in odd, idiosyncratic, illogical, and fragmented language, even when that member is not present. Topics of conversation often drift or abruptly change direction with a lack of closure. This characteristic style of family communication has been labeled *communication deviance* (CD; Singer, Wynne, & Toohey, 1978). It is particularly intriguing that this distorted form of communication is highly reminiscent of the communication style that typifies the actual schizophrenic individual. Research by Goldstein and his colleagues indicates that parental CD precedes onset (Goldstein, 1987) and is therefore an excellent predictor of schizophrenia among premorbid adolescents (see Goldstein & Strachan, 1987, for a review).

In a masterful program of research, Miklowitz and his associates examined the disrupted verbal interactions of schizophrenic patients and their family members (e.g., Miklowitz et al., 1995; Miklowitz et al., 1986; Miklowitz et al., 1991). Their work shows that aspects of CD, such as idea fragments (e.g., "But the thing is as I said, there's got ... you can't drive in the alley"), contradictions and retractions (e.g., "No, that's right, she does"), and ambiguous references (e.g., "Kid stuff that's one thing but something else is different too") distinguish parents of schizophrenia patients from parents of healthy control subjects (see Miklowitz et al., 1991, for additional examples and CD constructs). As if to make a potentially disruptive family situation worse for the schizophrenic patient, it appears that families that are high in EE are also high in CD (Miklowitz et al., 1986). Consequently, patients may be dealt a double dose of problematic interactional exchanges with their family members. It is little wonder that patients discharged to parents high in EE, who are also likely to express unclear, odd, and fragmented ideas, are at such a high risk for relapse.

The disruptive potential of relationships with high CD family members has been documented in a longitudinal investigation that followed a sample of at-risk, but nonpsychotic, adolescents over a period of 5 years (Doane, West, Goldstein, Rodnick, & Jones, 1981). Adolescents whose parents exhibited high CD and interpersonal aspects of EE, such as criticism, guilt induction, and intrusiveness, at Time one were more likely to develop schizophrenia-spectrum disorders as young adults than those from low CD and EE families.

The work on family EE and CD is best summarized as follows: Family EE is a good predictor of relapse among schizophrenic patients in remission; family CD is a good discriminator between families of schizophrenic persons and families of healthy controls (Miklowitz, 1994). Although neither EE nor CD are specific to families with a schizophrenic member, each represents a potent risk factor for the course and possible onset of the disorder.

Personal Relationships and Schizophrenia

Finally, it should be noted that problematic interpersonal relationships extend beyond the realm of family relations for the schizophrenic patient. Schizophrenic patients typically have smaller social networks and report that they have fewer close friends than healthy controls or even other psychiatric patients (Erickson, Beiser, Iacono, Fleming, & Lin, 1989). Importantly, Erickson et al. observed a negative correlation between number of family members in the schizophrenic patients' social networks and their prognosis, whereas a greater number of friends and acquaintances was associated with better outcomes. In addition to potential disruption of friendship relations, schizophrenia is also associated with less closeness and more conflict with siblings (Lively, Friedrich, & Buckwalter, 1995). Participants in Lively et al.'s study expressed a considerable degree of grief and stress associated with their attempts to cope with the ill sibling.

DEPRESSION

Major Depressive disorder is a pervasive illness with a lifetime risk of 10% to 25% for women and 5% to 12% for men (DSM–IV; American Psychiatric Association, 1994). The disorder is associated with a dangerously high mortality rate, as 15% of its victims die by suicide. Depressive episodes are marked by nearly constant depressed mood, diminished interest in any activities, significant weight loss or gain, sleep disturbance, psychomotor agitation or retardation, fatigue, feelings of worthlessness and guilt, difficulty concentrating, and recurrent thoughts of death or suicidal ideation (American Psychiatric Association, 1994).

Depression and Social Skills

An early interpersonally oriented approach to depression appeared in the form of Lewinsohn's Behavioral Theory of Depression (Lewinsohn, 1974, 1975). As part of this theory, Lewinsohn stressed that depressed people often exhibit disrupted social skills, this makes it difficult for them to obtain positive reinforcement from their relationships with other people.

At the same time, poor social skills make it difficult to avoid negative outcomes in social relationships. The inability to produce positive—and avoid negative—social outcomes is thought to precipitate episodes of depression. A considerable body of literature is generally supportive of the notion that depressed people have social skills problems that can create relational difficulties for them (see McCann & LaLonde, 1993; Segrin, 1990, Segrin & Abramson, 1994, for reviews). Poor social skills have a strong association with interpersonal rejection from others (Segrin, 1992). Therefore, depressed people with poor social skills would be expected to experience difficulty in establishing and maintaining rewarding interpersonal relationships.

Depression and Interpersonal Rejection. A substantial body of evidence indicates that an important interpersonal problem for people afflicted with depression is rejection from others (e.g., Amstutz & Kaplan, 1987; Gotlib & Beatty, 1985; Gurtman, 1987; Siegel & Alloy, 1990). Much of the research on this phenomenon is guided by Coyne's *Interactional Model of Depression* (Coyne, 1976a, 1976b). According to this model, depressed people are hypothesized to induce a negative mood in their interactional partners through a process of emotional contagion. This hypothesis is predicated on the assumption that it is an irritating, negative experience to interact with depressed people. As a consequence of this negative mood induction, others are expected to move from initially offering nongenuine reassurance and support to outright rejection and avoidance of the depressed individual. Depressed people appear to be quite aware of this rejection (Segrin, 1993a), and such negative interpersonal feedback exacerbates their negative mood states (Segrin & Dillard, 1991).

Numerous attempts to experimentally test Coyne's Interactional Model of depression have often failed to demonstrate the hypothesized negative mood induction effect (e.g., Gotlib & Robinson, 1982; McNiel, Arkowitz, & Pritchard, 1987; but see Coyne, 1976a), although this effect may become more evident over repeated interactions with the depressed target (Hokanson & Butler, 1992). However, the rejection of depressed persons by their interactional partners appears to be a reliable and robust phenomenon (e.g., Amstutz & Kaplan, 1987; Elliott, MacNair, Herrick, Yoder, & Byrne, 1991; Gurtman, 1987) and holds up across different cultures (Vanger, Summerfield, Rosen, & Watson, 1991) and age groups (Connolly, Geller, Marton, & Kutcher, 1992; Peterson, Mullins, & Ridley-Johnson, 1985; Rudolph, Hammen, & Burge, 1994).

This interpersonal rejection effect associated with depression appears to be moderated by a number of different variables. For example, depressed males elicit more rejection from others, especially other females, than do depressed females (Hammen & Peters, 1977, 1978; Joiner, Alfano, & Metalsky, 1992). Some evidence also indicates that friends are less rejecting of depressed persons than strangers (Segrin, 1993a; see Sacco, Milana, & Dunn, 1985), that other people who assume a helper role are less rejecting (Marks & Hammen, 1982), and that those who rely on advice giving and joking with the depressed person are more rejecting (Notarius & Herrick, 1988). Other potential moderators of the depression–rejection effect include physical attractiveness of the depressed target (less rejection of attractive targets; Amstutz & Kaplan, 1987) and self-esteem of the target; depressed people who are low in self-esteem and seek reassurance from their partners are especially prone to eliciting rejection (Joiner et al., 1992).

A meta-analysis of the literature on interpersonal responses to depression indicates that the phenomenon of interpersonal rejection of depressed persons is very reliable and moderate in magnitude across studies (Segrin & Dillard, 1992). However, the extent to which depressed people create a negative affective state in others, through social interaction, is weaker and more sporadic. Research conducted since this meta-analysis continued to produce results that generally are consistent with this conclusion (e.g., Connolly et al., 1992; Joiner et al., 1992; Marcus & Davis, 1993; Rudolph et al., 1994; Segrin 1993a). Interested readers may wish to consult Coyne (1990), Coyne, Burchill, and Stiles (1990), Coyne, Kahn, & Gotlib (1987), McCann (1990), and Segrin and Dillard (1992) for more in-depth reviews of this literature.

Personal Relationships of Depressed Persons.   The personal relationships of depressed people are characterized by dissatisfaction (Burns, Sayers, & Moras, 1994), diminished influence and intimacy (Nezlek, Imbrie, & Shean, 1994; Patterson & Bettini, 1993), and diminished activity and involvement (Gotlib & Lee, 1989). Some evidence indicates that the quality of social interaction with others is more strongly associated with depression than the sheer quantity (e.g., Rotenberg & Hamel, 1988). As might be expected, the availability of a confidant with whom one can self-disclose and engage in rewarding conversation is negatively associated with depression. It is the case, however, that many depressed people lack a close intimate relationship altogether (Brown & Harris, 1978; Costello, 1982). This finding is particularly important in that lack of a close confiding relationship appears to create a heightened vulnerability to experiencing depression (Brown & Harris, 1978).

Research on the personal relationships of depressives leads one to question the worth of their relational partners. For example, in Fiske and Peterson's (1991) investigation, depressed participants complained of dissatisfaction and anger with their romantic partners as well as increased quarreling relative to nondepressed participants. These same respondents reported being hurt or upset by their romantic partners more frequently than did nondepressed controls, despite (or perhaps as a cause of) their greater desire for more love in the relationship. Depressed people also perceive their intimate partners as more hostile than nondepressed persons do (Thompson, Whiffen, & Blain, 1995). One recently studied group of depressed women reported that they received less social support from their confidants than did a group of nondepressed controls (Belsher & Costello, 1991). The confidants of these depressed women exhibited more depressogenic speech (e.g., "I can't do anything right anymore" or "I'm never going to find a job") than did confidants of either nondepressed or psychiatric controls. One might speculate that these friends actually contribute to the depressed person's aversive psychological experience. Findings such as these are one illustration of how being in dysfunctional, hostile, and unsupportive relationships that are wanting in intimacy precipitate depression and other undesirable affective states (Coyne & De-Longis, 1986; Coyne, Kessler, Tal, Turnbull, Wortman, & Greden, 1987).

If it is the case that depressed persons typically find themselves in low quality, interpersonal relationships, it is necessary to at least contemplate the extent to which the relationships are actually better than the depressed person makes them out to be. Depressed people have a tendency to be overly negative in evaluating their interpersonal relationships (Hokanson, Hummer, & Butler, 1991) and estimating the frequency with which negative interpersonal events occur (Kuiper & MacDonald, 1983). Undoubtedly, many depressed people are in dysfunctional or dissatisfying interpersonal relationships. However, there is reason to suspect that at least some of the variance in these reports of aversive and dissatisfying interpersonal relationships is due to the depressed person's general tendency toward negatively biased assessments of such relationships.

Depression and Family Interaction. In addition to the experience of disrupted personal relationships, depression is also associated with problems in marital interactions and relationships (see Beach, Sandeen, & O'Leary, 1990; Coyne et al., 1987, for reviews). Repeatedly, this research shows that depression and marital distress go hand in hand (Beach & O'Leary, 1993; Beach et al., 1990; Hinchliffe, Hooper, & Roberts, 1978). Estimates indicate that 50% of all women in distressed marriages are depressed (Beach et al., 1985) and 50% of all depressed women are in distressed marriages (Rounsaville, Weissman, Prusoff, & Herceg-Baron, 1979).

The communication between depressed people and their spouses is often negative in tone and tends to generate more negative affect in each spouse than that of nondepressed couples (Gotlib & Whiffen, 1989; Kahn, Coyne, & Margolin, 1985; Ruscher & Gotlib, 1988). Biglan and his coworkers suggested that depressed persons and their spouses often find themselves in dysfunctional vicious cycles of interaction (Biglan et al., 1985; Hops et al., 1987). Their findings indicate that depressed persons are often rewarded by their spouses for emitting depressive behaviors in that the depressive behaviors tend to inhibit the hostile and irritable behaviors of the spouse (see also Nelson & Beach, 1990). McCabe and Gotlib (1993) showed that over the course of a 10 to 15 minute marital interaction, the verbal behavior of depressed wives became increasingly negative. It is therefore not surprising that this study demonstrated that couples with a depressed spouse viewed their marital interactions as more hostile and less friendly than did the nondepressed couples.

In an impressive program of research, Hinchliffe and her colleagues investigated a number of specific marital communication problems experienced by depressed people (Hinchliffe, Hooper, & Robert, 1978; Hinchliffe, Hooper, Roberts, & Vaughan, 1978; Hinchliffe, Vaughan, Hooper, & Roberts, 1978; Hooper, Vaughan, Hinchliffe, & Roberts, 1978). These investigations reveal that when interacting with their spouses, depressed persons exhibit distorted patterns of responsiveness such that there is a lack of synchrony between the husband and wife. This is evident through increased self-focus and decreased responsiveness to the partner's states and opinions among couples with a depressed member. In addition, depressed people tend to be most expressive with their spouses when they are discussing issues that are negative in nature. It is interesting to note that in one study, acute depression was associated with a tendency to control and influence the other spouse (Hooper, Baugh, et al., 1978). These and other investigations indicate that the marital interactions of depressed persons are not always withdrawn and avoidant; they can take on a hostile and manipulative tone well.

A variety of other investigations of marital interaction find depression to be associated with poor communication during problem-solving interactions (Basco, Prager, Pite, Tamir, & Stephens, 1992), negative self-evaluations and statements of negative well-being (Hautzinger, Linden, & Hoffman, 1982; Linden, Hautzinger, & Hoffman, 1983), verbal aggressiveness (Segrin & Fitzpatrick, 1992), and problems in establishing intimacy (Basco et al., 1992; Bullock, Siegel, Weissman, & Paykel, 1972). Given all of these negative communication behaviors and marital problems, it is easy to understand why depression and martial distress are so powerfully related. Some evidence indicates that these communication problems are the result of marital distress more than depression per se (Schmaling & Jacobson, 1990). However, the similarity of these findings with those of depressed persons' other personal relationships points to obvious and pervasive interpersonal problems across a variety of different relational contexts.

Depressed persons experience as many problems in their role as a parent as they do in their role as a spouse. In numerous investigations, depression was linked to disrupted and dysfunctional parenting behavior (e.g., Hamilton, Jones, & Hammen, 1993; Hammen et al., 1987). In general, the parenting behavior of depressives is characterized by similar negativity, hostility, complaining, and poor interpersonal problem solving that is associated with their other relationships. Apparently, as a consequence of this disrupted parenting behavior, the children of depressed parents are at a much higher risk for behavioral, cognitive, and emotional dysfunction than are those of nondepressed parents (e.g., Lee & Gotlib, 1991; Whiffen & Gotlib, 1989; see Downey & Coyne, 1990; Gelfand & Teti, 1990; Morrison, 1983, for reviews). Among the problems experienced by children of depressed mothers is depression itself (Hammen et al., 1987; Warner, Weissman, Fendrich, Wickramaratne, & Moreau, 1992). Although the effects of maternal depression received much attention in the literature, evidence suggests that paternal depression also has ill effects on children (Forehand & Smith, 1986; Thomas & Forehand, 1991).

Children of depressed mothers typically exhibit a behavioral pattern indicative of rejection. During interaction with their parents, children of depressives express negative affect, are generally tense and irritable, spend less time looking at their parent, and appear less content than do children who interact with their nondepressed parents (e.g., Cohn, Campbell, Matias, & Hopkins, 1990; Field, 1984).

Finally, it appears that many depressed people experienced difficulties in their families when growing up. Consistent results indicate that people who are depressed typically describe their family of origin as rejecting (Lewinsohn & Rosenbaum, 1987) and uncaring (Gotlib, Mount, Cordy, & Whiffen, 1988).

Comorbidity of Depression and Loneliness

It is difficult to examine the relational well-being of depressed people without noting the prominent association between this state of distress and loneliness (Rich & Bonner, 1987; Weeks, Michela, Peplau, & Bragg, 1980). It has been argued that these two psychosocial problems have such similarity in features, especially in the domain of interpersonal problems, that the prototype of loneliness is literally nested within that of depression (Horowitz, French, Lapid, & Weckler, 1982). In short, the social withdrawal that is characteristically symptomatic of depression undoubtedly prompts feelings of loneliness. At the same time, chronic loneliness can be emotionally taxing and can easily cascade into depression (Rich & Scovel, 1987; see Segrin, (1998) for a more in-depth analysis of the comorbidity and overlapping interpersonal features of depression and loneliness). In the following section, a very similar constellation of problems with personal and family relationships is evident among those who are lonely.

LONELINESS

Like the literature on depression, research on loneliness illustrates numerous social and interpersonal problems associated with the condition. Given that loneliness is a discrepancy between a person's desired and achieved level of social interaction (Peplau, Russell, & Heim, 1979), it is perhaps a foregone conclusion that lonely people have problems with interpersonal communication and relationships.

Loneliness and Personal Relationships

Perhaps the most substantial affliction experienced by lonely persons is a lack of intimacy in their social and personal relationships (e.g. Hamid, 1989; Revenson & Johnson, 1984; Vaux, 1988). This may be explained by the fact that lonely people have a difficult time making friends (Medora & Woodward, 1986) and experience poor communication with family members (Brage, Meredith, & Woodward, 1993) and low social integration (Vaux, 1988). The most common type of problem that lonely people experience is inhibited sociability, manifested through difficulties with introducing the self to others, making friends, participating in groups, and making phone calls to others to initiate social activity (Horowitz & French, 1979). These problems with social behavior are perhaps best understood as the consequences of disrupted social skills that are prevalent among those who are lonely (Jones, 1982; Jones, Hobbs, & Hockenbury, 1982; Segrin, 1996; Spitzberg & Canary, 1985).

Loneliness appears to be tied to feeling a lack of control over personal relationships. For instance, Schulz (1976) constructed a 2-month long, social contact program between students and institutionalized elderly. Some elderly residents chose when they had this contact and/or predicted its frequency and duration. Other elderly participants were just dropped in on periodically. In each condition, the student–elderly contacts were of equal duration. However, it was the elderly who had some control or predictability in these relational contacts that felt less lonely. The importance of controllability also appears prominently in the literature on loneliness and social cognition. The tendency to make uncontrollable attributions for outcomes of interpersonal events, as well as internal attributions for interpersonal failures and external attributions for interpersonal successes, was demonstrated to be a strong correlate of loneliness (Anderson & Arnoult, 1985; Horowitz, French, & Anderson, 1982).

Involvement in personal relationships offers numerous benefits, or provisions, such as attachment, social integration, guidance, and reassurance of worth (Weiss, 1974). Operating from this social provisions framework, Kraus and her colleagues demonstrated that lonely subjects felt that they had less access to these social provisions from their relationships with others (Kraus, Davis, Bazzini, Church, & Kirchman, 1993). This is understandable in light of the fact that feelings of loneliness in this study were also associated with fewer friends, fewer activities with friends, and less perceived quality of friendship.

Gaining access to the social provisions of personal relationships may be especially problematic for lonely people because they tend to hold negative views of other people, including relational partners. Student participants in a study by Wittenberg and Reis (1986) exhibited a tendency to provide more negative evaluations of their dormitory roommate—and be less accepting of other people, in general—as a function of their own loneliness. With such negative views of those who are in a position to dispense the social provisions that appear to ameliorate loneliness, many lonely people create a self-fulfilling and perpetuating interpersonal problem for themselves.

The Ineffectiveness of Family Relations to Ameliorate Loneliness

What appears to be particularly lacking for the lonely person are meaningful and intimate friendships. Quality relationships with family members, on the other hand, do little to prevent or ameliorate the experience of loneliness (e.g., Jones & Moore, 1990). In fact, Jones and Moore found that the more social support students had from their family, the more lonely they were. Although the increased family social support may be a result of the students' loneliness, it is clear that these types of relationships do little to help the lonely person's situation. In a study with truly mind-bending results, Andersson and his colleagues further explored the role of family relationships in the experience of loneliness (Andersson, Mullins, & Johnson, 1990). He obtained retrospective reports of parent–child relationships from a large sample of elderly women in their 70s and 80s. Children who had an excessively close, warm, and nurturing relationship with at least one parent were significantly more lonely as elderly adults than a group of controls. Andersson et al. (1990) concluded that the effects of overinvolvement from parents can be as noxious as underinvolvement or neglect when it comes to producing lonely children. This is due in part to the fact that parental overinvolvement can create a sense of narcissism in the child. One reason that family relationships and involvement might be so ineffective at buffering against loneliness is because they are relationships of obligation. Consequently, lonely people find little solace in social support from persons who they feel are obligated to offer it.

One might additionally hypothesize that extremely close parent–child relationships build great expectations that other relationships chronically fail to meet. Such a phenomenon could easily create a sense of dissatisfaction and longing for greater intimacy in one's interpersonal relationships. Finally, excessive closeness and interaction with parents displace the interactions that children have with peers. This leads to a corruption of the processes that lead to peer–referent social skills. An individual lacking in such social skills would again experience difficulty in establishing and maintaining satisfying social relations.

Additional suspicion about the ill-effects of relationships with the family of origin have been raised by results of a recent investigation from Henwood and Solano (1994). These authors surveyed a sample of first-grade children and their parents and found that children's loneliness was significantly correlated with that of their mothers (see also Lobdell & Perlman, 1986). Whether parental loneliness is transmitted via genetics, environment, socialization, or a combination of these factors, the family does not appear to be a source of buffers against the loneliness experience.

Loneliness and Social Anxiety

One possible cause of the lonely person's problems in establishing intimate relationships involves social anxiety. There is a powerful link between loneliness and the experience of social anxiety (e.g., Moore & Schultz, 1983; Segrin, 1993b; Segrin & Kinney, 1995; Solano & Koester, 1989). The socially anxious tend to approach social interactions with discomfort and nervousness and in more severe cases, avoid them altogether. As a consequence, other people typically respond rather unfavorably to these awkward and reserved interactions. Many people cope with the experience of social anxiety by avoiding those situations that prompt the anxiety. For the lonely person, this may result in evading others before ever having a chance to develop relationships with them. It is easy to see how the experience of social anxiety creates barriers to establishing meaningful relationships with others.

ALCOHOLISM

Alcoholism is a specific class of the more general diagnosis of substance dependence. Defining features of *alcohol dependence* include tolerance (i.e., need for increased amounts to achieve the desired effect or diminished effect with same amount), ill effects associated with withdrawal (e.g., hyperactivity, hand tremor, insomnia, nausea, or anxiety), ingestion of larger amounts over longer periods of time than intended, a persistent desire or unsuccessful efforts to reduce or control intake, spending a lot of time obtaining the substance, and diminished or disturbed social, occupational, or recreational activities as a result of persistent alcohol use (DSM–IV, American Psychiatric Association, 1994).

Contact with clients at the VA center in Jackson, Mississippi led Foy and his colleagues to note that many of the alcoholics seeking treatment reported having interpersonal problems (Foy, Massey, Duer, Ross, & Wooten, 1979). In particular, these clients appeared to have difficulty with their coworkers and bosses that caused job-related problems. Observations such as these come as little surprise to the individual acquainted with an alcoholic. Interpersonal problems are fairly pervasive among those with serious drinking problems. Problematic relationships clearly have the potential to trigger the onset of problem drinking in some people. Once the pattern of problem drinking is established, interpersonal relationships typically suffer.

Insight into the origins of alcoholics' interpersonal relationship problems may be gleaned from research on the interpersonal traits associated with alcohol dependence. For example, continuous (versus episodic) alcoholics can be characterized by elevated cynicism and distrust in interpersonal relationships (McMahon, Davidson, Gersh, & Flynn, 1991). Although it is not clear if these traits antedated the alcoholism or proceeded from it, each possibility has intuitive appeal.

Alcoholism and Family Relationships

The toll of alcoholism on interpersonal relationships is very evident when studying alcoholics and their spouses. Suman and Nagalakshmi (1993) found spouses of alcoholics to be low in extraversion and high in neuroticism. These same spouses were significantly more inhibited and withdrawn in interpersonal relationships than spouses of nonalcoholics. Nagalakshmi also found alcoholics to describe themselves as more loving, affectionate, and understanding than nonalcoholics (Neeliyara, Nagalakshmi, & Ray, 1989). However, their spouses sharply disagreed with the alcoholics' self-perceptions, perceiving them as less loving and more aggressive. Such differing perceptions among intimates are a potent recipe for distress.

In a pioneering study of marital relations and alcoholism, Gorad (1971) placed marital pairs in a game simulation in which they could win money individually through competitive moves or collectively through cooperative moves. Gorad also included a possibility in which partners could secretly compete with each other without making their competitive moves known. The alcoholic men in this study made more secretly competitive moves than their wives or any of the nonalcoholic men. This finding is thought to be characteristic of alcoholics' attempts to avoid taking responsibility for their behavior in close relationships—where alcohol provides an external, uncontrollable attribution.

In an extremely influential line of research, Steinglass demonstrated that the interactions of alcoholics with their spouses are actually more patterned, organized, and predictable while they are intoxicated (Steinglass, 1979, 1981; Steinglass & Robertson, 1983; Steinglass, Weiner, & Mendelson, 1971). Thus, the alcohol ingestion serves an adaptive function in the marital relationship through a stabilizing phenomenon. In one investigation of alcoholics and their family members (Steinglass et al., 1971), the expression of previously inhibited positive affect between family members became extremely pronounced during drinking periods. Observations such as these prompted Steinglass et al. to suggest that there is an *alcoholic system* in some families, in which drinking is an integral part of the family system that actually maintains and stabilizes the family. Unfortunately, in the majority of cases the intoxication provides only a temporary solution to the family's problems and often brings with it more serious, long-term ill effects.

Although drinking temporarily injects positivity into some family relationships, several laboratory investigations also documented negative effects associated with drinking. For example, Jacob had families with an alcoholic father discuss items from various questionnaire inventories (Jacob, Ritchey, Cvitkovic, & Blane, 1981). During their family discussions, the alcoholic couples expressed more negative affect during the drink versus no-drink conditions (see also Billings, Kessler, Gomberg, & Weiner, 1979). The nature of nonalcoholics' interactions was not effected by the drinking conditions.

The literature on alcoholism and marital and family relations (see Jacob & Seilhamer, 1987; Jacobs & Wolin, 1989, for reviews) clearly indicates that for at least some families, alcohol brings stability and temporary positivity. These outcomes contribute to a family maintenance of the alcoholism. Studies by Jacob and Billings are a reminder that increased negativity in family relations is also quite possible as a result of drinking (e.g., Billings et al., 1979; Jacob et al., 1981). An intriguing issue in need of further clarification is the extent to which distressed family relations contribute to problem drinking, as well as the extent to which problem drinking deteriorates family relationships. Currently, there appear to be no data that directly disconfirm either of these causal routes.

Children of Alcoholics

Children of alcoholics (COAs) received a great deal of research attention as an at-risk population (e.g., Sher, 1991; Windle & Searles, 1990). Concern with this population stems from the belief that parental alcoholism leads to disrupted and dysfunctional family environments that have ill effects for those who grow up in them. These ill effects are driven by parental modeling of dysfunctional and destructive behaviors, corruption and deterioration of parenting behaviors, or an amalgamation of both processes. Indeed, results of a large sample, cross sectional study with rigorous sampling techniques indicate that COAs exhibited significant differences from non-COAs in greater involvement in alcohol use, more drug dependence, more depression, agoraphobia, social phobia and generalized anxiety, less behavioral control, lower self-esteem, lower scores on tests of verbal ability, and lower academic achievement (Sher, Walitzer, Wood, & Brent, 1991). It should be noted that differences between COAs and non-COAs in this investigation were small to moderate in magnitude. Other findings indicate that COAs are more depressed, less satisfied with their marriages, and more likely to drink for coping purposes than non-COAs (Domenico & Windle, 1993). Findings such as these suggest such pervasive deficits among COAs that it is a wonder they are even minimally functional.

The problem most strongly linked with being a child of an alcoholic parent is a risk for alcoholism (Pollock, Schneider, Garielli, & Goodwin, 1987). Children of alcoholics are far more likely to have alcohol problems themselves than are members of the general population. Consideration must certainly be given to the influence of genetic mechanisms in the familial transmission of alcoholism. At the same time, however, it is plausible to assume that social learning processes also contribute to the phenomenon. Children who observe parents using alcohol as a means of relaxation, coping with stress, celebration, and so forth naturally are expected to imitate this behavior that their parent(s) regularly modeled during the formative years.

Notwithstanding some of the significant problems that appear to be associated with being a child of an alcoholic, a nontrivial body of literature is emerging that questions the distinctness and at-risk status of the COA population. For example, studies found no differences between COAs and non-COAs in alcohol-related problems; suicidal ideation; personal control;

perceived social support (Wright & Heppner, 1991); state anxiety; mood (Clair & Genest, 1992); social skills (Segrin & Menees, 1995); social maladjustment (Dinning & Berk, 1989); personality traits of expressiveness, alienation, and defensiveness (Havey & Dodd, 1993); object relations deficits, compulsive behavior (Hadley, Holloway, & Mallinckrodt, 1993); or depression (Reich, Earls, Frankel, & Shayka, 1993). The list of such studies is too long and the breadth of dependent variables too extensive to dismiss these findings to sampling error or other artifacts. Such findings are interpretable as good news for the COA. Although alcoholic parents raise children with psychosocial problems of their own, this is not a deterministic relationship. Researchers are beginning to note that COAs are a complex and heterogenous population, and dysfunction may be more evident in those COAs seeking attention through self-help groups and professional contacts (Hinson, Becker, Handal, & Katz, 1993; Sheridan & Green, 1993). In addition, some models of the influence of parental alcoholism on children's adjustment suggest that variables, such as marital strain, social isolation, role reversals, and medical problems, for example, moderate this relationship (Seilhamer & Jacob, 1990).

EATING DISORDERS

The American Psychiatric Association recognizes two distinct subtypes of eating disorders: anorexia nervosa and bulimia nervosa (DSM–IV; American Psychiatric Association, 1994). Obesity is currently considered more of a medical condition than a mental health problem. The defining features of *anorexia nervosa* include a refusal to maintain a normal body weight, an intense fear of gaining weight, and a disturbance in body-image perception. *Bulimia nervosa* is defined by recurrent episodes of uncontrolled binge eating, inappropriate compensatory behaviors to control weight gain (e.g., self-induced vomiting, and misuse of laxatives or diuretics), and an undue influence of body shape and weight on self-evaluations. A chief difference between the two disorders is that individuals with bulimia nervosa are able to maintain their body weight at or above normally prescribed levels. Similar to depression and alcoholism, this is a disorder with a lethal component. The long-term mortality for those afflicted with eating disorders is estimated to be over 10% (American Psychiatric Association, 1994). Descriptions of these disorders in the DSM–IV contain references to interpersonal problems. Associated features of Anorexia Nervosa include social withdrawal and diminished interest in sex. Episodes of binge eating associated with Bulimia Nervosa are often triggered by interpersonal stressors.

Research on interpersonal relationships and eating disorders are typical of the work on interpersonal relationships and, more generally, mental health. The recognition of some type of relational difficulty associated with the disorder predates current investigations by at least a century (Laseque, 1873). One of Laseque's more notable contributions was the suggestion of *parentectomy*—hospitalization of the patients to remove them from exacerbating parental forces. Family relationships, in particular, have been a focal point of this line of work (see Kog & Vandereycken, 1985; Vandereycken, Kog, & Vanderlinden, 1989; Waller & Calam, 1994; Wonderlich, 1992, for reviews). Finally, the proliferation of studies on this associated feature of eating disorders is particularly evident in the past 25 years.

In a recent longitudinal investigation, 51 diagnosed anorexics were followed for a period of 5 years (Gillberg, Rastam, & Gillberg, 1994). One of the most notable features of those who did not recover over the course of the investigation (53%) was unsatisfactory family relationships and problems making personal contacts outside the family. Findings such as these are suggestive of the important role played by social relationships in the course of the disorder.

Dysfunctional Family Relationships and Processes

Interest in the interpersonal relationships of people with eating disorders focused largely, but not exclusively, on family relationships. The work of Minuchin and associates was at the forefront of this approach (Minuchin, Rosman, & Baker, 1978). These authors observed dysfunctional patterns of interaction among families with an anorexic patient. Their interactions, which often minimize conflict and adaptability, were argued to be entwined with the symptoms of the disorder.

Family relationships continue to receive a great deal of attention by those who seek to explain the origins and course of eating disorders (e.g., Strober & Humphrey, 1987; Wonderlich, 1992). Examples of this can be found in the investigations on family cohesion and adaptability. Systems-oriented researchers emphasized family adaptability and cohesion as two dimensions of family relationships that are crucial to healthy family functioning, provided that neither are too extreme (Olson, 1993). A series of recent studies indicate that eating disorders are associated with perceptions of low family cohesion (Blouin, Zuro, & Blouin, 1990; Humprey, 1986; Steiger, Puentes-Neuman, & Leung, 1991; Waller, Slade, & Calam, 1990). Although this finding is relatively stable among child and parent reports of family cohesiveness (e.g., Attie & Brooks-Gunn, 1989; Waller et al. 1990), eating disordered children give lower ratings to their family's cohesiveness than do their parents (Dare, le Grange, Eisler, & Rutherford, 1994). Regardless of which family member's perception is actually correct, the fact that the parent and child with an eating disorder differ in their view of the family's cohesiveness is perhaps itself diagnostically significant.

Investigations of family adaptability yielded less consistent results than those of cohesion. Some evidence indicates a negative association between family adaptability and symptoms of eating disorders (e.g., Dare et al., 1994; Waller et al., 1990). However, a study by Humphrey (1986) found more chaos, less organization, and more poorly defined boundaries in the family—all suggestive of greater adaptability—among patients with eating disorders. However, in most studies, the families appeared to be extreme in their adaptability (either too much or too little), indicating potentially detrimental family relations.

As in schizophrenia, family EE is beginning to emerge as an important family process variable in the eating disorders literature (e.g., LeGrange, Eisler, Dare, & Hodes, 1992; van Furth et al., 1996). The van Furth et al. investigation indicated that aspects of maternal expressed emotion during family interactions with eating disordered patients explained 28% to 34% of the variance in the patients' eventual outcome and response to therapy. The extent to which mothers made openly critical comments during the family interaction assessment was a stronger predictor of patients' outcomes than a host of other impressive predictors such as premorbid body weight, duration of illness, body mass index, and age at onset.

Other family process variables that were indicated in the eating disorders phenomena include disturbed affective expression (Garfinkel et al., 1983), excessive parental overprotectivness (Calam, Waller, Slade, & Newton, 1990; Rhodes & Kroger, 1992), and excessive parental control (Ahmad, Waller, & Verduyn, 1994; Wonderlich, Ukestad, & Perzacki, 1994). This later variable has particular significance in that the symptoms of eating disorders may be an overt manifestation of a struggle for control. Although the locus of this struggle may be with the parents, there is reason to believe that it may extend to others with whom the anorexic or bulimic is in a relationship.

Mother–Daughter Relationships

The ratio of females to males suffering from anorexia is approximately 10 to 1 (Lucas, Beard, O'Fallon, & Kurland, 1988). This may be due to the greater concerns with body image, dieting, and weight control among women compared to men (Hsu, 1989). Perhaps owing to the widely held importance of the relationship with the same-sex parent in a child's development, there has been a great deal of attention granted to mother–daughter relationships among anorexics. Girls with eating disorders have been known to describe their mothers as overprotective (e.g.,

Rhodes & Kroger, 1992) and less caring (Palmer, Oppenheimer, & Marshall, 1988). In light of such findings, it is not surprising to discover that mothers of eating disordered daughters express a desire for greater family cohesion than what they currently perceive (Pike & Rodin, 1991). A group of eating disordered young women retrospectively reported maternal relations that involved more emotional coldness, indifference, and rejection, compared to a sample of controls (Rhodes & Kroger, 1992).

Some evidence suggests that dietary restraint may be passed on from mother to daughter. Hill, Weaver, and Blundell (1990) found an $r = .68$ correlation between mothers' dietary restraint and that of their adolescent daughters. In another investigation, mothers' satisfaction with their body sizes correlated $r = .77$ with that of their daughters (Evans & le Grange, 1995). This particular sample of mothers had a history of eating disorders.

A more sinister view of the mother–daughter relationship emerges from those investigations of mothers' attitudes toward their daughters' body image. Mothers of eating disordered girls in one study thought that their daughters ought to lose significantly more weight than mothers of a group of noneating disordered girls (Pike & Rodin, 1991). Sadly, these same mothers rated their daughters as significantly less attractive than the daughters rated themselves. This is particularly amazing given that people with eating disorders typically have low self-esteem and a negative body image (Attie & Brooks-Gunn, 1989), and hence, are unlikely to inflate ratings of their own attractiveness. Data provided by mothers in an interview study indicate that mothers of bulimics were more controlling and held higher expectations for their daughters than control mothers (Sights & Richards, 1984). The effects of being in a relationship with a mother prone to such negative and excessive evaluation could be extremely caustic for an adolescent girl (see, e.g., Pierce & Wardle, 1993).

It should be noted that the attention granted to mothers of eating disordered children has been criticized by feminist scholars as "mother-blaming" (Rabinor, 1994). Rabinor, for example, argued that the tendency to see mothers as causally related to childrens' problems is a legacy of the psychoanalytic school that overemphasized mothers' roles and devalued the influence of fathers. At the same time, however, psychodynamically oriented theorists argue that many eating disordered girls use food as a means of fighting a battle (both interpersonally and intrapsychically) with an overprotective, but nonempathic, mother (Beattie, 1988). The data on mothers' roles in the pathogenesis of eating disorders are alluring. Whether they represent a disrespectful and misguided focus or a theoretically and etiologically meaningful domain of inquiry will best be resolved through future empirical investigation, particularly with comparative collateral data from fathers.

Comorbidity With Other Mental Health Problems

Given the often disturbed parent–child relationships associated with anorexia and bulimia, it is not surprising that a number of other mental health
problems tend to covary with the disorder. Chief among these are depression (Blouin et al., 1990; Wonderlich & Swift, 1990b), borderline personality disorder (Waller, 1994; Wonderlich & Swift, 1990a; Wonderlich et
al., 1994), and substance abuse (Watts & Ellis, 1992). It is important to
note that these related mental health problems may in some cases be
secondary to the eating disorder and more strongly associated with poor
family relationships than the eating disorder per se (see, e.g., Head &
Williamson, 1990). The elevated incidence of borderline personality disorder among anorexic and/or bulimic patients, which runs as high as 40%,
is also notable in that symptoms of this disorder include difficulties with
personal relationships, poor anger control, impulsivity, and affective insta-
bility. This suggests that eating disorders reside in a nomological network
that also holds problematic interpersonal relationships and functioning in
close proximity.

Disturbances in Nonfamilial Relationships

As noted earlier, not all research on the interpersonal relationships of
people with eating disorders focused on the family context. The personal
relationships of eating disordered patients also appear to be problematic
(e.g., Herzog, Pepose, Norman, & Rigotti, 1985). O'Mahony and Hollwey
(1995) recently conducted an intriguing study in which they compared
interpersonal problems of 31 anorexic patients to those of 105 women who
had an occupation or hobby that stressed physical conditioning and appearance (e.g., dance, athletics, or professional models) as well as 96 women
from the general public. The anorexic group in this study scored significantly higher on a measure of loneliness than either of the comparison
groups. In addition, the correlation between loneliness and eating problems
was higher in the anorexic group ($r = .65$) than did either the weight-con-
cerned group ($r = .47$) or the general public ($r = .28$).

A study of bulimic women indicates that such individuals perceive less
social support from friends as well as family members (Grissett & Norvell,
1992). These women felt less socially competent than did a group of
controls in a variety of social situations, particularly those that involved
seeking out social encounters and forming close relationships with others.
Some of these interpersonal problems stem from distorted views of
personal relationships by people with eating disorders. Some evidence

indicates that characteristics of eating disorders are positively associated with a possessive, dependent love style and negatively associated with a relatively more healthy, passionate, and friendship-based love style (Raciti & Hendrick, 1992). Taken as a whole, currently available evidence paints an equally disturbed view of the personal relationships of people with eating disorders relative to their family relationships.

Theoretical Accounts of Problematic Social Relationships in Eating Disorders

The role of parental, particularly maternal, modeling in the etiology of eating disorders was highlighted by several writers (e.g., Silverstein & Perlick, 1995). *Social Learning Theory* (Bandura, 1977) indicates that people can learn behaviors through imitation of a model. This process of learning is enhanced when, among other features, the model is perceived to hold high status and is similar to the target. Each of these conditions is in tact in the typical mother–daughter relationship. Findings reviewed earlier indicate that daughters' concerns with dieting and body image are strongly associated with those of their mothers (see also Paxton et al., 1991). Mothers of eating disordered daughters often have symptoms of eating disorders themselves. According to Social Learning theory, girls observe their mothers' restrictive eating behaviors and imitate them, perhaps because they perceive that their mothers were rewarded for such dieting. No student of communication could ever rightfully overlook the possibility that the media also plays a powerful role in this process of social learning, whereby unusually thin and attractive models are commonly depicted as the recipients of social rewards.

Psychodynamically oriented theories (including Object Relations and Attachment theories) continue to occupy a conspicuous presence in the eating disorders–family relations literature (e.g., Beattie, 1988; Dolan, Lieberman, Evans, & Lacey, 1990; Rhodes & Kroger, 1992). These accounts emphasize the symbolic significance of food in the adolescent girl's struggle for control in her relationship with her mother. Abuse of food is seen as a means of covertly expressing dissatisfaction with the mother–daughter relationship. Refusing to eat food represents a rejection of the mother's overprotectiveness and overinvolvement in the child's life. Rhodes and Kroger (1992) contributed further to this approach by suggesting that the adolescent girl with an eating disorder is struggling with a second separation–individuation process, similar to that which infants are hypothesized to experience in their relationships with their mothers. They present some supportive data indicating that eating disordered women had higher levels of separation anxiety and lower healthy separation scores, while experiencing greater maternal overprotectiveness than their nondisordered counterparts.

Among current approaches to understanding the role of the family in eating disorders, perhaps the most widely accepted is a variant of the diathesis-stress model. According to this model, some people harbor a predisposition, or *diathesis* to develop a mental health problem. These predispositions are latent and range from biological markers to early childhood learning experiences, to cognitive vulnerabilities. When such individuals experience a significant degree of *stress*, this diathesis develops into full blown distress or disorder. This position draws heavily on the literature that documents disturbances in personality traits and temperaments associated with bulimia and/or anorexia (e.g., Brookings & Wilson, 1994; Steiger, Stotland, Trottier, & Ghadirian, 1996; Vitousek & Manke, 1994). These pathological traits may be passed on from the parent to child (Steiger et al., 1996) and create a predisposition or vulnerability to the eating disorder. The ultimate manifestation of the eating disorder is thought to be triggered by (among other things) disturbed family relations (e.g., Strober & Humphrey, 1987). Thus, it is the interaction of predisposing traits and temperaments, along with problematic family and social relationships that ultimately bring about the eating disorder.

CONCLUSION

The mental health problems of schizophrenia, depression, loneliness, alcoholism, and eating disorders all share a common correlate: problems with interpersonal relationships. For some problems, such as schizophrenia, depression, loneliness, and perhaps eating disorders, the problematic relationships appear to antedate the disorder. At the same time, there is some evidence to indicate that the symptoms of schizophrenia, depression, alcoholism, and eating disorders may themselves disrupt interpersonal relationships.

When one considers, at a more general level, the literature on interpersonal relationships and mental health problems, it is reasonable to conclude that the two influence each other in a recursive fashion. Interpersonal relationships that are dissatisfying, violent, emotionally distant, bizarre, and abusive can easily precipitate mental health problems. Evidence reviewed earlier clearly shows that living with a depressed, alcoholic, schizophrenic, and so on. individual is taxing. Dealing with their chronic symptoms, complaining, aggressive behavior, struggles for interpersonal control, dysphoric behavior, delusional speech, and the uncertainty of their mood states can stress even the most stable personal relationships. Thus, there is a significant potential for a downward psychosocial spiral whenever mental health problems or significant relationship problems exist. The two are so strongly linked that one is often an inevitability given the other. This may explain why interpersonally oriented therapeutic regimes are used to treat some psychological problems (e.g., Jacobson & Bussod, 1983; Weissman, Klerman, Rounsaville, Chevron, & Neu, 1982).

A phenomenon that emerged repeatedly in every mental health problem reviewed in this chapter is problematic family relations. Dysfunctional relations in the family of origin while growing up appear to contribute to a wide variety of mental health problems. Our society as a whole typically holds a very positive view of family relations. However, findings reviewed earlier clearly indicate that there is a dark side (or dark sides) of family relations (see also Stafford & Dainton, 1994). When they entail too much cohesion or adaptability, overprotectiveness, intrusiveness, and are marked with communication deviance, high EE, neglect, or rejection, very serious mental health problems result. Although scientists have known for decades that the family can be a breeding ground for mental health problems, the general public appears less aware or less willing to accept this fact.

There is a remarkable similarity in the interpersonal correlates of the metal health problems reviewed in this chapter (e.g., problematic family interaction and dissatisfying personal relationships). At the same time, there is a pronounced dissimilarity in the symptoms and defining features of these various disorders. Perhaps the most likely metatheoretical account of the relationship between these different disorders and similar interpersonal correlates can be found in the diathesis-stress models (e.g., Abramson, Alloy, & Metalsky, 1988; Monroe & Simons, 1991).

Clearly, disturbed and barren family and personal relationships constitute a significant stressor for most people. At the same time, a subset of the population harbors a diathesis or predisposition to develop a mental health problem. When these individuals experience significant stressors—that may be interpersonal in nature—symptoms of the disorder begin to emerge. The dysfunctional interpersonal environment surely serves as a breeding ground for further development and worsening of the symptoms.

The key to explaining the similar interpersonal features and differing mental health outcomes lies in the proposition that differing predispositions that interact with the same type of stressor (i.e., destructive interpersonal relationships) leads to differing mental health outcomes. The person who harbors a diathesis for developing schizophrenia may in fact experience the disorder after prolonged exposure to an overintrusive and conflictual family environment. On the other hand, a person who has a vulnerability to eating disorders may ultimately experience this type of problem as a result of exposure to a very similar family environment. Likewise, two different people might react to dissatisfying social relationships with depression in one case and alcoholism in another, depending on the particular diathesis that each retains.

Because interpersonal problems are not always causally involved in cases of mental health problems, it should be noted that different mental health problems lead to similar negative interpersonal consequences. This is because the symptoms of psychological distress repel and/or stress other people who are in contact with the mentally ill individual. Most people react negatively to those who are experiencing mental illness—be it schizophrenia, depression, or alcoholism.

Finally, one might wonder if there is a bright side to any of these problems in the midst of what is otherwise obvious negativity and misery. Bearing in mind the provisional nature of conclusions based on anecdotal data, there appears to be an elevated incidence of problems such as depression, loneliness, and alcoholism among history's greatest artists. An optimist might suggest that out of mental anguish and concomitant disruption of social relationships comes at least occasional creativity, motivation, and insight. For the problem of depression, considerable scientific evidence indicates that many perceptions, including those that are social in nature, are more accurate among the depressed relative to those who are not depressed (Alloy & Abramson, 1988; Dykman, Horowitz, Abramson, & Usher, 1991; Lewinsohn, Mischel, Chaplin, & Barton, 1980). Nondepressed people tend to overestimate the quality of their performances, degree of control over events, their social skills, and so forth, whereas depressed people appear to have more realistic views. Because of their lack of this illusory, ego-enhancing bias, Alloy and Abramson (1979) described depressed people as "sadder but wiser." Regardless of the potential positive aspects associated with these disorders, it is doubtful that those afflicted with them find these to be much consolation or solace.

Human beings are among the most social animals on the planet. By definition, this means that we treat with great importance, and are strongly influenced by, interpersonal relationships. The psychological importance that we attach to these relationships can easily mutate into a full-blown psychological disorder when these relationships with family, friends, coworkers, and spouses are distressed and maladaptive. Although other contributory mechanisms to mental health problems such as genetics, neurochemical disturbances, cognitive and behavioral deficits, and environmental stress, are undeniable, the inseparable tie between problematic interpersonal relationships and mental health problems is sure to remain as long as humans maintain their social orientation.

ACKNOWLEDGMENTS

Thanks go to Heather Bunker for assistance in identifying sources for this review and Eve Lynn Nelson for helpful comments on an earlier version of this chapter.

REFERENCES

Abramson, L. Y., Alloy, L. B., & Metalsky, G. I. (1988). The cognitive diathesis-stress theories of depression:" Toward an adequate evaluation of the theories' validities. In L. B. Alloy (Ed.), *Cognitive Processes in Depression* (pp. 3–30). New York: Guilford.

Ahmad, S., Waller, G., & Verduyn, C. (1994). Eating attitudes among Asian schoolgirls: The role of perceived parental control. *International Journal of Eating Disorders, 15,* 91–97.

Alloy, L. B., & Abramson, L. Y. (1979). Judgment of contingency in depressed and nondepressed students: Sadder but wiser? *Journal of Experimental Psychology: General, 108,* 441–485.

Alloy, L. B., & Abramson, L. Y. (1988). Depressive realism: Four theoretical perspectives. In L. B. Alloy (Ed.), *Cognitive processes in depression* (pp. 223–265). New York: Guilford.

American Psychiatric Association. (1994). *Diagnostic and statistical manual of mental disorders* (4th ed.). Washington, DC: Author.

Amstutz, D. K., & Kaplan, M. F. (1987). Depression, physical attractiveness, and interpersonal acceptance. *Journal of Social and Clinical Psychology, 5,* 365–377.

Anderson, C. A., & Arnoult, L. H. (1985). Attributional models of depression, loneliness, and shyness. In J. H. Harvey & G. Weary (Eds.), *Attribution: Basic issues and applications* (pp. 235–279). New York: Academic Press.

Anderson, C. M., Reiss, D. J., & Hogarty, G. E. (1986). *Schizophrenia and the family.* New York: Guilford.

Andersson, L., Mullins, L. C., & Johnson, D. P. (1990). Parental intrusion versus social isolation: A dichotomous view of the sources of loneliness. In M. Hojat & R. Crandall (Eds.), *Loneliness: Theory, research, and applications* (pp. 125–134). Newbury Park, CA: Sage.

Angst, J. (1992). Epidemiology of depression. *Psychopharmacology, 106,* S71–S74.

Anthony, J. C., Warner, L. A., & Kessler, R. C. (1994). Comparative epidemiology of dependence on tobacco, alcohol, controlled substances, and inhalants: Basic findings from the National Comorbidity Survey. *Experimental and Clinical Psychopharmacology, 2,* 244–268.

Attie, I., & Brooks-Gunn, J. (1989). Development of eating problems in adolescent girls: A longitudinal study. *Developmental Psychology, 25,* 70–79.

Bandura, A. (1977). *Social learning theory.* Englewood Cliffs, NJ: Prentice-Hall.

Basco, M. R., Prager, K. J., Pite, J. M., Tamir, L. M., & Stephens, J. J. (1992). Communication and intimacy in the marriages of depressed patients. *Journal of Family Psychology, 6,* 184–194.

Bateson, G., Jackson, D., Haley, J., & Weakland, J. (1956). Toward a theory of schizophrenia. *Behavioral Science, 1,* 252–264.

Beach, S. R. H., Jouriles, E. N., & O'Leary, K. D. (1985). Extramarital sex: Impact on depression and commitment in couples seeking marital therapy. *Journal of Sex and Marital Therapy, 11,* 99–108.

Beach, S. R. H., & O'Leary, K. D. (1993). Marital discord and dysphoria: For whom does the marital relationship predict depressive symptomatology? *Journal of Social and Personal Relationships, 10,* 405–420.

Beach, S. R. H., Sandeen, E. E., & O'Leary, K. D. (1990). *Depression and marriage.* New York: Guilford.

Beattie, H. J. (1988). Eating disorders and the mother–daughter relationship. *International Journal of Eating Disorders, 7,* 453–460.

Beglin, S. J., & Fairburn, C. G. (1992). Women who choose not to participate in surveys on eating disorders. *International Journal of Eating Disorders, 12,* 113–116.

Belsher, G., & Costello, C. G. (1991). Do confidants of depressed women provide less social support that confidants of nondepressed women? *Journal of Abnormal Psychology, 100,* 516–525.

Biglan, A., Hops, H., Sherman, L., Friedman, L. S., Arthur, J., & Osteen , V. (1985). Problem-solving interactions of depressed women and their husbands. *Behavior Therapy, 16,* 431–451.

Billings, A., Kessler, M., Gomberg, C., & Weiner, S. (1979). Marital conflict-resolution of alcoholic and nonalcoholic couples during sobriety and experimental drinking. *Journal of Studies on Alcohol, 3,* 183–195.

Blouin, A. G., Zuro, C., & Blouin, J. H. (1990). Family environment in bulimia nervosa: The role of depression. *International Journal of Eating Disorders, 9,* 649–658.

Brage, D., Meredith, W., & Woodward, J. (1993). Correlates of loneliness among midwestern adolescents. *Adolescence, 28,* 685–693.

Brookings, J. B., & Wilson, J. F. (1994). Personality and family-environment predictors of self-reported eating attitudes and behaviors. *Journal of Personality Assessment, 63,* 313–326.

Brown, G. W., & Harris, T. (1978). *Social origins of depression.* New York: The Free Press.

Brown, G. W., Monck, E. M., Carstairs, G. M., & Wing, J. K. (1962). Influence of family life on the course of schizophrenic illness. *British Journal of Preventative and Social Medicine, 16,* 55–68.

Bullock, R. C., Siegel, R., Weissman, M., & Paykel, E. S. (1972). The weeping wife: Marital relations of depressed women. *Journal of Marriage and the Family, 34,* 488–495.

Burns, D. D., Sayers, S. L., & Moras, K. (1994). Intimate relationships and depression: Is there a causal connection? *Journal of Consulting and Clinical Psychology, 62,* 1033–1043.

Calam, R., Waller, G., Slade, P., & Newton, T. (1990). Eating disorders and perceived relationships with parents. *International Journal of Eating Disorders, 9,* 479–485.

Carson, R. C. (1983). The social-interactional viewpoint. In M. Hersen, A. E. Kazdin, & A. S. Bellack (Eds.), *The clinical psychology handbook* (pp. 143–153). New York: Pergamon.

Clair, D. J., & Genest, M. (1992). The children of alcoholics screening test: Reliability and relationships to family environment, adjustment, and alcohol-related stressors of adolescent offspring of alcoholics. *Journal of Clinical Psychology, 48,* 414–420.

Cohn, J. F., Campbell, S. B., Matias, R., & Hopkins, J. (1990). Face-to-face interactions of postpartum depressed and nondepressed mother–infant pairs at 2 months. *Developmental Psychology, 26,* 15–23.

Cole, R. E., Grolnick, W., Kane, C. F., Zastowny, T., & Lehman, A. (1993). Expressed emotion, communication, and problem solving in the families of chronic schizophrenic young adults. In R. E. Cole & D. Reiss (Eds.), *How do families cope with chronic illness* (pp. 141–172). Hillsdale, NJ: Lawrence Erlbaum Associates.

Connolly, J., Geller, S., Marton, P., & Kutcher, S. (1992). Peer responses to social interaction with depressed adolescent. *Journal of Clinical Child Psychiatry, 21,* 365–370.

Costello, C. G. (1982). Social factors associated with depression: A retrospective community study. *Psychological Medicine, 12,* 329–339.

Coyne, J. C. (1976a). Depression and the response of others. *Journal of Abnormal Psychology, 85,* 186–193.

Coyne, J. C. (1976b). Toward an interactional description of depression. *Psychiatry, 39,* 28–40.

Coyne, J. C. (1990). Interpersonal processes in depression. In G. I. Keitner (Ed.), *Depression and families* (pp. 31–54). Washington, DC: American Psychiatric Press.

Coyne, J. C., Burchill, S. A. L., & Stiles, W. B. (1990). An interactional perspective on depression. In C. R. Snyder & D. R. Forsyth (Eds.), *Handbook of social and clinical psychology* (pp. 327–349). New York: Pergamon.

Coyne, J. C., & DeLongis, A. (1986). Going beyond social support: The role of social relationships in adaptation. *Journal of Consulting and Clinical Psychology, 54,* 454–460.

Coyne, J. C., Kahn, J., & Gotlib, I. H. (1987). Depression. In T. Jacob (Ed.), *Family interaction and psychopathology* (pp. 509–533). New York: Plenum.

Coyne, J. C., Kessler, R. C., Tal, M., Turnbull, J., Wortman, C. B., & Greden, J. F. (1987). Living with a depressed person. *Journal of Consulting and Clinical Psychology, 55,* 347–352.

Dare, C., Le Grange, D., Eisler, I., & Rutherford, J. (1994). Redefining the psychosomatic family: Family process of 26 eating disorder families. *International Journal of Eating Disorders, 16,* 211–226.

Dinning, W. D., & Berk, L. A. (1989). The children of alcoholics screening test: Relationship to sex, family environment, and social adjustment in adolescents. *Journal of Clinical Psychology, 45,* 335–339.

Doane, J. A., Goldstein, M. J., Miklowitz, D. M., & Falloon, I. R. H. (1986). The impact of individual and family treatment on the affective climate of families of schizophrenics. *British Journal of Psychiatry, 148,* 279–287.

Doane, J. A., West, K. L., Goldstein, M. J., Rodnick, E. H., & Jones, J. E. (1981). Parental communication deviance and affective style: Predictors of subsequent schizophrenia spectrum disorders. *Archives of General Psychiatry, 38,* 679–685.

Docherty, N. M. (1995). Expressed emotion and language disturbances in parents of stable schizophrenia patients. *Schizophrenia Bulletin, 21,* 411–418.

Dolan, B. M., Lieberman, S., Evans, C., & Lacey, J. H. (1990). Family features associated with normal body weight bulimia. *International Journal of Eating Disorders, 9,* 639–647.

Domenico, D., & Windle, M. (1993). Intrapersonal and interpersonal functioning among middle-aged female adult children of alcoholics. *Journal of Consulting and Clinical Psychology, 61,* 659–666.

Downey, G., & Coyne, J. C. (1990). Children of depressed parents: An integrative review. *Psychological Bulletin, 108,* 50–76.

Dykman, B. M., Horowitz, L. M., Abramson, L. Y., & Usher, M. (1991). Schematic and situational determinants of depressed and nondepressed students' interpretation of feedback. *Journal of Abnormal Psychology, 100,* 45–55.

Elliot, T. R., MacNair, R. R., Herrick, S. M., Yoder, B., & Byrne, C. A. (1991). Interpersonal reactions to depression and physical disability in dyadic interactions. *Journal of Applied Social Psychology, 21,* 1293–1302.

Erickson, D. H., Beiser, M., Iacono, W. G., Fleming, J. A. E., & Lin, T. (1989). The role of social relationships in the course of first-episode schizophrenia and affective psychosis. *American Journal of Psychiatry, 146,* 1456–1461.

Evans, J., & le Grange, D. (1995). Body size and parenting in eating disorders: A comparative study of the attitudes of mothers towards their children. *International Journal of Eating Disorders, 18,* 39–48.

Field, T. (1984). Early interactions between infants and their post-partum depressed mothers. *Infant Behavior and Development, 7,* 517–522.

Fiske, V., & Peterson, C. (1991). Love and depression: The nature of depressive romantic relationships. *Journal of Social and Clinical Psychology, 10,* 75–90.

Forehand, R., & Smith, K. A. (1986). Who depressed whom? A look at the relationship of adolescent mood to maternal and paternal depression. *Child Study Journal, 16,* 19–23.

Foy, D. W., Massey, F. H., Duer, J. D., Ross, J. M., & Wooten, L. S. (1979). Social skills training to improve alcoholics' vocational interpersonal competency. *Journal of Counseling Psychology, 26,* 128–132.

Freud, S. (1966). *Introductory lectures on psychoanalysis.* New York: Norton. (Original work published in 1917)

Fromm-Reichmann, F. (1960). *Principles of intensive psychotherapy.* Chicago, IL: Phoenix Books.

Garfinkel, P. E., Garner, D. M., Rose, J., Darby, P. L., Brandes, J. S., O'Hanlon, J., & Walsh, N. (1983). A comparison of characteristics in families of patients with anorexia nervosa and normal controls. *Psychological Medicine, 13,* 821–828.

Gelfand, D. M., & Teti, D. M. (1990). The effects of maternal depression on children. *Clinical Psychology Review, 10,* 329–353.

Gillberg, I. C., Rastam, M., & Gillberg, C. (1994). Anorexia nervosa outcome: Six-year controlled longitudinal study of 51 cases including a population cohort. *Journal of the American Academy of Child and Adolescent Psychiatry, 33,* 729–739.

Goldstein, M. J. (1987). Family interaction patterns that antedate the onset of schizophrenia and related disorders: A further analysis of data from a longitudinal, prospective study. In K.

Hahlweg & M. J. Goldstein (Eds.), *Understanding major mental disorder: The contribution of family interaction research* (pp. 11–32). New York: Family Process Press.

Goldstein, M. J., & Strachan, A. M. (1987). The family and schizophrenia. In T. Jacob (Ed.), *Family interaction and psychopathology: Theories, methods, and findings* (pp. 481–508). New York: Plenum.

Gorad, S. (1971). Communicational styles and interaction of alcoholics and their wives. *Family Process, 10,* 475–489.

Gotlib, I. H., & Beatty, M. E. (1985). Negative responses to depression: The role of attributional style. *Cognitive Therapy and Research, 9,* 91–103.

Gotlib, I. H., & Lee, C. M. (1989). The social functioning of depressed patients: A longitudinal assessment. *Journal of Social and Clinical Psychology, 8,* 223–237.

Gotlib, I. H., Mount, J. H., Cordy, N. I., & Whiffen, V. E. (1988). Depression and perceptions of early parenting: A longitudinal investigation. *British Journal of Psychiatry, 152,* 24–27.

Gotlib, I. H., & Robinson, L. A. (1982). Responses to depressed individuals: Discrepancies between self-report and observer-rated behavior. *Journal of Abnormal Psychology, 91,* 231–240.

Gotlib, I. H., & Whiffen, V. E. (1989). Depression and marital functioning: An examination of specificity and gender differences. *Journal of Abnormal Psychology, 98,* 23–30.

Grissett, N. I., & Norvell, N. K. (1992). Perceived social support, social skills, and quality of relationships in bulimic women. *Journal of Consulting and Clinical Psychology, 60,* 293–299.

Gurtman, M. B. (1987). Depressive affect and disclosures as factors in interpersonal rejection. *Cognitive Therapy and Research, 11,* 87–100.

Hadley, J. A., Holloway, E. L., & Mallinckrodt, B. (1993). Common aspects of object relations and self-presentations in offspring from disparate dysfunctional families. *Journal of Counseling Psychology, 40,* 348–356.

Hamid, P. N. (1989). Contact and intimacy patterns of lonely students. *New Zealand Journal of Psychology, 18,* 84–86.

Hamilton, E. B., Jones, M., & Hammen, C. (1993). Maternal interaction style in affective disordered, physically ill, and normal women. *Family Process, 32,* 329–340.

Hammen, C. L., Gordon, D., Burge, D., Adrian, C., Janicke, C., & Hiroto, D. (1987). Communication patterns of mothers with affective disorders and their relationship to children's status and social functioning. In K. Hahlweg & M. J. Goldstein (Eds.), *Understanding major mental disorder* (pp. 103–119). New York: Family Process Press.

Hammen, C. L., & Peters, S. D. (1977). Differential responses to male and female depressive reactions. *Journal of Consulting and Clinical Psychology, 45,* 994–1001.

Hammen, C. L., & Peters, S. D. (1978). Interpersonal consequences of depression: Responses to men and women enacting a depressed role. *Journal of Abnormal Psychology, 87,* 322–332.

Hautzinger, M., Linden, M., & Hoffman, N. (1982). Distressed couples with and without a depressed partner: An analysis of their verbal interaction. *Journal of Behavior Therapy and Experimental Psychiatry, 13,* 307–314.

Havey, J. M., & Dodd, D. K. (1993). Variables associated with alcohol abuse among self-identified collegiate COAs and their peers. *Addictive Behaviors, 18,* 567–575.

Head, S. B., & Williamson, D. A. (1990). Association of family environment and personality disturbances in bulimia nervosa. *International Journal of Eating Disorders, 9,* 667–674.

Helzer, J. E., Canino, G. J., Yeh, E., Bland, R. C., Lee, C. K., Hwu, H., & Newman, S. (1990). Alcoholism—North America and Asia: A comparison of populations surveys with the diagnostic interview schedule. *Archives of General Psychiatry, 47,* 313–319.

Henwood, P. G., & Solano, C. H. (1994). Loneliness in young children and their parents. *Journal of Genetic Psychology, 155,* 35–45.

Herzog, D. B., Pepose, M., Norman, D. K., & Rigotti, N. A. (1985). Eating disorders and social maladjustment in female medical students. *Journal of Nervous and Mental Disease, 173,* 734–737.

Hill, A., Weaver, C., & Blundell, J. E. (1990). Dieting concerns of 10-year-old girls and their mothers. *British Journal of Clinical Psychology, 29,* 346–348.

Hinchliffe, M. K., Hooper, D., & Roberts, F. J. (1978). *The melancholy marriage.* New York: Wiley.

Hinchliffe, M. K., Hooper, D., Roberts, F. J., & Vaughan, P. W. (1978). The melancholy marriage: An inquiry into the interaction of depression. IV. Disruptions. *British Journal of Medical Psychology, 51,* 15–24.

Hinchliffe, M. K., Vaughan, P. W., Hooper, D., & Roberts, F. J. (1978). The melancholy marriage: An inquiry into the interaction of depression. III. Responsiveness. *British Journal of Medical Psychology, 51,* 1–13.

Hinson, R. C., Becker, L. S., Handal, P. J., & Katz, B. M. (1993). The heterogeneity of children of alcoholics: Emotional needs and help-seeking propensity. *Journal of College Student Development, 34,* 47–52.

Hokanson, J. E., & Butler, A. C. (1992). Cluster analysis of depressed college students' social behaviors. *Journal of Personality and Social Psychology, 62,* 273–280.

Hokanson, J. E., Hummer, J. T., & Butler, A. C. (1991). Interpersonal perceptions by depressed college students. *Cognitive Therapy and Research, 15,* 443–457.

Hooley, J. M. (1985). Expressed emotion: A review of the critical literature. *Clinical Psychology Review, 5,* 119–139.

Hooper, D., Vaughan, P. W., Hinchliffe, M. K., & Roberts, J. (1978). The melancholy marriage: An inquiry into the interaction of depression. V. Power. *British Journal of Medical Psychology, 51,* 387–398.

Hops, H., Biglan, A., Sherman, L., Arthur, J., Friedman, L., & Osteen, V. (1987). Home observations of family interactions of depressed women. *Journal of Consulting and Clinical Psychology, 55,* 341–346.

Horowitz, L. M., & French, R. D. (1979). Interpersonal problems of people who describe themselves as lonely. *Journal of Consulting and Clinical Psychology, 47,* 762–764.

Horowitz, L. M., French, R. D., & Anderson, C. A. (1982). The prototype of a lonely person. In L. A. Peplau & D. Perlman (Eds.), *Loneliness: A sourcebook of current theory, research and therapy* (pp. 183–205). New York: Wiley.

Horowitz, L. M., French, R. D., Lapid, J. S., & Weckler, D. A. (1982). Symptoms and interpersonal problems: The prototype as an integrating concept. In J. C. Achin & D. J. Kiesler (Eds.), *Handbook of interpersonal psychotherapy* (pp. 168–189). New York: Pergamon.

Hsu, L. K. G. (1989). The gender gap in eating disorders: Why are the eating disorders more common among women? *Clinical Psychology Review, 9,* 393–407.

Humphrey, L. L. (1986). Family relations in bulimic-anorexic and nondistressed families. *International Journal of Eating Disorders, 5,* 223–232.

Jacob, T., Ritchey, D., Cvitkovic, J., & Blane, H. (1981). Communication styles of alcoholic and nonalcoholic families when drinking and not drinking. *Journal of Studies on Alcohol, 42,* 466–482.

Jacob, T., & Seilhamer, R. A. (1987). Alcoholism and family interaction. In T. Jacob (Ed.), *Family interaction and psychopathology: Theories, methods, and findings* (pp. 535–580). New York: Plenum.

Jacobs, J., & Wolin, S. J. (1989). Alcoholism and family factors: A critical review. In M. Galanter (Ed.), *Recent developments in alcoholism* (Vol. 7, pp. 147–164). New York: Plenum.

Jacobson, N. S., & Bussod, N. (1983). Marital and family therapy. In M. Hersen, A. E. Kazdin, & A. S. Bellack (Eds.), *The clinical psychology handbook* (pp. 611–630). New York: Pergamon.

Joiner, T. E., Alfano, M. S., & Metalsky, G. I. (1992). When depression breeds contempt: Reassurance-seeking, self-esteem, and rejection of depressed college students by their roommates. *Journal of Abnormal Psychology, 101,* 165–173.

Jones, W. H. (1982). Loneliness and social behavior. In L. A. Peplau & D. Perlman (Eds.), *Loneliness: A sourcebook of current theory, research and therapy* (pp. 238–252). New York: Wiley.

Jones, W. H., Hobbs, S. A., & Hockenburg, D. (1982). Loneliness and social skills deficits. *Journal of Personality and Social Psychology, 42,* 682–689.

Jones, W. H., & Moore, T. L. (1990). Loneliness and social support. In M. Hojat & R. Crandall (Eds.), *Loneliness: Theory, research, and applications* (pp. 145–156). Newbury Park, CA: Sage.

Kahn, J., Coyne, J. C., & Margolin, G. (1985). Depression and marital disagreement: The social construction of despair. *Journal of Social and Personal Relationships, 2,* 447–461.

Klerman, G. L. (1986). Historical perspectives on contemporary schools of psychopathology. In T. Millon & G. L. Klerman (Eds.), *Contemporary directions in psychopathology: Toward the DSM-IV* (pp. 3–28). New York: Guilford.

Kog, E., & Vandereycken, W. (1985). Family characteristics of anorexia nervosa and bulimia: A review of the research literature. *Clinical Psychology Review, 5,* 159–180.

Kraus, L. A., Davis, M. H., Bazzini, D., Church, M., & Kirchman, C. M. (1993). Personal and social influences on loneliness: The mediating effect of social provisions. *Social Psychology Quarterly, 56,* 37–53.

Kuiper, N. A., & MacDonald, M. R. (1983). Schematic processing in depression: The self-based consensus bias. *Cognitive Therapy and Research, 7,* 469–484.

Laing, R. D. (1965). Mystification, confusion, and conflict. In I. Boszormenyi-Nagy & J. L. Frano (Eds.), *Intensive family therapy* (pp. 343–363). New York: Harper-Collins.

Laseque, E. C. (1873). On hysterical anorexia. *Medical Times Gazette, 2,* 367–369.

Leary, T. (1957). *Interpersonal diagnosis of personality.* New York: Ronald.

Lee, C. M., & Gotlib, I. H. (1991). Adjustment of children of depressed mothers: A 10-month follow-up. *Journal of Abnormal Psychology, 100,* 473–477.

LeGrange, D., Eisler, I., Dare, D., & Hodes, M. (1992). Family criticism and self-starvation—A study of expressed emotion. *Journal of Family Therapy, 14,* 177–192.

Lewinsohn, P. M. (1974). A behavioral approach to depression. In R. J. Friedman & M. M. Katz (Eds.), *The psychology of depression: Contemporary theory and research* (pp. 157–185). Washington, DC: Winston-Wiley.

Lewinsohn, P. M. (1975). The behavioral study and treatment of depression. In M. Hersen, R. M. Eisler, & P. M. Miller (Eds.), *Progress in behavior modification* (Vol 1, pp. 19–64). New York: Academic Press.

Lewinsohn, P. M., Mischel, W., Chaplin, W., & Barton, R. (1980). Social competence and depression: The role of illusory self-perceptions. *Journal of Abnormal Psychology, 89,* 203–212.

Lewinsohn, P. M., & Rosenbaum, M. (1987). Recall of parental behavior by acute depressives, remitted depressives, and nondepressives. *Journal of Personality and Social Psychology, 52,* 611–619.

Lidz, T., Cornelison, A., Fleck, S., & Terry, D. (1957). The intrafamilial environment of schizophrenic patients: 2. Marital schism and marital skew. *American Journal of Psychiatry, 114,* 241–248.

Linden, M., Hautzinger, M., & Hoffman, N. (1983). Discriminant analysis of depressive interactions. *Behavior Modification, 7,* 403–422.

Lively, S., Friedrich, R. M., & Buckwalter, K. C. (1995). Sibling perception of schizophrenia: Impact on relationships, roles, and health. *Issues in Mental Health Nursing, 16,* 225–238.

Lobdell, J., & Perlman, D. (1986). The intergenerational transmission of loneliness: A study of college freshmen and their parents. *Journal of Marriage and the Family, 48,* 589–595.

Lucas, A. R., Beard, C. M., O'Fallon, W. M., & Kurland, L. T. (1988). Anorexia nervosa in Rochester, Minnesota: A 45-year study. *Mayo Clinic Proceedings, 63,* 433–442.

Marcus, D. K., & Davis, K. K. (1993). Depression and interpersonal rejection: The role of anticipated interaction. *The Journal of Social Psychology, 134,* 251–252.

Marks, T., & Hammen, C. L. (1982). Interpersonal mood induction: Situational and individual determinants. *Motivation and Emotion, 6,* 387–399.

McCabe, S. B., & Gotlib, I. H. (1993). Interactions of couples with and without a depressed spouse: Self-report and observations of problems-solving interactions. *Journal of Social and Personal Relationships, 10,* 589–599.

McCann, C. D. (1990). Social factors in depression: The role of interpersonal expectancies. In C. D. McCann & N. S. Endler (Eds.), *Depression: New directions in theory, research, and practice* (pp. 27–47). Toronto: Wall & Emerson.

McCann, C. D., & LaLonde, R. N. (1993). Dysfunctional communication and depression. *American Behavioral Scientist, 36,* 271–287.

McFarlane, W. R., & Beels, C. C. (1988). The family and schizophrenia: Perspectives from contemporary research. In E. W. Nunnally, C. S. Chilman, & F. M. Cox (Eds.), *Mental illness, delinquency, addictions, and neglect* (pp. 17–38). Newbury Park, CA: Sage.

McMahon, R. C., Davidson, R. S., Gersh, D., & Flynn, P. (1991). A comparison of continuous and episodic drinkers using the MCMI, MMPI, and ALCEVAL—R. *Journal of Clinical Psychology, 47,* 148–159.

McNiel, D. E., Arkowitz, H. S., & Pritchard, B. E. (1987). The response of others to face-to-face interaction with depressed patients. *Journal of Abnormal Psychology, 96,* 341–344.

Medora, N., & Woodward, J. C. (1986). Loneliness among adolescent college students at a midwestern university. *Adolescence, 82,* 391–402.

Meyer, A. (1957). *Psychobiology: A science of man.* Springfield, IL: Thomas.

Miklowitz, D. J. (1994). Family risk indicators in schizophrenia. *Schizophrenia Bulletin, 20,* 137–149.

Miklowitz, D. J., Goldstein, M. J., & Neuchterlein, K. H. (1995). Verbal interactions in the families of schizophrenic and bipolar affective patients. *Journal of Abnormal Psychology, 104,* 268–276.

Miklowitz, D. J., Stracham, A. M., Goldstein, M. J., Doane, J. A., Snyder, K. S., Hogarty, G. E., & Falloon, I. R. (1986). Expressed emotion and communication deviance in the families of schizophrenics. *Journal of Abnormal Psychology, 95,* 60–66.

Miklowitz, D. J., Velligan, D. I., Goldstein, M. J., Nuechterlein, K. H., Gitlin, M. J., Ranlett, G., & Doane, J. A. (1991). Communication deviance in families of schizophrenic and manic patients. *Journal of Abnormal Psychology, 100,* 163–173.

Minuchin, S., Rosman, B. L., & Baker, L. (1978). *Psychosomatic families: Anorexia nervosa in context.* Cambridge, MA: Harvard University Press.

Monroe, S. M., & Simons, A. D. (1991). Diathesis-stress theories in the context of life stress research: Implications for the depressive disorders. *Psychological Bulletin, 110,* 406–425.

Moore, D., & Schultz, N. R. (1983). Loneliness at adolescence: Correlates, attributions, and coping. *Journal of Youth and Adolescence, 12,* 95–100.

Morrison, H. L. (Ed.). (1983). *Children of depressed parents: Risk, identification, and intervention.* New York: Grune & Stratton.

Mueser, K. T., Bellack, A. S., Wade, J. H., Sayers, S. L., Tierney, A., & Haas, G. (1993). Expressed emotion, social skill, and response to negative affect in schizophrenia. *Journal of Abnormal Psychology, 102,* 339–351.

Neeliyara, T., Nagalakshmi, S. V., & Ray, R. (1989). Interpersonal relationships in alcohol dependent individuals. *Journal of Personality and Clinical Studies, 5,* 199–202.

Nelson, G. M., & Beach, S. R. H. (1990). Sequential interaction in depression: Effects of depressive behavior on spousal aggression. *Behavior Therapy, 21,* 167–182.

Nezlek, J. B., Imbrie, M., & Shean, G. D. (1994). Depression and everyday social interaction. *Journal of Personality and Social Psychology, 67,* 1101–1111.

Notarius, C. I., & Herrick, L. R. (1988). Listener response strategies to a distressed other. *Journal of Social and Personal Relationships, 5,* 97–108.

Olson, D. H. (1993). Circumplex model of marital and family systems: Assessing family functioning. In F. Walsh (Ed.), *Normal family processes* (2nd ed., pp. 104–137). New York: Guilford.

O'Mahony, J. F., & Hollwey, S. (1995). Eating problems and interpersonal functioning among several groups of women. *Journal of Clinical Psychology, 51,* 345–351.

Palmer, R. L., Oppenheimer, R., & Marshall, P. D. (1988). Eating-disordered patients remember their parents: A study using the parental bonding instrument. *International Journal of Eating Disorders, 7,* 101–106.

Patterson, B. R., & Bettini, L. A. (1993). Age, depression, and friendship: Development of a general friendship inventory. *Communication Research Reports, 10,* 161–170.

Paxton, S. J., Wertheim, E. H., Gibbons, K., Szmukler, G. I., Hillier, L., & Petrovich, J. L. (1991). Body image satisfaction, dieting beliefs, and weight loss behaviors in adolescent girls and boys. *Journal of Youth and Adolescence, 20,* 361–379.

Peplau, L. A., Russell, D., & Heim, M. (1979). The experience of loneliness. In I. H. Frieze, D. Bar-Tal, & J. S. Caroll (Eds.), *New approaches to social problems* (pp. 53–78). San Fransisco: Jossey-Bass.

Peterson, L., Mullins, L. L., & Ridley-Johnson, R. (1985). Childhood depression: Peer reactions to depression and life stress. *Journal of Abnormal Child Psychology, 13,* 597–609.

Pierce, J. W., & Wardle, J. (1993). Self-esteem, parental appraisal and body size in children. *Journal of Child Psychology and Psychiatry, 34,* 1125–1136.

Pike, K. M., & Rodin, J. (1991). Mothers, daughters, and disordered eating. *Journal of Abnormal Psychology, 100,* 198–204.

Pollock, V. E., Schneider, L. S., Garielli, W. F., & Goodwin, D. W. (1987). Sex of parent and offspring in the transmission of alcoholism: A meta-analysis. *Journal of Nervous and Mental Disease, 173,* 668–673.

Pyle, R. L., Neuman, P. A., Halvorson, P. A., & Mitchell, J. E. (1991). An ongoing cross-sectional study of the prevalence of eating disorders in freshmen college students. *International Journal of Eating Disorders, 10,* 667–677.

Rabinor, J. R. (1994). Mothers, daughters, and eating disorders: Honoring the mother–daughter relationship. In P. Fallon, M. A. Katzman, & S. Wooley (Eds.), *Feminist perspectives on eating disorders* (pp. 272–286). New York: Guilford.

Raciti, M., & Hendrick, S. S. (1992). Relationship between eating disorder characteristics and love and sex attitudes. *Sex Roles, 27,* 553–564.

Reich, W., Earls, F., Frankel, O., & Shayka, J. J. (1993). Psychopathology in children of alcoholics. *Journal of the American Academy of Child and Adolescent Psychiatry, 32,* 995–1002.

Revenson, T. A., & Johnson, J. L. (1984). Social and demographic correlates of loneliness in late life. *American Journal of Community Psychology, 12,* 71–85.

Rhodes, B., & Kroger, J. (1992). Parental bonding and separation-individuation difficulties among late-adolescent eating disordered women. *Child Psychiatry and Human Development, 22,* 249–263.

Rich, A. R., & Bonner, R. L. (1987). Interpersonal moderators of depression among college students. *Journal of College Student Personnel,28,* 337–342.

Rich, A. R., & Scovel, M. (1987). Causes of depression in college students: A cross-lagged panel correlational analysis. *Psychological Reports, 60,* 27–30.

Roscoe, B., & Skomski, G. G. (1989). Loneliness among late adolescents. *Adolescence, 96,* 947–955.

Rosenfarb, I. S., Goldstein, M. J., Mintz, J., & Nuechterlein, K. H. (1995). Expressed emotion and subclinical psychopathology observable with the transactions between schizophrenic patients and their family members. *Journal of Abnormal Psychology, 104,* 259–267.

Rotenberg, K. J., & Hamel, J. (1988). Social interaction and depression in elderly individuals. *International Journal of Aging and Human Development, 27,* 305–318.

Rounsaville, B. J., Weissman, M. M., Prusoff, B. A., & Herceg-Baron, R. L. (1979). Marital disputes and treatment outcome in depressed women *Comprehensive Psychiatry, 20,* 483–490.

Rudolph, K. D., Hammen, C., & Burge, D. (1994). Interpersonal functioning and depressive symptoms in childhood: Addressing the issues of specificity and comorbidity. *Journal of Abnormal Child Psychology, 22,* 355–371.

Ruscher, S. M., & Gotlib, I. H. (1988). Marital interaction patterns of couples with and without a depressed partner. *Behavior Therapy, 19,* 455–470.

Sacco, W. P., Milana, S., & Dunn, V. K. (1985). Effect of depression level and length of acquaintance on reactions of others to a request for help. *Journal of Personality and Social Psychology, 49,* 1728–1737.

Schmaling, K. B., & Jacobson, N. S. (1990). Marital interaction and depression. *Journal of Abnormal Psychology, 99,* 229–236.

Schulz, R. (1976). The effects of control and predictability on the physical and psychological well-being of the institutionalized aged. *Journal of Personality and Social Psychology, 33,* 563–573.

Segrin, C. (1990). A meta-analytic review of social skill deficits in depression. *Communication Monographs, 57,* 292–308.

Segrin, C. (1992). Specifying the nature of social skill deficits associated with depression. *Human Communication Research, 19,* 89–123.

Segrin, C. (1993a). Interpersonal reactions to depression: The role of relationship with partner and perceptions of rejection. *Journal of Social and Personal Relationships, 10,* 83–97.

Segrin, C. (1993b). Social skills deficits and psychosocial problems: Antecedent, concomitant, or consequent? *Journal of Social and Clinical Psychology, 12,* 336–353.

Segrin, C. (1996). The relationship between social skills deficits and psychosocial problems: A test of a vulnerability model. *Communication Research, 23*, 425–450.

Segrin, C. (1998). Interpersonal communication problems associated with depression and loneliness. In P. A. Anderson & L. A. Guerrero (Eds.), *Handbook of communication and emotion: Research, theory, applications, and context* (pp. 215–242). New York: Academic Press.

Segrin, C., & Abramson, L. Y. (1994). Negative reactions to depressive behaviors: A communication theories analysis. *Journal of Abnormal Psychology, 103*, 655–668.

Segrin, C., & Dillard, J. P. (1991). (Non)depressed persons' cognitive and affective reactions to (un)successful interpersonal influence. *Communication Monographs, 58*, 115–134.

Segrin, C., & Dillard, J. P. (1992). The interactional theory of depression: A meta-analysis of the research literature. *Journal of Social and Clinical Psychology, 11*, 43–70.

Segrin, C., & Fitzpatrick, M. A. (1992). Depression and verbal aggressiveness in different marital couple types. *Communication Studies, 43*, 79–91.

Segrin, C., & Kinney, T. (1995). Social skills deficits among the socially anxious: Loneliness and rejection from others. *Motivation and Emotion, 19*, 1–24.

Segrin, C., & Menees, M. M. (1995). The impact of coping styles and family communication on the social skills of children of alcoholics. *Journal of Studies on Alcohol, 57*, 29–33.

Seilhamer, R. A., & Jacob, T. (1990). Family factors and adjustment of children of alcoholics. In M. Windle & J. S. Searles (Eds.), *Children of alcoholics: Critical perspectives* (pp. 168–188). New York: Guilford.

Shean, G. (1978). *Schizophrenia: An introduction to research and theory.* Cambridge, MA: Winthrop.

Sher, K. J. (1991). *Children of alcoholics: A critical appraisal of theory and research.* Chicago: University of Chicago Press.

Sher, K. J., Walitzer, K. S., Wood, P. K., & Brent, E. E. (1991). Characteristics of children of alcoholics: Putative risk factors, substance use and abuse, and psychopathology. *Journal of Abnormal Psychology, 100*, 427–448.

Sheridan, M. J., & Green, R. G. (1993). Family dynamics and individual characteristics of adult children of alcoholics: An empirical analysis. *Journal of Social Service Research, 17*, 73–97.

Siegel, S. J., & Alloy, L. B. (1990). Interpersonal perceptions and consequences of depressive-significant other relationships: A naturalistic study of college roommates. *Journal of Abnormal Psychology, 99*, 361–373.

Sights, J. R., & Richards, H. C. (1984). Parents of bulemic women. *International Journal of Eating Disorders, 3*, 3–13.

Silverstein, B., & Perlick, D. (1995). *The cost of competence: Why inequality causes depression, eating disorders, and illness in women.* New York: Oxford University Press.

Singer, M., Wynne, L., & Toohey, M. (1978). Communication disorders and the families of schizophrenics. In L. C. Wynne, R. L. Cromwell, & S. Matthysse (Eds.), *The nature of schizophrenia: New approaches to research and treatment* (pp. 499–511). New York: Wiley.

Solano, C. H., & Koester, N. H. (1989). Loneliness and communication problems: Subjective anxiety or objective skills. *Personality and Social Psychology Bulletin, 15*, 126–133.

Spitzberg, B. H., & Canary, D. J. (1985). Loneliness and relationally competent communication. *Journal of Social and Personal Relationships, 2*, 387–402.

Stafford, L., & Dainton, M. (1994). The dark side of "normal" family interaction. In W. R. Cupach & B. H. Spitzberg (Eds.), *The dark side of interpersonal communication* (pp. 259–280). Hillsdale, NJ: Lawrence Erlbaum Associates.

Steiger, H., Puentes-Neuman, G., & Leung, F. Y. K. (1991). Personality and family features of adolescent girls with eating symptoms: Evidence for restricter/binger differences in a nonclinical population. *Addictive Behaviors, 16*, 303–314.

Steiger, H., Stotland, S., Trottier, J., & Ghadirian, A. M. (1996). Familial eating concerns and psychopathological traits: Causal implications of transgenerational effects. *International Journal of Eating Disorders, 19*, 147–157.

Steinglass, P. (1979). The alcoholic family in the interaction laboratory. *Journal of Nervous and Mental Disease, 167*, 428–436.

Steinglass, P. (1981). The impact of alcoholism on the family. *Journal of Studies on Alcohol, 42*, 288–303.

Steinglass, P., & Robertson, A. (1983). The alcoholic family. In B. Kissin & H. Begleiter (Eds.), *The biology of alcoholism: Vol. 6. The pathogenesis of alcoholism: Psychosocial factors* (pp. 243–307). New York: Plenum.

Steinglass, P., Weiner, S., & Mendelson, J. H. (1971). A systems approach to alcoholism: A model and its clinical application. *Archives of General Psychiatry, 24,* 401–408.

Strober, M., & Humphrey, L. L. (1987). Familial contributions to the etiology and course of anorexia nervosa and bulimia. *Journal of Consulting and Clinical Psychology, 55,* 654–659.

Sullivan, H. S. (1953). *The interpersonal theory of psychiatry.* New York: Norton.

Suman, L. N., & Nagalakshmi, S. V. (1993). Personality dimensions of alcohol dependent individuals and their spouses. *NIMHANS Journal, 11,* 95–98.

Thomas, A. M., & Forehand, R. (1991). The relationship between parental depressive mood and early adolescent parenting. *Journal of Family Psychology, 4,* 260–271.

Thompson, J. M., Whiffen, V. E., & Blain, M. D. (1995). Depressive symptoms, sex, and perceptions of intimate relationships. *Journal of Social and Personal Relationships, 12,* 49–66.

Vandereycken, W., Kog, E., & Vanderlinden, J. (Eds.). (1989). *The family approach to eating disorders.* New York: PMA Publishing.

van Furth, E. F., van Strien, D. C., Martina, L. M. L., van Son, M. J. M., Hendrickx, J. J. P., & van Engeland, H. (1996). Expressed emotion and the prediction of outcome in adolescent eating disorders. *International Journal of Eating Disorders, 20,* 19–31.

Vanger, P., Summerfield, A. B., Rosen, B. K., & Watson, J. P. (1991). Cultural differences in interpersonal responses to depressives' nonverbal behaviour. *The International Journal of Social Psychiatry, 37,* 151–158.

Vaughn, C., & Leff, J. P. (1976). The measurement of expressed emotion in the families of psychiatric patients. *British Journal of Clinical and Social Psychology, 15,* 157–165.

Vaughn, C. E., & Leff, J. P. (1981). Patterns of emotional response in relatives of schizophrenic patients. *Schizophrenia Bulletin, 7,* 43–44.

Vaux, A. (1988). Social and emotional loneliness: The role of social and personal characteristics. *Personality and Social Psychology Bulletin, 14,* 722–734.

Vitousek, K., & Manke, F. (1994). Personality variables and disorders in anorexia nervosa and bulimia nervosa. *Journal of Abnormal Psychology, 103,* 137–147.

Waller, G. (1994). Borderline personality disorder and perceived family dysfunction in the eating disorders. *Journal of Nervous and Mental Disease, 182,* 541–546.

Waller, G., & Calam, R. (1994). Parenting and family factors in eating problems. In L. Alexander-Mott & D. B. Lumsden (Eds.), *Understanding eating disorders: Anorexia nervosa, bulimia nervosa, and obesity* (pp. 61–76). Philadelphia: Taylor & Francis.

Waller, G., Slade, P., & Calam, R. (1990). Family adaptability and cohesion: Relation to eating attitudes and disorders. *International Journal of Eating Disorders, 9,* 225–228.

Warner, V., Weissman, M. M., Fendrich, M., Wickramaratne, P., & Moreau, D. (1992). The course of major depression in the offspring of depressed parents: Incidence, recurrence, and recovery. *Archives of General Psychiatry, 49,* 795–801.

Watts, W. D., & Ellis, A. M. (1992). Drug abuse and eating disorders: Prevention implications. *Journal of Drug Education, 22,* 223–240.

Watzlawick, P., Bavelas, J. B., & Jackson, D. D. (1967). *Pragmatics of human communication.* New York: Norton.

Weeks, D. G., Michela, J. L., Peplau, L. A., & Bragg, M. E. (1980). Relation between loneliness and depression: A structural equation analysis. *Journal of Personality and Social Psychology, 39,* 1238–1244.

Weiss, R. (1974). The provisions of social relationships. In Z. Rubin (Ed.), *Doing unto others* (pp. 17–26). Englewood Cliffs, NJ: Prentice-Hall.

Weissman, M. M., Klerman, G. L., Rounsaville, B. J., Chevron, E. S., & Neu, C. (1982). Short–term interpersonal psychotherapy (IPT) for depression: Description and efficacy. In J. C. Anchin & D. J. Kiesler (Eds.), *Handbook of interpersonal psychotherapy* (pp. 296–310). New York: Pergamon.

Whiffen, V. E., & Gotlib, I. H. (1989). Infants of postpartum depressed mothers: Temperament and cognitive status. *Journal of Abnormal Psychology, 98,* 274–279.

Windle, M., & Searles, J. S. (1990). *Children of alcoholics: Critical perspectives.* New York : Guilford.

Wittenberg, M. T., & Reis, H. T. (1986). Loneliness, social skills, and social perception. *Personality and Social Psychology Bulletin, 12*, 121–130.

Wonderlich, S. (1992). Relationship of family and personality factors in bulimia. In J. H. Crowther, D. L. Tennenbaum, S. E. Hobfoll, & M. A. P. Stephens (Eds.), *The etiology of bulimia nervosa: The individual and familial context* (pp. 103–126). Washington, DC: Hemisphere.

Wonderlich, S. A., & Swift, W. J. (1990a). Borderline versus other personality disorders in the eating disorders: Clinical description. *International Journal of Eating Disorders, 9*, 629–638.

Wonderlich, S. A., & Swift, W. J. (1990b). Perceptions of parental relationships in the eating disorders: The relevance of depressed mood. *Journal of Abnormal Psychology, 99*, 353–360.

Wonderlich, S., Ukestad, L., & Perzacki, R. (1994). Perceptions of nonshared childhood environment in bulimia nervosa. *Journal of the American Academy of Child and Adolescent Psychiatry, 33*, 740–747.

Wright, D. M., & Heppner, P. P. (1991). Coping among nonclinical college-age children of alcoholics. *Journal of Counseling Psychology, 38*, 465–472.

Wynne, L. C. (1981). Current concepts about schizophrenics and family relationships. *Journal of Nervous and Mental Disease, 169*, 82–89.

VI

MUSINGS

12

Investigating the Positive and Negative Sides of Personal Relationships: Through a Lens Darkly?

Karen S. Rook
University of California, Irvine

PERSONAL RELATIONSHIPS AND EMOTIONAL HEALTH: PARADOXICAL FINDINGS

A paradox exists in research that seeks to understand how our relationships with friends, family members, and others influence our health and well-being. On the one hand, it is abundantly clear that most people are strongly motivated to form close relationships (Baumeister & Leary, 1995) and that they care deeply about the quality of their relationships. Moreover, personal relationships appear to represent a critically important source of psychological well-being. For example, when Klinger (1977) asked people to indicate what gave their lives the greatest sense of meaning, most responded with a reference to their personal relationships; few cited work or other life domains as a centrally important source of meaning. Research on the perceived quality of life confirms that the caliber of people's personal relationships is a more powerful predictor of their happiness and life satisfaction than is the caliber of their lives in most other domains (Argyle, 1987; Campbell, Converse, & Rodgers, 1976). An extensive body of evidence documents the important role that others play in helping to limit the toll that stressful life events take on emotional and physical health (e.g., Cohen & Wills, 1985). Research on loneliness and bereavement also provides ample evidence of the anguish, longing, and despair experienced by people who either lack or have lost close relationships (Peplau & Perlman, 1982; Stroebe, Stroebe, & Hansson, 1993). In addition, large, well-controlled prospective studies indicate that people who have few social ties experience an increased risk of morbidity and mortality, and this increased risk cannot be attributed to potentially confounded factors, such as socioeconomic status (SES), health-risk behaviors, use of health services, or prior health status (Burman & Margolin, 1992; Cohen, 1988; House, Landis, & Umberson, 1988; House, Umberson, & Landis, 1988).

On the other hand, it is clear that personal relationships can function as a source of conflict, strain, and disappointment, and troubled personal relationships threaten health and well-being. For example, complaints about personal relationships have been found to be among the most common concerns expressed by individuals seeking psychotherapy (Horowitz, 1986; Pinsker, Nepps, Redfield, & Winston, 1985), and criticism and emotional overinvolvement by family members have been linked to an increased risk of relapse among recently discharged psychiatric patients (see review by Segrin, chap. 11, this volume). Efforts to provide social support to people experiencing major stressful events often backfire, aggravating (rather than alleviating) the recipient's difficulties (Dakof & Taylor, 1990; Dunkel-Schetter, 1984; Wortman & Lehman, 1985). Studies of common everyday stressors suggest that those of an interpersonal nature (e.g., demands from others and conflicts and tensions in one's relationships) arouse more distress than do other kinds of stressors (Bolger, DeLongis, Kessler, & Schilling, 1989; Veroff, Douvan, & Kulka, 1981; Zautra, Burleson, Matt, Roth, & Burrows, 1994). In addition, the adverse effects of interpersonal stressors persist over several days, whereas the effects of other stressors dissipate more quickly (Bolger et al., 1989). Tensions in close relationships have been associated not only with worse psychological health (Segrin, chap. 11, this volume) but also with worse physiological outcomes, such as increased cardiovascular reactivity and depressed immune functioning (e.g., Ewart, Taylor, Kraemer, & Agras, 1991; Kiecolt-Glaser et al., 1993). The chapters in this volume, and in an earlier companion volume (Cupach & Spitzberg, 1994), present compelling evidence of the unintended (or sometimes intended) harm that people can inflict on those who are close to them.

Thus, although several different lines of research have documented the rewards and benefits of social relationships, several other lines of research have documented their costs or hazards. This apparent paradox has stimulated the emergence of a small but growing literature that focuses on the question of whether positive or negative aspects of personal relationships have greater significance for human health and well-being (see Rook, 1992a). This literature has begun to coalesce around a dominant methodological approach that typically entails the use of survey methods (questionnaires and telephone- or in-person interviews) to collect self-report measures of emotional health, supportive social interactions (or ties), and problematic social interactions (or ties). The associations between these interpersonal variables and health-related outcomes, such as depression, are typically examined cross-sectionally, using multiple regression methods or other analytic methods that assume linear associations. These analyses often include controls for gender, marital status, income, physical health, and personality factors (e.g, extraversion or neuroticism) that might influence the associations of interest. A few researchers have examined these associations longitudinally (e.g., Finch & Zautra, 1992; Holahan, Moos, Holahan, & Brennan, 1997; Lakey, Tardiff, & Drew, 1994; Lepore, 1992; Pagel, Erdly, & Becker, 1987; Vinokur & Van Ryn, 1993); other researchers have supplemented participants' self-reports with reports obtained from significant others (Abbey, Andrews, & Halman, 1995; Vinokur & Vinokur-Kaplan, 1990).

Without oversimplifying the findings that have emerged thus far from this literature, it is fair to say that many studies have yielded evidence of what has been referred to as a *negativity effect*—evidence that negative social exchanges exhibit stronger or more reliable associations with well-being than do positive social exchanges (see Ingersoll-Dayton, Morgan, & Antonucci, 1997; Rook, 1990b, 1992a). For example, in an early study that documented a negativity effect, Rook (1984) asked a sample of elderly women about the extent to which various members of their social networks engaged in positive exchanges, such as providing support and companionship, as well as negative exchanges, such as taking advantage of them or invading their privacy. Analyses that included controls for the women's age, education, and physical health suggested that the negative exchanges significantly detracted from their morale, whereas the positive exchanges only weakly or nonsignificantly contributed to morale.

This pattern has been replicated in cross-sectional studies based on larger, representative samples (e.g., Ingersoll-Dayton et al., 1997; Schuster, Kessler, & Aseltine, 1990) and in longitudinal studies that have included controls for baseline psychological functioning (e.g., Pagel et al., 1987; Vinokur & Van Ryn, 1993). The longitudinal studies help to address the concern that the adverse impact of negative exchanges represents a mere artifact of participants' state of psychological adjustment. For example, depressed individuals might be more prone to perceive or precipitate negative exchanges with others. Pagel et al. (1987) used a short-term, longitudinal design in a study of caregivers to determine whether changes in negative social exchanges predicted changes in caregivers' depression levels. Controlling for initial depression levels and for age, sex, and health status, they found that participants who reported an increase in negative exchanges over a 10-month period also reported an increase in depression; no parallel finding emerged for changes in positive exchanges. Further analyses revealed that participants' initial depression levels did not predict their later exposure to problematic exchanges. Similarly, initial mental health did not predict subsequent exposure to negative exchanges in longitudinal studies of unemployed individuals (Vinokur & Van Ryn, 1993) or elderly widows (Morgan, Neal, & Carder, in press).

Moreover, negativity effects have been documented in relation to physiological, as well as psychological, outcomes. For example, Kiecolt-Glaser et al. (1993) assessed changes in immune functioning among newly married couples engaged in a discussion of marital problems. They found that hostile behaviors exhibited during the discussion predicted decrements in immunological functioning and elevated blood pressure during the next 24 hours, whereas supportive behaviors were not related to either immunological or blood pressure changes. Ewart et al. (1991) similarly found that clinically significant increases in blood pressure during a marital problem-solving task were related to hostile behaviors, but were unrelated to supportive behaviors.

This pattern of findings across a number of studies has led to an emerging conclusion that the negative aspects of personal relationships are more consequential for health and well-being than are the positive aspects (Rook, 1992a, 1992b). This conclusion has gained credence from parallel findings in other literatures that have documented the potent effects of negative information and events (e.g., Cacioppo, Gardner, & Bernston, 1997; Taylor, 1991). For example, research on life stress has shown consistently that negative life events detract from well-being, whereas positive life events rarely have the corresponding effect of enhancing well-being (Taylor, 1991). In a related vein, stress researchers have presented evidence that the potential loss of resources (material, interpersonal, or intrapersonal) is more emotionally and motivationally arousing than the potential acquisition of resources (Hobfoll, 1989). Research on person perception indicates that negative traits are given more weight than positive traits in the formation of overall impressions of others (e.g., Skowronski & Carlston, 1989; Vonk, 1993). Similarly, studies of judgment under conditions of uncertainty indicate that preference-inconsistent (negative) information is processed more deeply and exerts greater influence on judgments and behavior than does preference-consistent (positive) information (e.g.,

Ditto & Lopez, 1992). A substantial body of evidence also suggests that people exhibit an aversion to risk in decision-making tasks; that is, potential losses are more influential than potential gains (Kahneman & Tversky, 1984).

Thus, negativity effects have been documented in nonsocial as well as social domains (see Kanouse & Hanson, 1972, for an early review). The emergence of such effects across diverse literatures—using quite diverse methodologies and investigating diverse populations—suggests the possibility of common underlying dynamics. Indeed, it is the very possibility that these diverse negativity effects share similar cognitive, emotional, and motivational underpinnings that has prompted researchers to frame questions about the relative significance of positive versus negative interpersonal experiences in terms that might otherwise seem perplexingly broad.

In view of these converging lines of research, interest in the darker side of social relationships, although not new, is gaining momentum. This interest partly developed as a reaction against what is regarded as an unrealistically positive view of social relationships that has tended to dominate social scientists' writings (Duck, 1994; Heller, 1979; Spitzberg & Cupach, this volume). If the lens through which personal relationships were once viewed was too rosy (Duck, 1994; Spitzberg & Cupach, this volume), it now appears to be turning a decidedly darker hue. This corrective emphasis is understandable and may well lead to more balanced, integrated analyses of both the light and dark sides of social relationships, as Duck (1994) and others (e.g., Coyne & DeLongis, 1986; Heller, 1979; Rook, 1990a, 1990b, 1992a) have urged. Achieving a balanced view, however, requires that the empirical lens through which we scrutinize personal relationships be free of distortion. The major premise of this chapter is that some methodological limitations, largely overlooked, may have distorted the comparisons of positive and negative social exchanges in prior research. These methodological limitations call into question the notion that negative exchanges are more consequential for health and well-being than are positive exchanges.

The purpose of this chapter is to take a critical look at the evidence that has been mustered to date for negativity effects and, in particular, to identify methodological problems that may have hampered efforts to evaluate the relative impact of positive and negative experiences in personal relationships. A number of methodological requirements must be met in order to conduct a fair evaluation of the relative effects of these positive and negative interpersonal experiences. These requirements, and the implications of ignoring them, constitute the central focus of this chapter. This chapter emphasizes methodological concerns that have not yet been widely discussed; other important concerns, such as the problems associated with self-report data or cross-sectional designs, have been discussed more fully elsewhere (e.g., Finch & Zautra, 1992; Lepore, 1992; Rook, 1990a), including the chapters in this volume (e.g., Segrin, chap. 11, this volume; Sillars, chap. 3, this volume). The final section summarizes recommendations for future research that flow from the discussion of methodological problems.

BOUNDARIES AND DEFINITIONS

Before beginning, it is important to identify the boundaries that limit this analysis. It is also important to clarify at the outset what is meant by the terms *positive* and *negative social exchanges*. The boundary conditions and definitional issues are addressed below.

Boundaries of the Analysis

The literature to be discussed has focused primarily on what might be regarded as a class of "everyday" negative social exchanges, such as criticism, demands, insensitivities, intrusions, and interference (e.g., Ruehlman & Karoly, 1991). Thus, this work generally has examined a narrower range of negative interpersonal experiences than that considered in this volume, which includes such disturbing experiences as jealous rages, fatal attractions, sexual coercion, and relational obsession and stalking. It is possible, of course, that some research participants in the studies to be reviewed may have had exactly such disturbing experiences in mind when they reported that members of their social networks invade their privacy or provoke their anger. In general, however, the findings that have emerged from this literature and the methodological issues they raise should not be assumed to generalize to research on the darker and more deeply troubling side of close relationships.

The impact of positive and negative exchanges in the work to be discussed has been gauged most often with reference to emotional health outcomes, although similar patterns have emerged in studies of physical health outcomes. The discussion in this chapter regarding the relative impact of positive and negative exchanges, therefore, is based primarily on work that has examined psychological well-being. The patterns that have emerged from this work cannot be assumed to generalize to other outcomes, such as relationship decisions and behaviors. In addition, this work has focused largely on the psychological well-being of a focal person who is the target of others' positive and negative deeds. Unlike much of the research reported in this volume (e.g., Guerro & Anderson, chap. 2; LePoire, Hallett, & Giles; Segrin, chap. 6; Canary & Messman, chap. 5; Sillars, chap. 3; Spitzberg & Cupach, Introduction), this work generally has less to say about reciprocal and contingent patterns of positive and negative exchange between two or more individuals.

Most of the work to be discussed has focused on nonclinical populations, although the interpersonal processes and outcomes that characterize nonclinical populations may differ less than is typically assumed from those that characterize clinical populations (personal communication, Henderson, May 10, 1990; Stafford & Dainton, 1994). Efforts to extrapolate from the work to be reviewed to clinical populations should be undertaken with caution.

Finally, the work that is the focus of this chapter typically has evaluated the effects of positive and negative exchanges on well-being by aggregating the negative and positive exchanges that occur in an entire social network (e.g., Ingersoll-Dayton et al., 1997; Pagel et al., 1987; Revenson, Schiaffino, Majerovitz, & Gibofsky, 1991; Rook, 1984) or in subgroups of the network, such as family members or friends (e.g., Abbey, Abramis, & Caplan, 1985; Holahan et al., 1997; Schuster et al., 1990). Such aggregated data have relevance to this volume because analyses indicate that the network members most likely to be named as sources of troublesome interactions are spouses, family members, friends, and neighbors (e.g., Rook, 1984). With some exceptions (e.g., Manne & Zautra, 1989), however, this work generally tells us less than does the work presented in this and the previous volume about the dynamics of problematic exchanges that occur in specific dyadic relationships.

Definitional Issues

Following Vinokur and Van Ryn (1993), *positive social exchanges* are defined as actions by members of a person's network that involve the expression of positive affect toward or positive evaluations of the person as well as efforts to facilitate the focal person's pursuit of personal goals. This includes the various types of emotional support and assistance that social support theorists have emphasized (e.g., House, 1981; Wills, 1985) as well as the affection, humor, and shared activities that others have emphasized (e.g., Bolger & Eckenrode, 1991; Buunk, 1990; Rook, 1987). *Negative social exchanges* are defined as actions by members of a focal person's social network that involve the expression of negative affect toward the person, devaluation of the person's worth, or actions that undermine the person's pursuit of personal goals (Vinokur & Van Ryn, 1993). This emphasis excludes some of the conventional costs of relationships that have been discussed by social exchange theorists (Homans, 1974; Thibaut & Kelley, 1959), such as time, money, and material goods that may be required to maintain a relationship or the displacement of opportunities to engage in alternative activities. This chapter concentrates, instead, on actions that people tend to regard as misdeeds or transgressions and that customarily cause distress. This admittedly broad definition subsumes instances of clumsy but well-intended support or miscarried support (Coyne, Ellard, & Smith, 1990; Coyne, Wortman, & Lehman, 1988; Wortman & Lehman, 1985), but encompasses other kinds of troublesome social exchanges as well—such as criticism and demands.

COMPARING THE IMPACT OF POSITIVE AND NEGATIVE SOCIAL EXCHANGES: METHODOLOGICAL ISSUES

The sections that follow discuss a number of methodological issues that may have influenced the conclusions derived from studies that have sought to compare the effects of positive and negative social exchanges on psychological well-being. These issues include potential problems related to the samples studied, the assessment of positive and negative social exchanges, the choice of outcomes used to gauge the effects of these exchanges, and the analysis and interpretation of data regarding these effects.

Sampling

Levels of Stress in the Sample. Some researchers have suggested that the impact of positive and negative social exchanges on emotional well-being may depend on the extent to which study participants are experiencing life stress (Rook, 1990a; Shinn, Lehmann, & Wong, 1984). The *stress-buffering hypothesis* posits that social support exerts the greatest effects on well-being among stressed individuals, presumably because it encourages more benign appraisals of the stressful situation and facilitates more effective coping responses (e.g., House, 1981; Wills, 1985). Indeed, strong versions of the stress-buffering hypothesis suggest that social support exhibits a weak or nonsignificant association with well-being among non-stressed individuals (Cobb, 1976). A parallel *stress-exacerbation* (or stress-amplification) *hypothesis* has been posited, which predicts that conflictual social interaction has the greatest influence on well-being among stressed individuals (Rook, 1990a, 1992a; Shinn et al., 1984), presumably because it adds to the individuals' existing emotional burdens, drains coping resources, and undermines self-esteem.

Ingersoll-Dayton and her colleagues (Ingersoll-Dayton et al., 1997) recently argued that many of the studies that have yielded evidence of a negativity effect were conducted with samples experiencing high levels of life stress. For example, negativity effects have emerged in studies of elderly widows (Rook, 1984), spousal or familial caregivers of individuals with Alzheimer's disease (Fiore, Becker, & Coppel, 1983; Kiecolt-Glaser et al., 1988; Pagel et al., 1987), victims of sexual assault (Davis, Brickman, & Baker, 1991), pregnant adolescents (Barrera, 1981), and unemployed persons (Vinokur & Van Ryn, 1993). Ingersoll-Dayton et al. (1997) suggested that the results of such studies, by virtue of being based on vulnerable groups, may have exaggerated the evidence for negativity effects. They tested this idea in a large, representative sample of middle-aged and older adults by comparing the effects of positive and negative social exchanges among more- versus less-stressed individuals (defined by a median split on a measure of stressful events experienced within the past five years). Their analyses revealed evidence of a negativity effect only among the more-stressed individuals; among the less-stressed individuals, both positive and negative exchanges were significantly related to well-being.

Other studies that have examined the influence of life stress, although in nonrepresentative samples, have yielded a different pattern of findings. In a study of older adults, Okun, Melichar, and Hill (1990) found that negative interactions were strongly associated with psychological distress, regardless of the participants' level of life stress (measured in terms of recent daily stresses). Similarly, Finch and his colleagues (Finch, Okun, Barrera, Zautra, & Reich, 1989) found that problematic social ties were strongly associated with emotional health not only among elderly individuals who were recently bereaved or physically disabled, but also among matched controls who had not experienced recent life stress. Negativity effects have emerged, moreover, in samples that could not be categorized on a priori grounds as distinctly stressed, such as college students (Abbey et al., 1985) and married couples (Schuster, Kessler, & Aseltine, 1990). Finally, although Ingersoll-Dayton et al. (1997) were correct in noting that negativity effects have been documented in some studies that have focused on vulnerable groups, the stress-buffering hypothesis suggests that it is exactly such groups that are likely to benefit from social support. By this logic, positivity effects should be as likely to emerge as negativity effects in vulnerable groups.

Thus, neither the available evidence nor the existing state of theorizing about the conditions that create susceptibility to negativity effects allow us to estimate with confidence the extent to which the samples studied to date have yielded exaggerated evidence of negativity effects. This possibility warrants attention in future research, however, and researchers should be prepared to consider the implications of sampling procedures that yield samples with skewed distributions of life stress.

Levels of Social Integration in the Sample. The levels of social integration represented in a sample also have implications for the results of efforts to compare the effects of positive versus negative social exchanges. In much of the research conducted to date, true social isolates are unlikely to have been included in the samples studied. Socially isolated individuals are difficult to locate and to recruit to research projects (e.g., Pilisuk & Minkler, 1980), yet comparison of isolates and nonisolates are more likely than other comparisons to reveal the benefits of social ties (a point discussed more fully in a subsequent section; see also House, 1981). Statistical provisions for contrasting participants who cluster at empirically defined "low" versus "high" points in a distribution of social integration scores do not solve this problem if the low point omits individuals who are truly isolated (cf. Finney, Mitchell, Cronkite, & Moos, 1984). Given the difficulty of accessing and recruiting isolated individuals, this problem will not be easy to overcome in future research, but the potential limitations of truncated sampling should be considered when inferences are derived about the impact of positive versus negative social exchanges.

Assessment of Positive and Negative Exchanges

Adequacy of Domain Sampling. The adequacy with which the domains of positive and negative social exchanges are sampled in a given study has implications for the evidence that emerges regarding negativity effects. Table 12.1 shows a range of exchanges that could be sampled in each domain. (This table does not include serious interpersonal threats and violations because, as noted earlier, the focus of this literature has primarily been on commonplace negative exchanges.) Many of the existing studies appear to sample the negative domain fairly well, assessing a diverse set of negative exchanges. In contrast, the assessment of positive exchanges has been less comprehensive, typically emphasizing emotional and instrumental social support and excluding shared leisure and simple companionship, as shown in Table 12.1. The enjoyable, hedonic forms of social interaction make important, independent contributions to health and well-being (e.g., Bolger & Eckenrode, 1991; Buunk, 1990; Rook, 1987; Thompson, Futterman, Gallagher-Thompson, Rose, & Lovett, 1993), and their omission clearly can yield results that underestimate the effects of positive exchanges.

Extremity. An unbiased comparison of the effects of positive and negative social exchanges also requires the two kinds of exchanges assessed

TABLE 12.1

Sampling of Positive and Negative Social Exchanges

Positive Exchanges	Negative Exchanges
Emotional support	Denial of Support
Appraisal support	Criticism
Informational support	Rejection
Instrumental support	Deception or betrayal
*Affection or intimacy	Demands or control attempts
*Shared activities	Interference
*Shared storytelling or humor	Exploitation

Note. The Positive Exchanges (denoted with an asterik) are often omitted from researchers' inventories.

to be of roughly equal extremity. Evidence of a negativity effect that is based on comparisons of extreme negative exchanges (e.g., public ridicule) and mild positive exchanges (e.g., problem-solving discussions) would not be especially compelling. Such a comparison is obviously likely to favor the conclusion that negative exchanges are more consequential for well-being. The extremity, or intensity, of positive and negative stimuli has been a central concern in other literatures in which negativity effects emerged, such as the person perception literature (Wojciszke, Brycz, & Borkenau, 1993), but this has not been true in the literature on personal relationships. Although the work conducted to date does not appear to have been plagued by systematic differences in the extremity of the positive and negative social exchanges assessed, this problem may have been present to some extent and warrants greater vigilance.

Interestingly, studies of impression formation and decision making, in which negativity effects have emerged, indicate that the disproportionate impact of negative stimuli is not simply due to their extremity (Skowronski, & Carlston, 1989); that is, negative stimuli exert an effect that is independent of their extremity. This may hold true in the realm of personal relationships as well (cf. Berscheid, 1983). It is difficult to determine this, however, without greater attention to the extremity of the positive and negative relational experiences that are assessed. Efforts to equate the extremity of the positive and negative exchanges studied does not mean that measures need to be forced into a degree of parallelism that is artificial or that overlooks the "darker" relational experiences examined in several of the chapters in this volume. If constructing parallel measures is unduly restrictive, concerns about extremity can be addressed by exercising care when the positive and negative relational experiences are aggregated for statistical analysis and when inferences about their relative effects are derived from these analyses.

Time Frames. The time frames specified or implied in measures of positive and negative exchanges are also likely to influence the evidence that emerges for negativity effects. For example, consider the two different time frames implied in the wording of the following items: "In the past week, did anyone act too busy or make excuses when you needed help?" "Does anyone tend to act too busy or make excuses when you need help?" The latter phrasing, unlike the former, suggests a chronic or recurring pattern of disregard. A serious problem would arise if the items assessing positive exchanges were largely phrased in terms of discrete events or transactions, but the items assessing negative exchanges were phrased in terms of recurring or chronic patterns. Doing so would clearly introduce a bias in favor of finding evidence of negativity effects.

A related asymmetry would arise if positive social exchanges were assessed in terms of potential transactions, but negative exchanges were assessed in terms of actual transactions (e.g., Lepore, 1992; Rook, 1984). Many of the positive exchanges assessed in this literature address study participants' access to various kinds of social support (a point that is later explored more fully). As a result, items are often phrased in a way that asks participants to consider who they could turn to for support in time of need. For example, participants might be asked "Is there anyone you could turn to if you needed to discuss a personal problem?" The phrasing of items about negative exchanges, in contrast, often suggests ongoing patterns of interaction (e.g., "Is there anyone who refuses to provide help when you need it?"). Access to others with whom social exchanges have the potential to be enacted presumably have weaker effects on well-being than does the actual enactment of such exchanges with others (see Sarason, Pierce, & Sarason, 1990; Sarason, Shearin, Pierce, & Sarason, 1987; Turner, 1992, for an alternative view of the health-related effects of perceived versus received support).

Systematic asymmetries such as these in the phrasing of items used to assess positive versus negative social exchanges compromise the validity of analyses designed to compare the effects of the two kinds of exchanges. Such asymmetries in phrasing do not appear to be a rampant problem in the existing literature, but may have been present in some studies and, accordingly, may have helped to inflate the evidence for negativity effects.

Assessment of Outcomes

Valence. A fair test of the relative importance of positive versus negative exchanges also requires attention to the choice of outcome measures used to evaluate the effects of these exchanges. Many studies have examined outcomes that reflect emotional distress, such as depression or anxiety (Abbey et al., 1985; Finch & Zautra, 1992; Fiore et al.,

1983; Kiecott-Glaser et al., 1988, Lepore, 1992; Pagel et al., 1987; Revenson et al., 1991; Schuster et al., 1990). Proponents of a two-factor theory of well-being, in contrast, have argued for a basic distinction between positive and negative dimensions of psychological health (e.g., Diener, 1984; Lawton, 1983; Zautra & Reich, 1983). That is, these theorists argue that emotional health is more than the absence of distress. They argue, further, that different causal factors influence the positive and negative dimensions of emotional health (Lawton, 1983; Zautra & Reich, 1983). The factors that contribute to happiness, for example, may differ from those that help to alleviate depression. Some researchers have extrapolated from these theories to predict that positive and negative social exchanges are equally important, but for different dimensions of emotional health (Finch et al., 1989; Ingersoll-Dayton et al., 1997). Specifically, they reason that positive and negative social exchanges are linked to congruent dimensions of well-being, with positive social exchanges predicting positive affect, for example, and negative social exchanges predicting negative affect (*outcome-specific effects*). From this perspective, studies that link participants' interpersonal experiences only to negative aspects of emotional health would tend to yield inflated estimates of the significance of negative experiences.

Only a few studies have incorporated this distinction in seeking to contrast the effects of positive versus negative social exchanges, and these studies have yielded inconsistent results (Finch et al., 1989; Ingersoll-Dayton et al., 1997). Ingersoll-Dayton et al. analyzed data from a national sample of adults aged 50 years and older. Their data set included information about the respondents' supportive social interactions, troublesome interactions, and levels of positive and negative affect. In analyses that controlled for respondents' demographic characteristics and health status, the researchers found (as predicted) that positive interactions were related to positive affect but were not related to negative affect. The reverse was true for negative interactions: They were related to negative affect but not to positive affect.

A somewhat different pattern of results emerged in a study by Finch and his colleagues (Finch et al., 1989) that assessed older adults' positive social ties, negative social ties, and two aspects of adjustment—psychological well-being (assessed with a measure of perceived quality of life) and psychological distress (assessed with a measure of psychiatric symptoms). The researchers expected positive social ties to be primarily related to psychological well-being and negative social ties to be primarily related to psychological distress. The results only partially confirmed their expectations: Positive ties were related solely to psychological well-being, but negative ties were related both to well-being and distress. Finch et al.

concluded that negative interactions are so salient to an individual that their effects spill across various affective domains (a *crossover effect*).

To determine whether negativity effects, outcome-specific effects, or crossover effects are more common (Rook, 1992b), researchers must assess positive and negative dimensions of emotional health as well as positive and negative aspects of social network involvement. Only a limited number of studies have met these requirements thus far.

The suggestion that a differentiated conception of well-being yields fairer tests of the relative significance of positive and negative exchanges need not be limited to distinguishing between positive and negative dimensions of emotional health, but rather, may be extended to distinctions within these two broad dimensions. For example, some researchers have argued that problem-focused support (such as helpful advice about a vexing personal problem) may be most relevant to outcomes that reflect relief from distress (such as reduced anxiety) and preservation of self-esteem (e.g., Felton & Berry, 1992, Wills, 1985). Felton and Berry (1992) noted that such problem-focused support serves primarily "compensatory functions or functions that offset stressful circumstances and the negative emotions that tend to accompany them" (p. 96). The role of shared leisure and other forms of companionship, in contrast, is less remedial, and companionship may be singularly important in sustaining or enhancing life satisfaction, happiness, and other positive outcomes (Argyle, 1987; Rook, 1987). More generally, theoretically anchored distinctions among emotional health outcomes provide the basis for more complex predictions about the associations between social network involvement and psychological functioning, predictions that may guide us to a more even-handed search for positivity and negativity effects.

Stability.   The stability of the outcomes assessed also has implications for the findings that have emerged to date. Evidence suggests most people exhibit only modest shifts in psychological functioning over time (e.g., Costa et al., 1987; Monroe & Johnson, 1992). That is, their psychological health generally fluctuates modestly around a fairly stable mean level. For some, this relatively stable, personal level of functioning is marked by few symptoms of psychological distress, whereas for others this personal level will be marked by numerous symptoms of more or less chronic distress. Access to reliable social support in an earlier life stage may well operate, as attachment theorists (Bowlby, 1969) and others (e.g., Sarason et al., 1990; Sullivan, 1953) have argued, to help establish these personal mean levels of psychological health. Negative social exchanges, in contrast, may play a greater role in accounting for fluctuations around these mean levels (cf. Berscheid, 1983). If so, then the prevailing research strategies in this literature may be ill-equipped to detect the developmentally important, stabilizing function of supportive social bonds.

Moreover, some clinical outcomes of interest, such as depression, follow various trajectories of onset, development, exacerbation, remission, and possible recurrence (Monroe & Johnson, 1992) that are not reflected in a person's score on a measure of psychological health at one point in time. That is, the same score could indicate, for different people, any of several qualitatively different states. For example, a score of 25 on a widely used measure of depressive symptoms, such as the Center for Epidemiological Studies-Depression scale (Radloff, 1977), is often regarded as suggesting the presence of clinically significant depression, but it is impossible to know from such a score alone whether this represents the first onset of disorder, a recurrence of disorder, or an improving or deteriorating trajectory in an already-established disorder. Positive and negative social exchanges may be differentially important in the onset versus maintenance of emotional disorders, but prevailing research designs that indiscriminately mix together newly symptomatic and consistently symptomatic individuals may fail to reveal such distinctive roles (Monroe & Johnson, 1992). Thus, greater attention to the chronicity, or stability, of the emotional health outcomes under study and to the meaning of shifts in psychological functioning over time might lead to different conclusions about the relative importance of positive and negative social exchanges for emotional health (see Cohen, 1988, for a discussion of similar issues regarding the role of interpersonal processes at different stages in the course of physical illness.)

Data Analysis and Interpretation

Nonlinear Associations.   An important data analysis issue that has received little attention concerns the possibility of nonlinear associations between the health-related outcome of interest and either positive or negative social exchanges (Veiel, 1992). Some support researchers have argued that the association between levels of social support and psychological health should be conceptualized and evaluated as a nonlinear association, with the greatest benefits of support appearing when individuals who have no supportive relationships are compared with individuals who have at least one such relationship (Coyne & DeLongis, 1986; House, 1981; Kahn & Antonucci, 1980). That is, a critical threshold may exist beyond which increased levels of support contribute little to a person's psychological well-being. This contrasts with the more conventional prediction of a simple linear association between positive social ties and psychological health. A parallel critical threshold could be predicted (although with less certainty) regarding the effects of negative social exchanges, such that the largest differences in emotional health would be observed in comparisons of individuals who have no (or few) problematic social relationships with individuals who have one (or more) such relationships.

Few studies have tested for such nonlinear patterns (Finch & Zautra, 1992). This is worrisome because when researchers have reported the distributions of positive and negative interactions in their samples, a sizable number of respondents have disclaimed having any negative interactions with others. For example, in some studies of older adults, as many as 25% to 30% of the respondents have reported that they have no problematic interactions with members of their social networks (e.g., Rook, 1984). In contrast, very few respondents report having no supportive interactions with members of their networks. Higher figures have been reported in other studies, with as many as 58% or more of respondents disavowing any problematic interactions (Okun, Melichar, & Hill, 1990).

These differences in the clustering of respondents at the low end of the distributions of positive and negative exchanges could partly account for the finding that negative exchanges have a disproportionate impact on psychological functioning. That is, the data collected in these studies may have included the critical threshold for negative exchanges (to the extent that one exists), but may have excluded the critical threshold for positive exchanges. If so, this would not disconfirm the significance of negative exchanges, but it would cast doubt on the inference that negative exchanges have more powerful effects than do positive exchanges.

Cumulative Effects.   Another important analytic issue concerns the interpretation of regression coefficients that emerge in tests of positivity and negativity effects. Negativity effects are typically assumed to be present when the regression coefficient linking negative social exchanges to an outcome of interest is significantly greater than the corresponding coefficient linking positive social exchanges to the outcome. This pattern has been construed as indicating that negative social interactions have a greater impact than do positive interactions (i.e., that a negativity effect is present). Yet, as Morgan and Schuster (1992) recently pointed out, these regression coefficients really tell us about the average contribution to psychological health of each additional negative exchange and each additional positive exchange. Although this incremental effect of each additional negative exchange exceeds the incremental effect of each additional positive exchange in many studies, respondents typically report few negative exchanges and many positive exchanges (Finch et al., 1989; Revenson et al., 1991; Rook, 1984; Schuster et al., 1990), as noted earlier. Thus, the cumulative effect of positive exchanges may exceed the cumulative effect of negative exchanges. This would be true if the positive exchanges were sufficiently numerous to offset their comparatively weak individual (per exchange) effects. Vinokur and Van Ryn (1993) commented in this regard, "Compared with the volatile and extreme effects of social undermining, those of social support appear weaker but more stable" (p. 350).

Morgan and Schuster (1992) reanalyzed published regression results from several studies, showing that findings initially interpreted as revealing a negativity effect actually reveal a positivity effect when the cumulative effect of the weak-but-numerous positive exchanges is taken into account. From a phenomenological perspective, this would mean that when negative exchanges occur, they may be more potent or salient than positive exchanges (Rook & Pietromonaco, 1987), but when aggregated, negative exchanges may be less consequential for psychological health precisely because they occur infrequently. That is, the potent-but-scarce negative exchanges may have less cumulative impact on well-being than do the comparatively weak-but-common positive exchanges. This suggests a need to be more circumspect in the interpretation of negativity effects that emerge from conventional regression analyses.

How many positive exchanges are required to offset the deleterious effects of negative exchanges in ongoing relationships is an interesting question. Gottman (1994) suggested, based on his extensive research on marital interaction, that couples need to maintain a ratio of at least 5 positive exchanges to 1 negative exchange in order to preserve marital satisfaction. In unhappily married couples, a 1 to 1 ratio is more common (Gottman, 1994). Relationships that offer few hedonic rewards, or too few rewards to offset the costs, are likely to terminate (Carstensen, 1993; Thibaut & Kelley, 1959), although several of the contributors to this volume point out that even manifestly dysfunctional interaction patterns sometimes serve functions that help to perpetuate both the pattern of negative exchanges and the relationship itself (e.g., Le Poire et al., chap. 6; Segrin, chap. 11).

Magnitude of Effects Over Time. A final analytic issue concerns the relative magnitude of negative versus positive effects over time. When researchers have suggested that negative social exchanges are more consequential for well-being than positive social exchanges, they imply that the greater effects of negative exchanges endure over time. That is, they assume that negative exchanges produce a greater displacement from a baseline level of functioning and this effect endures over time, as illustrated in the upper panel of Fig. 12.1. In this figure (showing hypothetical data), the curve plotted for negative exchanges suggests that these exchanges produce a greater departure from baseline well-being than do positive

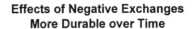

Effects of Negative Exchanges
More Durable over Time

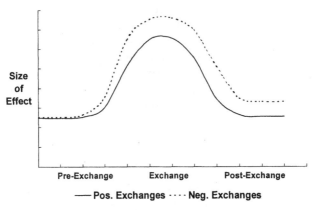

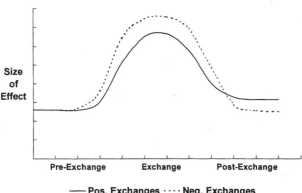

FIG. 12.1. Alternative models of the relative magnitude of the effects of positive versus negative exchanges over time.

exchanges, and this effect persists over time. It is possible, however, that negative exchanges have greater impact only in the short run (e.g., Vinokur & Van Ryn, 1993). This possibility is portrayed in the lower panel of Fig. 12.1. In this alternative model, negative exchanges have a greater initial impact than do positive exchanges, but the effect of negative exchanges decays more dramatically over time. This second model mirrors Taylor's (1991) analysis of the effects of positive versus negative life events over time. She argued that negative life events evoke strong initial psychological responses that subsequently become dampened as people actively seek ways to minimize or undo the impact of the events. No comparable minimization process applies to positive events, and their long-term impact, therefore, is ultimately greater.

The virtual dearth of longitudinal studies that explicitly compare short-term versus long-term effects of positive versus negative exchanges makes it difficult to evaluate these two competing models. In analyses of data from a sample of older adults that span a 1-year period, Lewis and Rook (1991) obtained preliminary support for the idea that negative interactions have more substantial effects in the short run, but positive interactions have more substantial effects in the long run. Finch and Zautra (1992), however, reported findings from a study spanning a period of several months that support the idea that negative exchanges have more powerful effects both in the short run and the long run. In a large study of unemployed persons, Vinokur and Van Ryn (1993) found that negative social exchanges had a strong adverse impact on participants' psychological health at baseline, and decreases in negative exchanges were related to improved psychological health at follow-ups that took place 2 and 4 months later. Positive interactions in their study were only related to concurrent psychological health at baseline.

Thus, the available data are limited and conflicting, but it is important to bear in mind that negativity effects have been most often documented in studies that have examined concurrent associations between psychological functioning and positive versus negative social interaction. These cross-sectional approaches can detect initial negativity effects, but cannot reveal whether, or how rapidly, such effects decay over time. As a result, the predominance of cross-sectional approaches in the work conducted to date may have tended to inflate the evidence for negativity effects.

RECOMMENDATIONS AND CONCLUSIONS

The literature discussed in this chapter is concerned with the question of how, on balance, the "good" and the "bad" (though perhaps not the "ugly") aspects of personal relationships influence well-being. Interest in this question has been stimulated, in part, by an apparent paradox in research on the health-related effects of social bonds, with some work suggesting that close relationships contribute, and may even be essential to, health and well-being (Baumeister & Leary, 1995; House et al., 1988) and other work suggesting that the negative aspects of close relationships tend to cancel or outweigh their positive aspects (Rook, 1992a). If the analysis presented here is correct, then the latter view rests on an empirical base that suffers from some methodological limitations that have received relatively little attention. Specifically, the evidence for negativity effects, although intriguing in its implications and its resonance with similar findings in other literatures (Cacioppo et al, 1997; Kahneman, & Tversky, 1984; Kanouse & Hanson, 1972), may have been overstated. The idea that negative social exchanges substantially detract from emotional health has been well-established, but the inference that negative exchanges generally matter more for emotional health than do positive exchanges appears to require stronger empirical support.

Several recommendations for future research follow from the discussion of methodological limitations in this chapter. First, consideration should be given to the implications of sampling plans for the distributions of life stress and social integration in the resulting samples. Second, the positive and negative social exchanges assessed in our studies should adequately capture each domain, should be of roughly comparable extremity, and should reflect comparable time frames. Third, the emotional health outcomes assessed should reflect a differentiated view of emotional health and an awareness of the temporal course of the outcomes studied. Fourth, data analyses and interpretations should probe for possible nonlinear associations, should differentiate incremental versus cumulative effects, and should distinguish between short-term and long-term effects. Attention to these methodological issues is unlikely to reverse the conclusion that negative social exchanges cause considerable emotional distress, but it may provide the basis for more tempered conclusions about the relative importance of positive and negative exchanges.

These recommendations were derived from a methodologically oriented review of a circumscribed body of research, and they can be elaborated considerably with the ideas and insights presented in other chapters in this volume. A number of intriguing themes recur across these chapters that suggest directions for expanding our understanding of the relational dynamics, individual differences, and cognitive-behavioral processes that surround positive and negative social interactions. For example, the irony that many of the very traits and behaviors that provide the basis for initial attraction contain the seeds for subsequent conflict and even repulsion (Bratslavsky et al., chap. 10; Felmlee, chap. 1) was largely unexplored in this chapter. The processes that lead from early harmony to later discord and disaffection involve dialectic tensions, contradictions, ambiguities, and biases in perceptions and communication that are discussed in detail by the contributors to this volume (LePoire et al., chap 6; Sillars, chap. 3; Spitzberg & Cupach, Introduction). Similar processes may underlie the transformation of problematic behavior from merely annoying to deeply disturbing or even threatening behavior (Cupach & Spitzberg, chap. 8). Avenues for further inquiry are suggested, as well, by the contributors who observed that seemingly dysfunctional interaction patterns sometimes serve a function (though not necessarily an adaptive one) in the social relationships or groups in which they occur (Guerrero & Andersen, chap. 2; Le Poire et al., chap. 6; Segrin, chap. 11). As a result, dysfunctional relational patterns are reinforced and perpetuated, and efforts to change them often meet resistance (Le Poire et al., chap. 6; Segrin, chap. 11). The bidirectional nature of these associations—between dysfunctional interaction and psychological disorder (Segrin, chap. 11) or between miscommunication and emotional distress (Sillars, chap. 3)—has not been fully explored in the literature reviewed in this chapter. Several contributors also remind us that historical and cultural contexts influence how people experience and attempt to manage the problematic interactions that occur in their close relationships (Bratslavsky et al, chap. 10; Guerro & Anderson, chap. 2; Spitzberg & Cupach, Introduction). These contributions significantly enrich, and illustrate how we might extend, our current understanding of the troubling aspects of personal relationships.

REFERENCES

Abbey, A., Abramis, D. J., & Caplan, R. D. (1985). Effects of different sources of social support and social conflict on emotional well-being. *Basic and Applied Social Psychology, 6*, 111–129.

Abbey, A., Andrews, F. M., & Halman, J. (1995). Provision and receipt of social support and disregard: What is their impact on the marital life and quality of infertile and fertile couples? *Journal of Personality and Social Psychology, 68*, 455–469.

Argyle, M. (1987). *The psychology of happiness*. London: Methuen.

Barrera, M. (1981). Social support and the adjustment of pregnant adolescents: Assessment issues. In B. H. Gottlieb (Ed.), *Social networks and social support* (pp. 69–96). Beverly Hills, CA: Sage.

Baumeister, R. F., & Leary, M. R. (1995). The need to belong: Desire for interpersonal attachments as a fundamental human motivation. *Psychological Bulletin, 117*, 497–529.

Berscheid, E. (1983). Emotion. In H. H. Kelley, E. Berscheid, A. Christensen, J. H. Harvey, T. L. Huston, G. Levinger, E. McClintock, L. A. Peplau, & D. R. Peterson (Eds.), *Close relationships* (pp. 110–168). New York: Freeman.

Bolger, N., DeLongis, A., Kessler, R. C., & Schilling, E. A. (1989). Effects of daily stress on negative mood. *Journal of Personality and Social Psychology, 57*, 808–818.

Bolger, N., & Eckenrode, J. (1991). Social relationships, personality, and anxiety during a major stressful event. *Journal of Personality and Social Psychology, 61*, 440–449.

Bowlby, J. (1969). *Attachment and loss: Vol. 1. Attachment*. New York: Basic Books.

Buunk, B. (1990). Affiliation and helping interactions within organizations: A critical analysis of the role of social support with regard to occupational stress. In W. Stroebe & M. Hewstone (Eds.), *European review of social psychology* (vol. 1., pp. 293–322). Chichester, UK: Wiley.

Burman, B., & Margolin, G. (1992). Analysis of the association between marital relationships and health problems: An interactional perspective. *Psychological Bulletin, 112*, 39-63.

Cacioppo, J. T., Gardner, W. L., & Bernston, G. G. (1997). Beyond bipolar conceptualizations and measures: The case of attitudes and evaluative space. *Personality and Social Psychology Review, 1*, 3–25.

Campbell, A., Converse, P. E., & Rodgers, W. L. (1976). *The quality of American life*. New York: Russell Sage.

Carstensen, L. L. (1993). Motivation for social contact across the life span: A theory of socioemotional selectivity. *Nebraska Symposium on Motivation, 40,* 209–254.

Cobb, S. (1976). Social support as a moderator of life stress. *Psychosomatic Medicine, 38,* 300–314.

Cohen, S. (1988). Psychosocial models of the role of social support in the etiology of physical disease. *Health Psychology, 7,* 269-297.

Cohen, S., & Wills, T.A. (1985). Stress, social support, and the buffering hypothesis. *Psychological Bulletin, 98,* 310–357.

Costa, P. T., Jr., Zonderman, A. B., McCrae, R. R., Cornoni-Huntley, J., Locke, B. Z., & Barbano, H. E. (1987). Longitudinal analyses of psychological well-being in a national sample: Stability of mean levels. *Journal of Gerontology, 42,* 50–55.

Coyne, J. C., & DeLongis, A. M. (1986). Going beyond social support: The role of social relationships in adaptation. *Journal of Consulting and Clinical Psychology, 54,* 454–460.

Coyne, J. C., Ellard, J. H., & Smith, D. A. F. (1990). Social support, interdependence, and the dilemmas of helping. In B. R. Sarason, I. G. Sarason, & G. R. Pierce (Eds.), *Social support: An interactional view* (pp. 129–149). New York: Wiley.

Coyne, J. C., Wortman, C. B., & Lehman, D. R. (1988). The other side of support: Emotional overinvolvement and miscarried helping. In B. H. Gottlieb (Ed.), *Marshaling social support: Formats, processes, and effects* (pp. 305–330). Newbury Park, CA: Sage.

Cupach, W. R., & Spitzberg, B. H. (Eds.). (1994). *The dark side of interpersonal communication.* Hillsdale, NJ: Lawrence Erlbaum Associates.

Dakof, G. A., & Taylor, S. E. (1990). Victims' perceptions of social support: What is helpful from whom? *Journal of Personality and Social Psychology, 58,* 80–89.

Davis, R. C., Brickman, E., & Baker, T. (1991). Supportive and unsupportive responses of others to rape victims: Effects on concurrent victim adjustment. *American Journal of Community Psychology, 19,* 443–451.

Diener, E. (1984). Subjective well-being. *Psychological Bulletin, 95,* 542–575.

Ditto, P. H., & Lopez, D. F. (1992). Motivated skepticism: Use of differential decision criteria for preferred and nonpreferred conclusions. *Journal of Personality and Social Psychology, 63,* 569–584.

Duck, S. (1994). Stratagems, spoils, and a serpent's tooth: On the delights and dilemmas of personal relationships. In W. R. Cupach & B. H. Spitzberg (Eds.), *The dark side of interpersonal communication* (pp. 3–24). Hillsdale, NJ: Lawrence Erlbaum Associates.

Dunkel-Schetter, C. (1984). Social support and cancer: Findings based on patient interviews and their implications. *Journal of Social Issues, 40,* 77–98.

Ewart, C. K., Taylor, C. B., Kraemer, H. C., & Agras, W. S. (1991). High blood pressure and marital discord: Not being nasty matters more than being nice. *Health Psychology, 10,* 155–163.

Felton, B. J., & Berry, C. A. (1992). Do the sources of the urban elderly's social support determine its psychological consequences? *Psychology and Aging, 7,* 89–97.

Finch, J. F., Okun, M. A., Barrera, M., Jr., Zautra, A. J., & Reich, J. W. (1989). Positive and negative social ties among older adults: Measurement models and the prediction of psychological distress and well-being. *American Journal of Community Psychology, 17,* 585–605.

Finch, J. F., & Zautra, A. J. (1992). Testing latent longitudinal models of social ties and depression among the elderly: A comparison of distribution-free and maximum likelihood estimates with nonnormal data. *Psychology and Aging, 7,* 107–118.

Finney, J. W., Mitchell, R. E., Cronkite, R. C., & Moos, R. H. (1984). Methodological issues in estimating main and interactive effects: Examples from coping/social support and stress field. *Journal of Health and Social Behavior, 25,* 85-98.

Fiore, J., Becker, J., & Coppel, D. B. (1983). Social network interactions: A buffer or a stress? *American Journal of Community Psychology, 11,* 423–439.

Gottman, J. M. (1994). *What predicts divorce? The relationship between marital processes and marital outcomes.* Hillsdale, NJ: Lawrence Erlbaum Associates.

Heller, K. (1979). The effects of social support: Prevention and treatment implications. In A. P. Goldstein & F. H. Kanfer (Eds.), *Maximizing treatment gains: Transfer enhancement in psychotherapy* (pp. 353–382). New York: Academic Press.

Hobfoll, S. E. (1989). Conservation of resources: A new attempt at conceptualizing stress. *American Psychologist, 44,* 513–524.

Holahan, C. J., Moos, R. H., Holahan, C. K., & Brennan, P. L. (1997). Social context, coping strategies, and depressive symptoms: An expanded model with cardiac patients. *Journal of Personality and Social Psychology, 72*, 918–928.

Homans, G. G. (1974). *Social behavior* (2nd ed.). New York: Harcourt Brace.

Horowitz, L. (1986). The interpersonal basis of psychiatric symptoms. *Clinical Psychology Review, 6*, 443–469.

House, J. S. (1981). *Work stress and social support.* Reading, MA: Addison–Wesley.

House, J. S., Landis, K., & Umberson, D. (1988). Social relationships and health. *Science, 241*, 540–545.

House, J. S., Umberson, D., & Landis, K. (1988). Structures and processes of social support. *Annual Review of Sociology, 14*, 293–318.

Ingersoll-Dayton, B., Morgan, D., & Antonucci, T. C. (1997). The effects of positive and negative social exchanges on aging adults. *Journal of Gerontology: Social Sciences, 52*, S190–S200.

Kahn, R. L., & Antonucci, T. C. (1980). Convoys over the life course: Attachment, roles, and social support. In P. B. Baltes & O. G. Brim (Eds.), *Life-span development and behavior* (pp. 253-286). New York: Academic Press.

Kahneman, D., & Tversky, A. (1984). Choice, values, and frames. *American Psychologist, 39*, 341–350.

Kanouse, D. E., & Hanson, R. L. (1972). *Negativity in evaluations.* In E. E. Jones, D. E. Kanouse, H. H. Kelley, R. E. Nisbett, S. Valins, & B. Weiner (Eds.), *Attribution: Perceiving the causes of behavior* (pp. 47–62). New York: General Learning Press.

Kiecolt-Glaser, J. K., Dyer, C. S., & Shuttleworth, E. C. (1988). Upsetting social interactions and distress among Alzheimer's disease family caregivers: A replication and extension. *American Journal of Community Psychology, 16*, 825–837.

Kiecolt-Glaser, J. K., Malarkey, W.B., Chee, M., Newton, T., Cacioppo, J. T., Mao, H.-Y., & Glaser, R. (1993). Negative behavior during marital conflict is associated with immunological down-regulation. *Psychosomatic Medicine, 55*, 395–409.

Klinger, E. (1977). *Meaning and void: Inner experiences and the incentives in people's lives.* Minneapolis: University of Minnesota Press.

Lakey, B., Tardiff, T. A., & Drew, J. B. (1994). Negative social interactions: Assessment and relations to social support, cognition, and psychological distress. *Journal of Social and Clinical Psychology, 13*, 42–62.

Lawton, M. P. (1983). The varieties of well-being. *Experimental Aging Research, 9*, 65–72.

Lepore, S. J. (1992). Social conflict, social support, and psychological distress: Evidence of cross-domain buffering effects. *Journal of Personality and Social Psychology, 63*, 857–867.

Lewis, M. A., & Rook, K. S. (1991, November). *Positive and negative social ties: Short-term vs. long-term effects on psychological distress.* Paper presented at the annual meeting of the Gerontological Society of America, San Francisco, CA.

Manne, S., & Zautra, A. J. (1989). Spouse criticism and support: Their association with coping and psychological adjustment among women with rheumatoid arthritis. *Journal of Personality and Social Psychology, 56*, 608–617.

Monroe, S. M., & Johnson, S. L. (1992). Social support, depression, and other mental disorders: In retrospect and toward future prospects. In H. O. F. Veiel & U. Baumann (Eds.), *The meaning and measurement of social support* (pp. 93–105). Washington, DC: Hemisphere.

Morgan, D., & Schuster, T. L. (1992, July). *Assessing the impact of positive and negative relationships in social networks.* Paper presented at the biennial meeting of the International Society for the Study of Personal Relationships, Orono, ME.

Morgan, D. L., Neal, M. B,. & Carder, P. C. (in press). Both what and when: The effects of positive and negative aspects of relationships on depression during the first three years of widowhood. *Journal of Clinical Geropsychiatry.*

Okun, M. A., Melichar, J. F., & Hill, M. D. (1990). Negative daily events, positive and negative social ties, and psychological distress among older adults. *Gerontologist, 30*, 193–199.

Pagel, M. D., Erdly, W. W., & Becker, J. (1987). Social networks: We get by with (and in spite of) a little help from our friends. *Journal of Personality and Social Psychology, 53*, 793–804.

Peplau, L.A., & Perlman, D. (Eds.), (1982). *Loneliness: A sourcebook of current theory, research and therapy.* New York: Wiley.

Pilisuk, M., & Minkler, M. (1980). Supportive networks: Life ties for the elderly. *Journal of Social Issues, 36*, 95–116.

Pinsker, H., Nepps, P., Redfield, J., & Winston, A. (1985). Applicants for short-term dynamic psychotherapy. In A. Winston (Ed.), *Clinical and research issues in short-term dynamic psychotherapy* (pp. 104–116). Washington, DC: American Psychiatric Association.

Radloff, L. S. (1977). The CES-D scale: A self-report depression scale for research in the general population. *Applied Psychology and Measurement, 1*, 385.

Revenson, T. A., Schiaffino, K. M., Majerovitz, D., & Gibofsky, A. (1991). Social support as a double-edged sword: The relation of positive and problematic support to depression among rheumatoid arthritis patients. *Social Science and Medicine, 33*, 807–813.

Rook, K. S. (1984). The negative side of social interaction: Impact on psychological well-being. *Journal of Personality and Social Psychology, 46*, 1097–1108.

Rook, K. S. (1987). Social support versus companionship: Effects on life stress, loneliness, and evaluations by others. *Journal of Personality and Social Psychology, 52*, 1132–1147.

Rook, K. S. (1990a). Parallels in the study of social support and social strain. *Journal of Social and Clinical Psychology, 9*, 118–132.

Rook, K. S. (1990b). Stressful aspects of older adults' social relationships: An overview of current theory and research. In M. A. P. Stephens, J. H. Crowther, S. E. Hobfoll, & D. L. Tennenbaum (Eds.), *Stress and coping in later life families* (pp. 173-192). Washington, DC: Hemisphere.

Rook, K. S. (1992a). Detrimental aspects of social relationships: Taking stock of an emerging literature. In H. O. F. Veiel & U. Baumann (Eds.), *The meaning and measurement of social support* (pp. 157-169). New York: Hemisphere.

Rook, K. S. (1992b, April). *Social relationships and emotional health: A reconsideration of positivity and negativity effects.* Invited address presented at the annual meeting of the Western Psychological Association, Portland, OR.

Rook, K. S., & Pietromonaco, P. (1987). Close relationships: Ties that heal or ties that bind? In W. H. Jones & D. Perlman (Eds.), *Advances in personal relationships* (Vol. 1, pp. 1-35). Greenwich, CT: JAI.

Ruehlman, L. S., & Karoly, P. (1991). With a little flak from my friends: Development and preliminary validation of the Test of Negative Social Exchange (TENSE). *Journal of Consulting and Clinical Psychology, 3*, 97–104.

Sarason, B. R., Pierce, G. R., & Sarason, I. G. (1990). Social support: The sense of acceptance and the role of relationships. In B. R. Sarason, I. G. Sarason, & G. R. Pierce (Eds.), *Social support: An interactional view* (pp. 97–128). New York: Wiley.

Sarason, B. R., Shearin, E. N., Pierce, G. R., & Sarason, I. G. (1987). Interrelations of social support measures: Theoretical and practical implications. *Journal of Personality and Social Psychology, 52*, 813–832.

Schuster, T. L., Kessler, R. C., & Aseltine, R. H., Jr. (1990). Supportive interactions, negative interactions, and depressed mood. *American Journal of Community Psychology, 18*, 423–438.

Shinn, M., Lehmann, S., & Wong, N. W. (1984). Social interaction and social support. *Journal of Social Issues, 40*, 5–76.

Skowronski, J. J., & Carlston, D. E. (1989). Negativity and extremity biases in impression formation: A review of explanations. *Psychological Bulletin, 105*, 131–142.

Stafford, L., & Dainton, M. (1994). The dark side of "normal" family interaction. In W. R. Cupach, & B. H. Spitzberg (Eds.), *The dark side of interpersonal communication* (pp. 259–280). Hillsdale, NJ: Lawrence Erlbaum Associates.

Stroebe, M., Stroebe, W., & Hansson, R. (Eds.), (1993). *Handbook of bereavement: Theory, research, and intervention.* Cambridge, England: Cambridge University Press.

Sullivan, H. S. (1953). *The interpersonal theory of psychiatry.* New York: Norton.

Taylor, S. E. (1991). Asymmetrical effects of positive and negative events: The mobilization-minimization hypothesis. *Psychological Bulletin, 105*, 131–142.

Thibaut, J. W., & Kelley, H. H. (1959). *The social psychology of groups.* New York: Wiley.

Thompson, E. H., Futterman, A. M., Gallagher-Thompson, D., Rose, J. M., & Lovett, S. B. (1993). Social support and caregiving burden in family caregivers of frail elders. *Journal of Gerontology: Social Sciences, 48*, S245–S254.

Turner, R. J. (1992). Measuring social support: Issues of concept and method. In H. O. F. Veiel & U. Baumann (Eds.), *The meaning and measurement of social support* (pp. 217–233). New York: Hemisphere.

Veiel, H. O. F. (1992). Some cautionary notes on buffer effects. In H. O. F. Veiel & U. Baumann (Eds.), *The meaning and measurement of social support* (pp. 272–289). New York: Hemisphere.

Veroff, J., Douvan, E., & Kulka, R. A. (1981). *Mental health in America: Patterns of help-seeking from 1957 to 1976.* New York: Basic Books.

Vinokur, A. D., & Van Ryn, M. (1993). Social support and undermining in close relationships: Their independent effects on the mental health of unemployed persons. *Journal of Personality and Social Psychology, 65,* 350–359.

Vinokur, A. D., & Vinokur-Kaplan, D. (1990). "In sickness and in health": Patterns of social support and undermining in older married couples. *Journal of Aging and Health, 2,* 215–241.

Vonk, R. (1993). The negativity effect in trait ratings in open-ended descriptions of persons. *Personality and Social Psychology Bulletin, 19,* 269–278.

Wills, T. A. (1985). Supportive functions of interpersonal relationships. In S. Cohen & S. L. Syme (Eds.), *Social support and health* (pp. 61-82). Orlando, FL: Academic Press.

Wojciszke, B., Brycz, H., & Borkenau, P. (1993). Effects of information content and evaluative extremity on positivity and negativity biases. *Journal of Personality and Social Psychology, 64,* 327–335.

Wortman, C., & Lehman, D. R. (1985). Reactions to victims of life crises: Support attempts that fail. In I. G. Sarason & B. R. Sarason (Eds.), *Social support: Theory, research, and application* (pp. 463–489). The Hague, The Netherlands: Martinus Nijhoff.

Zautra, A. J., Burleson, M. H., Matt, K. S., Roth, S., & Burrows, L. (1994). Interpersonal stress, depression, and disease activity in rheumatoid arthritis and osteoarthritis patients. *Health Psychology, 13,* 139–148.

Zautra, A. J., & Reich, J. W. (1983). Life events and perceptions of life quality: Developments in a two-factor approach. *Journal of Community Psychology, 11,* 121–132.

Author Index

Subject Index